A View of New Orleans As Seen from the Plantation of Bernard Marigny. Painted in November, 1803 by Bequeto deWoisarie. Note Marigny's formal garden at lower left, and the stockade or Fort St. Charles at right of center. (Courtesy of the Chicago Historical Society)

TO MY DAUGHTER MILDRED

New Orleans
the Glamour Period, 1800-1840

A History of the Conflicts of Nationalities, Languages, Religion, Morals, Cultures, Laws, Politics and Economics During the Formative Period of New Orleans.

by
ALBERT E. FOSSIER, M.A., M.D.

A FIREBIRD PRESS BOOK

PELICAN PUBLISHING COMPANY
Gretna 1998

Manufactured in the United States of America

Published by Pelican Publishing Company, Inc.
1000 Burmaster Street, Gretna, Louisiana 70053

FOREWORD

The most interesting period in the history of New Orleans is that included in the first four decades of the nineteenth century. During these years, the city emerged from the status of a small town which, for nearly a century, had been neglected by both France and Spain. Subjected to the whims of foreign masters, a pawn of the politics of a war-torn Europe, New Orleans before the Purchase although the capital of a vast empire, was never much more than a village. But when it became a part of the United States, New Orleans soon grew into a metropolis which attracted the attention not only of the Nation but of the world.

Increasing in population rapidly, New Orleans soon ranked with the largest cities in the country. It became a city of fabulous wealth whose commerce was extensive and in whose port, vessels of many nations displayed their flags. New Orleans was then a place of adventure, of pleasure, of opportunity and of easily acquired fortune. It was also a city plagued by epidemics, for nowhere else had any city a more appalling mortality — a mortality that depleted its population nearly every year. It was a haven for political refugees, as well as the haunt of adventurers and the rendezvous of filibusterers. It was the sanctuary of criminals and, above all, the dream of fortune seekers — all contributing to make it then (as it is now for other reasons) the Nation's most interesting city.

Before the Purchase life in the small colonial city of New Orleans bordered by a swamp, practically isolated from the rest of the world though sometimes plagued by calamities, was comparatively serene; for there were no conflicts of nationalities; language, customs, religion and culture. Its population was homogeneous. The mingling and the intermarriage of the flower of French and Spanish nobility with many of more humble origin resulted in a proud, genial, gentle, and urbane people. It cannot be said that their culture was either French or Spanish, or even a combination of the two, for they had evolved one of their own, which must be called Creole. These were the people who became American citizens under the provisions of the Louisiana Purchase. They are referred to in this history as the Ancient Population, Creoles, Gallo-Americans, the Creole and French faction, and the Indigenous Population.

The first four decades of the nineteenth century were of the greatest importance in the history of New Orleans. The crowning events of that time were the acquisition of Louisiana by the United States, the Battle of New Orleans, the advent of the steamboat and of the railroad, the Anglo-Saxon infiltration, the building boom and the city's remarkable growth.

The ceremonies of the Transfer, the Battle of Chalmette, l'affaire Wilkinson and the Aaron Burr conspiracy are not included in this work. Not only would the description of these events in themselves fill a volume, but their inclusion would be a useless repetition, since they have been authoritatively recorded by other historians.

The Lafittes have fallen into the realm of romance, so much so, that it is impossible today to determine where truths ends and fiction begins. The only factual works on that subject may be said to be those of the historian Stanley Faye of Aurora, Illinois, who devoted practically a life time in intensive research on the activities of the privateers in New Orleans and Barataria. His contributions on that subject were published in the Louisiana Historical Quarterly and many other historical publications.

I have, therefore, omitted any extended reference to Lafitte and his privateers.

An historian must be thoroughly acquainted with the period he is recording, he must fully familiarize himself with the events and customs of the time, and he should not permit his imagination to glamorize or obscure the truth. Above all, he must be factual. He must study the individuals about whom he writes — their personalities, their motives, their successes, their frustrations, their ambitions, their prejudices and their hatreds, as well as the causative factors which guided their actions — with all the zeal, astuteness and pertinacity of a scientist, for, as Plutarch said, "so very difficult a matter is it to trace and find out the truth of anything in history."

The author has tried to present an authentic picture of life as it was lived in New Orleans during the first years of the last century. For more than thirty years during spare moments he has scrutinized old manuscripts and letters, read and abstracted every available newspaper of that time, both French and English, critically studied the works of travelers who then visited the city, and consulted the archives of the municipality, State Legislature and the courts. Needless to say, a maze of contradictions was encountered, for opinions differed and observations varied, some authors censuring and other praising. Some depicted the city as a place of iniquity, of impiety, of godlessness and of depravity. They called it "the pest-hole of the world", "the city of the wet grave" and lamented the callousness of its ignorant population. Again, others were profuse in their praise. They extolled the beauty of the women, their social grace, elegance and virtue. They also lauded the charity, hospitality, and the *savoir faire* of the population, and, because of its culture, many proclaimed New Orleans the Paris of America.

In order to properly appraise this diversity of opinion among the visiting contemporary chroniclers, it is necessary to ascertain their sources of information. We must also examine their motives, their religious beliefs, their nationalities and their innate prejudice and intolerance to anything that did not conform to their own code of ethics. Many visiting writers of Puritan convictions, were unable to reconcile themselves to the gayety, frivolity and easy way of life of the pleasure-loving Latins which they considered sinful. Some were honest in their convictions, whilst others wrote with the malicious intent of popularizing their books by sensationalism. Yet their criticisms, exaggerated or biased as they might be, undoubtedly had some basis of truth, and have increased our understanding of how the people of that time lived and of what they did.

Richard Whately said, "History gives us the extraordinary events and omits just what we want, the every day life of each particular time and country." The author has attempted to supply this deficiency in the usual New Orleans history by depicting the every day life of those who lived amidst the many conflicts that made the period from 1800 to 1840 so interesting. New Orleans at that time was a crucible containing the elements of hatred, bigotry, religious intolerance and national prejudices as well as political rivalry which eventually fused into the homogeneity that made it a great American city. It can truthfully be said that this chapter of its history is unique in the annals of the country.

Most of the material on which this history is based is derived from the fading and musty files of contemporary newspapers which are fast deteriorating. They are the depository of much unrecorded history, for the facts were published as they were seen by these reporters of long ago, and they have given us a glimpse of what happened backstage in that drama of human events. Controveries were carried on and strong differences of opinion are found in their editorial columns, but, whenever this occurred, both sides of the argument were presented to the reader so that the truth can usually be discerned.

All quotations are verbatim and translations from the French are literal, for no effort has been spared to make this work as authoritative as possible. The reader will notice that all footnotes have been omitted since the author feels that these small-print references at the bottom of the pages are not only distracting but are infrequently read. He also feels that any quotation worthy of mention should be included in the body of the text.

The names of so many of the pioneers who labored and suffered with such devotion to promote the advancement of their city during its formative years have fallen into oblivion, They deserve a better fate, for no matter how humble may have been their role, they left a heritage of which their many descendants may well be proud. It has been my pleasure to bring them to life again.

The quotations from old newspapers, as well as those from other early writers, were often written in a turgid and affected style, and sometimes make "hard" reading. But I have not attempted to paraphrase them and have inserted these excerpts without change as they reflect the spirit of the age.

The author is grateful for the many courtesies extended to him by Miss Elizabeth Hugh during the course of writing this work. He also expresses his sincere thanks to his friend, Dr. Lucien Fortier, for the interest and encouragement he has manifested during the compilation of this history, and especially for his laconic observation that "at your age time is short". How right he is, for having lived three quarters of a century, there is no time left for procrastination. So due to his friendly admonition, to this volume has been appended the word FINIS.

A. E. F.

CONTENTS

Chapter		Page
	Foreword	VII
I	New Orleans As It Was	1
II	The Marvelous Thirties	10
III	The Levee, the Arks, and the Steamboats	23
IV	The Advent of the Rail Road	36
V	Expanding Commerce	45
VI	Banks, Booms and Depressions	59
VII	Municipal Affairs	76
VIII	Political Squabbles	92
IX	The Three Municipalities	119
X	Postal Service and Mail Routes	138
XI	The Judiciary and the Bar	143
XII	Police, Traffic Violations, Prisons, Executions	161
XIII	The Fourth Estate	175
XIV	The Militia	193
XV	A University Is Born	204
XVI	Hospitals and Infirmaries	218
XVII	The Progress of Education in Louisiana	229
XVIII	Libraries, The Historical Society and Lyceums	238
XIX	Orphans and Orphanages	247
XX	The Heterogeneous Population of New Orleans	255
XXI	Creoles	266
XXII	The American Infiltration	279
XXIII	Catholicism	294
XXIV	The Schism in the Catholic Church	310

CONTENTS

XXV	Pére Antoine	326
XXVI	The Rise of Protestantism	336
XXVII	Reverend Joel Parker	348
XXVIII	Quadroons and Quadroon Balls	356
XXIX	Slaves and Free Persons of Color	366
XXX	Morals and Vice	381
XXXI	Yellow Fever	394
XXXII	The Cholera Epidemic of 1832	404
XXXIII	City of the Wet Grave	419
XXXIV	Funerals and Memorial Ceremonies	429
XXXV	Measuring Swords and Exchanging Shots	440
XXXVI	Amusements — Refined and Vulgar	452
XXXVII	The Theatre	467
XXXVIII	Patriotic Celebrations	485
XXXIX	Lafayette Visits New Orleans	490
XL	Napoleon's Death Mask	497
	Appendix	502

— Chronological Table

— Governors of Louisiana

— New Orleans Members of Legislature

— Mayors of New Orleans

— Members of City Council

Bibliography

Index

LIST OF ILLUSTRATIONS

View of New Orleans, 1803 (Frontispiece)	....Opposite Title Page	
The Government House, 1815	Page	4
Custom House, 1815	"	5
Street Scene, New Orleans, 1828	"	7
Banks' Arcade, 1938	"	15
Merchant's Exchange, 1836	"	17
Markets of New Orleans	"	19
City Exchange (St. Louis Hotel), 1838	"	22
Verandah Hotel	"	22
"Maid of New Orleans" — Steamboat, 1820	Op. "	48
Dock Scene at New Orleans, 1828	" "	48
Port of New Orleans, 1833, by Pinistri	" "	49
Exchange Hotel (St. Charles Hotel), 1838	"	35
Orleans Cotton Press, 1838	"	52
Carrollton Hotel	Op. "	80
Magazine Street, 1834	" "	80
Station, Carrollton R.R., 1834	" "	81
City Pound, 2nd and 3rd Districts, 1835	" "	81
Station of Projected Rail Road, Poydras St.	" "	81
Commercial Bank, 1838	"	72
Atchafalaya Bank, 1838	"	72
Waterworks designed by Latrobe, 1815	"	81
Hand Fire Engine, 1835	"	85
Map of Three Municipalities, 1840	"	120
Map Showing Legal Boundaries of Three Municipalities	"	121
Old Parish Prison, 1836	Op. "	144
Old Citizen's Bank Building	" "	144
Banks of New Orleans, 1838	" "	145
Churches of New Orleans, 1838	" "	176

LIST OF ILLUSTRATIONS

American Theater and Arcade Baths, 1838	Op.	"	177
Sugar Refinery	"	"	177
Levee Steam Cotton Press	"	"	177
Charity Hospital, 1815		"	220
Charity Hospital, 1832		"	224
View of Place d'Armes, 1820	Op.	"	240
Same, 1836	"	"	240
Bond of the First Municipality, 1837	"	"	241
Franklin Infirmary, 1838		"	227
Orleans College, 1815		"	230
Ursulines Convent, 1815		"	236
Old Houses of New Orleans	Op.	"	272
More Old Houses	"	"	273
View of River Front by Garneray, 1835	"	"	336
Collapse of Planter's Hotel, 1833	"	"	337
A Lady of Fashion Out for a Drive	"	"	337
Cartouche from Tanesse Map of 1815		"	347
St. Charles Theatre	Op.	"	368
St. Charles Theatre Interior	"	"	368
Scene, Corner Rampart and Esplanade Streets	"	"	369
Cenotaph for Memorial Ceremonies		"	433
Funeral Cortege, Memorial Ceremonies		"	435
View of Chartres Street and the Cathedral about 1830	Op.	"	432
River Front Scene, New Orleans in early Forties	"	"	433
St. Philip Theatre, 1815		"	468
Orleans Theatre, 1815		"	470
Camp Street in 1830, showing the American Theatre		"	478
The Charity Hospital around 1830	Op.	"	464
Port of New Orleans, 1841	"	"	465

CHAPTER I

NEW ORLEANS AS IT WAS

New Orleans grew slowly from the time it was established to its acquisition by the United States. The original settlement comprised only a few hovels, a church, a warehouse and a public square situated on relatively high ground fronting the river, surrounded by practically impenetrable swamps. The settlers were tortured continuously by swarms of mosquitoes and were in constant danger of attacks by alligators and poisonous snakes. Their mortality was great, their ranks were frequently depleted only to be replenished by new immigrants, many of whom died soon after arriving. Despite all, little by little this village emerged into a town, better homes were built, a few public buildings were erected, and life became more tolerable. The indomitable courage, endurance and persistence of these people were further tried by two great holocausts which practically reduced their city to ashes.

The Chevalier Guy Soniat du Fossat, who was a witness, gives the following graphic description of the great conflagration that almost destroyed the town. He wrote:

> On Good Friday of the year 1788, a fire caused by the negligence of a woman who thought of proving her devotion by making a small altar in her house. She left several candles burning around it and went off to take her dinner. During her absence, a candle fell on some ornaments which took fire and the house in an instant was in flames, which communicated to the adjoining house, and the wind which was strong at that time spread the fire to the balance of the city, which in two hours was consumed.
>
> The powder which the merchants had in their stores for daily use contributed largely to accelerate the conflagration and rendered it more dangerous to those who wanted to save the remaining buildings. It would be difficult to depict the despair of the poor unfortunate persons whose properties had suffered from the fire; these unhappy creatures who, two hours before enjoyed vast and commodious lodgings with enough affluence to make one's life agreeable and easy, saw themselves and their children in a moment without resource. Some of them were obliged to take refuge in the woods without necessary provisions and clothes. Some slept without cover under the broad canopy of the heavens.

Governor Miro opened his house to all who were seeking shelter and he dispensed succor to the distressed families, caused the royal stores which had excaped the flames to be opened and he distributed the provisions therein contained.—All these cares and attentions gave the necessary comfort to those who had lost their belongings, but could not place them in the same condition they were before. Poverty stared them in the face and these conditions brought all the inhabitants to a state of consternation which was followed by the death of one-sixth of the citizens.

Eight hundred fine and commodious houses valued on an average at three thousand dollars each, were destroyed in that conflagration without any prospect on the part of the owners of ever recovering anything except perhaps the bare hope of receiving some day relief from the King.

Henry E. Chambers was of the opinion that "it is doubtful if such a loss proportional to population was ever inflicted upon any American city as that from which New Orleans suffered in 1788." The population at that time was 5,338. He stated that "856 houses were consumed by the fire that swept through the heart of the town from the front to the rear. Among the buildings destroyed were the Cathedral, the arsenal, the prison and a number of public buildings."

The bouyant spirit of the colonists immediately made itself manifest, for out of the smoldering embers of their former homes, a new city rose which again was partly destroyed in 1794 by another holocaust. This time, although causing great property loss and human suffering, it was not as devasting as the previous one.

Again the people were not discouraged, for with grim determination they again rebuilt their homes. Dire as were these catastrophies they were not without their advantages. A new city rose from the ashes, more substantial buildings were erected, a new style of architecture originated, a new cathedral, a presbytery, a cabildo and many stately homes were built which to day are a precious heritage. Even at that time despite so many faults, New Orleans had charm and distinction. Such was the city acquired by the United States in the Louisiana Purchase.

The only glimpses of the city as it was at the turn of the nineteenth century and during the next forty years of marvelous growth are to be had from the writings of travelers and from the files of the newspapers.

The city was protected from any possible assault by a rampart surrounding it, which included the area of what is now known as the *vieux carré*. There were five large bastions, two abutting the river, and three in the rear of the city. There were also five intervening redoubts. The city was further fortified by Governor Carondelet, who had a ditch eighteen feet wide dug around its entire circumference with ramparts of earth and palisades nearly six feet high along the inner side.

Major Stoddard who visited the city in 1812, gave the following description of these fortifications:

> Each bastion had a banquet, rampart, parapet, ditch, covered way and glacis. A small redoubt or ravelin was placed in in the center of each bastion, sufficient size to admit sixteen embrasures, four in each face, three in each flank and two in the gorge facing the city.

He noticed that they were badly supplied with ordnance, for few bastions had more than four or five pieces of cannon, but that those on the east and lower end of the city were pretty well supplied. He remarked that "they seemed to be mounted in places least vulnerable and least subject to an attack." The gates for the Pontchartrain road were formed of palisades from ten to twelve feet long. They were shut every night and after 9 o'clock no one was allowed to enter.

Stoddard described the barracks as having been located at the lower end of the front street. The buildings were of brick and one-story high with a shingle roof and large enough to accommodate 1500 men. They were built by the French and had a spacious arcade both front and rear. A large parade ground was between the buildings and the river surrounded by a brick wall. Adjacent to it was the King's Hospital. It was a military hospital dedicated to the care of the sick soldiers and sailors. It must not be mistaken for the Charity Hospital which administered to the destitute, then located in the rear of the city. Then came the Convent of the Ursulines, a spacious brick building, two stories high and with a shingle roof. It had a large garden, producing fruits and vegetables. In close proximity was the old Government house built by the French. It stood about one hundred feet from the river, a two-story building surrounded on all sides by galleries and arcades. Stoddard claimed that "this structure is indifferent, both as to architecture and convenience." In the same square were the lodges and stables of the regular dragoons, and the gardens belonging to the Government House. Then came the public stores,

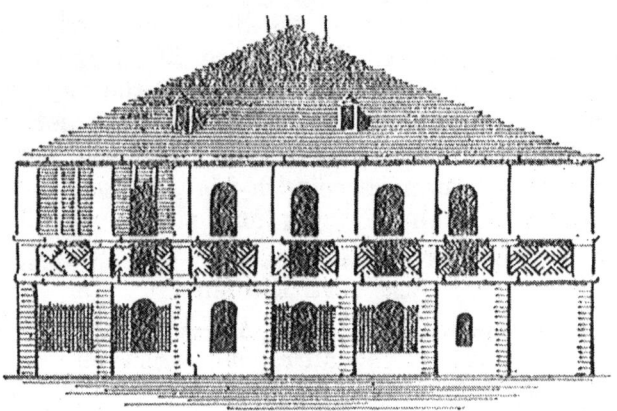

GOUVERNEMENT   année 1761

The Government House at the corner of Levee and Toulouse Streets. Built by the Franch in 1761 it survived the fire of 1788. Destroyed by fire in 1827. (From the Tanesse drawing of 1815)

---

also built by the French. These buildings were of brick, one-story high. They were 35 ft. wide by 200 feet in depth and on the opposite side were the artillery yard and ordnance department. Close by was the market. These buildings were among the very few to miraculously escape the conflagration which practically destroyed the city.

Major Stoddard gave the following description of the buildings built after the fire of 1794:

> They were composed mostly of cypress wood and generally covered with shingles or clapboard. Among them is an elegant brick house covered with tile. Several of them were two stories high and two in the same quarter three stories high. One of them cost $80,000.00 and the rest from $15,000.00 to $20,000.00. They are all plastered on the outside with white or colored mortar; this, as frosts are seldom severe in the climate, lasts many years; it beautifies the buildings and preserves the bricks, which from the negligence or parsimony of the manufacturers are usually too soft to resist the weather.

The Cathedral flanked by the jail and the Capuchin rectory was totally destroyed by the great fire. The church was rebuilt on its original site, together with the Cabildo and the Presbytery both originally two stories high and with a flat roof. The *place d'armes*, an open space with only a few shrubs, was ornamented by a cannon which gave a martial appearance to the drill ground. It was unattractive but presented an unobstructed view of the river. The sight evidently must have pleased Latrobe, for he wrote: "The public square which opens to the river has an admirable general effect and is infinitely superior to anything in American Atlantic cities, as a water view of the city." Such was New Orleans at the time of the Louisiana Purchase. It had then approximately 8000 inhabitants and 1000 dwellings.

Immediately after its acquisition by the United States, the city awoke from its lethargy and its growth was not only very rapid but phenomenal.

Even as early as 1817, Wm. Darby wrote prophetically that "no city of any great extent can easily rise in the vicinity of New Orleans; its concentrated advantages will allure population and commercial capital into its own bosom and prevent the increase of other towns within the sphere of its attraction. Some place on or near the Mobile River will no doubt become of considerable importance, but a ratio will exist between the cities situated on the respective streams on similar scale with that between the Mississippi and Mobile rivers."

Benjamin Henry Latrobe described New Orleans as it was at the end of the second decade of the nineteenth century. He remarked that the city has "at first sight a very inspiring and handsome appearance beyond any other city of the United States in

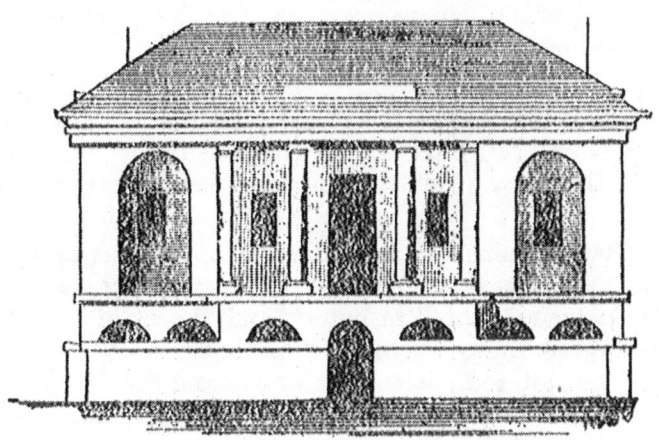

DOUANE   annee 1809

*The Custom House on Levee Street. Built in 1809.
(From the Tanesse drawing of 1815)*

which I have as yet been." He gave a very interesting description of the square (the Place d'Armes, now Jackson Square) and of the two streets fronting it, St. Peter and St. Ann, stating that the square was neglected, the fence ragged and in many places open, and paving stones heaped up in it.

He wrote that the Presbytery, which then belonged to the Church, was divided into seven stores with apartments above and that they brought a high rental. Besides the Cathedral, the Cabildo and the Presbytery, the most pretentious building facing the square was Tremoulet's hostelry. It was located at the corner of St. Peter and Levee (now Decatur). According to Castellanos, it was a lodging house and restaurant and one of the select hotels of that time, yet Latrobe affirmed that it was "by far the filthiest which I have ever inhabited, but my room is kept clean by an excellent servant I had bribed to attend me particularly."

The cuisine must have been excellent for Tremoulet had been a cook, upon which fact Latrobe commented that it was "an excellent station from which to rise to the dignity of the master of a large hotel."

The architecture of the Hotel was French. The lower story abutted upon the street, and there was an entresol where the store keeper lived or rented out to other families. Surrounding a court yard 20 by 30 feet, was a fine "range of apartments." Externally the house had a very pleasing appearance and Latrobe commented that "if the whole square were thus built up it would be one of the handsomest in any country."

"In the interior, the court gives light to all the stores, but it is reserved only for the use of the principal story and is entered by a porte-cochere. Part of the entresol is also appropriated to the use of the hotel which thus becomes very roomy and commodious."

All that remains today of the Place d'Armes and of its surrounding buildings of the first decades of the nineteenth century are the Cathedral, the Presbytery and the Cabildo. Even these have undergone many changes. The Cathedral was enlarged and its facade was altered. Both the Cabildo and the Presbytery at that time were two stories high with a flat roof, surrounded by a wooden balustrade. Later another story was added, giving them their present appearance. The Baroness de Pontalba demolished the buildings facing the square on St. Ann and St. Peter Streets, and erected the luxurious structures known as the Pontalba buildings, which were at that time reputed to be the finest exemplification of apartment architecture in the United States. Even the name "Place d'Armes" was changed to Jackson Square.

The residential section of the city extended from Royal Street toward the swamp. Latrobe noted that most of the houses retained the old architecture.

He wrote in his journal:

> Nearly 88% of the homes are one-story with high roofs covered with shingles or tiles which project five feet over the sidewalks which allowed the water to drain into the gutters, the height being hardly ten feet and the eaves often not more than eight feet from the ground. In summer the walls are perfectly shaded, and pedestrians are protected from the sun and rain.

The interiors of these buildings were simple, the two front rooms had French doors which opened upon the streets, on one side were the drawing rooms and on the other the chambers. Many of these old buildings which have resisted the ravages of time still stand with but slight alterations in the Vieux Carré today.

After the Battle of New Orleans the Anglo-Saxon Americans arrived in ever increasing numbers and overtaxed the housing facilities of the city proper. Already overcrowded this caused the expansion of the city beyond Canal Street, thus originated the

Street scene in New Orleans. Drawn from a sketch at the Louisiana State Museum made by Leseuer in 1828.

American section, or faubourg St. Mary. The houses were different for they were based on the English style of architecture. Latrobe stated that in the faubourg St. Mary and wherever the Americans built:

> ... the houses have flat brick fronts with a sufficient number of holes for light and entrance. The only French feature is a balcony in the upper story. The French stucco the front of their buildings and often color them, the Americans have red, staring brick-work, imbibing heat through unshaded walls. The old English side-passage house with stairs at the end is taking the place of the porte-cochere, which carrying you quite through the house, leads to the staircase at the back where it takes up no room from the apartments and is protected by a broad and convenient gallery.

Gayarré wrote:

> Until the year 1796 the City of New Orleans had never been lighted at night except by the moon, and had been guarded by occasional patrols only when circumstances required it. But on the 30th of March of that year, the Baron de Carondelet wrote to his government that, considering the frequent and almost inevitable robberies which were perpetuated in a city of 6000 souls by a multitude of vagabonds of every nation, he had as proposed before imposed a tax of 9 reales a year [$1.12½] on every chimney to provide for a body of 13 *serenos* or watchmen, and established 80 lamps; that the cost would be $3,898.00 per year.

The lanterns were suspended from a rope stretched from buildings diagonally opposite at each street corner. Mayor Roffignac reported that during his administration the city was lighted by 306 lamps. In 1833 gas lighting was introduced by Caldwell.

Karl Pöstl in 1826 stated that, although the inhabitants of New Orleans for 80 years could not venture 100 paces beyond its gates "without utterly sinking to the breast in the mud or being attacked by alligators, it has become in the space of twenty years [1806-1826] one of the most beautiful cities in the Union, inhabited by 43,000 persons who trade with half the world."

He wrote that in four years more than 700 brick houses were constructed, and he estimated that there were at least 6000 buildings, and that "because all building materials were imported, they were very expensive." He noted also that the houses were rapidly changing from the uncouth Spanish style to more elegant forms. He claimed that in the city proper "most of the houses are three stories high, having a summer room enclosed by blinds. They all have galleries. In the lower suburbs the houses were of frame construction with Spanish roofs." Pöstl stated that two thirds of the residences were superior to those of the Northern cities of equal population, but the public edifices were inferior both in size and execution. He further asserted that "the city has improved in an astonishing degree during the 23 years that it has been incorporated with the United States; indeed much more than any other town of the Union in spite of yellow fever and the myriads of mosquitoes; and it has become one of the most elegant and wealthy cities of the republic."

In the early twenties, Fort St. Charles, the last of the old bastions, situated at the foot of Esplanade Avenue on the site of the former United States mint building, was demolished and the ground on which it stood was levelled and converted into a public square, which was named in honor of General Jackson. The public square, or Place D'Armes, was decorated and fenced in with an iron balustrade. The wooden gutters were replaced with stone, and arrangements were made to flush them with river water. Many low spots in the city and suburbs were filled and the question of taking the town out of mud by paving was agitated. Many streets were opened and a town clock installed in the steeple of the Cathedral. Two new markets and several buildings were erected by the city. Eight fire engines were purchased for protection against that intractable enemy, fire—so constantly dreaded by the citizens.

The city had outgrown its limits, the ramparts which surrounded it were leveled, the moats were filled and the swamps were drained. The city expanded up the river, down the river and towards the lake. Plantations were subdivided into building lots and faubourgs and suburbs sprung up nearly over night in the surrounding swamps.

These were the formative years of New Orleans which set the stage for the marvelous thirties.

CHAPTER II

THE MARVELOUS THIRTIES

In the eighteen-twenties, New Orleans grew beyond its original boundary. The arrival of new people was so rapid and so great that the original city could no longer house the population. It was the boom town of the Nation; but its crowded condition did not become acute until the thirties. This marvelous increment in population was due to the influx of migrants from all parts of the nation. Because of necessity and inclination, the English speaking inhabitants congregated in the faubourg St. Mary. There Anglo-Saxons made their homes and established their businesses. New Orleans was then really a twin city separated by Canal Street. The two sections of the city were distinctly different in their language, culture, ideals and religion. They were foci of prejudices and jealousies, yet their rivalry redounded to the phenomenal advancement of the city. Each section strove to out-do the other in erecting new buildings, beautifying their properties and increasing their commercial facilities, even to the point of useless duplication. This state of affairs reached its peak when the city was divided into three separate municipalities.

New Orleans was built on a bog, and was frequently referred to as a city of mud—of impassable streets and sidewalks. It was not until in the late twenties that any effort was made to remedy that deplorable condition. In the *Louisiana Gazette*, May 19, 1823, appeared an article on the cost of paving the streets. It stated "large stones would cost $4.00 per ton and small ones $2.00, and the curb stones, fifty cents per square yard", and its issue of June 16, "30,000 feet of curbing was offered for 25 cents." The paving stones were procured from the Northern States and from Europe, and the sand from Lake Pontchartrain and Pensacola. Even the workmen were imported from the North. For a long while it was thought that it would be impracticable to pave the streets with stones because of the character of the soil.

On November 18, 1824, the City Council passed an ordinance authorizing the paving of Levee Street from Conti to Esplanade. Mayor Prieur reported in his message of April, 1829, that sidewalks had been laid as far as Royal Street. He recommended the paving of all the streets, and that the squares of Gravier, Washington and Jackson (then situated on the site of the U. S. Branch Mint) be "filled up, enclosed and edged with sidewalks."

In March 1828, the City Council passed an ordinance stipulating that "for a number of years the property owners would pay for the cost of the pavement." A meeting in opposition was held at Globe's Coffee House in Chartres Street. The legality of the ordinance was contested in the courts, and in April, 1830, the Supreme Court decided "that the City had a right to enforce payment of the paving already done, by the owners of lots fronting the streets that had been paved." Lislet and Soulé were the attorneys for the city.

The *Courier* of February 20, 1832, reported that a meeting of citizens of the 5th and 7th wards took place at the Planter's Hotel on Saturday the 18th, to consider the necessity of paving the streets of New Orleans generally; E. Morse, Esq., was the Chairman and Peter Laidlow, the Secretary. A committee composed of John Linton, A. R. Taylor, B. Livermore, Thomas Banks, F. Gaiennie, D. F. Burthe, E. Yorke, J. B. Plauché and J. B. Freret, was appointed to draft plans for "the most expeditious mode of paving the streets of New Orleans."

The *Bee* of April 23, 1835 reported that from April 8, 1932, to April 7, 1835, the following streets had been paved:

    Royal: all its length.
    Levee: from Ursuline to Esplanade.
    Gallatin: from Ursuline to Esplanade.
    Clinton: between Bienville and Custom House, Sidewalks bricked.
    Magazine: from Canal and Poydras.
    Poydras: from St. Charles to New Levee.
    Camp: between Gravier and Poydras.
    New Levee: from St. Joseph and Roffignac.
    Esplanade: from Royal to Levee.
    Canal: from Royal to Levee.
    Basin: from St. Peter to 126 feet to Toulouse.
    Custom House: from Royal to Levee.
    Barracks: from Royal to Levee.
    Hospital: from Rampart to Levee.
    Ursuline: from Royal to Levee.
    St. Philip: from Royal to Levee.
    Dumaine: from Royal to Levee.
    Bienville: from Royal to Levee.
    Madison: from Conde to Levee.
    St. Ann: from Royal to Conde.

Orleans: from Royal to Conde.
St. Peter: from Royal to Chartres.
St. Louis: from Royal to Chartres.
Conti: from Royal to Chartres.
Frenchmen: from Esplanade to St. Vister.
Victory: from Esplanade to Enghein.
Moreau: from Elysian Fields to Enghein.
Chartres: from St. Peter to St. Ann.
Conde: from St. Peter to St. Ann.
Conde: from Barracks to Esplanade.
Tchoupitoulas: from Poydras to Delord.
Gravier: from Tchoupitoulas to Levee.
Girod: from Tchoupitoulas to Levee.
Notre Dame: from Tchoupitoulas to Levee.
Commerce: from Notre Dame to Girod.

An editorial in the same newspaper, dated April 29, 1835, complained that the "present system of paving is insufficient and burdensome considering the quality of the soil, which being marshy requires preparation before being paved." It further suggested that "drainage was necessary, and that the streets be paved with wooden blocks as in London and other European cities."

The *Bee* also complained that the "paving now being done is disgraceful to the contractors. Not the slightest care is taken to prepare a bed for the stones, which are hammered down at random" and "it feared that these pavements as laid cannot endure more than a few weeks."

The city spent in 1835 nearly $300,000.00 and had, since its incorporation, invested nearly $5,000,000.00 for the pavement of its streets. It was said that the amount of paving laid during these few years was truly impressive and was a good indication of the growth and the fabulous progress of New Orleans.

The streets were well illuminated, and the Gaslight Company was charted, granting it the exclusive privilege of lighting the city and its environs. The names of the streets were placed at the appropriate intersections, and this convenience was stated to have been unequalled by any other city of the nation. Imposing residences, and splendid commercial and public buildings were constructed. In 1832 the new building of the Charity Hospital was ready for occupancy, it was located on the same site of the present institution.

Stately bank buildings rose in the 1st Municipality. Today the only bank buildings remaining are those of the Bank of Louisiana and the Louisiana State Bank situated at the corners of Royal and Conti Streets. Both edifices attract the attention of tourists, one particularly for its high vaulted ceiling. It is now an antique emporium. The other is a two-story building enclosed by an ornamental iron fence. The Planters Bank was located at the corner of Royal and Toulouse; the Merchants Bank of New Orleans on Bienville and Royal; the Improvement Bank at No. 153 Chartres Street and the Bank of Orleans on Canal and Exchange Place. In the upper section were the City Bank located at No. 13 Camp Street and the Commercial Bank of New Orleans on Magazine and Natchez ... The Union Bank building at the corner of Custom House (Iberville) and Royal has recently been demolished to make way for a commercial establishment. The Citizens Bank building was a magnificent exemplar of Grecian architecture and it had all the dignity of an Ionic Temple. Its ruins are still remembered by the older inhabitants. These buildings added to the grandeur of the city a century ago.

In the faubourg St. Mary, which a short while before had been a swamp and the paradise of hunters interpersed with only a few scattered shanties, there were being constructed at a rapid pace imposing residences and commercial houses. Camp and St. Charles Streets became imposing thoroughfares; the progress of the latter, to a large extent, must be attributed to the vision and the enterprise of James Caldwell. His theater, the St. Charles which was erected in 1835 at a cost of $350,000.00, was not only the largest, but the most magnificent structure of its kind in the country. It was soon followed by other magnificent edifices.

In the early thirties, New Orleans had many small hotels and boarding houses, yet it was altogether unprepared to accommodate the influxe of migrants which invaded it during the winter months. Lodging was at a premium and the cost of living during the winter was exhorbitant. These hotels were called exchanges, and there political rallies were held and meetings to discuss the affairs of the city. In the early thirties the two largest hotels were the Strangers and the Orleans, both in Chartres Street. The ground floor of the latter was occupied by the store of Judah Touro. The Strangers was built in 1818, and provided accommodations for seventy guests. The Orleans accommodated one hundred.

The need for new hotels was acute, and soon plans were made for the building of two large hotels, one in the 1st and the other in the 2nd municipalities. The construction of the Exchange Hotel on the same site as the present St. Charles Hotel, began in 1835, and two years afterwards it doors were opened. The original hotel was an imposing structure. Its architecture was elegant—a Greek portico with columns surmounted by a superb large white dome which dominated the skyline of the city. Constructed at a cost of $800,000, its size, its luxury, its elegance, its sumptuous cafe, its unexcelled cuisine ad its excellent service made it the rendezvous of discriminating travellers.

The magnificent edifice is thus described: Fronting on St. Charles Street were six Corinthian columns, 14 feet high, with a pediment on the stop and four similar columns on each side of the portico. In the back of this, there was a gallery, 139 feet by 15 feet, paved with large granite blocks supported by iron beams which served as a ceiling for the lower floor under the portico, and above, provided a delightful promenade with marble steps leading to the saloon. The entrance to the bar room was under the portico. In the rear was a bathing establishment which had fourteen bath rooms supplied with hot and cold water. There was a grand spiral staircase, surrounded on each floor by a gallery, which reached the dome where there was a veranda eleven feet wide, surrounded by a colonnade, from which an unobstructed view of the city was had. The dome was 46 feet in diameter and was supported by fluted pillars. The men's dining and sitting room faced Gravier Street. It was 129 feet long by 50 feet wide, and its height was 22 feet. It could accommodate five hundred diners. The ladies room was 50 feet by 36 feet. Besides there were drawing rooms for the ladies and for gentlemen, the former was 40 feet by 32 feet and the latter 38 feet square. There were nine private parlors on the second floor with bedrooms attached. The same accommodations were provided on the upper stories. It had 350 rooms which were supplied with 88,000 cubic feet of water from four large cisterns. It was elegantly furnished at a cost of $150,000.00. In 1851 the Exchange was totally destroyed by fire.

About the same time the Verandah Hotel was built opposite the Exchange, on the corner of St. Charles and Common, at a cost of $300,000.00

It was more of a family hotel and frequently served as an annex to the Exchange Hotel. It was renowned for having the finest dining room in America. Its size was 85 feet long by 32 feet wide with a ceiling 27 feet high consisting of three beautiful elliptic domes from which hung the chandeliers. A statue of Venus adorned the ladies private entrance on St. Charles Street.

Not to be outdone by the Americans of the 2nd Municipality, the residents of the French section broke ground in 1836 for the construction of the St. Louis Hotel on St. Louis and Royal Streets. The rivalry between the Creoles and the "Americaines" was such that one could not endure to be surpassed by the other, so a larger and more magnificent building resulted. Constructed at a cost of $1,500,000.00 it possessed great architectural beauty and was the last word in hotel construction. It was called at first the City Exchange. With a ground floor dimension of 300 by 120 feet, the architecture was Tuscan and Doric. It was planned to provide an exchange, a bank, large ball rooms, and stores, as well as the usual hotel rooms. The main entrance had six Doric columns from the portico to the vestibule of the exchange. There was a hall measuring 127 by 40 feet, in which meetings were held and private business was transacted. It was said that the rotunda was one of the most beautiful in the country. There was a side entrance on St. Louis Street which gave access to the second floor where there were several ball rooms.

The grand ball room was magnificent both in its size and decor. The murals and the ceiling decorations were unsurpassed in America. In 1841 the hotel was destroyed by fire, but shortly afterwards from its charred ruins arose a larger and finer edifice.

Banks' Arcade was another place of interest, located on Magazine Street between Gravier and Natchez. Its designer was Chas. F. Zimple, and the proprietor Thomas Banks. The building was three stories high and had a glass roof. The ground floor furnished offices for lawyers, notaries, editors, brokers, etc., as well as

At left—*Banks Arcade, built in 1833 (from Gibson's Directory, 1838).*

shops, a restaurant and a coffee room with a floor space of 100 by 60 feet and a ceiling 36 feet high. Adorned with paintings and engravings, this room was frequently used for political meetings and for civic discussions. It could easily accommodate 5000 persons. History was frequently made there. On the second floor was the armory of the Washington Guards and a billiard room.

New Orleans because of its Vieux Carre' stands unique among the cities of this country, for a city without ancient buildings, is a city without a history, a city without legend. In old New Orleans each portico, each porte-cochére, each patio, each narrow street, each crumbling wall, each iron lace balustrade, each gallery, has a history of its own, and enshrines the lore of past grandeur, culture, urbanity and a genteel way of life. Some of the buildings which have resisted the ravages of time are gems of architecture. There are some modernists who advocate the razing of the Vieux Carre' and rebuilding it with unsightly so-called modern structures. Let it be hoped for the sake of posterity that such vandalism will never occur.

The thirties saw the advent of the steam railroad. The first was the Pontchartrain Railroad. It connected the city with the lake. Shortly afterward the upper section of the city built the Carrollton Railroad to compete with the first. A resort and hotel were constructed at its terminal in Carrollton.

The canal, (old basin) dug by Governor Carondelet, which connected Bayou St. John to the rear of the then city limits, possessed commercial advantages because of the trade with the parishes on the northern shore of Lake Pontchartrain and also from the Gulf coast as far as Pensacola. During the thirties that traffic was steadily increasing and was most profitable expecially to the merchants of the city proper. The tradesmen of the 2nd Municipality, desiring to improve their facilities, organized the Canal Bank, which was chartered by the Legislature on March 5, 1831 for the purpose of digging a canal from the lake to the river. This canal (New Basin) originated at West End and terminated at Rampart Street. The original plan of connecting it with the river never materialized. Having served their purpose, both basins have recently been filled.

The hope was expressed in the *Bee of* April 7, 1835, that "New Orleans would equal New York in twelve years." It asserted that during "the past 4 years the most gigantic strides had been made in its onward career," and stated that "in the north western, or the American quarters, the waterworks were now in fair state of being put into operation". The *Bee* pointed out that the city was being lit with gas; that the land in the rear of the city was being drained; that the part of the port allotted to the steamboats was extended; that steamboat companies were chartered for navigating the Mississippi and the western waters, opening an inland communication by turnpikes of railroads with Nashville and then across to the Atlantic. "The operations of the Pontchartrain railroad were extended in order to have an eligible outlet with Lake Borgne and then to the Gulf of Mexico". It made the assertion that "There were few states in the Union where capital embarked, can produce more profitable dividends." It expressed the hope that the progress of New York would be arrested by "railroads hence to Nashville and the chartering of steamboats on the Mississippi."

In 1833 faubourg Lafayette (the garden district) was granted the status of a town.

That year the Belgian, Theodore Pavie, wrote that "what is most ravishing and most appreciable is to find shade at every step, and especially ice, which is brought in by sea from Boston, Philadelphia, Providence, in fact from everywhere."

Another topic of controversy between the citizens of the upper and lower sections of the city was the selection of a site for a branch of the United States Mint to be located in the city.

Let us go back a few years. The Congress of the United States on the 20th of April, 1818, passed an Act "authorizing the dispo-

At right — Merchants Exchange. Built in 1836 at a cost of $100,000. Dakin was the architect. The Exchange opened on both Royal Street and Exchange Place with marble fronts. At one time the U. S. Post Office. Used as the Federal Court Room. Walker was tried here. Now occupied by Gluck's restaurant.

sal of certain lots of public ground in the city of New Orleans and the town of Mobile": Section 2 reads a follows:

And be it further enacted, That the President of the United States is hereby authorized as soon as, in his opinion the public interest will permit, to cause the Fort St. Charles to be demolished, and the Navy Yard in said city discontinued, and the lot of ground on which the said Fort is erected shall be appropriated to the use of a public square and may be improved for that purpose by order of the corporation of same city.

That plot of ground was then converted into a park, the original Jackson Square. Little effort was made to beautify it, in fact it was one of the dumping grounds of the city.

On April 27, 1835, in a report of the City Council is the following:

Mr. Allard presented two resolutions to the retrocession of of Jackson Square to the United States. The first resolution was to authorize the Mayor to cede by a notarial act to Mr. Martin Gordon, on behalf and in the name of the general government, for the purpose of building the branch of the United States Mint, the ground known as Jackson Square, the privilege of using, which as a public square was formerly ceded by the Congress to the Corporation.

The second was to permit the general government to erect any other buildings on any part of said square.

Mr. Grailhe said by the cession of Louisiana, the ground in question became the property of the U.S. Government, and was then occupied by Fort St. Charles. By an Act of Congress on the 20th of April, 1818, permission was given to the Corporation to use the ground as a public square—the general Government retaining the right to vested property. During the last session of Congress, an Act was passed establishing in this City, a branch Mint, and in persuance of that act, Mr. Gordon had been appointed superintendent, with power to select a location for the site. Mr. Gordon applied to the member of the 8th Ward, requesting him to prevail on the City Council, the right of usage formerly granted. But in this renouncing the privilege of using the ground as a public square, they renounced the right of no property, for the property continues to be that of the United States. All that is required of the City Council is that instead of using the ground as a public square, they will permit it to be used for the building specified. As a public square it is of no use to the City; and its filth and infection render it a perfect nuisance, etc. Mr. Schmidt moved an amendment that the city should always maintain jurisdiction over the square, to whatever purpose applied. Adopted.

A resolution was passed in accordance with the suggestion

HALLE DES BOUCHERIES construite en l'année 1813

Washington Market (from Gibson's Directory, 1838).

St. Mary's Market, Tchoupitoulas Street (from Gibson's Directory, 1838)

French Market, Meat and Vegetable (from Gibson's Directory, 1838).

At Left—Meat Market, built in 1813 (from Tanesse's Map of 1815)

of the Mayor, to grant to the General Government the use of Jackson Square to build thereon a Mint, but to retain the use, if said Mint be not there built, and recover it should the Mint close operation.

The next day the following editorial appeared in the *Bee*:

The City Council resolved to restore the use of the ground now called Jackson Square, to the general Government for the purpose of building a branch of the U.S. Mint. Rather than let the ground lie wasted and unimproved. Congress permitted the Corporation to use it as a public square. Congress still retains possession of it and the right to revoke the use when proper and convenient. The corporation never had more than permission to use the ground as a public square, and only to use it for that purpose. The right conceding the using the U. S. property as a public square is asked to be renounced. Baldwin is the only member who opposed same in the City Council.

On April 29th, in the advertisement section of the newspapers bids were solicited for the construction of the building. It was built at a cost of $300,000.00.

The report of Joseph Pilié, City Surveyor, to the City Council on April 8, 1835, is most illuminating as it depicts the great expansion of the city. He reported that the "dirty footways and cross bridges which were indeed receptacles for filth, had disappeared throughout the whole of the incorporated limits, to make way for proper and elegant trottoirs to cover sewers and paved ways offering all conveniences." Streets were paved and sidewalks bricked to Claiborne Street, as well as to the Elysian Field. In the 2nd Municipality, new streets were opened and others extended, and the sidewalks bricked and streets paved. The city was extending in every direction. The report stated that the market in the faubourg Marigny was improved, the meat market was repaired and whitewashed and the vegetable market renovated, that the St. Mary suburb-market, which was located on the square bounded by Delord, St. Joseph, Peters and Tchoupitoulas Streets was enlarged by 127 feet. Baronne Street was extended across the basin Gravier, and "the stinking sewer created by said basin has been filled up", and Phillipa and Baronne Streets have been filled up from Poydras to Julia Streets. Ground was prepared for a railroad to carry corpses to the new burial ground at the foot of Esplanade Avenue. Better fire protection was provided by the purchasing of new fire engines and a complete assortment of ladders. Trees were planted in the streets and the "brilliant light of gas has in some of our streets been substituted for the common lamp." The suburbs were lit with new lanterns. The port facilities were increased by the building of new wharves. Fifteen were built between St. Louis and Enghein Streets. One in St. Mary suburb, above Poydras Street, 321 feet long by 100 feet in width, one opposite Notre Dame Street between Girod and Julia Streets, 300 feet long, another opposite Julia Street, 213 feet in length, and one opposite Enghein Street for the purpose of disposing of the garbage and filth of the city into the river. The neutral ground on Canal Street was beautified and enclosed by an iron chain supported by ornamented iron standards.

Pilié in his report stated that "the canal along Canal Street was widened and cleaned on a length of about eleven acres."

The first proposal for the building of a bridge across the river at New Orleans was presented to the State Legislature at its session of 1826. The matter was referred to the Committee of Commerce and Manufacturers, which reported as follows:

> The Committee of Commerce and Manufactures, to whom was referred the petition of Mr. Gerome, praying to be authorized by the Legislature of this State to build a bridge across the Mississippi is of opinion after having examined the plan and had several interviews with the petitioner, that his project cannot be put into execution; and that, whatever advantage the State might derive from the construction of so useful a monument and, notwithstanding the desire of your committee to see the project of Mr. Gerome put into execution, still they do not think that the Legislature of the State ought to act upon the petition, because the project seems to be impracticable, but also, because the petitioner has not been able to give your committee any information which might convince them of the possibility of his procuring the necessary funds for the undertaking.

Jn. Bte. Labatut, Chairman.

The specifications for this bridge called for stone construction.

The cultural aspect of New Orleans kept pace with its physical progress, for more money was appropriated for educational purposes, and the children were provided with better and more schools. New colleges were opening their doors and the medical college was established. Lyceums were organized, the Louisiana Historical Society organized, and many attempts made to provide an adequate library.

NEW ORLEANS — THE GLAMOUR PERIOD, 1800-1840

The population of New Orleans increased from 29,737 in 1830 to 102,193 in 1840, an increase of 243.7% and this accession in population was made despite the depletion of its people caused by two cholera epidemics and several yellow fever epidemics. Commerce made great progress in spite of a severe panic and depression which not only afflicted the city but the whole financial world. It was a marvelous decade.

What more appropriate portraiture of New Orleans can be shown than the word-picture painted at that time by the Belgian, Theodore Pavie:

> New Orleans is populated like a capital of Europe, as rich as a city of the Indies, gay as a town in Italy, and as brilliant as an Oriental one.

The City Exchange on St. Louis St. from Chartres to Royal. Later known as the "St. Louis Hotel". The first building at the right on Chartres St. is the "Stranger's Hotel" and next to that the "Orleans Hotel". (From Gibson's directory of 1838)

The Verandah Hotel on the corner of St. Charles and Common Streets. (From a drawing in Gibson's Directory of 1838)

CHAPTER III

THE LEVEE, THE ARKS AND THE STEAMBOATS

The levee at New Orleans was a p i c t u r e s q u e scene. The bustle, the babble of many tongues and dialects, the mingling of bankers, merchants and sailors of all nationalities with the Negroes and Indians peddling their wares, the slaves and the roustabouts basking in the sunshine waiting for boats to moor, a congregation of all kinds of people from every stratum of society and of many nationalities and of different colors, presented a panorama unexcelled anywhere else in the world. The scene, not only appealed to the eye, but defied the most vivid imagination. At no time did it present such a marvelous spectacle as in the first four decades of the nineteenth century. The levee was the mart where the business of the city was transacted.

Immediately after the transfer the port was opened to all navigation, both domestic and foreign. The former restrictions to the trade on the Mississippi and its tributaries were lifted. And in a very short while the city had a phenomenal expansion in its commerce. In ever increasing numbers, flatboats and keelboats, loaded with produce and other commodities floated down the streams and rivers west of the Allegheny Mountains to find a ready market at the Port of New Orleans. The levee was lined with tiers of flatboats, arks, keelboats and barges. The extent of that commerce is not known today because of the lack of statistical records, for it was not until 1812 that any attempt was made to appraise that tonnage.

After the Battle of New Orleans came the steamboats, although their number increased rapidly, the trade on the river was so great that it did not i n t e r f e r e with, or diminish the traffic of the flatboats, but on the contrary, for many years they grew in size and number. It was not until many years later that they were superseded by the faster self-propelled, smoke-belching gigantic, luxurious steamboats, which in considerable numbers churned the muddy waters of the Mississippi River. The only aspect of New Orleans about which the m a n y travellers, chroniclers and diarists expressed a unanimity of opinion was the levee. They thrilled at its sight, were profuse in their praises, and expressed amazement at the extent of its commerce.

Captain Basil Hall of the Royal Navy, a Scotsman, who travelled in America during the years of 1827 and 1828, observed that there were thirteen large steamboats lying along the banks of the river facing the city. He wrote that:

> Abreast of the town a little further down the stream, alongside of the levee, lay about one hundred very odd looking crafts as I ever saw afloat in any country—called arks—from forty to ninety feet in length and ten to fifteen in width. They were all made of rough planks, pinned together with wooden bolts or tree nails as they were technically called. The arks generally drop down the stream in pairs, lashed side by side. During the day they are kept as nearly to the middle of the river as possible, in order to profit by the strength of the current. At night they make themselves fast to a tree. Four, five or six men are generally found on each of these rude barks, for it requires several hands to guide them into the proper channel by means of enormous oars fashioned in a rough way out of straight trees.

He also reported that there were a row of Pride-of-India trees lining the levee facing the market.

During the year 1821, the records show that 267 steamboats, 174 barges and keel boats and 441 flat boats landed at New Orleans.

The flat boats and the keel boats were the Kentucky boats of that time, nicknamed "Arks", and were steered, but not propelled, by large oars. They floated down the river.

The keel boats were of light draft and long and of narrow beam, having a capacity of fifteen to thirty tons. On their return voyage they were propelled by oars and with favorable winds, by sail, and frequently by poling and even by tow-line dragged by men w a l k i n g along the shore. In times of high water, by "bushwacking", that is by edging the boat up stream by pulling on the bushes growing at the waters edge.

The scows used for traveling down stream were of various sizes and were covered with a roof.

The flat boats from Kentucky were about fifteen feet wide and from fifty to one hundred feet long. They were built of massive timbers and were of sturdy construction, holding from two to four hundred barrels, besides the live stock and other farm commodities. Some, again, were family boats, fitted with compartments for the accomodation of the ladies and their servants, but in the same bottom, and under the same roof were the quarters for cattle, horses, sheep, dogs and poultry. The boats were navigated from the roof which covered the cabin, and they were manned by Kentuckians and Tennesseans. In the early eighteen-thirties they were as long at 150 feet and with a beam of 24 feet and a capacity of three hundred tons.

These boats, as a rule, made only one voyage down stream. After having unloaded their cargoes, they were demolished and with the salvaged lumber, many homes were built and many streets and sidewalks laid.

In 1829 tug boats attempted to tow these crafts up stream, but that was found to be impracticable.

In that same year the first coal barges reached New Orleans, consigned to the Labranch sugar plantation, located a short distance above the city.

The first ferry to cross the river was a catamaran type vessel called a horse boat. The two keels were connected by a platform on which a horse treaded in a circle, thereby turning the wheels which propelled the vessel. This form of propulsion was soon displaced by steam.

The rapidity of the growth of the river traffic is shown by E. W. Gould, who said that by the year 1832, it was estimated that approximately four thousand flatboats descended the Mississippi River annually with a total tonnage of 160,000. In 1834 there were 230 steamboats aggregating 39,000 tons. When it is considered that approximately only two-thirds of these craft ever reached their destination, the loss of the boats, and their cargoes must have been tremendous, and the number of the boatmen and their passengers who perished will never be known. During the decade of 1822 to 1832, the loss of steamboats and flatboats and their cargoes, caused by snags, amounted to $1,743,500.00.

The gazettes were replete with news of steamboat disasters caused by boiler explosions, fires, sinkings by snags or being blown ashore by storms; but scant notice was given to disasters suffered by the flat boats. The only inkling of such tragedies was the failure of the boatmen to return to their homes.

To meet the competition of the growing number of steamboats, the flatboats increased correspondingly, not only in numbers, but in size as well.

Josiah Condon, a Londoner, gave his impression of the port as it was at about 1830, as follows:

> The first object that presents itself is the dirty and uncouth backwood's flatboat. Hams, ears of corn, apples, whisky barrels, are strewn upon it, or attached to poles to direct the attention of the buyers. Close by are the rather more decent keel boats with cotton, furs, whisky and flour. Next, the elegant steamboat, which by its hissing and repeated sounds, announces its arrival and departure; sending forth immense columns of black smoke that form into long clouds above the city. Further are all the smaller merchant vessels, the sloops and the schooners from Havana, Vera Cruz, Tampico; then the brigs and lastly the elegant ships, appearing like a forest of masts.

At the foot of the market were a large number of small boats which arrived during the night, loaded with produce from the various plantations from above and below the city.

As the commerce of the port grew to tremendous proportions, so did the city enjoy a phenomenal expansion, not only in wealth, but also in population. A graphic picture of the levee as it was in 1834, was written by both Richard Bache, the son-in-law of Benjamin Franklin, and Tyrone Power, Esq. Both were visitors at approximately the same time. Bache wrote:

> ... there were as many as 1500 flat boats at one time, along the upper part of the city, and opposite the center of the city, 40 steamboats may sometimes be seen, and they come and go at every hour. There were powerful steam tow-boats which escorted ships two or three brigs and two or three sloops. If one casts an eye down the river he may see a whole fleet, sometimes, coming up without sail stretched, or an oar manned, all carried along and that at not a slow pace, but by a steam towboat of tremendous power. It was the Grampus tow-boat, marching up, having two large ships grappled to her side, two or three brigs at a cable's length behind and still further in the rear, one or two schooners and two or more sloops.

He continued:

> This is one of the most wonderful places in the world. A survey of the river shows as far as can be seen, flat boats from every point of the Mississippi river, laden with flour, corn, meats, live stock, cattle, hogs, horses, mules, etc. Some full with Negroes, some with "Old Monongahela" whisky. Along the whole line are the owners of flat boats trading with the citizens, merchants and shop keepers. And then such crowds (especially along the levee which is opposite the market house) of Negresses and

quadroons carrying on their bandananed heads, and with solemn pace, a whole table—or platform as large as a table—crowned with goodies, such as cakes and apples and oranges, figs, bananas, pine apples, cocoanuts, etc.

The following interesting description of the port is from the pen of Tyrone Power:

> For three miles of this, the Levee is bordered by tiers of merchant shipping from every portion of the trading world, and close against it, those of the greatest tonnage, having once chosen a berth, may load or unload without shifting a line; a facility derived from nature that no other port in the world can rival.
>
> Along the whole extent of this line, situated below the levee, but at a distance of 400 feet runs a range of store houses, cotton presses and shops connected by tolerably well flagged side walks; and certainly in no other place is such accommodations more absolutely required, the middle space or street so-called, being, after a rain, a slough to which that Despond, as described by Bunyan, was a bagatelle; and floundering through a pond in which, are lines of hundreds of light drays, each drawn by 3 or 4 mules and laden with the great staple cotton.
>
> At both extremities of the tiers of shipping, but chiefly at the South, lie numberless steamboats of all sizes; and yet again flanking these are fleets of the rude rafts and arks constructed by the dwellers on the hundred waters of the far West; and thence pushed forth, freighted with the produce of their farm, to find after many days, a safe haven and sure market here.
>
> The appearance of the Levee during the season is most animated. At the quarter occupied by the great western steam boats, the landing and discharging cargoes seldom cease during the busy months, when each hour appears to be grudged if not devoted to toil. At night, fires marks the spots where work is most brisk and the warehouses along the line are frequently illuminiated from the street to the upper story; crowds of laborers, sailors, bargemen and draymen cheer and order and swear in every language in use amongst this mixed population; and, above all, at regular intervals rises the wild chorus of the slaves laboring in gangs, who, if miserable, are certainly the merriest miserables in the world.
>
> No scene is more like to impress a stranger with a full knowledge of the vast deal of trade transactions here in a few months than the prolonged bustle at a time when the rest of the city sleeps; and as he pursues his way amongst tens of thousands of bales of cotton that actually cover the Levee for miles, he will cease to doubt of the wealth which he learns is on all hands accumulating with a rapidity almost partaking of the marvelous.

The type of the traffic on the river did not change very much during the next ten years. The only difference was in its great increase. Didimus, in his book "New Orleans as I Found it" in 1845 wrote:

Hundreds of long narrow black, dirty looking, crocodile like structures, without moorings, upon the soft batture, and pour out their contents upon the quay; a heterogeneous compound of the products of the upper Mississippi and it tributaries. These rafts or flat boats as they are technically called and covered with a raised work of scantling, giving them the appearance of long, narrow cabins, built for the purpose of habitation, but designed to protect from the weather a cargo often of the value of 3,000 to 15,000 dollars. They are guided by an oar at the stern, aided with an occasional dip of two huge pieces of timber which move on either side like fins, and float with the stream at the rate of three miles an hour.

Their number has not been diminished by the steamboats. Hundreds are lost by sudden squalls, only two-thirds reach New Orleans and the Insurance Companies look upon them as unsafe bottoms. Kentucky, Indiana, Illinois, Missouri, Arkansas and the Republic of Texas, send more than 20,000 horned cattle here, also horses, mules, sheep, corn in sacks and in bulk, and upon the cob—apples, cider, cheese, potatoes, butter, chicken, lard, hay, grease, pork alive, in barrels, fresh and salted. Flour from Virginia and Ohio, whisky from Missouri and tobacco from Kentucky.

He described the flat boat as a . . . long narrow trough, 50 feet from stem to stern, with a beam of 12; the floors and sides were made with thick planks, doubled and cross laid and well caulked and tarred in the seams; the whole covered with a high raised work of scantling. A man of ordinary height might have stood erect beneath its roof. Small cabin in prow for the captain.

The keel boat in ascending a stream is propelled by means of poles from 20 to 30 feet in length. The boatmen ranging themselves in equal numbers on either side of the craft, thrust one end of their sticks into the mud and placing the other against the right shoulder, apply force sufficient to move the heavy mass on which they stand.

The boatmen travelled back on foot along the coast road to Natchez, or crossing Lake Pontchartrain to Madison, they started the return journey to their homes.

A new era was ushered in New Orleans by the arrival of the first steamboat on January 10, 1812. It was the steamboat *New Orleans*, a craft of 371 tons, with a low-pressure boiler. It had a length of 116 feet and a beam of 30 feet. James Hall in his book "Notes on the Western States", wrote that the *New Orleans* was the first boat built for use on the Western waters, and that she was launched at Pittsburgh, from which port she sailed in December 1811. Hall was inaccurate as to the date of its arrival, for the local papers of that time definitely set the date as January 10, 1812, which must be accepted as authoritative. The *New Orleans* was constructed by Fulton at a cost of $38,000.00; her owner was Nicholas Roosevelt and her Captain, J. Baker. The crew consisted of the Pilot, the Captain, the engineer and six deckhands. Upon reaching the Crescent City they were given a royal reception, and enthusiasm rose to great heights when the population realized what this new means of transportation would have on the future greatness of the port. A new era had indeed dawned in which a great surge of prosperity would make New Orleans the wonder city of the world.

Excursions to English Turn and back were advertised in the papers, the fare was $3.00, the *New Orleans* would leave at 10 o'clock in the morning and return at 3 in the afternoon. The advertisement warned that "passengers who desired to dine before that hour will kindly carry their provisions." This was the first harbor sight-seeing trip in New Orleans.

The Steamboat *New Orleans* then made regular trips to Natchez, covering the distance in an average of seventeen days. She was in operation for a little more than a year when on her upper passage she was wrecked by striking a snag near Baton Rouge. But the *New Orleans* had proved that steamboating could be a profitable business, for during that short while she showed a net profit of more than $20,000.00.

Hall claimed that "there is no account of more than seven or eight [steamboats] built previously to 1817, from that period they have been rapidly increasing in number, character, model and style in workmanship.

During these five years, optimism as to the ultimate practicability of the steamboat waned, further accentuated by the monopoly held by Livingston and Fulton which discouraged the building of many new steamboats. It was only when Captain Shreve made the famous trip, in the year 1819, from New Orleans to Louisville, in the incredibly short time of twenty-five days and back in forty-five days with the Steamboat *Washington*, that confidence was restored. From that time on, the number of steamboats increased at a rapid pace.

The second boat, it was said, to land at New Orleans, was the *Comet*, in view of the fact that the wharf register of the port makes no mention of it, there may be some doubt as to its arrival. Hall stated that the *Comet* had a capacity of twenty five tons and that it was built in Pittsburg, that it was a stern wheeler and had a "vibrating cylinder"; that it made the trip from Louisville to New Orleans in the spring of 1814 and after two voyages to Vicksburg, it was sold and its engine was used in a cotton gin.

The *Comet* made history because it was the first steamboat to be propelled by a stern wheel. It was devised by Daniel French in order to circumvent the monopoly of Livingston and Fulton, based on the patent held by the latter on side-wheelers, which gave them an exclusive control on all river packets. This monopoly became so oppressive that it eventually was dissolved by a court order. In course of time, the stern wheelers proved to be more effective for river navigation, particularly on shallow streams.

The *Vesuvius* arrived in New Orleans on May 16, 1814. She was constructed at Pittsburg and was a 340-ton boat. Frank Ogden was captain. He was subsequently replaced by Captain R. DeHart. She was a packet boat which plied between New Orleans and Vicksburg until she was burnt to the waters edge near the city. She was salvaged and later resumed her regular route for quite a while.

The *Enterprise*, commanded by Captain Henry M. Shreve, landed in December 1814.

The *Etna*, a 340 ton boat, left Pittsburg in March 15, 1815, and arrived in New Orleans on April 24. John DeHart was the captain.

The *Dispatch*, Captain John DeHart, was launched in 1815 and arrived at New Orleans on February 13, 1816. She was wrecked in 1820.

The *Franklin*, 125 tons, Captain Henry M. Shreve, reached New Orleans on February 10, 1816. In 1819 she sank near St. Genevive.

The *General Pike* reached port on October 2, 1816. Ben Booth was the captain.

The *Washington,* commanded by Captain Shreve, arrived on October 7, 1816. In March, 1817, she made the round trip from Louisville to New Orleans in 45 days.

From 1817 to December 10, 1819, thirty four new boats, according to the wharf register at New Orleans, arrived at that port.

An article in the *Gazette* on June 12, 1818 stated that "the steamboat ceased to be a novelty on the Mississippi and because of this, became a recognized agent of the commerce of the valley". It noted also that the Steamboat *Franklin* made the trip from St. Louis to New Orleans in about eight days.

From the beginning of 1820 to the end of 1821, forty more vessels were added to that fleet of steamboats plying between New Orleans and the ports on the Mississippi river and its tributaries. This traffic not only brought great wealth to the port but also prosperity to many towns and cities along these waters. There was a ship building boom in the Middle West where shipyards sprung up over night at Brownsville, Indiana, and other small towns bordering the rivers. Steamboats, flatboats, keelboats, rafts were being built by the thousands; there was an insatiable demand for these craft to carry the ever increasing amount of produce to be transported all over the world. Because of its geographical location near the mouth of the river, New Orleans was the small end of a funnel through which that enormous commerce had to flow in order to find an outlet to the sea. That port, which depended principally upon its exports, with the advent of the steamboat soon enjoyed a flourishing business in its imports, for at last foreign goods could be shipped to the North economically.

Gould reported that the S. S. *Sea Horse* arrived in New Orleans from New York, and the S. S. *Maid of Orleans* from Philadelphia on February 12, 1819 and that they were "probably the first steamboats that ever performed a voyage of any length on the ocean".

In 1819 the steamboat *United States* was launched at Jeffersonville, Indiana. Its owner was Edmond Forstall of New Orleans and Samuel Hart its master. It was the largest craft at that time on the river, with a registered tonnage of 645 tons. Its planking and timbers were of immense thickness, twenty inches of solid walls, so as to make her snag proof. Her engines were imported from England. She plied between New Orleans and Louisville. Because of her heavy draft and her slow speed she was a financial liability. In the year 1823 she was sunk by the caving of the batture where she was moored. It was not until 1832 that a steamboat of similar tonnage was built.

The fabulous increase in the population of New Orleans must be attributed to the advent of the steamboat. The migration was to the west of the Alleghenies, a new frontier was opening, new states were admitted to the union and many trading posts soon bloomed into cities. The more refined and cultured element came from the Eastern seaboard on ocean going vessels and packets, whilst the more adventurous frontier men braved the hardship and dangers of the long, tedious and perilous voyage down the Mississippi in flat boats, the chief means of transportation until the advent of the steamboat.

With each passing year steamboats were built larger, faster, and more palatial in appointment; thus began an era of luxurious travel on the Mississippi. The competition for the passenger trade became very brisk. Every delicacy the market could afford was served, and the cuisine was exquisite. The dining tables were spread with the finest silverware, glassware and linen, and not excelled by the most renowned of restaurants. The service was luxurious to a superlative degree. These magnificent steamboats were the delight of gourmets, the joy of travellers and the paradise of professional gamblers. The experience of one of these trips was one long to be cherished.

Basil Hall reported that the "passage from New Orleans to St. Louis, before the steamboat, took nine weary months of rowing and warping — now 9 to 15 days and once was made in 8 days and 2 hours. The S. B. *Philadelphia* made the passage in 11 days 3 hours and average of five and a half miles an hour". He mentioned that the passenger fare to Louisville was $35.00 and that he had two staterooms adjoining the great cabin for $120.00 which accommodated three grown persons and one child for about $10.00 per day.

At that time there was a diversity in the cost for traveling up or down the river which was evidently due to the disparity in time consumed, for example the fare from New Orleans to Natchez was $25.00 and from Natchez to New Orleans, $15.00

Because of the unmarked channels, the unchartered course of the river, the hidden snags, the log jams, the changing mud banks, the constant danger of fire and exploding boilers, there were many river tragedies and many lives lost. Today we can only marvel at the skill of these early pilots who navigated their craft under the greatest difficulties, groping their way through the dangerous waters in utter darkness, illumined only by the flare of burning pine boughs in iron buckets slung on both sides of the upper deck. They were men of instant decision and of iron nerve.

Didimus describes the flatboatmen of the Mississippi:

> ... strong, hardy, rough and uncouth, savage, wild and lawless. ... six feet tall, with broad shoulders and breast fatless but well strung and muscular. Their posture stooped and their heads project a foot beyond their breasts. They wear their hair long and shaggy which falls disheveled about their ears. Their feet and hands are very large. Their eyes are swollen, red and watery, due to their prolonged exposure to the weather. Their eyelashes are scant and their eyebrows long, thin and shaggy. Their mouths large and their nose large and prominent, having a "warm whiskey hue." They wear a large felt hat *a la slouche* with an immense brim, from which the rains of heaven have long since extracted the glue. It looks for all the world like an old lady's cap-ruffle on a Sunday morning They wore a linsey-woolsey jacket with short sleeves and trousers of stout Kentucky jeans.

These men from Kentucky and Tennessee were called *Kentucks* by the people of New Orleans, but they bombastically misnomered themselves "Half horse and half Alligator".

They were the first frontier men of the trans Appalachian migration. They settled along the Ohio and Tennessee rivers and their tributaries. They opened up a new territory in the primeval forests and along the unchartered streams or rivers. They were allured by the wild open spaces of a new frontier. They were the pioneers who contributed so much to the development of the great Middle West.

Long before the Louisiana Purchase these settlers cleared their land and cultivated it. As their numbers increased there was a demand for a market for their product. The only outlet was the Port of New Orleans.

The heroism and stamina of these stalwart river boatmen, who braved lurking dangers at every bend of the river, snags, mud flats, storms and the treacherous attacks by Indians and river pirates showed that they were men of steel and the finest example of the pioneers who helped to make this country great. The adventures of these uncouth, brawling, lawless, adventurous and whisky drinking Kentucks form a most interesting chapter in our history. It is the saga of the Father of Waters. The flatboat was the forerunner of the covered wagon in the development of the West.

The following verse by an unknown poet, which so vividly portrays the trade of the levee, appeared in the *Louisiana Gazette* of November 11, 1821:

Once more Brother Jonathan has opened his shop
On the Levee where he offers to sell or to swap
Free of license or rent, the whole stock of truck
For cotton or sugar, leaf tobacco or cash,
He has whale oil and whiskey & rats home & onions
Rye coffee, sperm candles, soil leather & spun yarns
Wooden bowls, patent bridles, gigs, harness and teas
And a splendid assortment of good white oak cheese.
Boston rum, bricks, potatoes, tar mustard and flax,
Clyster, pipes, Dandy cravats and other Nick Nacks,
Guilt watch chain and seals, not charged at too high rates,
Swords, pistols and dirks, fit for soldiers or pirates,
Smoked herring and lumber, brogans and goose quills,
Blank books of all sorts, mackerel, cotton cords and corn
 shellac
Domestic straw bonnets and yankee made bellows
Brads, bibles, hay, playing cards, ready made clothes,
Drays, ready made clerks, whips and plantation hoes,
Shirts, feathers, ploughs & warm woolen caps.
Oak staves and oak oars, bristles, tripes and rat traps,
Coffins, hoop-poles and house frames, boots, stockings and
 shoes,
Paving stones, nests of boxes, small spars, iron screws,
Shot, bale-rope and vinegar, brooms, brushes and hats,
Knives and forks, plug tobacco, fresh butter and mats,
Mineral water and muskets, gun powder, white beans,
Most excellent things when a man would raise means.

Tin ware & loaf sugar, shooks, codfish & saddles,
Peas, penknives, oats, helmlock, joist, bed-ticking, cotton bagging
Linseed oil, plaids and stripes, seersuckers, pants and chairs,
Tubs, fish hooks and pickles, apples, grindstones and pears.
Prussic acir, bran chocolate, cranberries, flour,
Wooden clocks that keep time by the minute or hour,
Lee's pills, cargo beef, nails, molasses and mess-pork,
Exchange from Boston, Philadelphia and New York,
And many more notions too numerous to detail.
All of which he'll sell cheap by wholesale or retail.

Exchange Hotel on St. Charles St. from Common to Gravier. Built in 1836. Later this hotel was known as the "St. Charles". (From a drawing in Gibson's Directory of 1838). It was burned in 1851, rebuilt and burned again in 1894. Again rebuilt the St. Charles Hotel still stands on the original site. The church at the left is the First Presbyterian Church which at that time was on the uptown river side of Gravier and St. Charles Streets.

CHAPTER IV

THE ADVENT OF THE RAILROAD

The difficulty of travelling to and from that large and rich territory which bordered the Mississippi River and its tributaries had to a large extent been solved. The long, tedious and oft times, very dangerous voyage by keel and flat boat had been supplanted by the majestic and luxurious steamboat. The time consumed on these journeys had been reduced by weeks and months and besides, the journeys were made in relative safety and in great comfort. But how to expedite the over-land communication between New Orleans and the large commercial cities of the East was a problem which constantly faced the merchants of the City. Public meetings were frequently held, suggestions were proposed and petitions were sent to the Post Master in Washington in the hope to hasten the delivery of the mail. The difficulties were such that but little progress could be made. It was not until November, 1836 that the possible maximum speed for that time was attained, the express mail traversed the distance of fourteen hundred miles from New York to New Orleans in seven days. And that was only achieved by post riding day and night at top speed. But such a journey was impractical, or it should be said, impossible for travelers. The journey had to be made by post-chaise, frequently over almost impassable roads through primeval forests, and over mountain ranges, with rivers and streams to be crossed — a journey which none but the most interpid traveler would undertake. There was only one solution to that difficulty and that was the newly invented steam locomotive. In a few years people had seen the marvelous accomplishments of the steamboats, and they wondered hopefully whether the rail road would prove to be the dawn of a new era.

Over night the population of New Orleans became railroad conscious. They were enthused when they saw in the following notice in the Courier of July 17, 1828: "The friends to internal improvements are requested to meet at Hewlett's Coffee house on Monday the 28th of July, at noon, for the purpose of deliberating over adopting the necessary measures to erect a railroad from the Mississippi to Lake Pontchartrain."

The meeting was held as announced, T. W. Montgomery was Chairman and Louis Daunoy, Secretary. N. Morse, Esq., proposed the following resolution:

Resolved: That a committee composed of six persons be named for the purpose of obtaining the necessary information and making the necessary surveys in order to ascertain the exact distance and the most suitable route for the construction of a rail road from the Mississippi to the Lake Pontchartrain and at the same time to ascertain as near as possible the expense of constructing said road and that they make their report to a general meeting to be called by the Chairman of this meeting on the 2nd day of November next.

Resolved that B. Marigny, Samuel White, N. Morse, Matthew Morgan, W. Hoffman, and James Hopkins compose the above Committee.

Signed: W. W. Montgomery, President; L. Daunoy, Secretary.

This was the first step taken toward the building of the Pontchartrain Railroad. The rails were soon laid and for a short time the trains were pulled by horses, and it is said that with favorable winds, sails were used.

On May 15, 1830, the *Courier* carried the following communication signed "Mechanic":

There is in the City, now exhibiting at No. 27 Conti St., a miniature railroad, with a small steam engine, with an elegant car attached, in which any visitors may with perfect safety take a ride. I have visited the exhibition and must confess I have never witnessed so interesting a work of art.

There is in it no fiction.—All is wonderful reality and perfection—and exhibits at the same time the almost deified genius of man and the incalculable advantages which may result from this particular invention.

This was the first steam propelled vehicle ever displayed in the City.

The following announcement by the Pontchartrain Rail Road was published in the papers:

The road will be opened for passengers on Saturday the 23rd of April, (1831) at 4 o'clock in the afternoon. Until further notice the cars will leave the City at 3 o'clock, half past 4 and 6 in the afternoon.

On Sundays, every 2 hours commencing at 5 o'clock in the morning. Tickets can be had at the ticket office at the head of the road. A car will be provided for free people of color.

The elegant car "Louisiana" will run in the morning, any day in the week, leaving at 6, at 9 or 12 o'clock, on previous applications at the ticket office of the Company.

Traffic was discontinued from January 4th to be resumed again on February 19, 1832 because of the necessary repairs to the rails for the advent of the steam locomotives. The *Courier* carried the editorial, "The Steam Car Pontchartrain," on September 5, 1832:

This beautiful machine was put in motion this morning to ascertain if the steam joints were tight. It passed playfully up and down the road in front of the Washington Hotel, under complete control as any Hackney Coach. The power of the locomotive was completely tested before it left England. In the ensuing week our City will be visited by this wonder of the age, and we doubt not the stranger will receive a hearty welcome.

In the same journal of Wednesday, September 19, 1832, appeared an article which stated that: "A train of four cars with passengers and mail were taken to the Lake this morning in $12\frac{1}{2}$ minutes, several ladies were among the passengers. The mail coming in was met at the lake and brought up in 15 minutes."

The first railroad accident to occur in this city took place on October 7, 1832. A Negro, whilst crossing from one car to another, fell and his arm was crushed by the wheels.

Another accident occured on October 9, 1833. A Negro carrying boxes was run over by the train and killed instantly. And on June 24, a Negro slave was crushed to death. The frequency of these casualties aroused the ire of the *Bee*, which called loudly for their prevention through the "interference of the public authorities."

In June 1835, Dr. Lorton was struck by the train and his leg was amputated at the Luzenberg Hospital, and shortly afterwards an employee of the Rail Road was instantly killed.

Because of the frequency of these accidents the press clamored for better precautions for the public safety and especially for an ordinance demanding that headlights be placed on the locomotives.

The first attempted derailment of a train took place on January 28, 1833. Two men were caught in the act of placing pieces of wood across the tracks by the engineers and were jailed.

An interesting item was the riot which took place on the train on July 29, 1833, about which the *Courier* gave the following report:

Last evening a gang of ten to twelve colored men, taking the seats reserved for whites instead of Negroes. The Superintendent did all he could, but without effect. A fight ensued between white and blacks, the Negroes made a desperate resistance, but were overpowered. Two shots were fired by the Negroes. The leader was taken, beaten and put in jail.

By January the rail road was in full operation and offered service for freight as well as passengers.

An additional train the *Creole* made her first trip on May 16, 1833, her construction was "on a plan different from the steam car now running."

The City Council at a meeting in April of that year, authorized the Pontchartrain R. R. to extend its tracks down Levee to Enghein Street and above as far as the Ursulines. It was stipulated that the roadway would lie between the river and the trees and a speed limit was fixed at four miles per hour. There was a $25.00 fine for the violation of that ordinance.

The following communication was published in the *Bee* of August 6, 1834:

> The Rail Road must resort to horse-power, both engines are disabled at one and the same time. The President of the Company said that it was due to "accident". Attempts to mislead the public ought to be exposed. The facts are: The tires around the drive wheels are worn out from use and up to the very moment of stopping, no steps were taken by the President to provide others. He was repeatedly advised by the engineer some months ago that the engine would not run much longer without tires, but so limited was the knowledge of that gentleman of the affairs of the Company, that he was under the belief, until one of the engines was laid up, that extra wheels had been included in an order sent to England a year ago. Tires of the very dimension required have, for more than a year, been advertised in the R.R. journals as for sale in Philadelphia; but are now ordered.

The fare was twenty five cents.

The popularity of the Lake as a pleasure resort was greatly enhanced by the facility which the new system of transportation provided. Bath houses were rented to the ladies for a fee of twenty five cents each and even furnished with curtains to be hung during the day to protect bathers being seen by persons on the wharf.

"The Lake has its charms, but the rail road system of getting there must operate very much against its ever becoming a fashionable retreat for the female portion of the community. The facility thus afforded persons of every kind to visit it, will soon drive from the Lake those who prefer quiet and seclusion to the noise and tumult of a mixed assembly." Thus commented editorially the *Courier* on May 24, 1832 and it further amplified: "Persons visiting the Lake will find the most attractive accommodations. No expense has has been spared in fitting up the Washington and the Lee Hotels by their respective occupants, which, in connection with the bathing, furnished a more attractive and pleasant place of resort and recreation than is possessed by any other City in the Union."

The keen rivalry that existed between the population of the upper and lower sections of the city was the spur which hastened the promotion of another railway in the upper district with a terminal in Carrollton. Consequently a meeting was held on July 7, 1832 at Bishop's Hotel. Maunsel White was the Chairman and N. C. Schmidt, Secretary protem.

The purpose of the meeting was to receive the report of the Committee as to the expediency of constructing a rail road from the Faubourg St. Mary to a point on the river at or near Macarty's plantation. The report stated that such a "project was not only expedient but of the utmost importance, and that ground was examined by Zimple, your engineer, whose plan of the route we have the honor to lay before you".

The same paper remarked that the Carrollton Hotel became an agreeable resort. For the entertainment of its patrons there were floating baths in the river, shooting galleries, bowling greens, a cricket club and a ten-pin alley.

In the French section of the *Bee* of November 18, 1835, appeared an article entitled "A visit to Carrollton." It read:

The steam engine is excellent, manufactured by one of the best foundries of England . . .

The Carrollton Hotel is one of the finest establishments we have as yet seen in the environments of New Orleans. The house is spacious with large galleries surrounding it which contribute greatly to the comforts of its guests. It is dominated by a supurb belvedere, from which an unobstructed view can be had of the neighboring country. The Deschapelles point appears in all its glory and the vast plantation of Mr. Lucien Labranche offers to the eye of the spectator a panorama of one of the largest cane fields on the coast. The Hotel is well managed.

On every Sunday there were concerts by the musicians of the St. Charles and Camp Street Theaters.

There was quite a controversy between the Directors of the Rail Road and the City Administration. The right of way proposed by the Company did not meet with the approval of the Aldermen. The proposed plan of giving to the railway a right of way along the bank of the river from Race to Canal Streets, was strongly opposed by the Citizens, and it was advocated instead that it be routed on Magazine Street from Canal to Race Street.

A petition was signed by Maunsel White, D. F. Burthe, Chas. F. Zimple.

The following committee was appointed: M. White, J. B. Byrne, D. F. Burthe, L. Bouligny, F. Delachaise, Ben Chew, L. Millaudon, J. Slidell, C. F. Zimple, M. W. Hoffman, C. Derbingy, J. Kahn, D. T. Walden, Capt. Chase, J. Baldwin, W. L. Robeson, Major Spotts and J. Maybin.

The Carrollton Railroad began its operation on Saturday September, 26, 1835. It was the second railway carrying freight and passengers to be established in the City.

On September 28, the *Bee* gave the following account of the inaugural trip:

Carrollton: Distance by railroad $4\frac{1}{2}$ miles: Passes through a level and beautiful country, very high and dry, and arable lands; and affording one of the most pleasant drives in the southern states. It passes through the limits of an ancient forest of oaks, particularly interesting as being one of the very few of its kind remaining in the South. Probably this was the wood visited by Mrs. Trollope as the "Cynthia of the Minute" although she does not inform us of her sacrifice here.

There were various improvements along the drive. The fare is 25 cents on the Pontchartrain rail road, it is $37\frac{1}{2}$ cents for the same distance and the drive to Carrollton is more agreeable.

Refreshment for two hundred people. We ascended to the observatory and were much pleased at the view presented of the Mississippi and its winding course; although we were surprised at the red appearance of the water.

An editorial in the *Bee* of June 24, 1835, sheds light on the difficulties encountered by the railroad. It said:

The Rail Roads in the upper Faubourg have singularly incurred the displeasure of the City Council. The citizens of these parts have but nominal streets allowed them for travelling—often impassable.

Facilities afforded for traffic by the railroads in Magazine and Baronne Streets are likely to be as great and serviceable as for travelling, and an improvement which can promote such facilities should not be lightly regarded. As there are various streets parallel to these of Magazine and Baronne, through which carts may travel, the occupation of those two streets by the Rail Roads cannot interfere with the public thoroughfares in any sensible manner.

A fair proportion of the revenues of the Carrollton railroad was provided by the transportation of freight, principally from produce of the Carrollton section. To further facilitate that trade the Company proposed the building of a market, this again met the disapproval of the City Administration. Again we are indebted to the *Bee* for a glimpse on the then existing condition. It reported in November, 1835, on the 11th day, that it was "puerile play of the Council, granting permission to construct a railroad in the streets and then ordering them to be demolished when the Company had suffered large outlays in their construction."

Shortly afterwards the tracks were removed from Magazine Street.

> The article continued: We smile in very sadness at the meaness of the request divulged in the City Council, to think that a company of American Citizens should prostrate themselves, their rights and property at the footstool of the corporation, where they have been previously reviled and trampled on.
>
> And for what? It acquired permission to construct a market house on their lot in Poydras Street, they were willing to cede their property in that lot to the Corporation. Did not the Directors of the Carrollton Rail Road Co., know that the Corporation has but to permission itself to construct one or more market house, that the Council has no authority to interfere in the legitimate disposition of property by any individual company, when such uses would not obstruct the streets or highways of the City, and the authority could constitutionally be given them to that effect. The Council cannot interfere in the erection of any kind of market houses that may be erected, or for sale of any kind of provisions. They have indeed the privilege to appoint inspectors of their own markets, or of any market houses that may be erected, to see whether the food sold is consistent with the cleanliness and health of the City; but beyond that the charter gives them no power whatsoever.
>
> Why then the Carrollton Co. should have degraded themselves and attempted to purchase the conciliation of the Council and permission to do what the latter have no right or power to prevent, it is to us a matter of surprise. If the Directors of the Company sometimes study their own interest, they will immediately erect a good market on their premises on Poydras St., conceding only the legal privilege of inspection without control of the Corporation.

Their railroad cars will be enabled then at all times to bring provisions cheaply and early to market, and if they form a proper landing at Carrollton for flatboats and pirogues, they can enjoy superior advantages and additional revenues.

Shortly after this editorial the Mayor objected to the building of a market on a part of the old Canal Gravier. He said:

Prospects of New Orleans have a more favorable aspect now since there are several railroads and canals in the vicinity and three more harbors on Lake Pontchartrain for steamboats and schooners to trade with the eastern part of Louisiana, Alabama and Florida, that of the Canal and Banking Co. for the upper municipality, the Orleans Navigation Co. for the Central and the Pontchartrain Rail Road for the lower

The *Bee* reported this on April 28, 1836. It also commented that . . .

. . . the railroad from the Mississippi river through the Champs Elysées to Lake Pontchartrain, in operation three or four years, had an income of about $100,000.00 annually — which however is unfortunately forfeited by the Company in consequence of the bad construction of their harbors and the enormous expenses attending its entrance. The same Company has been bound to construct another railroad from the City to Lake Borgne; and to effect that they have procured banking priviledges with an additional capital of one million. This will shortly be commenced and will effect a direct communication with Lake Borgne — the navigation of which has been so supinely, so shamefully neglected, although it presents many facilities and advantages vastly superior to those of Lake Pontchartrain for coastwise and foreign trade. But unfortunately the neighborhood of Lake Borgne lack energy, capital and knowledge.

The railroad along the coast to Carrollton has been completed, but may be continued to Bayou Sara — were it not for the ignorance and perversity of some planters through whose ground it must pass. This evil being however partially abbreviated by the grant of public lands by Congress to Company for the work, the object may be constructed and then the railroad on the Eastern bank between New Orleans and Natchez.

The Mayor also mentioned the horse car which ran from the continuation of Orleans Street along the Girod canal to the Bayou St. John. It was constructed by Mr. Arrowsmith and "appropriately leading from the prison to the grave." Its objective was to furnish transportation to the New Cemetery, (St. Louis No. 3). It also provided a funeral car to transport the corpses and the mourners to the graveyard.

The Committee for the investigation of the affairs of the Carrollton Railroad and Banking Co., on April 5th 1836, presented the following financial report:

Stock paid in	$828,175.00	
Expenses of the Carrollton Hotel	36,390.97	
Rail Road	297,12.15	
Purchase of Real Estate independent of track	89,010.75	
In Banking operation	408,488.13	
Receipts—Hotel	3,125.35	
Railroad	40,516.85	$43,840.70
Expenses		20,236.28
Net Gain		23,403.42

The railroad to Carrollton and its branches are in full operation, yet it is only the beginning of the great work, its beneficial effects are beyond calculation. It runs through the most commercial part of the City; gives life to the industry of thousands, and a tenfold value to the lands bordering the tracks.

Real estate would in itself yield an enormous profit on its original outlay and if during the winter months the receipts have produced upwards of $43,000.00, it is but reasonable to expect double that amount during the spring and summer months.

The report showed the assets of the bank:	$1,633,858.47
Cash responsibilities of the Bank:	1,154,720.84
Surplus within the immediate reach of the Bank:	479,125.63

The stock holders congratulate themselves on having the most favorable charter ever granted by the State of Louisiana.

(1) The payment of a bonus of $100,000.00 in yearly installments:

(2) The payment of $500.00 per annum for 10 years to the male asylum:

(3) The donation of the rail road at the end of 74 years, the benefits:

(1) Perpetual charter for banking operations.

(2) Exclusive privileges, under certain conditions of constructing a railroad from this City to Bayou Sara, with no other penalty than forfeiture:

(3) An exemption of taxes for three years.

The *Bee* on May 21, 1836, carried the following notice:

Prize: A premium of $500.00 is offered per advertisement, by the Pontchartain Rail Road Co., for any invention which will prevent the emission of sparks in the flues of their locomotive engines:

Will not the Carrollton Company make the same generous offer?

CHAPTER V

EXPANDING COMMERCE

New Orleans during its colonial period was altogether dependent on the bounty of the mother countries. Its population, because of the indifference and disinterestedness of both the French and Spanish governments, grew slowly, and the colonists had little incentive and not much encouragement to develop the agricultural resources of the rich land adjacent. The commerce of the city was stagnant, impeded by the restriction placed on trade with the far upper reaches of the Mississippi and by limitations imposed on communications from abroad. New Orleans was practically isolated. It was not until 1795 that a treaty between the United States and Spain was signed, conceding to the former the right of free navigation on the Mississippi River. Not until then did the products of the newly opened frontiers of the West begin to trickle to that port. An article, which appeared in the *Louisiana Gazette* of March 5, 1825, stated that "at New Orleans twenty-five years ago [1800] only two or three square rigged vessels, or three or four schooners could do all the business of the city, and convey to the market all the surplus products of the valley of the Mississippi."

It was only after the Louisiana Purchase that all barriers were really raised, and in a few years the growth of the commerce of New Orleans was phenomenal. The city became a beehive of activity, fortunes were quickly amassed, the rumors of which, frequently exaggerated, reached the four corners of the world and attracted countless numbers of fortune hunters.

New Orleans had no manufacturers worthy of the name; the extent of her commerce depended on agriculture, and what small factories there were scarcely sufficed the needs of the community, nor did they give employment to many of her people. These factories made cordage, hair powder and vermicelli. There was a shot tower, and in the vicinity there were about a dozen distilleries making around two hundred thousand gallons of tafia, (rum distilled from molasses) and a refinery having a capacity of 200,000 pounds of sugar loaf. Naval stores, ship timber, lime, charcoal, cattle and other produce, were brought in small schooners and sloops, from the Gulf Coast as far as Pensacola, as well as from Lakes Pontchartarin and Maurepas. That trade found its way to the city by way of Bayou St. John and the Carondelet Canal. Shortly after the Purchase the exports at New Orleans were estimated as follows: flour, 50,000 barrels; salt beef and pork, 3000 barrels; cotton, 54,000 bales; sugar, 4000 hogsheads; molasses, 800 hogsheads; also peltries, naval stores, lumber, potash, Indian corn, meal, lead, cherry and walnut planks, hemp, masts, spars, hams, butter, lard, peas, beans, ginseng, garlic, hides, staves and tobacco in carrots; making a total of 40,000 tons.

In 1829, according to Richard Bache, the following commodities reached New Orleans by river craft: 2,868 hogsheads of bacon, 13,472 pieces of bagging, 3,995 kegs of butter, 5,505 barrels of beef, 795 barrels of besswax, 15,210 pounds of buffalo skins or robes, 275,128 bales of cotton, 6,849 barrels of corn meal, 91,882 barrels of corn in ears, 157,323 barrels of flour, 110,206 kegs of lard, 142,203 pigs of lead, 2,940 barrels of linseed oil, 6,215 packs of deer skins, 159 packs of bear skins, 28,732 hogsheads of tobacco, and 4239 bales of tobacco stocks.

Flint observed that in the early 1830's the commerce of New Orleans was immense and constantly growing. At the levee steamboats were arriving and departing every hour and fifty of them lined the docks at one time. The newspapers carried the advertisements of forty, or more vessels, announcing their departure for Liverpool or Havre. From the upper reaches of the river there came from five to six thousand boatmen. Flint commented: "No place in the United States has so much activity and bustle of commerce crowded into so small a space in the months of February and March. During the season of bringing in the cotton crop, whole streets are barricaded with cotton bales. The amount of domestic export from the city exceeds $12,000,000.00 a year, being greater than that of any other city of the Union, except New York, and nearly equaling that. The greatest items that make this amount, are sugar and cotton."

The total imports from foreign countries for the year ending September 30th, 1831 were $9,761,588.00. The total exports were $27,170,651.00 of which $15,752,029.00 went to foreign countries and $11,418,662.00 to coastwise ports. In that year 36,132 hogsheads of tobacco, 568,271 bales (300 pounds) of cotton and 55,351,420 pounds of sugar were exported.

The tremendous increase in the business of the port depended mostly on the agricultural expansion, not only of the neighboring parishes but also of the Middle West. It may be said that New Orleans, directly and indirectly, acquired its wealth from two major commodities, sugar and cotton, all others were of secondary importance.

Due to climatic conditions and to the ravages of insects, the culture of indigo, the main money crop of the colonists, was subjected to failures resulting in financial losses so great and so continuous that its culture had to be abandoned. Attention was then drawn to the cultivation of sugar cane with the hope of converting cane juice into sugar. In 1785, Soles, a Spaniard from Terre aux Boeuf, (St. Bernard Parish) imported a wooden mill from Havana, and he was the first in Louisiana to successfully convert the cane juice into molasses. He subsequently sold his mill to Mendez who eventually succeeded in making sugar. As the venture was financially unsuccessful it was soon abandoned. Interest did not wane, for under the continuous prodding of the enthusiastic San Domingans, some of the planters, including Jean Etienne DeBoré, were induced to resume the search for a method of granulating sugar. DeBoré persevered in his experiments despite great financial difficulties and frequently discouragement and braved the taunts and ridicule of his critics, but his perseverance was rewarded. In 1795, for the first time, he successfully converted cane juice into sugar. The news spread all over Louisiana and planters turned to the cultivation of sugar cane. The State entered into a period of great prosperity, for within five or six years there were seventy-five sugar houses, and in 1800 over fifteen million pounds of the commodity were manufactured. It was the beginning of a new era for New Orleans.

In 1829, The Agricultural Society of Baton Rouge reported the production of 100,000,000 pounds of sugar, an invested capital of $50,000,000.00, and that 33,000 slaves were employed in the cultivation of sugar cane.

Along the banks of the Mississippi, both above and below the city, and on the many bayous, in fact wherever navigation was then possible, lands were cleared for sugar plantations. In what was often a former wilderness there arose the majestic residence of a planter, surrounded by an arbor of stately oaks and fragrant magnolia trees and gardens of exotic flowers. In a setting of verdant fields of cane, as far as the eye could see, each plantation was a settlement in itself. The life of a prosperous plantation owner was one of ease and luxury. Aristocratic in outlook, the planters had a society of their own, and moved in the highest social circles of New Orleans, where many of them maintained a stately domicile. They lived a glamorous life which has long ago ceased to exist.

According to Richard Bache, in the early eighteen-thirties, a plantation, having a capacity of 400,000 pounds of sugar and 10,000 gallons of molasses, required an investment of $170,000.00, expended as follows:

1500 acres of land at $50.00 per acre	$75,000.00
90 slaves at $600.00 each	54,000.00
40 pairs of working oxen at $50.00	2,000.00
40 horses at $100.00 each	4,000.00
Horizontal sugar mill	4,000.00
2 sets of boilers, $1500.00 each	3,000.00
Buildings of all descriptions	25,000.00
12 carts	1,200.00
30 ploughs	300.00
All other utensils, etc.	1,500.00

A capital investment of $170,000.00.

The annual expenditures were:

Provisions of all kinds	$ 3,500.00
Clothing of all sorts	1,500.00
Medical attendance and medicines for slaves	500.00
Annual losses in slaves	1,500.00
Taxes	500.00
Losses in horses and oxen	1,200.00
Repairs to buildings	700.00
Repairs to ploughs, carts, etc.	300.00
Salary of overseer	1,000.00

A total of $10,700.00.

With sugar selling at 5½ cents a pound and molasses at 18 cents a gallon, the gross proceeds were $23,000.00, which gave a net profit of $12,300.00, or 7% on the invested capital.

Depending on fluctuations in the price of sugar, the inclemency of the weather, the extent of the success or failure of the crops, the net profit of a sugar plantation was estimated to be from 6% to 11%.

Pöstl claimed in 1826, that failure in sugar crops never occur, but "the planter however cannot expect anything in the first year from his sugar fields, the canes yielding produce only eighteen months after having been planted."

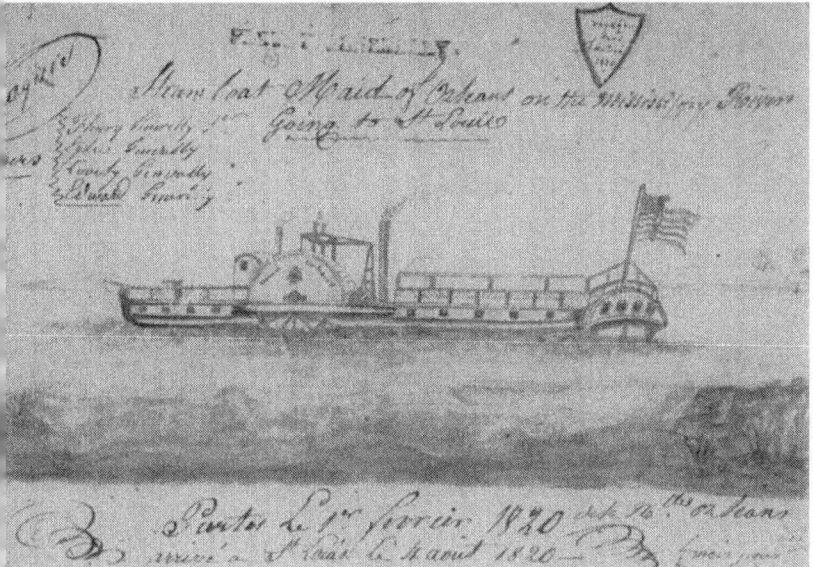

Steamboat "Maid of Orleans" on her way to St. Louis from New Orleans in 1820. This was an enterprise of the Generelly family, still known here. The "Maid of New Orleans" left New Orleans on Feb. 1, 1820 and arrived at St. Louis on August 4, 1820. She must have encountered engine trouble, too much high water or other difficulties to have taken such a long time for the trip. The passengers were Fleury Generelly, Eghe Generelly, Lovely Generelly and Edward Generelly. (Courtesy Howard-Tilton Library)

Dock scene at New Orleans with Latrobe's waterworks in the background. From a Leseuer drawing of 1828. (Courtesy of the Howard-Tilton Library)

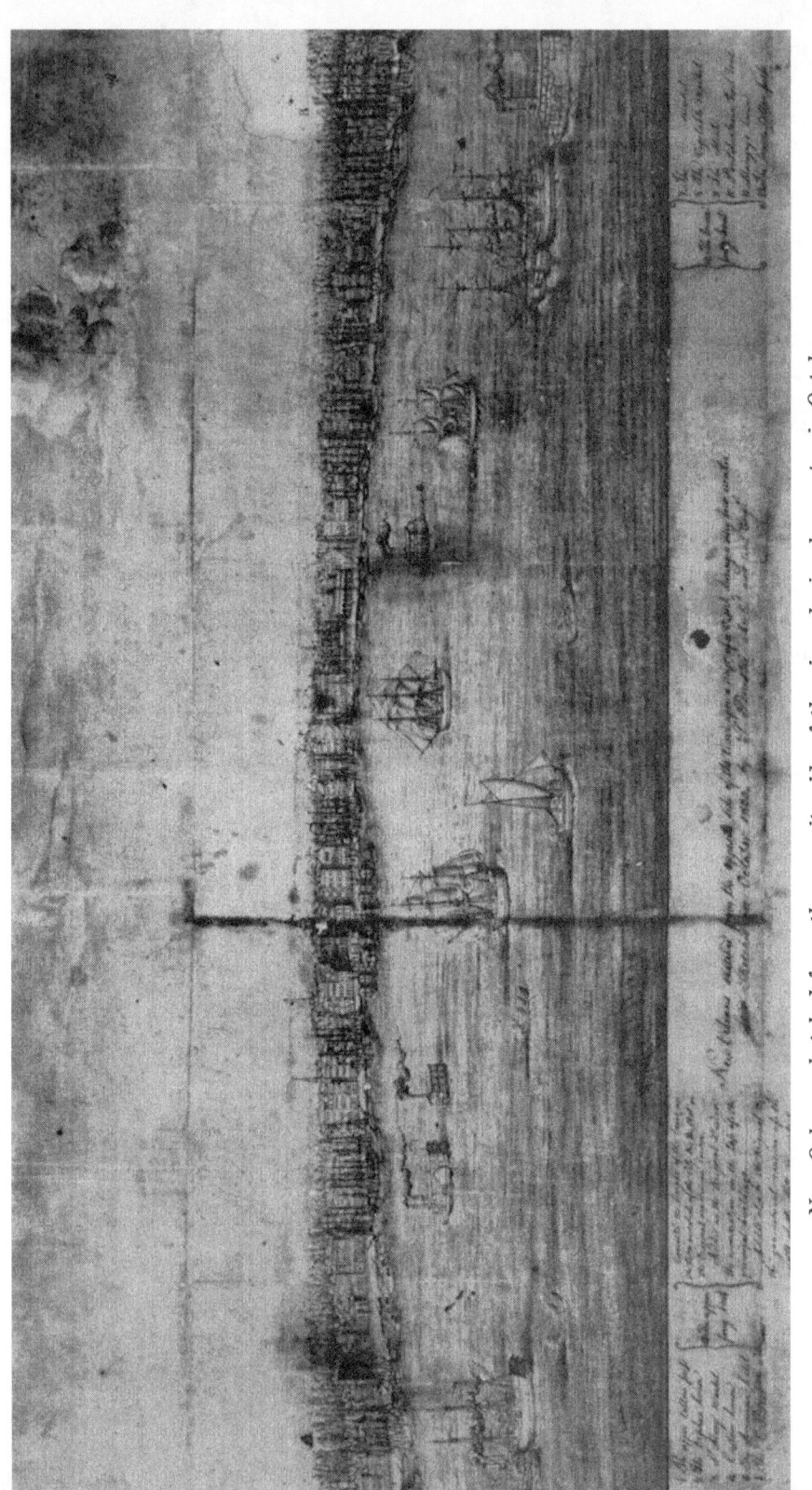

New Orleans sketched from the opposite side of the river during low water in October, 1833 by S. Pinistri, architect and engineer. The important buildings are numbered

The ribbon cane was introduced into Louisiana in 1825. It was said that it had many advantages over the old cane, "for it is larger and less liable to be injured by cold, being one month earlier. It takes also a firmer hold in the ground, and so better stands a gale of wind. Sugar from it is of a superior quality."

The cultivation of cotton made great strides in the early nineteenth century and was a dominant factor in making New Orleans one of the ascendant ports in the world. Cotton thrived in the warm sunshine of the deep South. It was easily harvested and crop failures were exceedingly rare, if any, a good market was always available, and its price was most renumerative to the farmer. It was a money crop. Pöstl tells us that a "cotton plantation may be established on $10,000.00." That 1500 to 2000 acres of the fertile red lands of the Red River Valley and those bordering on the Mississippi, may be bought for $3,000.00, and ten slaves for cultivating them could be had for $5,000.00. The first fifty acres can be easily cleared, thirty bales of cotton can be raised on twenty-five acres, valued at $1,500.00, and the following year the yield could be doubled, giving the planter a yearly return on each slave of three hundred dollars.

The following tables taken from *Niles Weekly Register* for September 17, 1825, show the wonderful increase in the growth of cotton, and a large decrease in the cultivation of tobacco for the years 1815 to 1825, as shown by the arrival of these commodities in New Orleans.

Bales of Cotton

Year	Surplus from previous year	Louisiana & Mississippi	Alabama & Tennessee	Mobile & Florida	Total
1815-16...					46,000
1816-17...					65,000
1817-18...					87,000
1818-19...					90,000
1819-20...					114,000
1820-21...		120,728	20,000		140,000
1821-22...	1,697	154,283		12,000	167,980
1822-23...	11,950	112,241	42,805	7,303	174,360
1823-24...	2,869	73,320	51,976	17,279	145,444
1824-25...	1,505	129,168	68,966	7,791	207,426

The total growth of cotton in the United States for the year 1824, was estimated to have been 571,000, and for the year 1825, 690,000 bales of 300 pounds each.

The following statistics taken from the same source, and for the same period, give the number of bales exported from New Orleans and the countries to which they were consigned:

Year	Great Britain	France	Total of Foreign ports	Coastwise	Grand Total
1815-16	18,840	1,164	33,921	12,079	46,000
1816-17	31,115	2,852	50,485	14,515	65,000
1817-18	50,959	1,298	74,314	12,689	87,000
1818-19	45,125	2,322	76,415	13,585	90,000
1819-20	64,950	1,274	94,234	19,766	114,000
1820-21	48,168	3,395	98,662	40,379	139,041
1821-22	64,457	3,844	104,600	51,430	156,030
1822-23	100,685	5,363	131,837	59,584	171,431
1823-24	61,624	1,076	97,124	46,819	143,943
1824-25	86,846	773	117,451	68,026	186,471

Governor Roman, in early 1835 reported to the Legislature that the value of Exports from New Orleans was $35,819,185.00 and noted that it was "almost double the value of exports from the whole United States in 1760." He estimated that exports for the year 1835 would amount to $40,000,000.00 including 500,000 bales of cotton, 100,000 hogsheads of sugar, 25,000 hogsheads of tobacco. This was the beginning of the reign of King Cotton in the South. Even at that early period, the number of bales shipped to New Orleans had increased fourfold, adding greatly to its prosperity.

That same article stated that "it appears that the amount of cotton grown on old lands rapidly decreases. Often it has been successively planted on the same ground for several years, but it becomes diseased and engenders caterpillars and other insects destructive to it." But more and more virgin soil was reclaimed for cultivation and its production increased astoundingly. In 1826 cotton was offered for 12½ to 13½ cents a pound. The price of cotton was not always stable, the commodity was subject to wild fluctuations, and some times the price dropped to as low as 8 cents per pound.

It will be seen from the following table that the total exports of tobacco both domestic and foreign, in eight year declined from nearly 36,000 hogsheads in 1817 to 14,413 in 1825.

TOBACCO EXPORTS (HOGSHEADS) FROM THE PORT OF NEW ORLEANS

Years	Coastwise	Great Britain	France	Gibraltar Spain	North of Eur.	West Indies	Total
1817-18	11,728	5,637	3,205	6,520	8,299	606	35,997
1818-19	13,547	9,086	3,440	2,962	6,171	867	36,073
1819-20	14,118	5,252	1,128	3,024	3,404	1,602	28,538
1820-21	14,624	1,339	867	6,018	4,037	738	27,623
1821-22	14,639	2,371	37	837	3,614	497	21,995
1822-23	12,666	6,506	40	1,145	8,409	484	29,250
1823-24	14,618	2,782	154	2,613	4,217	951	25,335
1824-25	9,136	2,521	76	2,355	1,102	223	14,413

It was estimated that about 10,000 hogsheads of tobacco were required for domestic consumption.

Governor Roman, in his message to the State Legislature at the beginning of the year 1934, gave the following estimate of the exports from New Orleans:

Cotton	450,000 bales @ $55.00	$24,450,000.00
Tobacco	30,000 hogsheads @ $40.00	1,200,000.00
Sugar	70,000 hogsheads @ 65.00	4,550,000.00
Molasses	3,500,000 gallons @ 20 cents	700,000.00
Western Produce		5,000,000.00

A total of $36,200,000.00.

The following year the Governor estimated the exports would total $40,000,000.00, comprising 500,000 bales of cotton, 100,000 hogsheads of sugar and 25,000 hogsheads of tobacco.

Most of this trade was transacted on the river front. The goods were exposed to rain and sunshine, and were bunched in lots with a pennant indicating the name of the owner. Only the most perishable goods were covered with a tarpaulin.

In the upper portion of the city in close proximity to the river there were large cotton presses, many occupying a whole square, enclosed on the four sides by huge sheds built of brick facing the streets.

The *Louisiana Gazette* of June 6, 1825 had this to say about the expanding business of the city:

> It has been well remarked by our respectable Mayor, that the great prosperity of our city, is in a great measure to be

Orleans Cotton Press, at South Peters between Terpsichore and Thalia. (from Gibson's Directory, 1838)

ascribed to the cultivation and increasing products of the Western country, and the rich countries on the banks of the Mississippi, and its tributary streams.

The upper faubourgs and the upper part of the city are covered with spacious, magnificent and costly buildings for the reception of every species of produce, it is there that merchants and others, chiefly connected with the upper country, have located themselves, and it is from thence that spring and must continue to spring, the vast resources of our flourishing city.

Yet according to the *Bee* of October 27, 1835, a "comparison of expenditures and revenues of the upper and lower cotton presses, the upper cost nearly double than the lower, yet it can scarcely pay the interest due on its debts less than one third of its costs—while the lower has made more in money and property for its stockholders than the dividends of any banking stock in the city."

John F. Condon, in his "Annals of Louisiana" appended to Francois Xavier Martin's History of Louisiana, rated the year 1833 as one of the most interesting in the annals:

The exports of New Orleans were estimated at this time to be about thirty seven million dollars, twenty million of which were the produce of Louisiana alone. Sugar was a large element in the productive industry of the state, and the continued prosperity of this industry depended in no small measure upon the tariff policy of the general government. The first blow to the agricultural industry of Louisiana was from the new tariff, providing for a gradual reduction of duties on foreign goods to 20 percent, taking off every two years one-tenth of all there was above that, as fixed by the former tariff. The minimum was to be reached, on the first of July, 1842. The effect of this change would be to diminish the price of foreign sugars, and consequently, that of the domestic article. The first few years but little alteration took place, and the sugar trade was in a highly flourishing condition. On the strength of the tariff of 1816, fixing the duty on imported sugars at three cents, the culture had been greatly extended and the crop had increased since 1828 from fifteen thousand to forty five thousand hogsheads. At that time there were more than three hundred sugar plantations, with a capital of thirty four million dollars, twenty one thousand men, twelve thousand heads of working cattle, and steam engines equal to sixteen hundred and fifty horse power, being employed in this branch of industry; and from this time to 1830, nearly four hundred new establishments were formed with a capital of six million, making the whole number of sugar plantations no less than seven hundred, with a capital of forty million. Louisiana already furnished half the sugar consumed in the country, and bade fair to supply the rest. The sugar planters were at this time looked upon as the most prosperous class in society.

Yet fortune did not always smile upon the sugar and cotton planters. Frequently wealth was dissipated as quickly as it was amassed. The financial depression of May 13th, 1837 was partly responsible for the failure of a large number of sugar planters, and according to the same author:

> Another cause of the existing distress was the new tariff, which had depreciated the value of American sugar in proportion as the duty had been reduced on the foreign article. At a former period the culture of cotton had been abandoned for that of sugar. The contrary was now the case; cane was destroyed and cotton planted in its place. One hundred and sixty-six sugar plantations were given up and cotton alone was destined to restore prosperity in Louisiana. The large profits that had been realized increased the rashness of the speculators and their eagerness to purchase raised the price to 18 and 20 cents. These prices were wholly unwarranted by the state of the markets in Europe, and the losses were immense. Numerous bankruptcies followed, some of great amount.

The following statistics of the exports and imports of New Orleans from September, 1804 to 1835 included, are those of Levi Woodbury, Esq., Secretary of the Treasury. Previous to 1821, the records do not show the imports.

Year	Exports	Year	Exports	Imports
1804	$ 1,800.363	1820	$ 7,596,157	
1805	3,371,545	1821	7,272,172	$ 3,379,717
1806	3,887,323	1822	7,978,645	3,817,238
1807	4,320,555	1823	7,779,073	4,283,125
1808	1,261,101	1824	7,928,820	4,539,769
1809	1,541,952	1825	12,582,924	4,890,034
1810	1,890,952	1826	10,284,380	4,167,531
1811	2,650,050	1827	11,728,997	4,531,545
1812	1,060,471	1828	11,947,400	6,217,881
1813	1,045,153	1829	12,386,060	6,857,209
1814	1,387,191	1830	15,488,695	7,599,082
1815	5,102,610	1831	16,761,989	9,766,693
1816	5,092,812	1832	16,530,930	8,871,653
1817	9,024,812	1833	18,981,377	9,590,505
1818	12,924,309	1834	23,759,607	13,781,809
1819	9,768,753	1835	36,242,226	17,516,049

The great increase in imports can only be attributed to the advent of the steamboat. Before, only a small quantity of goods could be transported up the river by keel boats then propelled by manpower and consequently the freight rates were exhorbitant. The river packets greatly reduced these costs, and made it possible for New Orleans to compete for the business on which before then the Atlantic seaboard had an absolute monopoly. Ballast was gradually replaced by cargo on ships arriving from foreign ports.

The following tableau gives a graphic picture of the growth of business in New Orleans from 1828 to 1834:

Number of	1828	1834
Merchants	60	272
Retailers	542	721
Keepers of taverns and cabarets	340	471
Brokers	46	67
Apothecaries	30	51
Billard Halls	39	55

The total revenue from taxes derived from the same was $55,506.00 and $73,285.00.

The trend of business is shown in the following table in which is computed the relative increase in the various districts:

Years	1828	1834	1828	1834	1828	1834	1828	1834
	Assessed value		Number of		Number of		Number of	
Districts	of land		Merchants		Retailers		Brokers	
1st	$6,989,897	6,960,300	60	105	476	397	46	12
2nd	2,649,650	4,260,300		4	63	98		2
3rd	1,339,175	1,419,800			3	10		1
4th	299,000	2,954,890				4		
5th		7,934,890		163		201		52
6th		3,809,250				11		

The boundaries of the districts were the 1st, between Canal and Orleans Streets; 2nd, between Orleans and Esplanade Streets; 3rd, faubourg Marigny; 4th, Bayou St. John and the lower limits of the parish; 5th, faubourg St. Mary; 6th, faubourg Annunciation, Lacourse and other upper limits.

The trend of business was decidedly above Canal St., for in a very few years assessed property values in that section were on a par with that of the original city and it had doubled the number of merchants and brokers, while the Vieux Carré maintained its supremacy in retailers.

The *Bee* on November 9, 1835, commented as follows on the great increase in business during that year:

> The quantity of goods of every description imported coastwise into New Orleans, during the present season, has been immense. The levee has been crowded during the last three or four weeks and there are now 123 brigs, ships, and schooners in port, four of which are British, nine Mexican, and all others American. Only one of these is a regular packet ship.
>
> During the present season, the supply of cotton as compared with the same period of time last year, is only half as great. The quantity received is 45,404 bales of which 14,700 have been exported.
>
> But the quantity of tobacco has been greater than in the same period in the last year; 1,497 bales have been received, and 756 exported previous to Saturday last.
>
> The sugar trade has been very dull up to the present. Cotton sells usually for 16 to 16¼ cents a pound; and sugar from 8 to 8¾ cents.
>
> It is now feared that the cotton and sugar crops will be under the average estimate.

In the early part of the next year, cotton was selling at eighteen cents for choice, and seventeen cents for prime quality. 146,852 bales were exported during that season, 63,167 to Great

Britain, 61,660 to France and 8,266 to other parts of Europe, and 13,259 coastwise. The stock on hand was 32,451 bales.

The current prices of commodities for the year 1822 were: Bricks, $10.00 to $14.00 per thousand; Lumber, $15.00 to $20.00 M. ft.; Cypress, $35.00 to $40.00 M. ft.; Shingles, $4.00 to $6.00 per thousand; Iron, $90.00 per ton; Nails, 7½ per pound; Lead sheets, 8 to 9 cents a pound; Hams, 10 cents a pound; butter, 14 to 20 cents a pound; Lard 6¼ to 15 cents a pound; Pork mess, $16.00 per barrel; Rice, $3.00 a hundred pounds; Sugar, 9 to 10 cents a pound; Molasses, 20 to 25 cents per gallon; Coffee, 30 cents a pound; Oats, 40 to 50 cents a bushel; American cigars, $2.00 per thousand; Brandy, $1.50 per gallon; and Cotton (prime), 16 cents a pound. The price of bread was fixed by law according to the cost of flour. In the spring of 1837 flour sold for $12.50 a barrel and bread 25 ounces for one bit (12½ cents), while in the fall of that year flour brought $8.75 per barrel and bread 34 ounces for one bit. These prices were advertised in the newspapers.

The Tremoulet Hotel advertised meals at 75 cents and board for $40.00 a month. Hot baths, 50 cents each or $8.00 per month.

Chartres Street was then the retail center of the city. Because of its many resplendent stores, the richness and variety of their wares, their artistic displays, their latest styles in ladies apparel, their gorgeous dry goods, their talented modistes, their superb glass and table wares and their exquisite jewelry, mostly all imported from France, visiting writers were fascinated, and pronounced New Orleans the Paris of America. Towards the end of the eighteen-thirties many of the stores moved to the lower section of Canal Street which soon displaced Chartres Street as the retail center of the city and Chartres Street began to lose its glamour. Little by little its appearance changed, and its stores, its magnificent cafés and its exchanges were converted into more prosaic establishments.

Royal Street was the main artery of the city and afterwards of the First Municipality, through which coursed the business of the day. It was renowned for its banking establishments, its exchanges, its hotels and its cafes, interspersed with magnificent residences and their exotic patios. To a large extent that street has escaped the ravages of time, its architecture is practically the same as it was in the beginning of the nineteenth century. Its fame has spread the world over, and today it is a Mecca of tourists.

Yet there has been a change. Because of the uniqueness of its shops, the type of goods sold and their unusual display, Royal Street may be said to be a resurgence of Chartres Street as it once was. By a strange coincidence articles sold in Chartres Street are now on display and being re-sold in the antique stores in Royal Street.

Bourbon, previously a street of shanties occupied mostly by Negroes, was soon transferred into an elegant residential section of the city, housing many of the socially prominent and distinguished members of the community. These former mansions recently have been profaned by becoming night clubs and establishments of questionable repute, and their illfame is widespread.

The Faubourg St. Mary is now what it was first intended to be, the commercial center of the city. Its growth in the twenties and thirties was rapid. There gathered the commission merchants, the exporters and importers, the wholesalers and the cotton and sugar speculators. This trade was conducted wholly by Anglo-Americans and as their wealth was easily acquired it had to be quickly displayed. From the swamps above Canal Street arose a new city in definite contrast to the old town — in architecture, in customs, in language and in culture. St. Charles and Magazine Streets were quickly built up with residences, public buildings and commercial houses. Unlike the Vieux Carré today they retain no vestige of the past.

Isidore Lowenstern of Liepsig, in 1837 observed that in New Orleans are found a collection of the most beautiful as well as the most precious merchandise from France and Great Britain, and there may be seen stores surpassing in elegance those of any other city of America, and that their stocks of luxury merchandise stand comparison with those of Paris and London. He also remarked that the tailors and shoemakers constitute a large portion of the laboring class in the French section of the city.

In the thirties women invaded the retail market, especially in the field of female apparel and notions. Among shops run by women, most in vogue were those of Madame Cochran, which specialized in styles for women, situated at No. 54 Chartres St.; Madame Fortunati's, ladies hats, No. 259 Royal St.; Madame Fryer, modes; and Mamade Brigot, notions. Madame Marion, formerly a dealer in fashions and a modiste of Paris with dressmakers from that city, had a store at No. 54 Royal St. between Bienville and Customhouse Sts., and Mrs. Docteur, specializing in fancy goods was located at 112 Royal St. between St. Louis and Conti Sts.

Many of the wealthiest merchants had been needy adventurers, arriving here without a dollar in their pockets. Many were peddlers at the market or on the levee, who in a short while acquired a considerable fortune.

The city was plagued by a swarm of retailers and vendors of notions, who sold their goods without paying either a license or store rent. Their manner of doing business drew numerous protests in the newspapers. They would flock here in the middle of autumn and vanish at the approach of summer.

The commission trade was very lucrative, especially for the French, English and Spanish traders, many of whom had an income of more than fifty thousand dollars a year. The bulk of that business was transacted from the late fall to late spring. The port was then a beehive of activity. The sugar season was in full blast, cotton had been picked, tobacco ready for shipment, and the crops for the North were being gathered and loaded on river craft, headed for New Orleans. In June, and even a little earlier, the port was practically deserted, all activities were reduced to a minimum, the yearly exodus had begun, and the steamboats were crowded with passengers leaving New Orleans.

Many of these traders returned home wealthy, others impoverished, but despite their frustrations, most had an overwhelming desire to return the next season to recoup their losses. The boatmen had demolished their barges and were returning to their homes, some with their hard earned cash, and too frequently others with only a memory of good times in New Orleans. After squandering their money in gaming houses, they were often robbed or even duped by unscrupulous adventurers who infested the city. They began their long overland trek to the far North, frequently to be waylaid, robbed or even assassinated by gangs of highwaymen who ambushed them along the trail.

None but the most intrepid visitors would remain to brave the impending dangers of a yellow fever epidemic. Many of those who stayed died of the scourge, but a large number of those who recovered from the disease of the black vomit made New Orleans their domicile.

In summer serenity prevailed, the streets were deserted, business was at a standstill and the native population resumed its even tenor of life.

CHAPTER VI

BANKS, BOOMS AND DEPRESSIONS

During the first forty years of the nineteenth century, New Orleans enjoyed an unprecedented growth both in population and commerce. Yet during that period of boom there were times of depression and even of panic, in which the credit of the city was greatly shaken, and ruin faced many of the most stable financial institutions. Money became scarce, the rate of interest, even with the best collateral rose to prohibitive heights, and loans were only begrudgingly granted, if made at all. Many fortunes were liquidated overnight, bankruptcies were a daily occurence, property values were greatly depressed, and destitution because of the scarcity of employment was acute. Millionaires of one year became the clerks of the next, and suicides were reported in the newspapers. These depressions were attributed to unrest, not only in the Union, but in Europe; to over-capitalization and its concomitant lowering of credit security; to the greed of speculators and to over-expansion of business. However, these periods of depression, though frequent, were of short duration. The bouyant temperament, which characterized the inhabitants of New Orleans, helped them surmount the most dire calamities. They realized that hard times would be followed by better times and that by redoubled efforts they would soon recoup their financial losses.

Shortly after the Louisiana Purchase the depreciation of the currency caused great uneasiness and distrust on the part of the inhabitants. The Spanish certificates (liberanzas), the then medium of exchange, had greatly depreciated. Their worth, no matter how small, was uncertain, and the use of American currency for liberanzas was confusing to the inhabitants and did not immediately gain their confidence. Martin in his History of Louisiana gives the following account of how that difficulty was met:

> Considerable distress was felt from the great scarcity of a circulating medium. Silver was no longer brought from Vera Cruz by the government, and the Spaniards were not very anxious to redeem a large quantity of Liberanzas, or certificates, which they had left afloat in the province, and which were greatly depreciated. Claiborne sought a remedy for this evil by the establishment of the Louisiana Bank, the extension of the capital of which, was allowed to two millions of dollars; but the

people being absolutely unacquainted with institutions of this kind, heretofore emitted in the province, were tardy in according their confidence to the Bank.

A petition signed by nearly everyone in the city and the territory, was presented to Governor Claiborne requesting him to institute a bank with Evan Jones as president and Paul Lanusse, a Creole, as secretary. An ordinance was passed with Claiborne's approval on March 12, 1804, chartering the Bank of Louisiana, the first bank to be established in New Orleans, stipulating that it should issue one thousand shares, that its board should comprise fifteen members, and its charter should run for fifteen years. This bank did not meet with the approval of the National Government, for Claiborne was censured by the United States Secretary of the Treasury for having established it.

The Louisiana Bank was formally organized in January, 1805. The president was Julien Poydras; cashier, Stephen Zacharie; and the tellers, James Fitzgerald and John Thibaut. The directors were Paul Lanusse, James Pitot, Julien Poydras, Daniel Clark, Michel Fortier, John Soulie, Thomas Harman, Thomas Urquhart, William Donaldson, John F. Merieult, Francois Duplessis, James Garrick, John McDonogh, John B. Labatut and Nicholas Girod. The directors were divided among the American and French elements with the latter predominating, as they were a majority of the merchants and business men of that time. A more representative list of directors could not be found in the city. Julien Poydras was the wealthiest man from among the Creoles and John McDonogh of the Americans.

The Louisiana Bank should have succeeded, but in spite of its important directorate, there was mismanagement and it was forced into liquidation a year before its charter expired.

In 1805, the same year the Louisiana Bank began operations, the United States Bank of Philadelphia opened a branch in New Orleans with Evan Jones, the original president of the Louisiana Bank, as president. The local directors were: Evan Jones, Benjamin Morgan, Thomas Callender, John Palfrey, Whitten Evans J. B. Provost, William Brown, Cavalier Jennier, Beverly Chew, John W. Gurley, Joseph McNeil, William Kenner and George T. Phillips. This was distinctly an American institution which paid no attention to the French population as far as the directors were concerned. This bank came to an end in 1811 when Congress refused to renew the charter of the Bank of the United States.

The Planters' Bank and the Orleans Bank, were chartered by the last Territorial Legislature at its sessions of January, 1811. The charter of the Planters' Bank was to remain in effect for fifteen years, and its authorized capital was to be $600,000.00 payable in specie. The capital of the Orleans Bank to be $500,000.00 "payable in lawful money or notes payable to the directors."

The late 1810 was a period of financial uncertainty and difficulty; but not one of major catastrophy. Victor Debouchel, a contemporary, wrote an excellent depiction of the prevailing conditions:

> The directors of the banks, the merchants and the speculators, committed themselves to gigantic enterprises, some were successful and again others failed and suffered considerable losses. In order to cover up the deficits, and to forestall bankruptcies, a large amount of paper money was issued, which became so discredited, that when the First Bank of the United States, asked in 1811 that Congress renew its Charter, it was refused. Many years of tribulations and bankruptcies have since passed. The sugar industry of Louisiana because of its prosperity was practically not affected. Agriculture gained new strength, the planters from other states, attracted by the fertility of the soil, arrived in crowds with numerous slaves. The value of the land increased each day, sugar commanded a lucrative price, it was the principal crop of Louisiana. The value of the sugar houses reached in a short while, forty million dollars. Despite that state of agricultural prosperity, commerce did not rise from its lethargy till only at the end of 1819. Only then there was a rebirth of confidence, which, is so timid and prudent after having been once betrayed.

This "rebirth of confidence" was of short duration for the *Louisiana Gazette* in an editorial entitled "employment" in its issue of October 3, 1820, did not recollect any period when so many persons were without employment, not only mechanics and farmers, but clerks and professionals. It explained the causes for that lack of employment:

> The great resources of the country and the active springs of commerce induce many of the early settlers to become merchants; and such has been the success of our policy, that more persons have embarked in commerce than could possibly succeed. A few merchants, it is true, made great fortunes, and this has led many others to experiment, with the same view; hence we have double the number we require.
>
> Professional men have also increased in ratio not called for by the extent of the population, and thus do we account for

so many persons who are idle, and have not the capacity to earn their living.

Heads of families, in selecting pursuits for their children, have heretofore been governed by a false pride, the effects of which are now severely felt. They have with a laudable spirit, endeavored to give their children a good education, which is beneficial whatever may be of their future career, but in the avidity of gain, persuance of what is miscalled a genteel profession, they make their children, clerks, merchants, lawyers, and physicians, and the consequence is, that we are now overstocked with them. These genteel professions produce nothing; men are idle, their families and themselves in want, while the shoemaker, tailor, blacksmith, carpenter and mason have sufficient work to do, not only to support their families, but to lay up something for a future day. This charm must be broken — men must consider the mechanic art as genteel, and parents must bind their sons to trades, instead of making gentlemen of them. The pursuits of agriculture are equally neglected. Our country abounds in rich and unimproved lands, and thousands of acres are selling for a small sum, and young men with industry, economy and perseverance, may make a comfortable living out of them. Their farms can produce all the essentials of life, and luxuries they must forego. It is useless to cry out against the times, without an effort made to lighten our burdens.

I fear the time will grow worse, and the epoch must be expected and be provided for, by giving a spur to industry, and every encouragement to economy.

We can produce everything our wants require, and men who are pursuing losing games, in hope that the time will mend, had better stop at once, and change the nature of their pursuits. Many persons who are unemployed in cities, will find it to their interest to remove to the country, and try a different pursuit.

According to the *Louisiana Gazette* of October, 1820, the exports of the first nine months of 1820 were $10,302,972.00, as compared to those of the first nine months of 1818, $15,365,227.00, a loss of about 33 percent. This loss was attributed to the decrease in the price of cotton by more than one-half, and a proportionate depreciation in the price of tobacco and flour.

Again in the same gazette, on November 18 of the same year, appeared the following written by "Feuillton", in French:

On the Levee, three breads for a picayune. The theatres are empty. Everywhere you hear of proverty, of failure and of misery. No one pays, it is said, and how can this happen?

The country did not suffer a calamity, the rich proprietor is not any poorer than in former years, the crops have not failed, yet no one has a cent! Yet, let's wait for the carnival and

and the balls, the hidden money will show itself and the powerful incentive for pleasure will return in commerce.

The Louisiana Bank got into difficulties by 1819, and on March 3rd of that year the State Legislature passed an act to compel its liquidation to be completed by March 13, 1822, later extended to March 1823, when it was completed.

An explanation of the troubles of the Louisiana Bank, based upon a report of the committee which investigated the affairs of the bank of date of May 29th, 1820, was published in an article in the *Louisiana Gazette* on July 20, 1820:

> The disappearance of a considerable capital from the Louisiana Bank during the period when that institution and those who administered it were in the full enjoyment of public confidence, and the sparing light thrown by the members of the late board on the facts, which have lately been disclosed to the stockholders; are circumstances well calculated to excite suspicion, and to justify the inference that a mismanagement of some kind, either neglect or fraud or perhaps both, might be traced to its doors.
>
> Stockholders wanted information, but individuals, whose spotless reputation were momentarily compelled to meet single handed the breath of suspicion or the eye of reproach, wanted justice.
>
> It commenced on the same day that gave birth to the Louisiana Bank, and like the deformities of the human body, has grown up with a vicious organization. Skillful hands might have checked its progress, but skill is the result of perseverance, study and a long experience only, and the establishment of a bank at the time when the Charter of the Louisiana Bank was granted, proved as great a novelty as the principle and civil forms of our blessed constitution were, when this territory was annexed to the great American Family. The Louisiana Bank began its operation in the month of April, 1805, Mr. Julian Poydras being appointed President, and the late Mr. S. Zacharie, cashier. The committee have heard it stated from an authority entitled to credit that a useful offer of assistance in organizing its books had been made by an experienced hand, but owing probably to feelings of ill-directed pride, or of petty jealousies from which new committees are so seldom free. Mr. Zacharie was not permitted to avail himself of it, and he had to look for precedents to his own experience, which the result will show, was but limited.
>
> At the death of Mr. Zacharie, an examination of the situation of the Bank took place by a committee composed of the

late Mr. Donaldson, Mr. Jean Soulié, and Mr. Richard Relf. The two last gentlemen have not been able to remember any particulars as to the mode in which it took effect, but from the report they made to their fellow directors, it appears that a deficit of $335.25 was discovered in Mr. Zacharie's account of cash, which resulting from some mistake, was carried to profit and loss.

There were on that occasion, of $50,935.00 in bank notes, torn and injured, which were burnt on the 8th of September, 1807, by the aforesaid three gentlemen, thus reducing the actual amount of notes in circulation at the death of Mr. Zacharie, to $1,194,495.00. On the same day, the late Mr. J. B. Fitzgerald was cashier, — Mr. Poydras continued as President until the 7th of March, 1809, when he resigned. Mr. Thomas Urquhart was appointed in his stead. All was well until May 25, 1810 — an emission of $105,000.00 in notes of $500.00 and $5.00 were not entered in the debit of cash account on the ledger, then kept by Mr. Pacaud.

The entries on the ledger during the month, evince other instances of incorrectnes, and on the 9th, a sum of $33,117.84, to the debit of cash account was entered for only $23,117.84; on the other hand there is a difference of $100.00 in the credit side of the account, a sum of $27,171.50 being entered for $27,071.50 only, thus establishing an actual deficit of $114,900.00 in the cash account, notwithstanding which Mr. Fitzgerald and Pacaud found means to agree in their balance by the simple process of reducing, in the same proportion, the amount of general desposits, which it will be perceived from the evidence in the appendix, were never once examined during Mr. Fitzgerald's cashiership.

On the first of March, 1815, the Board of Directors met, and appointed a committee of three members, to wit — Mr. Nott, Mr. Lanusse and Mr. Soulié, for the purpose of examining the situation of the Bank. Mr. Pacaud then laid before the Board his last fictitious balance sheet, and showed a sum of $356,215.64 in deposits. On the 7th of March, the above named three gentlemen, reported to the Board, that they had been arrested in their progress of their examination by the indisposition of Mr. Pacaud, but on the 10th, they declared that they had discovered the thread of Mr. Pacaud's fraudulent entries, from which it appears there existed a deficit of $145,759.79.

Mr. Pacaud acknowledges himself accountable for $100,000.00 overdrafts only, but the actual deficit was $172,773.11. On the fifth of March, 1815, Mr. Harman succeeded him as cashier.

This commentary was resumed in the issue of the next day, which said:

It will be perceived that from the defective mode of destroying notes*, the means of tracing the extra emission, if any, has really taken place to a pointed period, are out of the committee's power. But they have acquired the certainty that as far as respects the extra emission of the $500.00 notes, it is well nigh impossible that it could have occurred during Mr. Harman's cashiership — and when Mr. Harman assumed the cashiership, the errors and vices of Mr. F's administration were unknown to him, and as soon as he was acquainted with them his whole attention was devoted to sift matters.

It arose in part from overdrafts which had been permitted, and by omission of sundry deposits to the credit of individuals, such as the Widow Doisiere for $7800.00

The board acted on the advice of its counsel, Mr. Lislet. In May, 1818, the bank had a capital of $485,000.00, "when the account of d i s c o u n t s was in the proportion of four to one, say $2,093,287.59, and the average amount of discount for the whole year, was $1,538,184.00 with a capital of $482,300.00. The bank was then in a precarious position and the Board should be censured."

The *Gazette* expressed the opinion that it was not likely that the stockholders' loss would be more than ten to twelve percent of

---

*Questions at Examination of Mr. Sel — Late Receiving Teller of the Louisiana Bank 9th June, 1820.

Question — Please to inform the committee in what manner the burning of the unsigned notes remaining in the Bank was conducted after Mr. Girod had made the motion to burn such notes.

Answer — the said notes were first begun to be burnt in a regular manner — that is to say, in presence of several directors of the Bank on one of the fixed discount days. The first day or the day after, but most certainly on a day not fixed for the meeting of the directors, Mr. Girod repaired alone to the Bank, and inquired if the notes were to be burnt that day. On his being answered in the negative, he expressed the greatest impatience and without waiting for such of his colleagues as had, doubtless, been appointed to assist him in the operation, he took himself a very large bundle of said notes, and threw them into the stove, which is in the hall of the Bank, where they were consumed. Mr. Girod was constantly in a hurry to terminate his operation. On another occasion, he put into the stove a very large bundle of said notes. Mr. Harman, the Cashier of the Bank, surprising him at the operation, begged him not to burn so large a quantity at a time, as he might set fire to the house, but Girod replied that he longed excessively to see the operation finished, and that the notes must be burned.

their capital. As far back as March, 1811, Pacaud and Fitzgerald knew these defalcations.

The Louisiana State Bank was authorized by an act of the Legislature passed on March 14, 1818. Its capital was $2,000,000 and the charter stipulated that one-fourth the stock was to be reserved to the State, which was to subscribe $100,000, and that six out of the eighteen directors were to be appointed by the State. This bank in 1819 took over the old quarters of the Louisiana Bank at 417 Royal Street in the building still standing where is now located the "Patio Royal". The Louisiana State Bank had branches at Donaldsonville, St. Francisville, Alexandria and St. Martinville.

"Boats arrived — more expected, laden with flour and other production of the Western States", was the headline in the *Louisiana Gazette* of December 21, 1820, and it commented that: "In the meantime the market is forestalled by the shipment lately made from the Atlantic border. What are the merchants and farmers of the West to do in this conjunction? God only knows. As to ourselves, between non-intercourse with our best customers in the East Indies, and restrictions on the trade with France, the prospects before us are not very brilliant. We might have some hopes of better times, were the trade with Mexico opened by the Cortes; but who knows even then, whether the good folks at Washington would not hit on some mode of knocking this also on the head. The prospect of establishing a desert on this frontier, and the late cession of the rich lands in the upper part of the Red River country, argues ill for much regard for the interests of these questions".

Despite agricultural prosperity it was only by the end of 1820 that business arose from its lethargy and only then, there seemed to be a renewal of confidence, and it took three years to achieve it. In 1822, there was a slight recession, and in 1825, the crisis in England had some repercussions in America, but it was of short duration. After that time both commerce and agriculture made giant strides, there was a renewal of wild speculation and the promotion of unsound enterprises, fortunes were made on paper, all paving the way for the frightful financial crash of 1837.

"The year 1822, has been very peaceful, and yet there never were a more trying twelve months" commented the *Louisiana Gazette* in its edition of November 6, 1822. It declared that the Northern and Eastern States have in many places suffered from a great drought, which was attended by diseases, and the Western countries had been cursed with rags instead of money. The Southern States were the victims of a pestilence and a hurricane which not only resulted in the loss of thousands of lives, but in money as well". The item further stated that this was not all, that "gangs of pirates have repeatedly fastened upon the trades, and they are without any reasonable hope of a stop being put to such iniquities." It predicted that many sugar plantations will produce at a loss, and that cotton will sell below the cost of production.

But despite that pessimistic outlook, the article made the following prediction: "New Orleans however will have attractions sufficient for a crowd of strangers to visit it during the approaching winter. We shall not be surprised at seeing fifty large vessels, under foreign flags alone moored at one time in our harbor. The opening of free trade to the whole of the West India Islands, South America and Mexico, will certainly give additional facilities to mercantile speculators, and the centralization of a vast commerce will certainly offer a stimulus to all branches of industry among us."

The Bank of the State of Louisiana was chartered on April 7th, 1824, but its name was changed that same year to Bank of Louisiana. It had a fixed capital of $4,000,000.00, one-half of which was to be owned by the State, to be paid by bonds of the value of $100.00 bearing the rate of 5%. The amount subscribed by the State was $301,000.00. Of the eighteen directors, six were to be appointed by the Governor. The Legislature of March 24, 1827, passed an act ordering the bank to purchase bonds with the profits and "place them in a sinking fund for the redemption of the original issue", and it also provided that the State seat seven directors out of thirteen. These legislative orders seem to have been ignored, for in an act of March 7, 1834, it directed the Attorney General to institute suit against the bank and to compel it to place to the credit of the state, "as available means on July 1st next, the amount the state was entitled to in gains and profits made by the bank on the sale of State bonds; such portion as the State might be entitled to in the balance in the profit and loss account, and any other claims and amount which the Attorney General may think was due the State."

The Consolidated Ass'n. of Planters was incorporated on March 6, 1827, with a capital of $2,000,000.00.

The first savings bank in New Orleans opened on April 26, 1827. It was located at the office of the Louisiana Fire Insurance Co. on Chartres Street between Bienville and Conti Streets. Peter Derbigny was the president and the committee "for the present month": Joseph Roffignac, Tobias Bickle and Martin Gordon. A. M. Kennedy was the accountant. This information is found in the *Courier* of April 27, 1827, and the by-laws of the New Orleans Savings Bank were printed in the April 28th issue of the *Courier*.

New town-sites were developed in the vicinity of the city, in which lots were sold from ten to a hundred times their originial value. The demand for loans was so great that money became scarce, the rate of interest increased from fifteen to twenty per cent, even on the best of security, and bankruptcies became common. Ominous clouds were hovering over the financial horizon. The *Bee* of January 21, 1837 wrote:

> Some years ago $1200.00 per annum was considered an excellent salary for a chief clerk, or a bookkeeper in a large commercial house or bank. Now a young man of ability, as an accountant does not consider himself adequately compensated under $2000.00 per annum. In fact it is quite common at the present day, for mercantile houses to give $3000.00 and upwards, to their principal clerks. It requires much larger sums now to procure the necessities of life than a few years ago, and the laborer exacts higher wages than he ever did before. What one dollar could purchase in 1830, now requires two. Public officials as a rule are inadequately compensated. Scarcely a bank cashier who does not get more pay than the City's Treasurer. The Secretary of State gets less than the Secretary of a railroad or insurance company. Clerks are better paid than clerks of either houses of the Legislature. Judges, too little, and with great difficulty a single eminent lawyer can be induced to quit his practice to take a seat on the bench, and it is anticipated that when the present able Parish, Probate and District Judges go out of office, none but briefless lawyers will apply for the station, unless the salaries are increased.
>
> Yet, ten years ago the reverse was the case, it was the public officers, then to have compensation exceeding the rate of those in private life. But the latter have increased while the former have remained stationary.

In 1836 J. B. Perrault, the cashier of the Citizen's Bank, recevied a salary of $13,000, which with a house and other prequisites, amounted to $15,000 which was said to have been the largest salary paid in the country except that paid the President of the United States.

During that period of inflation and of wild speculation many banks were chartered, and many corporations were authorized by the State Legislature. The City Bank was incorporated on March 3, 1831, with a capital of $2,000,000.00. According to its charter that bank was subject to legislative inspection and was not allowed to issue notes of a lesser denomination than $5.00, and was not "to suspend redemption in current money of the United States, under a penalty of twelve percent".

At that same time the New Orleans Canal and Banking Company was chartered. Its capital was $4,000,000.00. Its purpose was to dig a canal from the lake to the river, later to be known as the New Basin. In 1832, the Union Bank of Louisiana was chartered with a capital of eight million dollars. Condon commented that "the State gave its bonds, and the subscribers to the bank gave mortgages on real estate, improved or unimproved, and slaves. How recklessly they borrowed and endorsed money in those days." Three banks were chartered in 1833, the Citizens Bank with a capital of $12,000,000.00, the Commercial and the Mechanics and Traders.

The purpose of the Canal Bank was to make loans to sugar plantation owners, holding as security a mortgage on their land, slaves and cattle, up to the amount of one-half of their appraised value. The loans were negotiated for a period of twenty years, at 6%, one-twentieth of the amount to be redeemable yearly. In 1835, three more banks opened their doors, they were: The New Orleans Gas Light and Banking Company, with a capital of $6,000,000.00; the Exchange Bank, capital $2,000,000.00; and the Carrollton Railroad Bank, with a capital of $3,000,000.00. To this large number of banks in 1836, was added the Merchants Bank with a capital of $1,000,000.00, and banking privileges were granted to the New Orleans Improvement Company and to the Pontchartrain Railroad Company.

In the meanwhile there was an orgy of speculation and wild financing. Condon wrote . . .

. . . the mania of speculation had seized on all minds, and turned all heads, and the effervescence of the people of Paris, excited by the Mississippi lands in the time of Law, had never been more violent. A state of affairs now existed in New Orleans of the most extraordinary character. An enormous value was placed on lands covered with water; towns were laid out in the midst of cypress swamps; prairies were set on fire, and speculators were ready to snatch at every islet. Some few, shrewder than the rest, or favored by fortune, succeeded in amassing enormous fortunes, but a far greater number were irretrievably ruined. To make the existing state of things in the end still worse, the banks were profused in their discounts, and did not scruple to issue paper to five times the amount of the available capital.

The value of city real estate rose to prodigious heights, so much so, that a bank purchased a site for a half million dollars that a short while before was worth $50,000 to $60,000. Money was diminishing in value, and the rate of interest was rising prohibitively. Everything pointed to an impending crash, but as long as the people were enjoying a false prosperity, laborers and artisans earning fabulous wages, clerks receiving constant raises in salaries and speculators gloating over their paper profits, no attention was paid to what the future might have in store, despite frequent warnings from the more conservative element of the community. In the search for the pot of gold at the end of the delusive rainbow, homes were mortgaged, lands hypothecated, and businesses pledged to procure funds to reinvest in highly speculative ventures.

In the eighteen-thirties New Orleans made stupendous gains both in population and commerce. There was an orgy of speculation, and in that flurry of easily acquired spurious paper money, the value of real estate pyramided to fabulous heights, the levee was glutted with goods, and the city was thronged with strangers. The unprecedented pseudo-prosperity of New Orleans amazed the world.

As early as February 1st, 1834, the *Niles Weekly Register* observed that "the money market in New Orleans is agonized and depressed, all products going there for sale feel the effect of the depression and sink in price. Cotton was down to 12 to 14 cents, and everything else in proportion." The conservative business men were aroused from their apathy and awakened to the realization that the trend could not be sustained, and that, unless it was arrested, severe consequences would ensue. The same journal of April 5, 1834, reported a meeting held at the Planter's Hotel on March 19, by the citizens and merchants of the city. S. W. Oakey, Esq., presided, and the following resolution was adopted:

> The people of New Orleans from a state of high prosperity are reduced to one of misery and distress by the pressure in the money market which has depressed the value of produce and of real property, and increased the rate of interest to eighteen to twenty four per cent per annum, which is grinding every por-

tion of the community, and unless relief is soon afforded, must be productive of the heaviest calamity.

It was stated that some loans had been negotiated at five per cent per month, and that payment was to have been made in this city on or before the third day of April, and these loans exceeded two million dollars and that one million dollars were due on real estate in the city or in the suburbs.

The newspapers of New York ascribed the bankruptcy of the house of Joseph, which precipitated the crisis there, to the failure of New Orleans merchants in their remittances, and for their not paying the balance due it.*

The *Bee* in an editorial denied the accusation by asserting that Joseph owed no less than $200,000.00 to one house alone in Canal Street and not less than $500,000.00 to different merchants in the City. It explained that "banks confided in the merchant, the merchant in the planter, the planter in his prospective crop, and the exporter in the market abroad. This may have been very indiscreet, but it was not criminal. The confidence prevaded all pursuits, and as its influence would be general when its operations should prove successful, so must to be more or less general when they fail. The evils are to be attributed to the errors of the system, not to the faults of the individuals."

The paper made the statement that failures were more widespread in the early eighteen-twenties than at the present time, but that "the notes and acceptances of every merchant who then suspended or stopped payment, were subsequently paid up in full by both planters and merchants."

On April 7, the *Bee* announced the negotiation of bonds of the Canal Bank, to the amount of one and a half million dollars by Hope and Company of Amsterdam, through the intermediary of Mr. Forstall, the then President.

From the beginning of that year the imminent crash was ap-

---

*The *Niles Weekly Register* in its issue of June 7, 1834, reported that "there had been some very extensive forgeries in New Orleans, and a large deficit had been discovered in the Consolidated Ass'n Bank, the cashier and two clerks have been arrested and held to $25,000.00 bail each.—but have since disappeared." In its June 28, issue it stated that "there has been a great deal of forgery and robbing of banks in New Orleans—and in exceeding large amounts. One person concerned has killed himself just after that event was known. Jaques Gaudauin, the porter of the Canal and Banking Co., robbed the Bank yesterday afternoon of about $41,000.00. This person has been caught and nearly all the money has been recovered."

parent to everyone, the newspapers were replete with conjectures, prophesies and diatribes about the banks and their management, some emitting dire pessimism and a few expressing a false optimism. Gloom hung over the city like a pall. The scarcity of money, the retrenchment by the banks, failures and rumors of failures, the lack of employment, the glut of commodities, the falling prices, and suicides, all were forebodings of the impending panic.

At long last the storm broke out in all its fury, and the city was in the throes of a panic. On Monday, the 13th of May, 1837, the Mechanics Bank, Carrollton Bank, Orleans Bank, City Bank, Louisiana State Bank, Louisiana Bank, Commerce Bank, Union Bank, Exchange Bank, Canal Bank and the Atchafalaya Bank suspended payment. The announcement caused a great deal of confusion and agitation. The city was in a uproar. Only the Citizens' Bank paid out in specie.

Debouchel, a contemporary writer in his "Histoire de la Louisiana" gave an excellent analysis of the causes which provoked the panic. He wrote:

> Fourteen banks in New Orleans, as well as the banks from other sections of the Union, suspended all payments by specie. Only the Consolidated Association and the Citizens Bank paid out in money. That announcement provoked a great agitation in the city, and on any other occasion, an infuriated people may

At Left — Commercial Bank. Built in 1833, costing $75,000. (Gibson, 1838).

At right—Atchafalaya Bank. Built in 1837, costing $125,000. (Gibson's Directory, 1838).

have demolished these failing institutions; but fortunately better judgement prevailed. In order to replace the small change which had disappeared overnight, the three municipalities issued certificates having a value of twenty-five cents to four dollars. Corporations, and even individuals, did the same, and the State of Louisiana was flooded with paper.

The total capital of the New Orleans banks was $55,032,000 and in less than three months the banks made loans to the amount of $11,500,000.00. Four firms owed them one million dollars each, and twenty-nine more, twelve millions. These loans were secured by mortgages on marshes, cypress swamps and flooded lands, and they had in their portfolios, worthless notes made for a term of six months to eight years. A bank with a capital of four million dollars was totally exploited by the directors for their exclusive b e n e f i t, and another to the amount of one third of its capital. Instead of banks they were only stock companies and instruments of usury.

The outstanding facility with which money was borrowed gave birth to unheard of speculations. The imports from Europe were greater than the exports. That system of credit increased the price of merchandise five fold, and made the United States appear as the Eldorado of importations.

The price of cotton rose from 18 to 20 cent a pound, but it did not command that price in Europe, which occasioned great losses and caused many bankruptcies. The sales of lands ceased, thousands of ephemeral fortunes lost, and only the usurers were the beneficiaries; loans on good security brought 24 to 30% per annum. The crisis was very severe in New Orleans, because the banks paid only with s c r i p t which destroyed confidence and crushed commerce.

These were agonizing days for the people of New Orleans.

The following postmortem appeared in the *Bee*, on Monday, June 13, 1837, saying that traders and mechanics had escaped the misfortunes that befell large business as well as the classified trades, such as dealers in dry goods, crockery, hardware, groceries and clothing, for they were able to maintain their credit, and as a result they "sustained little other loss than that arising from the stagnation of their business. Their credit is unbroken as to this day."

Continuing from the *Bee*:

The commencement of the present embarassment began in March last, banks had curtailed the amount of their business and materially contracted their issues; and henceforward they continued the system of curtailment with increased rapidity and energy.

Papers discounted on renewal for sixty days on payment of ten per cent of the amount of each renewal until December next, yet some of these institutions were obliged by the force of circumstance to require twenty per cent and sometimes forty per cent on renewal at sixty days, besides thwarting the wishes of the debtor to renew, by demanding all the names it was evidently impossible to obtain, and instances have occured for three names in good credit being refused as endorsers, instead of one that could not be procured! The consequence of which, was that the trader was obliged to take up all such paper without renewal — and all papers not discounted were also of necessity paid in full. Under these circumstances it will readily be perceived that the trading class paid into the banks three quarters of all sums received by those institutions, and that too, without other aid than such as could be obtained under the system of renewing at sixty days, deducting ten per cent.

It also stated that the banks "confined their loans to a few houses in a particular business, and most of them have fallen under their kindness".

The *Bee* of Saturday, July 1, established a pattern between the crash of 1820, and the one of 1837, as far as the banks were concerned. It asserted that the bank manifesto of the May 13th was the same as the one in 1820. The following quotation from that article is most interesting:

They said the specie in their possession was rapidly disappearing, being carried off to Barataria to purchase goods from Lafitte's smugglers, but they declared their affairs to be perfectly solvent, and that they had abundant means in their portfolio to meet all their engagements, which assurance afterwards proved to be delusive with respect to two of the banks. These too wound up a few years afterwards with a total loss to the stockholders of the one, and a loss to the other, of seventy five percent. But this is not precisely the point at which we would arrive. So far was the specie from being retained in the coffers of the banks by their refusal to pay, that at the end of the same year in which the suspension commenced the whole three were unable to raise $5,000.00 in gold or silver, and such, we are convinced worse will be the condition of most of the suspended banks of New Orleans in less than one year, unless they are compelled by force of public opinion, or of Legislative enactment, either to close their doors or to make preparations for the prompt resumption of legal payment.

The bankers were publicly accused of being "chartered libertines".

The resilience of the people was such that in a short while confidence was gradually restored. Optimism replaced despondency, losses were recouped, business was not only restored but was on the ascendency. Promoters, traders, speculators and adventurers arrived in droves, steamboats and river craft of all kinds landed with merchandise to be trans-shipped to all parts of the world. Again prosperity reigned.

In less than seventeen years, New Orleans, had been through two major depressions, plagued by epidemics of yellow fever, and preyed upon by that most devastating of all diseases, cholera. This city, which because of the inclemency of its clime could transact its commerce only during six months of the year, not only survived but grew to faublous heights both in population and in commerce.

Indeed, New Orleans was a city of destiny!

CHAPTER VII

MUNICIPAL AFFAIRS

During the French domination, the City was governed by a Superior Council, which upon the acquisition of Louisiana by Spain, O'Reilly abolished and in its stead, established the Cabildo, which was the form of government common to all Spanish towns. Pierre Clement de Laussat, who was appointed the colonial prefect of Louisiana and who was commissioned by the French Government as its representative for the transfer of the colony in accordance with the treaty of San Idlefonso, arrived in New Orleans on March 26, 1803. One of his first acts was to establish a City government more in keeping in form and character with the municipalities of the United States. He organized a city administration composed of a Mayor, two deputy Mayors, twelve Councilmen and a Secretary. He appointed Etienne de Boré, the Mayor, and Destrehan and Sauvé, deputy Mayors. The Council was composed of Livaudais, Petit, Cavalier, Villeré, Evan Jones, Fortier, Donaldson, Faurie, Allard, Watkins and Labatut. Pierre Derbigny was the Secretary and J. B. Labatut, the Treasurer. Their duties were as follows: Livaudais and Villeré, Supervisors of streets and levees; Fortier and Faurie, Supervisors of Markets, street-lighting and street-cleaning; Watkins and Allard were given charge of the hospitals and bakeries, and the superintendence of public health; Donaldson, Petit, Jones and Tureau were Justices of the Peace, both criminal and civil. This choice of officials proved to be a wise one, for many laws and regulations were passed which were conducive to the welfare of the City. Unfortunately their tenure of office was very short. This was the first City Council of New Orleans.

The City was incorporated on February 7, 1805, and its charter was signed by Julien Poydras, the President of the Council, with the approval of Governor Claiborne. It provided that the Governor would appoint the Mayor and the Recorder, and that the Aldermen would be elected. The Treasurer was to be chosen by the City Council, as well as minor officials. James Pitot was the first Mayor of the incorporated City. He served but for a short time for he resigned in order to be inducted as Judge of the

First Probate Court of the Territory. He was succeeded by John Watkins. In 1811, an amendment to the Charter provided that the Mayor would also be elected by the people. Nicholas Girod was then elevated to that office, his is the distinction of being the first elected Mayor of New Orleans.

It was not until the eighteen-twenties that New Orleans became the boom city of the Union. Previous to that time the Creoles and the French faction dominated the politics of the City, for to a large extent the bulk of the population was still contained within the confines of the original city. But that political control was fast dwindling away, for with the ever increasing influx of English-speaking migrants of all classes and professions from every part of the country, a strong and vociferous party developed determined to control the city. The newcomers smarted under the idea that the ancient population was a foreign element, and as such, should not have any influence whatsoever over the affairs of the city; that they were interlopers and should not hold any position of trust, and that any allotment of public funds should not be allowed for the benefit and improvement of the city proper. In the twenties that resentment and rivalry rose to such a pitch that eventually New Orleans was divided into three separate municipalities.

The *Louisiana Gazette* in an editorial entitled the "Financial Condition of the City" which appeared in its issue of February 25, 1823 had this to say:

> The treasury is empty, with a deficit not clearly certain, but said to amount to a very large sum. Borrowing resorted to under the pretext of paving the city, and the public money lent to men who always put off pay day, or else paid to useless efforts. Already the receipts of one of the best branches of revenues, those of the market house, have been mortgaged to the interest of the great loan; and this of itself will cause a deficit in the revenue that must eat up the borrowed money, and then called for new supplies. Paving of fifteen squares on two sides has nearly exhausted $100,000.00. The contractor was authorized to sell script of the Corporation for $150,000.00 — redeemable in ten years — and in the meantime bearing an interest of 7% per annum.
>
> Now what right had the corporation to stake their credit against that of an individual?
>
> It was loudly proclaimed by the City Council, but a fortnight ago, that the best notes were discounted at 30% and yet they consented to receive them at 8½%.

It was a custom of the time for both the State and the City to make loans to corporations and in many instances to individuals. The editorial continues:

> Referring to the resolution of the council introduced by Mr. Morse granting a delay to John Davis, owner of the Theatre d'Orleans, of 1, 2, or 3 years for paying what he owes the corporation, and lending a sum of $6000.00 to Mr. Caldwell, proprietor of the St. Charles Theater, on a similar credit.

Caldwell repaid the City the $20,000.00 it had loaned him, but the municipality was not so fortunate in the case of the Presbyterian Church for it lost $5,000.00 on a loan having no security whatsoever. The City made a loan of $12,000.00 to Davis to enable him to finish building his theater.

In the summer of the same year the city built five stores next to the Water Works, which it rented to grog shops for approximately $2,000.00 a year.

In May, 1824, Mayor Roffignac released a report, from which the following is abstracted: He stated that the only drawback to the City was the scourge (yellow fever). He recommended that stone gutters be substituted for the wooden ones which were "in a constant process of putrefraction," and that all low places be supplied with river water. He also recommended that wharves be built similar to the one at the foot of Conti Street.

He mentioned that in 1824 the resources of the City were $151,000.00 as compared to $119,050.00 in 1820, an increase of $61,950.00 in three years.

He cited the following accomplishments: Several streets were paved, the waterworks was purchased, the city was lighted by 306 lamps. Many streets were opened and 4000 trees were planted. Two new markets as well as several buildings were erected by the city. The public squares were decorated and fenced in with iron fences, a city clock was placed in the steeple of the Cathedral and the prison was enlarged, new canals were dug and eight fire engines were purchased. The old market was paved, Fort. St. Charles was demolished, and the ground on which it stood levelled. A road was constructed along the Canal Carondelet to the Bayou St. John, and two sites for cemeteries were purchased.

In August of that year the City Council authorized the digging of the St. Bernard Canal.

At the end of 1824, the City Council made public the following list of the City personnel and their salaries:

J. Roffignac, Mayor	$ 4,000.00
D. Prieur, Recorder	500.00
Moreau Lislet, Counselor	1,000.00
Gallien Preval, Secretary of the Council	1,200.00
Guichard, Sergeant at Arms	300.00
Chas. Blache, Treasurer	4,000.00
A. Lafferranderie, Bookkeeper to Treasurer	1,000.00
J. Davezac, Secretary to Mayor	1,800.00
P. A. Poillon, 2nd Secretary to Mayor	1,200.00
Ed. Montegue, Clerk to Mayor	600.00
J. H. Pilie, City Surveyor	1,800.00
L. D. Ferrier, Syndic of the Lower Banlieu	300.00
J. Griffon, Syndic of the Bayou Banlieu	300.00
Marigny d'Autrive, Syndic of the Upper Banlieu	300.00
Ed. Cardinaud, Capt. of the Guards	1,080.00
Chas. Dutillet, 1st Lieutenant of the Guards	720.00
Esquin de Miropaix, 2nd Lieut. of the Guard	600.00
Jacob Hart, Sergeant of the Guards	480.00
2 Corporals for Guards at $35.00 per month	1,260.00
40 Men of City Guard at $30.00 per month	14,400.00
Jean Macouin, Constable to Mayor	420.00
Corporal of lamp lighters	480.00
15 lamp lighters at $30.00	5,400.00
Lalaune Beaumaris, Commissary of Police	960.00
Gaspard Dupuy, Commissary of Police	960.00
Eng. Rousset, Commissary of Police	960.00
Ralph Plye, Commissary of Police	960.00
F. Penne, Commissary of Police	960.00
Pre. Duverges, Commissary of Meat Market	960.00
J. H. Blache, Commissary of Vegetable Market	960.00
Chas. Grandpre, Commissary of Faubourg St. Mary	960.00
Simon Meilleur, Jail Keeper	800.00
A. S. Coulter, Engineer Waterworks	1,800.00
Ane Beaujean, City Blacksmith	960.00
Jn. Bourg, City Storekeeper	720.00
F. Momus, Overseer of City laborers	720.00
Jean Ruelle, City Gardener	720.00
A. Bordeaux, Repairer of Fire Engines	396.00
Vignaud, Repairer of Clock	180.00
M. Peralta, 1st Negro Driver (Picqueur)	720.00
4 Drivers at $40.00 per month	1,920.00
TOTAL	$61,936.00

A Committee was appointed to study a reduction in these salaries, and the feasibility of abolishing some of the offices.

The receipts and expenditures for the Parish of Orleans from April 10, 1825 to April 10, 1826 were:

Taxes, etc.	$16,308.86
From arrears in taxes	5,783.07
Rent of Halls of Supreme Court, District Courts and Courts of Probates	2,750.00
Amount of notes drawn by Mme. Poeyfarre and discounts	5,216.66
Note to order of J. H. Holland for keeping and maintaining the prison	10,397.63
From Treasurer of State	500.00
Amount of receipts	$40,908.22
Expenditures, Salaries of Judges	$41,376.61

The *Courier* of April 24, 1828, published the message of Mayor Roffignac, which is quoted in part:

As you gentlemen, as well as myself, have seen for a long time, that the commercial grandeur of this city must follow the rapid and increasing population of the rich and happy states which empty their rivers into and mix into the Mississippi, I hardly need remind you that by means of emigration from the eastern to the western ones, I have heard has in every ten years since 1794, nearly doubled itself, but a long time must have elapsed before this particular state could have supplied all the wants of its first settlers, as well as those of the numerous emigrants from the eastern states. Many years therefore, must have passed away without producing any great disposable commercial exports. So that the imports were comparatively inconsiderable until the year 1823, when the Council began to interest themselves, particularly by improvements favorable to commerce, it then annually increased in every way, so that we had in the Port in October 1827, 204,408 tons of shipping, whereas in the same month of 1824, we had about 142,179:

The City debt amounts to about $253,600.00, it having already paid $150,000.00 into the sinking fund on account of the loan negotiated with W. Nolte and Co., for $300,000.00 and the further sum of $7,500.00 also paid with the sinking fund towards the liquidation of other loans contracted for continuing the paving of the new levee, and the enlarging of the sidewalks of the body of the City.

Revenues of the City for this year, which in 1820 was but $119,000.00, amount to $200,379.00. The current expenses were

Carrollton Hotel. First built in 1836, destroyed by fire in 1841 and rebuilt in 1842. (From the Louisiana Historical Quarterly)

Magazine Street in 1834, when a railroad was projected for this street. From plans in the Archives of the City of New Orleans. (Courtesy of the N.O. Public Library)

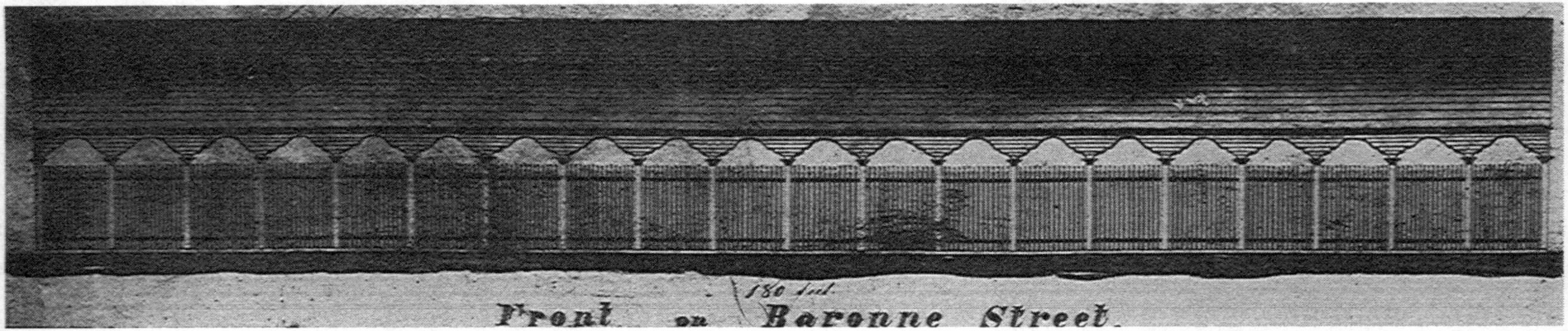

Rail Road Station for terminus of Carrollton Rail Road, 1834. (Courtesy of N.O. Public Library, Dept. of Archives)

Below (right)—Station of projected railroad to be located on Poydras Street. (Courtesy of N.O. Public Library, Dept. of Archives)

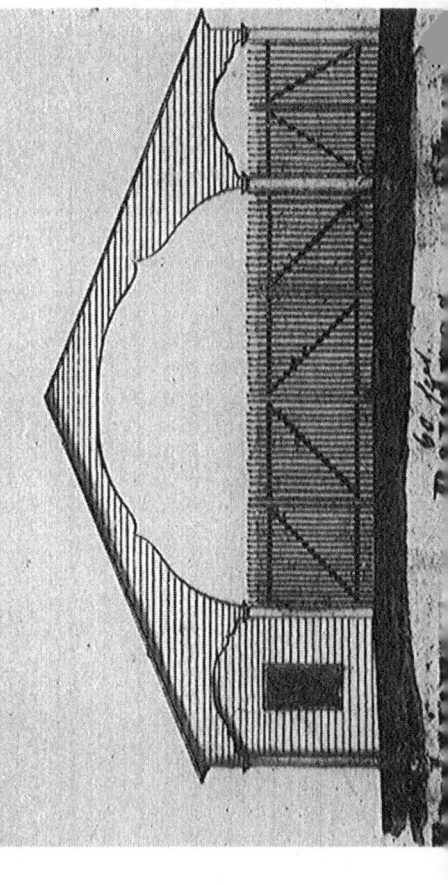

POMPE À FEU en l'année 1813
Waterworks, Levee and St. Philip Sts., built in 1813 (from Tanesse's Map of 1815).

$171,000.00; the interest account $5,334.00, leaving a net balance of $29,656.00.

The improvements carried into execution on the 19th of August, 1826 have cost, $565,437.00 for additional lamps, paving of the new levee, construction of wider brick sidewalks and stone gutters in the principal streets. Raising and covering the levees with shells, from Esplanade to Common Street. These recent improvements must have cost at least $90,000.00, which added to $565,437.00 equals $655,437.00.

Roffignac was elected Mayor for the first time in May, 1820. He held that office for eight years.

The *Argus* tried to disparage the achievements of Mayor Roffignac's by giving credit to others for the improvements made during his administration. It claimed that "it was Mr. Montgomery, who in June 1821, moved in the Council a resolution to plant trees around the city, and that he also urged the necessity for paving. Through him the City called Mr. Scott who first undertook the paving of the City." It also asserted that the

> . . . first levee is the work of Mr. Girod, who drew upon himself the ire of the Council as they did not approve of the measures perhaps on account of the embarrassment in finances. Mr. Girod obstinate in his purpose, declared that he would pay the expense, if the City treasury was unable to do so—and the Levee was made.

Mr. Roffignac received in 1821, a letter advising him that twelve lamps with reflectors, which were intended to be sold to the City. Council appointed a committe to investigate—authorized the purchase. It was by that means that all the city lamps were procured.

At the same time that article was profused in its praises for Prieur, who was Mayor, then not quite a year. It mentioned his accomplishments as follows: "Beautiful levees in Suburb St. Mary. In suburb Marigny the filling of the levee, so long contemplated and so long postponed, now offers to sea vessels an extensive commodious landing. The widening of sidewalks continue, Circus Square embellished by a new railing, and the vegetable market enlarged. And the City Guard increased to forty-five men."

In 1829, the office of the treasurer of the parish was moved to St. Peter between Royal and Bourbon.

J. Moreau Lislet, one of the leading lawyers at that time, shed further light on the debt owed by Davis to the City. This letter addressed to St. Romes, the editor of the *Courier*, appeared in that paper on April 2, 1830:

> Sir: I have seen it stated that one of the papers of New Orleans, in which are reported the proceedings of the City Council, that I had recommended the adoption of the proposals made by Mr. John Davis, proprietor and Manager of the Orleans Theatre, to pay to the corporation the sum of $13,000.00 and some hundred dollars on his note at one, two, three, and four years, with a good endorser, as a final settlement of what he might be indebted to the city. If it is as attorney of the corporation that it is pretended I made the recommendation, it is a complete mistake. It is true I deemed it my duty as Counsel for the corporation, to transmit to the Mayor, the written proposals which Mr. Dom Seghers, attorney for Mr. Davis, had handed me, because I always was of the opinion that the duty of a counsellor is to communicate to his client all proposals for arrangement made to him, in order to avoid reproach. It is true, also that as an individual I have told the Mayor and Mr. Peters, Chairman of the Committee on Finance, that as the business had been hanging for more than eight years without being brought to a conclusion, it might be proper to make sacrifice in order to bring it to a termination. All I added as an attorney, in speaking to Mr. Seghers, as well as to the Mayor, is that if I were consulted by the City Council about the proposal of Mr. Davis, I should certainly advise them not to subrogate an endorser to the mortgage which existed in favor of the corporation, but on the contrary to preserve as surety both the endorsement and the mortgage. Nor is it correct to say that according to the first arrangement Mr. Davis was to be exempt from the payment of the interest, if by that is understood

the interest on the delay of one, two, three and four years, solicited by him, since those interests were to be added to the notes to be furnished as well as I can remember.

No doubt the Committee of Finance have rendered a great service to the public in obtaining from Mr. Davis $18,000.00 instead of $13,000.00, but it is also to be considered that twelve years are granted to Mr. Davis instead of four years to pay the balance due by him. At all events, the happy results of the operation of the Committee of Finances in that affair, shows that the Mayor was right when he said in his message, that whatever might be his opinion of the proposal of Mr. Davis, he would submit to the wisdom of the council.

The Committee on levees, composed of John J. Miller, Frs. Gaiennie and Samuel J. Peters, Chairman, appointed by resolution of the City Council on April 12, 1830, submitted the following report:

Receipts:	Taxes on vessels in 1828.........	$ 32,241.13
	Taxes on vessels in 1829.........	32,171.53
	Taxes on vessels in 1830.........	32,900.00
	Taxes on steam boats 1828.......	8,675.00
	Taxes on steam boats 1829.......	8,500.00
	Taxes on steam boats 1830.......	9,950.00
	Taxes on flat boats 1828.........	7,206.00
	Taxes on flat boats 1829.........	9,883.00
	Taxes on flat boats 1830.........	8,875.00
	Pirogues in same years..........	2,055.00
	TOTAL	$152,456.66
	Expenditures	44,673.49
	Balance	107,783.18

The *Courier* of April 13, 1831 reported that the message of the Mayor did not exhibit the finances of the city to be "in the most flourishing condition", and it suggested a "more rigid economy".

The public improvements for that year were the building of wharves, enclosing and filling up of the public squares and the paving of streets. The expenses for the current year were $244,150.00; the receipts $246,367.00 and the loans $300,000.00.

The City Treasurer, Fleytas, in his report on the financial condition of the City for the year 1832, gave the following statement: Amount received, $714,596.72, and expenditures, $697,904.99, leaving a balance of $16,691.73.

J. Pilié and H. Fry were appointed by the City Council to suggest a plan by which the City could be protected from inundations from the waters of Lake Pontchartrain. They submitted the following recommendation in which they estimated that it would cost $64,000.00, and that the money could be raised by forming a Capital Stock Co., in which the proprietors of the low and marshy lands would subscribe to shares according to the valuation of their lands in their actual condition. This same land would be sold, after it was drained, at a considerable profit.

In the month of October, 1834, the bar adjoining the council chamber provoked severe criticism from the press. Objections were made to the City's paying for drinks and dinners for the aldermen. An editorial stated that the "Cafe in the City Hall paid for drinks for 18 months, $1,729.00, which amounts to about $1.75 per alderman for each meeting" and laconically observed "in the library are bottles and carafes instead of books". The Mayor, taking cognizance of the abuse, addressed a communication to the Council advocating the use of drinking water.

Despite all, the abuse still continued and it was not until December that public indignation was aroused. A communication appeared in the French section of the *Bee* of December 9, 1834 entitled "About the Bar in the City Council" brought that issue to a focus. It said:

> The odor of brandy must have something very seductive for certain members of the honorable Council, that neither the orders nor the request of the President could induce them to leave. In that chamber which touches the Council Chambers, is a library of demijohns, bottles and carafes, the bar is still there and the citizens are paying for it.
>
> The Council should expel the three aldermen for the little respect they held in that bar, from which neither order or requests could induce them to leave.
>
> May those to whom we are addressing these reflections remember that they have been elected to the Council to defend the interests of their constituents, and not to drink their money.

The following is taken from the report to the City Council:

> Dixon, Hyde and McFarlane had retired into the buvette, an establishment of which we have before spoken, from whence the loudest voices are heard.
>
> The absence of these gentlemen having broken up the quorum and put a stop to business, the recorder directed the Sergeant-at-Arms to call them to their seats. Several reiterated calls were subsequently made, but without success, when Mr.

F. Labatut retired. The Recorder declared that since the members would not absolutely hear reason, he would feel obliged to adjourn the Council; he accordingly did so to Saturday next.

At a special session of the City Council held on October 9th, 1834, upon the motion of Mr. Pritchard it was resolved that the seat of Mr. Schmidt be declared vacant.

The *Bee* on April 7, 1835, made a comparison between New York and New Orleans and expressed the hope that New York would be exceeded within twelve years: "During the past four years the most gigantic strides have been made in this onward career" the editorial stated, "eligible improvements were made in the City, in the northwestern or the American quarters, the water works now is in a fair state of being put in operation." It also enumerated many improvements to begin during the year among which are: amelioration of lands in the rear of the City; lighting the streets with gas; extension of that part of the port allotted to steamboats; chartering steamboats companies for navigating the Mississippi and Western waters; extending operations of the Pontchartrain Railroad so to have an eligible outlet to Lake Borgne and thence towards the Gulf of Mexico.

It also claimed that there were few states in the Union where capital can produce more profitable dividends. The exports of the city almost equal or exceed those of New York, and the banking capital of the State approximated $60,000,000.00.

Pilié, the City Surveyor, reported that from April 8, 1832 to April 8, 1835 the Levees were repaired, the ground was sloped toward the river from St. Peter to St. Louis, from Poydras to Girod, and from Elysian Fields to Enghein. Three new fire engines were purchased with a complete assortment of ladders. The

Double-decker hand fire-engine. Type used by Companies No. 13, No. 14 and No. 22.

vegetable market and the City Hall were completely repaired. The City square, which was a depot for the materials of the City, and Canal, Franklin, Treme and Customhouse Streets were filled in. Lots were purchased to extend St. Bernard and Canal Streets. Esplanade was extended beyond the former property of Plauché to that of Josephine Peyroux. And brilliant gas light in some streets replaced the common lamps.

A footway paved with bricks was laid around Gravier Square, Lafayette Square, and Washington Square. Anthony square was bordered with curb stone gutters.

The following was the estimated revenue of the city for 1835:

Rent of Meat Market	$ 36,000.00
Rent of Vegetable Market	18,000.00
Rent of Pirogues	1,365.00
Rent of St. Mary Market	13,000.00
Rent of stands for the sale of oysters	9,000.00
Duties of the Levee	45,000.00
Duties of Steamboats	20,000.00
Duties of Drays	22,000.00
Duties of Hawkers and Peddlers	18,000.00
Duties of Cabarets	60,000.00
Duties of Balls	400.00
Duties of Jails	8,500.00
Rent of Jail	2,000.00
Other Rents	22,000.00
Taxes for 1834	42,500.00
Prices of Licenses	2,600.00
Magazine	5,000.00
Rents, Taxes, etc.	5,000.00
Interest and Extraordinary Receipts	4,000.00
Fines	4,000.00
Loan to the Commercial Bank	100,000.00
Redeeming Funds No. 1	4,175.00
Stocks in Bank	38,028.00
Notes on hand due this year	15,692.00
Refund for Paving ($40,000.00) cash on hand	40,000.00
TOTAL	$556,070.00

The "Refund for paving" was explained by the budget committee as follows: "This sum ($40,000.00) will appear small when you consider that far more than a million dollars were expended by the City for paving and the treasury has not as yet recovered more than $132,000.00, which leaves yet to be received a sum of $260,000.00".

It is interesting to note that the estimated revenues to be derived from cabarets, $60,000.00, were greater than those from taxes ($42,500.00) or an excess of $17,500.00.

The estimated expenses for 1835 were:

Notes to be paid	$159,896.33
City Works	110,000.00
Salaries	30,000.00
Lighting of the City	21,000.00
City Guards	43,000.00
Cleaning of the City	15,000.00
Office Expenses	1,400.00
City Council Expenses	700.00
Legion	2,000.00
Male and Female Orphans	2,260.00
Magazine	2,200.00
Fire Engines ($8,000.00) Water works ($4,000.00)	12,000.00
Interest on Loans and Current Interest	80,000.00
Cross bridges	4,000.00
Commissioners	13,000.00
Police Expenses	6,000.00
Bayou bridge and dam	510.00
Steeple and clock	200.00
Liberties of the 8th District	600.00
Cost of suits (Legal)	6,600.00
Secret police	1,000.00
Repairs to City property	5,000.00
Indemnities	2,000.00
Printing expenses	500.00
Acts before notary public	2,000.00
Unforeseen expenses	2,000.00
Charitable purposes	12,000.00
Charity Hospital	2,100.00
Redeeming Funds No. 1	1,000.00
Redeeming Funds Generally	36,320.00
Jail expenses	6,000.00
TOTAL	$589,626.33

Total improvements ordered:

New Jails	$ 60,000.00
New Wharves	40,000.00
Carondelet Road	7,000.00
Paving	50,000.00
Levee in upper faubourg	50,000.00
Extending upper market	13,000.00
TOTAL	$779,626.33

The Mayor in his message to the City Council stated "That loans since 1830, amounted to $1,573,500.00 and that they were payable up to the year 1884."

J. Pilié, the City Surveyor, reported that fifteen new wharves were built by the City from St. Louis Street to Enghein Street. One wharf, 321 feet in length by 100 in width, in the suburb St. Mary above Poydras, also one 300 feet long at Notre Dame Street between Girod and Julia, one 213 feet at Julia and another at Enghein Street for the disposal of garbage into the river were built. He also reported that the canal along Canal Street was widened and cleansed.

That ever recurring contention between the upper and central municipalities as to the allotment of funds by the City, for their improvements was again agitated in an Editorial in the *Bee* of May 9, 1835. It claimed that the amount spent on paving in the upper suburb, $177,000.00, was partly true, but asserted that as to April 7, that amount should have been $252,553.30, while the lower suburbs only received $66,175.44. It commented that "this is no trifling difference when we consider that the upper faubourg paid very little taxes during the period of this expenditure." The editorial continued:

> Since 1830, only $15,000.00 was expended for wharves in the city proper, while $133,943.39 was spent by the upper faubourg for the construction of wharves, breakwater and filling.
>
> The City's disbursement in the upper faubourg was $366,396.82 to $81,175.49 in the lower. A difference of $295,175.49.
>
> Let our citizens ask now who are instigated with sectional feelings [it reproved] those who are indebted to the corporation and clamor still like the horseleech, give!! give! Careless how they involve the City Treasury, and the indifference that others should enjoy the same and similar measures:—or those who are the creditors of the corporation, and do not claim even their own rights. The upper faubourg is deeply in debt to the lower.

On July 9, of that year, a petition was presented to the City Council praying that they open Esplanade Street to the Bayou and form a straight line from Rampart Street to the Bayou. It was predicted that Esplanade Street would become one of the most agreeable thoroughfares in the City.

The Orleans Drainage Company proposed to drain the section bounded by Bayou St. John, Carondelet Canal and Bayou Road.

The *Bee* of September 23, 1835 proposed that the City Hall should be enlarged so that it would be more comfortable and expressed the pity "to see such a small cabinet consecrated to serve as the office and the tribunal of the Mayor, where seven or eight prisoners were led to be interrogated by our first magistrate, some men of the City guard, two or three commissioners of police, whose presence is always necessary, and the different employees of the Mayor, just about fill that room. The Council Hall is too small, and should be enlarged, and located in the center of the building."

A communication displaying great prophetic vision appeared in the *Bee* of March 6, 1836 under the heading "About widening of streets". It is here quoted in its entirety:

Let all the houses on the swamp side of Bourbon Street be thrown back thirty feet, such an arrangement could make Bourbon Street seventy feet wide, which is the width of Poydras Street, fifteen feet for banqettes on each side, and forty for carriages. I am aware how startling such a proposition is to the ancient population and proprietors in that street. If it was an Anglo-American population, the course of such a proposition could be easily foreseen. At first there would be a great outcry, a party for and a party against it. In a short time they would be satisfied of its advantages and all would cry for it. It would connect the faubourgs. All the retail stores and shops, dry goods, jewelers and milliners, etc., would assemble there. It would be the Broadway of New Orleans, and rents would soon be higher than that in Chartres Street; two, three, or four thousand dollars would instantly be added to the value of every lot.

To persons not accustomed to these operations the difficulties appear great, but on close examination they would vanish. The owners of lots on the river side of Bourbon Street would have to contribute towards the expenses. There are but few good houses on Bourbon Street, a three story brick houses can be moved back thirty feet, replaced on a good foundation for one thousand dollars, and the one story for $250.00 each. A contractor would undertake it for these prices.

All the difficulties of corner lots, etc., have been fully considered and could be met. It would cost $20,000.00 and add $500,000.00 to $750,000.00 to the value of the lots.

Let us look forward 50 to 100 years. Let us consider the advantages of the whole city and of the faubourgs. Let those who are not familiar with these preparations consult and advise with those of their fellow citizens in whom they confide and who have visited other cities, and have experienced the advantage of such improvements. The sincerest friends of the whole city, and who regards the interest of all, could not suggest any feature more beneficial to the incorporated city of New Orleans. You have what I advise—think, consider, ponder upon it —then act promptly and efficiently for your own interest.

Signed: W.

It is most unfortunate that the writer of this letter did not identify himself, evidently he was a man of vision.

The *Bee* gave its whole hearted support to the proposition in an Editorial published on May 13, it said:

> Were Bourbon Street widened, some 10 to 15 feet, by casting down all houses on the lower side, it might be made one of the finest in the City. Elegant ranges of stores, for drygoods and other retailers might be erected from Canal to St. Louis or even to Esplanade.
>
> This system of widening streets have been attended with most happy effects in London and other European cities; and while it has afforded superior conveniences and attractions, it has greatly enhanced the value of real estate in the improved districts. Property owned principally by colored persons, who cannot improve it, and will not sell.
>
> Capitalists are willing to embark in such projects, but they cannot purchase a square, and they are reluctant to erect elegant edifices for respectable tenants in the immediate neighborhood of Negro hovels.
>
> In the upper municipality this is not the case, and hence whole squares are purchased and simultaneously built on.

The property value of New Orleans for the year 1835 was estimated at $31,918,185.00. The tax was one dollar on every thousand dollars.

The following appropriations were made by the City Council at its meeting held on April 16, 1836, $30,000.00 for the purchase of three fire engines, two for the City square and one for the eighth ward. A grant of $1,000.00 to the New Orleans Lyceum, and $500.00 to the Commercial Library. One thousand dollars was allotted to the trustees of the Catholic Orphan Asylum, Messrs. A. Blanch, E. Cannon and others.

From the *Bee* of April 21, 1836 we learn that there were sixteen hundred carts and drays in the city. Of this number about three hundred were employed by the City to furnish water to families and to transport brick and other materials for public constructions, the other thirteen hundred were employed by the Commerce of the port.

1835 was one of the most remarkable years in the history of New Orleans. It is inconceivable how a community which had just emerged from the worse possible calamity that could afflict mankind, the co-existence of cholera with yellow fever, could have prospered, both in the manifold increase in its population and the growth of its commerce. During that period and especially in 1835, improvements were everywhere in evidence. The city had outgrown its original boundaries, the surrounding swamps were drained and filled, her streets were paved and well lighted, not only by the oil lamps but by gas light.

New Orleans was indeed a City of destiny.

CHAPTER VIII

POLITICAL SQUABBLES

During the colonial period, the colonists were the absolute subjects of the French and Spanish monarchies and they were denied the right of self-government. The Governors and their retinue of subordinates were chosen by the mother countries, unbeknown to the settlers and without their consent. They had no voice in the administrative affairs, and it may even be stated that to a considerable extent the very evistence of the colonists depended on the bounty and generosity of their Royal Majesties.

Three times they were the victims of French and Spanish machinations, the last when Louisiana was purchased by the United States. During colonial times the colonists preserved an unswerving loyalty to France, which even the many years of Spanish domination was unable to change. Their language, culture and devotion were always of and for la belle France, despite the fact that that country treated them with indifference and contributed very little to their welfare, while Spain, although in a meager way, did more to promote their well-being. Yet throughout the years the inhabitants nurtured the hope that someday France would redeem its former colony.

The announcement that the United States had puchased Louisiana was received by the colonists with mixed emotions. To say that they were disappointed is to put it mildly. The were overjoyed when they heard that they were again to be subjects of their beloved France, but their exultation was soon dissipated in profound disappointment.

It took but a short while for the significance of sudden transition from being subjects of foreign governments to that of full citizenship to dawn upon them. Although there were a few malcontents, all eventually became reconciled to the new status. The ancient population became true and patriotic citizens. They glorified in being Americans, and prayed that soon Louisiana would became a state of the Union. To them the privileges of citizenship were not to be taken lightly. They felt a moral responsibility for electing as their leaders men of the highest integrity, and who were the best fitted to govern them. Politics as such, did not enter into the picture till Louisiana was admitted to statehood.

William Charles Cole Claiborne, a native of Sussex county, Virginia, was appointed Governor of the Territory of Orleans, by the Congress of the United States on March 25, 1804, and the oath of office was administered by James Pitot, Mayor of New Orleans on October 2, 1804. On December 4th of that same year a legislative council was organized and Julien Poydras was elected President.

In his first proclamation Claiborne announced the acquisition of Louisiana by the United States, and promised that the inhabitants would be incorporated in the Union as soon as possible according to the principles of the federal constitution; that they would have all the rights and privileges, and in the meantime, they would be maintained in the free enjoyment of their liberty, property and religion, and that the laws and municipal regulations in effect at the time of the cession by the late government would still remain in force. During his term as territorial Governor, Claiborne had absolute power to make all political appointments and he was accountable to no one but the President of the United States. The beginning of his administration was turbulent because of the mutual distrust between the French population and the Governor. Claiborne held the opinion that the Louisianians were unfit for a representative Government, while the ancient population felt that they were discriminated against, and were not given a proportionate participation in the affairs of the administration. This is evidenced in the communications of Claiborne to Secretary of State Madison, of date January 10, 1804, quoted in part:

> The credulity of the people is only equalled by their ignorance, and a virtuous magistrate, resting entirely for support on suffrage and good will of his fellow-citizens in this quarter would at any time be exposed to immediate ruin by the machinations of a few base individuals, who with some exertion and address, might make the people think and act against their interest.

And again, in another official letter, he further expressed his anxiety, for he wrote:

> The population is composed of so heterogeneous a mass, such prejudices exist, and so many different interests to reconcile, that I fear no administration or form of government can give general satisfaction.

Chambers in his History of Louisiana stated "that the Louisianians were credulous and easily led was due to a large part to certain grievances which they held against the American rule. They believed Claiborne to be totally ignorant of all matters connected with the territory—inhabitants, language and laws. The English system of jurisprudence as followed in the United States was unpopular with them. The employment of the English language was irritating. His supposed partiality for Americans was a subject of their animosity."

These accusations of partiality were repudiated by Claiborne, who asserted that the Mayor and a majority of the City Council were composed of Ancient Americans, that Mr. Derbigny was clerk of court, and Mr. Lewis Herr, the sheriff; the four notaries were equally divided. Not a single "Modern Louisianian" held an appointment in the militia, as well as his aides-de-camp.

The historian Henry Adams wrote that "Louisiana received a government in which its people, who had been solemnly promised all the rights of American citizens, were set apart, not as citizens, but as subjects lower in the political scale than the meanest tribe of Indians whose right of self-government was never questioned." This contumely was voiced in the House of Representatives by Dr. Eustis, the Congressmen from Boston who harangued: "I am not one of those who believe that the principles of liberty can be grafted suddenly upon a people accustomed to a regimen of a directly opposite hue. I consider them as standing in the same relation as if they were a conquered nation." Chambers wrote that the ancient population's opinion of the Americans, based largely upon "their contacts with rude, breezy, turbulent, flat-boatsmen and adventurers who had come among them, was that which the patricians of Ancient Rome had for the invading barbarians. And yet these uncouth ones of the states from which they came, enjoyed the priceless boon of the franchise which, they, the Louisianians could not have". "The ancient population," so designated by Gov. Claiborne, resented these indignities and injustices and voiced their resentment in no uncertain terms.

"It may be said that in time these principles were so admirably grafted and a political w i s d o m so effectively developed", wrote Chambers, "that Louisiana sent a member of the family to which the voicer of the foregoing sentiments belongs to the United States Senate in the person of James B. Eustis who at the end of his senatorial service was sent as America's first Ambassador to the Court of France."

The same author wrote:

The United States in accepting t i t l e to the province as sold by Napoleon, had pledged that Louisianians should be admitted to all rights, advantages and immunities of citizens of the United States. To the people whose land had been sold this meant that Louisiana as a whole was to be admitted as one state. It also meant the immediate institution over them of a form of government under which they could derive without delay all the benefits of a self-governing citizenship and all the advantages of trade and commerce enjoyed elsewhere in the Union. Their awakening was therefore a rude one. The treaty with France had turned out to be one of these scraps of paper, which diplomatic history has too often recorded. Instead of holding their domain intact, even as in after years Texas was to hold its great area together as one, they found it ruthlessly dismembered with no regard to their rights and wishes in the matter. As to being admitted to the privileges, advantages and immunities enjoyed by citzens of the United States, the treaty promise to that effect could not have been made more ineffective had it been written on ice instead upon parchment with great names as signatures.

Derbigny, Sauvé and Destrehan, were selected by them to voice their justified complaint in Washington. They were men of distinction, refined, learned and cultured to say the least, they were in courtly manners and savoir faire, the equal of any dignitary in Washington. Chambers wrote "that they proved a revelation to the senators and congressmen with whom they mingled with perfect self-possession. Easterners who had obsessed themselves with the idea that Louisianians were all of a mongrel type had their eyes opened to their error."

They were royally entertained and every possible attention was shown them, and by their demeanor they greatly enhanced the prestige of Louisiana. Senator Plummer of New Hampshire wrote the following, which coming at that time from a New Englander must be considered flattering:

> They are all Frenchmen. Two of them (Derbigny and Sauvé) speak our language fluently. They are all gentlemen of the first respectability in that country — men of talent, literature and general information, men of business and acquainted with the world. I was much gratified with their company. They had little of French flippancy about them. They [more] resembled New Englanders than Virginians.

The first officers of the Territory were: Claiborne, Governor; Brown, territorial secretary; Dorciere, Flood, Mather, Pollock, Cantrelle, DeBuys, Dow, Kenner, Morgan, Poydras, Roman,

Watkins, and Wilkoff on the legislative council; Dupenceau, Prevost and Kirby, judges of the Superior Court; D. A. Hall, district judge; Dickenson, district attorney; Lebreton d'Orgenois (Dorgenois), Marshal of the District.

Such a government was not one to be called conciliatory to either the Creoles and the English-speaking element of the population. It gave birth to two political parties, one of the Creole, French and St. Domingan, and the o t h e r , the so-called Native American or the English-speaking faction.

Claiborne weathered the storm which threatened to engulf him, he steered his course with courage, firmness, moderateness, tolerance, justice and patience. He gained the confidence and respect of the Creoles, and he divested himself of the prejudices and misjudgements which permeated the North. This is attested to in his letter to Madison of July 7, 1809, in which he wrote:

> The Louisianians have as little mischief in their disposition, and as much native goodness as any people I have ever lived among, but unfortunately they are exceedingly credulous and their general sentiment and conduct may be easily directed by a few designing men. I find among the Louisianians considerable jealousy of their American brothers — viewing themselves as a distant and acquired branch of our family. They seem to think that they are not secure in the affections and confidence of the government. Of this circumstance also, designing men avail themselves to excite fear and suspicion, but I am persuaded that a little experience under American Government will give rise to very different impressions among the body of the people, and that in a few years the Louisianians will be among the most grateful of our citizens, and sincere admirers of our Union and Government.

Claiborne had all the powers of a despot for he was accountable to no one but the President, yet at no time did he abuse that authority.

On February 17, 1805 New Orleans was incorporated and its first charter was adopted by the Council under the signature of Julien Poydras, its President, and on March 4, of that year, the first election was held for aldermen. The Mayor and Recorder were appointed by Claiborne, the treasurer was elected by the council and all subordinate officials were chosen by the Mayor. James Pitot was the Mayor and Dr. John Watkins, the Recorder.

The City was divided into seven wards and the following were the first elected aldermen: Felix Arnaud and James Garrick for the first ward; Col. Bellechasse and Guy Dreux, second ward;

La Bertonniere and Antoine Argotte, third ward; Joseph Faurié and Francois Duplantier, fourth ward; T. L. Hannan and P. Lavergne, fifth ward; J. B. Macarty and Dorville, sixth ward; Poree and Guerin, seventh ward.

In 1811, Nicholas Girod was the first to be elected Mayor of New Orleans.

The last territorial legislature was held in January, 1811. At that session an act was passed granting Livingston and Fulton a monopoly on river navigation by steamboats. The act stipulated that they should have the "sole and exclusive right to build, construct, make, use, employ and navigate boats, vessels and watercrafts, urged or propelled through water by fire or steam, in all the creeks, rivers, bays and waters whatsoever within the jurisdiction of the territory during eighteen years from the 1st of January 1812." Other states bordering the waters of the Mississippi and its tributaries had promulgated similar laws. Such an all inclusive control of river navigation met with great opposition and was soon voided by the courts.

The reign of Claiborne as Territorial Governor was soon to end, for the census of 1810 gave the Territory of Louisiana a total of 76,566 inhabitants which then entitled it to statehead. On February 20, 1811 the Congress of the United States authorized the framing of a constitution and the forming of a state government. Louisiana's first constitutional convention assembled on November 4, 1811. Julien Poydras was its president and Eligius Fromentin, the secretary. The constitution was adopted on January 22, 1812, and it was approved by the President of the United States on April 8 with the stipulation that the act would become effective on April 30. Louisiana became the eighteenth state of the Union.

William C. C. Claiborne was elected the first governor of the State of Louisiana. His elevation to that office attested to the high esteem in which he was held by the two elements of the population. It was a tribute to his popularity and the seal of approval of the people who had learned to appreciate the difficulties of his administration and the tact and wisdom displayed by him in solving so many intricate problems. Because of his administrative ability his term of office was comparatively serene and devoid of the serious factional conflicts which were soon to arise. Gov. Claiborne was inaugurated on July 31, 1812. The following were the first state officials: L. B. MaCarty, Secretary of State; L. Montegut, Treasurer; Thomas B. Robertson, Representative to the Congress; Allan B. Magruder and J. Thomas Posey, U. S. Senators; Dominick A. Hall, George Mathews and Pierre Derbigny, Judges of the Supreme Court; Julien Poydras, President of the Senate; P. B. St. Martin, Speaker of the House.

In one of the salient passages in his inaugural address Gov. Claiborne sensed the impending battle of New Orleans. He pleaded:

> War is not the greatest of evils — base submission to aggression would have been a greater curse. It would have entailed dishonor, cowardice, vassalage upon our posterity. The recourse to arms may increase the pressure; but let it be recollected, that whatever sacrifice we make, is offered on the altar of our country — a consideration which will reconcile a faithful people to every privation. Let every man put himself in armor. Age itself should be prepared to advance against an invading foe. Our young men should hasten to the tented fields, and tendering their services to the government, be in readiness to march at a moment's warning to the point of attack. In such a contest, the issue cannot be doubtful. In such a cause, every American should bare his bosom. Where justice is the standard, Heaven is the warrior's shield.

At the completion of his term of office, Claiborne was elected to the United States Senate. He died shortly afterwards at the age of 42.

Jacques Philippe Villeré succeeded Claiborne to the governorship. He was elected in 1816 and served a full term of four years. He was the scion of a distinguished Creole family which played a most important role both in the colonial and American periods.

Villeré's election is of historical importance because it initiated the great political rivalry with all its discord, vituperation, jealousies and hatred which existed between the Creole, French and St. Domingans and the native American factions. His opponent was Joshua Lewis who sensed that, though the newly arrived Anglo-Saxons would vote in a body for him, their numerical strength was not sufficient to elect him. To attract some of the votes of the Ancient Louisianians he issued the following platform:

> Resolved, that we view our union with the American Confederacy as the only true foundation of our happiness; as having raised up from colonial vassalage, from subservience to for-

eign tyranny, avarice and caprice, into the dignity and happiness of a sovereign state.

Resolved, that penetrated with this sentiment, we view with deep regret any measures tending to draw the line, American citizens, native of Louisiana and American citizens native of other States of the union, as measures springing from a spirit hostile to the stability, prosperity and tranquility of the State.

Resolved, that it is contrary to the spirit of the constitution and an affront against the sovereign power of the state to endeavor to disregard the possible voice of the people in the election of governor.

This platform, which has been said to be the first published in the State, proved to be a political faux pas. Its intent and purpose failed to beguile even the most naive of voters, for instead of allaying the existing distrust, it only intensified it. Villeré was elected by a majority of 169 votes. Out of 4,459 votes cast in the State, he received 2,314. Lewis carried 10 parishes and Villeré, 16. An analysis of these results show that Lewis carried the parishes Ouachita, Lafourche, St. Tammany, St. Helena, Rapides, Catahoula, E. Baton Rouge, Feliciana, St. Mary and Concordia. In St. Helena, Catahoula, Feliciana and Concordia, not a vote was cast for Villeré. The parishes of Natchitoches, Opelousas, St. James, Pointe Coupe, New Orleans, W. Baton Rouge, St. Charles, Avoyelles, Plasquemines, Iberville, Assumption, Ascension, St. Martin, St. Bernard, St. John Baptist, and Suburban New Orleans gave Villeré a mapority. Lewis did not receive a vote in St. John Baptist. The Creole carried New Orleans by a vote of 590 to 292.

Villeré, sensitive to public opinion, was subjected to a great deal of calumny. His lack of knowledge of the English language was constantly criticized, his dependence upon Mazureau exaggerated and ridiculed, but no one decried his fairness and justice in the management of his administration.

The third governor of the State of Louisiana was Thomas B. Robertson. He was a Virginian, and had been a resident of the State since 1805. He served the territory first as attorney-general, then as its secretary, and afterwards as its Congressman. He was not only capable but also a man of great integrity. He was opposed by Pierre Derbigny, J. N. Destrehan and A. L. Duncan in the election which took place on the 3, 4 and 5 of July, 1820. The results were as follows:

Robertson received 1,903 votes; Derbigny, 1,187; Duncan, 1,039 and Destréhan, 627. As no candidate received a majority of the votes cast, the election was thrown into the halls of Legislature. That body had to choose between the two having the greatest number of votes. But Derbigny, having an unusual sense of propriety (although his chance of being elected was favorable) decided to eliminate himself because he felt that the wish of the electorate, which had given Robertson a plurality, should not be ignored.

This election had been hotly contested, and all the subterfuges and machinations known to political intrigue were employed by the different factions. The Creoles learned that idealism and respect for the sanctity of the ballot, as well as the idea of voting for the best qualified candidate, did not always win elections, and that in order to survive politically they had to adapt themselves to the electioneering customs of the Americans.

The first public protest against unfair practices to influence voters was voiced in *The Louisiana Gazette* of July 7, 1820:

> The results of the late election in the city, has clearly demonstrated the futility of occupying the public papers with long winded panegyrics on one candidate, and no less tedious diatribes against others. The gentleman in whose favor least was published, has obtained a majority of the whole number of votes, although there were three other competitors. The fact is that rich and influential men, determined to spare no pains, willing to stoop to all manner of cajolery and solicitations, have procured for their favorite more votes on that ground, than all the press of the world could have done otherwise.
>
> It was amusing to me to see these gentlemen pounce upon some well meaning, but good-natured citizens, examine their tickets and if not to their liking, substitute another in their place. Nor was this all, coaches were used to transport them from the dwelling of the distant voter. By this means and their prayers did they overcome their laziness or indifference, by this means even the sick and lame were brought up to vote, many of them no doubt having their little vanities tickled by such flattering mark of attention as a visit in a coach by a great man.
>
> There is another remark to be made while on this subject, the paucity of number of those who voted. In a city as populous as this, only 875 votes to be taken is somewhat surprising: in part it may be attributed to the number of rich absentees at this season. We wish some means could be found of keeping them at home, at least until the elections should be over.

In the same edition appeared the following article written in

French by "Feuillton" deploring the manner in which the last election was conducted:

> I am curious to know who won the last election, or who is the one who had received the most votes in the city if they had not employed all these small means, worthy heritage from the English, for it is only by imitating them, that our elections have become as ridiculous as theirs. Do you think that I conscientiously could think that I was the choice of the people, and deserving of their confidence, if I were elected by these small leaders? It is certain that at least one hundred persons did not know for who they voted! Do you think that these political jugglers work to choose a governor capable and worthy of Louisiana? Absolutely no! But these leaders answer, well! they have voted . . . Ah, the beautiful conclusion! It is like the gamblers who cheat who say it does not matter for we have won.

The following excerpt from a Georgia paper printed in the *Baton Rouge Gazette* of October, 1822, gives an interesting insight into the motives, prejudices, dissensions, hatreds and intolerance which permeated the politics of that time:

> The following will shed light on the origin and the causes of dissension which pervades the heterogenous population of Louisiana. The federal party in that State had but few friends, with but few exceptions and the population is sincerely republican and loyal to the administration of the present government.
>
> There are two parties which do not extend beyond the limits of Louisiana, and these are the American and the French parties.
>
> The people of Louisiana since it was established by the French, had been governed by the civil law, somewhat modified to meet the needs of the locality, and having been Catholic, were and are today opposed against the adoption of any other code or religion. They do not want the common law of England, nor the religion practiced by the people with which that law is incorporated.
>
> Vain attempts were made by the American members of the territorial legislature to substitute the common for the civil code, but without avail. At that period the number of Americans in Louisiana was not considerable, so the Louisianians had no fear that their antagonists would triumph, but with the increasing number of immigrants from other parts of the Union, the Louisianians became more suspicious and more careful. Although their party had acquired additional strength because of the arrival in New Orleans of a large number of Frenchmen from the isles of Cuba and St. Domingo, who immediately became allies of the Creoles because of the homogeneity of language, religion and culture. United as were the members of that party, the election of the first governor of the State caused a

momentary division. The French refugees were grateful to Governor Claiborne because he assumed the responsibility of allowing their slaves to enter the State, they together with the Americans supported him and opposed the Louisianians who wished to elect one of their own, and Governor Claiborne was elected. This break between the indigenes and the French refugees was of short duration, for after Governor Claiborne had terminated his term of office, they were again united in opposition of a number of Americans, whose aim it was to abolish their religion and the civil code.

Thus united in a common cause, together with the support of educated Americans, such as Robertson, Brown and Livingston they maintained their balance of power in the State.

The last war with England caused a rupture between the two parties. The refugees and the Creoles, and great many Americans, under the leadership of Edward Livingston, agreed to defend New Orleans to the last extremity, they all helped General Jackson, and contributed to the expulsion of the English from Louisiana. The general became their idol, but it was not so of many who considered themselves American citizens, but were more devoted to England. The arrest of Judge Hall by General Jackson furnished these men with a pretext to openly show their animosity for the General and those around him. The most influential Americans at first favored the common law, but experience taught them that all attempts to revoke the status quo whould be futile, and that it would be wiser to modify the principles of the civil code, in a way that they will be in accord with the system of government of the State, as well as of the Union.

A large majority of the citizens of New Orleans wished that the seat of government should remain in their city, while the American party, in the hope of greatly increasing their influence, at every session of the Legislature, advocated a change of location. But wherever may be the seat of government, the majority governs, and that majority is too strong at present, to be crushed, except by numerical superiority.

This graphic commentary gives a clear picture of the political issues of that time, and of the animosity and intolerance, then existing in the city, but one important factor was overlooked and that was the prevalence of the French language. The Anglo-Americans (so-called for convenience) were determined to suppress the French tongue in all civil, legislative and legal procedures, nay, some even wanted it abolished. They were not actuated by a noble spirit of patriotism, but one of self interest, because the indigenous population would be disfranchised, their lawyers would not be able to plead before a bar of justice, nor would they be able to hold a position of public trust. They were to be relegated to the status of foreigners, and be deprived of the rights and privileges of American citizenship. But it must be said that the more intelligent and cultured among them, who established their domicile there, espoused the cause of the Creoles, even to the point of incurring, not only the displeasure, but the enmity, of their fellow Anglo-Americans.

Politics was comparatively quiet for the next two years. In 1822 an election was held for a senator, and a member of the House of Representatives, as well as for members of the State Legislature. The same two political parties supported candidates for these offices. On June 22, 1822, the *Louisiana Gazette* reported that the French, Creole, and American faction, supported Edward Ligingston for the United States Senate, and L. Moreau Lislet for Congressman; and for State Representative, W. W. Montgomery, J. R. Grymes, L. St. Blanchard, P. E. Foucher, E. Mazureau and P. L. Morel. The American party endorsed for the State House of Representatives, E. W. Ripley, J. R. Grymes, P. E. Foucher, and A. Davezac. Edward Livingston received 645 votes for the Senate and L. Moreau Lislet 643 votes for Congress. The following representatives were elected; J. R. Grymes, 599 votes; E. Mazureau, 548 votes; P. E. Foucher, 492 votes; A. Davezac, 467 votes; F. Grima, 463 votes; C. Maurian, 453 votes. The unsuccessful candidates were E. W. Ripley with 169 votes; L. St. Blanchard, 158 votes; W. W. Montgomery, 151 votes; P. L. Morel, 135 votes; F. Meance, 98 votes; J. L. Saul, 34 votes; F. L. Percy, 33 votes; F. Delachaise, 32 votes and J. Mercier, 18 votes.

Grymes and Foucher were supported by both factions, while Mazureau and Davezac were the candidates of the opposing parties. Grima and Maurian were not the choice of either, and yet they were elected by a splendid majority. Evidently the votes were cast for the individual instead of the party.

Some objections were voiced in the papers about the large number of lawyers elected to the legislature, and that with the exception of Mr. Foucher, all were members of that profession, and the doubt was expressed that any lawyer, especially a young one, without experience, had the necessary qualifications.

In 1824, the election for Governor attracted considerable attention. It was an acrimonious conflict between the French and English-speaking segments of the population, and the beginning of the practice of electing a governor from a part of the State other than New Orleans. Long before the campaign opened, a Creole for Governor was made the issue by the American party. Friends of Villeré were then styled the "Mazureaunian Party". On January 22, 1824, the following item appeared in the *Louisiana Gazette*: "Let every one who it not blinded by party rage, take up the files of the *Advertiser* from the month of August last, and say whether it has had a tendency to widen the breach which factionists have made between the Creole and American population."

There were five candidates for the Governor's chair to wit: Villeré, Marigny, Johnson, Thomas and Butler. Villeré and Marigny were prominent Creoles and Johnson had been a resident of Donaldsonville since 1811. Villeré had been governor from 1816 to 1820, Johnson represented the State in the Senate of the United States for six years, General Thomas was the Senator from Baton Rouge, and Marigny, a prominent Creole of New Orleans.

In July, the election was held, 6,525 votes were cast in the State, including 1,037 in the city. Marigny carried New Orleans by 511 votes. Johnson received 257 and Villeré, 252. A tabulation of the total votes showed: for Johnson, 2,847 votes; Villeré, 1,831; Marigny, 1,427; Thomas, 236; Butler, 184. Out of 37 parishes and districts, Johnson carried eleven; Villeré, eight; Marigny, seven; and Thomas, only Baton Rouge, his home parish.

Most of the parishes in the southern part of the State gave majorities to Villeré and Marigny, while those in the northern sections were carried overwhelmingly by Johnson. As Johnson did not have the required majority, in November a joint meeting of the two houses of the Legislature was held, attended by thirteen Senators and forty-four Representatives. Johnson received forty-one votes; Villeré, fifteen; and one blank. Johnson was proclaimed Governor, and in December he was inaugurated.

Dominick Bouligny was at that same session elected to succeed Johnson as Senator. On July 3rd, 1824, Thomas Urquhart, C. G. DeArmas, A. Morphy, J. Mercier, J. R. Grymes, Gen. J. B. Labatut were elected State Representatives for the City of New Orleans.

The *Louisiana Gazette* of April 8, 1824, lamented "that the electioneering campaign by Johnson and Butler was conducted with so much violence and acrimony."

That same journal on March 17, 1824, gave the following

biographic sketch of Thomas Butler, and proclaimed him a virtuous partriot:

> His father served this republic in all the wars of the first thirty years of our national existence. He died in Louisiana and was much loved and respected by all who knew him. The annals of the wars give the names of General Percival Butler and five gallant sons and nephews, all distinguished as brave, faithful and patriotic . . . judge of the people of the Florida, who five years afterwards by an almost unanimous suffrage, made Thomas Butler, a member of Congress, where he served for three years.

Johnson accused Butler of being a traitor because he was with Aaron Burr. The article acknowledged the connection but explained that "while the idea held out that the destination was Mexico, and the object to aid a people struggling for liberty, he did not abandon him, (Burr) but as soon as Mr. Butler suspected any part of the enterprise was directed against his own country, he deserted Burr and settled among us."

One of the most interesting personages in Louisiana History is General Philemon Thomas. This soldier, patriot, statesman, adventurer and planter has never been given the recognition he has so richly deserved. The following sketch of his life shows the respect and admiration in which he was held by his contemporaries. On March 24, in the same newspaper he was extolled as follows:

> He enrolled himself as a volunteer in the army of our country in the year 1779, era of revolution, then only sixteen years old. Served with General Lincoln and Green, until the close of the war. Then went to Kentucky, — in 1784, he fitted out and loaded a boat with the produce of the State, and in the true spirit of adventure, descended the Ohio and the Mississippi in search of a market. On the fifth of May he arrived in New Orleans and remained in the City until the Fall, when with a single companion, he embarked at the Bayou St. John, crossed the lake and returned home by land.
>
> The result of the General's expedition was such as to produce about five years afterwards, an almost direct trade between Kentucky and New Orleans, which was seriously commenced by General Wilkinson and others.
>
> He then decided to make Kentucky his home; was at war against the savages until 1806.
>
> He rose in Kentucky from many ranks to grade of General; served in Legislature eleven consecutive years.
>
> Gen. Thomas removed then to Louisiana and settled in East

Baton Rouge, then under the Government of Spain. The tyranny and oppression of the Spanish Government was at this period so great, as to induce the inhabitants to call a convention, and that convention gave to General Thomas, then a Colonel-Commandant, the authority to command Florida as far as the Pearl River; and afterwards feeling that the Governor was not sincere, and in fact intended to deceive them, gave authority to General Thomas to possess himself of the archives and fort at Baton Rouge. On the twenty-third of September, 1810, a little before daylight, this duty was performed by him in a manner that will eternally honor him as a soldier and a man. Having completed this part of his duty, he m a r c h e d to St. Helena, where with much address, he quieted the apprehension of every description of persons, and ably executed the orders entrusted to him.

He was described as a man with clean unaffected manners, but not without a share of urbanity.

Gen. Thomas was a planter in Baton Rouge, and served six years in the Legislature and forty years as a public servant.

"What education does Mr. Villeré possess?" asked the *Louisiana Gazette* of April 3, 1824. "It is well known he is deficient on that point, but his countrymen make no reproach for this defect; it is enough for them to know that he embraces and combines what they adore — honesty, firmness of character and good sense."

The unfair criticism of his political enemies as to the manner in which he conducted his office of Governor, was rebuked by the *Gazette* of May 10, as follows:

It was said that Villeré was only nominally Governor, and that he suffered himself to be governed by the then Secretary of State, Mr. Mazureau, who (they say) claimed the right of managing him, and of disposing of all his patronage; it is well known that Mr. Mazureau is a gentleman of preeminent talents and having accepted the office of Secretary of State, it is not improbable that with a fitness of the office, peculiar to himself, he personally transacted much of the business and thereby saved his principal a great deal of trouble, but that Mr. Mazureau ever interfered with the Governor, but when his opinions were put in requisition, would be ridiculous to suppose. In point of patriotism, Mr. Villeré yields to no citizen of the State, is an honest man, a good neighbor and is sincere in his friendship and professions.

The press was relatively silent concerning the qualifications of Messrs. Johnson and Marigny.

Such were the issues on which that campaign was waged, and it is doubtful that in all her history, Louisiana had had five candidates for the Governorship as distinguished, or better qualified.

On May 5, the *Gazette* published the following eulogy of Mr. Marigny:

> We are not in communication with him in any way, or have anything to say of, or to do with him, but as a public man, Mr. Marigny has served with credit in Legislature, quitted it two years since as President of the Senate. He has never committed any great public offense. His private life possesses many admirable qualities for hospitality, in itself a virtue. He has always been distinguished, his house and table was always opened, as well to foreigners as to fellow citizens, always kind to new destitute arrivals.
>
> He has no desire for gain, as his fortune would render the salary of Governor a matter of little consideration. He has no wish for patronage, he has no relations or dependents whom the same fortune is not sufficient to succor. He is objected by some because they say he is not a man of talents. But excepting Mr. DeWitt Clinton, we have of late heard of but few Governors that have turned out to be great philosophers or conjurors, so he is on a par with his fellow contemporary Governors.
>
> He has an ordinary share of intelligence, grounded upon integrity, and a degree of self-possession and firmness.
>
> He is objected to because he is not a lawyer, here where lawyers are plentiful as mosquitoes (one or the other operating upon us in the same way, the former easing us of our spare cash, in the same ratio as the latter do of our superfluous blood.) he has no enemies among lawyers.
>
> He is a c c u s e d of not being a good republican, and a staunch royalist, a retainer of Louis the eighteenth, and an aristocrat in disguise, but these we treat as mere electioneering squibs, as charges growing out of the present contest. He only made occasional visits to the land of his ancestors, and as a man of fortune, mingled in gay circles in Paris, and was well received by the King of France. We see nothing anti-republican in this.
>
> He wrote a book, and from his personal and political enemies, has incurred the reputation of being a bad author, but what then, the offence carries it own punishment with it, and Mr. Marigny has made himself responsible at the bar of public criticism, indeed, convicted or not, he is already under the last. Mr. Marigny, however, having no reputation as a writer, goes without risk before the public; and although his work should

be damned, still he has no chance of losing his civil right, or his fair claim upon his follow citizens.

Only a taxpayer could vote in the State, and many were challenged at the polls as to their qualifications. The accusation was made that this was done to exclude American voters. The following protest was voiced on December 9, 1825 by the *Louisiana Gazette*:

> It is stated to be a fact, that there are great numbers of persons in this city holding property to a considerable amount, who are known to be the powers that be, or in other words, are Americans by principle, who have never been called on for the payment of taxes, for no other purpose than to prevent them from exercising their right of sufferage. If the views of a faction are thus to be protected by the officers of the State Government, and the rights of Americans are not thus trampled on, it is time that some more decided means than unnoticed remonstrances should be employed.

On May 20, 1824, a Jackson-for-President party was launched by J. R. Plauché, B. Grima, J. B. Labatut, W. Withers, L. T. Preston, Esq.

The first meeting was held on June 6th. It was presided over by F. Girod; General Plauché was vice-president, and Alfred Hennen the secretary. Addresses were made by S. R. Harper, Esq., A. Davezac, Esq., General Ripley and L. T. Preston, Esq. The Committee on Publicity was composed of L. T. Preston, A. Davezac, S. H. Harper, J. B. Wiltz, Sr., DeLaronde, L. Lacoste, D. C. Ker and General J. B. Labatut.

The *Louisiana Gazette* voiced its opposition to the election of General Jackson in the following editorial in its issue of June 29, 1824:

> The idea of making a President of the United States of General Jackson, is a soap bubble inflated by boys, and will soon explode.
>
> We should be the last to deny General Jackson's gallantry, or to derogate from his desert. But why inhume him alive, under a load of honors, which he cannot sustain? Why whelm him, with a flood of commendations to which he has acquired no title?

The editorial predicted that Mr. Adams' chance of success was more promising because Henry Clay would s u p p o r t him. Adams was elected.

In November, 1822, Governor Robertson resigned to accept the appointment of the Judgeship of the United States District

Court. He was replaced by Mr. Thibodeaux, the president of the Senate, and L. M. Lislet was appointed president protem.

Early in January, 1825, at a meeting of both houses of the Legislature, Edward Livingston was defeated by J. S. Johnson for Congress.

The *Louisiana Gazette*, on January 21, 1825, in an article entitled "Puff in the *Argus* about Mr. Livingston" wrote as follows:

The article intimates that the Majority in the Legislature have been actuated by envy or a want of reflection, etc., in their preference for Josiah Johnson.

Of the eminent talents of Mr. Livingston there is no question, the professional powers he has displayed in involving in litigation in the United States, the State of Louisiana and City of New Orleans, and an immense number of the inhabitants of our State, has justly made him dear to the members of the Bar, and ranks him first among his coadjutors. There is little doubt that the people of Louisiana will approve of their representation for the preference they have given to the unassuming Josiah Johnson.

Would it not be well to let the work appear before we attempt to forestall public opinion, on a subject we are so little acquainted with. We make no objection to giving time to complete his work, and a few more thousands to feed his midnight lamp, but we do wish the people to see the work before they be required to swallow it.

The burning of the code may be a public loss, but really it does not appear to us, that, if in that conflagration had been included, all the contradictory mass of law that has been completed since Louisiana became a state, it would not in the slightest degree have affected the security of property.

It further quoted the Editor of the *St. Francis Asylum*, a staunch supporter of Johnson, and the political voice of the Anglo-Americans, which said: "We are pleased to discover, in this act of our Legislature a disposition to bestow on intelligence and integrity, the reward they merit; for seldom have we seen these virtues displayed than in the public conduct of Josiah S. Johnson."

The year 1826, and 1827 were one of relative political tranquility and harmony.

In April 1826, Edward Livingston and P. E. Foucher offered themselves for Congress, and General Philemon Thomas announced his candidacy for the Governorship.

On Monday, May 3rd, elections were held for City officers: Joseph Roffignac was elected Mayor and Prieur, Recorder; and the following were elected aldermen: General Ripley, S. Livermore, Doctor Thomas, Baccas, Davezac, Montreuil, B. Marigny, Lacoste, F. Finke, Palfrey, J. Freret, Foucher and Fleitas.

On the third of July 1826 the general election was held, and Edward Livingston was elected to Congress. L. Maureau Lislet was made State Senator, and the following were chosen for State Representatives: Maurian, Waggaman, Morphy, Grymes, Landreaux, and Allard.

The following day, the *Gazette* reported that "considerable activity was observed during the whole time the polls were opened, which manifested the deep interest the people feel in the result of the elections."

And in a editorial two days afterwards, it reported that during the period of the election there was much excitement, and observed:

> We could not perceive, nor do we believe there was much collusion between the population who spoke the French and English languages.
>
> In truth there is no difference in interest or of feeling between the two populations. They are all anxious for promoting the general good. Americans by birth, in principles, and in feeling, it is a misconceived policy that would produce dissension. Indeed the election which terminated yesterday is the best refutation of the slander that Louisianians who speak not the English language are hostile to our institutions.

At the end of February, 1828, the following were appointed Jackson Electors from the State of Louisiana:

1st District	General John B. Plauché, New Orleans
2nd District	Theo W. Scott, East Feliciana
3rd District	Trasimond Landry
4th District	Alexander Mouton, Lafayette
5th District	Placide Bossier, Natchitoches

A Jackson meeting was held at Davis Hall in New Orleans on April 15th, Doctor David C. Ker presided, and J. J. Mercier, Esq., was the secretary. Resolutions were presented by J. R. Grymes. The following candidates were endorsed for the State Legislature: Generals J. B. Labatut and J. B. Plauché, John B. Grymes, G. DeArmas, Francis Gaiennie, Louis Allard and Martin Gordon.

That year t h e r e were acrimonious communications to the papers, particularly in the *Argus*, about the refusal of commissioners at the polls in not allowing certain individuals to cast their votes. They protested the decision as contrary to the constitution of the State, which provided that "in all elections for representatives every white male citizen of the United States, who at the time being had attained to the age of 21 years, and resided in the country, in which he offers to vote, one year preceeding the election, and who in the last six months prior to the said election, shall have paid a state tax, shall enjoy the right of an elector."

Again Marigny was a candidate for Governor, this time opposing Derbigny, the former staunch supporter of General Jackson, while the latter espoused the cause of President Adams. Marigny was the target of venomous diatribes in the *Argus*, an anti-Jackson, a pro-Adams and pro-American party organ. The *Courier* of July 3, 1828, published the following communication signed "A Jacksonian":

> These gentlemen Adams' men are aware that the election of Mr. Derbigny to the office of Governor, is perhaps the most fatal blow that can befall the cause of Jackson in this State; they are convinced that if they can now succeed to place the cause of Adams under the aegis of the powerful influence of executive authority, their party now desperate must assume new strength, and be enabled to maintain, with more chance of success, the electoral strength of the month of November. A proscription will be pronounced against every honest mind who shall ever show gratitude towards the Hero who saved Louisiana.

Some of the most prominent and distinguished citizens of the city contested the election held on July 7th, 8th, and 9th; their petion read as follows:

> Gentlemen: Notice is given to protest the election as member of the House of Representatives — of 2nd Senatorial district, on the following grounds:
>
> (1) Election illegally held and void because Felix Grima, Esq., presided and acted as Judge of Commissioners of said election, he, the said Felix Grima, Esq., not having been duly commissioned as presiding Justice of the City Court of New Orleans, his commission is null and void, having been signed and issued by the Governor, while the said office was filled by Edward D. White, and before he had resigned, and before there was a vacancy, "in violation of the constitution of Louisiana". Said commisssion was signed on the 6th of July 1828, in truth not granted before July 8, 1828:
>
> (2) That undue attempts were made by the candidates, or by persons, at their instance, etc., to influence and control the Parish Judge of City and Parish of New Orleans, in the appointment he should make or had made of the persons he had a

right to appoint to act as Ass't. Judge and Commissioners of said election, that he was illegally and unduly influenced in the matter. Also like influence was exercised to induce Gallien Preval, Esq., to resign, and decline to act as judge and commissioner of said election a f t e r being appointed by the Parish Judge.

(3) Many voters were refused the right to vote, under the pretense that said persons were not assessed for taxes on the tax list of 1827, but were assessed in 1828, and exhibited the receipts of the Treasurer of the State of Louisiana, and even offered to prove on their oaths:

Tax list of 1827 arbitrarily adopted.

(Signed) Generals J. B. Labatut and J. B. Plauché, J. R. Grymes, G. C. DeArmas, F. Gaiennie, L. Allard and M. Gordon.

Evidently this protest was inspired by the following item entitled "Another insult to Naturalized Citizens," which appeared in the *Courier* on July 8th: "Yesterday the venerable Judge Workman, a gentleman no less distinguished by his learning than his patriotism and philantrophy, who has resided in the United States for more than twenty-five years, who has held the office of Probate Judge of this City, and who has uniformly voted since he lived in Louisiana, was required by an Adams' man at the polls, to swear that he is a citizen of the United States. This was done, not only because Judge Workman is a friend of the people's cause, but because he is an Irishman by birth."

In April, 1829, the following persons were elected Aldermen: Martin Gordon, F. DeArmas, Rodriguez, S. Cucullu, J. P. Freret, M. White, N. Gaiennie and E. Blanc.

Dennis Prieur was then Mayor, and J. M. Fleitas, Recorder. The following were the officers of the City Council:

G. Preval	Secretary of the Council
J. Pilie	Court Surveyor
P. Deverges	Commissary of the District
F. Peuve	Commissary of the 1st District
Favre Daunoy	Commissary of the 1st District
R. Montegue	Commissary of the 1st District
F. D. Henry	Commissary of the 1st District
J. Hubert	Syndic of the upper banlieu
Theord Lewis	Syndic of the lower banlieu
E. Blanc	Syndic of the Bayou St. John Banlieu
Soniat	Syndic of Gentilly banlieu
Capt. Gumble	Wharfinger for flats and Steamboats

C. Durillet .... Captain of City Guard
B. Monseigneur .... 1t Lieut. of City Guard
Mirepoix .... 2nd Lieut. of City Guard
Jacob Hart .... 3rd Lieut. of City Guard
Simon Meilleur .... Keeper of the City Jail

M. D. Augustin was appointed Secretary of the City Council, replacing G. Preval, who resigned the last days of May.

Bernard Marigny and S. D. Dixon were candidates for the House of Representatives to replace W. C. C. Claiborne who had resigned. At an election held early in January 1832, the results were: S. D. Dixon, 624 votes and B. Marigny, 623 votes. This election was nullified by a vote of 30 to 8 by the House of Representatives and another election was ordered to take place in a few days for the following reasons published in the *Courier* of January 6, 1832:

In counting votes, it appeared that one of the tickets contained two names, Mr. Dixon's and another. Although there was only one member to elect, that vote had been admitted in in favor of Mr. Dixon owing to which he has obtained over his competitor, Mr. Marigny, a majority of one. Another reason is adduced, and it is that only 1242 voters came to the poll; whereas the box contained 1250 tickets, three of which were rejected because they were double.

At the end of the month, a second election was held, and that time Marigny was opposed by S.J . Peters, a large property owner in the upper faubourg. Again the line was drawn; the Americans against the Creoles. This election aroused great interest and partisanship. In the first election 1247 electors went to the polls, while in the second, 1550 ballots were counted. This time the Creole won by a substantial majority. The results were 836 to 708 votes. The election lasted three days.

At the end of that year, the Governor appointed George Eustis, Secretary of State to succeed McCaleb, a victim of the cholera. Etienne Mazureau was made Attorney General, Pierre S. Landreaux, Recorder of Mortgages for the parish of Orleans; Wm. McQueston, Tobacco Inspector of New Orleans; Cotton Henry, Flour Inspector of New Orleans; Jos. T. Blache, Gauger; F. Tricou, Auctioneer; C. W. Morgan, Sheriff of New Orleans; and I. L. McCoy, F. Dutillet, J. Lecarpentier, T. Mossey, Auctioneers; Chas. May, Gauger of the City of New Orleans.

An interesting personality in the political field was Colonel H. D. Peire. At the beginning of the year, 1832, he announced his candidacy for Mayor. A communication in the *Courier* of March 10, of that year gave an interesting sketch of his distinguished career, it said:

Colonel H. D. Peire took part in the battle of 1813. He was a major of the Orleans Volunteers, Aide de Camp to General Wilkinson. He went on an expedition ordered by the general government, for the occupation of the City of Mobile. On arriving in front of the place, he was dispatched to the General, the Spanish commander of Fort Charlotte, for the purpose of summoning him to surrender the fortresses. The General being anxious to avoad the effusion of blood, instructed his aid, to attain the delivery of the place by means of negotiations. In this Major Peire fully succeeded, and concluded the convention, by virtue of w h i c h , the port was occupied by United States troops. (This convention is contained in full in General Wilkinson's memoires.)

In the year following, Col. Peire having been appointed Major of the 44th regiment of the United States Infantry; and being then on recruiting services in Tennessee, received from General Jackson an order to meet him at Mobile, and to bring along with him all the forces he could unite, in order to undertake the expedition against Pensacola. Having reached the vicinity of that place, he was sent with a flag of truce to require the surrender of Fort St. Miguel; but he was fired upon by the British forces, who then formed a part of the garrison of that fort. Then General Jackson resolved to take the place by storm. Major Peire at the head of a battalion under his immediate command, and a battalion of the 3rd Regiment, U. S. Infantry, was ordered to lead the attack against the town. The promptness and gallantry with which the order was executed, were such, that the enemy had no time but to make a single discharge, which killed or wounded but few men. After the taking of the town, the General left the Major in command of it, with order to reduce Fort Miguel, either by negotiation or by force. It was obtained by the former. The inhabitants of Pensacola, many of whom are now living in New Orleans, remember the judicious and humane measures taken by Major Peire to prevent disorders, and to secure the safety of the citizens and their property. General Jackson on being informed of the attack which the British contemplated a g a i n s t New Orleans, repaired immediately to this place with Major Peire. The high opinion he entertained for that officer, after having witnessed his conduct at Pensacola, induced the General to entrust him with the command of the 7th regular U. S. Infantry, whose commanding officer was disabled by a wound. It was at the head of that gallant corps that Major Peire led the attack against the British, on the ever memorable night of 23rd of December 1814. He met the enemy with very inferior forces, and by his spirited conduct, gave time to our brave militia to reach the field of battle. This brilliant action, which by many, is considered as the principal one of the whole campaign, reflected much honor upon Maj. Peire. General Jackson mentioned his name on that occasion in the most flattering terms, and it was to his conduct in that affair, as well as in all others during the seige of New Orleans, that Major Peire earned the brevet of Lieutenant-Colonel. which the President of the United States caused to be delivered to him, accompained by the most honorable and complimentary expressions. Colonel Peire was distinguished by his zeal and punctuality in the performance of his duty throughout the whole campaign, and particularly on the 8th of January 1815.

In July Major H. D. Peire was appointed superintendent of the Port of New Orleans.

The *Argus* accused Peire of grasping at every office, one of the sneaking, meddling and crawling place hunters, who are outstanding candidates for every commission, whether in the gift of the people or the Executive. This was vehemently refuted by the *Courier*.

After the Battle of New Orleans Peire became an adventurer and a soldier of fortunes. Stanley Faye, in his authoritative article entitled "Commodore Aury" which appeared in the Louisian Historical Quaterly of July 1941, wrote about this interesting episode in the history of New Orleans:

Anglo-Saxons in Creole Louisiana were prominent in the New Orleans Associates, [a very secret society, of 1815-1816 in which the members were designated by numbers] with which Commodore Aury [the privateer] in Hayti allied himself by correspondence. At the head of the group stood Edward Livingston from New York. Among Livingston's chief aides were John Randolph Grymes of Virginia, late federal attorney; Abner L. Duncan, former territorial attorney-general in Natchez; Duncan's business partner, the merchant John K. West; Customs Collector Pierre Le Breton Duplessis from Philadelphia; the bank president Benjamin Morgan: Aury's agent, Francois Dupuy, who preferred to be known as a planter; Captain Henry Perry, quartermaster and ordnance officer in New Orleans; and Brevet-Lieutenant-Colonel Henry D. Peire, a veteran of the late war against Great Britain. Daniel Tod Patterson, commodore of the New Orleans naval station, acted as a member of the Associates to the extent that his official position and orders from Washington both authorized him and permitted him.

The party among the Associates dreamed of capturing the two Floridas and selling them to the United States for the price (about $2,000,000) that President Jefferson had earlier empowered James Monroe and Robt. Livingston, Edward Livingston's brother, to offer Spain for the provinces. By letter to Commodore Aury in Haiti the Associates proposed, first an attack upon Tampico, port of export for the Mexican silver mines. To Aury they offered the command of the sea forces; Colonel Peire would command the soldiers who would be disembarked from transports. Meanwhile a temporary port was needed. Inspection of the uninhabited and almost unknown coast of Spanish Texas resulted in decision to occupy Galveston Bay, just beyond the Texas—Louisiana border.

Nothing more is known of this remarkable organization and its presumably abortive attempt to capture the Mexican silver and buy Florida.

On May, 1834, the following office holders were appointed by the City Council:

M. J. Pilié and M. A. D'Hemecourt, Surveyor and Deputy surveyor.

F. Gogust and C. Durel, Syndic for vegetable market.

M. P. Eyratta, Commissioner for vegetable market.

S. Daunois and J. Dutillet, Commissioners of police for portion of the City, between Levee, Rampart, Canal and Orleans.

M. R. Montegut, Commissioner of police for faubourg Marigny,

M. G. St. Vilmes, Commissioner of police for faubourg Treme.

Bonseigneur, Captain of Police

M. Hart, 1st Lieutenant of Police

E. String, Commissioner of Police for boats, etc.

J. Wales, Superintendent of steam boats.

E. Mailleur, Jailer

M. G. Correjolle, Commissioner of the meat market

M. Communé, Commissioner faubourg St. Mary.

The campaign for governor was one of vituperation, crimination and recrimination. As early as April, J. D. Dawson and Edward D. White announced their candidacy. The *Argus* declared for White and the *Bee* announced its support for J. D. Dawson.

The issue was raised in the *Bee*, of May 12, 1834 in an article with the following headline: "Things to be remembered at the Polls". It said:

Remember that Edward D. White voted in favor of law calculated to bring distress and ruin upon the great flourishing interest of the State: Remember that we sent him to Congress to advocate our rights, and to represent our wants. Remember that he sold the one and mocked the other: Remember that John D.

Dawson was raised among us, that he never deceived the confidence of his fellow-citizens, in fact, that he has ever been respected as a gentleman, loved as a man, and honored as a judge.

The slogans were "Bank and Aristocracy against People" and "Dawson with Custom House gang and Jackson."

A song was composed for the occasion entitled "Le Whiski", a satire on Mazuerau, who in a speech, declared that the supporters of Dawson, "as a class of men who could be purchased for a glass of whiskey". The *Bee* retorted on June 28, 1834, with the following: "Mr. Mazureau's assertion dishonors his judgment or his candor, and is a gross libel on a majority of the voters of the State."

The polls were closed in the afternoon of July 9th. In New Orleans 1510 votes were cast, and it is reported that "much excitement prevailed, more in fact than has been displayed on any similar occasion." White was nominated Governor, and carried the City by the overwhelming majority of 958 to 552 votes.

According to the law of 1825 there could be only one Alderman for each 60 voters in each district of the City. In 1827 the law was changed to provide one Alderman for every one hundred and fifty voters.

The following were the Aldermen in 1835: McFarlane and Schmidt, Felix Labatut, A. Grailhe, A. W. Pichot, L. V. Gaiennié, Caldwell, Berry, Joshua Baldwin, Louis Allard.

In May, 1835 an election was held for State Representative to succeed the former incumbent, the deceased Mr. Ducros. Again Marigny was a candidate, and this time he was opposed by McFarlane. This contest is of interest because it again shows the rivalry that existed between the American and Creole sections of the city. The upper faubourg gave McFarlane 299 votes to Marigny's 44, but the city proper, Marigny received 442 votes to McFarlane 74, and in the lower faubourg Marigny received still a larger majority over his adversary, the vote being 164 to 9. The total giving Marigny a majority of 268. McFarlane had, in the French section only 83 votes, and Marigny polled in American section only 44.

The *Bee* of October 17, 1835 commented:

> It is seriously agitated by most influential citizens, to have a law passed by the Legislature to prevent the eligibility of any person to the election of Mayor for more than two terms, that is four years.
>
> Those who are aware of the extent of the executive patronage possessed by the Mayor of New Orleans, in consequence of

the number of appointments in his power, which generally gives him the almost absolute control of about 380 votes, will admit the propriety of such ineligibility in the election and appointments to the executive authorities of the State, who are in office only for four years.

In the State Legislature of 1836, the proposal to increase the salary of the Governor was debated, the opposition was based on the fact that the salary of the Governors of New York and Pennsylvania was $4,000.00, where in Louisiana it was $7,500.00.

The following Aldermen were elected in April, 1837:

1st Municipality: First District: Thomas Duplessis, Edward Duplesis, J. Armitage, Paul Tulane, Frederick Durrive, F. R. Stringer, G. B. Faures.

2nd District: J. Guillot, Jr., Ursin Wiltz, Solomon High, Felix deArmas, C. Lesseps.

3rd District: Manuel Cruzet, P. Davis, Jr., G. Brusle, J. Reynes, C. Morel, F. Lefebre.

4th District: E. A. Cannon, G. Preval, F. Lefebre.

5th District: Anthony Fernandez, F. Coquet, Jr., P. Plauché.

2nd Municipality: First District: James P. Freret, Spencer G. Loyd, C. C. Meux, James Caldwell.

2nd District: Samuel J. Peters, Edward Yorke, Henry Lockett.

3rd District: C. L. W. Shaumburg, Robert H. McNair, Samuel Huart.

3rd Municipality: 1st Precinct: G. Montgomery, Louis Feraud.

2nd Precinct: Bernard Marigny, John R. Bertrand.

3rd Precinct: John Kilshaw.

4th Precinct: Louis Duvignaud.

On October 30, 1837, the *Bee* reported an attempt made by Shaumburg "to banish the French Language" and labelled it "the boldest effort of its kind". It made the following comment: "Nor can the indigenous population of Louisiana, the Creoles, be excluded from municipal employments, or be deprived of the relations they hold in regard to magistrates elected by themselves. Shaumburg is a Creole. It is an election ruse to exclude any member of the ancient population from office of Mayor. This project is destroying the French language."

The resolution was vetoed by the Mayor. A short while afterwards Shaumburg announced his candidacy for the mayoralty.

CHAPTER IX

THE THREE MUNICIPALITIES

At the beginning of the nineteenth century the population of New Orleans was composed principally of the colonists of the French and Spanish dominations, refugees from San Domingo and French emigrants. They were bound together by a bond of language, culture, mutual understanding, social amenity and of religion. The new San Dominigan arrivals quickly amalgamated with the Creoles, became a component part of the French speaking population and soon formed a dominant political party in the city. Their numerical superiority controlled the elections. Only for a short while everything was serene, but this serenity was soon dispelled by the ever increasing migration from the North and West. These new comers, mostly of Anglo-Saxon origin, were still imbued with the concept of superiority, anti-Papal prejudice and the disdain, distrust and hatred for any one else but English-speaking people. They brought with them the predilection and bias inherent in their forebears of pre-revolutionary days, which persisted long after they had achieved their independence. At the same time the Creoles and the French maintained all their native characteristics. They were zealous in admiration for their origin, their language and their culture. Each group professed a superiority over the other, and each was indomitable in retaining its way of life irrespective of the consequences. The indigenous population vigorously protested against any infringement on the rights and privileges accorded them by the Purchase. They retaliated with social ostracism. Whilst they would mingle as equals in business, their homes were closed to all except the more distinguished and cultured Anglo-Saxons. They resented the attitude of the Americans who considered Louisiana a conquered nation, one to be exploited for their personal benefit, and for regarding its inhabitants as foreigners and unworthy of the dignity of citizenship, and who should not even be allowed to vote.

Another factor was the rapid growth of the city proper. It was over populated and over built and there was no room for further expansion. It had to be extended beyond its original boundaries, so either through necessity or by choice, the recently arrived

The three municipalities of New Orleans as shown on Norman's map of 1848.

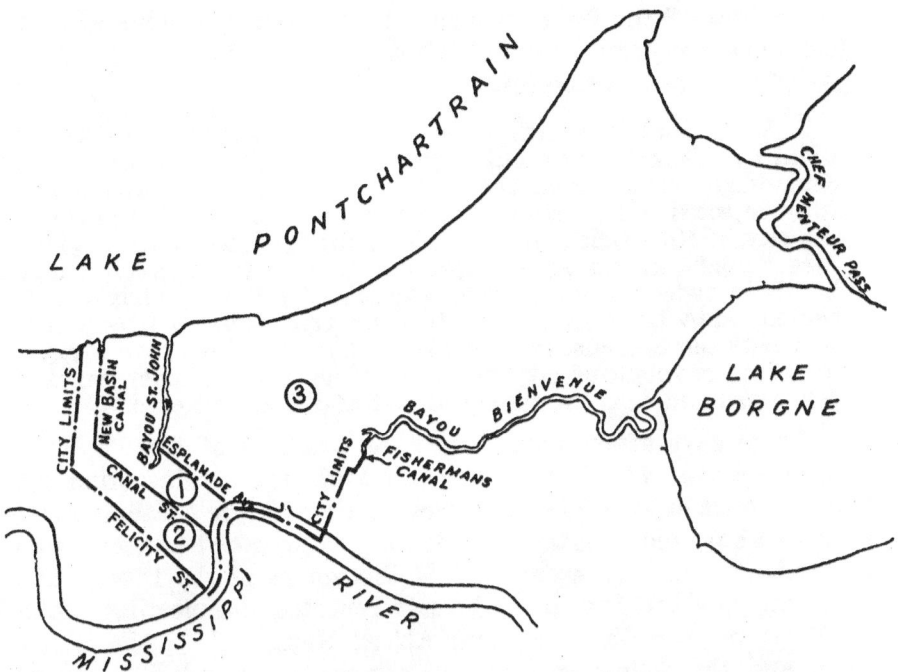

Map of the three municipalities in accordance with their legal boundaries as defined in the legislative act of incorporation, March 8, 1836

Americans, especially those who came with the intention of residing in the city permanently, congregated in the newly established faubourg St. Mary above Canal Street. Its growth was rapid and a community emerged entirely different in nationality and culture. In the section below Canal Street French was the prevalent tongue, whilst in the other only English was heard. The city was then divided into areas inhabited only by two conflicting irreconcilable elements. This led to its eventual apportionment into three distinct and independent municipalities.

As early as 1820 there were indications that a storm was brewing, but it was not till 1825 that it broke out in all its fury. The first foreboding of the impending clash was sounded in *Niles Weekly Register* of August 17, 1822, it reported:

> It appears that much irritation prevails between what is called the American and French parties at New Orleans. The former has succeeded in electing Mr. Livingston to Congress. But great complaints are made that the nationals of France and San Domingo have a monopoly on the posts of profit and honor.

An idea of the issue involved is had from a communication which appeared in the *Mercantile Advertiser* on January 25, 1825, signed "A Citizen" which said:

> What occasioned the loss of North America to Great Britain? Taxation without representation. The colonies often demanded redress from the mother country, which was scornfully rejected. The citizens from the great commercial parts of the city of New Orleans have twice petitioned the State Legislature demanding an equal representation in the Council which has been twice rejected. They say the city is not fairly represented. How are they to remedy their grievances, not by a civil war between citizens, but they maintain that they have a right to refuse payment of city taxes until the principle they contend for is granted to them, which is just and constitutional.

Three days afterwards, a meeting was held at Elkin's Hotel in Canal Street, for the purpose of taking into consideration the "late conduct of such of our representatives in the State Legislature who have aided in the rejection of the proposed law, and who allowed an equal representation of the voters of the City." The following day the *Louisiana Gazette* reported the meeting. John A. Fort was the Chairman and Alfred Hennen Esq., the Secretary, and the following resolutions were presented by General Ripley:

> Resolved: That our republican institutions rest upon the basis of an equality of rights in the whole community. For this sacred principle, the Patriots of the Revolution encountered perils and hardships. They have transmitted to it the present generation as our richest inheritance.
>
> Resolved: That the conduct of a majority of the Senate of this State in rejecting a law to equalize the representation in the City Council, has in our opinion denied the rights of a large portion of the inhabitants of this city. In adopting this conclusion, we are constrained to say that we are not actuated by any factious or turbulent spirit; feel no hostility to any portion of our citizens, and the prosperity of the city in which our interests are so intimately interwoven is a pledge that our only object is the good of the community.
>
> Resolved: That it is with painful feelings we are obliged to enumerate the oppressive measures of the City Council towards the commercial quarter of the City (faubourg St. Mary) and particularly to all those parts between the Custom house and the head of the steam boat landings—Our streets in this quarter have been neglected—the vast sums expended for paving have been distributed in sections where commerce is scarcely seen; while the spot above mentioned, which receives the rich

productions of our interior country, has been suffered to remain in so miserable a state that it has been scarcely possible for days to transverse it. Remonstrances have been made, but without effect, and there can exist no hope of a change unless it is produced by the dignified firmness of those citizens who are compelled to contribute to improvements in all parts of the city.

Resolved: That the 1st, 6th and 7th wards (Canal to Conti —Faubourg St. Mary—Faubourgs above St. Mary) being those by the system of oppression, form, in our opinion, a majority of our taxable voters, we believe, pay by far the greatest portion of taxes. Were the bill before the Senate, to pass, it would give the majority a right governing the minority; whereas, under the present system the rule is reversed and the minority now actually govern the majority. So palpable an absurdity calls for our loudest remonstrances.

It is bringing in an enlightened age, the doctrine of rotten boroughs; it wages war with the first principle of Republican Government and inflicts a deadly blow upon the rights of a free country.

As American citizens we detest it as a violation of all the principles which we hold sacred and we call upon society to join us in all constituted measures to destroy a system which holds us in a vassalage as base as it is repugnant to the spirit of freedom.

Resolved: That it is recommended to the wards above enumerated to persevere in their effort to change the present basis of the representation of the City Council and to procure one more congenial to our equal rights.

Senator Urquhart was voted a resolution of thanks. A committee of 20 was named by the Chairman consisting of J. A. Fort, J. Linton, D. Urquhart, P. E. Ploucher, L. Henderson, N. Morse, H. Carlston, General Plauché, R. Calgue, J. M. Reynolds, R. Morgan, B. Story, Burthe, J. H. Shephard, B. Montgomery, Judge Turner, A. Hennen, M. Toledano, J. Thomas and J. Hogan.

The committee submitted the following resolution which was unanimously adopted:

Resolved: That the meeting enter its solemn protest against the City Council being authorized by the Legislature to effect any loan for the paving of the city until such time as there shall be an equal representation in the City Council. We are frank to avow that under the present system of representation in the City Council, we feel no security for the impartial application of Loans for objects of general and common utility.

Eloquent and appropriate addresses were made by Mr. Morse, General Ripley and Mr. Harper.

A subsequent communication published in the *Louisiana Gazette* of June 30, 1825, gave an interesting picture of the discord then existing in the city, and appealed to the Legislature to pass an act authorizing the division of the city into two separate municipalities, claiming that it would prove to be important to the native born Americans. It said:

> Our habits, manners and education forbid us to associate ourselves with others in a municipality where our wants are not heeded, our complaints disregarded and all our exertions frustrated, when dedicated for the public good. The large majority of Americans here are men who have taken up their permanent abode with us, without having an interest any where else; and it seems to be the settled policy of the Corporation of New Orleans to consider them in a light of intriguers. This State having come into the possession of our General Government by an effort of Congress, and, we as citizens of the United States, having our citizenship solemnly guaranteed to us, as citizens of the United States—yet it must sound strange, having the greatest portion of wealth in our hands and comparatively as large a share of native talent, that still, we can find no representation in our municipal government. One of the strongest bonds that can unite a people together in a community is similarity of language; yet we here find the English language the only language of Americans, openly prescribed by the municipal authorities. The proceedings and records, in open violation of the Act of Congress for the admission of the State of Louisiana in the Union, are kept in the French Language. It will require a small share of penetration to discover that any law was binding upon the then Territory of Orleans, must now be actually so upon the City of New Orleans. By that only circumstance, the Charter of the City is virtually annulled. And in obtaining a new one, time to look out for ourselves. The population of the upper Faubourg, or a line dividing Bienville or Customhouse Streets, from the lower part of the City, is exclusively American and in point of numbers, highly respectable.
>
> Better be separated if their wishes are not accorded.
>
> Signed: Civius.

A foot note by the editor stated that "if the discussion exists to such an extent, no reason why any upper faubourg should not be separated in a separate municipality."

The temper at that time is historified by Farnell Hale in the following communication in the *Louisiana Gazette* of July 29, 1825:

> Our pockets have been drained to the lowest ebb to promote the value of Mr. Marigny's property in the lower faubourg. In point of health they have already made it a Golgotha; not con-

tented with that when they find they cannot drive us out of the jurisdiction by disease; they would strip us of all our money to increase the value of their own property.

We have a right recurred to us by the constitution of the United States to take up our residence in New Orleans; always conducting ourselves as becomes good citizens; in pursuing our lawful business and as their only object is to get us out of the country by their stupid legislation, we unhesitatingly declare we will not remove and above all, we will not consent to remain under their yoke any longer.

A diatribist in the *Louisiana Gazette* of August 10, 1825, charged the City Council with malappropriation of the people's money and stigmatized it as follows:

From the vgetable market to the saw mills above the streets contiguous running as far back as Royal in the City and Camp in faubourg St. Mary, embrace the center of commerce.

The city should be divided in the vicinity of Conti Street, below which with the exception of the small part from thence to the vegetable market, and that on the Levee, there is but little necessity for the enormous expenditures in ornamental improvements, continually progressing to the exclusion of the commercial sections. T'is notorious that there are whole streets paved where a dray is scarcely seen to move except in the morning on the way to its stand. The daily operation thereon excludes a just division of labor.

Loans have been effected by individuals for private benefit out of the City funds and even sincecures from men of large possessions, by a system closely bordering on the feudal, and once acted therein (facts will come out), their exertions are to self aggrandizement and opposition to every measure which tends to the amelioration of the constituents of those in the minority who are generally the representatives of the commerial interest. A prominent instance is exhibited in the election of Mr. Marigny, this man possesses no mental qualifications to entitle him to the suffrage of the constituents except to possession of wealth, and yet he is made a rallying point around which party concentrates, and he generally carries his point. Mr. Marigny is aware that his sway must eventually end, and t'is his object before such an event to secure for his faubourg all the improvements he can, and would not be sorry to have his yard paved at the City's expense. He knows that the uncomfortable current of the Mississippi, by sweeping around the bend on the other side, at every high water makes alluvial deposits opposite and above Canal St., in the very center of commerce, and also, that as property increases in value above, it must diminish below, and he loses no opportunity of diverting trade from its proper location. The new city pays for it. When once a division is effected, a measure which will, no doubt be strongly deprecated by every one below the division line, as much as it will be advocated above, planters will not be compelled to pay one dollar per bale for handling cotton through a morass, empty drays will not stall in our most frequented streets, our western brothers will not lose their hard earned pittance in paving transportation or suffer their perishable commodities to spoil in the impossibility of transporting them at all; the citizens will not pay for hauling wood as much as the wood itself costs, members of the Legislature will not come from the steamboats up to their knees in mud. Canals built, houses erected, etc., New Orleans will become the first City in the Union, now degraded, as she is, by the narrow policy of her council.

Men of large property easy in their circumstances, extensive house holders, reflect, but little, on the inconveniences their tenants suffer, in consequence of the bad administration of the city funds, exacting high rents, they leave to those who are compelled to pay them, the Herculean task of correcting the abuse of power.

Governor Johnson, sensing the imminence of a rupture within the city, called attention to the impending conflict in his message to the Legislature in January 1826, and warned:

Those symptoms of discord which to the mortification of every friend of this country, manifest themselves on some occasions in this our favored city, are no where perceptible in the circumjacent country, and even in the city, they are circumscribed and chiefly confined to the columns of gazettes, and perhaps a few persons of intemperate feelings, or whose views do not extend beyond the mere surface of things.

A reader assuming the sentiments of some of our city journals as a criterion, would be apt to deem it a singular anomaly that an assemblage of persons united by the bond of common interest, living under the same laws, professing equal devotion to the institutions of their choice, and who in the trying hours have stepped forth with one accord to defend with their blood, took occasion from mere imaginary distinctions, to express an asperity of feeling toward each other calculated to derogate from the character and consideration above.

This laudable attempt to conciliate the conflicting factions was categorically opposed by the *Louisiana Gazette,* the organ of the English population. In an editorial in its issue of January 7, 1826, it stated that the Governor's message "meets our unequivocal disapprobation," and it further asserted that "we defer also from his Exellency's opinion relative to the symptoms of discord in the city being "confined chiefly to the columns of gazettes but think it may be found to exist more in the spirit, that we are sorry to observe, is prevalent in opposing and depressing every thing American."

This same journal returned to the charge and continued its diatribe in an editorial dated January 12:

> As we are told, in order to apply politics to our State it should be remodelled according to the views of those whose only idea of Liberty are imbibed from the monarchial institution from whence they emigrated. No! we trust that there is a forlorn hope left among the American members of the Legislature who will manifest, by their example that whatever may be the choice of others, they at least will be faithful to the trust reposed in them by their constituents. In accordance to these views, feelings of disappointment must necessarily have arisen when this sacrifice of principle to ephemeral prosperity was made, so contrary to public expectations.
>
> We would ask: From what other country but France was this doctrine imported, that a chief magistrate of the people must necessarily attach himself to a party and one whose only object is hostility to the wishes of the people? And in this case, to crown the whole, there is not even a moderate chance of his ever becoming its head—for such is the smallest hope for any new convert rising to distinction in their ranks.

Early in 1827 an Act to divide the Parish of Orleans was introduced in the State Legislature and given serious consideration. In April the number of Councilmen for the city of New Orleans was reduced from 28 to 10. The following aldermen were then elected to the City Council:

1st Ward: N. Morse, M. Gordon; 2nd Ward: G. Bocas; 3rd Ward: M. Cruzat; 4th Ward: J. Lanna; 5th Ward: J. F. Cannonge; 6th Ward: F. L. Turner; H. W. Palfrey; 7th Ward; Don Burthe; 8th Ward: E. Blanc.

For nearly four years there was apparent peace. Passions seemed to have been calmed and a more conciliatory attitude existed in both factions. It was a lull before the storm which with redoubled fury rended the city asunder. The rumbling that presaged the outburst of hostilities, manifested itself in a communication, initialed "A. C. E." in the *Courier* of November 3, 1831, which said:

> All good citizens have witnessed with regret the proceedings of the City Council and the result of their labors since the opening of the present session, that is to say, since the last election of Aldermen.
>
> They now anxiously ask one another, what shall be the fate of a city whose representatives seem to have made it a point

to revive recriminations which appeared to be extinct, and the extreme violence of which reveal their tenacity.

To whom ought those dissensions of a deliberative body, whose labors are a vital interest to the City of New Orleans, particularly to be attributed? Let us not hesitate in saying it: they are the work of certain men, who enslaved by their hearty passions and consulting no other but their private interest, do not blush to sacrifice the public interest, the defense of which was intrusted to them by their fellow citizens as an homage paid by the sovereignty of the people to their principles.

What is at present the state of things, or rather the situation of minds? A rivalship which formerly seemed to have abated has now broken forth into open hostility. Its action is felt throughout all classes of society from the wealthy speculator down to the mechanic who lives by his daily labor; for it is the essence of a popular administration to affect at once the rich and the poor, the laboring man and him who has a settled income. It must therefore, be fairly proclaimed; that deplorable debates of our City Council are the result of a flagrant partiality, of which the aldermen of the upper part of the city have given sad examples. In fact, in a number of instances we have seen them opposing with a resistance which might be styled animosity, improvements required by the interests of the lower part, by a strict injustice or by most imperious necessity.

Enormous sums have been expended for that part of the City and of the other suburbs, and yet we have seen those very men, whose applications in behalf of other constituents were never refused, opposing at all times, by all possible means, the generous efforts of a resolute minority, who never despaired of a cause, the triumph of which becomes more certain every day.

A new era has begun for the lower part of the city and for all the precincts beyond suburb Marigny. The previous part of a popular and flourishing city, has too long been kept down by the oppression of a compact and systematic majority. Only reflect to what value property, situated below the square of the city, has lately risen and say whether that value is merely nominal, as is most perfidiously insinuated by the detractors of the new establishments, which progress with so much activity throughout the whole of the lower precincts. Who is the speculator who, laying any claims to intelligence and good faith, could deny in that respect the salutary influence of a few distinguished citizens, among whom they affect to cite an alderman of the

5th Ward, [Cannonge] as if it was a crime of him to devote his talents to the defense of the citizens who honored him by their choice.

It is essential that the public should be informed of certain facts of the highest importance, with regard to the reciprocal conduct of the Mayor and City Council; and those two powers ought also to be justly and distinctly appreciated, in relation to their respective conduct.

In these several respects the public expectation shall not be deceived. Precious information shall be furnished by the Alderman of the 5th Ward whose noble mind has just been put to the trial and who, strong by his conscience and of the sentiment of his duties, has not been afraid of assuming the highest responsibility. At the next sitting of the City Council the impartial citizens of New Orleans, shall have occasion to praise the conduct of these aldermen, who in order not to succumb, had no other resource but to oppose the *vis incentiae* to their adversaries. Not an efficient remedy, but as a palliative vigorously necessary.

It will hardly be believed and no one would have suspected it, but it will be proved, and by means of official documents too, that since the opening of the session, that is to say, since April 1st last, no sum has been specially appropriated for the use of the lower suburbs, not even for that of the City proper. How then could it be denied that there are in the City Council men whose partiality is truly revolting? Nay, several works, the completion of which has for a long time been ordered for that part, have not yet been executed, although for no other cause than the tenacious opposition of a few individuals. Nevertheless the enormous sum of $100,000.00 has been appropriated for the use of the suburb St. Mary.

The system adopted by the Mayor will likewise be the subject of our inquiries.

These diatribes continued unabated for some time in the City's gazettes. Many communications appeared in the *Argus*, the *Bee* and the *Courier* demanding an investigation of the City Council. The City Administration was championed by the Editor of the *Mercantile Advertiser*, whose bias was said to have been influenced by having been chosen city printer.

The *Courier* of December 11, 1832 reported that a meeting to consider the separation of the faubourg St. Mary from the city, and for the establishment of an independent corporation for "the government of its municipal affairs," was held at Bishop's Hall.

Judge Harper was chairman and P. Laidlow the Secretary. The following resolution was presented by Samuel Laidlow and seconded by Col. Thos. H. Hearsey:

Resolved: Separation of Wards 6 and 7 from the city would conduce to the general good of the city and by the additional stimulus given to the improvements in every section, be also productive of great advantages to the planting interests of the State:

The Petition to be presented to the Legislature requesting an act of incorporation.

The following committee was appointed to draft the petition; Samuel Livermore, Chas. Genois, Levi Pierce, John Linton.

The committee to procure signatures was composed of Joshua Baldwin, J. F. Freret, Thomas Banks, J. P. Genois, J. P. Tourne, J. W. Lavillebeuve, Thomas Soulet, Henry Norton, Peter Laidlow, L. Dubourg, Fred Caillou, Chas. Diamond, D. C. Hotchkiss, Chas. Byrnes, A. Fourcher and P. Riviere.

Another meeting was held on February 4, for the purpose of incorporating wards 6 and 7, and to present the proposed charter to the Legislature. The meeting was called to order by Joshua Baldwin, Esq. The Honorable Samuel H. Harper was Chairman, and Frank W. Lee and Peter Laidlow, Secretaries.

The following committee was appointed to appear before the Legislature: John Linton, Stephen Henderson, Chas. Genois and John Nicholson.

This acrimonious dispute between the downtown and uptown sections which had lasted for more than ten years was gradually approaching the hour of decision. In every place where men congregated—in the streets, in exchanges, in the cafés, in the theaters and ball rooms and in the home—the sole topics of conversation, with frequent heated arguments were the division of the city, the paving of the streets and the beautification of the two sections of the city, the foreign influence of the French population and the arrogant usurpation of the political control of the city by an overwhelming influx of Anglo Americans. Motives were impugned, insults were hurled, staunch friendships destroyed, canings were frequent and even duels were fought. For many years there had been men from either faction of sober judgment, who held prominent and influential positions in the community, who did their utmost to conciliate the dissenting elements, but they now gave up their Herculean task, and reconciled themselves to the inevitable. The only solution to the problem would be to divide the city.

Meetings were held, petitions distributed, orators rose to sublime heights, land speculators appraised their potential profits, and politicians cowed to a small but powerful minority. The final act of that inter-city conflict was staged in 1835 and 1836.

The *Bee* of May 13,1835, in an editorial, bewailed the fact that the agitation to divide the City would "engender sectional feelings necessarily producing personal animosities", and that the motives were improper, injudicious and unjust. It regretted that "antipathies and animosities are engendered and embittered among the residents of the same place"

The following day in another editorial the *Bee* noted that:

> We have distinctly and defintely proved that the expenditures of the Corporation for works of paving done in the upper Faubourg since its incorporation, have exceeded those done within the same period in the lower faubourg by the enormous sum of upwards of $285,000.00.
>
> On considering that the city revenues from the upper faubourg during the time of this expense fell far short of the expenditures incurred,, we fairly inferred that the faubourg was in debt to the Corporation.

In a communication to the *Bee* of May 21, 1835, entitled "UP TOWN and DOWN TOWN signed "Keep Cool" regretted that:

> ... These terms are so often repeated, and at each repetition give birth to such disagreeable feelings among our good citizens, that a service should be done to the community if by any means these terms should be used without creating sentiments of hostility between different portions of the City.
>
> We freely admit that there will always exist, both uptown and down town, small bands of grasping speculators who should desire that all public improvements should go in the immediate vicinity of their property and raise a cry of partiality and injustice, when favors of any kind fall upon any portion of the city in which they are not directly interested.

He further asked, "shall these knots of speculators forever divide our city into two unnatural parties against each other, abusing one another and occasionally fighting each other."

Another incident which further fanned the flames of resentment to a high pitch was the *PASSE DROIT* made by the Anglo-Saxons to the Creoles. It excited the animosity of the *Bee* in its issue of July 1, 1835, entitled "4th of July Celebration". It read:

> Desirous as we are of lending our influence to promote efficiently the celebration of the 4th of July, we cannot approve the choice made by the Committee of Arrangements for assem-

bling at Mr. Clapp's Church; and for dining at the Lake.

It is a species of insult to the central and lower part of the city to prefer the above church situated in a faubourg, to the Cathedral, situated in the center of the City—where certainly more persons would willingly meet and could conveniently be accommodated. If the Committee desire that their procession shall not be supported by the Creole population, they have acted well to secure their design.

A dinner at the Lake must necessarily prevent many (otherwise disposed) from participation in the festivals.

Ceremonies began at 8:30 A.M. and a portion of that Church was reserved for the ladies.

In answer to that protest it was explained that the choice of Mr. Clapp's Church was made because "it offered better opportunity for the orators to be heard; and gives greater convenience for the accommodation of the ladies."

At the last minute the names of Col. Shaumburg, Wm. Christy and General Labatut were added to the list of Presidents and H. B. Cenas and F. B. Daunoy to that of the Vice-Presidents.

Reverend Mr. Clapp made the invocation and the oration was delivered by C. P. Jackson. Bernard Derbigny delivered the address at the dinner held at Washington Hotel on the Lake.

The animosity against the French speaking population was further intensified by the advent of the Association of Native Americans, whose purpose was exposed in the following communication, written in French, in the *Bee* of July 22, 1835:

> Only American Citizens (indigenous or otherwise) born outside of Louisiana, are the only ones who have a real right to power. This privilege was unanmiously adopted at a meeting held behind closed doors in the church of a Reverend Doctor which without adverse opinion, passed the following resolutions:
>
> (1) No Creole can and from now on, be allowed to exercise any political function, either in New Orleans or in the State of Louisiana.
>
> (2) The same to be applied to any individual naturalized whatever may be his origin, to whom English is not his natural tongue.
>
> (3) Only those Americans born any where else in the Union may hold public office, even though they have established their residence in Louisiana for only 8 days.
>
> (signed) A Converted American.

The *True American* of July 23 reported that the Native Born American, on July 4, took an oath not to vote for any foreigner for any office whatsoever.

The following incident which occurred in the City Council is a good indication of the rivalry and jealousies that existed between the two sections of the City. In the message of Acting Mayor Jno. Culbertson to the City Council was the following:

> The fountain which is to be erected on the Place d'Armes [now Jackson Square] by Mr. Albert Stein, has arrived from the North on board of a vessel moored opposite Julia St. According to the opinion of the City Surveyor, it will be proper to erect on the Place d'Armes a temporary shed for that fountain until it is fixed in its proper place, which can be done according to Mr. Stein before two or three months. I wish you would authorized me to do it, if you do not think it proper to dispose of it otherwise. Mr. A. Stein has drawn on the corporation, previous to the arrival of the fountain, for the sum of $1,000.00. I have accepted his draft in conformity with your resolution of March 21, present year.

Mr. Thomas authorized the Mayor to place the fountain in the Place d'Armes. Mr. Caldwell moved that another be ordered for Lafayette Square. Mr. McFarlane moved that the fountain be placed in Lafayette Square. Whereupon Mr. F. Labatut showed that it had been especially ordered for the public square and could not be alienated. Mr. McFarlane then moved that the Mayor take custody of the fountain until those ordered for the other public squares shall have been received, and that all shall be simultaneously erected. That motion provoked discordant discussion and was lost by a vote of 8 to 3. Messrs. Barry and McFarlane voting in favor of it.

In January 1836, a petition was posted for signatures in Banks' Arcade, directed to both houses of the Legislature, asking it to create a separate municipality for the upper district.

The *Bee*, on January 16, made an impassioned plea to repel that tidal wave of intolerance, jealousy and cupidity, which threatened to engulf the city and eventually lead to its disintegration. It voiced its protest as follows:

> We are anxious that union and unanimity should prevail among all classes of our population and districts of the City; and because we are persuaded that all the petty differences which have hitherto prevailed can be adjusted or terminated by the republican resort of the ballot box.
>
> The ballot box is the best and surest remedy for all political evils which may afflict society in the United States; so long as republicanism is triumphant, and it is resolved that the will of the majority shall prevail.

The memorialists contend that more improvements have been made in the lower part of the city and more of the public funds expended during the present year than in any part above Canal Street — and that the port and paving of the upper faubourg has been neglected.

We are not prepared to deny this; for we have few motives or arguments to support the conduct of corporate management of the present council. We have ourselves repeatedly called on them to improve the port and extend the paving in the upper faubourg — knowing that policy as well as justice required them. But they prefer wrangling with the Mayor and others, as well as among themselves, rather than attend to the true interests of their constituents.

Still is there a legitimate remedy to cure and remove the disease without resorting to amputation. Remodel radically the municipal government of the city, so as to have it in the republican style, two councils for corporate legislation. Divide the city into 8 or 10 wards, let an alderman be elected from each ward for the upper council, and members elected for the lower; one for every 100 duly qualified voters.

New Orleans would be deprived of the glory of her name in all of her commercial transactions. There would be a division of the port as well as the city, and same name would not be applicable to separate municipalities; so that in all consignments to the port of New Orleans the greatest confusion will prevail. Separate the faubourgs from the City, their port is no longer than that of the city — and the port of New Orleans is alone declared by Congress to be a port of entry and delivery. A Community of name, interest, port and municipality is therefore essential for the welfare of the public;: and probably for the welfare of the individual merchants also, who transact business with other states and nations.

But a singular fatuity attends the citizens of the upper faubourg. The members are becoming annually increased; and yearly they are acquiring a greater control of the municipality. Yet now when they have almost obtained numerical superiority; and may soon be supposed enabled to obtain a balance of control, they are disposed to be contented with the government of a part, when they might direct the government of the whole.

Nay, in order to act more foolishly they will incur their quota of the debt of the city, in order that the ends of an aspiring few may be advanced and load themselves with more debt by obtaining loans on their own credit, when they might obtain it on the credit of New Orleans, aye, on the credit of those they accuse of oppression and injustice, but whose control in two or three years will be but the subject of remembrances. They are resolved that their supposed enemies shall continue their control in a separate government; and have an *Inperium in Imperio* to prevent to coalescence of both classes of our population.

Let the serious and disinterested in the western suburbs reflect dispassionately on the topic, and they will never again advocate a division of the city to acquire an exclusive control of a part, when they might have auperior command over the whole.

This logical intercession fell on deaf ears, for on Thursday January 19, a petition for the dismemberment of the city, signed by citizens of the 6th and 7th wards, was presented to the House of Representatives. It was printed in both languages and referred to a committee composed of Messrs. Davidson, Freret, Dixon, Augustin, Labatut, Barrow and Lewis.

A bill was introduced by Mr. Labatut to divide the city into three separate municipalties, under one Mayor and a general city council. It provided that the central municipality would comprise all the wards between Canal and Esplanade Streets, the second municipality, all those above Canal Street, and the third, all those below Esplanade. It further stipulated that each municipality should have a recorder and alderman on the basis of "the present corporation and they shall possess separate and distinct corporate rights within its precincts. The qualifications and duties of the recorders and aldermen shall be as present; but each recorder shall be a magistrate, having cognizance within its jurisdiction of all violations of city ordinances, or State laws, or any other violations of justice of the peace."

The city was to have but one Mayor, he was to be exempted of magisterial duties and without power to appoint any official of the separate governments, each municipality was to appoint its own. In each municipality a census was to be taken and one Alderman elected to represent each 100 qualified voters.

The aldermen of each municipality shall meet on the first Monday of May, as a common City Council, at which the recorder of the central station shall preside, and as often during the year as the Mayor or two of the Municipal government may require. This common council shall have exclusive jurisdiction in all that relates to imposing taxes on ships, boats and other vehicles; to fix the prices of all licenses to taverns, cabarets, pedlers, hawkersmen, the salary of the Mayor and its own Secretary; to organize a city guard and make all police regulations of a general nature — so that all taxes etc., shall be uniform throughout the city. But the council shall make no appropriation whatsoever, as the receipts of taxation shall be at the disposal of each municipality within its own jurisdiction and all the regulations relating to paving, lighting and watering, markets and wharves, each to have a separate treasury and treasurer, with all other officers necessary.

Offenders may be brought before the recorder of the district where the offense was committed, or where the offender resides, but the jurisdiction of the city court shall not in any manner be affected, and the prison shall be common to all sections, each paying a pro-rata proportion of all general expenses of whatever kind.

The property of the corporation, as streets, squares and wharves shall belong to the municipality in which it is situated; but the use will be common to all districts. The real estate and revenues arising from it shall be distributed among the municipalities according to stipulation. The credits of the present corportion in the various banks and the shares it posses in the various corporates or other institutions are to be equally apportioned among the three districts.

This bill met with the approval of the discordant elements, whilst the more conservative citizens had their misgivings as to the ultimate results.

The *Bee* of March 2, 1836, announced that is had passed the House by a majority of 6 to 1, and that in the Senate there appears to be a majority of 5 to 1. It commented that "its friends have no apprehension of its non-passage: It's enactments may be enforced April next at the coming city election, and by May 1st we may expect to find regularly organized the council of the three municipalities."

This amendment to the Act of February 17, 1805, incorporating the city was signed by Alcee Labranche, Speaker of the House; F. Derbigny, President of the Senate, and was approved by E. D. White, the Governor, on March 8, 1936.

Thus ended a turbulent decade of a furious conflict, of dissension and antagonism, of selfish interests, jealousy, prejudice and intolerance. The Creoles, the indigenous portion of the population, many of who were direct descendants of the founders of their city, glorifying in their American Citizenship, who in the defense of their country had had their baptism of fire under Jackson, smarted with indignation at being treated as aliens by a recent migration from the North, East and West, which with its overwhelming numbers wished to deprive them of their innate right of suffrage. They accepted the inevitable. The Anglo-Americans were victorious.

Immediately after the division there was a great boom in all the three municipalities. Property values rose to prodigous heights, speculation became rampant. Fortunes were made or lost overnight. New Orleans was the El Dorado of the World.

The *Bee* of March 28, 1936, commented that the property owners in the central municipality will neither sell or improve, that real estate in the upper municipality is selling greatly beyond its intrinsic value, and that purchasers would buy lots in the central section if they were put up at auction. Lots in the rear ward, which a short while ago sold for $300.00, are now selling for $2000.00 and soon resold for $7000.00.

The *Bee* of May 21, 1836, reported that: "Speculation in real estate has advanced to such a pitch of extravagence in the upper district of the city, that the purchase money of some sales made, particularly near Carrollton, cannot be realized in less than 20 years, and such a period is a little too long for one to lay out his money. At auctions property sells for 30 times what a property cost three years ago, on his own notes, with mortgage on the property; he sells out a few weeks afterwards for the notes of others—forgetting the risk incurred, but speculating nowa-days has little foresight—like prejudice, it is purblind."

The State Legislature in 1852 adopted a new charter for the city of New Orleans, under which the three municipalities were reunited under one city government.

CHAPTER X

POSTAL SERVICE AND MAIL ROUTES

The mail in the early eighteen hundreds was of slow delivery. Letters from the Eastern seaboard arrived in New Orleans by sailing vessels or overland by post riders, and from Europe after long and sometimes perilous trans-oceanic voyages. The deliveries were uncertain and the letters were frequently lost in transit. But conditions were such at that time that but little could be done to expedite the dispatch of the mail. In the beginning of the eighteen twenties, when New Orleans was emerging from the status of a town to that of a large city, and was entering a period of great commercial importance, its population was increasing manifold, the need of a quicker, better and more efficient mail delivery was demanded by its merchants and bankers. Complaints were frequently voiced, meetings held, protests sent to Washington and many attempts made by influential citizens to improve the service. This fight on the post office makes an interesting chapter in the history of the city.

The first recorded organized protest against the inadequate service by the Post Office took place at Elkin's Exchange on October 12, 1823.

Colonel William Boyd presided and L. Lesassier, Esq. as Secretary and the following resolution was adopted:

> Resolved: That a committee of five persons be appointed to draft a memorial to the Post Master General, on the subject of the bad management of the Post Office of this City and also to suggest to him the improvements which are practicable in transporting the mail to and from the City.

R. Relf, H. Dandreau, P. Laidlow, Wm. L. Robeson, Wm. Y. Lewis, were appointed on that committee to whom all resolutions were referred and they were requested to report on Tuesday evening at 7 P. M. at the same place. The meeting was held and the report of the committee was unanimously adopted. It was read in French and English. The following committee was appointed to solicit signatures: C. E. Russel, G. Crosey, H. Landreau, Joseph Le Carpentier. The following grievances were voiced:

> That the utmost time allowed by law for opening the mail is one hour, continually violated in this City, mail seldom

opened after its arrival—for two hours, and even four hours, the doors are closed. The office is seldon opened on Sundays—and on other days of the week is kept closed for an unreasonable length of time. Commercial letters are detained to the injury of the one addressed. Sometimes two days before the letters are delivered from ship to the post office.

Those who have no boxes have difficulty in obtaining their papers, in consequence of the clerk neglecting to work them, even they are finally lost.

That your committee know of no law authorizing (in the absence of a regular mail) the charge of 14 cents on a ship letter and in particular for double letters ,which is demanded in this office.

First: Eastern mail be brought by way of Columbus direct to Madisonville—on the military road—instead of the route to Natchez, in favor of New Orleans—300 miles.

Second: In transporting mails from the Atlantic States on horseback, letters are defaced by the rains, etc, as to be illegible—recommend that they be carried by carriage.

Third: Three days now between mails: City entitled to a mail daily.

Signed: Peter Laidlow, Wm. L. Robeson, Honoré Landreaux

In 1824, Pulman Skipwith, Esq., of Baton Rouge was appointed Post Master

In 1826, the mail from Washington to New Orleans was routed through the parishes of Washington and St. Tammany to the Rigolets, then ferried to Pine Island and from thence to Chef Menteur.

Major D. R. Hopkins, resigned from the State Legislature to become Post Master.

The time consumed in transporting the mail was a subject of continuous controversy and dissatisfaction, and it was not till 1829 that home ameliorations were proposed by the post office department. The delivery of the mail from the North was increased to three times a week and the time was further shortened by routing it from Mobile to Pascagoula by stage and from there to New Orleans by steamboat.

The following was the schedule:

Arrive at Mobile on Mondays, Tuesdays and Saturdays, at 2 P. M., leave Mobile every Monday, Wednesday and Friday at 10:30 A. M.

Arrive at New Orleans, every Tuesday, Thursday and Saturday at 4 P. M.

A counter proposal was made in a commnication in the *Bee* of June 8, of that year, entitled "The Mails".

Seventeen years since the first steamboat arrived in New Orleans :and we have seen no attempts made to profit by the most rapid of all carriers, except some almost abortive essays to convey the mails between New Orleans and Mobile.

Let two steamboats be chartered for carrying passengers and mail, with engines strong enough to propel them at least nine miles per hour against current. One should leave every other day and arrive in Natchez in twenty six hours. It could stop at every post office on the river. One hour delay at Bayou Sarah, Baton Rouge, Donaldsonville, etc., while a quarter hour would be all that is necessary to change mail in minor places.

Would cost $40,000.00 per annum, the passenger fees would make that sum.

Signed: Creole

The *Courier* of November 14, 1831 announced that the Western Mail will be transported from this City by steamboats, so far as Memphis, thence to Nashville, Louisville, Cincinnati, with accelerated speed. A tri-weekly line of stages will begin shortly to run from Nashville by way of Jackson and Madisonville, for mail and passengers. "These arrangements will open, between this city and the great commercial points of the mighty West, a rapid and certain communication".

The *New York Courier and Enquirer*, in March 1832, advocated a daily mail delivery between New York and New Orleans, the route to be through the Southern States then to Mobile and Lake Ponchartrain by steam boats. It claimed that in good weather it would only take twelve days to cover the distance.

Most of the delays and difficulties encountered in mail deliveries were between Mobile and New Orleans. For years meetings were held by the business men of the City requesting that the mail be expedited and that the prevalent abuses be eradicated. The Government acknowledged that the difficulty was between New Orleans and Mobile, and that the steamboat companies under contract to carry the mail had suffered severe losses because of the failure of the boilers in the new boats and that "high pressure engines will not answer for salt water, for they are laboratories of salt which constantly corrode the metal and impair the works!"

The cost of carrying mail in the Southern States was 87½ cents per mile.

Another meeting of protest was held on the 28th of July 1834, again to "consider the mail between this City and Mobile". Objections were voiced against the new arrangements of the Post Office Department, which improved the service from Georgia to Mobile, while at the same time ignoring that of Mobile to New Orleans. The committee recommneded that the "daily mail be transported between this City and Mobile by steamboat, avoiding altogether the portage between Pottersville and Mobile, because the land carriage, during the greatest part of the season is difficult to accomplish—is invariably tedious: consumes much more time than a good boat would require to perform the route by water."

It further suggested that three boats would be necessary and two should be continuously working. It also condemned the route to Mobile by way of Madisonville, because it was at times impassable and passed through an unimproved part of the country.

A Congressional report for the year 1832 gives the following figures on the revenue of the post office for one year: The total for the United States was $1,471,371.04. The amount of postage sold in New Orleans, $37,288.03; New York, $160,203.32; Boston $62,270.20; Philadelphia, $106,930.86; and Baltimore $54,923.03.

The *New York Courier and Enquirer* reported in April of 1832, that in good weather the daily mail could make the distance between New York and New Orleans in twelve days. The route was through the Southern States to Mobile, thence by steam boats to Lake Pontchartrain. It was the record speed up to that time. It was not until November 23, 1836, that the Northern mail was expedited to the satisfaction of the merchants, for the express mail reached the city from Washington, in eight days and seven hours and from Baltimore in seven days; an unprecedented speed. Yet four days afterwards it was announced that the New York mail reached New Orleans in only seven days and that to traveled a distance of 1400 miles, "despite the practically impassable roads in some sections, the deserted country, the many rivers and estuaries to be forded or to be crossed by boats and that the greatest part of the journey was made in the darkness of the long nights of that season".

In 1834, the post office in New Orleans was situated at the corner of Royal and Canal Streets and in 1835 it was moved to the corner of Customhouse (Iberville) and Exchange Alley, between the Union Bank and the New Exchange. But there was no increase in accommodations for the public. The post master was Wm. H. Kerr.

Postal Regulations

Rates of postage were for a single letter composed of one piece of paper for any distance not exceeding 30 miles, 6 cts.; over 30 miles and not exceeding 80 miles, 10 cts.; over 80 and not exceeding 400, $18\frac{3}{4}$ cts.; and anything over 400 miles, 26 cts.

A letter composed of two pieces of paper is charged with doubled the rates; if three pieces, with triple; and if four pages quadrupled. One or more pieces of paper mailed as a letter and weighing one ounce shall be charged with quadruple postage and at the same rate should the weight be greater.

All express mail between New Orleans and New York closes at 10 A.M., all letters must be paid in advance and marked Express. Letters will be charged triple postage. No letter containing money or letter exceeding half an ounce in weight will be sent by the Express Mail.

CHAPTER XI

THE JUDICIARY AND THE BAR

Lured by the elusive pot of gold at the end of the rainbow, professional men, lawyers particularly, from every part of the Union and from Europe rushed to New Orleans to open offices. They believed that in that city of golden opportunity success would immediately smile on them, and with exuberant energy and undaunted hope, they waited for their first clients and for the chance to display their forensic brilliancy. But many were of limited ability, or lacked the culture and education to make a successful lawyer. Some left the city of their frustration, others spent their meager funds and found themselves stranded, whilst others entered the field of politics. With all the fury of desperation they became the dissenters, the agitators and the rabble rousers, who under the cloak of patriotism advocated the abolition of the French language, the disfranchisement of every one with a Gallic name, whether a native or naturalized, and that only English-speaking Americans be permitted to exercise the franchise of citizenship.

There were many great lawyers at that time in New Orleans, renowned for their erudition, eloquence, culture, distinction and legal ability. Some of them were Anglo-Saxon Americans and others either French or Creoles, but it must be said that among those distinguished gentlemen a greater spirit of camaraderie existed than was evidenced among physicians. Their names are still remembered today, and they have emblazoned a shining spot on the escutcheon of the legal profession of New Orleans.

The State Legislature adopted a jurisprudence based on the laws of Spain and France as well as on the Napoleonic code. This was not acceptbale to many Anglo-Saxon Americans. They wanted the State to adopt the common law existing throughout the country. It was a long and bitter fight, but eventually that conflict was won by the efforts of some of the English-speaking lawyers and those who spoke French, under the leadership of Edward Livingston, with the assistance of Lislet L. Moreau and Pierre Derbigny. They revised the old Code of 1808. In 1825 they presented the new code known as "Civil Code of Louisiana" which became effective that same year. Fortier wrote:

"Their work resulted in the so-called Civil Code of Louisiana. The Code of Practice was enacted April 12, 1824 and was promulgated Sept. 3, 1825. It repealed all former rules of practice and such parts of the Civil Code as conflicted with it. The Code of Criminal Law, prepared by Edward Livingston, was completed in 1828 and was a large work of 800 pages. It embraced five divisions—a Code of Crimes and Punishments, a Code of Procedure, a Code of Evidence, a Code of Reform and Prison Discipline and a Book of Definitions. DeBow called the work a 'good book but one of little practical utility'. On the other hand, Magnet, the French historian, said: '(Livingston) has composed a book that recommends itself to the attention of philosophers as a beautiful system of ideas and to the use of nations as a vast code of rules".

An interesting story of a contempt of court case was related by Saxe-Weimar:

A resident lawyer named Lloyd, whose reputation stood very low, had, on the preceding day insulted the presiding Judge Turner in the streets for which reason the judge had him taken in custody by the sheriff and thrown into prison. The injured judge presided in his own suit and in this manner was both judge and party. I was informed that Mr. Turner was insulted in his individual capacity, but that he decided as a judge in the name of the State of Louisiana.

The explanation did not satisfy me, the distinction between a person and his office may be correct in theory, it is however, very hardly so in practice and on this account the proceeding to me appeared arbitrary. Further, Mr. Lloyd wished to defend his own cause, he was ,however, half intoxicated, and attacked the judge so grossly from time to time that he [the judge] ordered him frequently to be silent. The examination of the witnesses consumed so much time that I was obliged to leave the court before the termination of the case. I heard afterwards that Mr. Lloyd had been adjudged to provide two securities for his good behavior during one year, each in a penalty of $100.00 and since he was not able to find these securities immediately, to be remanded to prison.

This observation of Saxe-Weimar was based on only part of the facts, but the impression he conveys as to the dictatorial powers of the judges in this city is fallacious. In *Niles Weekly Register* of June 3, 1826 is found a report of what actually happened:

During the trial of a criminal on Wednesday last, or more properly in passing sentence upon him, the judge had occasion to make some severe observations on the conduct of two members of the Bar in regard to the prisoner, before his trial. The same afternoon one of them (Mr. Lloyd) met the judge in the upper Faubourg and accosted him in abusive and menacing language.

The old Parish Prison on Orleans Street. Built in 1836. (From photograph owned by Stuart O. Landry)

The old Citizens Bank Building on Toulouse Street between Royal and Chartres Streets, downtown side. (From collection of Stuart O. Landry)

(Bank of Orleans.)

(Union Bank of Louisiana.)

(Canal Bank.)

(From Gibson's Directory of 1838 — Courtesy N. O. Public Library)

On Thursday the judge issued his warrant against him and he was lodged in prison during that night. Yesterday he was brought to court and after hearing a variety of testimony in relation to the conversation between him and the judge, he was ordered to find security to keep the peace during one year, in two securities of $1,000.00 each and to be committed till he finds such securities. He was accordingly conducted to prison.

This is not an uncommon incident, for too often these traveling diarists and reporters perverted the truth and wrote stories and observations derogatory to the reputation of the city.

Flint, writing in 1832 about the administration of justice in New Orleans, made the following complimentary statement:

> The municipal and criminal courts are prompt in administrating justice; and larcenies and brawls are effectively punished without any just grounds of complaint about the law's delay.

During that period the court procedures were conducted both in the French and English languages. This presented many difficulties but they were unavoidable, for the French could not learn English, or rather many would not, and the Anglo-Sazons had a contempt for anything Gallic, and certainly would not speak that tongue.

As the population at that time was about evenly divided between those who spoke French and English, it was inevitable that all court transactions should be conducted in the two tongues. It did cause confusion, delay and increase in cost to the litigants, because it was frequently necessary for both sides to employ both French and English lawyers, but despite all, justice was well administered. It was many years before the English tongue became the official language of the courts.

Charles Gayarre gave a graphic description of a court scene in his article "The New Orleans Bench and Bar in 1826."

> It was a forensic contest between two, great lawyers Etienne Mazureau, a native of France, a shining light of the New Orleans Bar, representing the defendant a Creole, and Alfred Hennen, a New Englander, who was equally as prominent, for the plaintiff.
>
> Here a struggle ensued between the two lawyers about the composition of a jury. Hennen challenges as many of the Creoles and naturalized French as he can and Mazureau does the same with the Americans. At last the jury is formed—nine of the Latin race and three of the Anglo-Saxon. On Mazureau's lips may be seen a smile of satisfaction. Hennen has a troubled look.

Let us give a little of our attention to the manner in which the jury has been sworn.

Clerk to the first juror: "you swear that"—

First Juror: "Je n'entend pas. Parlez Francais." (I do not understand. Speak French.)

Clerk: "All right."

And the oath is administered in French.

Second juror approached to qualify.

Clerk: "Vous jurez que"—

Second juror: "I do not understand. Speak English."

Clerk: "All right".

And the second juror, duly sworn in his vernacular, takes his seat, and so on to the last of the twelve, each one insisting on being addressed in his own maternal tongue.

Judge: "Mr. Augustin Macarty, I appoint you foreman of this jury!"

On hearing which, Mazureau allows again an expression of approval to beam over his face. Macarty is of an ancient and hightone family. He has served several years as mayor of the city and is uncompromisingly conservative in all his views and feelings, the very embodiment of the old regime.

The jury gave a verdit to the defendant.

Hennen: "May it please the Court, I beg leave to file my motion of appeal from this extraordinary verdict."

Mazureau approached Hennen, who is handing some papers to his clerk. They look at each other face to face and both laugh heartily. They seemed to be much amused at something.

Mazureau pulls out his watch: "Oh! Oh! already four o'clock. It is dinner time. Hennen, my house is close by. I have today a fat turkey aux truffles and some exquisite claret just arrived from Bordeaux. Suppose you join me?"

"Willingly."

And the two eminent lawyers went away arm in arm.

Gayarré relates the following interesting incident:

It was in the latter part of June and exceedingly hot. When Grymes for the plaintiff rose to address the jury in English, one of the members of the jury, who did not understand a single word of that language, speaking in the name of such of his colleagues as were in the same predicament, begged the judge on that ground to allow them to leave their seats and be permitted to inhale the fresh air under the arcade of the building in which the court held its session. This was graciously permitted, and during one hour that Grymes spoke the Gallic portion of the jurors enjoyed their promenade and their cigars in the cool breeze that came from the river. When Grymes had done and Seghers, on the same side, rose in his turn, the voice of the sheriff was heard crying loudly, "Gentlemen of the jury who are outside, please come into court." They immediately filed in and gravely resumed their seats. Seghers had hardly said a few words in French when the Anglo-Saxon jurors, on the application for a similar favor were also permitted to stretch their legs under the same arcade and to pass their time as comfortably as they could. The repetition of this scene took place when Livingston and Moreau Lislet spoke alternately. This was of daily occurrence at that epoch.

After a little while everybody became reconciled to what at first had been thought an intolerable inconvenience or annoyance. In the course of time the high-spirited and light limbed Latin genet and the massive, slower tempered horse, being both harnessed to the car of justice, learned to pull together and contrived by some means or other to make its wheels work smoothly, not withstanding the natural difficulties of the road. The qualifications to be a juror were then of higher order than those which have been since required, and if the echoes which are wafted to me in my retreat from our courts of justice are faithful expressions of the public sentiment on the subject, I must come to the conclusion that trials by jury then, notwithstanding certain eccentricities from which they were not free, gave rise to fewer complaints than those of the present day.

In 1835 there appeared a controversy in the local press relative to the use of the French language in court procedures. The *Bee* of December 8, protested that:

In a very improper attempt to inculpate ourselves on account of an assertion made in an article concerning jurors and trial by jury, yet it must have been evident to any candid mind that when speaking of the French language in the courts of justice only much valuable time would be saved to all concerned and the ends of justice be as efficiently and more speedily attained. If we were in error, our columns were opened to refutation. But none should have presumed to assert that we wished to have abolished the French language among our citizens—an assertion not only unwarranted and presumptuous in our assailants, but one which shows that he either did not understand us or that he designed willfully to misrepresent.

The conduct of the courts was frequently attacked by the gazettes, the ability of the judges was questioned, and their lack of judicial responsibility was attributed to the "low grade of lawyers who became judges because the poor pay prevented the better ones from seeking the position."

There were many criticisms of the way the judges presided over their courts, among which may be mentioned the one on July 31, 1835 in the *Bee*:

Although we are aware that the civil code of Louisiana equals, if not exceeds, that of any other state of the Union, although we may be persuaded that the code of practice and criminal code are merely tantamount in their efficient operation to those of any other state, we are credibly informed that there is no state in which there is less efficency and more diversity in the administration of the laws.

The fact is—judges badly paid and are perfectly irresponsible—To secure the services of honest and intelligent lawyers for the duties of judges, they should receive a salary as commensurate with the fees of practicing barristers: and they should be subject to impeachment.

Our judges withhold sessions of their courts as they please ... and their conduct in most respects is *ad libitum*, without responsibility, governed chiefly by the dictates of judgecraft and the formulas of office rather than by the covenants of law. So is it with their colleagues, the prosecuting attorneys — in whose hand the administration of justice become a mere shuttlecock— banded as they best can "raise the wind."

Hence the citizens of the State are ncessarily compelled per se, to administer justice, the laws are inoperable and violated with impunity. The judges connive at the failures of the attorneys and the attorney must in turn shelter the judges; between whom suitors are arrested or sacrificed without redress to themselves or to the community.

It seems that this maladministration of justice was as prevalent in other sections of the State as in the City. For the *St. Francisville Gazette* on November 1832, complained:

There is not a Louisianian who would not necessarily consent to pay an additional expense for judges to be assured of his life and property: and to throw off the odious yokes which absolute judges (holding the power to oppose them by the terror of their names and the difficulty of language) imposed upon the unfortunate Louisiana. But it requires a person who has been in the remote counties of the state to judge of the desolation which has been occassiond to families that have suits pending in a tribunal where they were not understood and where the judge was an entire stranger to their usages and languages. That officer, clothed by common law, from which he differs only in form, and which he may twist as he may think proper, rarely awards a judgment in favor of a Louisianian when an American is the defendant.

Opinion is so strongly established among the unfortunate Creoles against those judges that they prefer abandoning their established rights than to be judged by an American.

That deplorable condition was not typical of Louisiana, for

it prevaded the whole country. The *Bee* on August 3, 1835, published the following interesting communication:

> People are compelled to take the law in their own hands on account of the bad judiciary—(Lynch Law). A reform in the judiciary is indispensable to correct the evils; and that reform should be radical.
>
> Thomas Jefferson wrote to J. Taylor: "The judicial is seriously anti-republican." And in a letter to W. T. Barry, he admonished: "We already see the power installed for life, responsible to no authority (for impeachment is not even a scarecrow) advancing with a noiseless and steady pace to the great object of consolidation!"
>
> "Before (he continued) the canker has become inveterate, before the venom has reached so much of the body politic as to get beyond its control, a remedy should be applied—Let the future appointments of judges be for four to six years and renewable by the president and senate.
>
> "That there should be a public function independent of the nation,—whatever maybe their demerits—is a solecism in a republic of the first order and inconsistency."

And on August 6 of that year the *Bee* editorially asked for radical reform in the judiciary because, it said, that it was more necessary in Louisiana than in any other State of the Union.

There were many judges in the city, men of integrity and ability, whose memory lingers in this day. The very papers which were so vociferous in demanding the reform of the judiciary were also generous in their praises for certain gentlemen of the bench.

The following resolution was passed by the City Council eulogising Judge James Pitot, who passed away on the 4th of November 1831: It said:

> One of the most distinguished and respectable citizens: His memory ought to be endeared to us by the service he rendered as judge, it ought no less to be so for the services he has rendered as first magistrate of this city.

He was succeeded by Judge M. Maurian who was replaced by Charles Gayarré.

On June 4, 1832, Judge Joshua Lewis died. He had presided with honor over the first district court for thirty years. He was succeeded by Judge Chas. Watts: In December of that year Hon. Henry A. Bullard was appointed judge of the Supreme Court, replacing Judge Alexander Porter, who had been elected to the Senate.

The *Bee* of February 8, 1836, carried the following item:

The city court has been so well conducted under Judge Bermudez that our citizens have so reaped the advantages of the attention and energy displayed in determining their cases that they have laudably as well as properly endeavored to extend his jurisprudence and benefits.

They have therefore applied to the Legislature that it should have cognizance of all suits not involving greater amount of $1000.00, and have committed the petition in the Senate to the charge of Mr. Hoa.

We have occasionally endeavored to do justice to the intrinsic merits of the gentleman, because we find him indefatigable and intelligent, and are proud as well as pleased that the numerous and influential merchants of New Orleans, who have signed his memorial, partake of our opinion by entrusting it to his charge. Last session he affected a very material amelioration in the city court, and we hope that this year he will forward and follow his efforts in the same judicious course.

The *Bee* of August 3, 1835, complimented Judge Maurian as follows:

Judge Maurian has too much to do—he is well adapted to his judicial station, gifted by nature with a clear and comprehensible mind, quick and correct judgment and having a full knowledge of laws. He is an honor to this adopted state.

On October 1st, 1832, the distinguished jurist and philanthropist, Judge Workman, died a tragic death. The *Bee* recorded his demise as follows:

The venerable Judge Workman, one of our most distinguished and respected citizens, has disappeared from among us. We learn that on Monday, he left the Bay of St. Louis (where he had been spending the summer) in a small boat with two Negroes for the purpose of dining with Judge Harang at Pass Christian. Not finding the judge at home, he set out to return, since which time he has not been heard of and no trace of the Negroes or the boat was discovered.

Rev. Mr. Clapp wrote that he was "a superior linguist and well versed in the original scriptures."

In February 1825 all justices of the peace were abolished, and in their stead the State Legislature organized the Municipal Courts. The officers of the courts appointed by the Governors were:

Judge E. Smith—Poydras and Girod—Faubourg St. Mary
Judge Bermudez—Between Bienville and Customhouse Streets
Judge Gallien Preval—Between St. Peter and St. Ann Streets
Judge A. Dubourgh—Between Canal, Marigny and Esplanade
Judge E. D. White—In The Government House in the Senate-room.

The following is the number of cases on the docket of the District Court as of November 1st, 1837:

Circuit cases at issue	249
Jury cases at issue	341
Court cases on promissory notes	34
Number of cases that will be put at issue in 40 to 45 days, about	150
Jury cases on promissory notes	34
Total	825

Of this number it is considered that about 200 are old obsolete cases, which are either settled or will never be tried. But even substracting this amount, there will still remain upwards of 600 cases. Now, these, it will be remembered, that leaving Sundays and holidays, motion days, etc. out of the calculation, there will not remain more than 100 days for the determination of cases. Some conception may be formed of the arduous nature of the duties of the court. We understand that the prevailing judge has directed the docket of the cases to be printed in a pamphlet for the use of the gentlemen of the Bar.

Debouchel in his "Histoire de la Louisiane" stated that in 1808 a lawyer who fomented a suit or who is a party to an agreement in which a portion of the property in litigation is accorded him, or who appropriates the money of his client is disbarred. And also, if because of his negligence or if he fails to appear for the trial thereby losing his case, he must pay the court costs as well as the damage he may have caused his client. The schedule of fees was $16.00 per case pleaded before the superior or circuit courts of the territory and $5.00 in the parish courts. In 1809 the fees were indiscriminately fixed at $11.00.

The *Bee* of January 21, 1837 commented that the Judges were underpaid and that it will be "with great difficulty a single eminent lawyer can be induced to quit his practice to take a seat on the bench and it is anticipated that when the present able Parish, Probate and District Judges go out of office, none but the briefless lawyers will apply for the station unless the salaries are increased. Yet ten years ago the reverse was the case—it was the public officers then, whose compensation exceeded the rate of those in private life. But the latter have increased while the former have remained stationary."

Frequently the press deplored that too many lawyers, doctors and clerks were arriving in the city to ameliorate their condition or in quest of fortune and that it was "estimated that not less than one hundred attorneys were in the city who have not been able to clear their current expenses. Too many physicians here, too many lawyers, too many accountants, yet those will throng here to be disappointed and impoverished or turned their talents to ways of raising the wind." To which an attorney replied that there were only a few over a hundred members of the New Orleans Bar and that many have retired and that the number of practicing lawyers numbered less than a hundred, to which the Editor curtly replied "the premises are not quite accurate; but the inference is almost irresistible."

Yet at that time there was a galaxy of legal luminaries whose brilliancy of intellect, astuteness, eloquence, and profound knowledge of the law have never been eclipsed. These men have emblazoned a golden page in the history of the legal profession of New Orleans. They were the originators of a code of law which is still the law in Louisiana. They successfully practiced their profession under conditions that would be intolerable today. They wielded tremendous power in the Legislature, and their profound knowledge of the law commanded the respect of the court. Their eloquence, whether in the political arena or in the forum of civil affairs, commanded the attention and admiration of the population.

The four greatest legal stars of the era may be said to have been Edward Livingston, Etienne Mazureau, Moreau Lislet and John R. Grymes. They were the giants of the Bar. Yet, among others slightly less lustrous, were S. E. Cannon, Pierre Soulé, Christian Roselius, Issac T. Preston, Alfred Hennen, Domingue Seghers and Albert Hoa. All belonged to that golden period of legal resplendency.

Gayarré tells us that among the Americans who had come to New Orleans, none was so distinguished as Edward Livingston:

> He was of an illustrious family and before emigrating to the extreme South, he had been mayor of the city of New York. He had not been long in the place which he had chosen for his sphere of action before he gave ample evidence of his superior talents. He at once became one of the leading members of the bar, notwithstanding his having enemies who spread evil reports against him, and his having incurred a great deal of unpopularity in consequence of the part he took in the famous "batture case" which gave rise to riot in New Orleans, and to an acrimonious controversy between Thomas Jefferson and himself, in which he showed that he was at least equal, if not superior to his great

adversary. He, however, manfully and successfully battled against numerous obstacles. He was possessed of too much genius and firmness of nerve to be kept down and prevented from rising up, eagle like, to the altitude where he could freely expand his wings and breathe in his native empyrean element. Conquering prejudices, calumnies and envy, as he became better known and appreciated, the esteem and confidence of his fellow citizens in his newly elected home grew rapidly and he was sent to represent Louisiana in the Senate of the United States.

Livingston became Secretary of State under President Andrew Jackson, and later was the Minister Plenipotentiary to France.

Gayarré wrote further of Livingston:

He was a profound jurist and an accomplished scholar. Which of the two predominated, it would have been difficult to tell. He managed his cases in court with admirable self possession. It was the calm consciousness of strength; it was the serene majesty of intellect. There was no sparring, no wrangling, no browbeating. When he rose to speak, the attention of the judge, jurors, members of the bar and everybody in court was instantly riveted. There were no flashy declamations, no unbecoming carpings, no hair-splitting, no indecorous claptrap, no tinsel ornament, no stage thunder, no flimsy sophistical argumentation, no idle straggling words. His discourse was compact and robust; his language was terse and pure. His eloquence was of the classical order and uniformly elegant. It would in forensic debates, flow at first with the modesty of a gentle stream, but by degrees, swelling and rushing like the mighty tide of the ocean, it would overflow far and wide and leave the opposition not an inch of ground to stand upon.

Livingston's counter-part was Etienne Mazureau, a Frenchmen. Both were men of extraordinary ability and both were exceedingly able advocates, so much so, it was quite a controversial subject among the contemporary biographers as to which one was the most learned or the ablest lawyer. Their judgment seems to have been influenced by their affiliation with either the Anglo-Saxon or the French group. But suffice it to say that both men were brilliant stars in the legal firmament.

Etienne Mazureau left France at the age of twenty four and soon afterwards became a resident of New Orleans. He arrived in the city at the very beginning of the nineteenth century, where he remained for the balance of his life. He was very active in the politics of the City and State and was one of the leaders of the French faction which was the subject of so much acrimony from the newly arrived Anglo-Saxon Americans. He was the

Attorney General of the State and was frequently elected to the State Legislature.

In the early eighteen-twenties, Mazureau held the dual office of legislator and Attorney General. This dual office-holding was contested, on the basis that it was unconstitutional. Mazureau argued for three days that the holding of both offices at the same time was sanctioned by the constitution and the law. He won. It is said that the "appearance in the court room of a large basket of champagne borne on the shoulders of a perspiring Negro was to the Bar an unfailing prognostic that the ex-Attorney General is retained in a case on that day."

Gayarré, Mazureau's contemporary, writes of him:

> He is an adroit and most powerful logician, but on certain occasions his eloquence becomes tempestuous. He delights in all studies appertaining to his profession and possesses a most extensive and profound knowledge of the civil law from the twelve tables of Rome and the institutes of Justinian to the Napoleon Code. He is deeply versed in the common law, which, however, when the opportunity presents itself, it is his special pleasure to ridicule and treat with spiteful depreciation.
>
> He is particularly elated when in his forensic conflicts he triumphs over an Anglo-Saxon member of the bar to whom he happens to have taken a special dislike.
>
> His voice is supurb, now calmly argumentative, now tremulous with passion and frequently derisive with sneers and sarcasms as sharply pointed as the savagest arrow.
>
> He is equally great and successful in civil and criminal cases. Hence his income is very large.

Mazareau was of medium size, stocky, with flashing dark eyes, black hair, and a brown complextion; he was a perfect specimen of the Southern type, as of the manner born.

His name is tradition among the Creoles of the City. He inspired a stanza, in that most popular song of the ante-bellum Negroes which is still remembered today:

> Monsieur Mazureau
> Dans son vieux buro
> Sembalit crapo
> Dans la baille dolo
> Boo! boom! Boo! Doom!
> Danse Calinda
> Boo! Boom! Boo! Boom!
> Danse Calinda.

A literal translation would be: Mr. Mazureau in his bureau, resembles a big frog which fell in a tub of water. Dance Calinda, Boom Boom!

Such is the penalty of fame.

Another colorful personality was John R. Grymes, a Virginian who migrated to New Orleans in the early nineteenth century. He was proclaimed by one of his biographers as being the "most eminent advocate of Louisiana and perhaps in the South West." He volunteered his aid to General Jackson at the Battle of New Orleans, and it is said that he was the one who persuaded the General to pardon the Lafittes and their men. He was appointed District Attorney of the United States at the age of twenty five.

Grymes is perhaps best remembered for his association with the Lafittes and for his defence of these freebooters in several suits against them by the Government. The many stories written about his visits to the lair of the pirates, which the fictionists have embroidered to please their readers, made Grymes a legendary character. The following excerpt from an article written by a contemporary in the *Courier* of May 12, 1843 must be considered as factual:

> In the several suits of the Government against that notorious freebooter, which circumstances have given rise to many ridiculous stories, to which we need not allude to than to pronounce their falsehood. In one of these suits, as the story goes, Colonel Grymes was associated with Edward J. Livingston, and they were to receive a contingent fee of $5000.000 each. By some flaw of the indictment over defect of proof, they cleared the pirate, who being released, invited his lawyers to his retreat at Barataria where he could pay their fee. Mr. Livingston distrusted his client, and sold his fee to his brother counselor for one half.
>
> Accordingly Col. Grymes and Lafitte set sail for Barataria. When they arrived at the Pirate's home, the distinguished advocate was received in a most elegant tent, and regaled with all the luxuries and elegance which wealth could procure in a tropical clime. After spending two or three days in royal plenty and abundance, the Colonel was sent back to the city in one of Lafitte's vessels with the snug sum of $10,000.00 in his trunk.
>
> Many other stories, more aprocryphal than this, are told of the connection of the distinguished counsel with his distinguished client.

It was said that he never wore the same suit for more than two consecutive days and that he "changed his colors often and as rapidly as the chameleon. Today he is in full black, apparently in mourning — tomorrow, he will surprise the public with a green cockney coat with foxhead buttons, buff pants, white hat, red neckerchief — the next day he will appear in full spotless white and so on through all the changes in the tailor's calendar."

He was a member of the State Legislature and also served in the United States Senate, where he took rank with the Calhouns and the Bentons. It was said that his addresses were always remarkable for a certain equability and dispassionateness of style, even on subjects of a party nature.

Grymes was not very effective as a popular orator. Of this he was fully aware. He seldom addressed public assemblages, and when he did he was generally brief, for his style was too dignified and didactic, too statesmanlike for these occasions.

An episode is related about the reluctance of Grymes to engage in public speaking. In 1840 Hon. S. S. Prentiss, spoke at a meeting at the St. Charles Theatre, and Grymes was called to answer him the following evening at a meeting held at the Orleans Ball Room. After a few sentences he pleaded indisposition and begged to be replaced by some more competent orator.

Grymes was a master lawyer, and it is written of him that "there are many men of our bar more learned, many more eloquent, many more profound, but few in such perfect and efficient harmony, the requisite of an able and successful lawyer. In fact, he displayed admirable skill, tact and judgment." Te enjoyed an immensely lucrative practice, in one suit his fee was $60,000.00 He was one of the best paid lawyers in the United States.

Grymes lived luxuriously and was an enthusiastic gambler in horse racing, cock-fighting and cards. Gayarré said that "he would not brook the shadow of a word of disparagement, and on a point of honor would immediately like all Southern gentlemen, appeal to the arbitration of the duel."

Niles Weekly Register of February 26, 1835, records the following interesting incident:

> An encounter lately took place in the House of Representatives of Louisiana which produced a great sensation in New Orleans. On the 3rd instant, about 10 o'clock, a little before the usual time of the meeting of the House, Mr. Grymes, a distinguished lawyer of New Orleans, entered the hall and advancing toward Mr. [Alceé] Labranche, the speaker of the House, who was standing near the clerk's desk, raised his cane

and struck him, whereupon Mr. Labranche drew a pistol and fired at Mr. Grymes. The ball passed through the lapel of Mr. Grymes' overcoat.

Immediately upon being fired at, he dropt his cane, drew a pistol, and returned the fire of Mr. Labranche, who was retreating through the clerk's door, and fell near it wounded. The wound, we believe, is not dangerous. Mr. Grymes was summoned to the bar of the House to be tried for the assault on the Speaker. He commenced by protesting against the power of the House to arraign him, asserting the only power of this nature granted it by the constitution was that of punishing its own members by expulsion or otherwise. The question whether the House had jurisdiction in this affair after being warmly debated, was decided in the affirmative. Mr. Grymes acquiesced in the decision, and answered the interrogations put to him, admitting that he had shot the Speaker, but that he had not drawn his pistol until he was shot at, and denying that he had violated any of the privileges of the House . . . The result of the trial was that Mr. Grymes was reprimanded.

Another brilliant star in that galaxy was Moreau Lislet. He was a good natured rotund Frenchman, his hands small and plump, his body was soft and his flesh quivering. His physical condition belied his mental stamina and often lulled his legal opponents into a false security. So much so that Gayarré said that: "He does not look formidable, does he? No. Well, you had better beware of him."

His legal ability is best portrayed by that historian who pictured him as follows:

He is an artesian well of legal lore — deep, very deep. He is one of those two or three jurists who were entrusted by the Legislature with the work of adapting the Napoleon Code to the wants and circumstances of Louisiana under her own institutions. He is a very great favorite with the judges, the clerks, the sheriffs, the jurors, the members of the bar — in fact with every body. He is so kind, so benevolent, so amiable in all his dealings and sayings, His bonhomie is so captivating! Of so sympathizing a nature is he that for instance, he sometimes takes his adversary's side of the question, admits that there is a good deal in his favor and says it and shows it, too. He will even go so far as to present it to the court in its very best aspect, But after having acted with such kindness and impartiality toward his opponent, he pathetically apologizes for destroying all his hopes and illusions, regrets that his claim is not founded on the law and evidence applicable to the case, demonstrates it beyond the shadow of a doubt and finally exterminates the poor fellow with a sigh of compassion over his hard fate. Ho! Ho! beware of Mr. Lislet and of his bonhomie!

No mention is made of E. E. Cannon by our historians, yet as a lawyer and legislator he deserves to be remembered as one of the greats of New Orleans. A native of France he was a highly respected and esteemed member of the Bar. His anonymous biographer said of him, in the *Courier* on May 19, 1843, that "with him party is subservient to principle; and no consideration can induce him to sacrifice any of his principles."

The following interesting story is told about an altercation he had with Judge Turner. Cannon, who had been rather brutally treated by that Judge, retaliated in turn in language which was regarded by the Judge as contempt of Court. He was accordingly imprisoned. Upon his release, Cannon presented the judge with a cartel which was declined, upon which Cannon published him everywhere as a disgrace to his station.

Pierre Soulé left an uneffaceable imprint on the scroll of the learned advocates of New Orleans. He was the son of poor shepherds in the Pyranean Mountains. At an early age he became a scholastic at the Jesuit's seminary in Toulouse. For some reason he renounced the vocation he had embraced, and developed a strong hostility against that order. In France he became involved in the turbulent politics of that time, and in 1824 wrote articles for the Parisian papers. He then published *Le Nain*, and was accused of insulting the King and of publishing doctrines against religion. Leaving France Soulé landed in New Orleans in 1824, completely destitute. He proceeded to Kentucky where he learned to speak English and to read law. On his return to New Orleans in 1826, he was admitted to the Bar. It is told that as a lawyer he was distinguished for his energy and ingenuity, that he studied his cases and prepared them well. He was famous as a criminal lawyer.

The following word picture of Issac T. Preston, who came from South Carolina, is quoted in part from an article which appeared in the *Courier* on May 12, 1843:

> No one could possibly mistake that large, portly, plain-dressed, independent looking old gentleman, who shambles along our streets in easy slippers a "world too wide", with a market basket in one hand and an old law book in another.
>
> There is democracy in his very shirt color. — His extraordinary spectacle of the Att'y. General driving his own carriage, and that an old-fashiened one with the driver's box on one side. These are not affectations. Far from it — They

proceed from an exteme simplicity and a generous bounty of heart.

An effective speaker; style excessive plain and homely, in his popular addresses he displays figures and tropes, but they are always of the most clumsy structure and most glaring taste either too extravagant and hypercritical, or carried into the most unendurable of oratorical vices, the double metaphor.

As a lawyer he is distinguished for extraordinary skill and adroitness. In a hard pinch he has no superior. His ingenuity in setting a case, in giving the facts and evidence is unparalleled. As a constitutional lawyer he is well versed in the history of our government and in its principles. He is not literate, but self taught and a self made man.

Fortier in his history of Louisiana tells us that Christian Roselius, of Bremen, came to New Orleans as a redemptioner about the time of the Louisiana Purchase. But his biographer wrote in the *Courier* on May 23, 1843, that it is "not true that he ever was a redemptioner." That anonymous writer was a contemporary of Roselius' and his statement should be considered factual.

Young Roselius, arriving in the city when he was sixteen years old, was a printer's apprentice and type setter, and soon wrote for the *Louisiana Advertiser* under the nom de plume, the letter "C". In 1826 he published the first literary journal in New Orleans — *The Halcyon*. His venture did not prove profitable. It lasted only 18 months. During that time he studied law in the office of the venerable James Workman and with August Davezac. He was admitted to the bar in 1827. At the beginning of his career, Roselius was not very successful, and had to depend on the support of his wife who was a school teacher. He later became the Attorney-General of the State of Louisiana.

It is said of him that "as a lawyer he had few superiors in legal acumen, strength of reasoning and powers of research."

Gayarré tells us that Alfred Hennen came from New England and described him in the following:

> He is invincibly self-possessed and no provocation can throw him off his guard in his fortress of cold and passionless reserve. Nothing can ruffle his temper; and if the attempt is made he turns it off with a good-natured laugh and blunts the edge of his adversary's weapon. He is an erudite, but plain, dry, plodding, practical lawyer who never aims at any flight of eloquence. He has a large and well-furnished library which he liberally puts at the disposal of his friends. He is laboriously industrious, and always comes into court with a long string of authorities which he uses as a lasso to throw round the neck of his oppon-

ents. He is not much addicted to urge upon the court the argumentative deductions from the broad principles of jurisprudence, but prefers relying on an overwhelming avalanche of precedents and numerous decisions.

Like all members of the legal profession from the other States of the Union, he much prefers the common to the civil law, the latter being looked upon by them as an abortive creation of the Latin mind which they hold, of course, to be naturally inferior to the Anglo-Saxon intellect.

Albert Hoa was born in New Orleans and died on February 15, 1844, in the prime of a brilliant career at the age of thirty-eight. He is better known as one of the most brilliant legislators in Louisiana. His career was an illustrious one, though short. His premature demise was a great loss to the State.

CHAPTER XII

POLICE, TRAFFIC VIOLATIONS, PRISONS, EXECUTIONS

New Orleans in the days of which I write was the refuge of criminals and unscrupulous adventurers from all over the world. Its port harbored the crews of ships flying the flags of every nation, as well as obstreperous river boatmen. The tribulations and the grind of a long, tedious hazardous voyage were soon forgotten as port was reached, for the crewmen were exhilirated by the anticipation of a long-dreamed of orgy without any restraint.

These men had a perfect contempt for civil authority. They did not respect, much less obey laws. They would flock to places of ill repute, and fill the grog houses and the gambling dens. They would brawl and fight among themselves. Their ruffianism was was not always limited to the riverfront and the disreputable sections, but was some times extended to the respectable quarters of the city.

The permanent residents were as a rule law abiding and crime was practically unknown among them. It was during the cold months, when the danger from yellow fever had subsided, and the population was doubled by the invasion of transients, which included all classes of society from reputable business and professional men to *chevaliers d'industrie* and those steeped in vice and crime. While respectable visitors were well received and accepted as an asset to the community, the advent of vagabonds and ruffians was a constant source of irritation and concern. There was always a fear that these malefactors would overrun the city. There are many recorded instances of tumults and riots when the doors of residences and commercial establishments had to be barricaded against the onslaught of a drunken mob. In some cases the police were powerless to cope with the situation, and had to be reinforced by groups of citizens and the militia. The life of a "gendarme" was hard and dangerous, and their numbers were at times not equal to the task of policing the city and its suburbs. The police were frequently censured by the press, yet they were occasionally commended by visiting diarists.

In 1823 Captain Alexander noted that the police regulations were excellent. He wrote that "some time ago it [New Orleans] was a lurking place for desperate assassins, and though there were two murders committed during my sojourn, yet in general, one may walk the streets in safety at all hours".

Josiah Condon observed in 1830 that "New Orleans, which twenty years ago was the lurking hole of every assassin, is now in point of serenity, not inferior to any city."

Flint, who visited the city in 1832, made the following observation:

> The police of the city is at once mild and energetic, and notwithstanding the boatmen and sailors, the multifarious character of the inhabitants collected from every country and climate.
>
> Notwithstanding the multitudes of boatmen and sailors, notwithstanding the mass of people that rush along the streets of the most incongruous materials, I have seen fewer brawls and quarrels here than in any city I have resided so long. For all the evils that arise among such a people, the municipal court finds a prompt if not a proper remedy. Nothing so effectively operates to prevent larcenies and brawls in such a place, as administering prompt justice. They do not complain here of the "Law's delay" in all these matters.

In 1833 Stuart wrote that "considering the number of strangers in the city, the police did not seem to be faulty." And the following year Tyrone Power commented that "the police of this place I should imagine at present is better than in the northern cities since the noise and disturbances in the streets is a thing unknown, and after ten at night everything is usually still and quiet, excepting upon the levee where work at that season appears to go on day and night."

A. A. Parker, a visitor at approximately the same time, was critical of law enforcement in New Orleans and was very derogatory in his remarks as to the efficiency of the police. He expressed his disapproval as follows:

> I must say that New Orleans does not show that order, neatness and sobriety found in other larger cities of the Union. Murders, robberies, thefts and riots, are too common to hardly elicit a passing notice. Man here seems to have become reckless of life, it is taken and given for "trifles light as air", with an indifference truly astonishing. The police is inefficient and shamefully negligent.
>
> The authorities of the city appear to stand aloof, and see the populace physically and morally wallowing in crime. It does appear to me, that if all the virtuous portion of the citizens would brace themselves to the work, the city might be greatly

improved in morals. Let the strong arm of the law be put forth fearlessly.

But it is indeed, too true, and whoever happens to visit, [New Orleans], that places a decent value upon life, or the goods of life, will be glad like me, to escape without injury, or loss of either. I could not however, feel at ease among such a set of plunderers and robbers.

As long as crime is sanctioned in New Orleans, so long will it be the general haunt of the knaves and vagabonds of the Union, and of the world.

The *Bee* on November 14, 1837, gave a graphic picture of the lawless element which thronged into the city. Under the headline of ABUSES, it observed:

What has certainly been the chief objection to a residence in New Orleans? Its licentiousness and insecurity! During certain seasons of the year, we have been the prey of sharpers and scoundrels, *chevaliers de'industrie,* and gamblers who all flock hither to exercise in tranquility their lawless vocations. Not all, but the influx of plunderers and cut-throats, the refuge of the jails and penitentiary, the scum of civilization and the pest of society, who find in New Orleans admirable and abundant opportunities for the practice of their profession. In summer the fatality of our climate affrights even them. The immediate instinct of self preservation is superior to the attraction of booty, and they leave us to have a season unmolested, but with the first frost they return to their cherished asylum. Now that Havana has cut them off, they consider this their dear, native home. The hordes of desperadoes that formerly found protection there, have been expelled by the ceaseless vigilance of inexorable discipline, and now gladly seek shelter among us. They chuckle at our weakness, and smile at our senseless rhodomontade. They lurk in secure and undiscoverable haunts during the day and do their work under cover of night's propitious shades.

This unwelcomed seasonal infiltration of that lawless and criminal element infringed on the serenity and security of a law abiding community.

The *Louisiana Gazette* on October 5, 1825, called for much needed reform and stricter discipline of the City Guards, claiming that they are "generally idle all day, and invisible during the night." The editorial suggested that "they should quarter by themselves and not be permitted to pursue their various trades and occupations during the day."

The *Courier* of April 7, 1829, called for more City Guards for the preservation of peace and tranquility within the City, and deplored the fact that citizens were obliged to guard and protect themselves. It proposed the following:

A plan to form a company of cavalry of police, to be named the Orleans Gendarmes, to consist of a Captain, one Lieutenant and twenty four privates, to wear a uniform, and to be armed with a broad sword and a pair of pistols.

Their horses to be kept in the same stable, and the men to be lodged under the same roof near the stable, and to be under the orders of the Mayor.

The twenty four men to get on horses at sunset and repair to the City Hall, from whence they will separate and patrol the city and suburbs until dawn light. Each man to have a whistle.

It was also suggested that they were to be paid, by voluntary subscriptions from the merchants and inhabitants of the city.

The *Bee*, in an editorial on January 22, 1834, again complained caustically of the inefficiency of the City Police:

New Orleans without exception, has the worse police of any city in this Union, and if the facilities for gaining an honest living were not so great, we do believe that for crime and midnight assassination, it would excel Havana in its worse days.

Only think of a body of seventy to eighty men, divided into two watches guarding a place as large in extent. The Council that would provide it with a suitable and effective watch, would immortalize itself with our citizens.

The City Guard was composed of a hundred and two men, divided as follows; the City Hall, forty two men, faubourg St. Mary, twenty-seven men; faubourg Treme, twelve men; faubourg Marigny, eleven men, and faubourg Lacourse, eleven men.

On February 12, 1834, the *Louisiana Advertiser* severely censured the police. It charged:

Our police establishment still remains a blot on the face of a free country, an ancient barbarism in a great commercial and republican city, an inefficient and utterly useless incumbrance, a system of petty sinecures, as well as a glaring remnant of despotism in a land of liberty. Where from the Gulf of St. Lawrence to that of Mexico, can you find a community more enlightened, more intelligent and more enterprising, than the majority of the people at this time in our City?

We have begun to draw a covering over the actual mud we have long wallowed in; let us wipe off the mire, the stain that adheres to our local institutions, produced by the existence of an armed band of foreign mercenaries. An unfeeling and almost irresponsible soldiery, paid by ourselves to maim and butcher at their own discretion the free citizens of a free and enlighted republic.

We blame not the "city guard" — we blame not the administrators of the law, but the laws themselves.

The *Bee* of July 2, 1835 published yearly salaries of what it called the "inefficient City Guard":

1 Captain		$1320.00
2 Lieutenants	each ($960.00)	1920.00
2 Sargeants	each ($480.00)	960.00
4 Corporals	each ($420.00)	1680.00
94 Privates	each ($360.00)	33,840.00

This was a total annual expenditure of $37,720.00.

The lamp lighters were also employed as night police.

The *True American* complained that the majority of the City guard did not speak either French or English.

The *Bee* of September 23, 1835, found it "ridiculous for the City Council to close all taverns, grog shops, and all houses of refreshment at 8 o'clock, which is so absurd, that the Mayor is obliged to permit them to remain opened until 9 o'clock at the present time, and during the pleasurable months of winter, till 10 or 11 o'clock."

It also remarked that "still the ordinance exists, although willingly and willfully violated."

The following year the Grand Jury of the Parishes of Orleans, Jefferson, St. Bernard and Plaquemines reported as follows:

> The general inefficiency of the police, the great and increasing number of grog shops and tippling houses, the public halls wherein white and colored persons of depraved character indiscriminately mix, the almost general practice of carrying deadly weapons, appear to the Grand Jury among the most prominent of these causes. The great number of free colored persons residing in the City, in contravention to law, requires immediate attention in the opinion of the Grand Jury, the prompt execution of the existing laws in relation to such individuals in a few instances, would produce the effect of much to be desired, and rid the State at once of this most vicious and most depraved of its population.

Samuel J. Peters: Foreman
New Orleans, February 26, 1836.

Again, violations of the speed laws were called to the attention of the public by the *Bee*, on April 20, 1836. The article protested that:

> Furious driving of drays and other vehicles in the streets has become an outrageous nuisance, and in consequence, not

only of increased number driven, but the bad condition of the streets, it is doubly obnoxious.

Some efficient remedy should be adopted to prevent the many evils almost daily occurring within this malpractice. No one can walk the streets without having their clothes bedaubed by the wheels of the drays, etc., flying past them, and most ladies make many complaints that they cannot perambulate without being endangered or bedaubed; they are constantly obliged to confine themselves at home, to the serious loss of haberdashers and other mrchants.

There are ordinances of the City Council on the subject, but they are inefficient and unenforced. The drivers contemn the laws because none take an interest in their fulfilment; and therefore the evils of rapid driving are now of serious magnitude.

Slaves and others stand up in their drays, and have not only personal recreation in furious driving, but personal amusement in witnessing the appearance of those, whose walking they delay or prevent, and those who they affright or bedaub. They feel an interest in displaying their importance, and are quite delighted in their feats.

Here then is the cause of the evil; and to this should the remedy be applied. We have never known of any law or ordinances effectual to prevent rapid driving, which did enjoin under penalty all drivers of drays and such like vehicles to walk by the side of their horses. It is true that drivers of hacks and omnibuses cannot be subjected to the system, but most of the evil of rapid driving in this City arises from the drays and carts. Their drivers stand up in them, and lash away as if their fortunes and fate depend on their fury. The slaves care little for their master's horses, if they are themselves amused, and if they by driving rapidly at one time are enabled to idle at an alternate period.

All drays and other public vehicles should be conspicuously numbered and then it should be easy to enforce the ordinances, by detecting and punishing the offenders.

The policemen, called *gendarmes*, were uniformed in blue coats and pants, with bell shaped hats with black leather cockades. They were armed with brass handle cutlasses, flintlock muskets and bayonets. For their protection they made their rounds in squads of four, and were mustered every evening in the Place d'Arms.

Even in those horse-and-buggy days accidents occured. The *Argus* reported the death of Dr. Buchanan due to an accident caused by a horse frightened by a kite, and of two more persons dangerously wounded in a like manner. It called attention to the fact that the ordinances against kite flying in the public streets were not observed, suggested that "in as much as the public authorities are so remiss in performing their duties, the citizens should take upon themselves to put a stop to the flying of kites, whenever the occasion offers."

The press in complaining of the inefficiency of the City Police, made frequent mention of laxity in enforcement of city ordinances. There were reports of traffic accidents, of the careless driving and the gross negligence of the teamsters, as well as their disregard for the safety of the pedestrains.

On June 4, 1822 the *Louisiana Gazette* complained about the Negro draymen galloping their horses dangerously and in violation of the law. On December 5, 1823, under the headline "Accident", it reported that Mr. Tricou was hurt by a dray which upset his carriage, and the paper suggested that laws be passed by the City Council prohibiting draymen from going faster than a trot.

Speed laws were again the subject of an editorial in the *Bee* of November 14, 1835, it offered the following suggestion:

> The fast driving of the drays and other vehicles through the streets have become an intolerable nuisance, despite the ordinances of the City Council, and in consequence of the negligence of the police Commissiaries.
> The most effectual law that we have known to prevent this nuisance were those ordered that all drivers should walk by the side of their horses or drays, or otherwise be fined.
> When drivers are permitted to ride in their carts it is of course for the pleasure to drive quickly, but when they are compelled to walk, the temptation to rapid charioteering is entirely conquered. Will the members of the City Council act on this suggestion?"

Another police regulation was debated by the City Council in June 1823 — whether the curfew should be announced by the shooting of a cannon or by the ringing of the bells of the Church at 9 P. M. It was decided that a cannon shot would signal the curfew.

An interesting communication about "Stray Dogs", signed "A Sausage", appeared in the *Louisiana Gazette* of July 28, 1823. It was a protest against the large number of dogs in the City allowed to make a kennel in the Butcher's market, and which added nothing to the cleanliness of the hall itself. It suggested:: "As this place seems to be the rendezvous for the half-starved and distressed stray dogs of the City, it is to be hoped, his Honor, instead of poisoning the more valuable species who have their masters, will give more attention to the curs."

The *Louisiana Gazette* of September 25, 1823 reported an attempted escape by the prisoners of the City jail, it stated that: "The Mayor, Police and members of the Volunteer fire companies were also prompt in assembling to aid the civil authorities in the execution of the laws".

At that time there were 160 prisoners of whom fifty were involved in the riot. There were but three persons confined for debt. In March 1824, an act was introduced in the State Legislature to abolish imprisonment for debt. A Committee of the Senate of which Moreau Lislet, was the chairman, made the following report:

> The State Prison is kept with all the cleanliness that the small extent of the place can admit of — that the prisoners are properly treated, and that the most exact discipline prevails among them. There were no complaint from the prisoners.

The committee proposed two plans for improving the jail:

> One, to purchase the lots that jam the back part of the prison as far back as Royal Street, which would amount to a ninety foot front on said street, by 100 feet in depth, and fronting St. Pierre Street, to erect thereon the necessary buildings for the improvement of the State Prison — could be purchased for about $45,000.00 and adding $55,000.00 to $60,000.00 for buildings. The State would have for the sum of $110,000.00 or $120,000.00, which could be borrowed in the other states, or from abroad, at the rate not to exceed 6 to 7%, an establishment that could suffice during fifteen or twenty years, whatever may be the progressive increase of the number of prisoners during that time, calculated at the present number.

> The second plan: To raise one story over the actual building of the public prison would suffice for the time being.

> J. H. Holland claimed that the raising of another story over the prison wouldn't cost much, and would contain enough room for a workshop, sufficiently large to employ all the convicts, at such labor as would not require many tools or much room, i. e., cigar making, shoe making, tailoring, etc.

> The buildings added last year to the prison, are so constructed as to render it less secure than before, there being in the center an open yard, out of which escape is not at all difficult, owing to the lowness of the walls. The defect may be corrected by raising the walls or putting a grating across the yard, and without impeding or obstructing the light.

The committee's recommendations never materialized, but were the incentive for the State to build a penitentiary in Baton

Rouge. Governor Roman in his message to the Legislature on January 2, 1832, stressed the necessity for the construction of a house of correction, he proposed that:

> The prison in which these persons are now detained, who have been condemned by our courts of justice, as well as that of the United States, was originally built for a police jail, and is in no manner fit for those to whom it is now appropriated. Experience has proved that it is not sufficiently strong to hold criminals, and from the small extent and the ill-judged distribution of this edifice, there must abuses necessarily exist, which all the zeal of the keeper of the prisoners cannot prevent.
>
> The convicts, whatever may be the nature of their crime, are crowded together during the night in the same apartment. These rooms which are too compact to be capable of containing the prisoners during the day, all open upon a narrow yard which is within the body of the building, and in which all culprits are kept together, without the distinction of age, crime or even color. The murderer, the thief, the forger, the swindler, and the vagabond are all confined together, and such an union cannot but increase their corruption. An association of this character forms a school of immorality and vice, where the least perverted are perfected in the arts of wickedness by those who have become hardened by long experience.
>
> It has been demonstrated by experiments that have been made in several States of the Union, that these houses once constructed, the annual expense of their support is more than covered by the proceeds of the labor of their inmates. The State receives no compensation for the labor by the criminals in the streets of New Orleans, and this kind of punishment is subject to more than one objection; the least of which, without doubt, is not the idea that must be awakened in a portion of our population at the sight of these men, loaded with chains and reduced to a species of slavery. Their support is to us an enormous burden, and we have moreover to pay rent for their safekeeping to the City of New Orleans.
>
> The amount drawn from the Treasury of the State, since the year 1819, (at that epoch when Governor Villere for the first time recommended the erection of a penitentiary) is $179,631.88.
>
> If a house of correction had been built, the difference which would have resulted from it in favor of the State up to the present period, would have been more than sufficient to pay the cost, which would have been occasioned for its erection.

On the thirteenth of March, of the same year, the Senate appropriated $50,000.00 for the purchase of a lot of ground in Baton Rouge for the purpose of erecting a penitentiary thereon.

The Louisiana penitentiary in Baton Rouge was soon built and put in operation. An article in the *Bee* of March 9, 1836, tells us that 104 cells were completed, and that 24 more were under construction, and 240 more were to be built. It had 116 inmates, 50 of whom were incarcerated during the last summer and of these 50, 10 were brought up for robbery, 30 for larceny, 1 for forgery, 2 for slave stealing, 3 for swindling, 8 for horse stealing, 1 for burglary, 1 counterfeiting, 1 for passing counterfeit money, 2 for receiving stolen goods, 1 for attempt to poison, I for maiming, and 2 for murder. Only two were natives of Louisiana, and one of them was a free-man-of-color.

The amount expanded since 1832 for the ground, building, and the maintenance of the convicts was $84,400.00, and $15,000.00 for the salaries of the officers.

"But the labor of the convicts is becoming profitable", the article continued, "that last year its value exceeded the current expenses by $3,076.29 net; not that the State made that sum on their labor, but saved it in erecting additional wings and cells. When the building shall have been completed, and the convicts have their workshops prepared and in use, the profits naturally arising from their labor will greatly exceed the cost of their maintenance. Perceiving the profitable nature of the convict labor, the committee recommended the confinement for terms of years proportioned to all offence, shall be the only punishment." It also recommended that capital punishment be abolished.

The report of the Grand Jury of the 1st District of the State of Louisiana to Judge J. F. Canonge, of the Criminal Court, asserted that the state prison in New Orleans was an infected hole.

> The building lacks in solidity, the rafters in the section reserved for women prisoners had rotted away, the gallery has no railings, and is dangerous to the children who live in the place with their mothers, and the stairs leading to that gallery have also rotted away and are without a balustrade.
>
> The infirmary, without being contradicted, can be said to be the least clean. A small room about fourteen feet square, had six patients having different diseases, which some could have been contagious, etc.
>
> H. Leaumont, President of the Grand Jury.

Two years afterwards the Grand Jury of the parishes of Orleans, Jefferson, St. Bernard and Plaquemines made the following report:

The number of persons confined in the Parish Prison when the Jury entered upon its duties, was much greater than the prison was calculated to contain; and even now the number is too great to ensure the cleanliness so essential to the health of the inmates.

The loathsome state of the prison is the more to be deprecated when it is considered that a portion of the inmates are there confined for no other fault than their inability to pay their debts. Such persons are forced to be companions and associates of the most depraved and hardened of our species.

The indiscriminate manner in which white and black females are associated, is another evil consequence on the limit and extent of the jail.

In June, 1834, the City Council adopted a motion by Felix Labatut to authorize the committee on construction, acting with the Mayor, to contract for a police and county jail.

The new Parish Prison was constructed on what is now the site of the pumping station of the Sewerage and Water Board on Orleans Street, in the rear of the Auditorium. On July 14, 1837, the Grand Jury inspected the jail which was then ready to receive prisoners from the old calaboose. The report said:

> We learn they will report that after burning charcoal in the different rooms and cells, they may be [the prisoners] removed on Saturday next, without detriment to their health. The building is certainly airy, commodious, well distributed and sufficiently capacious for the confinement of the prisoners, and has a great and indispensable advantage over the old prison, that the debtors are entirely separated from those who are imprisoned for crime. The debtor's rooms are as pleasant as they can be made with a due regard to security for escape. It is intended, we understand, to introduce the water from the water pipes as soon as it can be done conveniently, which will aid much to the comfort and cleanliness of those whose unfortunate lot may place them there. The old calaboose is a horrible residence for any human being, no matter what his guilt may be, but when we reflect that heretofore debtors, innocent men accused of no criminal offence and seamen suspected of a design to desert their vessel are mingled with convicts and the very dregs of the human race in a space much too limited for the whole number, we cannot help looking upon the complexion of the new prison as the consumation auspicious to humanity.

On October 25, of that year, the *Bee* reported that the Negroes had been transported to the new jail "as the old tenement is now only a useless and unsightly mass, and trust that it will soon disappear."

Another interesting report was made by the Grand Jury to the Criminal Court of the 1st District. Its investigation revealed that the 1st Municipality appropriated the old prison as a place of confinement for persons arrested by watchmen. The 2nd Municipality rented a suitable building instead of the horrible den heretofore used as their police prison.

The "lock up house" for the police of the first municipality is one of the "sinks or dens" strongly condemned.

A young man hanged himself within the walls, and filth and odors of the most abominable kind could induce a man to commit suicide.

The place has its entrance under the staircase of the "Principal" and justifies the jury in thinking that the nearer the public authorities the greater the neglect of those whose duty it is (or should be) to have a proper daily inspection of them. In this place the Jury understands all persons are confined who may be taken up during the night, for any offense howsoever small or great it may be and then they must remain mixed up with the criminals, of all degrees until morning. This should not be, there should be separate rooms.

On June 21st, the Jury investigated the temporary jail of the 2nd Municipality — a place of torture (not worthy of name of prison) worse than dreadful reports spread. Capt. Harper charged with the command of the police of this municipality, "dens worthy only of the Inquisition of former days", there are five dens. In the first den at 7 P. M. were eight prisoners, some of whom were sick and confined for some days—wooden room, about ten square feet, 7 or 8 feet high, only one grated aperture in the door about 12 by 15 inches, for air and light, there were night stools without covers, as many as seventeen have been shut up in that Hell, when the temperature out of doors was 90 to 95 degrees, that it is apparent none but one, and that one, the strongest prisoner, could breath through the only aperture, while the other poor and miserable sufferers were compelled to lie down from faintness and exhaustion in such a heat, and among such filth and abominable ordors, the only wonder is that some plague has not already broken out and desolated the neighborhood, or that instant death has not relieved the sufferers from such inhuman and questionable tortures.

The second apartment or den is similar to the first in every respect and is occupied by three slaves.

The third apartment contained eight women; seven slaves or free persons of color, and one white, "comment on such indiscriminate imprisonment is not thought to be necessary in this state".

The fourth apartment is occupied by six slaves or free persons (males) similar in size and arrangement.

The fifth apartment is the largest and lightest; chain gangs of fourteen slaves, lying naked from choice.

Whole of the temporary jail, was formerly the kitchen and outhouses of some of our citizens, who certainly never dreamed of placing in any one of the apartments more than two persons.

Balance of the establishment fronting Lafayette square is used as a guard house.

S. J. Peters and Freret, aldermen of the 2nd Municipality were on the spot and promptly took two sick men and the white woman to the Hospital.

The Recorder never visited the jail but once or twice, and it is high time to inquire who is the officer in charge? The prisoners should be transported to the new prison to wait for trial.

Guardhouse and jail of the 3rd Municipality: Rooms large, sufficiently aired, and apartments on ground floor, and the walls planked to guard against the damp. Favorable impression.

The report mentioned that there was a vast increase in crime, "due to liquor, use of knives, dirks, pistols and concealed weapons." It was signed: J. B. Lepretre, Foreman; E. Montegut, Clerk; and dated July 8, 1837.

The unfortunate suicide, mentioned in the report was arrested on a charge of theft, and was lodged in the prison of the 2nd Municipality. He ended his days by hanging himself with a handkerchief tied to a bar of the window.

This Grand Jury gave a graphic expose of the barbarity and deplorably treatment accorded to prisoners at that time. This inhumanity was soon to cease, better jails were constructed. The custom of chain gangs working on the streets was soon to be abolished, and the prisoners were to be given the consideration which a human being is entitled to. It was the beginning of a new era.

The *Bee* on April 30, 1837, gave a most dramatic report of an execution. It is quoted in full:

Yesterday a crowd assembled about the city prison to see a man named Thomas Tibbits, accused and found guilty of murder, led to execution. They seemed to be like the troubled ocean, and fixed their impatient gaze upon the door through which he was to pass to the fatal spot. At length he appeared, and so great was the curiosity to see him that the avenues to the prison were completely choked up. When he got into the cart, he bid adieu to all those by whom he was surrounded, and took with an apparent careless air his seat upon the coffin which was to cover his mortal remains. At the gallows he kept up the same indifference, renewed his farewell to the spectators. Addressing his hangman, he observed, "Since I am yours, do your duty, and put the rope around here", indicating the particular spot of his neck.

By a strange fatality, the hangman, who was probably unacquainted with his business, made the rope too large, and the culprit fell with great violence to the ground upon the plank being withdrawn. Surprise and indignation for a moment reigned among the crowd. Several denunciations were heard against the hangman for his unskillfulness, and justice was about to remedy this unlooked for circumstance, when upon examination it was found to be all in vain. The concussion was so great that the unfortunate wretch had broke his collar bone; and thus was the punishment of the law fulfilled.

We are assured that there never was a criminal who exhibited greater courage and self-possession. The number of persons present was immense, greater than was ever seen upon a similar occasion in this city.

CHAPTER XIII

THE FOURTH ESTATE

A printing press propelled by hand or foot, boxes of types, some reams of paper, frequently housed in a back room in an alley, and a newspaper was born. Such was the humble beginning of most of these old, musty and partly discolored newspaper files of more than a century ago. In their columns repose the disturbances, the conflicts, the bigotry, the hate, the animosities, the jealousies, and the distrust of an heterogeneous population. Were it not for those early journalists, the history of the formative period of New Orleans would be nebulous, its authenticity would be lost in a haze of traditions and legends, which as the time passes by, become more and more glamorized and exaggerated. It is true that the visiting chronicler, the diarist, and other authors — and they were many — wrote their impressions of the city and its people. But the shortness of their stays precluded their obtaining authentic information and limited the accuracy of their observations. Because of this many of these writers distorted the facts and too frequently reported sensational and dubious stories to increase the sale of their books. It is only through a perusal of the early newspapers that a balance between truth and fiction can be established.

Printers, some of them itinerants, with more or less literary ability, would become over night successful editors and publishers. Among them were often men of talent who soon gained the confidence and respect of the community. Others were doomed to failure and would dispose of their presses, or would ship their equipment to some other part of the country to start anew; for printing ink was in their blood and their hope to succeed was never dimmed.

News was scarce and whatever reached here was long delayed. The sources of information were ship captains, letters from abroad, visitors to the city and from newspapers from other cities, both domestic and foreign.

As a rule the journals were ethical in their editorials, and even in the heat of a political campaign were conservative in their appraisals of the candidates they supported or opposed. In reporting local news they limited themselves to simple statement of facts, no matter how sensational. There were few stirring headlines, nor any maudlin reporting of crimes, for fear of influencing the due process of law. There were no flamboyant advertisements nor any illustrations as we know them today.

The more controversial topics were discussed anonymously in communications or letters from the public, which was unfortunate, because the identity of only a few of these writers is known today. Even editors frequently resorted to pseudonyms.

Many of these communications were vituperative and insulting, and often provoked duels. Some of the most interesting bits of the history of the times came from the pens of those anonymous contributors.

At times errors, misrepresentations and even scandalous accusations would creep in, but they were challenged by competing editors, or by outraged correspondents, and from such controversies a fair evaluation of the truth may be made.

Many of these journals were published both in English and French, and occasionally a different point of view was expressed in the respective sections. Frequently, the English was ambiguous and involved, and written in the prevailing style of the day. The French was purer, concise and expressive.

The editors of that period had to be brave men. They were held accountable for the words they printed, for those whom they assailed demanded satisfaction on the field of honor, resorted to fisticuffs, or to attacks with walking canes. By a strange paradox, many of these encounters which took place were among journalists themselves, and each newspaperman would publish a report in his respective journal in justification of his brawl, which provided amusement for its readers.

The *Moniteur de la Louisiane* was the first paper published in New Orleans. It was established in 1794, and even during the Spanish Domination it was written in French. The first paper in the English language was the *Louisiana Gazette,* which made its appearance on July 27, 1804. It was bi-lingual and for many years it had the distinction of being the leading newspaper in Louisiana.

The *Louisiana Gazette* of March 13, 1820, announced the passing of Louis Brunner, one of its editors, and his replacement by Charles Guillaume Duhy.

In 1823, there were seven newspapers in Louisiana, six in New

(Second Presbyterian Church.)

(Methodist Episcopal Church.)

(Congregational Church.)

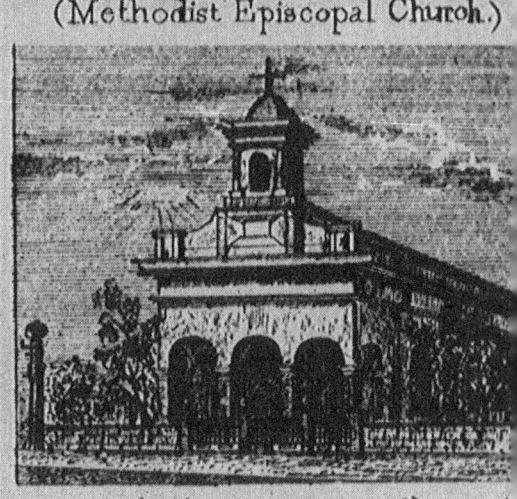
(St. Antoine's Chapel.)

(Ursuline Chapel.)

(Christs Church.)

(From Gibson's Directory of 1838 — Courtesy N. O. Public Library)

(American Theatre & Arcade Baths.)

(Sugar Refinery.)

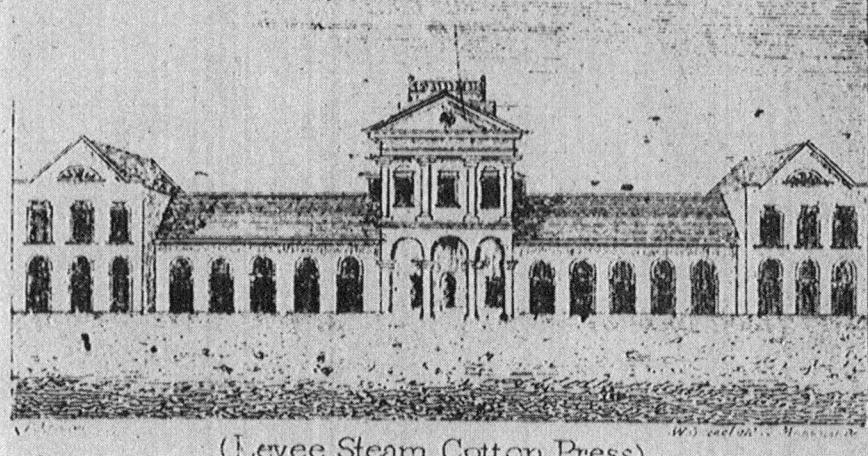
(Levee Steam Cotton Press.)

(From Gibson's Directory of 1838 — Courtesy N.O. Public Library)

Orleans and the *Baton Rouge Republican,* a new addition to the Journalistic field.

In the *Louisiana Gazette* of June 25, 1823, appeared the announcement of the the death of the most brilliant member of its staff, their Editor of the "Feuillton", Alexis Daudet, with the following obituary:

> He was a native of Paris and of very respectable family. He was once an actor, eighteen years ago, he had many parts in low comedy, and was often applauded by those who frequented the only theater of the city.
>
> He owned the *Lanterne Magique,* a weekly paper under his direction, which at one time was very much in vogue.
>
> Whilst editing the Feuillton of this paper, many abuses in our local police have been denounced and set forth in a light so ridiculous as to ensure their amendment, and yet the public were kept in good humor. In short the deceased was a man of wit and a lover of repartee, fond of a jest, and to nothing so much an enemy as to wordly thrift.

Daudet was the best qualified journalist of New Orleans at that time. His discernment, his blunt but always courteous denunciations, always fair, were written in terms of conciliation rather than reproach. In this work he is frequently quoted, but unfortunately some of the beauty of his language and expression are lost in the translation.

A "Feuillton" was the part of a newspaper devoted to literary articles. Duhy has the distinction of being the first commentator of New Orleans.

The *Louisiana Gazette* on August 1, 1823, chided Doctor Beardslee the Editor of the *Advertiser,* because he neither understood French nor loved Frenchmen, and further remarked:

> Doctor Beardslee is greatly irritated about the advice we gave the strangers here to leave town. He evidently fears that some of the voters on whom his masters depend, will not return to cast their votes at the next election. Certain factions desire so much to reign in Louisiana, that they fear any circumstances that may cause them to lose its supporters. Little matters the life of their equals just so, at any cost, the ancient population should lose its influence.

On September 1st, 1823, it was announced that Chas. Guillaume Duhy had sold the *Louisiana Gazette.* In his valedictory he gave the following reasons: "It is a ruinous competition that has reduced the price of advertisements to the point that the journals most in vogue will make just about enough to pay for the printing." The new editors were Richardson and Mead. The plant was located at Bienville and Chartres, and the price of subscription was ten dollars a year.

Shortly afterwards its headquarters were moved to 31 Custom House, corner Chartres, and Mr. Richardson who was from Ohio, became the sole editor. A. Chopotin was placed in charge of the French edition.

At that time Lowel K. Mead became the sole editor of the *Iris*, which provoked an acrimonious dispute between the editors of that paper and the *Gazette*.

Langley and Howard announced the publication of a new newspaper to be called *The Evening Star*, to be released on the first of May, 1824.

An amusing episode was the dispute between Bernard Marigny and C. De St. Romes, editor of the *Louisiana Courier*, which began on June 28th, 1824, under the title "Marigny accused of not being a purist":

> We have often said and we will say that Mr. Marigny does not know a word of French, and among thousand of proofs, which we could state, we shall merely cite the mistakes he committed in the signification of the word "Purist". A purist is a man who is nice in point of language, but whoever has read one phrase, a mere phrase of Mr. Bernard de Marigny, will confess that it would be ridiculous to say that he is a purist, for the word implies a perfect knowledge of one language, and although Mr. Marigny has had for his teacher, Mr. Thierry, Mr. Leclere and more recently Mr. Charbonnier, all of them men of parts, we shall certainly be the last to say that he is a purist, as we do certainly recollect certain pieces written by him, which we published in our paper, after having corrected the errors of all kind with which they were filled, and because we are convinced that notwithstanding his voyage in France, where he learned many fine things, he is still a very poor grammarian.
>
> Signed: C. De St. Romes

He was rebuked in the *Gazette* as follows:

> The pre-eminent Charles De St. Romes, compared with whom all other writers sink into insignificance, with a mind like his person, round as a ball, rolls in its rage, his press groans, his slaves fall prostrate, and his readers shudder as he advances to announce that B. Marigny is not a writer, and with his usual modesty declares that he has himself corrected his writings, and if you do not believe this you may ask Pluto! He had better refer his readers to Mr. Charles Maurian, who under the appellation of translator, washed his dirty linen for him for ten

years. He has asserted that Mr. Marigny has been bowing to obtain votes. In this art Mr. St. Romes is admitted to excel; for many years the members of the Legislature and of the City Council can bear testimony of his superior skill, they have all been accustomed to remark, when a printer was to be named.

When Mr. St. Romes applies to Mr. Marigny the title of Count, he forgets that he is himself so despotic that all around him feel the efforts of his tyranny—no apprentice can live with him to acquire his art, and if the Great Man should be called to heaven, the *Courier* would disappear, and if he should lose Mr. Maurian, he must close his office.

Signed: A. CITIZEN

As a parting shot he was further ridiculed in the *Gazette* on June 30, in the following pithy sentences:

1st: St. Romes engaged one day in a party to shoot with pistols. Went with his valet.
2nd: Was thrown from his mare.
3rd: Married men after him.

L'Amie des Lois, Journal Eclesiastique de la Nouvelle Orleans, made it appearance during that year.

The *Argus* was owned by Mr. Crozat, and Major Benjamin Buisson was the editor.

The *Louisiana Gazette*, which called itself the organ of the American people, was sold in May, 1825, to R. D. Richardson and A. T. Penniman, a printer from Boston. The publisher was James McKaraher. The announcement was made that the *Gazette* had purchased two presses of the latest and "most elegant construction", a sufficient quantity of types of a quality equal to any in the Union.

The competition between the six papers was so keen, especially during the summer months, when the city was deserted by so many of the transient population, that they were forced to bury their differences, and to enter into an agreement to publish their journals only three times a week, from the first of July to the first of November. That pact was signed by J. C. De St. Romes, M. Crozat, Richardson and Penniman, Beardslee and Penrice, Duhy and Stroud, and Benjamin Buisson and Company. The *Courier*, The *Louisiana Gazette* and the *Louisiana Advertiser* appeared on Mondays, Wednesdays and Fridays, and the *Argus*, the *Mercantile Advertiser* and the *Journal of Commerce*, on Tuesdays, Thursdays and Saturdays.

The newest arrival in the field of journalism was the *Journal de Commerce;* Prosper Foy was the editor.

On July 25, 1825, the *Louisiana Gazette* celebrated its twenty-second anniversary.

Although in the summer of 1825, the city was enjoying its seasonal tranquility, it was aroused from its lethargy by invectives in the papers against, one of its leading and well respected citizens, Bernard Marigny. This controversy was discussed both in the American and French quarters, and sold many papers, for many were the speculations as to the outcome of the contretemps.

On August 5, a questionnaire appeared in the *Louisiana Gazette,* directed at B. Marigny asking him about the 28th of December, 1814. He was asked:

> Has the testimony of Colonel DeClouet and Abner L. Duncan, Esq., been refuted? How the mock report of the Committee of the house served to convince the public, that you did not advise, as a member of the Senate, the surrender of the State to the British Army during the invasion?
>
> I must remind you, Sir, that these charges are still in the memory of the people. If this testimony is correct, was the motive dictating that course to you a desire of preventing your property from being sacrified in the cause of your country, rather than it should be possessed by the enemy? If so, we may give you more credit for your cold calculating prudence which should ever govern those who aspire the offices of trust from the people. Can you say the testimony alluded to is false, when you have General Jackson's letter to Governor Claiborne, dated February 6, 1815? An extract of which is as follows: "If a charge so injurious has been falsely made by any officer of my army, it is necessary that proper proceedings be immediately had against him, and the innocence of every member of the House, whom in the camp he has so vilely aspersed, be made apparent to the world; and on the other hand, if the charge be true as regard any member or members of the Assembly; it is equally necessary that proper proceedings be forthwith instituted against him or them, as well as that the innocent may escape suspicion, so that the guilty may receive punishment."
>
> Now sir, you know General Jackson's energy of character well, can you for a second establish Colonel DeClouet's guilt, he being an officer under General Jackson's command, that the General would have neglected to consign him to immediate punishment for that outrageous falsehood? Besides to show the General's opinion on the subject, we refer to the continuation of Reid's biography of General Jackson, by Mr. Eaton, his colleague

in the Senate of the United States from Tennessee, and written under the General's immediate inspection.

To show the indifference manifested by you, as regards the result of the glorious action, on the 8th of January, were you not walking to and fro, on the piazza of your house, only a short distance from the lines, after the action had commenced and the cannonade was distinctly heard? Did you not inquire of an officer riding express to the city by order of the Commander-in-Chief, what was the news at the lines? And what was the reply: "If you were there, sir, at the post of your duty, you should see what the news were".

In another letter Sir, I shall inquire whether the common report be true or not respecting your exertions to obtain a title of nobility from the French Government, also respecting your refusal to drink to the health of the illustrious Lafayette at the public entertainment.

A few days afterwards on August 10, the diatribe continued; the following is abstracted from a long communication on City Affairs:

As the City Council now exists, t'is a mockery of common sense. The majority of the members were elected from men of large possessions, by a system of closely bordering on feudal, and once seated therein, (facts will come out), their unremitted exertions are to self aggrandizement and opposition to every measure which tends to the amelioration of the conditions of the constituents of those in the minority, who are generally the representatives of the commercial interest. A prominent instance is exhibited in the election of Mr. Marigny, this man possesses no mental qualifications to entitle him to the suffrage of his constituents except the possession of wealth, and yet he is made a rallying point around which party candidates flock; and he generally carried his point. Mr. Marigny is aware that his sway must eventually end, and t'is his object before such an event occurs, to secure for his faubourg all the improvements he can, and would not be sorry to have his yard paved at the City's expense.

In subsequent editions the *Gazette* carried on its attacks against Mr. Marigny. It expressed the opinion that the "Legislature in 1815, would have capitulated to the British, had the measures taken by General Jackson (or Mr. Duncan) not been decisive." And among the more malicious: St. Rome accused Marigny of speaking his language incorrectly. "Governor Villeré cannot speak at all. When he once attempted to make a speech to both houses of the Legislature, he commenced by opening his mouth and ended with a yawn. We look yet, for a specimen of his writing." And the most dastardly of all: "Marigny identifies his slaves by branding them on the back with the letters B.M."

On September 12th, in the *Gazette* appeared another communication signed "Algernon Sydney" from which the following is quoted:

> Who but a faction would have unblushingly dared to propose B. Marigny for Governor? After the active part he took, in endeavoring to surrender the State to the enemy in 1815, and after he had bent his knee, at the footstool of French Royalty, measly begging for a title of nobility; after he had on a public occasion in France, where the beloved guest of the Nation, General Lafayette was present, refused to drink his health when publicly pledged by the company, because that illustrious friend of mankind was out of favor with the enthroned puppy, who, then wallowed under his crown. Who, but a faction would spend tremendous sums of money drawn from the pockets of the native Americans to adorn and embellish the private estate of this man.

In only two ways could that journalistic persecution end; one on the field of honor, the other in a court of justice. Two days afterwards we read in the same journal that Bernard Marigny had sued the Editors of the *Louisiana Gazette* for libel, and that Mr. A. T. Penniman was arrested The citation read as follows:

> Whereas complaint has been made on oath of E. A. Cannon before me, G. Preval, Associate Judge of the Civil Court of New Orleans.
>
> That Messrs. Richardson and Penniman, Editors of the *Louisiana Gazette*, have in the Gazette of the 12th inst., written and published a libel against Bernard Marigny. You are thereby commanded to take said Richardson and Penniman and bring them with a warrant before me, to answer to said complaint, and should they not be seen or found in three days from the date thereof, you will not fail to return immediately the warrant with what you have done, endorsed thereon.
>
> Witnessed my hand and seal, the 19th day of Sept., 1825
>
>   Signed: GALLIEN PREVAL
> Associate Judge of the City Court of New Orleans.

A few days afterwards an editorial entitled "Liberty of the Press" appeared in the *Gazette,* which said:

> The odds against us are dreadful, on the one hand, the public will have to behold, engaged in a suit, two printers fully occupied in earning their daily bread and with not time to give to other matters. On the other, a rich planter of more than consular dignity, with no other employment than that which the Coffee House, some houses of intrigue, and the gambling houses

may find for him, leagued with one of the greatest luminaries the bar ever produced, a personage notwithstanding his professional avocations, also of much leisure, besides a host of partisans behind the curtains, who are to supply by intrigue and council what Messrs' Marigny and Cannon, may fall short of by their operations in the open field. Cannon has, it is generally understood, been a constant guest at the Chateau Marigny, and has for years drunk his wine and cracked his nuts and his jokes at the expense of this august patron, and toad-eater like, has been anxious to show himself zealous in the cause of his truly great master.

Cannon is the most thorough-going swearer we have heard tell of for some years.

This seemed to have put a quietus on the dispute, for little more is to be found in the papers on the subject.

On October 19, in a communication in the *Gazette* from "perhaps the oldest American in New Orleans" is the following pertinent contribution to the history of journalism of the city, it said:

If I recollect aright, the first open attempt at hostility to the Americans by the Press, was made in 1822 in a paper that was established for the purpose of putting down the Americans, and promoting the views of the leading factions. This paper was effectively opposed by the lamented J.P.C. Sampson, Esq., the then editor of the *Louisiana Advertiser*, and the iniquity of their principles was completely laid open. It was from the same nursery of faction that the *Argus* owed its origin.

Scarcely a month had passed since the Marigny episode when R. D. Richardson, senior editor of the *Louisiana Gazette* found himself involved in a brawl with John Gibson of the *Argus*. The first inkling of that altercation was in the October 21st issue of the *Gazette*, which stated that an "infamous placard was circulated last evening denouncing the senior editor" and it requested the public to suspend their judgment respecting it, until he could set in type numerous documents establishing the private character of John Gibson as "infamous to the highest degree, and that of B. Grima and P. Guillot, as liars and cowards."

A meeting was held between Richardson and the two intermediaries of John Gibson, Major Grima and Mr. Guillot. P. K. Wogan and John Porter, who witnessed the scene, gave the following written testimony which was published in the *Gazette* of October 24th:

I was requested by Captain Richardson to come in and on entering I found Major Grima and Mr. Guillot, who appeared to be engaging in a rather anmiated conversation about a dispute between Capt. R. and Mr. John Gibson. In the course of said conversation Capt. R. remarked two or three times, that he would meet only gentlemen who espoused the cause of Mr. Gibson. Major Grima and Mr. Guillot were very pressing in their request to know why Capt. R. did not consider Mr. Gibson as a gentleman, to which request Capt. R. at length replied that he had heard some reports concerning Mr. Gibson's conduct at Covington, and until they were cleared up, he could not meet Mr. Gibson, as a gentleman; to which Major Grima and Mr. Guillot replied that they considered him (Mr. Gibson) as a gentleman, and would continue so to consider him, until he should prove him not to be such. Capt. R. again observed, that he would meet any gentleman who would espouse Mr. Gibson's cause.

Dated October 22, Signed: P.K. Wogan

That declaration was substantiated by John Foster, who further added:

"But in order that Mr. Guillot might perfectly understand the course necessary for him to take on the occation, you told Mr. Guillot that from everything you knew of him, you were induced to think favorably of him. I made up my mind at that time, from language and manner, that the expression was meant to signify that you were ready to accept his invitation to the field, in case he saw fit to espouse Gibson's cause.

I must also observe, that when you expressed your determination not to give Gibson any further satisfaction, Mr. Guillot took from his pocket a note, which I afterward understood was a challenge and stated that he would only allow you to read it, without retaining a copy of the original. You promptly refused to read it, or have anything to do with it, unless the note was left in your possession. Afterwards in a conversation between Messrs. Guillot and Grima, they concluded to leave it in your possession.

The provocation was an article which appeared in the *Gazette* on October 19, signed "Covington" which ended with the following phrases:

But perhaps they (the editors of *Argus*) are musing over some peculiar performances which took place at Covington in this State. The subject is a fruitful one, and properly suit their imagination better than writing newspaper paragraphs. Mr. Gibson to whom this referred, went immediately to see Mr. Richardson, accompanied by Mr. Grima. Mr. Gibson demanded the name of the writer of said article. Mr. Richardson said he would give the names only when the *Argus* would give the names of those who wrote against him in that paper.

Mr. Gibson stated he held himself responsible for "Theodoric", "Flagellator" was Dr. McFarlane who was also the author of "Dicky Sly Boots", "Puff Pennyless", and others. Mr. Richardson said "take me for the author of Covington".

Mr. Gibson then wrote the following note:

> R. R. Richardson, Esq.
> Sir:
> In the last paragraph of an article in your paper this morning, signed "Covington", I take the following phrase to be an insinuation intended to convey an opinion on the public mind, derogatory to my character as a gentlemen, and a man of honor, or not, and if so, will you state the impression you intend to convey.
> New Orleans, Oct. 19, 1825.   Your obedient servant,
> John Gibson.

Grima and Guillot were the bearers of the note, and Richardson promised a written answer the next morning. "These gentlemen withdraw after a moment conversation, in which Mr. Richardson endeavored to justify himself by very unsatisfactory reasons and in cajoling the gentlemen to whom he addressed himself."

The next day Richardson gave the following answer:

> John Gibson, Esq.
> Sir:
> In answer to your note of yesterday, I have to state, that owing to haste and when the communication, you allude to, went to press, a typographical error escaped detection. The quotation you have inserted in your note should read thus—"but perhaps they are musing over some peculiar performance which took place some years ago at Covington in the State. The subject is a fruitful one, and perhaps it suits their imgination better than writing newspaper paragraphs."
> As regards the effect to be produced at what you are pleased to term an "Insinuation", I have only to state that as the sentence now reads, as above, the only inference which can be admitted, is the plain grammatical construction of it.
> It may not be improper to observe here, that in the interview between us yesterday, you were pleased to say, that you would assume responsibility for those anonymous paragraphs that appeared in the *Argus* of the 15th inst., and your partner Mr. Guillot added to me yesterday afternoon, that they were written by Jos. H. Mead.
> I am Sir,
> R. D. Richardson

Gibson still insisted that Richardson give a positive assertion that there was no insinuation against his character as a gentleman and a man of honor. As Gibson did not receive an answer to his request, he addressed another note to Richardson:

R. D. Richardson, Esq.
Sir:

In so much as you refuse to give me the author of the article which appeared in your paper of this morning signed "Covington", and as you refuse to disavow any intention in that piece of insinuating anything against my character as a gentleman and a man of honor, I call upon you for such satisfaction as is due in such cases from one gentleman to another.

My friends Messrs, Grima and Guillot are fully authorized to act for me in this business, and to regulate with you or your friends the terms and manner by which satisfaction can be by you rendered.

New Orleans, Oct. 19, 1825   Your obedient servant
                                John Gibson

Richardson gave the following answer to the challenge:

John Gibson, Esq.
Sir;

In answer to your last note, I have only to state that as I have already referred stating that in the paragraph in the last *Gazette*, there was "no insinuation against your character as a gentleman and a man honor", the same views of that subject compels me equally to decline meeting you. In making this declaration, in justice it is due to myself to state, I will meet any gentleman, respected in society as such, who may espouse your cause.

It may not be amiss to observe also, the publicity which you have given to the determination which influenced you in your last note, in conversation and in repeated and unnecessary calls at my counting room and printing office, at a time when your friends were observed by hundreds of persons in the street, who surmised very correctely the object of their visit, would effectually prevent a meeting when there were no other obstacles in view.

Your obd't S
R. D. R.

Immediately aftrewards, Grima and Guillot met with Richardson, and the following is the published report of that interview:

There with all possible politeness they requested to be informed of the reasons which prevented him from considering him as a gentleman, this was asked of him several times and in the most pressing manner. Mr. Richardson answered that certain reports had circulated against Mr. Gibson during his residence in Covington, but that it was not convenient for him to repeat them; that he would not. Mr. Guillot then told him "You will not listen to our demand, you will not even give us any reason for refusing." Mr. Gibson will force you to it; we are his friends, we shall advise him as a man of honor, and we will consider him as such until we have some proof to the contrary, therefore, we here declare to you our intention to support him in any measure he may take, in any step he may make, to compel you to make the declaration which he has demanded, or to render him the satisfaction which he requires; we have the honor to wish you good day.

Gibson then placarded the city with hand bills, a custom of that time, usually employed when the aggrieved party was denied satisfaction on the field of honor.

John Gibson was a disturbing element in the community. He was pugnacious, insolent and arrogant. His villifications were contemptible, yet no gentleman would defile himself by crossing swords, or exchanging shots with him, or even soil his hands by attacking him, for according to the Code Duello, a gentleman could only meet his social equal on the field of honor. Gibson was not considered a gentleman. He was a leader of the agitators in the city. His opposition to the Gallo-Americans knew no bounds, he was not only one of the organizers, but the chief ringleader of the Native American Association. He was the frequent recipient of a caning. In his refusal to meet Gibson in a duel, Richardson acted according to the custom of the time. Despite all, Gibson was one of the most colorful journalists of New Orleans.

These lengthy qoutations reproduced verbatim from these newspaper files shed light on the customs of that time.

Shortly after that tempest in a teapot, following a disagreement between Penniman and himself, Richardson sold his share in the *Louisiana Gazette* to James McKaraher for $5000.00. This time Richardson refused to be drawn into any controversy.

On January 14, 1826, it was announced that James M. Bradford, who had been a resident of Louisiana since 1804, and who had been elected State printer, was the new editor.

On January 25, 1826 in his valedictory, Richardson wrote:

I have ever been the firm and fearless friend of American principles and American men; and if the stand I took, when on the 4th of July, a day above all others sacred to harmony, union, and a good feeling, a Major General, took upon himself the liberty to order a certain Major, then under arrest, and in the course of examination before a Court Martial, by which he was subsequently cashiered, to the command of the Legion, purposely to insult the pride and feelings of a Brigadier General proper, and of the American troops, generally, if the stand I took upon his occasion has caused feelings of ill will against me,

I cannot help it, and I know not how to mend it, at least in any other way than that I brought it upon myself.

That act of a French General, till when all had been comparatively harmonious and peaceful, opened a wound sore, very sore indeed, and which threatened the future tranquility of Louisiana, perhaps the peace of the general government.

In conclusion, I have more reason to regret having taken that stand, if I advert to the loss and sacrifices it occasioned me, than to any satisfactory result from it, but I do not regret it, and politically take my leave of the public.

The *Louisiana Gazette* announced its advertisement rate to be:

Each Square of 18 lines, three times.......$1.50
Each additional 5 lines................. .50
One square once....................... .75
Not exceeding 5 lines, each time.......... .25

The weekly *Louisiana Gazette* made its first appearance on July 25, 1826.

On December 5, 1825, Charles Lorrain, formerly one of the editors of the *American Advertiser*, died. It was said of him that the "American population will regret him whose political rights he was among the first to assert."

In October 1826, the *Orleans Evening Post,* a commercial paper made its appearance. James B. Ward was the editor.

On August 18, 1827, the editor and proprietor of the *Propogateur Louisianais* gave notice that "he would wish to make known that he has no connection, whatsoever with the projected French Journal, entitled l'Abeille." (*The Bee*)

The Franklin Typographical Society was organized in December, 1831. The journeymen printers demanded the following scale of wages: "All newspapers, book and job offices, $15.00 per week; by the piece, fifty cents per thousand; work done on morning papers after midnight, twenty-five cents an hour extra; all rule and figure work at $1.00 per thousand."

The *Bee* reported on March 18, 1824 that T. G. Joans, the senior editor and proprietor of the *Mercantile Advertiser*, had absconded after forging the names of Prieur, Duplessis, Culberton, and Holland as endorsements to note drawn by himself, and had succeeded in regotiating them. Joans was described as being a small man, with a remarkable physiognomy, and to be exceedingly plausible. He was an Englishman by birth, and a resident of the city for four or five years.

On September 1st, 1834, the *Bee* celebrated its seventh anniversary, it had then, thirteen hundred subscribers, which in the next year had increased to nearly two thousand.

In January, 1835, the *Journal Whiz*, alias *Argus*, was sold. P. N. Biron was the editor.

John F. Carter began the publication of the *New Orleans Union*, an independent Journal, on Monday, September 21, 1835. In May 1835, the *New Orleans Observer*, a religious paper made its appearance and in August, the *Daily News*, under the editorship of Robert J. Ker was soon afterwards established. The *Morning Post*, edited by Lawrence, a lawyer, began its publication on November 30, 1835.

The *Bee* laconically stated that "It is consolatory to find journals of New Orleans now respectably printed and in general ably edited, which could not certainly be said of them last year when Major Noah of the *New York Star* was obliged sarcastically to remark 'the New Orleans papers as well patronized, tolerably conducted and wretchedly printed'."

In 1829 there were nine newspapers in the State and in ten years their number had grown to eighteen weekly papers in the parishes, and to five daily, and five weekly or tri-weekly in the City.

On February 24, 1836, the *Bee* announced the discontinuation of the *Morning Post*. It said it was well edited and well printed, "but being chiefly a partisan paper, it could not live, even with the support of the Post Office and other ex-officio advertisements." The *Bee* observed:

> We are more surprised at the attempt to bolster up a journal of strictly party tendency in New Orleans than at the failure, considering that the general politics of the country are little understood in Louisiana, and seldom control the elections, and considering that the leading members of the Jackson party are disunited among themselves, and distrustful of each other, but more so considering that our citizens are merchants rather than politicians, much less partisans.
>
> Yet should we consider the number as well as the condition of the population, we might be more surprised at the number of daily journals published in New Orleans. There are probably 70,000 residing inhabitants during the greater part of the year, of which about 40,000 are colored persons, and 25,000 of the latter are slaves. Of the 30,000 who are white, we may suppose that not one in eight persons, are subscribers to newspapers, probably only one in ten. Many of these 3000, take

two or more journals, of which there are still four morning and two evening.

The *Bee* has about two-thirds of that number; the *Bulletin* has more than one half, but few of the other papers have the half of the half. The *Bulletin* is the most profitable journal in New Orleans, in consequence of its extensive advertising support, but the *Bee* has the greatest number of subscribers, and is daily increasing its list and advertising patronage. It has now nearly 2000 subscribers, and we are resolved to advocate any measure conducive to the general interest, to refrain from discussing irritating topics and to afford our readers all the commercial and other information possible and useful, we have humble, yet earnest, hopes of enhancing the value of our paper and will augment the number of the advertisers and subscribers.

Four months later the *Bee* announced that during the past twelve months it had almost doubled the number of its subscribers, and trebled the number of its advertisers.

In January, 1836 the competition for the State printing was keen. The competitors were Bayon of the *Bee,* Gibson of the *True American* and Rea of the *Bulletin.* On the second ballot, and by a majority of one, the State Legislature awarded the contract to the *Bee.*

It was argued by the *Bee* in an editorial in its issue of May 31, 1836, that advertisements were injurious to newspapers, and that the conditions were peculiar to America, due to the poverty of those who tried to establish a newspaper office. Such a situation did not exist in Europe. The editorial continued as follows:

In Atlantic cities compositors received about $8.00 a week, merchants and others contract for yearly advertisements of a square each day, continued or occasionally renewed or repeated, at the rate of $25.00. In New Orleans, merchants contract for $30.00, when compositors receive from $16.00 to $20.00 a week, and not only daily alter their advertisement, but daily augment them to four or five times the length originally agreed on and object to extra pay.

But they will not reflect that the advertisements which they send in a month cost more for compositors' labor alone, than what they pay for their contract in a year. The cost of setting up the advertisements in labor alone was $150.00 and the amount received was $30.00.

Newspapers languish and sink under the oppressive patronage of yearly advertisers, we write in sorrow rather than anger, trusting that this condition of affairs will soon be ameliorated.

On March 13, 1837 an agreement was entered into by the

proprietors of the New Orleans newspapers. The price to the subscribers were to be $12.00 per year for dailies, payable semi-annually in advance, and $10.00 for the tri-weekly editions (country) payable one year in advance.

The advertisement rates were to be $1.00 per square for the first insertion and one-half the price for each subsequent ones. For the yearly advertisements, merchants and traders — $40.00 for English only, $60.00 for both languages. Banks, Insurances, etc., — $50.00 in English and $80.00 for both languages. Marriages and obituary notices, $1.00 per square for the first insertion, for communications or advertisements of a personal nature the charges double and in advance. A deduction of 25% to Auctioneers, Sheriffs, Register of wills, Marshal and sale of real estate, in both languages, 50% in English alone, 10% on sales of other property. Theatres and other places of amusements — for the season, $100.00 for English alone and $150.00 for both languages. Announcements of candidates for political offices, charges double.

The agreement was signed by J. C. De St. Romes, J. Bayon, P. P. Rea, J. C. Pendegast, John Gibson and F. A. Lumsden.

In 1837 for some unstated reason the paper carriers were "unauthorized to sell papers in the street" for the newspapers were intended for subscribers only. Both the sellers and purchasers would be prosecuted for violating that decree.

On June 29, 1837, Robert J. Ker, resigned the editorship of the *Bee*.

On January 26, 1837, a new daily newspaper, *The Picayune*, made it appearance on the streets of New Orleans. It was a bold enterprise, because it was launched on a capital of four hundred dollars, and that money was borrowed. Its success was instantaneous, for in a very short while, it proprietors, two printers, George William Kendall and F. A. Lumsden acquired their own press, and moved to more pretentious quarters in Camp Street.

Although eventually *The Picayune* was merged 75 years later with the *Times-Democrat*, it has not lost its identity. It still lives as the *Times-Picayune* and is the oldest newspaper in New Orleans. Through the 120 years of its existence, it has had a steady and continuous growth. Today it is recognized as one of the leading and most influential papers of this country.

The second oldest publication, which ceased to function in

1918, was the *Bee (l'Abeille)*, then published exclusively in the French language.

The *Bee* of October 31, 1837, published the following:

The difficulty which took place between Messrs. J. Bayon and F. A. Lumsden has been amicably and honorably arranged to the satisfaction of both parties.

Signed: J. Bayon   F. A. Lumsden

Witnesses: A. D. Burt, John Hudout, P. Deverges, Rene Perdonville, New Orleans, Sept. 28, 1837.

Another journalistic dispute amicably settled.

The principal newspapers published in New Orleans in the early days were:

Le Moniteur de la Louisiana, began publication in 1794 and was published in the French language.

The *Louisiana Gazette*, its first issue appeared on July 27, 1804. It was the first English newspaper, its publisher was Eugene Mowry. For the first six years it was a semi-weekly, it made its first daily appearance on April 3, 1810, then for a while it was a tri-weekly. It was purchased in 1814 by David McKeehan who sold it to John Gibson in 1833. In 1835, its name was changed to *True American*.

In 1809, appeared the *La Lanterne Magique* and *The Friend of the Law* and the *Journal du Soir*. The latter in 1822 became the *Louisiana and Friend of the Law*. It was purchased in 1824 by Manuel Cruzat, who renamed it the *Argus*. In 1834, its name was changed to *Louisiana Whig*, and in 1835, it merged with the *Bee*.

The *Courier* was founded in 1809. The *Advertiser* was established in 1820. In 1825, it was published by James Beardslee, and in 1830 it was sold to John Peurice.

The *Bee* appeared Sept. 5, 1827 founded by Francois Delaup. It was published in French and English.

These printers, editors and publishers of the early nineteenth century have recorded the glamorous history of New Orleans during its fastest growing decades.

CHAPTER XIV

MILITIA

One of the first official acts of Claiborne after his appointment as Territorial Governor of Louisiana was the reorganization of the militia. His task was important and one which demanded a great deal of tact and discretion. Many of the officers were too young for their rank, having been chosen more for their social position than for their military experience. There were two companies of "free men of color" which presented him with a dilemma; if he re-commissioned the latter he would be severely criticized by the citizens of the State, and disbanding them, might incite resentment on their part and let loose on the community an armed mob capable of causing riots and perhaps the spilling of blood. The Governor sought the advice of the Department of State at Washington, and in the meanwhile, he let the matter rest. At the Battle of New Orleans these companies of "free men of color" distinguished themselves in the defense of their city.

The battalion of free men of color was then commanded by General Fortier, a rich white merchant, and Major Lacoste, also white, and a wealthy planter. Chambers tells us "that all the subordinate officers were colored. This battalion volunteered as a body at Claiborne's call and assured him that their numbers could be largely increased if necessary."

It was recognized by the military strategists of the early nineteenth century that the positions that the enemy would probably seize and occupy were the cities of New York and New Orleans, and that the latter "luckily possessed great natural strength." Evidently their surmise was correct, for the English attempted to capture New Orleans in order to establish a foothold from which they could invade the United States.

The invasion of the city was anticipated. Governor Claiborne foretold it in a message, and pleaded for a better and more active citizen soldiery, and in an impassioned exhortation appealed to the citizens to defend their homes at all costs, and to be prepared for all eventualities. Yet he was instructed by Washington to muster troops for service in the North. The militia composed principally of Creoles refused to respond for which Chambers tells us that their motives were impugned and their patriotism questioned. What actuated this opposition cannot be ascertained today, but it may be surmised that it was based on the probability of the impending invasion of their city and on their reluctance to deplete the scant manpower needed for the defense of their homes. Rumors of defeats and retreats, of apathy and the lack of will to resist on far-away battleflieds by Northern militia and citizen soldiery, infiltrated the city, and not only increased the anxiety of its inhabitants, but made them more determined to retain every man capable of bearing arms for the defense of their own section of the country. As events turned out, Washington was proved to be wrong and the militia of New Orleans was vindicated.

In the American Quarterly Review of September 1835, in an article on National Defense in which appeared documents accompanying the Message of the President (1834), the Reports of the Secretary of the State and the Secretary of the Navy complimented the militia of Louisiana, Kentucky and Tennessee "that manned the weak lines of New Orleans", and further stated that:

> There are, therefore, many of our present population who associate their ideas of the late war only with the glories of New Orleans, or the laurels of our navy, who know nothing of the disgraceful capitulation of Detroit, the expedition down the St. Lawrence, and the more fatal disaster when the flower of our youth of the Western States, fell beneath the knife of the savage ... Yet, as our militia is at present constituted it has been reasonably doubted whether the employment upon emergencies has been productive of more good or evil to the military character of our country. The same description of forces, which broke out at Bladensburgh upon the first fire, which refused to cross to Queenstown to complete a victory already gained, manned the weak lines at New Orleans from which a superior regular force of veterans retired completely beaten, and failed at Plattsburgh. Therefore, no reliance can be placed upon the effects a militia force as at present organized can produce.

According to that official report, the only bright page in the dismal chapter on the war of 1812, was the gallantry of the troops at Chalmette, composed to a large extent of Gallic militiamen, the privateers of Lafitte, the free men of color, and valiant frontiersmen of Tennessee and Kentucky, commanded by the great General Andrew Jackson. Even to this day this hallowed battlefield, after nearly a century and a half, is being desecrated by the rapid encroachment of industry.

Although it was a victory achieved after peace was declared, it must be considered decisive, for had the English captured New Orleans, the map the United States might be different today. But this is all within the realm of conjecture. Despite the gallantry and display of patriotism of the citizens of New Orleans at Chalmette, prejudicial rumors were circulated in the North that, in the event of war with France, the Creoles and the French inhabitants of that city would renounce their allegiance to the United States in favor of the former country. These charges of lack of patriotism on the part of Louisianians were repeated for years afterward. Such ugly accusations were strongly resented in an editorial in the *Bee* of October 22, 1835, which read as follows:

> We can assure them that France would not dare to make such an appeal and that there are none more devotedly attached to the Union than the Gallo-American citizens of Louisiana, for whatever predilections they may have for the social habits and for the people of France, such prejudicies cannot and shall never effect their loyalty to the United States.

During the eighteen twenties there was great activity in the militia, although the enthusiasm was marred by the political bickerings prevailing at that time.

An order was issued by F. Gaiennie, Commander of the 4th Regiment, on June 11, 1823, that "all the white male individuals liable to the militia service above 18 and under 45 years, residing within the limits of the 4th Regiment, and in this State six months since; which limits comprise the whole square from Canal Street to the extremity of Faubourg Wiltz, on each side of the river, will assemble on the 4th of July next, in Gravier Square, (Lafayette Square), at 10 a. m. to be reviewed, conformably to the law of 1820, under penalties prescribed by the assessing court."

An interesting meeting of the Louisiana Guards was held at Richardson's Cafe, on the 2nd of August, 1825, when the following resolution was passed:

> Whereas in our opinion it is contrary to the laws of the United States that a foreigner not naturalized should hold a military commission, and the decision of the United States Congress, in the case of General Bernard, confirms this opinion; as in the event of war, with the power of which such alien is a subject, his command must cease, and he be sent forty miles from tide water, and considered as a non-combatant, our prisoner, that it is hazarding the dearest interest of our country, and sacrificing the privileges and rights of American citizenship, is to appoint foreigners not naturalized to command: Therefore,

Be it resolved, that we whose names are herewith subscribed members as of the Louisiana Guards, solemnly pledge as a body and individually not to obey the orders of Major Cuvellier, or those of any other foreigner not naturalized, who may at any time be appointed to a command of the militia of Louisiana, or to any other state of which we may become citizens.

Signed: Edward Fenno, Captain; Robert Bell, 1st Lieutenant; Boswell Wooster, 2nd Lieutenant; David F. Cotter and M. McCoy, Orderly Sergeants; James Purdon, Thomas Johnston, Amos M. McCoy, Sergeants; C. Willard, 1st Corporal; George Palfrey, Henry Williams and S. D. Dixon, Corporals; Robert F. Confield, William M. Cowley, Thomas P. Hearsey, A. W. Breadlove, Frederick W. West, H. C. Cammack, Charles H. Taney, Curtis Clay, A. G. Worthington, A. H. Shade, William H. Hunter, Richard S. H. George, W. S. Brewer, Louis Tulane, C. Dame, Alfred Penn, H. S. Bennett, J. Boria, William A. Sheldon, John A. Paxton, William Swan, Lyman John Hall, William Covens, William T. Palmer, John T. Sanderson, John T. McCall, Stuart Hillhouse Lewis, Tomas Anderson, James Beardslee, James Coubrough, Lewin Philipe, Henry Beauchen, J. N. Folwell, L. Pitcher, S. H. Turner, G. V. Bright, Aaron Harper, William Taylor Lewis, H. Wilson, William Beardslee, William Rogers, S. Harris, William L. Tracy, Charles R. Rollinson, Robert G. Dixon, Washington Clark, F. Reynolds, Clem J. Clow.

Captain Edward Fenno died at sea on November 10, of that year. He was a merchant and a solider. William L. Robeson succeeded him.

On October 1st, 1823, a resolution proposed by Mr. Christy was passed by the City Council, to the effect that "any alarm of any kind, when necessary for military to assemble, firebells shall be rung three times, viz: three strokes in quick succession, pause of one-half minute, and then three more strokes, and pause, and so on for fifteen minutes."

The New Orleans Fensibles, about fifty in number, held its first parade in full uniform on December 29, 1823. The officers were Captain, John A. Fort; 1st Lieutenant, Samuel H. Harper; 2nd Lieutenant, George William Boyd; and David Griffith, orderly sergeant.

The rivalry, the jealousy, the political aspiration, and the intolerance which divided the population into two distinct factions, the French speaking element and the so called Anglo-American, pervaded the Legion as it did in all other social and civic activities. The standard for the recruiting in the several militia companies was the political affiliation of the recruit and the language he spoke, with resultant rivalry and bickering.

The Grima incident gives us an aperci of what transpired at that time. The following is quoted in part from an article which appeared in the *Louisiana Gazette* on September 9, 1825:

> This faction is composed of foreign Frenchmen, and refugees of St. Domingo, together with a few active recruits of the city. It is sowing seeds of discord and dissension in the city. It has three presses in the City, well organized for their purposes; some of them high in office and in our councils, and who were willing to surrender the State to the British under the parole and countersign of BEAUTY AND BOOTY.

The journal charged that they wished "to wrest the military command from General Robeson because he is an American." It further imputed that "patriots who prevailed on General Lacoste in the afternoon of the 3rd of July, when over their cups, and extorted a pledge from him that he would place Major Grima in General Robeson's command on the 4th [July] — which business was managed so artfully, that General Robeson knew nothing of it until he arrived on the parade ground, in company with General Lacoste."

Major Grima was accused of publishing a letter in the *Journal of Commerce* (which unfortunately is not available) in which he most emphatically denied having done so in a notice in the *Louisiana Gazette* of September 2, 1825, it reads:

> I postively declare that not only I am not the author of said piece, but that I never have written any article for any gazette, and assure you at the same time, that it is not through the medium of a newspaper, that I would seek satisfaction for insults.
>
> Signed: Grima

And in an editorial about Grima, it commented that:

> The hostility to everything American carried on with all the secrecy and policy imaginable until at length by organizing this faction to carry on mutinous plans into effect, they attempted to drive General Robeson from his military command. The American population could stand this no longer.

The court after finding the prisoner, Major Grima, guilty, recommended that he be restored to his command. And this was done by the Governor, when he should have disapproved of that part of the sentence of the court, and the Major should have been dismissed. No doubt the Governor's amiable and conciliatory disposition led him into error.

We still have no doubt that Mazureau will repent and become better, and that Marigny will co-operate with him for the good of the State. But in this he will find himself deceived.

Governor Johnson in his message of January, 1826, held a more liberal view and attempted to reconcile the differences existing in the ranks of the Militia, by making the following appeal:

> It is to be regretted that in the 1st Brigade, a corps distinguished for discipline, any collusion should have arisen. The Act is creating the Louisiana Legion, the primary object of whose protection was the defense of New Orleans, has received from some of the officers of that corps a different construction from that given to it by the General commanding the brigade. This diversity of construction has given birth to misunderstanding injurious to the service. The legion is composed principally of gentlemen who distinguished themselves during the late war, and who have equipped themselves at considerable expense.
>
> Their discipline — their fine martial appearance on all occasions — their frequent exercises, and consequent military proficiency, do them great credit.

In May, 1829, Colonel Francois Gaiennie was promoted to the rank of Brigadier General of the 1st Brigade of the Louisiana Militia. Lieutenant Colonel C. Cuvellier was promoted in rank to Colonel of the Louisiana Legion following the resignation of Colonel J. Roffignac; and L. Gally, Captain of the Artillery Battalion, was made Major.

Again dissension broke out in the ranks of the Militia, this time invectives were hurled against Colonel Cuvellier in the following notice "To the Public" which appeared in the *Courier* of July 23, 1831:

> However painful to men of honor, to put the public in the confidence of their own affairs, sometimes it becomes a duty to do so, and to shrink from that duty is cowardice.
>
> We the subscribers, therefore, think we owe it to ourselves, to society, and to the Louisiana Legion, a corps for which we profess the highest regards, to make known the villainy and infamy of one of its chiefs unworthy of the epaulete he wears, and of the sword which was confided to him, not to frighten women, but to be used in the defense of his country.
>
> We therefore, proclaim Colonel Cuvellier as a coward and a villain, holding ourselves ready to give an explanation to whosoever has a right to require it, and the officers of the Legion to whose rank he is not worthy to belong.
>
> Signed: Chalaron, E. D'Anfossy, J. Oblié, J. Puchen.

These insults were immediately answered by Colonel Cuvellier in the following public statement:

My conduct for the last fourteen years is a sufficient answer to the charges brought against me by men who have hardly known me since three months.

The four signers of the above publication assaulted me yesterday evening at 4 o'clock on the Levee. This morning at 9 o'clock one of them had received a message from me, and agreed to make me a reparation which is only accorded to men of honor. The public will be able to judge for what purpose the publication has been prepared, and on which side cowardice and perfidy are to be found.

Signed: Cuvellier

On July 27, the following communication from Cuvellier appeared in the same paper, it was addressed "To My Fellow Citizens":

I declare upon my honor that the relations which have existed for more than 12 years between Mrs. ——, her late husband and myself, never ceased to be of the most honorable description, and no one more deeply regrets, than I do, the unfortunate scenes which lately occured.

If the greatest sacrifices a man of honor can make could efface even the recollection of those melancholy incidents, that respectable lady would at all times find me ready to make them.

Signed: Cuvellier

The officers of the Legion that same night exonerated Cuvellier of all charges of cowardice and infamy, and published the following report:

The undersigned officers of the Louisiana Legion, having met in a committee to take under consideration a publication against Colonel Cuvellier, which appeared in the *Louisiana Courier* of Saturday last, declare as follows: The question must be divided into two distinct and separate points, to wit: (1st) Private quarrels. (2nd) An attack against the honor and reputation of Colonel Cuvellier, as a soldier and a citizen.

With regards to the first point, the subscribers declare that notwithstanding the wrongs which Colonel Cuvellier may have committed towards Mrs. —— the public reparation he tenders to her by the preceding article, and with which she has, in the presence of the Committee, who waited upon her in the name of the officers of the Legion, declared themselves fully satisfied, takes from us the right of pronouncing on an affair already settled.

As to the second point, the subscribers think that the epithet of coward and infamous can in no manner apply to Colonel Cuvellier, who, on the contrary has, in that respect, given incontestable proofs that he never ceased to merit the confidence of his comrade in arms.

Signed:

Chas. E. Daunoy, Lt. Col. of the Legion
Vignie, Lt. Col. of the Cavalry.
Gally, Major of Artillery
S. Saint Cyr, Major of Infantry
J. Saint Cyr, Captain of the Grenadiers
J. Dufour, Captain of the Voltigeurs
M. S. Cucullu, Captain of the Cassadores
S. S. Relf, Captain of Artillery
S. Alfred Ducors, Captain of Sapeurs
Hortaire Andry, Captain of the Lancers
Dr. Thomas, Physician
F. Correjolles, Lieut. of Chassers
Felix Labatut, Lieut. de Chasseurs a Cheval
J. S. Daunoy, Lieut. of the Casadores
F. Gener, Lieut. of the Casadores
Joaquin Viosca, Lieut. of the Casadores
Bigot, Lieut. of the Voltigeurs
L. Liautaud, Lieut. of the Voltigeurs
L. Lasalle, Lieut. des Tirallieurs
F. Nogais, Lieut. des Tirallieurs
D. Augustin, Lieut. of Artillery
S. M. Cohen, Lieut. of Artillery
N. Mioton, Lieut. of Grenadiers
A. P. Lanaux, Lieut. of Grenadiers
Fleury Generelly, Lieut. of the Dragons d'Orleans
J. Thompson, Lieut. des Lanciers
J. Guadiz, Aide Chirugien
J. Durdle, Adjutant d'Artillerie
F. Buisson, Lieut., Quartier Maitre d'Artilleries
Chas. Revaile, Adj.-Maj., lre Battalion d'Infanterie
Edward Caressol, Ensign de la Legion
J. F. Casteret, Cornette de St. Bernard
Aldophe Desforges, Porte drapeau d'Artillerie
F. Galien, Corneter

Rumors were evidently spread that Cuvellier was to leave the City, for in the *Courier* of August 15, appeared the following notice:

> Having been informed that misinformed persons are spreading the report that I am about departing to France, and therefore I intend to close my establishment and to resign the command of the Legion, — I have the honor to inform those whom it may interest, that the assertion is entirely unfounded, and that on the contrary, I am determined to settle forever in this country.
>
> C. Cuvellier

In 1833, J. B. Plauché was elected Brigadier General of the Legion of Louisiana.

On August 12, 1835, a court-martial was held in the City Council Chamber for the trial of Captains J. Viosca, J. Penas and Lieutenant Garnier, for having refused to take orders from Colonel Smith on the 4th of July. The disagreement was amicably settled. The court-martial gave the following recommendations: "The superiors were not to impose any unnecessary orders on their subordinates inimical to their personal feelings or prejudices, and that those in the ranks to be aware of the subordination essential in militia and military discipline."

In the French section of the *Bee* of August 14, appeared the following article entitled:

Legion of Louisiana

The charges made against Viosca, Penas and Garnier have been withdrawn by Colonel Smith after obtaining from these three officers satisfactory explanations concerning their conduct at the parade of the 4th of July.

On July 7, 1835, the *Bee* resented the vilifications against the Legion which appeared in the *True American* published by John Gibson, the inveterate vilifier of the Creoles and French and a Native American agitator:

We are not surprised at this, as it is but in unison with the assaults recently made by its conductors on the Creole population of the city ... That paper asserts that the Legion insulted the American party — that is the agitators of the upper faubourg.

Place the matter in its true position, and every gentleman, every man having the slightest honor in his composition, must admit that the Louisiana Legion and the Orleans Guard, acted as become the diginity and responsibility of their station. They were ever accustomed to celebrate the 4th of July and all anniversaries and public festivals of the city at the Cathedral and square, where time has now almost rendered sacred and inviolate their military habitudes and honors their prejudices and predilections. There their duties and remembrances of their affections are centered. — a violation of those must therefore be considered as the recklessness of ignorance, or the wantoness of insult; and when this violation has been preceded by other circumstances of an unequivocal tendency to aggravate or abuse, its object could scarcely be mistaken.

The gentlemen of the Legion and Guard have ever been desirous of defending liberty; and participating in every fete, festival or celebration in which their services were required, or could give effect or importance. Even on Saturday (the 4th) they verified their readiness so far as propriety permitted, in consequence of the limited courtesy extended to them. — They might have expected conciliation at least from those who had so long and repeatedly denounced them as the French party — ready to take arms against their country, if invaded by France, and they might have reasonably expected that prominence in commemorative arrangements to which their conduct and character entitled them. Silently though indignantly they heard the rude murmurs brooded against them; but when their sectional feelings aroused the semblance of prescription, should they tacitly acquiesce in their own disgrace and depreciation? And certainly that part of the arrangements excluding the Cathedral and central square, may be termed prescription.

Whose was then the insult? Those who aggressively prescribed the religious and military quarters of the Legion and Guard, or those who repelled the aggression by the only honorable means in their power.

But let the matter now subside. It was wrong for those who ridiculously term themselves the American party par excellence to exhibit sectional feelings and a want of conciliation and courtesy in a national celebration, to invite the Legion and Guard to participate in their own humiliation.

The *Louisiana Advertiser* published yesterday that the commanders of some companies actually forbid their men to join the celebration. We have made inquiries on this subject; and find the allegation groundless . . . Not content with aspersing the Catholic clergy; because they did not officially in their pontificals form part of the procession. We were not aware that any persons as clergymen of any denomination did; and we believe it is well known of Catholic clergymen to form part of no pageant, except funeral processions. But the insinuation is designed to lead to the conclusion that the Catholic clergy are opposed to our independence or liberty . . . There are none of our citizens more useful, respectable and liberal minded than our clergy of all denominations, and there are few more honorable and spirited than the gentlemen of the Louisiana Legion and Orleans Guard. Let therefore the vilifiers beware in time.

But according to the circumstances which provoked this affair it appears to us deserving of the general attention it provoked. Neither should it be tried to put an unfavorable light on the motives which actuated these officers to break rank before commanded by their superior officers, if they have done so they probably thought they could do it, and their motives must have appeared satisfactory since Colonel Smith cordially consented to drop any procedures concerning same.

But there is one incontrovertible fact, and that is, that there is a great lack of discipline in the Legion, which, it may be said, has existed since its organization. So in order to mend the prejudicies which this indiscipline can occasion, to maintain in the various companies which comprise that corps, that union and that spirit of fraternity which are so vital, the various chiefs who have successively commanded it, had to relax constantly their authority. Has this condescension, or rather this weakness, on the part of the commanding officers of the Legion, been productive of good results? No! For it has encouraged insurbordination in the ranks, to such a point, that besides the uniforms and the insignias which differentiate the soldier from his non-commissioned officer, the non-commissioned officer from the officers, and the officers from the captains, and every one of them can ask himself with surprise, who is the one who commands and from which one he should take his orders. In order to prevent the complete ruin of the legion it was necessary for the superior officers to possess that spirit of conciliation, which they have always manifested. It is time for this abuse to cease.

The militia is the palladium of our city; on her alone depends the public safety in a moment of danger.

In September, 1835, the Urban Guards was in the process of formation. The following recruits signed the roll: F. DeArmas, T. Lambert, P. Duberteaud, Tratour, J. J. Sigg, Girard, Dubois, L. Halbran, R. Toledano, Ferand, Chasette, G. A. Montmain, James Rooch, De St. Romes, P. A. Aubert, E. Bertus, A. Harrison, C. Herty, P. DeBuys, A. Noret, A. Droz, Surgi, A. Aicard, Fourché Cougat, Martin, A. Barenheidt, Dujay, Barthet, D. DeLaronde, A. Molier, E. Lafargue, J. Bayon, H. Jacquelin, Octave DeArmas, H. Legendre, E. Caillard.

That same month, the Germans and Swiss organized themselves into a company of Militia. The committee of organization was composed of Frederick, President; Suffert, Secretary; H. G. Schmidt, J. J. Sigg, J. Herzog, E. Weirauch, A. Wetzel, L. Dondelmoser.

And on October 6 it was announced that the Washington Guards were recruited with the following officers: C. F. Hosey, Captain; R. C. Palfrey, 1st Lieutenant; Geordy, 2nd Lieutenant.

At that time there were approximately two thousand citizen soldiers in the City.

In 1833, Theodore Pavie claimed that the militia of New Orleans was the finest in America, and Lowenstern, who visited the city in 1837, stated that it was organized according to the French pattern, and that it was much better than those of other sections of the Union; their uniforms were elegant, especially those of the Hulans — blue with red pantaloons — and that they were truly very attractive. He estimated that at least three thousand men were enrolled and uniformed.

CHAPTER XV

A UNIVERSITY IS BORN

It was not until the year 1834 that the Medical College of Louisiana was organized. It was the first medical school in the Southwest. During the summer of that year a few English-speaking doctors, realizing the need for a school of medicine in this section of the Union, decided to establish one. The *Bee* of September 29, 1834 made the following announcement:

We are highly gratified to notice the establishment in this city of a medical college. The gentlemen who fill the chairs of professorship are men of skill and experience and we hope that we may not be thought invidious when we point to Messrs. Hunt, Ingalls and Luzenberg, with whom our acquaintance is extended: The former two have been officiating in a like capacity in similar institutions and the latter has established a reputation of the highest degree as a surgeon.

In the same issue of the journal the prospectus of the Medical College of Louisiana was published in the French and English languages. It is quoted in part:

The undersigned practitioners in New Orleans, convinced of the want of scientific medical knowledge in the State and in several adjoining States, and of the non-existence of schools necessary for the diffusion of that knowledge, and aware too that an acquaintance with the peculiar diseases which prevail in this part of the Union cannot be made in Cincinnati and Philadelphia, but must be obtained by the students at the bedside of the patient; and anxious to advance the cause of science; and to disseminate rational principles so as to remove or alleviate human sufferings; and to put an end to the murderous practice of empirical arts of selfish speculators on the ignorance of vulgar credulity; and thereby to increase the happiness and prosperity of the country, have associated themselves as a Faculty for the purpose of delivering Medical Lectures in the city under the name of the Medical College of Louisiana.

The establishment of this school in the City of New Orleans, it is sufficiently obvious, must prove of the greatest benefit to the States of the Southwest generally. It will tend to excite professional emulation, to diffuse knowledge, to expose ignorance and to eradicate or arrest under scientific treatment, the disease of which thousands are now victims.

Nor will its effects end here. By removing the danger to death and the apprehension of disease, it will cause population to increase, agriculture to yield additional profits, trade and commerce to flourish and the arts and sciences to advance rapidly among us. In short, its operations will be to improve our national extraordinary advantages, to remove the obstacles in the path of our prosperity and under proper exertions, put New Orleans in a short time in medical knowledge with New York and Philadelphia.

The following reasons were given for locating the school in New Orleans:

1st. Because it is the largest and most populous town in the Southwest.

2nd. Because its hospitals, which will be opened for the purpose of instruction, are the largest in the Southern and Western States, so that practical medicine and surgery can be taught at the bedside of the patient.

3rd. Because it is a commercial town and more surgical accidents occur to seamen than to any other class of individuals.

4th. Because the study of anatomy can be prosecuted with more advantages and at a cheaper rate here than in any other city of the United States.

5th. Because in consequence of its great population, its hospitals are filled with patients, and

6th. Because students can get board at $25.00 per month.

The College inaugurated its first term of four months on the first Monday of January, 1835, with the following physicians on the faculty: Thomas Hunt, M. D., Dean and Professor of Anatomy and Physiology; John Harrison, M. D., Adjunct; Chas. A. Luzenberg, M. D., Professor of the Principles and Practice of Surgery; J. Monroe Mackie, M. D., Secretary, Professor of the Theory and Practice of Medicine; Thomas R. Ingalls, M. D., Professor of Chemistry and Pharmacy; Edwin B. Smith, M. D., Professor of Obstetrics and Diseases of Women and Children.

Demonstrations in practical anatomy were given daily by Adjunct Professor John Harrison and chemical lectures were held twice a week at the Charity Hospital.

This unexpected announcement was the cause of quite a furor in the city. It was the principal topic of conversation, provoking acrimonious discussions, not only among members of the medical profession, but among the educated public as well. The necessity for the *modus procedendi* for the formation of the new school, as well as the personality and the qualifications of the members of the faculty were the subjects of controversy in the home, in the streets, in the exchanges, in the coffee houses and in the newspapers. The announcement of the names of the faculty, composed principally of English-speaking physicians, a few of whom had only recently arrived in the city, incited expressions of critical opinion. Strenuous objections were voiced against the establishment of the College without first procuring the sanction of the Legislature or the authorization of Congress. It was also evident that the idea of "self appointed professors" was distasteful to many members of the local profession. The very youth of many of the organizers of the College created open hostility, for Hunt, Harrison, Luzenberg and Mackie were then only twenty-six years old. The following communications in the press are of the greatest historical importance because they voiced the strong opposition by many of the physicians of the city to the establishment of our first medical college. In the French section of the *Bee* of October 3, 1834 is this letter:

> Yesterday whilst I was reading your gazette, I was delighted, because I thought that Congress had legally created a college which would be so useful to the city and also that Louisiana, so happily situated for the study of the diverse branches of the art of healing, would acquire a regular school from which would emanate distinguished physicians, capable of imparting to our profession its well deserved lustre and to those who practice their profession, the amount of consideration of which they are deprived of a large portion by the numerous charlatans, who have shamefully arrogated to themselves, to the great shame of our tribunals, the right to practice medicine, either by the usurpation of titles that they at no time possessed, or by making a vile trade of the noblest of professions.
>
> I was greatly surprised to notice that the college was organized without legal authorization: In England, in Germany, in France and in fact in every civilized country, a school of medicine cannot be established without legal authority. The professors are appointed only by the Government or by an university. The aspirants for a chair must be at least a doctor of medicine in one of the principal faculties of the country . . . It is therefore that only the most learned professors be chosen.
>
> God is my witness, that it is not my intention to even insinuate that the honorable gentlemen who have signed the prospectus are not in the above category, but this is not alone sufficient because no matter what may be the extent of their education, they do not have the right to appoint themselves to these all important professorships. These chairs should be alloted

only after a competitive examination conducted before one of the leading faculties of the Union, or to physicians who have already graduated from one of these faculties, or from one of the principal universities of Europe. The professors should be at least thirty years old. These professorships should demand as much experience as knowledge. Do the signatories of the prospectus combine all the essential requisites, or even a majority of them? Without a shadow of a doubt, No! How then can they possibly teach in a Medical School?

I do not know to what extent liberty may be stretched in the United States. But I do not think that a medical school may be legally organized in the manner proposed by our honorable confreres, the future alone can determine this question.

I do not know whether any invitations were extended by the organizers of the new college to Creole or European-born physicians who practice their profession here, to join them in their enterprise. If they have not done so, they should have, and I am certain that the one to whom an invitation should have been extended, would have proved to the signers of the prospectus that a medical school should not be instituted *ad libertum*.

(signed) An American Physician

This opinion was evidently not shared by the Editor of the French section of the *Bee* for in the following issue he commented that "those who had the idea of founding here a medical college have undisputed rights to the gratitude of their fellow citizens in general, and also especially to the esteem of men fully capable of appreciating a similar benefaction". He further asserted that the public always hesitated before calling in a physician. And very frequently the disease has progressed considerably before it was decided to call in "a man of the art".

"What is the cause of the negligence? Is is because physicians in general do not inspire the necessary confidence?" he queried, and "Why do they not inspire that confidence?" "Is it because the public has so often been duped by charlatans who do not even have the necessary talents to be bootblacks? The ethical doctors have necessarily suffered from the maneuvers of these scourges of the human species." He welcomed the advent of the college because it promised a strong guarantee for the safeguarding of health, and because of the assurance that its students would possess the indispensable knowledge needed for the practice of their art.

The cudgel was taken up in the defense of the new college by a correspondent who signed himself "Humanitas". He asserted that the state legislature would be appealed to at its next session for the grant of a charter and for sufficient funds to accomplish the desired purpose, and he felt certain that many persons in the state would lend their aid. He further stated that the offer of a professorship was made to one of the most distinguished French physicians of New Orleans, which he declined after mature deliberation because he did not feel that he was sufficiently conversant with the English language.

"An American Physician" retorted, this time in English, in the *Bee,* of October 10. His letter in part reads thus:

> I am of the opinion that a faculty of medicine, instead of a local, is of a general interest, and that it never was contemplated by the writers of the prospectus that their students, on leaving the institution should be allowed to practice only within the limits of Louisiana, which however, must be the necessary consequence of a law passed by the Legislature, and if this ever happens that body might be expected to take the utmost care that the professors should give proof of their capacity before being allowed the right, if I am allowed to use the expression, to dispose of the lives of their fellow citizens.
>
> The author of the article pretends that I blame the faculty for not having invited some French physicians to aid in the formation of the institution. By Europeans, I mean English, German, Spanish, Italian physicians, a great number of whom can write and speak correctly the English language. I did say the Creole or European physicians, and add that had the founders of the college proposed it to them, they might have opposed it on the ground that such an institution cannot be self erected at the will of the proposers; which so far as I can see, has no other meaning than that the Creole or European physicians could not with any excuse have cooperated in the execution of the project ... I think the professors of such a college should not be self-appointed to such high functions, which to be successfully performed, must stand the test of public scrutiny, or otherwise have afforded proof of great medical and chirurgical requirements sufficient to entitle them to the honor of professorship.
>
> The Legislature should not grant them a charter, or give them money unless satisfied as to their attainment ... If as it is pretended, a distinguished French physician has refused to associate himself with the future faculty, this refusal corroborates what I have advanced on the subject. It confirms what I have said that no physician of whatever origin he may be, comprehending that he owes to his profession, will ever consent to support an institution which may be regarded as illegal,

notwithstanding the respectability of those who have given it unauthorizedly a local habitation and a name.

Although the new college was still a subject of controversial discussions, the plan of attack was changed. The editorials and communications in the daily press were now more constructive in tone, and a strong effort was made to have the lectures delivered in the French and English languages. At last the college was born after a long travail, and its establishment was accepted as a *fait accompli*. The curriculum proposed by the youthful founders of the medical college of Louisiana, was discussed, criticized, scrutinized, investigated and dissected, whenever and wherever doctors met. Prophesies were made as to the possibility of its success. The younger members of the profession, carried away by their undaunted enthusiasm, glorified its founders and predicted for the college a brilliant future. The more matured and gray-headed practitioners shook their heads and, although they acknowledged the necessity for such an institution, voiced the opinion that there would not be a sufficient number of students with an adequate education to qualify for the study of medicine. They ambitioned a college which would cast honor on the State of Louisiana, one which would graduate physicians the equal in learning, distinction and culture to those of the greatest medical centers in the old country. They prayed for a high standard of medical education and offered suggestions which, from their experience would prove most advantageous to the students of medicine.

An anonymous letter, appearing in the *Bee*, October 18, 1834, and written in French by a proponent of a higher standard of medical education asks: "Should the lectures be delivered in the French or English languages, or should they be given in both?" He thought the latter plan was feasible, but he doubted that the proposed professors could speak French and that even if they were able to do so, that they could conduct their courses of lectures in that idiom. Continuing:

> The American Physicians who have appointed themselves to the School of Medicine of Louisiana appear to be actuated of philanthropic sentiments, and the French doctors who practice their art here, doubtless, have the same sentiments. If such be the case, they should teach without an honorarium. Then the professors would not be a burden on the Government. The number of classes would be doubled and there would then be

two professors for each branch, one of whom would teach in French and the other in English.

But I do not think that a French physician would accept a chair if he had to teach according to the scheme proposed in the prospectus. Although the teaching staff would necessarily be divided, the school could be directed by one dean and housed in the same domicile. Separate days could be designated for the courses given in the French and the English language.

The writer then discussed the status of primary education and the necessity of a proper foundation for the study of medicine. The colleges established in New Orleans up to that time, he said, did not teach philosophy and but few of the humanities. He dwelt upon the necessity of founding a college in which the classics and philosophy would be included in the curriculum. He also proposed that this college be under the direction of the University. He submitted a plan of medical education which was far in advance of the requirements of the colleges of the time in the country. He suggested a course of four years, the first of which would be pre-medical. The course was to be opened only to students who had studied the classics and who were prepared for the study of philosophy. The third year Latin was to be reviewed, and philosophy was to be taught in the French language. The medical course for that term was to be limited to anatomy, physiology, chemistry, hygiene and medical physics. At the end of the first term, the students should pass an examination and "those whose merits and application deserved the confidence of their professors would be entrusted with the teaching of the new students". By following this plan, the number of professors for the second term would be augmented. During the second year internal pathology, botany and even pharmacy could be taught. During the third year special attention would be given the operative medicine, external and internal clinics, external and internal pathology. The fourth or graduating year should comprise internal clinics, medical jurisprudence, clinics and obstetrics. There should be a summer and winter term. He ended his communication with this statement: "Here is a course of medicine, I hope some day will be given to Creole students in the Medical College of Louisiana." It is needless to say that such an idealistic plan of medical education fell on deaf ears. It was far ahead of the time.

The editor of the French section of the *Bee* on October 21, 1834, deplored the fact that there was not in the city and its vicinity a college capable of giving a course of instruction befitting a student of medicine. He claimed "that was the greatest obstacle to the promotion of the new medical shcool; because before commencing the study of medicine, a student should employ a portion of his youth in preparatory courses, so that he will be thereby better able to understand that intricate science". He stressed the importance of having in this city an institution where students may be properly prepared for the study of medicine. He deplored the fact that such a school did not exist in the immediate South and that of necessity, the new school of medicine must draw its students from the northern state and from Europe. He appealed to the legislature of the State to assist in the promotion of the two colleges. He suggested that the College of St. James (Jefferson College) and the institution of Mr. Bellanger in New Orleans could, if they could procure special professors, offer a premedical course. He ended his editorial with the following admonition:

> The Medical College can give its course, it is their undisputable right. But what guarantee have we that the professors have the necessary qualifications if they are not legally instituted? And besides, how do we know that the young men who take their course are able to understand them? It is then absolutely necessary that the legislature must recognize officially the teachers, and that all students seeking admission to the medical school must pass a public examination. Such a serious undertaking demands the taking of all necessary precautions.

Speaking of the difficulties encountered by these pioneers of medical education in the Southwest, the *Bee* (April 29, 1835) editorially said: "The experiment was rather hazardous, as the establishment of a medical college was viewed with jealousy, if not suspicion. But the zeal and prudence of the gentlemen who united to form the faculty, nobly braved and conquered all difficulties."

The Medical College of Louisiana inaugurated its course of lectures on the first Monday of January, 1835. The minutes of the college state that Dr. Edwin R. Smith tendered his resignation of the Chair of Materia Medica on October 2, 1834, because of "the consideration arising from the loss of a very near and dear relative put it out of his power to retain the professorship with which he had been honored". Dr. Edward H. Barton was unanimously elected to succeed him. Dr. Smith, although one of the organizers never fulfilled the duties of his professorship. Dr. Barton was editorially commended by the *Bee* as "a gentleman of extended information, great experience as a physician, having resided more than fifteen years in Louisiana and in every way fully qualified for the trust."

The college did not own its domicile, some of the lectures were delivered at the homes of the professors, and others in the hall at No. 41 Royal Street and twice a week a lectures were held at the Charity Hospital. The course required two years, the sessions four months.

The first session was attended by eleven students, the greater number of whom were citizens of the neighboring states. The first course of lectures terminated on April 27, 1835. The professors were highly commended and it was stated that the lectures were well attended by the students as well as by "respectable persons of both sexes", the lectures being open to the public also.

The College was granted a charter by the Louisiana State Legislature on April 2, 1835. It was entitled: An Act to Incorporate the Faculty of the Medical College of Louisiana and the Medical School of New Orleans." The preamble of this Act reads:

> Whereas, the encouragement of learning is one of the first duties of an enlightened Legislature, and
>
> Whereas, Thomas Hunt, M.D.; John Harrison, M.D.; Chas. A. Luzenberg, M.D.; J. Monroe Mackie, M.D.; Thomas R. Ingalls, M.D.; Ed H. Barton, M.D.; Aug. H. Cenas, M.D. have associated themselves together and taken measures for the establishment of a Medical College in the City of New Orleans, and
>
> Whereas, the establishment of such a college would greatly advance the cause of science and produce most beneficial results to the people of the State, tending at once in the general preservation of health, the increase in population, the extension of trade and commere, the productiveness of culture and the rapid growth and promotion of the arts and sciences.

It was provided in Section one of that Act that they were thereby constituted a body corporate and politic under the name of "Faculty of the Medical College of Louisiana."

Section four provided that:

> The Faculty of the Medical College shall be and they are hereby authorized to make such regulations as they might think proper for the election of the professors, to remove or dismiss any professor from his professorship in the institution, and to fill, under any regulation that they may deem expedient any vacancy in the Faculty provided always that it shall require the concurrence of a majority of four-fifths of the members of said

Faculty, to elect any professor or to remove or dismiss any professor from his professorship in said Medical College.

It was also enacted in Section six that the Governor of the State, with the Judges of the Supreme Court, George Eustis, G. Mulligan, W. H. Sparks and John B. Dawson, be constituted the Board of Trustees of said College.

That same Act provided for the incorporation of the Medical College of New Orleans, whose Faculty shall comprise Drs. Labatut, Lemonier, Formento, Lambert, Fortin, Tricou, Conaut and others. Its Board of Trustees to be composed of the Governor, the Mayor, the Recorder and the members of the City Council of the City of New Orleans.

Although the Medical College of New Orleans was granted a charter, it never began to function. Apparently its promoters realized the futility of such an institution in a city which was rapidly increasing its English-speaking population, although the faculty of the contemplated medical school was composed of some of the most noted physicians in the South.

The Medical College of Louisiana during its first year, was rent with dissensions. The *Bee* on May 16, 1835, announced that Dr. Hunt, the founder and chief promoter and the Dean of the school and whose ability as a professor was highly respected, resigned not only from the chair of Anatomy, but also as the head of the institution. It gave no reason for Dr. Hunt's resignation, but only said: "We are pleased to ascertain that the resignation proceeded from the most honorable and disinterested motives." The *Bee* further elaborated:

> He [Dr. Hunt] had to encounter many difficulties from being placed in the vanguard of an institution, resembling one that failed, and nobly he surmounted those difficulties, till he obtained a charter for the college and the patronage of the public. Of his superior attainments and capabilities for a professorship in any faculty, there can be no doubt; this, his lectures alone delivered during the past session sufficiently attest.
>
> We can but surmise that only a very serious provocation would have induced Dr. Hunt to resign from an institution he labored for so assiduously during the most trying period of its existence.

The only intimation of the dissension is to be had from a few cryptic remarks in the press. The *Bee* of June 11, 1835, editorially commented:

We are indeed sorry that the Faculty has forfeited the aid of the acknowledged ability of Dr. Hunt. It was almost well that the organization of that College commenced *de novo* and that elections were consequently held for every deanship so constituted.

The chair made vacant by the resignation of Dr. Hunt was not immediately filled, for it was announced in the *Bee* of June 12, that "a successor to Dr. Thomas Hunt (as Professor of Anatomy) has not yet been selected; but the inquiry is made in every quarter for an efficient candidate".

On June 11, 1835, it was announced that Dr. Ingalls had vacated his professorship of Chemistry to which Dr. Powell was elected. On the following day Dr. Cenas tendered his resignation of the chair of Obstetrics and Diseases of Women and Children. He was replaced by Dr. Ingalls. Speaking of his resignation a contemporary newspaper laconically remarked: "Apropos, would not an old woman answer very well as professor of midwifery?"

The name of Dr. W. Byrd Powell, the newly appointed professor of Chemistry, was frequently mentioned in the news as well as in the advertisement columns. He was an itinerant lecturer on phrenology. His lectures in New Orleans were very popular; in fact the reputation he achieved therefrom elevated him to the chair of chemistry. Many testimonials he received attest the high regard in which he was held by the most prominent members of the clergy, the bar and of the medical profession. Amongst many of them were Henry A. Bullard, Benjamin Story, E. H. Barton and the Reverend Clapp. Dr. Powell taught in the medical school for only one year. The reason for the short tenure of his professorship is unknown today. He was the only one of the medical professors of New Orleans about whom there is any question of his ethical conduct. When he left the city, where he went, what he did or what became of him, is not known. Even the newspapers which had been so profuse in praising him and which had published so many of his advertisements were ominously silent on his departure.

The second session of the Medical College of Louisiana opened on December 7, 1835, with a lecture from Professor Luzenberg, the newly appointed dean. There were sixteen matriculants. It was customary in those days for the professors to extend through the medium of the press, invitations to the ladies and gentlemen of the city to attend the opening lectures. They even extended to the public, on the paying of a small fee, the privilege of attending certain courses intended for medical students. The French and English sections of the newspapers were replete with these invitations. These are not only interesting but are of historical interest. These press notices were always most flattering to the professors. To quote a few which appeared in the *Bee* for the month of December 1835:

Dr. Edward H. Barton will deliver a lecture this afternoon at 41 Royal Street—his introductory for the season. From his known ability in his profession and diligence in accumulating observations and statistical details, we have no doubt of his being highly interesting. He will probably glance at the climate of Louisiana and New Orleans, and the local causes assigned for endemic diseases, for he has collected a vast number of facts bearing on this subject; and therefore can do it more justice.

Among other advertisements is the following:

MEDICAL COLLEGE: Dr. Powell's course of chemical lectures will commence this evening at 5 o'clock P.M. in the hall of the institution and will continue every day except Sundays, till the first of April. To the first week of this course the ladies and gentlemen are invited. During this time those who desire to attend the course, or only the popular portion of it, will obtain tickets at the office No. 45½ Canal St. At 7 o'clock tonight, at the same place, he will deliver his introductory. The ladies and gentlemen are solicited to attend.

He that desires to acquire an accurate knowledge of man, of physiology and pathology, should attend the daily lectures given at the Hospital from 12 to 1, by Dr. C. A. Luzenberg. They are those of a master of his profession.

We have received as "Introductory Lectures on the Importance Derived from Medical Science in Improving the Physical Condition of a Country, etc." by Edward Barton, M.D., of the Medical College of Louisiana. The lecture is published in pamphlet form and can be obtained at any of the book stores. It contains much useful information—particualrly as regards Malaria and swamp lands and should therefore be read by all the intelligent of our citizens. We should promise to make extracts from it but that we wish our subscribers to purchase it.

The roster for the second session shows thirty matriculants. The first graduation exercises took place at four o'clock in the afternoon of April 5, 1836, in the Congregational Church in St. Charles Street. The orator was the Honorable Henry A. Bullard, the learned and distinguished Justice of the Supreme Court of Louisiana. The exercises were opened with prayer by the Reverend Theodore Clapp. The Dean of the Faculty, Dr. Luzenberg, delivered an oration in Latin, which was said to be in conformity with a custom more honored in the breach than in the observance. Mr. George Eustis, a prominent member of the bar and also a member of the Board of Trustees, spoke eloquently to the graduating class. After the conferring of degrees, the exercise terminated with a prayer. The degrees of Doctor of Medicine, the first conferred, not only in Louisiana, but in the Southwest were awarded to Messrs. M. M. Carpenter, M. A. Delatule, Alphonse Delavigne, Walter Fosgate, Alexander Hart, Albert Simon Kostki, Odgen D. Longstaff, John C. Lawhon, John H. Lewis, F. J. Romer, and Cornelius Traweek.

The second report of the College, of date, January 5, 1837, mentioned that "the present course (1837-38) was more numerous in students and that the majority came from the neighboring states." They expressed the regret at the departure of many students because of lack of proper facilities and suitable accommodations. Attention was called to the fact that they had "no apartments for lectures and for the deposit and preservation of anatomical preparations, collections and specimens of natural history, pharmacy, botany, minerology, drawings, books, models and every variety of chemical and surgical apparatus."

It was announced in that prospectus that the course would begin on the first Monday in December and end on the fourth Saturday in March. The tuition fees were:

Matriculation fee.......................$ 5.00
Price for tickets for each professor...... 20.00
Demonstrators ticket.................. 10.00
Graduation fee........................ 30.00

The total approximated to about $150.00 per session.

The following professors composed the Faculty for the session of 1838-39: Warren Stone, M.D., Professor of Anatomy; Ed H. Barton, M.D., Dean and Professor of the Theory and Practice of Medicine; John Harrison, M.D., Professor of Physiology; James Jones, M.D., Professor of Obstetrics and Diseases of Women and Children; J. Monroe Mackie, M.D., Professor of Materia Medica and Therapeutics; John J. Riddell, M. D., Professor of Chemistry and Pharmacy; Warren Stone, M.D., Professor of Surgery.

At that time changes were frequent, not only in the personnel of the Faculty, but in interchanges between the various chairs. The catalogue for the session of 1839-40 announced that Dr. James Jones relinquished the chair of Obstetrics and Diseases of Women and Children for the professorship of the Theory and practice of

Medicine, replacing Dr. Barton, who resumed the teaching of his original branch, Materia Medica and Therapeutics, previously taught by Dr. Mackie who had resigned. The new appointments were A. G. Nott, M.D., Professor of Anatomy, A. H. Cenas, M.D., Professor of Obstetrics and Diseases of Women and Children, and C. W. Morgan, M.D., Demonstrator of Anatomy.

It was announced that Doctors Nott and Cenas had returned from Europe after a stay of a few years devoted to preparing themselves for the teaching of their respective branches.

A School of Pharmacy was established by the Medical College of Louisiana on October 20, 1838.

It was not until the end of the year 1840, that the College acquired its domicile. It was a modest building in the immediate vicinity of the Charity Hospital, which at that time was in a comparatively retired location. For the first time the lecture rooms were under one roof.

The Medical College of Louisiana during the first ten years of its existence was of slow growth. The number of its students, although then slightly increasing year by year, was small and its graduates seldom exceed ten a year.

The first year of medical education in New Orleans was a hectic one. Not only its success, but its very existence was precarious. It was the ardor, the love of the profession, the steadfast determination and the unflagging spirit to overcome the seemingly overwhelming odds, as well as the fearless courage of these beardless youths, the organizers of the first medical college in the Southwest, which surmounted dissensions in their own ranks as well as the untiring opposition of obstructionists. They built well, for from their modest beginning, this college without a domicile, with only eleven matriculants, grew to become a great institution of learning whose influence is felt not only throughout the South, but the whole country.

The Medical College of Louisiana is today the Medical Department of Tulane University. Its contributions to the science and art of medicine and its achievements are known the world over. Its alumni are justly proud of their Alma Mater's distinguished heritage.

CHAPTER XVI

HOSPITALS AND INFIRMARIES

New Orleans' greatest monument is not the masterpiece of some eminent sculptor, nor a mass of granite perpetuating the name of some great warrior, prominent statesman or famed philanthropist, nor yet a magnificent edifice recording a great epochal event or a renowned historical achievement, but an institution dedicated to the greatest of charities, the alleviation of suffering and the healing of the sick—The Charity Hospital of Louisiana, founded by Jean Louis, a sailor, two hundred and twenty-one years ago.

On the 21st day of January, 1736, Jean Louis, a resident of New Orleans, passed away leaving an holographic will in which he stipulated that:

> My debts having been paid and the above provisions having been executed, a sale shall be made of all that remains, which, together with my small lot, I bequeath to serve in perpetuity to the founding of a hospital for the sick of the City of New Orleans, without anyone being able to change my purpose to secure the things necessary to succor the sick.

A site was chosen at the extremity of the town which, Governor Miro stated, stood on a portion of ground allotted to the city's fortification and today corresponds to the square bounded by Rampart, Basin, St. Peter and Toulouse Streets. Half of the money was expended for beds and the usual equipment. With the remaining 5,000 livres, augmented by the labor of the natives, a large brick hall was built. That building was forty-five feet in length by twenty-five in breath and fourteen in height and its construction began on the 29th of March, 1736. This, the original Charity Hospital, was named the *St. John* and was mentioned in the official legal records as "l'hôpital des Pauvres de la Charite." In the interesting memorial, dated May 20, 1737, to the Minister in France, written by Bienville and Salmon, they told that the hospital had five patients. Miro tells us that the devasting hurricane which played havoc with the city in the summer of the year 1779 converted the Jean Louis Hospital into a heap of ruins and that only the storehouse and kitchen escaped the fury of the storm.

The following is taken from the "Annuaire Louisianais pour l'anné, 1809, par B Lafon":

"The old hospital was founded by the French and was entirely destroyed by the storm of 1779, Don Almonaster y Roxes, Colonel of Militia of that town, Royal Alfares, perpetual Regidor and Knight of St. Charles founded the one which exists today, in the year 1786. It was entirely constructed at his own expense, he furnished it with all necessary implements necessary to help and alleviate the sick and gave to it five skilled slaves and transferred all the rentals of the shops at the corner of St. Peter and Levee. He also repaired at his own expense five small houses, the property of the former hospital." It also stated that "the donation was of twenty beds for the use of the sick who are neither incurable nor leprous and they must not only be destitute, but recognized as such." Dr. Blanquet was the physician and Juan Ximens, the Administrator.

The first Legislative Act referring to the Charity Hospital passed the first Legislature Assembly of the Territory of Louisiana on March 8th, 1808, is of historical interest because it was the initial step taken by the Territory of Louisiana to control that institution and also because it gives an interesting aspect of the condition and arrangement of the Hospital at that time. It is doubtful whether the provisions of this Act were ever enforced; for a few months afterwards, on the 23rd of September, 1809, the hospital burned to the ground. This Act, however, was premonitary to the fact that existing conditions in the direction of the Hospital could not endure and that the administration of same would perforce soon become invested in the Territorial Government. A subsequent Act enacted by the Legislature, three years after the passage of the original Act, can be considered the Charter of the Charity Hosiptal of the State of Louisiana.

The Jean Louis Hospital and the Military Hospital situated on Hospital Street, now General Nicholls Street, must not be confused for they were two distinct institutions and for different purposes.

For five years not a suitable place for the care of the sick was available, nor was it until the year 1814 that the square bounded by Canal, Common, Phillipa (now University Place) and Baronne was sold by the city to the Administrators of the Charity Hospital for the construction of a building. The construction of the new hospital was authorized by the Legislature on April 25th, 1811. The Board of Administrators consisted of Messrs. Felix Arnaud, Dow, Joseph Montegut, Butler, Bellechase and Fortier and on November

6th, 1811, Messrs. Robelot, Castenado and S. Henderson, members of the City Council, were elected administrators of the Charity Hospital in compliance with the law. These gentlemen constituted the first Board of Administrators of the Charity Hospital.

HOPITAL DE CHARITE const' en 1815

Charity Hospital at 147 Canal St. Under construction in 1815 when Tanesse drew his map. See Castellanos' drawing of complete buildings shown elsewhere.

The corner stone of the building was laid in 1815. The following description of the Hospital as it was in 1823, is taken from the City Directory of that year: — "The Charity Hospital, situated at No. 147 Canal Street, consists of two large buildings containing one surgical hall, two large fever wards, one dysentery ward, one ward for chronic cases, one for females, one for convalescents, one bathing room, one apothecary store and a number of other apartments for the families of the residents, officers, etc. The Hospital has lately undergone a complete repair and reform and is at this time as clean, wholesome, and well conducted as any institution of the kind in the United States. During the last year, about 1700 sick persons were admitted. 1,200 of whom were discharged well and the remaining died. One-half of which of yellow fever. The lot on which the building stands is laid off in a garden, poultry yard, etc. The whole appearance of this humane establishment at present indicates that the physicians and officers are very attentive to their duty . . . Dr. John Rollins is the House Surgeon and Apothecary at this time, who is assisted by physicians of the City who visit in turn. Sick persons who wish admission must apply to the Mayor or any one of the Administrative group. The Hospital is likewise an asylum for lost children who will be taken the very best care of until claimed. About 1,300 males and females were admitted during the year 1821 and as many as 130 persons received attention at one time."

From the above it may be seen the rapid strides made by the Hospital. In a few years it had grown from a 24 to a 120 bed hospital. That institution in equipment and management was second to no other in the country.

An Act passed by the second session of the Fourth Legislature in 1820, provided for the care of the insane in the following clause: "It shall be the duty of the Administrators to cause a separate building to be erected as an appurtenance of said establishment in order to receive and attend such persons as may have fallen into a state of insanity."

Dr. McConnell was the first House Surgeon and in the year 1823 he was succeeded by Dr. John Rollins. In 1831 Dr. William Picton was elected to that position. Dr. David C. Ker, a British Army Surgeon and a veteran of the Battle of New Orleans, who after the crushing defeat of General Packenham, true to the noblest tradition of his profession, permitted himself to be captured that he might administer to his wounded soldiers. This gallantry gained for him the admiration and respect of his former enemies. He made that city his home and in the year 1827 was appointed visiting physician to the Charity Hospital.

As there were no specific appropriations from the State, its revenues were derived from the levying of special taxes on amusements, gambling and the fines and penalties assessed in criminal cases, also from forfeited bonds and a passenger tax of $1.00 on foreign cabin passengers, $2.00 on steerage passengers and on United States passengers beyond Louisiana, fifty cents. James Burns in his "Historical Sketch of the Charity Hospital of New Orleans", wrote: "The managers of theaters at one time were required to give periodical benefit performances for the hospital, but not only did these never benefit the Hospital, but on at least one occasion the manager brought the Hospital into debt for his benefit." There was even resistance to the passenger tax, for in one year, eighty-three boats defiantly refused to pay it and one hundred and seventy-three landed their passengers in Lafayette [above the city] to evade its just impost. This was changed in 1838, each theater was taxed $500.00; each circus $150.00, each menagerie $50.00, each show $25.00, as Hospital Assessment. These taxes together with an occasional donation provided for its support. In 1832 the cost of maintenance is given as $31,295.00.

The great increase in population demanded a larger and more commodious institution and the Canal St. site and buildings were sold to the State of Louisiana for $125,000.00 for a state house.

The following abstract taken from the report of the Board of Administrators for the year 1832 is illuminating because it not only depicts its financial difficulties but proclaims the great extent of its philanthropy for the care and treatment of so many strangers who invaded the city, for they constituted a very great proportion of the patients, and that but relatively very few of the residents of the City were admitted. It can really be said that the scope of its charity was national instead of local. The report stated:

> Your committee need only state the number of patients received the last year from almost every state and nation and kingdom on earth, to exhibit in strong colors the wide-extended usefulness of this unfading monument of individual liberality and public benefaction. During the year 1832, 2,480 unfortunate fellow beings have shared the open-handed beneficence, of whom 1,545 have been restored to health, to friends and to society. Five hundred and sixty-nine had died, a number of which when we reflect on the wasting pestilence which has visited our city, in a character, from which it would seem as if we had been marked out as the peculiar object of its relentless violence, certainly does no dishonor to the skill of the gentlemen who have charge of the medical department. There were on the 1st day of January past 167 under treatment, producing an average number for the year of 180. We have much cause to congratulate ourselves that only forty of the whole number were citizens of Louisiana. Here, your committee cannot forbear to express their surprise that the peculiar situation of this institution and the unlimited dispensation of its charities have not attracted the attention and enlisted the interest and generosity of other States. The liberality of Pennsylvania, which we are always happy to acknowledge, furnishes a proud example which it is devoutly to be wished might be imitated by others. We doubt not that the generous spirit of the philanthropic state reaps a rich reward from the reflection that during the last year, her liberality contributed to the relief and comfort of all of their unfortunate fellow-citizens whom circumstances had removed far from their homes and their friends.

This report emphatically refutes the calumnious propaganda then circulated throughout the nation about the callous indifference and the inhumanity of the people of New Orleans.

The part of that report concerning the financial condition of the institution is interesting, it reads:

They (the committee) deeply deplore that an institution so laudible in its object, so extensive in its benefits and presenting so wide a field for the exercise of the highest and purest feelings of our nature, should depend on support on means extremely capricious in their duration and which cannot be advocated on principles of religion or on morals. The whole amount of money received by the institution for the year 1832 was $239,892.25: of this amount $190,119.20 have been realized from the sale of property of various descriptions. The sums of $16,169.78, embracing one legacy of $5000.00 and $50.00 collected by the marshall has accrued from premiums on State bonds, interest on State bonds and moneys invested, leaving a balance of $33,603.27 which had been derived from what is called the ordinary source of revenue. Of this ordinary revenue $31,041.00 have been received in shape of taxes on gaming licenses. Hence it appears how small a portion of necessary expenditures of this institution is derived from any substantial and permanent sources of revenue. The disbursements during the year including $14,550.45, due individuals on accounts of the preceeding year, and also $9,000.00, due the Louisiana State Bank for money loaned, amounted to $48,259.68 of which sum $31,407.70 were appropriated to the ordinary current expenses of the establishment. $86,885.62 were expended on the new edifice; $690.83 were paid for commissions and tax on estate; $2,600.00 were paid for four slaves for the use of the hospital, and $3,125.00 interest on State bonds, leaving a balance in favor of the institution of $91,682.65; from this sum we may deduct $15,000.00 for the completion of the building which is now rapidly progressing and we have $76,632.68 the entire productive capital of the institution. From this sum we may with some degree of certainty, anticipate a revenue of $7,600.00. The amount annually required to support the establishment considerably exceeds $30,000.00, and for upwards of $20,000.00 of which we are obliged to rely on the frail and unsubstantial resource of gaming licenses. Your committee much regrets that the law requiring all persons opening theaters in the City of New Orleans to give four representations per annum at the will of the Council of Administration, has not been carried into effect and that the law imposing a tax of ten dollars on each and every public ball has not been rigidly enforced. Your committee believes that by a watchful observance of these laws that the present revenue of the institution might be increased several thousand dollars.

The report mentioned that the new edifice would cost a little less than one hundred and fifty thousand dollars. It continued:

It is sufficiently spacious to accommodate four hundred patients, allowing the most liberal provision for offices and attendants. The apartments are large, neat, well ventilated and admirably well adapted to the peculiar object for which they were designed. It is hoped for the sake of humanity that the time is near when diseased indigence will occupy this vast structure. And it is believed that the superior comforts and advantages, which the peculiar structure of the building, the discipline and habits of the servants and the constant medical attention, hold out to invalid strangers, cannot fail to draw to it many who would gladly make a liberal compensation for such accommodations ... The justice of this plan will appear most palpable when we reflect that, of the number of patients received into the hospital during the last year, 1,709 were subjects of foreign government.

The new Charity Hospital was described as a building of great size, it was 290 feet in length and three stories high.

It is composed of a corps of loges opening into a spacious hall, intersected at right angles by another running lengthwise of the building on which the wards open. From this hall access is had by broad stairs to the upper stories which are similarly divided, and thus to the cupola from which there is a magnificent view of the city and environs. The lower story is occupied by the Library, Physician's room, Surgeons Room, Medical College, Lecture Room, etc. ,and the second and third stories into wards for the patients, twenty-one in number, as also into four other apartments designed as such; but owing to the plan not being carried out, now used one as a chapel and three others for the accommodation of the Sisters of Charity ... It is calculated to hold 540 patients.

The second floor was appropriated to the use of female patients and was divided as follows: a ward for women of good

Charity Hospital, 1832. (From Gibson's Directory of 1838)

character, another for those of bad and also one for the exclusive use of surgical and obstetrical cases. The grounds around it were enclosed with a substantial brick wall and were handsomely improved and always very neatly kept.

The Sisters of Charity inaugurated their long period of devotion to the sick and afflicted on January 6, 1834.

In the first issue of the New Orleans Medical and Surgical Journal, May 1844 is the following description of an insane asylum, a department of the Charity Hospital:

> In the rear of the main building is the lunatic asylum, built by an appropriation of the Legislature in 1841. The building is 103 feet long by 35 broad and three stories high. A gallery extends the whole length and height of the house in front and affords a fine promenade; a passage of 9 feet wide runs through the whole length of the building on each floor. On each side of these passages, the rooms open, 38 in number, well supplied with light and air and with doors and windows well secured. The stairs run at the end of the house and occupy but little space. At the opposite end from the entrance, on the ground floor, is the bathing room, in which is to be found an admirable apparatus for the shower bath, the use of which is often required in the treatment of mental diseases. The third story of the Asylum is divided into two spacious sleeping apartments. At each end of the building are large well-designed arbours, which are covered with vines, affording an admirable shade in warm weather. These with the grounds immediately around the Asylum are well adapted for exercise in the open air.

In addition of the Charity Hospital there was the United States Marine and Naval Hospital under the administration of Dr. J. S. McFarlane, who also owned the Orleans Infirmary at the corner of Circus and Poydras Streets.

There were also private infirmaries owned by some of the doctors of that time, the most famous was the Franklin Infirmary.

On March 26, 1834, the City Council received the following communication from the Mayor:

> A proposal was submitted by Dr. Luzenberg to construct, under certain conditions, a hospital to be erected in the faubourg Marigny, which was deeded to the corporation by Mr. Marigny for that specific purpose.

Unfortunately the minutes of the City Council for that year are lost, but in the French section of the *Bee* of April 24, is the following interesting editorial:

Proposal for the Founding of a New Hospital

The City Council for some time has been deliberating on the proposal of Dr. Luzenberg, a man who does not lack in savoir faire, which is so necessary for success, made what seems at first blush, a very attractive proposal, but its real purpose is seen bared after mature reflection. He proposes a loan to the City of $10,000.00 bearing 6% interest, which is predicated upon his having the management of the institution. The amount is to be repaid in ten years. He is to receive a fee of fifty cents per patient for the first fifty patients and seventy-five cents for those exceeding that number. It was advanced in the Council that Dr. Luzenberg was only actuated by a philanthropic motive. He was highly praised, although it was acknowledged by some that he was prompted by some speculative motive. This proposition is neither advantageous to the sick or to the City because it is not possible for fifty patients to receive the full attention of one physician, and besides such a hospital cannot be constructed for the sum of $10,000.00 when such an amount is to include the purchase of the furniture and equipment. The whole thing is a folly. It would be preferable to have twelve or more wards with a physician in charge of each. A class of men so useful to society is not dominated by selfishness. Certainly, twelve men among so many will offer their services. It is astonishing that the City Council has not consulted a few physicians or requested a report from them on such an important project. The City Council should reject the proposition.

Further light is shed on the Luzenberg proposal in an editorial in the *Bee* of September 4, 1835, which reads in part:

> It was built by Dr. Luzenberg at the instigation of the City Council's promise having been held out to him of acquiring the patients from the lower faubourg of the corporation. A resolution partially to that effect had been passed by the City Council, yet patients from the lower faubourg are too often sent to the Charity Hospital and Luzenberg has been hitherto deprived of the support promised and expected.

A substantial structure measuring 65 x 55 feet faced with an important portico was erected on Elysian Fields Avenue and Celestin Streets — now North Johnson. It was named the Franklin Infirmary. From the first day its doors were opened, it was crowded to capacity. Very seldom there were less than eighty to a hundred patients. The Franklin Infirmary was not only very extensively advertised in the press, but it received frequent commendatory editorial accounts.

The Infirmary was capable of comfortably accommodating one hundred patients. It was said that it had shady walks and was em-

The Franklin Infirmary, in Champs Elysees and North Johnson on Pontchartrain R. R., about two miles from the city. Built in 1835 by Dr. Charles A. Luzenberg. Had accommodations for 100 patrons. (Gibson's Directory)

bowered by luxuriant foliage and flowers. In the garden were bears, pelicans, reptiles and birds of various kinds and on the walls frescoes depicting the different ensigns and signals of every nation.

The following was the schedule of fees as advertised in the *True American* of July 10, 1838:

>Private room may be had by gentlemen at $5.00 per day, including attendance, etc.
>Terms in the ordinary wards $2.00 per day.
>Slaves also $2.00. Small-pox in the ordinary wards $5.00.

The infirmaries, all privately owned, administered practically exclusively to the floating population. The residents of the city were not only treated at, but surgical operations were performed in their homes.

The *Louisiana Gazette* carried the following advertisement in its issue of July 22, 1824:

> A Private Hospital or Infirmary
> Is open for the reception of patients at the corner of Levee and Marigny Canal — Spacious three story brick building belonging to Alexander Milne Esq. A convenient apartment with the necessary apparatus and instruments for capital operations in Surgery, will also be provided.
> Mr. John Rollins—Superintendent
> Dr. Davidson.

Objections were voiced by a large number of the inhabitants against the location of the Infirmary is a petition to the Mayor "who is required to act thereon agreeably to provisions of the ordinance concerning the public health of May 18, 1816." This was answered by a petition by Dr. Davidson in which he claimed that he was ignorant of that ordinance prohibiting hospitals within the City limits.

At the same time a motion was passed in the City Council that the Dr. Sanchez Hospital be inspected. Dr. Sanchez was ordered by the Mayor to admit no white persons in his institution, but a petition by the citizens of Faubourg St. Mary averred that they had no complaint concerning same and praised its order and cleanlinness and declared no accident resulted from it. Thereupon the Mayor's order was revoked.

Another private institution was Dr. Stone's Infirmary, or as it was commonly called *Maison de Santé,* situated on the corner of Canal and Claiborne Streets. It was an imposing building and was erected especially for the purpose, it was spacious and airy; "the rooms were arranged in such a manner as to render them equally pleasant and comfortable at every season". The terms of admission were as follows: Private rooms on the first floor, $5.00 per day; Rooms on the second floor, $2.00 to $3.00; and for slaves, $1.00. Its advertisement read that "the charges include all medical attendance, nursing, etc. Surgical operations charged for extra. Competent nurses, both male and female, are constantly in the service of the Infirmary. Medical gentlemen sending patients to the Maison de Santé, will be at liberty to continue their attendance; such attendance, however, not to interfere with the regular charge of the Institution."

CHAPTER XVII

THE PROGRESS OF EDUCATION IN LOUISIANA

Many travellers who visited New Orleans in the early nineteenth century made inviduous remarks about the lack of proper school facilities, the need of libraries and the illiteracy of its citizens. This indifference toward cultural pursuits they attributed to the indolent way of life of the pleasure-seeking Creoles and French immigrants, as well as to the avidity of the fortune-seeking Americans.

It must be acknowledged that some of those observations were partly true, yet practically the same conditions existed in other parts of the Union, especially in the middle West. However, there was a culture in New Orleans unsurpassed by any other city of the country. It was said that New Orleans was barren of authors, but this is disproved by the classic works of Gayarré, Martin, Debouchel and others whose erudition and perfection of language, in many instances, far surpasses the writings of those who criticized the cultural life of the city. Many of its orators, both French and English, were unexcelled.

As early as 1725, Father Raphael, Superior of the Capuchins, established a school for boys under the tutelage of a brother of that order.

Governor Claiborne in 1804, in his address to the Legislative Council, stressed the necessity for education in the following words:

> In adverting to your primary duties, I have yet to suggest one than which none can be more important and interesting. I mean some general provision for the eduaction of youth. . . . Permit me to hope that under your patronage, learning will prosper and means of securing information be placed within reach of each growing family. My advice, therefore, is that your system of education be extensive and liberally supported.

In 1805 the College of Orleans was established, the first educational institution to be incorporated by the Legislature. It was located at St. Claude and General Nichols Streets, in a building now occupied by the parochial school of St. Augustine Parish. Ficklen stated that whilst it enjoyed the title of College, it had degenerated to the grade of a secondary school, except for the

COLLEGE D'ORLEANS année 1812

Orleans College, 31 Bayou Road and St. Claude. Built in 1812. (Tanesse Map, 1815)

---

teaching of the classics. Gayarré, the historian, was its most distinguished scholar. French, English, Greek, Latin, Spanish and Mathematics were taught. Its first president was Jules D'Avezac, a brother-in-law of Edward Livingston and a refugee from St. Domingo.

Chambers thought highly of the refugees from St. Domingo, many of whom were well educated and excelled in the learned professions. D'Avezac, who was a lawyer, served but a short term as a teacher. He was succeeded by another St. Domingan, Rochefort, who was the professor of Belles Lettres.

Among the professors was Lakanal, one of the colorful personalities who sought refuge in New Orleans. He had been a defrocked Catholic priest who became a member of the National Assembly of France. One of the leaders of the French Revolution, who voted for the decapitation of Louis XVI.

On July 22, 1823, the *Louisiana Gazette* announced that Mr. Lakanal had just resigned the presidency of the college, and stated that it was rumored that the administration would replace him by an abbot strongly imbued with monarchical principles and a belief in the Divine right of Kings.

Its enrollment in 1823 was forty-four boarders and thirty-five day pupils. It was a pay school except for some who were destitute. Gayarré tells us that the sons of the latter were always dubbed "Charity students", and thus marked with the badge of poverty; they were treated as the plebes of the Institution.

Governor Robertson in his address to the Legislature in November 1824 stated that the college and schools were liberally endowed, and that nearly one-fifth of the State revenue was applied to the school fund. He reported further that the College of New Orleans had heretofore disappointed the hopes of the public, "while some changes in its organization and character has been lately brought by the directors, the services of respectable and learned professors have been obtained and assurances given which authorize us to look forward with confidence to its increasing prosperity and usefulness."

Governor Johnson in his report to the Legislature in January 1826 stated that the College of Orleans

> Does not according to the reports of the Administrators, appear to have attained the end to which it was erected. The number of students does not exceed twenty, nor has it been greater for some time past. The advantage of educating so small a number can hardly compensate the expense which the institution cost the State. Instead of such a college, which from the present prospect and many years experience, we cannot expect to rise much above the rank of a grammar school would it not be better to establish within the City of New Orleans a university where the science of law and medicine and the other branches of learning might be taught to those who have already completed their scholastic studies? There are some institutions of this kind in every great state of the Union. Louisiana should not be without hers. Our elementary schools and classical academies are excellent.
>
> I am still of opinion that one great object would be to diffuse the benefit of education among the poor and to render our country schools as assessible as possible.

The coup-de-grace was given by Moreau Lislet, who made a motion in the Legislature to consider the advisibility of closing the Orleans College. The motion read:

> If the truth must be told it has fallen from its anticipated efficiency because an American Gentleman, distinguished for his learning and piety, presided over the College and matures the minds of the youthful inhabitants, not because he is efficient or unskilled in any of his duties, but because a feeling, baneful to the peace, happiness and prosperity of the State prevails to the prejudice of whatever is American.
>
> This is the only institution for the promotion of the higher branches of knowledge which has been established by the constitution and authorities of the people and yet it has been suffered to languish, linger and droop, and now also its end is to be consummated.

It can be surmised that the same conflict of nationalities, language, politics and religion which eventually caused the City to be divided into three municipalities, was the basic factor in the abolishment of the College of Orleans.

In 1926, the historical institution of learning closed its doors. The *Journal of Commerce* published an article signed E. A. C., which asserted:

> This writer might trace the ruin of the College of Orleans to other causes than the enmity of the late Governor Robertson or the present incumbent. It can be found in its management a disposition of the people to give preference to other schools. We venture to say that the population of Louisiana called American, will never be found wanting in voting funds for the endowment of a literary institution in this city or elsewhere, which can give any promise of success.

Reverend Clapp gave a more accurate perception of the provocative factors which caused the discontinuance of the College. He wrote:

> From the beginning, all the presidents, professors and officers of the institution, had been of French extraction, either Creoles or foreigners. One of the most popular and efficient member of the Board of Administrators was an English gentleman of splendid talents and acquirements. It was his wish to place some Northern man at the head of the College "in order", as he said, "to Americanize the usages, studies and course of discipline".
>
> The pastor of the Presbyterian Church was recommended to him as a person qualified to fill the office. This was done without my knowledge or consent. It happened in the spring of 1824.

The person alluded to was Judge Workman, a native of Ireland and who for many years had been a citizen of the United States.

Pöstl in 1826 observed that the institutions of learning are inferior to those of any city of equal extent and of less wealth, such as Richmond and even Albany. The only literary institution in Louisiana was the Louisiana College. Free schools were being formed in the City. He commented that "excepting the elements of reading, writing, arithmetic and Latin, it affords no intellectual information."

He claimed that the best school was kept by Mr. Shute, rector of the Episcopalian Church, an enlightened and clever man, who fully deserved the popularity he had acquired. Reading, writing, geography particularly, and general history were taught under his tuition and in his rectory.

In 1826 the College of Louisiana was incorporated, it was

located on Victory Street in faubourg Marigny. The act provided that the salaries of the president were to be $3000.00, the professors, $1500.00; the prefects, $1000.00; and the grammar school teachers, $750.00. The tuition fees were $15.00 for the preparatory, $20.00 for the freshman class, $25.00 for sophmores, $30.00 for juniors and seniors, and for the French and English languages, $20.00.

In the *Courier* of April 5, 1828, a plea was made for better educational facilities in Louisiana, it read in part:

> Not an institution in the neighboring parishes: in fact in the whole State. There is not one institution which by its organization and the number of its professors may deserve that name, that there are indeed a few elementary schools, but nothing like what is called a college.
>
> In order to acquire that education they should send their children to Bardstown or to Baltimore, to France or England.
>
> The education which best suits a man is that which he receives in the country where he is destined to live. The mind of man is so disposed as to find it difficult to shake off early notions. It is but seldom that one does not preserve some prejudices in favor of the land where he acquired his first ideas, where his soul began, in a manner, to assume a shape or mould. — A Louisianian ought to be educated in Louisiana. But in Louisiana, that country so wealthy, so fertile, so liberal in the principles, as adverse to all kinds of aristocracy, save that of virtue and talents, what has been done? Every thing except what was necessary.

In the Eighteen-thirties, education made rapid progress. The public shook off its indifference and demanded better school facilities for its children. Boards of Regents were appointed and more money was appropriated by the State. There was a slow but gradual evolution in the educational field, but the main difficulty, the reluctance of parents to send their children to the free schools, remained unsolved. This was deplored by Governor Roman in his report on primary schools to the Legislature of January 2, 1832:

> Reports from the parishes offer some satisfactory results and prove at least that the money allowed by the State is not every where employed without profit. It is with regret that I must add that these parishes form but execptions and that the situation of schools in the greater part of the others demonstrates the inefficiency of the laws hitherto adopted for the education of indigent children.
>
> In some part of these parishes there are not more than

ten scholars instructed at the expense of the State; in others there are not even as many, although more than two hundred could be taught.

Suffice it to say that I still consider as one of the principal causes of the very partial success in our primary schools, the invincible repugnance felt by most of the parents to have their children educated entirely at the expense of the State. They cannot decide to send their sons into schools where they are exposed to be regarded as subject of public charity and as forming an inferior class, distinct from where those are placed whose education is paid for.

In 1832, the Board of Regents for the Central and Primary Schools was composed of J. E. Canonge, President; Hughes Lavergne, Secretary; Felix Grima, A. E. Canon, George Strawbridge, Thomas Urquhart, T. F. Caleb, Alonzo Morphy, George Eustis and C. M. Conrad.

The Board reported that the schools had resumed operation since the first of October. That of two hundred scholars who were to be admitted gratuitously, according to law, only one hundred and fifty availed themselves of the privilege.

In February 1834, the report of the Legislature on free schools showed that New Orleans had 217 pupils out of 1175 from the State at large. Fifteen hundred children, between the ages of five to fifteen were educated on an appropriation of $80,440.77.

The College of Louisiana was in a flourishing condition, having an enrollment of sixty-six students, and the amount expended was $14,812.50. It received $10,000.00 from the State.

In December 1833, Governor Roman in his message to the Legislature said "the law concerning public education passed at your last session is the first step towards a more extended organization of our system of elementary instruction." He also announced that Jefferson College would be opened in February next.

The report of the Board of Regents in February 1833, stated that the central school and one of the primary schools were domiciled in the old Ursuline Convent, but because at various times these class rooms were ceded to the Legislature to hold their sessions there, they were impelled to seek another location. The schools were then moved to the Union Hall on Ursulines between Dauphine and Burgundy. The three schools provided for 236 pupils, 82 in the primary school, 108 in the lower section, 82 in the upper section, and 48 in the central school.

From its incipiency, Jefferson College in St. James parish was a success. After its first year it had an enrollment of 250 students. The faculty consisted of C. Crozat, Dean and professor of mathematics; A. Crozat, Professor of Latin and Greek; Fletcher, professor of English; Debret, Professor of French; Galvez, Professor of Spanish; Kimball and Robin, Prefects and Masters of study and A. Chopin, Superintendent.

The College was incorporated by an act of Legislature in 1835 and was endowed for a period of ten years by the State to the amount of $15,000.00 per annum.

In 1836 The College of Jefferson had 135 students who paid a tuition fee of $230.00 each, and the faculty consisted of nine professors.

That same year the College of Louisiana had more than one hundred scholars. In 1842 it was destroyed by fire.

The first public announcement of the opening of Spring Hill College near Mobile, Alabama, is to be found in an advertisement in the *Courier* of November 6, 1830. That circular had the following headlines:

"College of Spring Hill, under the direction of the Rt. Rev. Dr. Portier, Bishop of Mobile." It said in part:

> The Institution which will be opened between the 1st and 15th of November inst (1830), under the appelation of the College of Spring Hill is situated on the great mail route from Washington City to New Orleans and seven miles west of the City of Mobile. — Though the Regency of the College be Catholic, yet no influence will be exercised upon pupils bred in the principles of other Christian denominations."
>
> The tuition for the scholastic year was fixed at two hundred and sixty dollars.

Spring Hill College was the Alma Mater of many of the most prominent and distinguished citizens of New Orleans and of Louisiana. Its contribution to the field of education in Louisiana was great. It is the only college of that period which has not only survived to this day, but has achieved a high standard among the institutions of higher education in the far South.

The Ursulines landed in New Orleans in July, 1727 and according to the Jesuit Father de Beaubois, on May 6, 1728, the school of the Ursulines had an enrollment of sixteen girl boarders and twenty five day pupils. "They kept gratis orphans who had

COUVENT DES RELIGIEUSES construit en 1733
Ursuline Convent, built in 1733(?) (Tanesse Map, 1815).

been entirely forsaken or were in very bad hands." Mére Transchepain was the Mother Superior. During the French and Spanish domination these good sisters taught the poor as well as the wealthy girls.

Amos Stoddard gives the following descriptions of the Ursuline Convent as it was in 1812:

> The Convent of Ursulines is situated on the upper side of the Barracks and beyond the Hospital (King's Hospital). It is of brick and covered with shingles. It is two stories high. An extensive garden is attached to it, extremely productive of fruits and vebetables. It will accomodate about fifty nuns and from seventy and eighty young females who resort to it for their education. Attached to the Convent is a small house containing three rooms divided longitudinally from each other by a double grating about six inches asunder, which apertures about two inches square where strangers may see and converse with the nuns and boarders on particular business. Near to the main school house where the female children of the citizens appear at certain fixed hours to be gratuitously instructed in writing, reading and arithmetic.

A large proportion of the Creoles ladies were educated by the Ursulines and a few by private tutors. The Protestant, or the American young ladies, were taught by school mistresses who were partly French and partly American. The better class of Anglo-Americans preferred to send their daughters to a Northern Institution where they would remain for two years before returning home.

The status of education was on a par, doubtless, with that of most of the States of the Union, and in some instances it was superior. Except in rare instances, women were not as well educated as the men, yet we read in the *Courier* of August 2, 1828, that the Seminary for young ladies of Grand Coteau, which was endowed by the Widow of Mr. Charles Smith, "provided for our daughters the proper means of female education unknown in our country." The curriculum advertised included: Cleanliness, reading, French and English, arithmetic, English Grammar, history, geography, domestic economy, needle work and medical attention. Music, dancing and the social graces were also essential for ladies' education.

Yet in the *Bee* of February 17, 1836 we find the following interesting comment:

> Knowledge in women is deemed to be actually a disgrace or derogation from their utility; as their sensibilities are of the keenest kind, they feel this — are careless to acquire and indifferent to display any sort of information which must have been obtained by assiduous study. They receive calumny if they are learned and contempt if they are not.

This must have been the concensus at that time for it was not then contradicted.

During the colonial times and in the early American period, the opulent Creoles sent their sons to France to be educated, especially in medicine and law. In a great number of instances, it must be said that these young men, who as a rule had an unlimited amount of spending money, occupied more of their time in the brilliant society of gay Paris than in the halls of the Universtiy. Many returned back home without the advantages which they went abroad to receive.

CHAPTER XVIII

LIBRARIES, THE HISTORICAL SOCIETY AND LYCEUMS

The neglect of literary pursuits in New Orleans during the early nineteenth century was deplored and censured by many of the travellers who visited the city at this time. They attributed that lack to the insatiable lust for wealth of the Anglo-Americans and the ardent passion for pleasure by the Creoles and the French.

For many years there were no public libraries in the City, but there were many private ones and many of its citizens of both nationalities enjoyed the pursuit of literature.

It was only when men of culture and education and men of the learned professions made New Orleans their permanent domicile that any thought of improving the general culture arose. As early as the Twenties, efforts were made to establish libraries and reading rooms and to organize lyceums and other cultural societies, but these were of short duration. Because of lack of interest they were soon abandoned. It was not until the late Thirties that real interest was manifested in these endeavors.

The following notice was published in the *Louisiana Gazette* of January 13, 1820:

> Notice is given to the share holders of the Library Society that the annual election of eleven directors thereof will take place in the Library room in the Government House, the 17th of January 1820, at 10 O'clock A. M. to 3 P. M.
>
> By Order of the Board of Directors
> J. B. Desdunes Secretary.

The same paper of February 12, 1824, mentioned a "Youth's Free Grecian Library", of which Judge Workman, Alfred Hennen and Dr. Davidson were the trustees, and that Colonel Starrett had presented to the Library one hundred volumes.

In that same year the Society Library was founded and Bellanger Desboullets was the Treasurer and Librarian. At the same time we read of the Touro Free Library at the Presbyterian Church. The directors were John Workman, Beverly Chew, Peter Laidlow, William Rose, Thos. B. Servass, Richard Davidson, Joseph Thomas, Maunsel White and J. A. Maybin.

In that same year the News and Reading Rooms were opened at No. 7 Camp Street. The fees were $1.00 per month, 50 cents per week.

The *Courier* of April 2, 1828 carried the following notice:

> The subscribers for the New Orleans Law Library will assemble at the Court Room of the Parish Court of the Parish of New Orleans, on Wednesday next for the purpose of choosing five directors for that institution.
>
> James Workman,
> On the part of the Commissioners

In the French section of the *Courier* of September 20, 1828, there is an article entitled "New Orleans Library," which said:

> Since the establishment of the New Orleans Public Library, this establishment was maintained with a great deal of difficulty because of the scantiness of its revenues. It was able to sustain itself because the hall it occupied in the Government House was rent free, and with the revenue from two small buildings accorded to it by the Legislature. The fire which destroyed these buildings not only deprived the library of some of its revenues, but destroyed a portion of its books.
>
> Must such an eminent and useful establishment so favorable to the propagation of learning, so necessary, it may be said, in a population as divided as this one. Shall New Orleans be the only large city in the Union without a library accessible to all those who wish learning or in search of pleasure, May God please that such a reproach will never be made to the Citizens of this city.
>
> About twenty five hundred volumes were snatched from the flames. Many excellent works are still complete and with some effort this institution can still be saved from total ruin.
>
> The first thing is to collect the dues in order to pay a debt of about $500.00. The new location of the Library will be on Chartres Street above the auction room of Mr. Le Carpentier. As in the past, books as well as money will be accepted as dues.
>
> The undersigned directors will spare no pains, not only to prevent its dissolution, but to make it more prosperous.

The officers were: J. Pitot, President; P. Derbigny, J. H. Holland, J. Chabaud, J. B. Manseau, Directors; Edward Louvet, Secretary.

In 1831, the City Council appropriated $500.00 to the Commercial Library of which S. V. Sickles was the president and Alfred Malard the Secretary.

The *Courier* carried the following announcement:

Commercial Library Society: Room above Wm. C. Norris Clothing Store, situated No. 38 Chartres St., and the same entrance as that of the *Louisiana Advertiser* in Customhouse St. Shelves, tables, lamps and all other articles necessary for the furniture of the library and reading room obtained. Now ready for books promised: Members entitled to introduce a stranger in the library.

On the table different papers of the City and best periodicals of the north.

Signed: A. Malard, Sec.

On July 25th, the library was opened for the circulation of books. The initiation fee was $5.00 and the annual dues the same. It was open every evening excepting Sundays.

"Henceforth the reading room of the Commercial Library is to be opened on Sundays," wrote the *Courier* in its edition of May 17, 1832:

The religious scruples of the Majority of the Directors, it appears, yielded to the conviction that they would rather be performing a laudable act in throwing open the doors of the institution on the Sabbath than violating the laws of God. Thus another resort is offered to the young man where he cannot be reached by the demoralizing example of the many who have selected that sacred day of rest as a time of dissipation and debauchery.

The churches are open, but for an hour or two and these once closed, the young clerk, fatigued with the labors of the week has heretofore had no other place to go, wherein he could meet with and enjoy the company of friends, than to coffee houses or the lake, where all the temptations that can be rendered to draw him from the practice of virtue are displayed in an innocent and attractive shape.

The *Bee* on October 18, 1837, stated that the Commercial Library had 5000 volumes and that it had achieved that size without municipal aid, that it "possessed no banking privilege", that it had no source of profit to enrich it and that it "depends upon support it meets with among the citizens in general".

The same journal of December 4th of that year reported the 6th annual meeting of the Library, and stated that there was strong opposition against the board. It said further: "This inveterate enmity is the more surprising when it is remembered that under the control of the present directors the affairs of the library have been ably managed and that amid the monetary embarrassments which distracts the community the institution has been maintain-

View of Place d'Armes — now called Jackson Square — about the year 1820. (Courtesy Howard-Tilton Library)

View of Public Square — now Jackson Square — 1836. (From an old print)

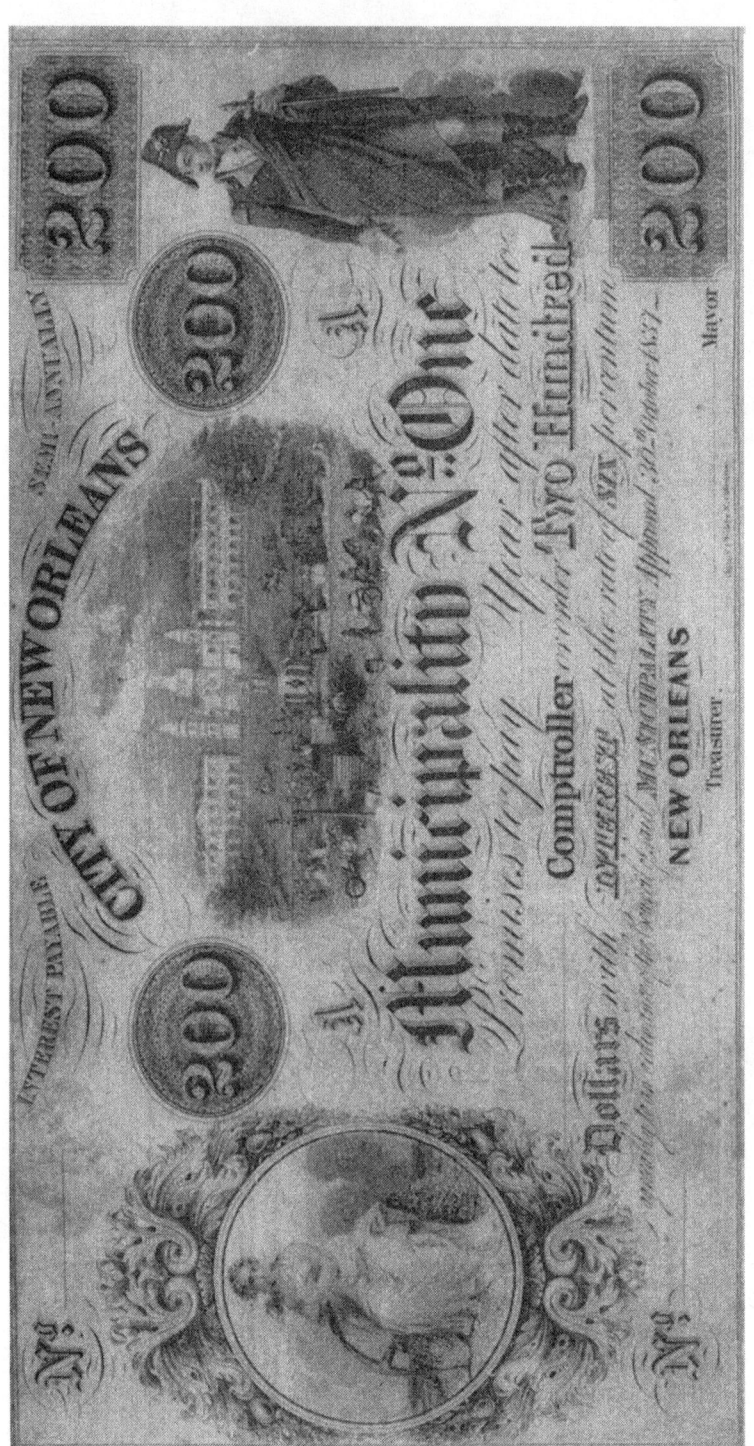

Reproduction of $200.00 bond issued in October, 1837 by the First Municipality of New Orleans. Actual size. (Collection of Stuart O. Landry)

ed in a position of comparative serenity; that at least one half of the present board consists of the original founders; that their interest was never flagged." The cause of the disagreement was the contemplated discharge of the librarian. The *Bee* wrote that "it will be found the Board was perfectly justifiable in the proposed ejection. Mr. Jore was guilty of dereliction of duty in various ways — 1st, in absenting himself from the rooms when they were visited by different members of the board; next, by numerous advertisements and notices without notice of the board and written in a style of grammatical inaccuracy and bombastic pedantry which only drew down public ridicule upon the institution. When resolutions were passed demanding punctual attendance at the library, except at meal hours, and on occasion of indispensable business, this gentleman became highly incensed and used impertinent and unjustifiable words to the Secretary. So he was discharged and the board was named tyrants."

James Stuart, who visited New Orleans in 1830, mentions in his book that a Miss Carrol had a public reading room conducted on a small scale, consisting of American and British reviews. Quoting him: "She had only fifty subscribers, so she could not afford a daily British newspaper, so got the *Scotchman* as the best of the twice-a-week papers. An advertisement in the New Orleans papers stated that the present indifference to her establishment discourages the ardent hopes of success cherished by the proprietor, who was faltered into the belief that the City of New Orleans was more than ripe for some species of common resort for useful information and regional entertainment."

Three years afterwards, an ad in the papers announced the auction of the books of Miss Carrol (then deceased) together with those of Reverend J. F. Hull and Reverend C. Leiris. "Such an extensive collection of books was never offered before in this city."

At the end of the year 1831, a meeting was held at the Commercial Library for the purpose of organizing a Lyceum. J. A. Maybin presided, and L. C. Duncan Esq., the Secretary, presented the following resolution:

> Resolved, that a committee of six, including the Chairman, be appointed to report upon the expediency of establishing a Lyceum in this City, on a plan similar to those now in successful operation in various parts of the United States.

Early in January, a constitution was submitted by Mr. Agnew and a committee of five was appointed to draft the By-Laws. The following officers were elected: J. A. Maybin, President; L. C. Cannon, Secretary.

Agnew, Evans and De la Plaine, were appointed a committee to "confer with the Commercial Law Ass'n on the expediency of uniting that Association with the Lyceum".

On January 25, Maybin delivered the inaugural address at the Presbyterian Church.

The *Bee* on November 30, 1835, wrote that the Lyceum was established in 1831 and was chartered in 1833: "but suspended in its operation since that time". The article said that it was likely to be reestablished and that at a meeting on the "last Saturday at the chambers of Mr. Maybin, the President of the Lyceum, additional members were enrolled".

The active members were Henry F. Leonard, Seth Barton, Esq. Winthrop, Jordon, Nixon and Pepin. It expressed the hope that "the Lyceum may be the nucleus of a Louisiana Institute to which the Physical and the Historical Societies, the former in suspension and the latter in embryo — might be attached, if our citizens evinced proper energy. But our literary gentlemen of the legal and medical professions must evidence more zeal and liberality in the cause of literature in order to succeed."

The dues of the Lyceum were $5.00 per year.

In 1836 the Lyceum was active and many literary meetings were held at Lyceum Hall, No. 41 Royal Street. The first was an address by Seth Barton, followed by a debate by Messrs. Hennen, Lucius Duncan, Barton and Maybin on the subject, "Should Capital Punishment be Abolished in Cases of Criminal Jurisprudence."

On another occasion Mr. Wharton delivered a good-natured lecture on the "Mental Incapacity of Women" which was followed by a debate. At a following meeting, Lucius Duncan lectured on the "Romance of American History".

At one of its weekly meetings the subject of "phrenology" was debated by Messrs. Winthrop, Leonard, Johnson, Barton and Andrews. The subject discussed attested the erudition of the speakers.

It is unfortunate that these lectures given at the Lyceum were lost, for had they been preserved they would have been a valuable contribution to the literature of the City.

On May 13, 1835, the *Bee* published an editorial on the "Historical Society of Louisiana":

> On last Saturday, many respectable literary gentlemen of This City assembled at the Supreme Court Room for the purpose of organizing a Historical Society of this State; the Hon. Henry Bullard was called to the chair and J. Burton Harrison, Esq. was appointed Secretary to the meeting.
>
> Resolutions were passed establishing the Society and defining its objects — research into the history of this part of North America under the aborigines, the Spaniards and the French.
>
> A committee was also appointed consisting of the honorable Alexander Porter and Henry Bullard and J. B. Harrison; With the instruction to report a project of a constitution for the society to be presented to an annual meeting convened for the 2nd of January next, — when it is intended to complete the the organization of the institution.
>
> The Secretary was directed to correspond with literary gentlemen in different parts of the State; the members engaged themselves to commence immediately an investigation of such subjects within the scope of the society, as they can compass during the summer; and Judge Bullard was requested to prepare and deliver a discourse at the first annual meeting.

The editorial further commented that "the literature of Louisiana has been too long and supinely neglected; but under auspices like those of this society, we have reason to hope that stigma will be effaced. Most of the eastern states have their historical societies which have elucidated in a material degree and in an authentic manner the annals of their respective localities and predecessors; and many of their works are deposited in the archives of the National or Congress Library".

On June 10, 1835, the *Bee* deplored the lack of interest given to literary pursuits by the more cultured members of the community, it lamented that "it may be true though trite to say that there is no city in the United States of similar magnitude and having similar resources where public education is so neglected as in New Orleans. Literature in general is at its lowest ebb and science and the fine arts have not as yet dared to make their appearance among us." It deplored the fact that "not one literary society has yet been organized; there are no literary meetings, no literary parties. There is not a single lyceum or public library of repute for higher classes of intellect, and a correct idea may be formed of the intellectual pretentions of our Legislators when it is known that there are only about twenty volumes in the library of the State Legislature and that these are chiefly copies of the legislative codes, enactments and proceedings. Yet even these volumes are not known to more than a dozen members, were not consulted by more than a half dozen members during the past session, and when a motion was first made to appoint a joint library committee, most of our legislators looked astonished and amused at the proposal".

The article enumerated the gratifying changes which had taken place in the past six months. It noted that a historical society was projected under the auspices of Judges Porter and Bullard, a medical school was then partly in operation under the superintendence of efficient physicians and that the Medical Society of New Orleans had been chartered, the Colleges of Jefferson and Jackson "whose objects approximate those of Universities, were established and that Franklin College would soon open its doors".

The editorial complained that "commercial transactions are indeed the prime objects of all our citizens not of the learned professions; and these have hitherto been so disunited among themselves as to be rather adverse to any combined plan of amelioration, for there is not one law library among us; and we all know too truly that there is not one library of any nature patronized by the professors of law, physics and divinity. The vacuum of professional leisure is therefore whiled away in idle gossiping or public carousing at balls, hotels and theaters — and too often and fatally, at banking games."

Again the *Bee* returned to the charge with a polemic in its issue of November 13, 1835, which because of its most interesting appraisal of a lack of literary pursuits at that time, must be quoted in full:

> We have occasionally lamented the deficiency of support for literature and the fine arts in Louisiana, not for the purpose of censuring the good people of the State, but for stimulating them to honorable exertions in so noble a cause.
>
> There is not a literary lyceum or society in New Orleans, nor is there any public or subscription library except upon a small scale for the benefit of the spirited and generous accountants — originated and maintained by themselves. They should enlarge their objects; and have a Lyseum attached to their institution as in the Atlantic Cities.
>
> Doubtless the deficiency arises from the all engrossing pur-

suits of trade and commerce. Yet as soon as our merchants are well informed, even on general topics — and as there are many members of the legal and medical profession among us who may wonder that there is not one law library nor one medical library in the City or State; not one library of a general nature.

Merchants are engrossed with their pursuits from morning to night, and their leisure moments are devoted to bar-rooms or theaters, or such places, and attorneys and physicians follow suit. Yet many of the latter possess considerable talent in their profession; but there it is concentrated and is restricted generally to their immediate practice.

We are not aware that an attorney of Louisiana ever wrote a general work on law or jurisprudence; and we believe that all their efforts have been confined to forming digests of statutory enactments or judicial decisions. And as for physicians, they will not write nor has the public any means to judge their attainments, but by their individual practice. Dr. Barton is, we believe, the only exception of older physicians, there are no statistical data preserved of the mortality, diseases, meteorology, nor of any scientific reminiscenses of Louisiana, the past few years, from personal observation.

With regard to the history of the State as preserved, it is a heterogenous mass of meagerness and wholly dependent on persons not born in the State; and but adventitiously attached. No Louisianian has taken the trouble to compile a history of the State; for the historical history of Gayarré is but a work for the schools and is chiefly an abstract of Martin's history. This latter is the only one of its kind in the English language; and who diligently digested from the French works on the colony of Louisiana. It is very inelegantly written and anomalous and defective in many respects. Yet Louisianians were indebted to a stranger for even its history. It is indeed time that a Historical Society of Louisiana has been projected, under the auspices of a young Virginian; but it is not yet organized and from the apathy of Louisianians to literary pursuits, may not for sometime.

Nor is the encouragement given to literary works of any kind very extensive. It is true that a few citizens subscribe for the Boston and Philadelphia reviews; and some for the *New York Albion* and *Mirror;* but scarcely beyond them does their generosity of knowledge extend — although some citizens from the Atlantic States may possibly subscribe for some periodical published in their former state or city. But no citizen of Louisiana, except by passing strangers, Darby and Breckenridge, have favored the public with what they learned of the State during a transient residence there; as did Charlevoix, LaHarpe and Ulloa before them. But strangers have been our historical and statistical writers.

Mr. Slidell, one of our citizens, now in the United States Army, has indeed written some works; but he is a star shining; one of the literary firmament of Louisiana, yet even his works are scarcely known here; and we have often in vain sought a copy of them.

There was an attempt made to get up a literary paper in this City; for the voluntary and eleemosynary contributions of our supposed literati, but the means employed produced its failure, and having dragged its existence through a year, almost unnoticed and unknown, the *Louisiana Recorder* is now on the eve of giving up the ghost.

It is unfortunately true that better prospects illuminate the horizon. A medical school has been established; it is likely that the Legislature will erect and endorse an university for the State: and that the increased number of citizens from other states will create a spirit of literary competition as well as of mercantile.

It is probable that the critical and unfair estimate of Martin and Gayarré, may have been inspired by the prejudices then existing between the two factions.

Xavier Martin was born in Marseilles, France in 1762, and became a newspaper man, a lawyer and a writer of laws. He emigrated to America as a young man, studied law in North Carolina and was admitted to the bar there in 1789. On the 21st of March 1810, he was appointed to the bench of the Superior Court of the Territory of Louisiana. His history was published in 1827.

Charles Gayarré, a Creole of Spanish and French descent, was born in New Orleans on January 6, 1805. He was a graduate of the College of Orleans, studied law in Philadelphia and was admitted to the bar of Pennsylvania. In New Orleans he became a member of the State Legislature, a Judge and a United States Senator, from which high honor he resigned on account of illness. He was later appointed Secretary of State by Gov. Johnson. Gayarré's first history, published in 1830, was written in French, his later historical work was in the English language.

Both historians were brilliant and served their State and City. They are to this day considered, and rightly so, not only the most illustrious, but the most authoritative historians of Louisiana, and their works are the bases for all such future historical efforts.

With that exception, what the *Bee* wrote was true, and without doubt was a much needed stimulant for greater literary efforts in New Orleans.

CHAPTER XIX

ORPHANS AND ORPHANAGES

It would seem that in a city which had such a high death rate the number of orphans would be tremendously great. However, that was not the case, because the majority of the thousands of victims of the epidemics were bachelors and the few who were married did not bring their families to expose them to the perils of a long and tedious voyage or to the dangers from disease in an unhealthy city. As a large number of the Creole families were interrelated and devoted to one another, they would, sometimes at a great sacrifices, adopt the orphans of their relatives and friends. As far as they were concerned, the orphanage problem was not pressing. There were, however, orphans who demanded the care of the community, especially after the catastrophy of 1832.

The Ursuline nuns were the first to provide an asylum for orphans. This they did to their utmost ability for nearly a century despite scant means and public apathy. For some reason or other that orphanage attracted the attention of the City Administration for on October 13, 1824, it adopted the following resolution:

> Mr. Girod stated that the orphan girls, whose board the corporation pays to the nunnery, were not treated in a proper manner and moved that the council adopt the necessary measure to withdraw said orphans and place them in the Poydras Asylum.

Davezac moved the appointment of a committee to inquire: first, in what manner the nuns treated the orphan girls entrusted to their care; second, whether the nuns on leaving the city had provided for the establishment of a school in town for the day scholars and finally, for what reason they hitherto never acquainted the Mayor with the choice of the girls destined to fill the vacancies happening among the girls whom the corporation places in the convent.

Davezac, Girod and Wiltz, who constituted the committee, made the following report:

> Gentlemen: Saw the girls at Ursulines Convent: Shown by the Mother Superior — only 14: — The others not yet repaired there on account of the removal of the convent. More

than ½ barefooted — dress very much neglected — Upon your committee observing that at this season of the year shoes were necessary to the preservation of health, or required by decency in a country where the want of them is in some manner one of the signs of slavery, the Mother Superior observed that they had all got shoes and that it was of their own choice not to use them, and, in fact, having been ordered to go and put on their shoes, they soon came back with shoes on, the greatest part of which were quite new.

Two ladies of the convent presided at the classes. One for French and the other for English: Education is not neglected. Taught — reading, writing and arithmetic. Two girls read with facility and correctness.

Asked about plans concerning the day school in town, she replied that the convent, having disposed in favor of the episcopal seat of their property, they thought themselves dispensed with continuing the establishment, but that they would receive with pleasure in their own dwelling place some of the young girls as would call there for the purpose of being instructed in reading and writing.

Food for the children consisted of: for breakfast, Indian corn boiled with salt; dinner, bread and boiled beef; supper, bread and sometimes butter. Change of clothes only once a week, even in the summer. They carry on the table the food of the boarders, in fact, perform all menial work.

There exists between the boarders and the orphans a difference of dress, food, education and occupation, no doubt necessary but which tends to degrade those unfortunates in their own eyes by subjecting them to continual humiliation.

At the following meeting of the Council, Mr. Davezac moved the withdrawal of orphan girls from the Ursuline Convent to the Poydras Asylum under the following conditions:

The Mayor shall pay the directors yearly $1600.00—payable quarterly—for 24 orphan girls—or fraction thereof. They must be taught French and English,—etc., as well as the elements of their respective religion. And that a standing committee be appointed to visit the girls from time to time.

Julien Poydras, a native of France, was an old resident of Louisiana who began his career as a peddler and who soon amassed a large fortune. He was a man of distinction, a merchant, planter, poet, statesman, philanthropist and a patriot. He founded and endowed a girls' orphanage which bore the name of Poydras Orphan Asylum.

Governor Robertson, in his message to the Legislature in 1824, stated:

The Charity Hospital and the Poydras Asylum continued to receive the previous attention of their benevolent directors: These institutions, particularly the last, has been liberally endowed by munificient patrons, whilst that for the relief of destute orphan boys having no reliance but upon the donations of philantrophistic individuals, must, without the aid of Government, remain for a long time incapable of rescuing from destruction this interesting portion of the rising hope of the republic.

In some circumstances such institutions may be prejudicial, in others of doubtful utility; but here in New Orleans, from the greater number of strangers overtaken by disease and death, leaving their helpless offspring to be brought up in misery and vice, or to perish from neglect and want, they may be considered as indispensable. It is a proud boast of Louisiana, so far as public charity is a virtue, that she clothes and feeds more naked and hungry foreigners in proportion to her population than any other country in the world.

Among more than one thousand individuals thus annually supported, there are not to be found thirty citizens and inhabitants of the state.

That same year the Council Committee reported that there were fifty-six girls varying in age from five to fifteen years, and that they were "united in one class". They were instructed in reading, writing and arithmetic, and that they were taught only English. They were nearly all well and cleanly dressed: "There was no elegance about them, but every thing was indicative of care and cleanliness."

Protestants were instructed in their religion and Catholics attended their church every Sunday and that "equality there reigns".

Their table is simple like their dress but their food is such as to satisfy the taste of their age and variated so to avoid disgust. All are in good health. Exemption from none of the domestic occupations and labor but they are all equally subjected to it.

Again the Governor's message to the Legislature in January, 1826 mentioned that "the Poydras Orphan Asylum which is now managed by a few ladies of high respectability and signal benevolence, has been endowed by its generous patron whose name it bears and who will ever be in grateful remembrance. It now contains ninety girls which are as many as the present building can conveniently accommodate. The increasing number of the orphans demands an augmentation of room in the Asylum, and to this end further Legislative aid will be required."

The joint committee appointed to visit the Poydras Asylum and the orphanage for destitute boys, reported to the Legislature on January 30, 1826, that the number of orphans had greatly increased and that they numbered one hundred. The total receipts were $6,029.00 of which $3,000.00 was appropriated by the state. The total expenditures were $4,898.00, which left a balance of $1,131.00. The committee reported that the sum donated was too small to build the necessary buildings.

In 1835, the Legislative Committee expressed their praise for the Sisters of Charity. The total receipt was $13,200.00, of which the State contributed $6,000.00 and the City $1,600.00.

An Editorial in the *Bee* of June 25, 1835, commended the Poydras Female Asylum as "an interesting institution". It reported that the orphanage was in the charge of eight Sisters of Charity who administered to about 106 children, that the dormatories were comfortable and well ventilated, but that they were not large enough and that the infirmary was too small and that the patients were compelled to sleep two in a bed.

On Sunday night, April 4, 1824, a meeting was held at the Presbyterian Church for the purpose of establishing a boys orphan asylum. Mr. Wm. Robert presided and S. Bretton Bennett was the secretary. The committee was composed of Gov. Robertson, Roffignac, Rev. Antoine, Rev. Mr. Hull, Dr. Gallegher, Gen. Labatut, Xenon Cavelier, Richard Relf and Peter Laidlow.

The first officers of the Asylum were James Workman, President; P. Laidlow, Treasurer; and A. Perlee, Secretary.

The property of S. Livermore, situated in the Fauburg Lafayette, was purchased, repaired and converted for the purpose intended. It was occupied in the following December. In the meanwhile, temporary provisions were made to place the orphans in the care of Mrs. Berton at No. 515 Tchoupitoulas Street, where six boys between the ages of five to thirteen were boarded free, clad and educated.

The necessary funds for maintenance of the home and for the care of the inmates were provided by private subscriptions. The Mayor was only authorized to subscribe $1,000.00 and to pay $8.00 per month for each boy in the institution.

The Governor in his Legislative message of January 1826, said:

> A number of gentlemen of this city of worth, who associated themselves for the purpose of establishing an Asylum for the re-

ception of destitute orphan boys, now have the gratification of seeing the institution in successful operation. They have obtained a valuable lot of ground and erected suitable buildings and have already received upwards of 40 interesting children, who were thrown hopeless and forlorn upon the world. These gentlemen not only devote much of their time but have also contributed largely to it in a pecuniary point of view. The debts due by this institution for its land and building may render some further aid expedient.

The orphanage was soon destitute of funds and more appeals to the public were made. The response was spontaneous. Collections were made in the churches, entertainments were given in its behalf, subscriptions were solicited and the Legislature was appealed to for more help. But as one of the papers expressed it "the graves of the strangers are here seen in exuberant abundance. The malady of our sickly season sweeps away the natural prop of the orphan and the object of all his youthful affection".

In 1825, the directors of the orphanage were James Workman, J. B. Labatut, Peter Laidlow, Geo. W. Morgan, Beverly Chew, Wm. Christy, L. Nicholson, and A. Perlee. The following year an appeal was made to the Legislature for more funds, and it was stated that there were forty-one inmates, "all kept in the best possible order. They receive an education, the expenses have exceeded the income and the need for more money is great".

Entertainments were given to provide the necessary funds. On June 15, 1826, a society of French and Creole amateurs performed on the boards of the Orleans Theater for the benefit of the Asylum. The following year J. Davis, the impresario of the same theater, presented the opera "Cendrilion" free of charge and expense. The total receipts amounted $1,000.00. On May 12, 1829, Edwin Forest gave a benefit performance which netted $1,300.00. In 1832, an amateur theatrical show given at the American Theater, grossed $1,028.00, from which was deducted $14.00 for printing and $300.00 for rent of the hall. There were many more benefit performances, both amateur and professional, which contributed greatly to the maintenance of the institution.

On November 24, 1832, a few days after the terrific catastrophy which annihilated one-sixth of the population in about ten days, Lucius C. Duncan ,the Secertary of the Asylum, made the following report:

> During the past season and autumn, the institution has not been visited by the pestilence which walketh in darkness and

wasteth at noonday, — although disasters and death in every form have entered almost every house in our devastated city and suburbs.

To the unremitted attention, day and night, on the part of the attending physician and of an efficient superintendent, to the health of the children and to the general comfort, cleanliness and convenience of the institution, more perhaps in a great measure, be ascribed their almost miraculous exemption from either of the epidemic diseases which has so fearfully and so fatally raged among us.

The number of inmates has increased and will, no doubt, shortly still further increase in a proportion quite equal to the extent of the mortality among those unfortunate classes whose claim upon the society are most urgent and most frequent.

There are ninety-five boys in that Asylum; thirty-one were admitted since August 4 last: Twenty-two during the present month: and all of this number the Board deems it neither improper nor disrespectful to their Hibernian friends and patrons and remind them that a very large proportion are native or the offsprings of native of the Emerald Isle.

The unexpected addition to their numbers has called for the erection of a new building to serve as a school and which the Board, relying upon the liberality of their fellow citizens, have determined to erect, though on their own responsibility.

The most generous benefactor was John Hogan who, in December 1834, after selling his land for a hotel to be built on St. Charles and Common, made the munificent donation of $6,000.00.

Chairman Beauvais of the Committee on Boys and Girls Orphan Asylums, in March, 1834, reported as follows to the Legislature:

We have visited the Male Orphan Asylum and cannot too highly commend the manner in which it is conducted and the great and praise-worthy attention of the gentlemen under whose direction it is conducted.

It appears from the report of the Directors herewith submitted, that they received 319 orphans of whom 48 have died, 65 have been placed out to learn different trades and professions, 119 have been reclaimed by their friends, leaving in the asylum 87.

During the year many of these unfortunates were received while ill of the prevailing epidemic and this fact accounts for the number of the deaths.

The means of the Asylum are derived from the following sources: Voluntary contributions and annual appropriation from the state and city: The Committee suggested an increase in appropriation for the funds are always exhausted. While at the same time, the directors and the attending physicians devote a great part of their time to the institution without any other compensation than that flowing from their own reflections of time spent in the cause of humanity, nor do they wish any other compensation.

Recommends: Granting the Male Orphan Asylum the further annual appropriation of $2,500.00 for the period of ten years.

In 1835, the Board adopted the following rules for the admittance and discharge of the orphans. No child was to be admitted unless weaned or over six years of age. "That none to be admitted in the institution having any relations able to provide for them, and they should not be kept past the fourteenth year. When a boy reached fourteen years of age, if not apprenticed, he should be given a certain sum and allowed to provide for himself. No single director should be allowed to admit a child and none received on the recommendation of any, without a certificate of destitution."

On March 11, 1837, the Journal of the Senate published the joint report of the two chambers on the condition of the Catholic Orphan Boys Asylum. It found the "Institution is a most flourishing condition that the limited nature of its means and resources will admit of," and that it was well conducted. One hundred and forty-three boys were received in the institution and at the time of the inspection there were eighty-seven. The Committee recommended an appropriation. It was signed by Jos. E. Johnson, Chairman of the Senate Committee and by Geo. K. Rogers, Chairman of the House.

The State Legislature was more liberal in proffering the much needed financial assistance than the City Administration, which was reluctant to extend to the Asylum any monetary relief. This is attested to in a communication published in the *Bee* on June 27, 1837, which reads as follows:

> We have been witnesses of the philanthrophy and humane exertions of Dr. Kindelon, a gentleman whose liberality and intelligence is known and appreciated throughout the whole city, in behalf of the interesting institution which is under his control and for whose advancement he has labored with an ardor that partakes eminently of the divine religion of which he is one of the most humble followers. It was therefore with regret that we saw the Mayor place his veto upon the resolution presented by Edward Duplessis which was conceived in a spirit of noble benevolence and designed to extend and promote one of the most useful charities that our city could boast.

It further stated that Mayor Prieur acted "with the best intention, thanks, however, to the perseverance of our estimable citizen, Gallien Preval, it has received help".

On October 17, 1837, the Council of the First Municipality passed a resolution directing its members to wear crepe on the left arm during thirty days as a token of respect to the memory of Rev. Father Adam Kindelon, "on account of his public philantrophy, long and unremittently exerted."

Today little is known about Father Adam Kindelon. He has not achieved fame. There is not an orphange which bears his name. No street was named in his honor, no great seat of learning bears his name, no monument was erected to perpetuate his memory and he has been ignored by historians, yet he was one of the great philanthrophists of New Orleans.

The urgent need for a foundling asylum was stressed in an editorial which appeared in the *Bee* on April 6, 1837. It was the first public appeal made to arouse the attention of the community to that most important and needed charity. It said:

> The infanticides which have so recently been committed in our city are calculated to arouse all our feelings of horror and pity and admonish us of a fatal increase.
>
> We must then penetrate higher into the mystery of infanticide, and although it is in the relaxation of morals that we are to find the cause that so many creatures are cast upon the world, it must be borne in mind that libertinage in its fatal course does not always leave its offspring without succor, for be it spoken to the credit of humanity most of the wretches who yield themselves up to prostitution recoil with horror from assassinating the fruits of their debauchery, but if there is an asylum the wretched mother will see herself no longer self-condemned to eternal remorse, and whatever may be the rigor by those by whom she is surrounded, she will feel there is less risk for her reputation in depositing her child in the asylum.

It will thus be seen that New Orleans was responsive to its obligations relative to the sick, the orphans and the dead. The city did everything in its power, under the most trying circumstances, not only to alleviate suffering, but to comfort unfortunates. Despite the obloquious comments by irresponsible, or it may even be said malicious reports of supposedly on-the-scene reporters, diarists and chroniclers at that time, the humaneness, the charity and the benevolence of the people of New Orleans were never equalled, much less surpassed by other communities in the Union.

CHAPTER XX

THE HETEROGENEOUS POPULATION OF NEW ORLEANS

The first hundred years of the history of New Orleans comprehends all the hardships that humanity can endure. The record of those years is an epic of courage, perseverance, endurance and an inflexible determination, which today challenges the wildest flight of the imagination. Nowhere else and at no other time, has the apothegm "survival of the fittest" been better exemplified. Despite sickness and pestilence, the excessively high death rate, the insalubrity of the climate and two devastating conflagrations, these pioneers never faltered, but with abounding faith in the future greatness of New Orleans, labored, suffered and died to attain their purpose. Withal they maintained their dignity, established a culture of their own, and the elegance and charm of their society attracted the admiration of many contemporary European writers.

During the colonial period, both French and Spanish, the growth of New Orleans was slow. The grandiose promotive scheme of John Law to colonize Louisiana had crashed and the impact had impoverished France.

Guy Soniat DuFossat reported that the John Law concession had shipped 6000 Germans to settle Louisiana. This number is verified by Hanno Deiler, who further observed that he had come to the conclusion "that of those 6000 Germans who left Europe for Louisiana, only about one-third, 2000, actually reached the shores of the colony. By this I do not mean to say that 2000 settled in Louisiana, but only that 2000 reached the shores and were disembarked in Biloxi and upon Dauphine Island, in the harbor of Mobile." Again the same author gives us a vivid picture of the suffering of these immigrants on that inhospitable shore. He wrote:

> Those poor immigrants were put on a land where there was more or less a famine, sometimes even starvation, and where the provisions which the concessioners had brought with them to feed their own engagés were taken from the ships by force to feed the soldiers, and the immigrants were told to subsist on what they might be able to catch on the beach, standing for the most part of the day in the salt water up to the waist — crabs, oysters and the like — and on the corn which the Biloxi, the Pas-

cagoula, the Choctaw, and the Mobile Indians might let them have.

Many of those who had survived the perils of a long sea voyage succumbed to diseases, exhaustion and starvation. The survivors went to the concessions granted them on the lower Arkansas River. Not succeeding there they later migrated to the German Coast, on the Mississippi river, a short distance above the city, and others became residents of New Orleans.

It is not within the scope of this work to delve deeply into the history of that period for that would necessitate the writing of another volume. It is only mentioned because these French and German emigrants were the first settlers of New Orleans. The city was founded by Canadian explorers with the help of French and German emigrants. The latter soon lost their Teutonic characteristics, in a short while they abandoned their native tongue and adopted the Gallic idiom. Even their names took a French pronunciation, which they have retained to this day. They intermarried with the French, and they soon forgot that they were of German origin. They are numbered among the Creoles of Louisiana.

In the early part of the present century at a meeting of the Louisiana Historical Society, Deiler electrified the assembly by categorically asserting that a large number of the Creoles of Louisiana were of German origin. That statement met with the disbelief, ridicule and even the enmity of many of the prominent Creoles in the audience. After the uproar had subsided he turned to his fellow historian Alcée Fortier and told him that he also had Germanic blood flowing in his veins. This Fortier vigorously denied. Whereupon Deiler produced documentary evidence proving beyond doubt that he was a member of the Labranche family and that they were originally Germans. In his relentless search of old documents he had discovered that the name of Labranche was originally Zwieg, and that John Zweig was one of the earliest German colonists in Louisiana. When asked his name by a French official he was questioned as to its meaning. He answered "a branch," whereupon he was told his name was Labranche, and it has remained thus ever since. Professor Fortier was still skeptical, and it was not until Charles Soniat, a prominent lawyer of that time, and a historian in his own right, and himself a member of the Labranche family, vouched for the authenticity of the archive and that Deiler's assertion was correct. The Labranche family was one of the most distinguished in Creole society. Deiler recounted this anecdote to the author, and stated that he considered it one of his greatest triumphs. This was the first fusion of nationalities in Louisiana.

Fifty-one years after its founding, the census of 1769 gave New Orleans a population of 3190 whites and 1265 slaves. Thirty years later during the Spanish domination it had increased to 5556 whites, of whom 3268 were males and 2288 females, an increase of 2466 or approximately 80 a year. At the time of the purchase its population was estimated to have been 8000 whites and blacks and that there were 1000 dwellings. Seven years afterwards, the census of 1810 showed a substantial growth for it recorded 17,224, of whom 6316 were whites and 10,911 were Negroes. It must be noted that the number of slaves and free-persons-of-color exceeded the whites by 3595. W. B. Warden, the American Consul at Paris, compiled the population of New Orleans for 1810 according to sex, age and color, as follows:

White males less than 10 years	697
White females less than 10 years	726
White males from 10 to 16 years	347
White females from 10 to 16 years	416
White males from 16 to 26 years	477
White females from 16 to 26 years	517
White males from 26 to 46 years	1315
White females from 26 to 46 years	709
White males from 46 and over	750
White females 46 and over	377
All other free persons, Indians excepted	4950
Slaves	5961

The first mass emigration took place in 1804, following the Negro uprising in San Domingo. M. Barbé Marbois wrote that "the executions of the whites began at the Cayes in February 1804, and continued from town to town to the Cape, where it redoubled in fury. The massacre lasted from the end of April to the 14th of May. Neither age or sex were spared and outrages against sex preceded death. The vicitms numbered 2,420." They sought refuge in the neighboring island of Cuba, where instead of finding a haven of hospitality, because of the hostilities then existing between France and Spain, they were objects of suspicion and hatred, and were forced to seek asylum in Louisiana. From May 19th to July 18th, 34 vessels sailed from Cuba for New Orleans with 5797 refugees, of whom 1828 were white, 1978 free black or colored persons and 1991 slaves. Because of their impoverishment, for they were only able to escape with their lives, a few faithful slaves and whatever property they were able to salvage from the ruins of their opulent estates, they were received with distrust by a large number of the population because of the fear that they would become a burden on the community, but this apprehension was of short duration. A large number of these St. Domingans became solid citizens and contributed greatly to the culture of the city.

The unrest in Europe during the years 1814 and 1815 forced many individuals to flee from their homes to seek refuge from political persecution, and many others to recoup their fortunes in more propitious climes. They emigrated to America and not a few of them landed in New Orleans.

In 1820, the population had increased to 25,214, of which 13,314 were whites—8000 were males and 5314 females—2900 free persons of color, 2400 males and 500 females; and 7500 slaves of whom 3000, were males and 4500 females. And in the parish of Orleans there were 14,391 inhabitants, of whom 3,576 were white males and 2,251 white females, 49 foreigners not registered, free persons of color, males 403, females 421, and slaves, 4622 males and 2969 females, for a total of 14,391.

Josiah Condon in 1826 estimated the population of New Orleans to be 39,350 and classified it as follows:

	Males	Females	Total
Whites	14,500	7,500	22,000
Free color	3,600	800	4,490
Slaves	5,500	6,300	11,800
Foreigners			1,300

The aggression and conquest of the West Indies, especially of Jamaica and Guadalupe, incited many of their French settlers to flee from the yoke of their hated enemy, and many of them sought refuge in the more congenial city of New Orleans.

A few years previous to, and in the beginning of the nineteenth century, the vast territory west of the Allegheny mountains and bordering the Mississippi river and its tributaries was wild and sparsely settled. Within a few years its growth was phenomenal. States were admitted to the Union. In isolated prairies and primeval forests, towns, cities, canals, roads, schools, colleges, churches and other improvements sprouted as if touched by a magic wand. In the year 1820 the western and southwestern states comprising Kentucky, Ohio, Indiana, Mississippi, Illinois, Louisiana, Missouri,

Alabama and the territories of Michigan and Arkansas numbered 2,233,880 inhabitants and the census for 1830 shows their population to have been 3,707,299; a gain of 1,473,419 in ten years or of 68.6 percent. Yet during the same period, the Atlantic States composed of Maine, New Hampshire, Rhode Island, Connecticut, Vermont, New York, New Jersey, Pennsylvania, Delaware, North Carolina, South Carolina, Georgia and the District of Columbia increased their population from 7,426,716 in 1820 to 9,135,403 in 1830, a gain for the ten years of only 1,723,687 or 25 percent.

During the years of 1820 and 1830 the total gain of population in the United States was 32 percent, while the South and West, during the same decade showed a gain of 68 percent. The great accession in the population of New Orleans was not typical, for in fact, the then Western States grew in corresponding proportion.

Since the founding of New Orleans its emigration was mostly of French origin, some Germans, comparatively few Spaniards, many Irish and a scattering from every nation of the world. After the Battle of New Orleans it was principally from the other states and territories of the Union, predominantly settled by Anglo-Saxons.

A synopsis of the nationalities of the emigrants entering the port of New York from December 1818 to December 1819, compiled by the Mayor's office of that City, quoted by the *Louisiana Gazette* of August 18, 1820, noted the arrival of 18,932 foreigners of whom 7,629 were English, 6,067 Irish, 1,942 Scotch, 372 Swiss, 590 Welshmen, 247 Spaniards and 54 Portuguese. It mentioned that there were usually more Irish than English. It further observed that the "Swiss made good farmers and were a handy, industrious, temperate race of people, and that the Welsh were temperate and good emigrants." This gives a fairly good index of the origin of the emigrants settling in northeast United States compared to those of New Orleans at that time.

Darby in 1817 observed that "no city perhaps on the globe, with an equal number of human beings, presents a greater contrast of national manners, language and complexion, than does New Orleans. The proportion between the whites and men of mixed casts or blacks, is nearly equal. As a native, the French among the whites are yet most numerous and wealthy, next will be the Anglo-Americans, thirdly the natives of the British Islands. There are but few Spaniards or Portuguese, some Italians and scattering individuals of all civilized nations of Europe."

James S. Zacharie wrote:

> All the various immigrations have left a particular imprint on our civilization. The French from Normandy who were mostly soldiers, brought a knightly temperament of high honor and a courtly refinement, and from Brittany came a sturdy and peaceful peasant class with a love of farming and profound religious sentiments. The Spaniards brought a love of order and form, with agricultural tastes of cattle ranching and sonorous language melting into a French tinged with a Norman and Breton patois to be handed down to us as a Creole dialect. From the West came those venturesome men, who, crossing the Allegheny mountain range had found homes in the forest and prairies and came to trade in "Orleans" and finally to settle there. From New England came enterprising yankees, and from New York and Maryland, men with great commercial and financial ideas who soon extended the commercial relations of the port, and transferred the town into a city, and who also have made the English language of the State so singularly pure and free from the peculiar accent and exaggerations that have crept into it in old England.

This flattering picture by Zacharie is contradicted by the vitriolic and perhaps biased observations of Karl Pöstl in his book AMERICANS AS THEY ARE, published in 1826. It is the most slanderous indictment of a people, based on faulty observation and obviously of a misunderstanding of a pioneer country. He stated that the French emigrants were numerous and included merchants, lawyers and physicians, etc., but that

> .... the greater part however, consists of adventurers, hair dressers, dancing masters, performers, musicians and the like. The French are of all men, the least valuable acquisition of a new state. Of a lavish and wanton temper, they spend their time in trifles which are of no importance to any but themselves. Dancing, fighting and riding are the daily occupation of these people. Their influence on a new and unsettled state, whose inhabitants have no correct opinion of true politeness and manners, is far from being advantageous. With neither religion, morality, or even education, they pretend to be the leaders of the bon-ton because they come from Paris, and they in general succeed. As for religion and principles, except a sort of *point d'honneur*, they are certainly a most contemptible set, and greatly contribute to promote immorality.

This may have been true of a small minority, but history has proved that many of these French emigrants made solid citizens, and have by their energy and industry contributed greatly to the upbuilding of their adopted city. Even to this day their names are revered and respected in this city.

He said that there were many Germans in New Orleans, and, without discrimination, points the finger of scorn on what proved to have been a valuable addition to the population. He wrote the following:

> These people, without being possessed of the smallest resources, embarked 8 or 10 years ago, and after having lost one-half or three-fourths of their comrades during the passage, they were sold as slaves, or as they were called Redemptioners, the moment of their arrival. These mixed with the Negroes in the same kind of labor, they experienced no more consideration than the latter and their conduct certainly deserved no better treatment. Those who did not escape were driven away by their masters for their immoderate drinking, and all, with few exceptions were glad to get rid of such dregs. The watchmen and lamp lighters are Germans, and hundreds of these people fell victims to the fever between the years 1814 and 1822.
>
> The rest of the white population consists of English, Irish, Spaniards, and some Italians amongst whom are several respectable houses.

Besides the advertisements in the newspapers there is little said about the redemptioners except that they were German. This abominable practice seems to have been in vogue in the 1820's. There are no clues to indicate how extensive that traffic was, or how many of these unfortunate individuals who sold themselves in bondage for a stated period of time to pay for their passage here, remained in this city, or were sent to the neighboring plantations. There is absolutely no indication as to their numbers or as to what role they played in the community.

The only specific information to be had is found in the advertisement section of the papers.

In the French section of the *Louisiana Advertiser* of January 17, 1820, appeared the following advertisement:

TO BE ENGAGED

A quantity of Germans, of both sexes and all trades, arrived from Bremen in Germany on the Brig, *Mississippi*, Captain Johanson. They wish to engage themselves in order to pay for their passage. They are of sound health and have good qualities.

The greatest number have their families.

Apply to the Captain on board or to A. F. Strass.

Another advertisement appeared in the issue of March 18, 1826:

GREAT ADVANTAGES

Are offered to the public in the employment of the following valuable mechanics and laborers, who will cheerfully serve any person disposed to pay their passage, ($70.00) each, in the *Galiote Fortune* from Bremen — Among whom will be found:

2 Blacksmiths, 2 Brewers, 3 Bricklayers, 3 Butchers, 2 Barbers, 2 Carpenters, 1 Carpenter and Joiner, 1 Cooper, 5 Gardeners, 1 Joiner, 1 Joiner and Upholsterer, 1 Laborer, 1 Miller, 1 Painter, 1 Rope maker, 9 Shoemakers, 6 Tailors, 2 Tanners, 1 Bleacher, 2 Single women — with whole families which should make them very serviceable on farms or unimproved lands.

The mechanics will serve for one year, the laborers, 18 months.

Apply to L. Jacobs and Co. No. 4 Conti St.

Also in the same newspaper on August 10th and September 5th is the following advertisement:

All persons desirous of taking Redemptioners are requested to apply to J. Ferrier at the Mayor's office where they will be accommodated on the most reasonable terms.

Their servitude was by law binding during the term of their contract. Those who escaped as well as those who contributed to the attempt, were subject to criminal prosecution. This is attested by the following notices in the French section of the *Louisiana Gazette* of April 14th and July 25th, 1820:

ESCAPED REDEMPTIONERS

A German family composed of the father, Andreas Thomas, the mother and four children have escaped from their master before they have served the time stipulated in their contract. Notice is hereby given that anyone who will give asylum to any of the said family, or would give them employment, will be prosecuted to the extent of the law. A reward will be given to anyone who will place the said Thomas in the hands of the Sheriff, who has the order for their arrest.

And also:

Has left the home of the undersigned, on the 12th inst., Charles Sutroth, German Prussian in nationality, age 35, about 5 ft. 4 in., face flat, blonde hair, reddish complexion. He has many scars on his head and on his right arm. The said Sutroth, engaged himself for two years. An honest reward to anyone who arrests him and have him put into custody in any jail of this State.

This voluntary human bondage was not typical of New Orleans or Louisiana, but was a well established practice in many other states of the Union, espeically those on the Eastern seaboard.

Another surge of emigrants who contributed greatly to the future prosperity of the city were the Irish. Driven from their homes by the ruthless persecution of their English masters and later by the potato famine, thousands upon thousands sought refuge in the United States. Although a vast majority of them disembarked in the northern ports, notably New York, and migrated to various places in that section of the country, many landed in New Orleans. There was a constant flow of Irish emigration in the beginning of the 19th century which reached its peak in the forties. The great majority of these refugees were paupers, unskilled, illiterate and fit only to do laborious work. Their lot was a hard one as they were subjected to the frequent epidemics, and their death rate was excessively high. Captain J. E. Alexander reported that it was "distressing to record that an average of 600 Irish perish yearly in and about New Orleans who had come in search of high wages, $1.00 a day. They are commonly employed trenching in the country and digging the foundations of houses in town."

The Irish encountered a certain amount of prejudice in the city but it was nothing to compare to the resentment shown in the North where it was bruited that they were "putting in jeopardy our civil liberties and sowing broadcast over the land the seeds of moral contagion and death." Even worse was their Catholicity. The Reverend Mr. Clapp exonerated them from the vile calumnies circulated not only in New Orleans but throughout the country, he wrote:

> I have seen much of the Irish in New Orleans in seasons of perils and disaster. I love them, however poor, for their generous and noble traits of character. I do not fear that their influence will be injurious to us, either in a political or religious bearing. But I am reminded that they bring to our shores degraded, dangerous characters and habits. If it were so, is to be wondered at, when we remember what scenes of the most atrocious despotism have been grinding them to the dust for a long series of ages. They are exiles seeking a refuge from want and oppression. It is not in my heart to speak of them in terms of contempt and bitterness. He who applies to them vile and oppobrious epithets virtually reproaches their Maker.

But some say that they are stupendously ignorant. Is it their fault if they are so? For more than 70 years, in Ireland, a Catholic schoolmaster was liable to be transported, and, if he returned, to be adjudged of high treason, barbarously put to death, drawn and quartered.

The most iniquitous law broke up their schools. The children of necessity grew up uneducated and must come here ignorant, if they come at all. I thank God that they do come; there is room for them all. For it is an encouraging, well established fact that, in general, Irish emigrants, as soon as they land among us, begin to improve, and rapidly to assume a more elevated character.

Some are afraid of their religion. It is perfectly safe in a free country to tolerate all forms of religion, because the principles of reverence in man, uninfluenced by coercion, can never lead to any species of immorality.

The progeny of these Irish emigrants became one of the most patriotic, respected and influential elements of the population, they are a power in politics and in the legislative halls, and have added to the culture, not only of Louisiana, but of the country as a whole.

Before the Louisiana purchase there were but few Anglo-Saxons in New Orleans, the population in the main was Latin. Before the Battle of New Orleans, the emigration from the other states of the Union was relatively small, and it was not until afterwards that the attention of the people of the United States was focused on that city. The fabulous wealth easily acquired, the ever increasing trade, the commerce of the port, the gayety and the easy way of life were the dreams of the adventurers and the golden opportunity of the industrious. They flocked to that city of opportunity in droves. Their numbers will never be determined, nor will their many casualties ever be known. These Anglo-Americans, some of them natives, others naturalized citizens, or even English emigrants, regarded Louisiana as a subjugated country, a foreign nation fit only to be exploited. The majority of them were contemptuous of the rights and privileges of the native population. They despised their language, their religion, their laws, their culture and their Gallic origin. Yet it must be said that among them there were men of distinction and learning. Doctors, ministers, lawyers, journalists, merchants and politicians made the city their home and integrated with the original population. They made a great contribution to the culture, prosperity and the greater development of their adopted city. This infiltration of Anglo-Americans was the greatest contribution to the remarkable growth of New Orleans.

The aggregate population of New Orleans taken from the United States census for 1830 was 49,826, composed of 21,221 whites, 12,600 males and 8,631 females; 11,906 free-persons-of-color, of whom 4,864 were males and 7,042 females; and 16,689 slaves, 6,988 males and 9,551 females. The *Bee* in an editorial on May 7, 1835, estimated the population to be 55,000 permanent and 25,000 transients. In 1840, the census gave a population of 102,162 classified as follows; 59,510 whites, 19,226 free persons of color and 23,448 slaves, a total increase in thirty years (1810-1840) of 77,529, comprising 51,519 whites and 26,011 negroes, free and slaves, a yearly average of 1,707 whites and 1,504 blacks.

These were the formative years of New Orleans.

CHAPTER XXI

CREOLES

The noun CREOLE has only one meaning and only one. The word is strictly French, although it has later found its place in our English dictionaries, and some of our lexicographers have given it an ambiguous definition, which leads to a false conception of its true meaning. This misinterpretation is shared by many who flatter themselves on their education and culture.

Webster's Twentieth Century Dictionary of the English language in 1936, gives the following description of the noun *Creole*: "In Louisiana, (a) a native of French or Spanish ancestry; (b) French speaking white, (c) a native black." An analysis will show that (a) is partly right and that (b & c) are categorically wrong.

Jean Bossu in his "Travels in North America" wrote in 1751: "The Creoles are those that are born here of a Frenchman and French woman or of European parents."

The Nouveau Dictionaire Francais, based on the Dictionary of the French Academy in 1792, defines the noun *Creole* as follows: "Nom qu'on donne à un Européen d'origine qui est né en Amerique." "Un Créole, Une Créole." (A name given to one of European origin born in America. A Creole). The "Dictionaire General et Grammatical des Dictionaires Francais," published in 1839, gives the same description as the above. In a comparatively recent work, Le Larousse Pour Tous, Nouveau Dictionaire Encyclopedique, defines the noun as "Personne de pure race blanche née aux colonies." (Persons of pure white race born in the colonies).

It would be just as incongruous to say "a Creole man" as to say "a Louisiana man." In the former case it would be absolutely incorrect. The noun Creole is always written with a capital C. The statement in Webster's Dictionary quoted above that a Creole is a native of French and Spanish ancestry (in Louisiana) must be qualified to include any European nationalist who settled in Louisiana during the colonization period. According to the classical thesis of Hanno Deiler, formerly professor of German at Tulane University, the early German settlers have every right to call themselves Creoles.

A French speaking white is not a Creole in any sense of the word, unless he is a direct descendant of an European parent born in Louisiana during the French and Spanish Domination. That fact is self evident. The noun *Creole* can never be applied to a black man no matter how light the color of his skin, because the word is applicable only to persons of pure white blood of European extraction.

The adjective *creole* has again a different signification. It qualifies anything pertaining to the State of Louisiana. It has been called the Creole state and rightly so, because for about eighty years it had been settled and developed by French and Spanish colonists. We speak of creole Negroes, of creole mules, of creole chickens, creole eggs, creole cooking, and so on — in fact, the term is applicable to everything pertaining to and raised in that state as differentiated from those from other parts of the country.

The Creoles have a proud heritage and have to a large extent maintained even to this day their language, their religion and their culture.

The *Courier* of October 25, 1831 published an interesting communication concerning the definition of the word "Creole"; it read:

"Creole" — A most singular and we think preposterous and absurd definition of the word, is contained in the *Emporium* of Wednesday; namely that none are Creoles but such that are born of European parents. I have always been called and so considered myself a Creole, notwithstanding my father and my father's father were called Creoles. We have also called the slaves born in this country Creoles — the horses raised there are also termed creole horses — nay even the chickens, the cane, the corn and rice of our own production have also been called under the appelation, universally command a finer price in the market, than the similar articles, the product of other states and countries. But it would seem that after the lapse of more than a century, we have discovered in this age of discovery that we know not the meaning of a word which had its origin with us. How kind and how modest is it in this literary and scientific editor of the *Emporium*, thus to inform us that we ourselves know not the meaning of the word which we have distinguished from those who have emigrated to this State. The word "Creole" is incorporated in our statute book; its meaning is there clearly defined: Our historians have also used the word to signify such as have been born in the country, whether white, yellow or black; whether they be children of French, Spanish, English or Dutch, or of any other nation.

And yet the modern Lexicographer of our city, gravely informs us that he has investigated the subject and that the result of his labor proves that Creoles are not the colored population but such alone as have been born of European countries.

A careful study of this anonymous communication makes it strongly suggestive that the writer wished to apply to himself the noun *Creole*, instead of the adjective. There were many free persons of color, even during the time of slavery, who appropriated for themselves the title of Creole. Many of these unfortunates, whose color of skin was light, were well educated, some acquired wealth and others even achieved distinction in the field of literature, in the cultural arts and in the professions. A book, "The Creoles of Louisiana," was written by one of them. Published in the North, it is a biography of those who had distinguished themselves — an exceedingly rare book because the copies were purchased and destroyed on coming from the press. Because they could not efface that unfortunate stigma in the city of their origin, many of these people migrated to other parts of the country, or to Europe where some married white women.

The slave, not having a surname, after the emancipation often took the family name of his former owner — some of the self-assumed names were the most distinguished in the history of the City. The slaves of the Anglo-Saxon Americans took the names of their previous owners, or of Jones, Smith, Jackson, Washington, etc.

There should be no controversy about the meaning of the noun, Creole. The unanimous definition in all French Dictionaries is "of European origin born in the colonies," and that precludes the admixture of African blood. Even during the early colonial times the amalgamation or mingling of the races was discouraged, and the priests were forbidden to marry blacks and whites. In 1761, Governor Vaudreuil issued a decree that "any Frenchman harboring a black slave for the purpose of inducing him or her to lead a scandalous life, shall be whipped by the public executioner and sentenced to the galleys for life." Miscegenation was never permitted by the laws of Louisiana.

Fortier tells us that in 1767, "when the Marchioness of Alrado came from Peru to marry Gov. Ulloa, to whom she had been previously betrothed, she brought with her a number of Peruvian women who were her personal friends. Owing to the dark complexions of these women, the white women (Creoles) of Louisiana took them for mulattresses, and for a time refused all social recognition to the Marchioness because of her association with those regarded as members of an inferior race. — It is neither proper nor just to apply the term *Creole* to any member of the colored race and the use of the word in that sense is very properly resented by the French and Spanish descendants of Louisiana."

The Creoles of Louisiana have never been conquered, although they had been betrayed and bartered by their mother country, France, and without any notification whatsoever, transferred to Spain, a nation they detested. Their love for France never cooled; after all they were French, and the hope that some day they would revert to their former status as French subjects lingered in their hearts.

They always resented their Spanish rulers, even to the point of rebellion. The Louisiana Creoles committed the first overt act of defiance against a European mother country and struck the first blow for the cause of liberty in this country. It antedated the Boston Tea Party by five years. They did not throw merchandise into the water from a ship in the harbor, but they slashed the mooring lines of the ship on which the newly appointed Spanish Governor Ulloa had arrived to take possession of the colony, allowing the vessel to drift down the river amidst the mocking cries of derision and defiance of an irate population. It was a bold action when it is considered that in the entire province, there was at that time a population of 5556 white individuals of whom 1893 were fit to bear arms. When Governor O'Reilly arrived here with an army of 4500 men and proclaimed to the inhabitants that he did not come to molest them, but only to take possession of the country in the name of the King of Spain, it was only with that assurance that he was permitted to land without any disturbance. The Creoles, true to their honor, kept their word, and never suspected the perfidy of the hypocritical Spaniard, veiled by public professions of friendship and promises of amnesty. He came to Louisiana to get blood and blood he got. Six of the most prominent Creoles, the leaders of the revolution were marked for vengeance.

Villeré was vilely assassinated and Lafreniere, De Noyan, Marquis, Joseph Milhet and Caresse were condemned to the gallows and to have their property expropriated. The only mercy extended them was that they met death before a firing squad rather than on the gallows.

The execution took place on the 28th of September 1769. All

the troops were ranged in battle formation on the Levee and the public square, (Place d'Armes). The gates were closed, the sentinels were doubled and troops patrolled the streets of a deserted city. The inhabitants left their homes in order not to witness the execution.

The five heroes met death with courage and resignation. They refused to be blindfolded. Milhet facing the Spanish guns made a dramatic speech of defiance, which should be perpetuated in our history textbooks, among the noblest in the history of our country:

> A thousand times I have braved death for an adopted country and I have never closed my eyes in the presence of her enemies. Let us die, my friends, as brave men. Death is not frightful.

With a sublime nonchalance he asked to be given some snuff and turning to his enemies said:

> And you Spaniards, know that we die because we have never ceased to wish to be Frenchmen. My heart is French, I have fought thirty years for Louis the Beloved and I glorify to know that my love for him is the cause of my death! Shoot, Ruffians!

Their plea before that biased tribunal was that they could not be considered rebels against Spain because the French flag still flew over the Colony; that they owed no allegiance to Spain before the receipt of official papers; and that the Prince had not as yet afforded his protection, and, therefore, had no right to condemn them. That plea fell on deaf ears. Their demand for an appeal to Castile was denied. O'Reilly wanted blood and blood he must have These martyred heroes were not executed, they were assassinated. Several of them left a large progeny in Louisiana. Their names emblazon a glorious page in the History of New Orleans, whilst O'Reilly's page is blotted with infamy; no wonder then even to this day he is known as "Bloody O'Reilly."

Although governed by Spain, the New Orleans people never were other than French. While the judicial and official language was Spanish, the prevalent tongue was French. Only a few, for official and business reasons, made any attempt to learn and speak the Spanish tongue. The Creoles maintained their own culture, originally French, but modified by colonial conditions. Although their priests were Spaniards, their sermons and their intercourse with their parishoners were in French. In other words, the Orleanians never ceased to be Frenchmen, and to nurse the hope that some day the country they loved would repossess the colony.

The Creoles were stunned at first when they heard the news of the American Purchase. One day they were under the Spanish Domination, then the next day they heard the news that France had acquired the colony, and very shortly afterwards, that it had been sold to the United States. Even the local Spanish Government had no intimation of what had transpired, and refused to believe the report until officially confronted with orders from Madrid. At first the Creoles suffered some trepidation, but they soon realized the advantages of American citizenship. They embraced Americanism with fervent devotion and glorified in the change of status from being a subject to that of being a citizen. From that time on they were loyal citizens. The Spaniards, and they were mostly officials and soldiers, left for Spain and other Spanish dominions.

During the territorial period the serenity of the life of the Creoles was not disturbed, their language, religion, and culture were unopposed. But that tranquility was soon rudely interrupted. The invasion of Anglo-Saxon Americans began. Many of these people had the impression that the native New Orleanians were foreigners, not entitled to the rights of American citizenship and only fit to be exploited. They were attracted here by wealth easily acquired. These strangers migrated to this city in great numbers, most of them without any intention of making it their permanent residence. It was then that the conflict of nationalities, language, religion, politics, law, and culture began.

The great melting pot in which a united people was to be fused began to simmer.

An editorial in the *Courier* of June 14, 1833, answering an article on New Orleans by Master Brooks, editor of the *Portland Advertiser*, reads:

> Most exceptional part of Mr. Brooks notes on our city is the contrast drawn between the French and American population and which it strikes us he has attempted to render unfavorable to the former. We allude of course to what is said with regard to their moral and religious obligations and all that concerns them as citizens. Whatever difference may seem to exist upon these points to the eye of the stranger, may be attributed to a difference of education which does not affect the character or moral worth of those it is supposed to lower in the scale of usefulness nor retard in the smallest degree the advancement of those interests which have for their object the promotion of individual and general prosperity and happiness.
>
> There is perhaps not upon the face of the globe a more pa-

triotic people than the Creole of Louisiana — none more ardently attached to the institutions of their country — none who look upon a menace of her destruction with more unqualified indignation. And yet, sensitive as they are upon this subject, they would suffer less, perhaps from a dissolution of the Union than the people of any other state composing it.

It will not be denied that the American population (and this, by the way is a distinction without a difference) are somewhat in advance of the natives in works of public and private improvements; but already have the latter been aroused to a sense of their interests and already are they vying with the former in the laudable competition of giving embellishment to the city and securing for it all the advantages and preeminence to which, from its locality alone, it may safely and confidently aspire. The spirit of improvement is confined and at present it is nowhere more conspicuous than in the city proper.

Mr. Brook has also run a little ahead of the fact in supposing that the almost magic growth of what is called the American part of the city is the exclusive work of Yankees if he means this term to embrace such only as were born in New England. The middle, western and southern states have all contributed their quota in the formation of those enterprises and industries, to which this part of the City is indebted for its beauty and grandeur. Europeans and Creoles also have assisted in imparting to the property and business of this division of the city much of the wealth and activity to which it so justly lays claim. Indeed it may be said that while the latter classes, for the most part, are permanently identified with whatever concerns the interest of the City, the former, in too many instances, to use Mr. Brown's own language "only alight to make money here," ultimately intending when they have accomplished their object, to return again to New England, whose hills and valleys they never lose sight of and at the mention of whose name their hearts throb with quickened emotion.

The view he has taken of the Creoles is such a one as would perhaps naturally impress itself upon the mind of strangers unaccustomed to the peculiar habits and manners which distinguish them from the rest of the Americans. If he has made it a reproach to the Creoles and French generally, that they disregard the laws of morality and religion by violating the sanctity of the Sabbath, he also accused the American of sacrificing decency and moral duty for mercenary considerations alone. So far, therefore, as a contrast has been instituted between the two classes that inhabit the City, the view presented is in our opinion, decidedly in favor of the French: for which he has exhibited the latter as the devotees of pleasure, pursuing their mistress in every channel where she is likely to be found, he has at the same time condemned the Amricans for their sordid feelings and for-

Above—This building at the corner of Ursuline and Charles Streets was built in 1740, and was probably the oldest building in New Orleans when it was demolished in 1926. (From the collection of Stuart O. Landry)

At right—Old tiled-roof house on Dumaine Street, photographed about 1890. (Collection of Stuart O. Landry)

Below—Old house in the Vieux Carré, typical of early New Orleans houses.

Old house at the corner of Orleans and Dauphine Streets. Note cobble-stone paving. Photographed about 1890. (Collection of Stuart O. Landry)

The Grima house at 820 St. Louis Street is typical of the finer homes that were built in the Vieux Carré from 1825 to 1840. (Photograph courtesy Richard Koch)

getfulness of these moral and religious duties which is the pride of New England to impress upon her sons. Thus according to Mr. Brown's own estimate, the French are less objectionable in some of the points in which he has been pleased to contrast them with Americans. The general accuracy of his remarks shows him to be a man not disposed to wilfully misrepresent, though from the cursory and superficial nature of his observations it is not surprising that he occasionally falls into error and exaggeration."

As early as 1814, Breckenridge in his Views on Louisiana, observed that "their language, [Creoles] every thing considered, is more pure than might be expected; their manner of lengthening the sounds of words, altogether languid and without the animation which the French generally possess, is by no means disagreeable."

The Duke of Saxe-Weimar, who visited New Orleans wrote in 1828 his impressions of the Creoles as follows:

The real Creoles are upon the whole a warm hearted generation and the people with whom I was least pleased here, were the Americans who are mostly brought only by the desire to accumulate wealth.

The best description of the Creole is the one in Flint's Geography, published in 1832, he represents them as follows:

The forefathers of the present race of Creoles were of a mild and peaceable race. The ancient inhabitants attached more importance to a criminal prosecution and felt more keenly the shame of conviction than the inhabitants of the present time.

We consider the Creoles generally as a mild and amiable people with less energy and less irascibility than the emigrants from the other states, the descendants of the French have all the peculiar and the instinctive traits of that people in all countries. They possess mild vivacity and show rather the ingenuity of successful imitation, than the boldness and hardihood of inventive minds. The parents of the present race were insulated from the rest of the world; were plunged in the woods, had no object of ambition; no political career before them; and they were content to hunt, make voyages in their canoes; and smoke and traffic with many of the savages. Many of them knew neither to read or to write. It is otherwise with their descendants. They are generally born to fortunes; have a career before them, and are early brought to perceive the necessity of being educated; and the children of the French are now as generally instructed as those of the Americans.

They are fond of shows, the theater, balls and assemblies; are extremely polite and generally more sober and moral than the Americans. The women are remarkable for becoming excellent wives and mothers; and are extremely domestic and economical in their habits. Many of the more wealthy planters cross the sea to spend the summer and to educate their children in France.

The planters are generally high minded, irascible, social and generous; much addicted to the sport of the turf and the gaming table. They are fond of hunting and keeping large packs of dogs. Having overseers for the most part over their lands and are too apt to become dissipated. There is a rising spirit of literature and a disposition to read among them, which will employ many of the hours that used to be spent around the gambling table.

The people generally are adverse to care, deep thinking, and profound impressions; and are volatile, gay, benevolent, easily excited to joy or sorrow; and a common maxim of a sickly climate where life is precarious, is "a short life and a merry one." — In many respect no people are more amiable. They carry the duties of hospitality to great lengths and extend the kindness to consanguinity almost as far as the Scotch are said to do.

The luxury of the table is carried to great extent. They are ample in their supply of wines; though claret is generally drunk. In drinking, the guests universally raise their glasses and touch them together instead of a health.

Tyrone Power, an American, tersely gave his impression of the Creoles, he wrote:

> They seldom mix. He inevitably conserves much of the air and appearance of la Belle France and can never be mistaken, offering according to his disposition, all the varieties of the original stock from the small deportment and companionable bonhommie of the well bred Frenchmen, to the fierce brusquerie and swaggering of the gallant of the estaminet.

The French, including the Creoles, were accused of having formed a fifth column to sabotage the campaign of General Jackson. This was a slanderous charge which had no foundation in fact. The following article in the *Bee* of June 1, 1936, throws light on the subject. It said:

> That the British expected to be joined by the Louisianians during their invasion of this State in the late war cannot be doubted; but it is not easy to ascertain on what they founded their belief of such assistance. Nor was the belief confined to England alone, in giving them confidence; but was unfortunately extended to General Jackson and created that suspicion in his breast which led to those marked actions towards the natives, for which he has been severely censured.
>
> But Secretary Cass has promised to redeem the character of the Hero of New Orleans in a second Article in the American Quarterly Review, by exhibiting the source of causes of his suspicion.
>
> Yet that the natives of Louisiana were true to the cause of

America, there can be no doubt, than that singular confidence was exhibited by the British General and as singular suspicion by the American, in their assistance. Jackson himself understood this before the action on the 8th of January and in many instances proved his confidence in them.

General Jackson sent a young Creole, then a cadet in his army, and only eighteen years of age, to Sir John Lambert for the liberation of some Negroes, slaves of planters here, — Was courteously treated by the officers of the British army, then stationed at Dauphin Island, and was invited to dine with them.

He then proceeded to fulfill a private commission to General Keane. Keane on the 23rd of December had taken Mr. Lacoste a prisoner, and, relying on the suspected assistance of the Louisianians, voluntarily promised to indemnify him and other natives for whatever cattle and provisions were taken from them for the British army. Lacoste sent his account for $350.00 with the young Creole to have it paid by Keane. It was presented when the General was leaning against a tree, as he had been wounded during the action of the 8th: General Keane replied that when he had made the promise to pay, he had expected to find Louisianians different from what they had proved to be — his friends and not foes — and that their conduct cancelled all debts.

The Creole rejoined, "I do not know why you expected to find them friends of the invaders of their country, you have found them as they are, warm defenders of their native Land and Americans in every instance. But I am not aware how their conduct can affect your honor which was solemnly pledged to pay this debt which I present. However, we shall know hereafter how to value the honor of a British General." The Creole bowed and withdrew.

But he had not gone one hundred yards till overtaken by an aid-de-camp of the General, who requested his return. "Tell your General (said the Creole, holding up his flag of truce) that if he wants me, he may find me on that ship at anchor." Shortly afterwards, General Keane sent the whole sum in guineas to him on board the ship.

It is not a little remarkable that Mr. Lacoste kept the sum till his death; and that about twelve months since, one of his heirs applied to have the coins exchanged into dollars.

The Creole militia contingent achieved glory by their support of General Jackson.

Despite the contempt which the Anglo-Saxons had for the Creoles and the French element of the community, the urbanity of the latter gradually refined the conduct of the more uncouth Americans who were absorbing the very things they derided. No less an authority than James Logan of Edinburg, a visitor in 1938, wrote about the jealousy that existed between the American and French population, who, he said, "cohabit very little," and that the "former holding the latter in contempt on account of their trifling manners and because they show a want of energy and enterprise in commerce. The French again dislike the Americans, who are somewhat coarse in their manners and because they considered them as intruders. Notwithstanding all this, the French politeness is imitated by the Americans who are more polished than those of the other Southern States." He observed that the American section has a French restaurant and "in many particulars adopted the customs of their neighbors, using napkins at dinner, for instance, and drinking with each other." Besides, in the large hotels the cooking was French and that they sit longer at their meals than in the north.

Nowhere is there to be found a derogatory remark about the Creole ladies. Their morals were never questioned. They were faithful wives and devoted mothers. They were devout Catholics. Divorce was practically unknown, no matter what may have been the provocation, they remained faithful to their spouses to the end, not only because of religious convictions, but also because of the stigma attached to divorce. Their charity was proverbial; during the periods of dire calamity they were ever ready to succor the unfortunates and to administer to the sick. "Feuillton" in the *Louisiana Courier* of August 17, 1821, records an incident of their charitable work:

> A Society of respectable Creole ladies who, because of their morals or their wealth, who in spite of the heat of the season make it a grim duty to visit the indigent and the sick. They give the poor their moral and physical assistance, none escape their vigilance nor their aid.
>
> These ladies have rented a house which they have furnished at their own expense; they furnish nurses to attend to the sick, the doctors and apothecaries are paid by them, nothing is left to chance in the care of those entrusted to them.

Karl Pöstl described them as having in general an interesting appearance.

> A black languishing eye, color rather too pale, figure of middle size which partakes of embonpoint and does not exhibit any waist, are the characteristics of the fair sex. With a great deal of vivacity they show, however, a proper sense of decorum. Adultery is seldom known among the better classes, notwithstanding, the many grounds afforded to them by the infidelity

of their husbands. As wives and mothers, they are entitled to every praise, they are more moderate in their expenses than the northern ladies; and though always neat and elegantly dressed, they seldom go beyond reasonable bounds. Several instances are known of their having displayed a high degree of fortitude. In sickness and danger they are the inseparable assistants and companions of their husbands.

In literary education, however, they are extremely deficient and nothing can be more tiresome than a literary tete-a-tete with a Creole lady. They receive their education in the Convent of the Ursulines where they learn reading, writing, some female work and the pianoforte. It is superfluous to observe; being descendants from the French, that they are the best dancers in the United States.

And now for the feminine point of view, Harriet Martineau, an English observer, wrote in 1838:

The division between the Americans and the French factions is visible even in the drawing room. The French complain that the Americans will not speak French, — will not meet their neighbors halfway in accomodation of speech. The Americans ridicule the toilette practice of French ladies, their liberal use of rouge and pearl powder. If the French ladies do this to beautify themselves, they do it with great art, I could not be quite sure of the fact in any one instance, while I am disposed to believe it from the clumsy imitation of the Art which I saw in the countenance of an American rival or two. I witnessed with strange disgust the efforts of a young lady of Philadelphia to make herself as French as possible by these disagreeable means. She was under twenty and would have been rather pretty if she had given herself a fair chance, but her coarsely painted eyebrows, daubed cheeks and powdered throat inspired a disgust which she must be singularly unwise not to have anticipated. If this were a single case it would not be worth mentioning; but I was told by a resident that it is a common practice for young ladies to paint both white and red, under the idea of accommodating themselves to the French manners of the place. They had better do it by practicing the French language than by copying the French toilette. New Orleans is the only place in the United States where I am aware of having seen a particle of rouge.

Except for the mixture of languages and the ample provisions of ices, fans and ventilators, the drawing room assemblages of New Orleans bear a strong resemblance to the routs and dinner parties of a country town in England.

The Creole's greatest fear was dishonor. His word was his bond and among themselves it was accepted as such. Loans and business transactions were frequently made without notes and securities, and rarely were they demanded. The safest collateral was a good name and but very rarely were these obligations defaulted. Even in their last wills and testaments they included the names of their creditors and the amounts due them, with specific instructions that before other legacies they be repaid. In many instances when this wish was impossible of fulfillment, because of insufficient funds, sons assumed the obligation of their fathers and at great personal sacrifice managed to liquidate it in order to protect their good name.

The Creoles were clannish. They intermarried and their genealogies will show that in many instances there were two or three alliances between the same families. Wealth was not a social requisite, the portals of the parlors of the richest amongst them were opened to their less opulent neighbors, providing they possessed the social graces, distinction and above all a good name. Even to this day among the old Creole families the phrase "c'est la distinction" denotes the acme of approbation.

The Creoles were a proud race, proud of their origin, proud of their honor, proud of their culture and proud to be American citizens.

CHAPTER XXII

THE AMERICAN INFILTRATION

The infiltration of Anglo-Saxon Americans began after the Battle of New Orleans. During the interval between the date of the "Purchase" and the memorable defeat of the English at Chalmette, the increase in the population of New Orleans, although steady, was relatively slight. The number of refugees from San Domingo, together with European immigrants principally from France, settling in Louisiana about equalled the number of immigrants who came from different sections of the Union, so the numerical balance between the Latins and the Anglo-Saxons was not too greatly disturbed.

The advent of steamboats, which greatly shortened the time of passage between the cities and towns bordering the Mississippi and its tributaries, induced thousands to visit New Orleans. Like migratory birds at the approach of Winter, they flocked to that city, only to return North at the approach of Summer. The number of these American visitors will never be known. They were not listed in the city directories, mentioned in the newspapers, or otherwise recorded. Of those who stayed many were victims of the ever recurrent epidemics and filled unmarked graves.

The reputation of New Orleans as a city of opportunity was so widespread that men of all classes, the cultured and educated as well as the dregs of humanity, braved perils and even death in their quest for the wealth so easily acquired. Some of them became permanent residents, but the larger number returned to their homes.

In the French section of the *Louisiana Gazette* of October 23, 1820, under the title of "American Emigration," is the following:

> The emigration of citizens from the North which visits us every year must have already commenced, if it has not done so already. In one of the recent papers of New York are found advertisement of at least eight vessels destined for New Orleans. They are welcome, that is to say, providing they are honest and hard working men, but the *chevaliers d'industrie* and the lazy, they could dispense us of their presence. Anyhow Louisiana must not be such a detestable country as has been proclaimed in

letters by certain individuals who have been here. How can we account for that great haste to visit it?

From Karl Pöstl, (1828) the following is quoted in part:

The central Government and the generality of Americans behave towards Louisianians in a becoming manner. But there is a character of American freedom, especially in the deportment of an American toward foreigners and strangers in his own country, something repulsive. It is not the pride of a nobleman accustomed to be obeyed, nor the natural pride of an Englishman who carries his sulky temper along with him and finds fault with every thing: It is rather the pride of an adventurer — of an upstart, who exults at his not being a runaway himself, although the descendent of one. Louisiana immediately after its cession, was admitted to the full enjoyment of all the advantages connected with the prerogative as one of the States of the Union and its white natives, the Creoles, were considered as citizens born of the United States. But the moment the cession was made, crowds of needy Yankees and what is worse, Kentuckians, spread all over the country, attracted by the hope of gain; the latter treating the inhabitants no little better than a purchased property. Full of prejudice towards the descendents of a nation they knew little more than the proverb "French Dog", they, without knowing, or condescending to learn their language, behave towards these people as if their lands as well as the inhabitants could be seized without ceremony. This was not, certainly, the way of thinking or the conduct of all the Northern new comers, there being amongst them many a useful mechanic, merchant, planter or lawyer; but a greater number come with a degree of presumption which was in an inverse ratio with their unbounded and absolute ignorance. The Creoles, with their proper sense of their own independence, naturally retreated from the intercourse of these intruders, on the other hand, the consequence of an oppressive colonial government, the natural effect of an enervating and sultry climate, could not fail giving to the character of the Creoles a certain tone of passiveness which make them an object of interest.

Americans from other parts of the Union may be considered as constituting 3/8 of the present populations of the State and of New Orleans.

Most of those who settled in Louisiana grew wealthy either as planters or merchants, and really the wealthiest families of Louisiana are at present Americans from other parts of the Union who likewise hold the most important public stations. The Government as well as the members of Congress and Senators have hitherto been Americans for the very natural reason that the Creoles could not speak the English language, although some very important offices were filled by the latter. Nothing can exceed or surpass the suppleness of the Yankee; and the refined Frenchmen with all their dexterity, may still benefit from them and their kindred.

Half of the inhabitants may be said to be regularly settled; the rest are half settlers. Merchants, store keepers, remain only until they have amassed a fortune answering their expectations and then remove to their former homes.

Some reside in winter and leave in summer which is the case with all Yankee commission merchants.

He further observed that the new comers in Louisiana were mostly planters, farmers, merchants and mechanics. "The farmers being more or less wealthy," he wrote, "come for the purpose of establishing themselves and usually buy sugar and cotton lands on the Mississippi or Red Rivers, which though in general, healthy, on the other hand, are a sure grave to those who neglect taking the necessary precautions. Planters descend upon Louisiana in the winter months; but as the heat increases every moment, and has a debilitating effect upon their bodies, accustomed to a colder climate, they attempt to counterbalance this weakness by an excessive use of spiritous liquors, to promote digestion."

The number of Americans who settled permanently in New Orleans has been estimated from three-eights to one-half of those who came to stay for a short time.

Condon, a Londoner, observed that "the better American families as soon as they have amassed a fortune answering to their expectations, prefer removing to the North."

Richard Bache, an American, in 1834 observed that "too many of the Americans who reside here and more especially those who make but a transient stay, are devoted to the exclusive subject of acquiring wealth and are so immersed in business as to neglect, it is to be feared, generally the interests of the mortal spirit."

A scurrilous communication appeared in the *Gazette* on October 30, 1822. It is self-explanatory:

> Turkey-buzzards: wild geese, ducks, pigeons and other useful birds of passage who annually arrive on our coast, are always sure of a welcome, but there are others of a more ravenous kind with the periodical visits we would willingly dispense — we allude to a species of birds called "Yankee Buzzards." The turkey buzzard is tolerated as an excellent scavenger. The Yankee buzzard cannot boast of these qualities. His character is opposite, he has ever been the locust to us — to him we are indebted to the host of "pistareens with heads on which cover the whole face of the earth so that the land is darkened." A buzzard of this

class, the other day, sold a barrel of potatoes to a citizen and received a bank note of $10.00; he put his hand into a well filled pouch and counted out 50 pistareens to pay $7.50, so that in place of receiving $2.50, (the price of his potatoes), he in fact sold them for $4.37½. This kind of speculation has been tolerated too long, — let the butcher in the market refuse to take the pieces for more than 20 cents and the evil will be remedied, let the City tax these persons who come sub-yearly and sell their property on the Levee only, and then the honest trader exposed to the climate both in summer and winter — who pays store rent — taxes and clerk hire will have some chance of getting a livelihood. The east winds have commenced and it is time for Locusts, ... Our traders are as much entitled to protection from foreign traders as are our manufacturers from foreign manufacturers. Give us then a protection tax.

signed: A. Aron Co.

The United States mint had established the value of the pistareen, an old Spanish coin, to be nearly seventeen cents. It was passed in New Orleans for twenty five cents.

That protest, in many respects was justifiable, for it was only one of many which deplored the abuse. Unfortunately, it was voiced in a provocative tone as to cause some indignation in the community. The following day in the same journal, appeared the following:

STRANGERS: In writing this communication, we are persuaded our correspondent had no intention of exciting those unfriendly sectional feelings which other writings in other papers of the city have, perhaps, acted a little to keep up. In coming among us with their potatoes, onions, cheese and other notions, our eastern fellow citizens are far from injuring. No: on the contrary, in so doing, they considerably contribute to the prosperity by lowering, one half perhaps, the prices of some of the first necessities of life. It is true that most of what they bring might be raised in Louisiana, but our planters have more profitable culture to which they devote all their forces and attention. It is alleged that the eastern folks injure regular traders by retailing on the Levee, now, they are not the only persons who retail on the Levee and are perhaps more culpable on that head than the scores of Ouachinangoes, free negroes, etc. If it hurts the standard store keepers, put a tax, but take care of the poor.

The slang of the present day as regards strangers is truly ridiculous in a country with a population like ours. The citizens of only a few years standing reproach him who came yesterday, as being a new comer; a stranger, a foreigner!

The article went on to say that the necessities of life for

some months back were fairly priced but with the winter months approaching they will rise in value. It also remarked the white population has greatly reduced because more than a thousand persons died of yellow fever during the past nine weeks.

The following communication gave the view point of an American who claimed to have been perhaps the oldest Anglo-Saxon American in Louisiana. It appeared in the *Gazette* of October 19, 1825: This article mentions the origin, rise and progress of the difficulties which existed between the two populations for a long time. The writer acknowledged that it was difficult to trace the precise time when

> a few interested factionists, among our foreign population, commenced their first usurpation of power; as well as all the instruments of intrigue by which they have so completely prostrated the American party. They thought that shortly after this State was taken over by the United States that the institutions of the State might be remodelled after the European governments. They found that this was not congenial to the American population. It was then a great object to put them down, which was first demonstrated in the attempts to dismember the State of the portion of the Territory which was represented exclusively by Americans. From that time (1810) to the present, they have with the most unwearied industry, made that object their rallying point; for a few years afterwards, when they found that the American population presented such a determined resistance to the measure, that same party became the most clamorous for the surrender of the State to the British in 1814, and which was eventually prevented by the energetic measures of General Jackson. Since which time although they appear much more humble, yet, still they show the most determined hostility to those who drew their first breath in our country; those who have since been prodigal of their blood for its defense and who identify their very existence with their liberties. If I recollect aright, the first open attempt of hostilities to the Americans by the Press was made in 1822, in a paper that was established for the purpose of putting down the Americans and presenting the views of the leading faction. This paper was effectively opposed by the lamented J. P. C. Samson, Esq, then the editor of the *Louisiana Advertiser*, and the inequity of their principles completely laid open. It was from the same nursery of faction that the *Argus* owed its origin.
>
> It was the same establishment that excited a body of American militia to place an alien at their head; and one who has been in the ranks of the enemy during the late war, and had thereby attempted the sacrifice of their liberties and our subjugation to the yoke of a foreign despot.

For approximately ten years the city was the field of a political revolution. The Americans were migrating in ever increasing numbers. They settled in the upper section, the faubourg St. Mary, and by sheer numerical strength they achieved political control; the conflicting elements were somewhat appeased when the City was divided. More and more of them made New Orleans their home. Through their indefatigable industry many acquired great wealth, others achieved eminence in their respective professions and in politics. Many of them as well as their scions, have added lustre to the culture of New Orleans.

The smoldering embers of jealousy, hatred, intolerance, animosity and greed burst into flames in the middle of the eighteen-thirties.

This time passions rose to a high pitch between those who proclaimed themselves native Americans and those of foreign birth or descent although citizens of the Union.

Public meetings were held which excited some of the population to near riots, hatred rose to a high pitch against the Gallo-Americans. Such an incident is reported in the *Bee* of September 4, 1835:

> For some time past in this City, sectional and national feeling of an improper tendency have been excited by remarks made on naturalized citizens as foreigners, so that the public mind was so strongly wound up on that subject as on another almost simultaneously excited — that of interference with slave property. Both are alike injurious to the peace, to the political and social order of the community; and most members of the legion were aggrieved by those remarks and the feeling improperly engendered against them by the same persons and parties that they would have been recreants to America had a war unfortunately occurred with France.
>
> They had negatively appeared on the 4th of July; and yesterday they might have been violently displayed but for the good sense and proper spirit of the members of the Legion.
>
> This was occasioned by some remarks in the *Louisiana Advertiser* of yesterday morning, the same paper in which many of the former animadversions of [against] our Gallo-American citizens were published; but which has since changed proprietors and editors, who have generally hitherto adopted a very different course and endeavored to assist the *Bee* in maintaining the rights and privileges of all classes of citizens distinct from birthplace or language.
>
> Yesterday, however, Dr. Verner singularly forgot his prin-

ciples of editorial policy and prudence and made some wanton comments — as specimens of wit rather than malevolent or designed calumnies — on the conduct of the Legion pending the riot of Saturday last: This was the same as casting a brand in a powder magazine. The members of the Legion had during four days given their time and means to preserve the peace of the City, and awe those who would have violated it under the semblance of Americanism in opposition to naturalized citizens enjoying offices and permanence in the country, or slaves or colored persons being taught mechanical trades.

Think then what must have been their feelings after having been voted a standard worth $2000.00, by the corporation; having palpably disproved the illiberal accusations made against them by interested agitators; and after having merited and received the approbation of a large majority of their fellow citizens — to be insulted by one who they had believed their friend.

Groups congregated to consider the matter; and the angry effects of wounded feelings preponderated. Many went to the *Louisiana Advertiser* for the purpose of apprehending the editor and preventing worse effects.

Found Pendergast, one of the proprietors — whom they compelled to escort them to the residence of Dr. Verner, the editor, but finding the Doctor had escaped, they brought Pendergast towards the police office — where he was very nearly in danger of being seized and being lynched, had it not been for the timely interference of the Mayor, the attorney general, the judge of Criminal Court and the Legion. The conduct of Prieur, Mazureau and Canonge deserves the highest praise. Pendergast was then put in jail and Verner escaped on the Rail Road to the Lake whither he was pursued — as yet in vain.

The proprietor was not responsible, only the editor was guilty. He should be liberated and an *amende honorable* to the Legion be required in the paper, etc.

Three days afterwards, the same journal had an article with the heading "The Causes of Disturbances Last Friday in the City," attributing them to, "the efforts wantonly made during the past six months to excite sectional and national feelings among different classes of our fellow citizens, yet cautiously refraining from indicating any individuals, associations or establishment." It rebuked the *True American* in the following: "Because the Governor preferred to the office a naturalized citizen from among the Gallo-Americans — did not that Editor (*True American*) in chagrin and chicanery assail all the Gallo-American citizens as would-be traitors of their adopted country, ridicule them as retaining any reminiscent predilection for la Belle France, endeavor to excite the citizens of the upper faubourg against the Creoles of the other part; and already proclaim that a division alone of the City by Canal Street could do justice to the Faubourg St. Mary, as the Creole citizens had clanned together for the purpose of monopolizing the City's revenues?"

It further accused that editor of personally assailing the Governor, and that the *True American* was instrumental in convoking the April meeting at Banks' Arcade, and having condemned the constitutional privileges and national justice and propriety by conferring any office of trust or emolument to Naturalized citizens.

The article accused George Pollock, who had been appointed Harbor master, of having been an armed foe of the Americans, and as having fought personally with the British invaders in the last war, when it was a brother of Pollock who had been in the war. The *True American's* attack on the Legion and the Catholic Clergy, relative to the 4th of July, fermented the leaven of discord against or among all Creoles, all Catholics, etc. Editor John Gibson of the *True American* "sought to establish a society of members which were secretly to pledge themselves to violate the Constitution and laws of the nation by denouncing naturalized citizens as foreigners."

It further stated the *True American* had only three to four hundred subscribers, and "that all that appears in it is invariably viewed with suspicion by the respectable and reflective portion of the community."

And of the editor, it said:

He seeks a division of the City that he may have a Mayor and corporation in his favor; and a dissension among natives and naturalized citizens, reckless of the feelings of the minor class, if he can excite the prejudice of the greater in number; and by their exercises obtain his selfish purposes. But he is known, suspected, shunned.

The *Bee* of September 4, 1835, reported that Pendergast was discharged from prison and that he was confined solely to protect him from the fury of the mob, and that the *Louisiana Advertiser* would soon resume publication. It requested that "those who have withdrawn their subscriptions from that journal should resume them, as Dr. Verner has left the establishment and precautionary measures will be taken to prevent hereafter the insertion of such remarks. It is well that general amnesty should be made as regards all persons concerned." It also published this letter of appreciation:

City Prison, Friday Morning.
To the Editor of the Bee:

Sir: In addition to the individuals enumerated in your paper of this morning, to whom I owe an incalulable debt of gratitude for the timely interference on my behalf, please give the names of Sheriff Buisson, Mr. Prats of the Legion, Mr. Labatut, Mr. Bell, Mr. Carpenter and Mr. Plauché.

signed J. C. Pendergast.

A few days later, that journal tersely announced that New Orleans was again tranquil and that the health of the city was good.

In its issue of April 17, 1835 the *Bulletin* stated that out of 38 appointments by Governor White, all were natives excepting seven: one a trustee of the Charity Hospital, one a regent of public schools, one a commissioner of drainage, one appraiser of that Company; all gratuitous. Of the remaining three, one an auctioneer was privileged to continue a special profession; only two derived any profit. There was an outcry about the appointment of Frenchmen, but there was one, Cruzel, a civil engineer who was appointed by Governor Roman at a salary of $5000.00 before he had come to Louisiana.

Thus it can be said that it was not the political preferment to the Gallo-Americans which precipitated the animosity of the so-called Native Americans, who at that time were in full control of the affairs of the State. These incidents were inspired and provoked by a small minority of undesirable agitators, trouble makers and unscrupulous adventurers. In the same issue at the *Bulletin*, there appeared an editorial which shed further light on the controversy:

We cannot indeed hide it from the public that there are not less than five to six hundred persons now in the City, that have been spewed out of the different counties of Mississippi and parishes of Louisiana; that have no legitimate means of support and are engaged in seeking where plunder may be made. These nightly leave their traces on the ships and crafts on the river, and the houses in the remote limits of the city, they harbor day by day under or about the wharves or the swamp — and go abroad at night for their prey.

The editor asked for better enforcement of the vagrant law.

The inhabitants of the City were not adverse to American migrants, on the contrary, they offered every inducement to industrious and respectable people to settle among them as attested by an editorial in the *Bee* of September 9, 1835:

> Machinists artisans are invited to come to the City as well as capitalists. They would have constant employment, good wages and many conveniences, — but we cannot think of inviting attorneys, doctors and accountants; for the market is already glutted with such. Many clerks arrived here last fall, of whom hundreds had been obliged to return almost penniless and wholly disappointed.
>
> If indeed there were three or four shipments of females to attended to the dry goods stores, etc., they would find a reckoning. Seamstresses and laundresses would do well to pay us a visit also. Indeed we believe what many ladies would find in their interest to emigrate hither, for our population in winter usually consists of five males in proportion to one female; a sad disadvantage to many young gentlemen well disposed to countenance the fair sex.

The apparent tranquility which followed the emeute of the previous fall was of short duration, for only a very short while afterwards the same accusations, criminations and recriminations broke out with renewed vehemence. Whilst the Native American Association was apparently inactive, it labored underground to confound its enemies, for it only waited for the proper time to renew the campaign of vituperation. The oath taken by the members was exposed in the *Bee* of February 10, 1836. It was:

> We solemnly swear before God's men and we appeal to the searcher of hearts for the truth of our declaration, that - - - - we are determined never to vote for any foreigner to any political office of trust or power, and to this resolve in the language of our departed patriots, we pledge our lives and sacred honor.

To which, in its French section the *Bee* appended the following:

> The last pamphlet published by the corresponding secretary of the Native American Ass'n. must have appeared to the peaceful inhabitants of New Orleans that now was the time for them to be on their guard and to oppose it with all their energy in order to prevent these catastrophies about to explode on the population.
>
> No one doubts that this pamphlet has resulted in a great exultation, it is then most important that true Americans, Louisianians by birth, and in general all the good citizens of the country, to unite themselves to convince the members of that

society that their inconsequent doctrine is frowned upon by the entire society, as it has for its purpose the union which should reign between the citizens in general; to form parties which eventually end in hostilities, and at least, what is most necessary to adopt suitable means to bring back to these wild spirits sentiments of justice and fraternity. With these motives, we must presume that the assembly on Thursday next, will be a large one, for then all citizens will remember that it is by only an imposing and respectable crowd that they will be able to prevent an impending catastrophy.

On that day and in the same journal, this time in its English section, appeared the following:

We have been requested to call a meeting to be held for the purpose of forming a society, as a counterpart to The Native American Association; and do so with reluctance and regret, as believing that such a society will be the means of strengthening the prejudices already existing, which lately threatened the peace of the city. It will be like creating one disease to remove another.

That the Native Americans Ass'n is the result of prejudice aided by self-interest, cannot be doubted and that the application or a charter of incorporation is objectionable, must be admitted even by those who apply precisely as it would be absurd or ludicrous to form an Ass'n of native Germans in Germany, Englishmen in England or Spaniards in Spain and apply for charters of incorporation.

But it is not necessary to denounce the members of that association, nor is it indispensable to defeat their object by counter association. When societies are based on the interests of prejudices influencing life, liberty and the pursuit of happiness — they are indeed an extended basis — as extended as the application of the first assertion of equal rights of all men contained in the Declaration of Independence. But such prejudices would be strengthened by combined opposition; and the worse results may be apprehended by dividing our citizens into classes such as those based on the supposed principles of the Native American Ass'n. If that opposition be confirmed, it may produce the most deadly feuds and personal encounters. It is better to nip the evil in the bud.

If the meeting called will only pass resolutions of a persuasive and reasonable nature, they may have a salutary influence, but if an opposition society is organized, Heaven preserve New Orleans.

NOTICE: A meeting of citizens of Louisiana who are now in the City of New Orleans is respectfully called for Thursday evening at 6:00 P.M. in Mr. Davis' Hall. The object of this meeting is to take into consideration and to propose a resolution in order to create an association of Loyal Americans and to pray for its incorporation by the State Legislature.

All the native citizens as well as the naturalized citizens and especially the Louisianians are requested not to fail to attend said meeting in as much as it is in their interest to put down an association which tends to disunion among us and to sow the seeds of discord through our ranks.

Editions of newspapers in New Orleans in favor of that patriotic call are respectfully requested to insert the above.

The *Bee* expressed the hope that the proceedings would be conciliatory, while firm, moderate in tone, resolute in the assertion of constitutional rights and legal privileges. The meeting of Loyal Americans was held, and it was said that "the purest patriotism, most conciliatory sentiments and honorable and liberal feelings prompted the meeting of that portion of the American people, united under the motto "Union and Brotherly Love."

Judge Gilbert Leonard of Plaquemines Parish presided. Ex-Governor Dupre from Opelousas attended. Judge Leonard made an impassioned address. A committee composed of the following gentlemen was appointed by Judge Gilbert: John R. Grymes, M. C. Cucullu, B. Marigny, Felix DeArmas, J. Bermudez, Gaston Brusli, W. F. Duplessis, Paul Lanusse, A. Blandeau, Armand Lanaux, Pierre Hoa, Aug. Delassus, Theo. Montreuil, Paul Delery, Pierre Jorda, Victor Poutz. Resolutions were proposed and adopted.

The Committee on resolutions was then appointed and was composed of: Dennis Prieur, Albert Hoa, B. Marigny, I. P. Preston, Felix Labatut, Donatien Augustin, J. R. Grymes, J. H. Holland, Jasques Dupre, Martin Gordon, Adolphe Mazureau and J. J. Mercier.

The following citizens composed the second committee: Edgar Montegut, P. J. Tricou, Justin Durel, Paul Bertus, Aime Guillot, Felix DeArmas, Wm. G. Hewes, Christian Roselius, Thos. Barrett, Pierre Soulé, Phil Power, Solomon High, J. F. Canonge, G. Leonard, T. Fitzwilliams, Dr. Cannon, Nicholas Sinnott, Joaquin Viosca, F. Tio, Judge Grivot, Michael Maher, General Plauché, N. J. Jourdon, Chas. Hilperens, A. D. Shenson, J. N. Cuddy, A. Phillips, Trasimond Landry, J. C. St. Romes, Jerome Bayou, Trigant deBeaumont, Major Relf, Armand Pitot, Jas. Guillot, Jr., F. Correjolles, A. Jeanfreau, Patrick Doherty.

A few days afterwards the *Bee* defended its policy of moderation, deplored the action taken at that meeting and pleaded for the restoration of peace in the community:

> Although the moderate course that we have of late pursued and are resolved to follow, evinces a disposition not to be champions or advocates of any particular party, section or society; our regard for the common welfare must induce us occasionally to notice that legitimately we consider as militating against the public peace and harmony of all classes — where society is as heterogenous as in New Orleans. During the course of the last summer, we deprecated the formation and continuance of the Native American Ass'n, because fully convinced of the evils which it was calculated to produce among us; without, however, denouncing its members or attributing unworthy motives to them — supposing that prejudice chiefly guided their conduct. The counter Ass'n of Native Louisianians is composed of good men, firm and resolute.
>
> This has been censured because it has taken the epithet of "Loyal" — that is acting in conformity of the law; but with what propriety is not apparent. Its meeting to be organized was public; its proceedings were published; and everything relating to it was open and avowed. Not so with the other association. The people have never been put in possession of its meetings, its proceedings and its organization.
>
> It is true that a protest was ushered into notice before its origin, and on which it was supposed to be based; but it is equally true that all connection with said protest by the association was denied publicly and privately. Our fellow citizens had therefore no means to judge of the conformation of the Society and finding it to be exclusive in its nature, that its proceedings were secret and that its members bound themselves together by oath, suspicion if not hatred was excited against it in the breasts of many native patriots as well as naturalized.
>
> Yet it was for a time passed over in silence till it should manifest itself by works; and when a singular pamphlet was published in the name of the Ass'n by its Corresponding Secretary, — when it was found that its members had applied to the Legislature for an act of incorporation, many of our fellow citizens believed that the latter was a stratagem to perpetuate what they felt to be contrary to the welfare of the Society and the harmony that should subsist between all classes of our population. They cast themselves on their reserved rights and formed a preservative and protecting society — different in almost every respect from the other. They are natives of Louisiana as well as citizens, they invite naturalized citizens to join them; they are not bound together by an oath, nor have their proceedings, nor principles or names been strenuously secreted. They are

among the most respectable portion of our community in intelligence, patriotism and influence.

The *Bee* is not with any party — But with controversy we are tired, as useless and obnoxious.

The *Journal of Commerce* published a communication signed "E.A.C." which said:

> This evident object is to revive the odious distinction of French and American party in the City. Every such object should be treated with merited reprobation. They ought not to be an American Party in Louisiana. Every citizen in the United States, whether native or adopted, be his language what it may, ought to unite in promoting the prosperity of the State. It is as unwise as it is ungenerous to excite discontent between the populations speaking different languages. It can be productive of no good.

At that very time an act was being considered in the State Legislature to divide the City into three distinct municipalities.

For a short time that underground activity was to all appearances dormant, but it soon manifested itself by its attempt to abolish the use of the French language in New Orleans.

In the *Bee* of October 20, 1937, is found an article stating that an attempt was made by Shaumburg to banish the French language. It was called "the boldest effort of its kind." The object was to disfranchise the native population because of their inability to speak English. It said:

> Nor can the indigenous population of Louisiana, the Creoles so called, be excluded from municipal employments or be deprived of the relations they hold in regard to magistrates elected by themselves. — Election ruse to exclude any member of the ancient population from office of Mayor. The project is destroying the French language.

This act of the City Council was vetoed by the Mayor.

In the early 1800's the trans-Apalachian migration began. New frontiers were opening in what was then the far West. Many of these settlers, who did not find that conditions met with their expectations, moved southward. The marvelous increase in the population of the West and South was possible only at the expense of the East. The *Cincinatti Advertiser* gave an interesting tableau of that trend. It observed that in 1820, the population of fifteen states: Maine, New Hampshire, Massachusetts, Rhode Island, Connecticut, Vermont, New York, Pennsylvania, Delaware, Maryland,

North Carolina, South Carolina, Georgia and the District of Columbia, was 7, 426, 716; and that in 1830 it had increased to 9, 153, 403—an accretion of 1, 732, 687 in ten years. Whilst in 1820 the nine western and south western states: Kentucky, Ohio, Indiana, Mississippi, Illinois, Louisiana, Missouri, Alabama, Territory of Michigan and Arkansas had a population of 2,233,880, in 1830 it numbered 3,707,299 inhabitants, an increment of 1,437,299.

New Orleans profited greatly from that great accession of population, in the West, for her commercial growth can be attributed to the trade from that region. Although many of the Western boatmen visited the City, but few remained to make it their domicile. They displayed all the characteristics of frontier men. Accustomed as they were to a wide open country, they could not adopt themselves to the ways of the city, nor would have they been welcome. The *Louisiana Gazette* of August 1, 1825, gave a facetious, though friendly description of these "boatmen designated by our honest inhabitants as *kentucks,* and by themselves as: horses, alligators, steamboats, snapping turtles and earthquakes — according as they are more or less terrible in the field of Mars' coach driver. They are the subject of horror and detestation of every planter and not much less avoided by town folks. The introduction of the steam boat changed the character of the boatmen."

Most of the cultured, refined and educated Americans came here from the North and East. They were the lawyers, doctors, ministers, capitalists and merchants. Many arrived there with the intention of remaining. Their distinction gave them an entré into the best society, and their untiring energy and outstanding ability made them an asset in the building of a greater New Orleans.

CHAPTER XXIII

CATHOLICISM

At the time of the Louisiana Purchase there were only two churches in New Orleans. One was the St. Louis Cathedral and the other the chapel of the Ursulines. All outward religious manifestation of any faith but the Catholic was absolutely prohibited by both France and Spain. During the colonial period there were only a few Americans in Louisiana, so the number of Protestants was relatively very small. But immediately after Louisiana became a territory of the United States and particularly after the Battle of New Orleans, there was an influx of Anglo-Saxon Americans. The way of life, the culture, the gaiety, the morals and the religion of the Gallic population were misunderstood. Altogether different from theirs, so much so were those customs and beliefs that a spirit of intolerance and suspicion was engendered in the new arrivals.

The religious intolerance and the national prejudices, which in the early nineteenth century were so prevalent in the North, inspired a distrust of and even a hatred for the people of New Orleans. This had its counterpart in the pre-revolutionary days. The colonists of New England displayed great animosity for their Canadian neighbors, for they, like the Gallic population of New Orleans were innately French, and what was more intolerable, they were Catholics.

Schlarman in his authentic book, "From Quebec to New Orleans" wrote:

When England took possession of Canada after the battle of the plains of Abraham and the Treaty of Paris, (1768) there were only 800 English in that country, while the French Canadians numbered 65,000. Quebec had a population of 6,700 and Montreal counted 4,000. The rural population amounted to at least 50,000. After the conquest the English population gradually increased: still, after a number of years the relative proportion of the inhabitants was English, 5% and French, 95%.

It is quite natural that Canada now being an English colony, attempts were made to Anglicize it in laws, language and even religion if possible. The 5% called themselves the "King's old subjects" and considered the 95% foreigners: the 5% clamored for institutions such as an Assembly which would have practically entrusted to them the government from which the 95%

were necessarily excluded because of the ridiculous and offensive oath of supremacy, with it odious fulminations against the Pope, which no Catholic could conscientiously take.

This state of affairs persisted until 1774 when the Quebec Act granted constitutional rights to the Canadians. Among other stipulations, it declared that "all questions concerning property and civil rights should be decided by the French law," and granted to the Canadian Catholics freedom of worship.

This concession by King George to the Canadians to practice unmolested their religion was vigorously condemned, and aroused the ire of the colonists further south, who loudly proclaimed him an apostate of the Anglican Church, of being a papist and a traitor to his crown. This helped to precipitate the war of the Revolution, for Parquet in his "Histoire du Peuple Americain," affirms that in 1774, Benjamin Franklin assured the Prime Minister of England, "that he had not met a single colonist, drunk or sober who aspired for independence from the yoke of England."

Again quoting Schlarman, the Rev. Daniel Barter, a former Congregationalist, wrote in 1827:

We are [were] all ready to swear that King George, by granting the Quebec Bill [that is, the priviledge to Roman Catholics of worshipping God according to their own conscience] had thereby become a traitor, had broken his coronation oath, was secretly a papist and whose design was to oblige this country to submit to the unconstitutional power of the English monarch and under his and by his authority to be given up and destroyed, soul and body, by that frightful image with seven heads and ten horns. The real fear of Popery in New England had its influence: it stimulated many people to send their sons to join the ranks. The common word then was: "No King, No Popery."

Alexander Hamilton fostered the same prejudice when he said:

Does not your blood run cold to think an English Parliament should pass an act for the establishment of arbitrary power and Popery in such an extensive country? If they had any regard for the freedom and happiness of mankind they would never had done it. If they had been friends of the Protestant cause they would never had provided such a nursery for its great enemy. They would never have given such encouragement to Popery. The thought of their conduct in this particular shocks me. It must shock you too, my friends. Beware of trusting yourselves to men who are capable of such an action. They may as well establish Popery in New York and the other colonies as they did in Canada. They had no more right to do it there than here. Your lives, your property, your religion are all at stake.

Schlarman wrote that "the Quebec Act with its broad concession to the French Canadians, gave Canada to Great Britian. Canada remained British by becoming French."

It may be said that were it not for the religious intolerance of the colonists, the Canadians most probably would have participated in the War of Independence.

This digression is only pertinent in so far as it establishes the reason for the contumely New Orleans was subjected to by the tories, who as yet had not become reconciled to the principles inscribed in the Constitution.

At that time Catholics were very much in the minority in the United States. In 1835 it was estimated that the population was 14,000,000, of which 590,000 were Catholics, or about 1/28 of the total population. Of other faiths, the Calvinistic Baptists were the most numerous. They numbered 2,743,452, or 1/16 of the total population. Of the Protestant faiths, the Methodist Episcopal was a close second with 2,600,000, or 1/8. The Congregational Orthodox with 1,600,000, or 1/12. The Protestant Episcopal and the Universalists had a little more than one million between them.

It is evident that in those days the Baptists and Protestants had a supremacy which was predominantly composed of Anglo-Saxon Americans, both natives and naturalized, who were imbued with all the religious and political prejudices and hatred for the Latin Countries. Especially were the English and New England writers, who left their impression of New Orleans, rabid censors of the morality and culture of a people they could not understand. They compared New Orleans with the infamous cities of the Bible. They branded it a city of godlessness and moral depravity. Their greatest complaint was what they called the profanation of the Sabbath, because of the trading and the patronizing of places of amusement, such as balls and theatres, on that day. Occasionally they deplored the small attendance of the Protestant churches, but when reference was made to the Cathedral, the concensus was that the Sunday services were well attended, principally by ladies with their children and slaves. They failed to understand that the doctrine of the Catholic Faith made it mandatory for its communicants to attend Mass on Sunday, and that after having worshipped their

Savior, they were at liberty to participate in any innocent pleasure. Many of the austere New Englanders with puritanical tendencies knew not tolerance, and anything counter to their views they castigated with a fanaticism beyond the bounds of reason.

Benjamin Henry Latrobe, who was an Episcopalian, and lived in New Orleans in the early nineteenth century, commented in his "Journal" on the observance of Sunday in New Orleans. He said you could tell it was Sunday, by the ships in the harbor hoisting their flags, the attendance at the Cathedral of all the pretty girls, the closing of the shops run by Anglo-Saxons, and the sound of guns firing in the nearby swamps where many went hunting. He noted that the shops as well as the theatres and ball-rooms were open on Sundays, but this did not seem to offend him as he wrote that if they were closed, "that day would be gloomy and *ennuyant* as elsewhere in the Union."

Hamilton has an interesting observation about religion and religious observances in New Orleans of that period:

> Both Catholic and Protestant agree in the tenet that all men are equal in the sight of God, but the former alone gives practical exemplification of his creed. In a Catholic church the prince and peasant, the slave and master, kneel before the same altar in temporary oblivion of all worldly distinctions. They come there but in one character, that of sinners; and no rank is felt or acknowledged but that connected with the offices of religion. Within these sacred precincts the vanity of the rich man receives no incense, the proud are not flattered, the humble are not abashed. The stamp of degradation is admitted to community of worship with the highest and noblest of the land.
>
> But in Protestant churches a different rule prevails. People of colour are either excluded altogether or are moved up in some remote corner, separated by barriers from the body of the Church. It is impossible to forget their degraded condition even for a moment. No white Protestant would kneel at the same altar with a black one. He asserts his superiority everywhere and the very hue of religion is affected by the color of his skin. From the hands of the Catholic priests the poor slave receives all the consolation of religion. He is visited in sickness and consoled in affliction, his dying lips receive the consecrated wafer, and in the very death agony the last voice that meets his, is that of his priest uttering the sublime words: "Depart Christian Soul." Can it be wondered, therefore, that the slaves in Louisiana are all Catholics; that while the congregation of the Protestant church consists of a few ladies, arranged in well cushioned pews, the whole floor of the extensive Cathedral should be crowded with worshippers of all colours and classes?

For all that I can learn, the zeal of the Catholic priests is highly exemplary. They never forget that the most degraded of human forms is animated with a soul, as precious in the eye of religion as that of the Sovereign Pontiff. — The arms of the Church are never closed against the meanest outcast of society. Divesting themselves of all pride of caste, they mingle with the slaves and certainly understand their character better than any other body of religious teachers.

I am not a Catholic, but I cannot suffer prejudice of any sort to prevent doing justice to a body of Christian Ministers whose zeal can be animated by no hope of worldly reward and whose humble lives are passed in diffusing the influence of Divine truth, and communicating to the meanest and most despised of mankind the blessed comforts of religion.

These men published no periodical enumeration of their converts. The amount and the success of their silent labors is not illustrated in the blazon of missionary societies, nor are they rhetorically set forth in the annual speeches of Lord Roden or Lord Bexley. And yet we may surely assert that not the least of these labors is forgotten. The record is where their reward will be.

Harriet Martineau, an English Protestant, in her book "Retrospect of Western Travel," expressed practically the same view point; writing of the Cathedral, she declared:

It is a place which the Europeans gladly visit as the only one in the United States where all men meet together as brethern.

Within the edifice there is no separation. Some few persons may be in pews, but kneeling on the pavement may be seen a multitude of every shade of complexion from the fair Scotch woman or German, to the jet black pure African — the Spanish eye flashes from beneath the veil; the French Creole countenance, painted high, is surrounded by the neat cap or the showy bonnets, while between them may be thrust a greyheaded mulatto, following with his stupid eyes the evolutions of the priest; or the devout Negro woman telling her beads — a string of berries, — as if her life depend on the task.

During the preaching a multitude of anxious faces, thus various in tint and expression, turned towards the pulpit, afforded one of these few spectacles which are apt to haunt the whole future life of the observer like a dream.

There are groups about the Cathedral gates, the blacks and the whites parting company as if they had not been worshipping side by side.

She also remarked that there was no strict observance of the Sunday and that "in the market there is traffic is meat and vegetables; and the group of foreigners make a Babel of the place with their loud talk in many tongues. The men are smoking inside their house; the girls, with broad colored ribbons streaming from the end of their long braids of hair are walking and flirting, while veiled ladies are stealing through the streets, or the graceful quadroon women are taking their airing along the levee."

Not only the Sundays, but the holy days of obligation were also observed by the Catholics. The *Gazette* mentioned that in 1822, All Saints Day (November 1st), drew large crowds in the Catholic Churches and that some parts of New Orleans were on a holiday and that it resembled more a city of Spain or Italy than a town of the United States. It reproachfully added that twelve to fifteen hundred persons had died within twelve weeks.

Yet, according to the Reverend Mr. Clapp, in New England they spoke about Louisiana in terms of "disparagement and vituperation." He related:

> Last summer a clergyman of Massachusetts observed to me that he could hardly conceive of a greater calamity than for a pious and enlightened minister to be compelled to spend his days in Louisiana where Christianity was encumbered by the corruption of the Roman Catholic Church.

This was the consensus relative to Catholicism in New Orleans. The intolerance, the bigotry and the hatred of the calumniators knew no bounds in their disapprobation. It sold books and newspapers which were avidly read by a biased public.

That campaign of hatred for the Catholic religion was not limited only to New Orleans, but prevailed as well, over the whole country. Clapp wrote about this, and he especially mentioned the Irish, because it was claimed that these people coming in crowds, would exert a most deleterious influence, "putting in jeopardy our civil liberties and sowing broadcast over this land the seeds of more moral contagion and death."

The Creoles were accused of being irreligious. If by that term is meant "not devout," it would have been true of many of their men, yet they were Catholics by heart and by conviction. They were baptised in their Church, married by their Church and at their hour of death fervently hoped to receive the last rites of their religion. They always insisted that their children be reared in the religion of their fathers and they encouraged the piety of their wives.

This did not apply to the French as distinguished from the Creoles. The former were usually political refugees from the disturbed conditions then existing in France. Some of them had atheistic tendencies and others were opposed to the practice of any religion. Most of the invectives against the clergy were from the pen of these men and as a rule were found in the French sections of the press.

The Catholic clergy was above reproach. The few scandalous remarks made about them do not deserve mention. The authors of these defamatory statements, and they were very few, always claimed hearsay from a dubious source.

The most opprobrious indictment of the Catholics of Louisiana and New Orleans, strange as it may seem, is found in the book "The Life and Times of John Carroll," written by Peter Guilday, Professor of Church History, The Catholic University of America. This work is considered most authoritative and adorns the shelves of nearly every Catholic library in the Union. It is quoted as follows:

> Many Catholics die without the sacraments, many children are unbaptized; others scarcely see a priest once in a life time; marriages are contracted without a blessing; Christian Doctrine is not taught, and such a decay of Catholic life is to be observed that within a few years the Catholic faith will be entirely obliterated. There is rife in the city of New Orleans, a spirit of unbelief or rather of godlessness which is gradually corrupting the whole mass. This plague is to be attributed to the coming of a great number of freemasons and hucksters of every description, to the spread of French maxims, to infrequent preaching of the Gospel, to love of lucre and pleasure, so much intensified by the climate and the number of female slaves; above all to the scandals given by the clergy.

That book was copyrighted in 1922 under the imprimatur of Patrick J. Hayes, D.D., Archbishop of New York.

It is evident that this baseless accusation is a composite of letters which were accepted as true by the author without considering their reliability, their motive, the reason of their hatred, if any, the opportunity for their observations, the character, and the mental and moral traits of the writers. In this respect he leaves us in the dark as to who these individuals were. It is the duty of an historian to investigate his basic material, to frankly expose the truth, publish the names of his authorities so as not to unqualifiedly perpetuate a scandal about individuals, a community, a culture and a civilization; much less the practitioners of a religion.

In the early decades of the nineteenth century, the communicants of the Catholic religion were almost wholly composed of the Creole or native element and a few Irish immigrants. The Anglo-Saxons were virtually all Protestants. Many of them were rabid anti-Papal, as well as the majority of the visitors who recorded their impressions of the City. Their darts of hatred and intolerance were hurled at the Creoles because of their culture, language and religion. The Creoles were the bulwark of Catholicism in Louisiana, and as far as they are concerned, it can be said unequivocally that they never nurtured "a spirit of unbelief or of godlessness which is gradually corrupting the whole mass" — a lie fabricated of whole cloth. The Creoles and their descendants have remained staunch Catholics to this day. After more than a century, the French speaking people of New Orleans and of South and Southwest Louisiana are predominantly Catholic, whilst the other sections of the State, which are mostly of Anglo-Saxon origin, are of Protestant conviction.

At that time the hucksters were migrants from the North, and were generally Protestants. Besides they exerted little influence in the religious affairs of the City, because their stay was usually of short duration. The French, the later migrants, were soon absorbed by alliances with Creole families, and soon were reconverted. So the assertion that the French who came over later were irreligious is not based on facts.

As to "the scandals given by the clergy," intensive research of that period reveals but little on that subject. On the contrary the records are most flattering. Their chastity was rarely if ever attacked, or their devotion to duty, their ministrations to the rich and poor and to whites and blacks, have been frequently commended as was mentioned in the quotations above.

Such a statement coming from such a source as Guilday is most unfortunate.

During the Spanish regime and in the early American domination the Capuchin Monks administered to the people of New Orleans, for Louisiana had been placed under their jurisdiction since 1721. Only once during the French and Spanish domination was that control challenged. Fortier in his book, "Louisiana," related that:

On March 9, 1752, Father Dagobert, the superior of the Capuchins, invited Father Baudoin, the Superior of the Jesuits, to give his benediction to the chapel of the hospital. The Jesuit Superior was quick to accept and soon afterward he set up the claim that by the publication of his letters patent as grand vicar and the giving of his benediction upon the request of the Capuchin Superior, he had been recognized as the vicar-general of lower Louisiana. This brought on what has become known in history as "the war of the Jesuits and Capuchins," which lasted for several years. In 1763, the French Government directed the suppression of the Jesuit order in all French territory. The Jesuits in Louisiana were accordingly expelled from the colony, and their property, amounting to about $180,000.00, was confiscated. Only July 21, 1773, Pope Clement XIV issued a Bull suppressing the order in all the states of Christendom, but in 1801 it was partially restored by Pope Pius VII and completely rehabilitated. The Jesuits returned to New Orleans in 1855.

The expulsion of the Jesuits ended the controversy. Father Dagobert, the Capuchin Superior, was then appointed vicar-general, which office he held for several years during the early Spanish domination. The Church which, during the time of the French colonization was a part of the diocese of Quebec, came under the jurisdiction of Bishop Echevarria of Santiago de Cuba. This diocese was divided in 1790 when the southern part of the island was made an archbishopric and the Floridas and Louisiana were attached to the diocese of Havana. On April 25, 1793, the two colonies formed a new diocese presided over by Bishop Don Luis de Peñalver y Cardenas. He remained in that See until June 26, 1802, when he was consecrated Archbishop of Guatemala. For a little over three years New Orleans was without a bishop. Shortly after the American purchase, the papal Bull of September 1, 1805, placed the diocese under the authority of Bishop Carroll of Baltimore, who appointed as his vicar the Very Reverend Jean Olivier, who was succeeded in turn by the Very Reverend Louis W. Dubourg, who came to New Orleans on August 8, 1812 bearing the appointment of Apostolic Administrator. Later, on September 24, 1815 the Pope at Rome consecrated him Bishop of New Orleans.

For some reason when Abbe Dubourg first arrived in New Orleans he was unpopular. When he preached his first sermon the congregation practically insulted him. They moved around restlessly on the benches, coughed and sneezed and spat on the floor "rubbing out their spittle on the floor with their feet," according to Latrobe.

He retrieved himself and won popularity by his conduct on the day of the battle of New Orleans on January 8, 1815, when he said a high Mass at the Cathedral with the ladies of the congregation present while all the able-bodied men were at the battle field.

Fortier gives an interesting account of the Abbé's patriotic endeavor and wrote: "General Jackson highly commended this action, and after the victory, requested Father Dubourg to hold a public service at the Cathedral. This was done on January 23, 1815. The Abbé met Jackson at the door of the cathedral and delivered a patriotic address [his flaming oration "a la Française," according to Latrobe, was long remembered] and Jackson in turn thanked the Abbé for the prayers offered in the church."

At his own request Abbé Dubourg was transferred to St. Louis, where he was able to display his great executive ability in furthering the propagation of his faith. What was St. Louis' gain was New Orleans' loss.

The diocese of New Orleans was established on July 18, 1827 when the newly ordained Bishop Rosati was appointed to that See. This he declined, and soon afterwards was made Bishop of St. Louis and apostolic administrator of the diocese of New Orleans.

Rev. Leon Raymond de Neckere, C.M., a native of Belgium, a member of the Lazarist order at the age of 30, was consecrated bishop on June 24, 1830. He soon after assumed his responsibilities as Bishop of New Orleans, where he administered the affairs of the diocese for a little more than three years. On September 5, 1833, he was a victim of yellow fever.

The following obituary appeared in the *Courier*:

> Bishop Leon de Neckere, Bishop of the Diocese of Louisiana, died yesterday from a disease lasting four or five days, and this morning his mortal remains were exposed in the Church of St. Louis. Mr. de Neckere is a Belge, and possessed all the qualities of heart and of spirit which endeared him as a Pastor. Learned, a good orator, virtuous and pious without bigotry, he fulfilled with honor the duties imposed on him as the chief of the Church amongst us. He has the esteem and the regrets of all classes and of all the sects of society.

It was not until November 27, 1835 that Monseigneur Blanc became Bishop of the diocese. In the interim the office was administered by Fathers Anthony Blanc and Ladaviere. Monseigneur Blanc was consecrated at the Cathedral, the first time that that ceremony was held in New Orleans. He was a native of France and died in New Orleans on June 20, 1860.

It might be said that the St. Louis Cathedral has a more interesting history than any other church in the United States.

About 1720, shortly after the founding of the City, Bienville dedicated a site for the building of a church and presbytery. The first church was constructed of wood and adobe, very primitive, but suitable to the use of the few settlers of that time. Destroyed by a tornado in 1720, it was replaced in 1724 by a more substantial brick building, which served that small congregation for more than sixty years. The conflagration which practically destroyed the City on Good Friday, 1788, reduced the church to ashes. It was rebuilt by Don Almonaster y Roxas at a cost of $50,000.00. The foundations of the building were laid in March, 1789, and after innumerable delays the edifice was opened for divine services five years afterwards.

The new building miraculously escaped the conflagration which swept New Orleans on the day of the fete of the Immaculate Conception, December 8, 1794.

In 1814 the façade of the Cathedral built by Almonaster was altered by the addition of two massive octagonal towers, and in 1834 by the addition of an imposing belfry.

The *Louisiana Gazette* of December 19, 1825, commented that "the Cathedral Church is undergoing extensive repairs. The elegance and taste displayed in its interior decoration does much credit to the ingenuity of the artist who has been engaged for the purpose."

On February 6, 1837, an Act for the purpose of incorporating the "Roman Catholic Congregation of the Church of St. Louis in New Orleans" was introduced in the Louisiana House of Representatives, authorizing said Church to borrow $200,000.00 for the purpose of rebuilding it. It was also stipulated that the "duration of the charter be extended till the year 1880 and that the present wardens be retained until 1840, when a new election is to be held."

In February 1850, a tower of the Cathedral collapsed causing great damage to the roof and walls. It is the prevalent, but erroneous belief, that the Cathedral was torn down and rebuilt in 1850. That is a mistake. When the wardens started to have the building repaired, they concluded to alter and enlarge the building to its present dimension and appearance. Steeples were raised on the old octagonal towers, and the façade was changed and made more imposing by the addition of columns and pilasters — the Cathedral as it stands today.

The following observation by 'Feuillton' in the *Louisiana Gazette* of August 23, 1821, deserves mention:

> The Father Jean Kuhn [Jean Pierre Koune] was carried to his last resting place last Tuesday by members of the Clergy of this city.
>
> The Abbé Jean has rendered many services without ostentation. It is not the question here to speak of his errors (if he had any) ; the saintly respect for the dead forbids all reflections; let it be said that hatred should end at the tomb. I, who never was one of his friends, it may be found extraordinary that I consecrate a few lines to his memory and would find it surprising that I am astonished like all reasonable persons that his remains were not placed in a private tomb. Father Kuhn [Koune] although not rich, leaves enough to defray his last expenses. How could the persons in charge of his last wishes ignore the duty due to his memory? These are painful reflections, I agree, if the reason is a fightful parsimony, they are to blame, but Father Kuhn [Koune] left enough friends who would gladly, in case of necessity, have contributed to that cause.

In June 1823, the first English sermon was delivered at the Cathedral by the Reverend Father Gallagher.

The *Courier* announced that the new Catholic Church, the St. Patrick, on Camp Street in the suburb of St. Mary, was opened for services on May 1, 1833, at half past nine o'clock A.M. Bishop de Neckere performed the ceremony, delivering his sermon in English. Pews were sold at auction on March the 28th, 1834. On the 17th of March 1856, St. Patrick's Day was celebrated by a high Mass and by a panegyric by Reverend Father L. L. Mullen.

The physical property as well as the management of the Cathedral, in the early days, was in the hands of the Marguillers, (wardens of the Church). They collected all revenues, established the fees for all services, such as funerals, weddings, etc., determined the salary of the pastors, assumed all financial obligations for the maintenance of the Church, and had a voice in the selection of their priests. In fact, they were the administrators of its affairs. Yearly elections were held by the congregation, and usually the most prominent Catholics, men of distinction and integrity, were elected to that office.

The *Courier* of March 31, 1927, ran the following notice.

The Roman Catholics, having a right to vote, are informed that an election of six trustees will take place on Monday the 3rd of April next, between the hours of 7 o'clock A.M. and 3 P.M., which will continue the following days at the same hours for the purpose of filling the vacancies occasioned by the expiration of the terms of service of Messrs. J. B. Labatut, S. Cucullu, T. Mosey, E. Girod, F. A. Blanc, A. Cruzat, and also to elect a seventh trustee in the place of Mr. F. Percy, who has resigned.

The election will be held in one of the rooms of the Fabrick, opposite the Sacristy of the Church.

By order of the President of the trustees.

Signed: H. Gastor

The *Bee* reported on April 6, 1834 that the following were elected wardens: F. Labatut, J. Bermudez, Edgar Montegut, H. Pedesclaux, J. Guillot, J. Bertrand, A. Pitot and W. F. C. Duplessis.

According to Guilday, a schism ensued in which Sedella (Pére Antoine) was upheld by Governor Claiborne. Again that author is, to say the least, most unfortunate in his choice of quotation, for he wrote that "Claiborne lent the whole influence of his position to break down the discipline of the Catholic Church and maintain in the Cathedral of New Orleans a man whose immoral character and neglect of duty [Pére Antoine] were notorious, and who would in any New England village have been consigned to jail."

This is denied by Chambers who wrote that "in one thing was Claiborne very careful and that was to do nothing detrimental to the Catholic faith or to arouse the resentment of the Catholic clergy. But one instance of internal strife over religious matters was brought to his attention from outside of New Orleans, and he handled this with such tact and reasonableness as to leave no resentment in its wake." The fact is that Father Sedella won the decision in the civil courts. That attack on the character of Father Sedella is scandalous and false, and unworthy of the pen of such a prominent writer. Slander, like cancer in its incipiency, is hard to detect. Both spread rapidly, one to destroy the body and the other, which is worse, the character, the reputation and as in this case, the sanctity of a man. The latter ends with death, the former haunts the hallowed grave.

The discord between the Marguillers (wardens) and the Church Authority persisted long after the death of Father Antoine in January 1827. The wardens collected all the revenues of the

Church, assumed all financial obligations and reserved to themselves a voice in the selection of their pastors. This usurpation of Episcopal prerogative based on the laws of the Church was strenuously resisted by Bishop Blanc, especially so, after the death of Father Moni, the curate of the Cathedral, and his appointment of Abbé Rousillion as his successor. The wardens immediately rejected that nomination, upon which Bishop Blanc issued a pastoral letter in which he censured the wardens and mildly suggested the possibility of excommunication, but that was as far as it went. He pacified the congregation by recalling the nomination of Abbé Rousillion and by appointing Father Maenhaut instead, who, shortly afterwards because of the disagreements between himself and the wardens resigned his post.

Because of this, on November 2, 1843, Bishop Blanc removed all the priests from the Cathedral and it was not until the following January that Father Bach became the curate. He died nine months afterwards. This time Bishop Blanc warned the wardens that he would not fill that vacancy unless they agreed that they would not interfere with the functions of their pastor. This they refused to do, and again the Cathedral was left without a curate. Thereupon the wardens instituted a damage suit for $20,000, against the diocese, which they lost in both the Parish Court and the Supreme Court. Thus ended a long controversy, which had lasted for approximately two generations, between the diocese and the congregation as to the title of the Cathedral and the insistence of the parishioners in having a voice in the selection of their pastors. No dogma of faith or morals was ever involved.

Monseigneur Blanc began his long pastorate as Bishop of the Diocese of New Orleans on February 20, 1837. His judgment, wisdom, understanding, patience and tolerance under the most trying circumstances, spell his greatness.

On the 21st day of April, 1833 Bishop de Neckere blessed a modest frame building on Camp Street. It was the first Catholic Church in the American section of the city. Because of the large number of Irish Catholic emigrants it was appropriately named St. Patrick. Shortly afterwards the tremendous increase in the congregation made it mandatory that a larger edifice be constructed.

The following advertisement appeared in the French section of the *Bee* of January 18, 1837:

NOTICE: The laborers [journaliers] of the 1st Municipality are invited to be present at a meeting to be held at the New York and Philadelphia Hotel on the Levee between Conti and Bienville, Wednesday, the 18 inst. at 7 P.M., to adopt suitable measures for the construction of the St. Patrick Church.

    Signed: James Roach, Thomas St. Leger, Wm. Mullowney, Thomas Bell, M. C. Tobin and Mich Callaghan.

The new church, which stands today was completed in 1837, and was blessed by Bishop Blanc. The plans were drawn by the renowned architect James Gallier. Father Kindelon, the founder of St. Mary orphanage, was the builder and the first pastor of the original church. He was succeeded by the well beloved Father James Ignatious Mullen.

    The frequent funeral processions, the tolling of church bells and the chants of the priests had a depressing effect on the morale of the population during the periods of epidemic. The City Council passed an ordinance prohibiting funeral ceremonies being held in the Cathedral. In order to overcome that objection, the Marguillers of the Cathedral decided to build a mortuary chapel in close proximity to the cemeteries. A plot of ground on Rampart Street corner Conti was purchased from the city, and the cornerstone of the Mortuary Chapel, then called the St. Anthony, was laid on October 14, 1826. The chapel was blessed on December 22, 1827. This edifice now known as the Church of Our Lady of Guadeloupe, has recently been renovated.

    At a meeting of the City Council held on February 13, 1836, Mr. Felix Labatut offered a resolution stating "that in case the trustees of the Catholic Church should bind themselves to the corporation to erect the edifice proposed by them, the corporation of New Orleans shall give to them the lot known as Anthony Square for its purpose." The resolution was passed as amended by Mr. Baldwin which provided that if the said church did not use it for that purpose it then should revert to the corporation.

    At the next meeting of the council Mayor Prieur vetoed it for the following reasons:

> In the contract passed on the 11th of March 1831 with the church congregation for the part of the square situated on the N.E. side which was authorized by the resolution of December 29, 1830, it was stipulated that the part of the ground so sold shall be employed to enlarge the square in the rear of the Church and that the corporation shall be bound to have the banquet

bordering on said portion of ground made at their own expense.
. . . . Again considering the question under another light, and supposing said cession to be possible, would it be just to concede gratis now to the church wardens the double of the ground which in 1931 they sold to the corporation at the very onerous term of $10,000. When the corporation found that such a lot of ground could not be useful to them, the congregation found out that it would be worth a price. Do you believe then that we ought to retrocede it gratis? I think not. . . . I think it impossible to change the destiny of Anthony's Square. Not only Dr. Thomas, but all the owners of property at the angles of Orleans Street have an unobjectionable right to oppose it.

D. Prieur, Mayor.

Labatut moved to override the veto. Dr. Thomas asserted that the ground was worth $60,000, and argued that the city had no more power to dispose of the square than to sell a portion of Orleans Street.

Labatut retorted that some years since that same spot was designated as the most appropriate for a flower market to cost $20,000. He stated that in 1794 when the present church was constructed the population amounted to 10,000, now it is 80,000, and that the building is by far too small to accommodate the church-going public.

Caldwell said that he would "vote to tear it down and rebuild another that would do honor to the State." The veto of the Mayor was overruled.

What spot more befitting for a monument to perpetuate the memory of New Orleans most beloved priest, Fray Antonio de Sedella, than La Place Saint-Antoine!

CHAPTER XXIV

THE SCHISM IN THE CATHOLIC CHURCH

Immediately after the Louisiana Purchase the Catholic clergy of New Orleans was in the throe of violent discord which soon resulted in a schism. It is only recently that we are able to learn the truth about this celebrated controversy. Documents and letters, edited and translated from the Spanish by Stanley Faye and published in the Louisiana Historical Quarterly of January 1939, shed a totally different light on the schism of 1805. These official papers of great historical importance were discovered by him in the Archivo General de Papeles de Cuba, Legajo [file] 179, catalogued "the Casa Calvo's retained copies of correspondence."

The following is a communication addressed to Don José Antonio Caballero, Spanish Minister of War by Don Santiago Calvo de la Puerta y O'Farrill, the Spanish-Irish Marqués de Casa Calvo, the Spanish Commissioner in New Orleans. This official document is quoted in full:

> The agreement and concord that, with such inspiration to the faithful had been preserved among the clergy for many months following the retrocession and sale of the province, is now disturbed in a scandalous way by the same priest who, with a kind of color of title [*titulo colorado;*] in canon law, that which has the appearance of validity, but suffers a hidden defect that makes it void happens to be here at the head [of church affairs] and who, forgetting the many things that he owes to the Spanish nation, has come to the point of giving the greatest proofs of ingratitude, persecuting with monstrous hatred the Capuchin friar His Majesty's pastor of the Holy Cathedral Church here, Fray Antonio de Sedella.
>
> This person is the Irish priest from the College of Salamanca, Don Patricio Walsh, who at the time of the translation of the Reverend Bishop Louis de Peñalver y Cárdenas to the archepiscopal see of Guatemala, remained as *teniente vicario* with the canon Don Thomas Hasset and — the latter dying, as also the only remaining prebendary, Don Francisco Guerrero — continued the ecclesiastical government of the province; because, despite the provisions of the Holy Laws, neither the Reverend Bishop of Havana nor he [the Bishop] of Baltimore — who, as the nearest prelates, could have taken charge of the Church —

did do so, because of the distance or because they felt that they lacked resources and means for such action.

I am informed that the Bishop of Baltimore replied to that effect almost at the very beginning, the point having been referred to him. . . . .

In the month of October, when it was patent what devotion for the good of the parishioners and what general estimation was enjoyed by Father Antonio de Sedella and the people were beginning to assert their decided desire to keep that friar here, although he had obtained from His Majesty permission to retire to his monastery — in reference to which in case of necessity the Catholics were intending to send a reverent petition to His Majesty — the demon of discord began to pour forth his furies and evil principles, which emanated from two European-French clergymen who were acting as assistant pastors and who, surprising the good faith of the Priest, Patricio Walsh, sowed the darnel [a poisonous grass] that so perniciously and harmfully has borne fruit.

The latter began to permit himself to violent acts of jurisdiction in contempt of the King's authority and of my commission and, what is more, is greatly endangering Religion and the peace of conscience of the faithful here.

Father Fray Antonio, His Majesty's pastor of this parish, he appointed as assistant pastor, requiring of him that he alternate weekly with the two European assistant pastors, who were heaping the former with injuries, interfering with him and ill treating him. Although here I lacked both power and authority, still I considered that I had enough for summoning the said Priest Walsh and exhorting him to take intervention and to arrange things in such a way that each might keep within the limits of his duties. As he had failed to present himself in the houses of my residence on the days when the Spanish people do so in order to show the gratitude and loyalty that they owe to the Sovereign, I sent to him the Priest Sebastian Gili, Chaplain of the Commission, and also the Secretary, Don Andrés López de Armesto, to the end that they with the greatest mildness and gentleness, might constrain him to bring back those unruly ones to reason and leave Father Antonio in quiet and peaceful possession of his pastorate, since the latter had even had the goodness to abandon to them the proceeds of the benefice in order that they might be appeased.

This has been asked of me by the same Father Antonio when he orally recounted those events.

The polite and courteous responses of the Priest Walsh, who at that time poured forth eulogies and encomiums of Father Antonio, tranquilized me and even for some time suspended my judgment, until the bomb exploded and on the eighth of this March the latter found it necessary to send me a complaint in writing, recounting the continuous ill treatment that he was receiving from the two assistant Fathers, Fray Juan Pedro Koune, paid by his Majesty, and the Priest Pedro Francisco L'Espinase, appointed and renumerated by the municipality, or city council. . . . .

In view of such proceedings I could do no less than take [an active] interest, being zealous although in a foreign land to preserve the respect that is owed to the Sovereign's orders, and in an *oficio* I inquired of the Priest Walsh if he was acting with authority from the United States; and, in that case, if he had decided to remain or to go, as had been ordered, to some other of His Majesty's dominions, in order that I might take action on my own part.

The response that the Priest Walsh gave me demonstrates the perverse or scantily respectful way in which, evading the point, he answered, ridiculing a matter that ought to have been treated with all seriousness.

Nevertheless for the sake of prudence and moderation and also the position I was in, I inquired a second time whether he was acting as a Spaniard or as an American, in order that, in the first case, he should conform to our wise laws and, in the second, that I might have recourse to those of the United States in addition to the powers that belong to me as Commissioner for the transfer of the province.

Time passed until the 16th without receiving a reply to the *oficio* sent on the 12th; but in this interim he did not omit carrying forward his design, since on that same 12th day Father Pastor Sedella forwarded to me two papers. In the first is shown the violent action that the Priest Walsh took in suspending the friar, and in the second the order that he gave him that he should put at his disposition the registers, ornaments, sacred vessels and other precious possessions of the Parish of St. Louis that were in his care.

These facts came to the knowledge of the people, and while I was seeking to calm their minds and to prevent the loud schism and scandal that was developing, all the Catholics of this parish arose as one and in a body, asserting that as things had come to such a pass they would make use of the privilege that the freedom of the American government permits them and would appoint a pastor of their own choice, since the Priest Walsh was not acceptable to them. So with the consent of the city council at the sound of the bell there gathered in the Cathedral Church more than four thousand souls, on Thursday the 14th, at ten o'clock in the morning, presided over by the Catholic aldermen; and although a large number were holding their votes in writing in order to put them in the locked box prepared to receive them, the impatience and desire of the people showed itself so unmistakably that they all, all, by acclamation elected Father Antoine, whom they went to seek at his dwelling and forcibly conducted to the Church, giving him the most complete satisfaction that he could wish for: and under these circumstances, after a courteous and polite discussion, this good friar decided to agree on condition that I as His Majesty's Commissioner consent, in view of the fact that he was preparing to go to Spain to enjoy the retirement that the King our Lord had conceded to him, and on condition that the Sovereign's approval should be forthcoming.

Thereupon the Catholics sent me a deputation in agreement with the city council — to which I replied favorably for the good of Religion and for that of the congregation — telling me that they would put a written memorial into my hands in order both to state the foregoing facts and to elucidate the points I am about to mention.

Thus they presented me the paper which, to save time, I referred to the consideration of the Judge-Advocate, who was on the point of sailing for Pensacola, causing him therefore to delay one day; and, at the same time asking a report from the Chaplain of the Commission, Don Sebastian Gili, meanwhile and in conformity with the advice that, in writing but informally, the same Judge-Advocate gave me I sent an *oficio* to the aforementioned Don Patricio [Walsh], telling him that if he considered himself a subject of our Sovereign I ordered him and exhorted him in His Majesty's name to remove immediately from Father Antonio the suspension that he imposed upon him, in order to calm those disorders and to avoid the greater disorder that was to be feared for Sunday the 17th, on which the people were determined that Father Fray Antonio would sing the parochial mass [Father Walsh had intended to say Mass on St. Patrick's day] and that all the other fathers should remain apart. Likewise, following the same advice, I required that he cease from the functions of ecclesiastical judge, [a quasi-governmental office under the *fuero* (extraterritorially) of the Church in Spanish dominions] adding for the sake of peace it would be well that he should go at the earliest possible moment to Havana to await the orders that His Majesty might be expected to give him.

While these two persons were preparing their report I became the recipient of a communication in which the Priest Walsh comments with ridicule upon my *oficio*, proceeding with the levity and scant courtesy that it demonstrates.

The reports of the said Judge-Advocate and the Chaplain of the Commission, who authorized me to respond to the delegates of the congregation of Catholics and to present them with certified copies thereof, to thank them for their good offices and to express appreciation of the importance of not leaving this Catholic community without the spiritual counsel that Father Fray Antonio de Sedella may bring to them by serving the pastorate of the parish Church here. I consented that he should remain until His Majesty, to whom I was reporting on the events, should deign to decide the future of that vassal, not doubting that in his generous Royal piety he would be pleased to give approval, because of his supreme usefulness that at present attaches to his functions in view of the circumstances in which the province now exists [a covert reference to the Spanish hope to regain Louisiana] and the confidence that the faithful among this flock have placed in that friar.

Since at the same time it was improper that the King's orders and my representative office should remain so scandalously ridiculed, for the third and last time I again asked the Priest Walsh on the 18th whether he considered himself a Spanish subject or a citizen of the United States, to which up to now he has not deigned to reply, although one of his friends has sought to persuade him to do so, with good and friendly arguments, which he rejects and treats with high disdain. Therefore, upholding what little Royal authority belongs to me, I informed him that it was proper to suspend his salary after the first of September, in view of the fact that *oficios* from the Royal Treasury had already said that all persons who should not leave the province should have no right to claim any salary after the last of August next since the Royal Treasury must not incur expenses that originate in procrastination for his own private ends, until His Majesty may decide upon the example to be made of this person if he should come into his dominions, now that there is no other means of arresting the force and suspending the violence of his illegal acts and relieving that friar, who is in every way worthy of piety and Royal clemency.

The results have been that Father Fray Antonio, not believing himself in conscience deserving of the punishment that the Priest Walsh, without authority and without reason, has decreed against him, and fortified by the opinion of the Judge-Advocate (the only jurist in canon law here at present) and by the report of the well informed Don Sebastian Gili, sang the parochial Mass before a large assemblage of people on Sunday the 17th, a larger number being present on the 19th, the day of the feast of St. Joseph, when I attended in order to contribute to the peace of mind of some who were letting themselves be carried away by the rumors of the [Ursuline] nuns, who were beginning to exert influence by means of the devout negro women, causing these latter to say that all those who attended Father Antonio's Mass were schismatists and were excommunicated.

The people here, acting on their own authority, have appointed with consent of the aldermen or city council — although that may not be necessary — five trustees of the Church property, who are to choose a treasurer from among their own number in order that, putting themselves in agreement with the pastor, they may arrange for supporting the Church, maintaining its ministers and managing the property of its endowment.

They have formally asked me for the transfer of the parish, to which I have consented, appointing the Secretary in order that he may take part in the inventory and transfer of registers, ornaments, sacred vessels and other precious possessions of the Church, and appointing the Priest Don Sebastian Gili for the same duties in respect to the ecclesiastical archives.

I do not doubt that we shall have to engage in a terrible struggle and to contend with numberless difficulties that will be raised by the mad passion of that Minister, who had passed as a moderate until the touchstone of superior authority revealed his true alloy; and I greatly fear that the city may be forced to take decisive action, as I myself should have done if it had been in my hands, in view of the fact that he is proceeding willfully, making parish Churches out of the Church of the nuns [Father Walsh later appointed the Ursulines Chapel as the only authorized place in the parish for the saying of Mass] and that of the Charity Hospital where it already appears that preaching has begun on the matter.

The French clergyman, Father L'Espinase, assistant pastor paid by the city, has resigned; but Walsh has immediately appointed another in order to carry out his design, and now more than ever in giving orders to all the parishes here and even to the two Floridas, without taking into consideration that the two canons of this Church have died and that this Church not only has had no bishop since the illustrious Peñalver, but even has been transferred to a foreign power, and that the two Floridas belong to the Bishop of Havana.

For the same reason and in order to enforce the respect owing to the Majesty of our Sovereign, I have likewise suspended the salary of Father Fray Pedro Juan Koune, who is paid on account of the Royal Treasury.

In order not to make this report more diffuse I have confined myself to the literal exposition of the facts supported by the documents that I enclose. I hope my conduct in this difficult situation may merit Royal approval and that His Majesty will deign to extend his favors to the Fray Antonio de Sedella, who is willingly sacrificing himself through his ministry to the wishes of his parishioners.

God keep Your Excellency many years.

New Orleans, March 20, 1805.

To His Excellency Don José Antonio Caballero.

Louis Peñalver, who had been the bishop of Louisiana since July 17, 1795, was translated to the archbishopric of Guatemala on June 20, 1802, which left the diocese of New Orleans without an episcopal head until September 1, 1805, when it was placed in the charge of Bishop Carroll of Baltimore. During that interim the See of New Orleans became vacant and the appointments of Bishop Peñalver became invalid and the administration of the diocese passed to the chapter of canons, which was composed of two members only, Fathers Hasset and Guerrero, who were appointed by royal acts of December 18, 1793 and August 6, 1794. In 1800 Canon Hasset was appointed vicar-general. Faye wrote:

> Thus jurisdiction would pass smoothly from bishop to vicar-general, and, upon vacancy, to the chapter of which Canon Hasset was a member. Apparently in order that, in case of Canon Hasset's death, the administration should be kept as long as possible from the inexperienced hands of Canon Perez Guerrero, Bishop Peñalver gave to Father Walsh, the experienced and capable *vicario foráneo*, appointed as vice-vicar-general (*teniente de vicario*). This would become effective only in case of Canon Hasset's death or disability. In any case Father Walsh's appointment, like that of Canon Hasset as vicar-general, would become void if the see should become vacant.
> When Canon Hasset died in 1804, predeceased by Canon Guerrero, the see had been nearly two years vacant by reason of Bishop Peñalver's translation to and occupation of the episcopal see of Guatemala. Therefore the appointment of Father Walsh as vice-vicar-general never went into effect.

Both Canons Hasset and Guerrero had appealed to the Bishop of Havana in 1802 for a clarification of the status quo. The reply of the Bishop to Father Hasset's letter is quoted in part:

> I believe that the jurisdiction in ordinary has reverted to the Chapter (Cabildo) in Louisiana — which you say has taken place because it has only two canons — because although when a Corps is composed of a much greater number the law requires at least three to constitute a Council (Capitulo), nevertheless when the Royal and Pontifical authority, as in this case, there are no more than two canons in one Church, just as these are the councillors ex-officio, of the Bishop while he lives, so without a doubt they will be his representatives and successors in his jurisdiction after his death or translation unless for some special reason another arrangement has been made as in the second case, which is that you exercise jurisdiction as [vicar-general] in the name of the translated prelate until his installation or assumption, which is the same as in the case of death.
> Thus I judge that you gentlemen should act in common accord, or each exercise a nonconflicting jurisdiction, or agree if possible that jurisdiction be exercised by one of you.

The following day the Bishop wrote to Canon Guerrero making the same appeal for amity and harmony, and exhorted that "if you are willing to cooperate harmoniously with that gentleman [Hasset] you and he can take counsel together and decide on what is best for your Church with respect to law and to the intentions of His Majesty and His Holiness."

These letters were signed Juan Jph, Bishop of Havana, July 30, and 31, 1802.

Evidently even at that time harmony did not prevail among the clergy.

A year and a half later, taking advantage of the vacuum then existing in the Church, Father Walsh assumed authority and named Fathers Jean Pierre Koune and Pierre François L'Espinase his assistants. The Spanish-Irish priest arrived in New Orleans in 1792. He was educated at the Spanish College of Salamanca. He was the chaplain of the Charity Hospital and later also of the Ursuline Convent. Father L'Espinase, a Frenchman, came from Jamaica.

Pere Antoine was accused of being the instigator of the schism of 1805, and that he was guilty, among other crimes, of insurbordination against his Church for inciting his parishioners to rebel against ecclesiastical authority. For more than a century and a quarter these accusations were never successfully refuted, for it is only but recently that the truth has come to light when Faye ferreted out official communications pertaining to the matter, buried in the files of the *Archives General de Indias, Papeles de Cuba*. These *oficios* are authoritative for they are from the pens of the principals in the controversy.

To an inquiry by Casa Calvo, the Bishop of Havana on July 28, 1804, gave the following reply:

> As to the question of spiritual jurisdiction, which is your Lordship's uncertainty and which ought not to embarrass you as much as me, the neighboring prelate .... I must tell you that I also felt uncertainty concerning the way in which the said jurisdiction was transmitted by its latest diocesan prelate to one of the canons there, as vicar (*teniente vicario*) and to another, who was not a canon, as vice-vicar (*teniente de vicario*), and concerning how the exercise of jurisdiction ought to have proceeded after the translation of the said prelate to and his assumption of another Church..... You may so inform the clergy there, to the end that they may apply to the proper place for their orphaned condition; which is as much as I can say in reply to Your Lordship's *oficio*.

That same day Bishop Juan Jph addressed a communication to Father Gili which is quoted in part:

> Relative to your ecclesiastical government of the bishopric where you are, which is no longer a bishopric of our domination since it is the duty of the governments, both political and ecclesiastical, respectively, to take suitable action, it is not my business to inquire whether the general ecclesiastical jurisdiction has been transferred or has ceased, and it should be enough for the parish priests and the others of the faithful to act wisely and discreetly and, whether through the principle of common error and color of title or through tacit delegation from the neighboring prelates in ordinary, to let things continue in the usual way, since they have a right in law to take things into their own care; for those reasons, I say, question cannot be raised concerning the validity of any act, internal or external, of jurisdiction in your territory until the exterior policy there shall be organized otherwise by the new nation to which it belongs and until the corresponding ecclesiastical authorities declare that the functions of the Spanish Ecclesiastical Ministers of your country have ceased or shall have ceased.

On March 5, 1805, Pére Antoine complained to Caso Calvo of the continuous ill treatment received by him from Fray Koune and the Priest L'Espinase, supported and incited by Father Walsh. In that *oficio* he objected to "the unnatural violence and scandalous action that results in humiliation of my duty and office."

The *oficio* continued:

> So that, Sir, when I was expecting he would have given the said assistants a reprimand for the scandals that they told to the assembled faithful on the fourth and fifth days of the aforesaid month, he refused to interfere at all, leaving me shamed and beaten and the others triumphant and victorious.
>
> These proceedings and the contents of his *oficio* make me fear that he may send me an order for the transfer of the books, archives and other things that are in my care as pastor of the aforesaid church; and I believe Your Lordship to be the sole and only one to whom belongs the duty of all transfers in this province, I hope you may be pleased to advise me what I ought to do in such an event, or if I ought to carry out any transfer without receiving an order from Your Lordship in due form, and to whom and how I ought to effect it, deciding what in contrary case might be Your Lordship's superior pleasure.

On the same day Pére Antoine complained to Father Walsh about "The continuous shameful insults and acts of disdain that I frequently received from the two Fathers, the Assistant Pastors, especially from the Priest L'Espinase, urge me to ask that you order me relieved from the pastorate that I now exercise as if in name only."

The only time he resorted to invective against his tormentors was in that *oficio* when he wrote:

> That the said Father L'Espinase should act thus towards me is not so strange, inasmuch as his irregular conduct made him quite notable and notorious in Jamaica, even to his being denounced by his superiors in public papers posted on the door of the Church there .... but what fills me with wonder is the conduct of the other [Father Koune] who is still receiving pay from His Catholic Majesty and intends to do so [similarly] paid to another of His Majesty's Dominion.
>
> I do not enter, Sir, into more details, since yesterday's scandal and that of today give witness to all I could say.
>
> I hope (and I beg of you) that you may give me a reply in order that on that basis I may confer with the Marqués de Casa Calvo (now the sole representative of the Spanish nation) and to the end that His Lordship may be informed of my final forced resolve.

The vile insinuations followed by scandalous public accusations from the pulpit inspired by Father Walsh against the beloved Pére Antoine were part of an ingenious, well laid plan for a coup d'état. On March 6, in an *oficio* to Fray Antonio, Walsh proclaimed "That from this moment I declare myself to be pastor (*Cura del Segrario*) of this Holy Catholic Church of New Orleans, and henceforth Your Reverence as well as the other ecclesiastical ministers engaged in my Church are to serve under my immediate orders and inspection as my assistant pastors. Of this I inform Your Reverence for your information and guidance, reserving to myself to give other and future orders at the proper time to Your Reverence for care and performance in the financial management and responsibility that you exercise."

The next day Fray Antoine replied that "as soon as occasion offers, I am determined to return to Spain to enjoy the favor that His Majesty has been pleased to grant me. For this reason I beg you to regard me as relieved of the pastorate of this Holy Catholic Church, although the assistantship to which you have been pleased to appoint me is not therefore to be understood as admitted, since I cannot degrade myself in contradiction to Sovereign authority and Spiritual authority in abandoning an office to which both elected me.

For this reason I beg you to forward to me the proper exeat, offering meanwhile (if you do not object thereto) to exercise the functions of my ministry, on condition that you regard these functions as of some usefulness; and observing for your guidance that, with the object of avoiding scandal I do not judge myself authorized to communicate your decision to the other ministers of the Church, nor do I oppose the action you have taken in assuming the office that I hold."

On the 9th of March, Casa Calvo in an *oficio* to Father Walsh protested "the unnatural, violent and scandalous action that you took, which results in humiliation of the duty and office of the said Fray Antonio." He further stated that:

> Zealous as I am that the Sovereign's orders be respected, as they ought to be, by His subjects, and in order to give information to superior authority concerning what has occurred, I hope you may tell me in reply if the powers you appropriate to yourself emanate from authority conferred by the government of the United States and, in that case, if you have determined to remain or to emigrate to some of His Majesty's dominions; dependent on your response, I shall take action incumbent upon me in order that the Reverend Fray Antonio, already relieved of his duties of pastor, may effect the formal transfer of what is in his charge as such.

Father Walsh immediately replied "that I wonder that Your Lordship should seek to appropriate to yourself powers that you either can or should possess or, consequently exercise." He then bombastically issued the following ultimatum:

> I say for Your Lordship's future guidance that I am provisor, [an office including that of Ecclesiastical Judge] Vicar-General of the Diocese of Louisiana and both Floridas, of the latter provinces, Vicar-General, Sub-Administrator-Apostolic-Military; and also of one of them, West Florida, Commissioner of the Crusade [vendor of indulgences for the support of missions] and I warn Your Lordship (I speak with respect) that it seems to me to be your duty to respect the office as such as chief ecclesiastic and that I am making and shall make vigorous complaint where and to whom it may seem proper, not only concerning all interference on your part concerning my ministry and against any proceeding of like nature I protest here and now in due form.

On March 11, Pére Antoine received the following *oficio* from Father Walsh:

> Being fully informed that Your Reverence is working evilly to raise the people here against their lawful Pastor and that the

darnel is already beginning to sprout among the weak of spirit, I have found it necessary to suspend Your Reverence (as I do by this present *carta de oficio*) from all ecclesiastical functions in this Bishopric, declaring you in the name of the Church (which I represent) to be irregular if you dare disobey this order (exercising functions of Sacred character) and subject to other penalties of law in case of resistance.

Immediately Casa Calvo advised Fray Antonio:

> In case that the Priest Patricio Walsh, persisting in the use of powers that are unknown to me, transfers or orders seized the Ornaments, Sacred Vessels, and the other valuables and things that were in your care pertaining to the Church, you will reply to him with the moderation that is your custom; that the transfer has to be effected with personal participation of the City Council and His Majesty's Commissioner; and as for what relates to me, you will refer to the provisions of Law 22, Section 2, Book I of the Code of the Indies and to the scandal and evil consequences that would follow so unconsidered a step. If nevertheless he should insist and take them from you by force, you will submit, afterwards making a report of all particulars that may have occurred, for my guidance and knowledge.

At a meeting of the parishioners held on March 14th, attended by three Catholic Aldermen of the city, Nicholas Girod, Charles Porée and Paul Lanusse, Pére Antoine was elected by acclamation Pastor and Ecclesiastical Judge of the Parish. The "condition set by the said Reverend Father for acceptance of the aforesaid nomination; and that was, that since he had been enjoying that same Pastoral benefice through the kindness of His Majesty and since he had also obtained from His Sovereign Piety permission to retire to Spain, he could not accept that office unless Your Lordship [Calvo] should first give permission." The report continued:

> Now we are confronted by another difficulty no less great and are on the eve of seeing ourselves without a Pastor and with no one to administer the Holy Sacraments; for this reason: Since in that meeting the aforesaid Reverend Fray Antonio de Sedella explained to us that, although he did not believe before God that he was suspended from his Ministry notwithstanding the order of Señor Don Patricio Walsh had directed against him, there were Doctors of Canon Law in this City who would pass on the matter .... and that he might exercise his duties without scruple of conscience and that the Christian faithful might likewise apply to the latter with full confidence and without doubts.

Immediately upon receipt of this communication, Casa Calvo sought the opinion of Señor Doctor Don Nicholas Marie Vidal, Lieutenant Governor and Judge Advocate of West Florida, former lay counsel of different Ecclesiastical Courts and likewise Counsellor of the Holy Court of the Inquisition de Indias, and also that of Father Gili of St. Bernard. The former on the eve of his departure for Pensacola wrote the following opinion:

I only said that I did not know on what authority or document he [Walsh] based it, [his authority] as in reality I do not know even now, and that I considered it as null if that which he was exercising was by virtue of the appointment by the Most Illustrious Señor Peñalver.

Coming now to the point of the suspension of Father Fray Antonio de Sedella, I will say that all the theologians and jurists agree that penalty cannot be imposed except for an offence of such importance; and all the people here are aware that Father Sedella has not committed the least offence and that on the contrary he is an exemplary clergyman, a tireless Evangelical Laborer, and that he has worked in the Lord's Vineyard at all hours of the day and of the night, in weather good and bad, alleviating the souls of rich and poor, such as in truth there are very few [who do;] whence arises the general regard that he enjoys and the high love and respect with which he is looked upon and acclaimed by all.

His having complained to what he regarded as Superior authority concerning the insults and vexations that, with notable scandal, were given to him by his own assistants, does not bear the appearance of a misdemeanor; yet it is he, the injured one, who has been punished, and the offenders and guilty ones left in impunity.

What the Priest Don Patricio Walsh set forth as the basis of the suspension was, that he went about inciting and provoking the people in his favor; and everyone knows that this is false and that on the contrary he has done what was possible on his part to calm the tempest that has been raised, and that the faithful Catholics have aroused themselves without urging from without, enthusiastically seeking his retention in the Ministry of the pastorate.

And lastly it is not a fault, nor does it contain anything of evil, that, when the Priest Don Patricio Walsh raised his voice to establish himself as Parish Priest and to name the other as his assistant, the latter should have used his rights in defense of his position and duty.

In view of this the aforesaid suspension appears no less unjust than unfounded, and it seems to me that Your Lordship may send an *oficio* to the said Don Patricio, telling him that if he is a subject of the King you exhort and command him, in the name of the King, to reveal to your Lordship and to the Catholic people on what he bases his authority, and to raise and remove immediately the suspension that he has imposed upon the aforementioned Father Fray Antonio de Sedella . . . . making the said Don Patricio responsible for the results both before God and man.

On that same day Father Gili answered Casa Calvo's *oficio* as follows:

> In order to respond with propriety on whether Father Fray Antonio de Sedella may exercise the functions of his Ministry notwithstanding the suspension that has been imposed upon him, I must previously consider whether the said punishment is legal and imposed by a legitimate jurisdiction, for which purpose I shall refer first to the word of Murillo, section 28 of the *Oficio Vivario*, paragraph 299, *pagini mihi 115*, which view is supported by Barbosa on the *Officio Episc, alleg 54, ex, No. 145*; and these are as follows:
>
> The jurisdiction of the Vicar expires by death, renunciation, entrance into a religious order, captivity, banishment, permutation, deposition, or translation of the Bishop for whom he is Vicar, even in legal processes begun, pending, &c.
>
> And so whatever the Vicar may do thereafter is null, because, since the jurisdiction of the Bishop and that of the Vicar are the same, when that of the former ends by his death, translation, &c., likewise that of the latter expires.
>
> And as it is not established that the jurisdiction that the Rev. Don Patricio Walsh has exercised up to now has any origin other than the commission that, in case of absence or death of the Canon Don Thomas Hasset, was given him by the Most Illustrious Señor Don Luis Peñalver y Cárdenas, former Bishop of this Diocese, it follows that, when the jurisdiction that the said Señor Peñalver exercised in this Province expired because of his translation to the Mitre of Guatemala, that which his Vicar exercised here likewise ceased, and in consequence it appears that the suspension imposed against the aforesaid Father Antonio must be null and void.
>
> But, even admitting that the Reverend Father Fray Antonio de Sedella may have given some reason for the unnatural procedure that he has suffered and that the Reverend Don Patricio Walsh may be legally exercising Ecclesiastical jurisdiction, the present circumstances of the Congregation of the Faithful of this City having by a unanimous vote asked that the Reverend Father Fray Antonio, who during more than twenty years past has with exemplary conduct and good results exercised the Ministry of Pastor, should continue his functions as such, and as the words in which the punishment was announced do not declare him "suspended-denounced" or "suspended-not-tolerated," it seems to me he may exercise them legitimately and without trespassing upon irregularity in Law.
>
> Such is the view of the expert in Canon Law, Vito Pickler, book 5, section 39, whose words I copy and translate for Your Lordship, from Latin into Spanish:

"The person suspended-tolerated, or not denounced, although he acts illegally in intruding into the exercise of the acts from which he is suspended, nevertheless acts legally, if he is sought and asked by others because of his usefulness, and the Faithful do not sin if with just reason they ask such acts of him, such as the Mass, Absolution and Communion; in which case of being asked, the suspended one does not trespass upon irregularity in exercising such acts."

The *oficios* of Vidal and Gili strengthened Casa Calvo's determination to end the schism for on March 18, he wrote to Father Walsh:

For the third and last time I put to you the question whether you consider yourself a subject of his Majesty and are you to continue as such, or whether you take the position of being a citizen of the United States, and I hope you will be pleased to reply to me categorically, since on your words will depend the steps that it will be proper in order that the Royal Treasury may not suffer undue charges.

On March 19, Paul Lanusee, Juan de Castañedo, Jean-Bâtiste Labatût, Bâtiste Durel, and Charles Porée were elected by the congregation as administrators and curators of the Holy Parish Church, "it being ordered at the same time to take stock thereof by formal inventory and likewise of the Registers, Ornaments, Sacred Vessels and other valuables pertaining to the cult that may be in the care of the Reverend Pastor Father Fray Antonio de Sedella, in whose possession they are to remain." "This schism made Fray Antonio, always a most loyal Spaniard, an American citizen," Faye wrote. "It threw Father Walsh into the reluctant arms of the American Courts. It caused Father Walsh within four months to enter even into the Burr Conspiracy and thus to justify if only in secret the action that Casa Calvo had taken against him."

This intrigue between Father Walsh and Aaron Burr is reported by Mathew Livingston Davis in his book, "Memoires of Aaron Burr, 1836-37."

On September 1st, 1805, a Papal Bull placed the diocese of New Orleans under the jurisdiction of Bishop Carroll of Baltimore, and it is significant that on the 21st of that month the office of Propaganda notified Father Walsh that he was relieved of the duties of Vicar-General.

These authentic official documents definitely establish Father Walsh as a master opportunist, a subtle strategist and an artful conspirator who seized the propitious moment for a coup d'état.

He planned well. He was the instigator and prime agitator of a cabal, organized for the purpose of defaming Pére Antoine thereby to usurp his pastorate.

This campaign of vituperation which not only reviled Father Antoine and the clergy, but the laity of New Orleans as well, was given full credence by the Office of Propaganda and the See of Baltimore. After the lapse of more than a century these derogatory letters are still accepted as the unqualified semblance of truth by many historians. Father Walsh, although frustrated in New Orleans, was triumphant in Baltimore.

The *Louisiana Gazette* of Friday, August 22, 1806, carried the following terse announcement of the passing of Father Walsh:

> DIED: This morning the Rev. Father Walsh, Vicar-General of Louisiana.

This was the extent of his obituary.

In an extraordinary session of the City Council held on August 22, 1806, the following resolution was adopted:

> Considering the petition presented by Messrs. Olivier and L'Espinasse [L'Espinase] — Priests of the Church of the Ursulines of this City, in which they requested the permission to bury in the Church of that Convent Mr. Patrick Walsh — Vicar-General of this diocese, who had often expressed to them the wish to be buried there;
>
> Considering likewise a letter from the Superior of the same Ursulines attached to the said petition and in which she informs that her community consents to fulfill the last wishes of the deceased if the City Council does not oppose it.
>
> The Council wishing on that occasion to pay, with the petitioners the just tribute of respect due to the memory of this virtuous ecclesiastic; Resolved that in his favor, they will act contrary to Article 32 of the Police Regulations, which forbids all burials within Churches and that the request of the petitioners shall be granted provided however, that the Sisters do not take advantage of the present to think themselves authorized in the future to plead exception to a rule so essential to the maintenance of the public health.

Father L'Espinase shortly after the death of Father Walsh disappeared from the scene and Father Koune who died in 1821, reposes in an unknown grave. The mortal remains of Pére Antoine were interred in saintly dignity in a vault at the foot of St. Francis' altar in the St. Louis Cathedral, the Church he loved so much.

CHAPTER XXV

PÉRE ANTOINE

Fray Antonio de Sedella, affectionately called Pére Antoine, was not only a colorful personality, but the most beloved priest New Orleans has ever known, despite the fact that he was much maligned and often not understood. His piety, his charity and his devotion to duty merited the love, the unswerving devotion and the genuine admiration, not only of the Catholics, but of the entire population of the city. Although he died 127 years ago, his memory, as a saintly man, is still revered by many of the old Catholics of New Orleans.

Pére Antoine was a Capuchin monk, sent to Louisiana by the Spanish Government to administer to the spiritual wants of its inhabitants. He arrived in the colony in the early spring of 1780 when he was thirty-two years old. Being a loyal subject of His Catholic Majesty, the King of Spain, he was later appointed a commissary of the Spanish Inquisition. He received this official appointment on December 5, 1788, and was ordered "to discharge his functions with the most exact fidelity and zeal, and in conformity with the royal will." In order to do so he requested Governor Miro to provide him with guards. Gayarré tells how his request was granted:

> Not many hours had elapsed since the reception of his communication by the Governor, when night came, and the representative of the Holy Inquisition was quietly reposing in his bed, he was aroused from his sleep by a heavy knocking. He started up and, opening the door, saw standing before him an officer and a file of grenadiers. Thinking that they had come to obey his commands in consequence of his letter to the governor he said: "My friends I thank you and his Excellency for his readiness of his compliance with my request. But I have now no use for your services, and you shall be warned in time when you are wanted. Retire then, with the blessing of God." Great was the stupefaction of the friar when he was told that he was under arrest. "What!," exclaimed he, "will you dare lay hands on a commissary of the Holy Inquisition?" "I dare obey orders," replied the undaunted officer, and the Reverend Father Antonio de Sedella was instantly carried on board of a vessel, which sailed the next day for Cadiz.

On June 3, 1789, Governor Miro in a letter to a cabinet minister, gave the following reasons for the expulsion of Father Sedella:

> When I read the communication of that Capuchin, I shuddered. His Majesty has ordered me to foster the increase of population in this province, and to admit in it all those that would emigrate from the lands of those rivers which empty into the Ohio. This course was recommended by me, for the powerful reasons which I have given in confidential dispatches to the most excellent Don Antonio Valdez, and which your Majesty must have seen among the papers laid before the Supreme Council of the State. This emigration was to be encouraged under the pledge, that the new colonists should not be molested in matters of religion, provided there should be no other public mode of worship than the Catholic. The mere name of the Inquisition uttered in New Orleans would be sufficient, not only to check emigration which is successfully progressing, but would also be capable of driving away those who have recently come, and I even fear, in spite of having sent out of the country Father Sedella, that the most fatal consequences may ensue from the mere suspicion of the cause of his dismissal.

Stanley Faye reports that event as follows:

> In the year 1789 Fray Antonio was vicar-general in the absence of Bishop Cirilio, when Acting Governor Miro exiled him and the Spanish Inquisition to Cadiz. Bishop Cirilio drew up an indictment against his vicar-general. The affair assumed the aspect of a disagreement between church-men. The diocese of Havana sent an inspector to investigate it, Fray Antonio returned to New Orleans high in the favor of the new bishop, the Most Reverend Louis de Peñalver y Cardenas, under whom he served again as pastor of the parish.

With Pére Antoine's return there never was any suspicion of an Inquisition in the Spanish Province of Louisiana.

It seems that the real story was only known to Father Antoine himself, and the secret was buried with him. However, after the lapse of more than a century documents have been found which shed altogether a different light on this famous controversy. The following quotation is taken from an article by Clarence Wyatt Bispham, S.T.M. which appeared in the Louisiana Historical Review for October 1919:

> A new theory accounting for Miro's retirement, however, is based upon certain documents which have recently come to light among the Papeles Precedentes De La Isla De Cuba.
>
> According to this theory Fra Antonio de Sedella did not come to Louisiana for the purpose of instituting the Spanish

Inquisition, but used that role as a mask to hide his real purpose, which was that of a secret agent of the King, sent to do a little private investigation of a political nature. He soon aroused the suspicion of Miro, who seized upon the Inquisition role as a pretext upon which to expel the good Fra from the province, and thus forestall whatever investigation Sedella might be bent upon.

Sedella upon his arrival in Spain was sent back to Louisiana, but was detained for a protracted period in Cuba, the inference being that it was through Miro's influence. A sharp letter conveying the command of the King of Spain himself, liberated Sedella and permitted him to go on his way to Louisiana, where from the time of his arrival to the end of his days he was the beloved Pére Antoine. Thus we have, as between the two, Miro repudiated and Sedella exalted, which was a sufficient last straw to add to the several other reasons for Miro's wishing to leave Louisiana.

In the preceding chapter the official documents, which must be accepted as factual, of the schism of 1805, definitely vindicate Pére Antoine of having incited that scandal in his Church, and definitely prove that he was the innocent victim of the wily Father Walsh and his cabal.

Father Walsh, having been frustrated in his attempt to discredit Father Antoine in New Orleans, changed his tactics and embarked on a campaign of vituperation not only against the good father but of the Catholics of New Orleans as well. He addressed his accusations to Governor Claiborne, to Propaganda and the See of Baltimore.

He wrote the following communication to Governor Claiborne on July 11, 1805:

> The interruption of the public tranquility which has resulted from the ambition of a refractory monk, supported in his apostasy by the fanatism of misguided populace, and by the countenance of an individual [Marquis de Casa Calvo] whose interference was fairly to be attributed less to zeal for the religion he would be thought to serve, than to the indulgence of private passions and the promotion of views equally dangerous to religious and civil order.

He further claimed that two men went to Havana for the purpose of enrolling monks to assist his "schismatic and rebellious conduct". Father Walsh solicited the aid of the Governor. That aid was refused. Yet it is evident that that letter had some effect on Claiborne, who was apparently duped, for in a letter dated October 8, 1805 to the Secretary of War, he complained that "we have a

Spanish priest here who is a dangerous man; he rebelled against his superiors of his own church, and would even rebel, I am persuaded, against the government whenever a fit occasion may serve. This man was once sent away by the Spanish authorities for seditious practices, and I am inclined to think that I would be justified should I do likewise. This seditious priest is a Father Antonio; he is a great favorite of the Louisiana ladies; he has married many of them, and christened all their children; he is by some citizens esteemed an accomplished hypocrite, has great influence with the people of color, and report says, embraces every opportunity to render them discontented with the American Government."

There is nothing in the history of that time to substantiate such baseless accusations. Evidently they were the result of the machinations of the wily Father Walsh. This communication of Claiborne planted the seed of scandal in the fertile soil of Washington and Baltimore. Its roots grew deep and wide and even to this day they are still spreading. Fray Antoine bore his martyrdom with resignation, fortitude and humility. His only consolation was the unbounded sympathetic understanding of the people of New Orleans who knew him best and loved him most.

On the afternoon of Monday, January 19, 1829, a pall of sorrow hung over the city—the beloved Pére Antoine de Sedella had passed away. With unconcealed emotion and uncontrollable tears the news spread. From the highest dignitary to the humblest slave, Catholics as well as Protestants, the non-religious and avowed atheists—felt that they had sustained an irrevocable loss. Their friend, their advisor, their counselor and their consoler in their hours of distress, was no more. Business was stopped, the courts recessed, and the affairs of Government were postponed.

The following day the *Courier* carried the news of his death:

DEATH OF FATHER ANTOINE DE SEDELLA
Funeral to take place on Thursday the 22nd inst, at 10 A. M.
Remains will be exposed at the Parochial Church

Notice by Church Wardens.

Yesterday at half past 3 o'clock P. M. the Rev. Ft. Antoine de Sedella, Curate of the Parish of St. Louis in N. O., died in the city at the age of 81. That event for which a long sickness ought to have prepared us, never-the-less has been sensibly felt by all classes of our population.

The death of the venerable pastor who for 50 years was the

support of the poor, the comforter of the afflicted, the example of toleration and piety. The death of such a man, we say, is a public calamity. Faithful to the principles of his Divine Master, he caused the religion, of which he was the faithful organ, to be beloved, and at his voice, the principles of the Gospel, of which his whole life was a constant practice, did penetrate the soul, and made every one anxious to fulfil his duties.

To honor his memory is to honor virtue and his remembrance will forever be dear to a country where he saw three generations succeed one another, of all of whom he justly enjoyed the love and respect.

TRIBUTE OF RESPECT (HOMMAGE A LA VERTUE)

In the District Court of the 1st District, Mr. Edward Livingston rose and addressed the Court as follows:

May it please the Court:—A revered Ecclesiastic has lately departed this life, who was endeared to the great mass of the inhabitants of the country by the most interesting collection of events from the cradle to the grave.

He conferred upon them in infancy that title from which they derive their hopes of happiness hereafter. In this life he united them in the bonds which secured their connubial felicity, and he it was who performed those solemn rites which connect his memory with the reverence due to that of their ancestors. He was the faithful depository of the most secret thoughts—their consoler in affliction—their resource in poverty—and their confidential friend in society. His charity, his kind feelings, were not confined to those of his own church; and his liberality, both of sentiment and action, were acknowledged by those of a different faith. This holiness, his virtues, should have entitled him to canonization, and if his title to that distinction were to be tried, as it is said to be in Rome, the advocate of the evil one would burn his brief and despair of showing one reason why he should not be received as a saint in heaven who led the life of one on earth.

The death of a man of this character, is a public loss and in order to show respect entertained by the constituted authorities for the memory of the Rev. Ft. de S., I move the following resolution be entered on the minutes:

"On motion of Mr. Livington, it is ordered that the Court will adjourn until Friday morning, for the purpose of giving to the Court and the Bar the opportunity of attending the funeral services of the beloved Father A. de S., a venerable ecclesiastic whose loss is lamented by the whole community, and that this resolution be communicated to the judges of the Supreme Court and of the other courts of this city, with an invitation to meet in the hall of this court for the purpose of attending the funeral together with the members of the Bar and officers of the court, at 10 o'clock this day.

Extracts of the minutes

Jno. L. Lewis, Clk.

The House of Representatives passed the following resolution:

The House of Representatives appraised of the death of the Reverend Father A. de Sedella, late curate of the Parish of St. Louis in New Orleans, and anxious to give to his fellow citizens worthy testimony of the respect they felt for the memory of the venerable father who for one half century has evinced no other ambition than of relieving the poor of every denomination, the afflicted in every condition, in life, of carefully watching over the peace and harmony of his flock and of presenting an example of virtue. On motion of Mr. Maurian, resolved that they attend the funeral in a body, etc.

The City Council also paid its tribute to Father Antoine. Mr. Kenny Laverty offered a resolution which unanimously passed in silent reverence:

Resolved: That the members of the City Council will wear crepe on their left arm for thirty days, as a mark of respect to the memory of the pious and deeply lamented Father A. de Sedella, and that this resolution be published in the different newspapers in the city.

The following notice appeared in the *Courier*:

That venerable pastor, as tolerant, as virtuous, as charitable, and enlightened, is not only regretted by an immense population, but he deservedly enjoyed the esteem and regard of the numerous class of our community, whose principles are founded on faith, hope and charity, those sacred dogmas which Father Antoine practiced as long as he lived.

Masons of all rites, and all degrees, to you we address ourselves. Remember that Father Antoine never refused to accompany to their abode the mortal remains of our Brethern, and that gratitude now requires that we should in our turn accompany him with all the respect and veneration he so well deserved.

Signed: A Number of Masons.

On Thursday the 22nd, at 10 A.M. the ceremonies began with the celebration of High Mass, followed by an eulogy, after which the cortege left the church in the following order:

The Legion
The Clergy
The mortal remains of Father Antoine
The physicians of the deceased

The Trustees
The Governor and the Secretary of State
The president of the Senate and the Senators
The speaker of the House of Representatives
The judges of the Supreme Court
The judges of the District, Criminal and parish Courts
The clerk of the City Court
The Consuls of Foreign Nations
The Mayors and the Recorder
The Aldermen
The Ministers from various Denominations
Members of the Bar
Citizens

The funeral procession proceeded from the Cathedral, down Condé St. to Dumaine, up Royal, then to St. Louis, from thence to Chartres, and down that street to the Cathedral.

The *Louisiana Advertiser* gave the following report of the ceremonies:

> The body of the revered patriarch, the spiritual father of the past and present generation, remained exposed in the building where the Catholic vestry holds its meeting, in Orleans St, from Monday, the day of his decease, t'il yesterday, when it was transferred to the Church.
> During that time, a crowd of people of all ages, sexes and colors flocked to pay their last tribute of respect to him, whom, when alive, they regarded as their guide, their father and friend. His features had preserved their mild and placid expression. Dealth had dealt gently with him, and laid a soft hand upon him. He seemed like a saint, rapt in holy meditation—nothing in his countenance indicating the age of sickness and the approach of decay. The silent tear, the sob of anguish, the prayer of the good, the blessing of the poor, attested that a whole life devoted to deeds of charity and virtue had received its only appropriate recompense — of sincere regrets of a grateful people.
> Early on Thursday morning, the firing of a cannon announced that the venerated remains were about to be removed to their last resting place. . . .
> The Cathedral was dressed in its insignia of deep mourning, the altar surmounted with lofty white feathers, on the right, opposite the main altar, an elevated platform had been erected, surrounded with steps, and covered with black cloth; on the angle of the structure and on all the steps, lighted tapers were placed. On the right, under the altar, consecrated to St. Francis, at whose shrine the deceased had daily for half a century paid

his devotions, the grave destined to receive whatever of him was mortal, stood open.

The Louisiana Legion, and the Lafayette Riflemen, were drawn up in front of the church, — the main portal of which was hung with black drapery, surrounded with the following inscription, admirable alike for its conciseness, its energy of expression, and the purity of its latinity:

PATRI
ANTONIA DE SEDELLA
Sac
Longoevus quamvis occubueris
Iggeus tamen nobis
Tui desiderium
Reliquisti

The executive officers of the State, the members of the Legislature, the judges, the members of the City Council, the gentlemen of the Bar, the foreign consuls and a vast number of gentlemen of all denominations, filled the church to overflowing. Father Monni, the successor of the deceased in his clerical functions, and in affection of the flock, officiated at the altar, surrounded by the whole body of the Catholic Clergy of this and neighboring parishes. The solemn effect of the High Mass on the crowd was enhanced by the grief depicted in the visages of the priests and the choiresters, and every heart seemed to respond to the mournful touching strains of the music, poured forth from the galleries above. When the Mass was finished and the music paused, Father Manhault ascended the pupit. He was eloquent without attempting to be so, for all that he said went to the heart of his hearers, he was the mere interpreter of everyone's thoughts, he did not panegyrize, he had nothing to extenuate, nothing to palliate, he drew a faithful picture of an original impressed on every mind: he spoke of the virtue of the departed, of his humility, of his indulgence to others, his severity to himself, of his universal good will towards men, and when he concluded by entreating all present to comply with the wishes of the dying saint, that his noble flock should join in prayer that his soul might soon "rest in bliss" — we are persuaded that fervent aspirations to that effect went forth to the Throne of Grace from the whole assembled multitudes.

The coffin containing the corpse was borne off on the shoulders of four young men, surrounded by eight pallbearers, friends of the deceased, and the procession moved from the Church.

On its return to the Church, two discourses were pronounced, one in French, the other in Spanish.

On Thursday, April 9th a memorial funeral service was held at the Cathedral in his memory. "The Philharmonic Society, the artists and amateurs of music were kind enough to cooperate in order to give to that august ceremony all the solemnity of which it was susceptible."

His will, executed only a few days before his death, was soon probated; the *Courier* of February 9th, carried the following notice:

> The Reverend Ft. Antonio de Sedella: having by his will, dated 27th of December 1828, left a legacy of $500.00, to be distributed among his godchildren (filleule at filleuls) without distinction of color, who may present themselves within the first six months after his death, at which time the division of said sum will be made among them by the undersigned testamentary executors. Notice is hereby given to all the godchildren of the deceased to make themselves known to the said testamentary executors by proving themselves to be really so.
>
> J. B. Labatut
Z. Cavelier

Thus passed away the most controversial personality in the history of New Orleans. He was denigrated by a few but powerful enemies, severely censured by his Church, yet he was the most beloved and revered priest which ever graced this community. Because of his piety, charity and humility, he enjoyed the unbounded affection and devotion of his parishoners, as well as of all the community. By a strange paradox the virtues which endeared him so much by those who knew him best were used as a pretext by his enemies to castigate him. He was accused of belonging to the Spanish Inquisition and of trying to introduce that nefarious institution into the colony, which calumny has been contradicted by documents that have come to light. He was said to have been an arch conspirator and that he plotted against the government of the United States, which accusation has no historical basis. He was accused of guilt by association with the Marquis of Casa Calvo, a ridiculous charge because Pére Antoine was then a subject of Spain, and Casa Calvo was the Spanish commissioner in charge of the transfer of the colony to the United States. That he plotted for the return of the territory to Spain was based on the unfounded suspicions of his arch enemies and not on factual evidence. It has even been said that he consorted with the Lafittes. If that be true, so did the most prominent merchants of the city. His very sanctity, his charity, his priestly devotions, were unscrupulously assailed.

It is not true that he instigated a schism in the Church and that he was guilty of insubordination. The chaotic conditions then existing in Europe, the virtual imprisonment of the Pope by Napoleon, the rapid and sudden changes of government in Louisiana, from Spain to France to America, and the bewilderment resulting therefrom, had its repercussions in the diocese of New Orleans. It is hard to believe that a man possessing so many virtues would maliciously flaunt his ecclesiastical superior unless he had a moral certitude that his course of action was correct. Now after a century and a half, passions having subsided, and the uncovering of documents from the Archives of Havana has shed more light on this mooted question.

From authentic testimony now available there cannot be any doubt that Pére Antoine had been badly maligned. The people of New Orleans, who lived with him, were his friends and knew him as no one else did, were all patriotic Americans who faced cannon fire in the defense of the Union. Patriots themselves they would not tolerate in their midst a traitor to their country, or one who would conspire for its overthrow. The trustees of his church and most of the Creoles as well as the new American residents, most of them Protestant, would not at his death have eulogized him, nor proclaimed his virtues, and mourned him as they did, if he had been anti-American.

Guilday, who proclaimed Father Antoine Sedella the *inimicus homo* of the diocese, should have said that he was the *amicus homo* of the Catholics of Louisiana.

CHAPTER XXVI

THE RISE OF PROTESTANTISM

The religion of Louisiana during the French and Spanish domination was Roman Catholic, and all outward manifestation of any other faith was prohibited. Whilst Protestants were not allowed to hold public services, there was not at any time religious persecution, and they could worship their God in the privacy of their homes without intereferences. The only churches in New Orleans were the St. Louis Cathedral and the chapel of the Ursuline nuns.

Immediately after the American flag was raised in the Place d'Armes, Governor Claiborne issued his first proclamation, in which he pointed out that the inhabitants were protected by the laws of the United States in the enjoyment of their liberty, freedom of speech and practice of religion. Freedom of religion was then established in Louisiana.

At that time the number of Protestants was few, but as the number of Americans increased, they formed congregations of various denominations. The first was Christ Church, established in November 1805. Its beginning was humble, but through a century and a half, it has grown and become a bulwark of Protestantism. Today Christ Church Cathedral is one of the major churches in New Orleans. It held the first religious service in English in New Orleans. Its first Pastor was Rev. Mr. Philander Chase, who afterwards became the Bishop of Ohio. He was the first Protestant minister of New Orleans.

The Reverend Theodore Clapp in his "Autobiographic Sketches" mentioned that the Episcopalian Church was built about the year 1813, but Paxton's Directory gave the date as 1818, and described it as follows:

"Neat brick octagon building with a cupola, corner Canal and Bourbon. Has an organ: The citizens of New Orleans to testify their respect for the virtues of W.C.C. Claiborne, late Governor of the State of Louisiana, have erected this monument in his favor." (It was situated in the Church yard.)

Again *Niles Weekly Register* mentioned that: "A new Episcopal Church, the first in Louisiana, was opened for public worship

River Front, New Orleans, around 1835. View by Garneray. (Reproduced by courtesy of Yale University Art Gallery)

Ruins of Planters' Hotel, 15 Canal Street (near Chartres). At two o'clock on the morning of the 15th of May, 1833 the roof and upper floors collapsed, burying 50 persons. Ten were killed and of the 40 who survived, many were injured. (Courtesy of the Chicago Historical Society)

A lady of fashion of the "glamorous thirties" taking her afternoon drive.

on the 14th of April last in New Orleans (1816). It contains 72 pews, 61 of which were sold for $13,000.00."

The second Protestant Church to be established in New Orleans was the First Presbyterian. It was opened for worship, according to the Reverend Mr. Clapp, on the 4th of July, 1819. The edifice is tersely described in Paxton's Directory as "a handsome brick building with a gothic front, situated in the suburb St. Mary, at the corner of St. Charles and Gravier. Has a belfry and striking town clock, has an organ."

The Reverend Mr. Clapp, the second pastor of that Church, gives the following description of its interior:

> On the lower floor there were one hundred and eighteen pews. Spacious galleries accommodating about four hundred people. Both sides of galleries free seats for strangers, and was called "Stranger's Church". The church was honored by the attention of the most respectable strangers during the winter season. Pews were taken by the residents of the city, and there were more applicants than pews.

It was said that strangers visiting the City never came to New Orleans without visting the American theater, the French opera, and Parson Clapp's Church.

At that time according to Picton, the Baptist congregations held their services in a school house on Burgundy below Canal Street. The Methodists did likewise.

Reverend Sylvester Larned was the first Pastor of the Presbyterian Church in New Orleans. He was born in Pittsburg, Mass. on the 31st of August 1791. His father was a Colonel in the war of the Revolution.

His biographer, R. R. Gurley, wrote that he entered Williams College in 1810, at the age of fourteen, "but the thoughtlessness and imprudence too natural in boys of his peculiar temperament at that age, led him into an incident which caused his removal by order of the faculty from the institution for a season. Indeed at this time he appeared to have wandered into dangerous paths, and to have thrown off in a great degree the restraints of conscience, authority and good example."

He then entered Middlebury College, where the President of that institution claimed that in composition and elocution, he surpassed any youth of his age, and that should he enter the ministry, he predicted, he would as a pulpit orator have no superior in the country.

He was sent to New Orleans "to examine the moral conditions, and to establish a Presbyterian Church, and to secure an able and faithful pastor." After thirty-five days of travel by sea Mr. Larned reached that city on the 22nd of January, 1817. He began immediately to build his church. He procured $12,000.00 in donations, with the stipulation that it would be raised to $15,000.00, and when $40,000.00 was collected the edifice to be erected. The city donated two lots worth $6,000.00 to the Church. The salary agreed upon for the new pastor was to be $4,000.00 per year or $3,000.00 with a home and garden.

To Larned's satisfaction he found "the moral state of things was indeed terrible, but not so bad as is thought in the Northern States. There is a very agreeable society of genteel, moral families."

Gurley describes him as follows:

> The body of Mr. Larned was the appropriate habitation of his mind, combining in just proportions, dignity, grace and strength. Art could have desired no finer model, and seldom, in her noblest statues, has she embodied the idea of a more perfect form. His countenance well expressed his soul — his voice was persuasive, and as he spoke, his eyes threw a fascinating brillancy upon the rich treasure of thought and sentiment, flung out from the depths and stores of his nature, so lividly around him.

Mr. Larned succumbed to one weakness, one he deeply regretted, and for which he atoned in a most dramatic manner. He had, under extenuating circumstances, deserted his post of duty during a yellow fever epidemic. He bravely faced his congregation, confessed his weakness, and professed his resolution never to leave again during a sickly season. The Reverend Mr. Clapp has recorded that dramatic moment:

> Last summer [said Mr. Larned] when the epidemic broke out, I followed the advice, (to leave the city) and ran away in the country. In my absence, both the French and English newspapers animadverted on the course which I took, and inquired if it were consistent with the character and obligation of a Protestant clergyman to desert his people in periods of calamity and general suffering. Catholic priests always remain at their posts, whatever perils assailed them. I felt in my heart that these criticisms were just, and resolved that I should never leave New Orleans again in a sickly season. I must adhere to this resolution. Duty is ours, events are God's. Surely a minister in his vocation should feel the ennobling principle and honor not less

acutely than a military hero. The soldier of the Cross should always act on the motto, "Victory or Death". It is as ingnominious for a clergyman to flee the approach of disease, as for an officer of an army to skulk on the field of battle.

During the next epidemic, in 1820, Mr. Larned applied himself assiduously to his ministrations, and for two months he attended funerals, visited the sick in their homes and in the Charity Hospital, despite the deep feeling of premonition that haunted him. He preached his last sermon on August 27, at 11 A.M. His text was: (Philippians 1-21,) "For to me to live in Christ, and die is gain."

Dr. Davidson, who was then present, recorded his discourse. After intimating that his own work on earth might be drawing to a close he said:

I am ready to meet a final hour; to take a last look at the countenances of beloved relatives and friends, to see the fair and glorious scene of sublunary shadows no more. For I have been made certain through Jesus, that the Universe of my Father stretches far beyond the islands, shores, and oceans of earth's spreading continents. As I see this audience with my bodily vision, so with the eye of faith do I now gaze upon these higher regions, where disembodied spirits are expiating over the verdant, smiling fields of an everlasting life — a life unassailable by disease, toil, pain, infirmity, sin, temptation or death. To me there is nothing dark or desolate in the entrance to a world of spirits. O, let me die, that I may go on and live forever! O, welcome, thrice welcome the hour when the portals of the tomb shall open to receive these mortal remains, and the light of a better world shall break in upon my forgiven, redeemed, and emancipated spirit!

He contracted yellow fever, and four days after that prophetic sermon he died on August 31, 1820.

In 1836, a plain white marble monument was erected to Larned's memory in Lafayette square, on which was inscribed his name, age, and date of his death, also the text of his last discourse.

Reverend Mr. Clapp wrote that he was admired for his personal accomplishments, genius, eloquence and noble bearing. "He died at a fortunate moment, both in reference to his clerical fame, and the prosperity of the Evangelical faith in New Orleans." As "he somewhat increased the displeasure of this congregation, for he scarcely so much as alluded to the distinguished doctrines of Presbyterianism in the pulpit. His sermons were generally homilies on the goodness of God, and the excellence and pleasures occurring from a religious life this side of the grave. He also manifested, they said, a fondness for worldy society, which seemed incompatible with the character of a devoted minister of Jesus Christ. The Deacons told me that they themselves, and nearly all of the communicants, had deserted the society in a body several days before the death of the late pastor."

The Reverend Theodore Clapp left Louisville in the winter of 1921, to succeed Mr. Larned. He was the second pastor of the First Presbyterian Church.

Shortly after the death of Reverend Mr. Larned, the Presbyterian Church got into financial difficulties with the City. In the *Louisiana Gazette* of February 24, 1823, appeared an article on "Money loaned by City to Presbyterian Church"; which stated: "The committee appointed to treat with the trustees of the Presbyterian Church reported that they had written to them, and offered to grant the Church a credit of one year, provided the vestry would give to the corporation their personal obligations bearing an interest of 10% — for the amount of what said church owed."

The next day the city attorney was directed to file suit against the Trustees of the Presbyterian Church for the sum of money they were indebted to the Corporation. In the same paper of March 3, appeared the following: "Some few days ago, three of the vestry of the Presbyterian Church had instituted an amicable suit in the Parish Court against said Church for $30,000.00 — the said vestry had gone into court and confessed judgment on the same day and thus by an act certainly very expeditious to say the least, the Church was likely to pass into other hands, without the corporation receiving satisfaction or security for its just claim. This said Mr. Morse is not right, and he moved that the Council should now instruct him to institute suit, in order to recover what the Church owes the City. Mr. Allard observed that as some of the vestry had thought proper to sue their own Church, the Corporation might as well do the same."

On March 24, the paper reported that the City had lost, by lending the Church $5,000.00 for it had no security at all. In May the City Attorney petitioned the City Council for $112.00, for law expenses incurred for a force surrender of the Presbyterian Church.

The following notice appeared in the *Gazette* on December 11, 1823.

"NOTICE: A meeting of the Presbyterian congregation, and all others who may feel disposed to join the same, are requested to meet this and tomorrow afternoon at half past 3 o'clock, at the ringing of the bell, at the church, where will be offered for rent the pews, for the purpose of ascertaining the amount which may be collected in that way, and if accepted by the proprietor of the building, those who engage will be confirmed in the selection they make."

Reverend Mr. Clapp asserted that the Church indebtedness was $45,000.00, and that there were "no assets and not one dollar in the treasury." The church petitioned the Legislature of the State for permission to operate a lottery, which it considered to be "a justifiable mode for raising money for charitable objects." The petition was granted, and the scheme was sold to Yates and McIntyre of New York for $25,000.00. In Mr. Clapp's words:

> The balance of the debt was raised by selling the Church to Judah Touro, Esq. a merchant originally from New England. The sale of the Church was looked upon as merely nominal, although it was purchased without any conditions, express or implicit, or any pledges as to the final disposition which should be made of it. All had confidence in the general character of Mr. Touro, and were very glad to have the Church put into his hands.
>
> It was a time of great business depression in New Orleans when Mr. Touro became the proprietor of the Church edifice and ground. Many of the society fell in the preceding epidemic. The friends of the institutions were few, feeble, impoverished, bankrupt, and pushed to the very brink of ruin. From that day down to its destruction by fire, he held it for their use, and incurred an additional expense of several thousand dollars for keeping it in repairs.
>
> He might have torn the building down at the beginning, and reared on the site a block of stores, whose revenues by this time would have amounted to half a million dollars at least. He was urged to do so on several occasions, and once replied to a gentlemen who made a very liberal offer for the property, that "there was not money enough in the world to buy it, there should be a church on this spot to the end of time."
>
> I have often heard Mr. Touro say, that although an Israelite to the bottom of his soul, it would give him the sincerest pleasure to see all the Churches flourishing in their respective ways, and that he was heartily sorry that they did not more generally fraternize with love, and help each other."

Attesting his generosity and philanthrophy, Mr. Clapp wrote

that besides allowing him to take nearly the whole income derived from the rent of the pews, Touro gave him in small acounts, from time to time, the sum of $20,000.00.

The Reverend Mr. Clapp was born on the 29th of March 1792 at East Hampton, Mass. In September 1812 he entered Yale College, after which he was a student at the Theological Seminary at Andover, Mass. In October 1817 he was ordained a minister of the Gospel. By a strange coincidence he was intimately acquainted with Mr. Larned, who was his class mate.

Before his arrival to New Orleans he labored under the impression that the Papal Church would be arrayed against him. He wrote: "One can hardly imagine how strong, blind and hateful were the prejudices against the Christian sect which deluded my mind when I began a professional life in New Orleans." He made the acquaintance of Catholic priests, and was pleased with the meeting. In many instances in his book he has avowed his respect, admiration and friendship for the Catholic clergy. He wrote that "besides performing clerical functions in Churches, Chapels, Convents, Asylums and Hospitals, they have founded and kept in vigorous operation numerous schools and seminaries of learning for both sexes. In their respective vocations they have displayed the most unflagging zeal and ardent, persevering industry. No Protestant minister in the United States, of any denomination, accomplishes as much hard service as they do. Morning, noon and night, at all seasons, whether healthy or sickly, they are engaged in the prosecution of the arduous and responsible labors. Apparently they live as if each day was their last, and as it becomes those to live who know not what a day, what an hour, may bring forth."

Mr. Clapp wrote further: In the cholera of 1832, I was the only Protestant clergyman that remained in the City, except the Reverend Mr. Hull of the Episcopal Church, who was confined to his house by a lingering consumption, and was unable to even leave his room. This gentleman never left the City in sickly seasons, but fearlessly continued at his post, however great and alarming the mortality around him. So it was that in the first cholera I had no coadjutors but the Roman Catholic priests.

The greatest hindrance to the spread of the Gospel in New Orleans is the peculiar condition of inhabitants. Nearly half of these are what may be called a floating population. They are there only for the honorable purpose of accumulating property. No one of them hardly looked upon New Orleans as his home. Of course, all are anxious to gain fortune as soon as possible.

What care they for New Orleans, provided their prospective personal schemes of profit and independence can be achieved? Hence the number is comparatively smaller than in places where the population is stable, who feel a deep abiding interest in building up churches, and other useful institutions. Those who favor such objects are singularly devoted and self sacrificing. The society is fluctuating and heterogeneous, almost beyond a precedent. It is constantly changing. In a short time, the settled pastor sees his pews emptied, and filled with new occupants. He has hardly time to form their acquaintance before they vanish, to be succeeded by another set of strangers. The disadvantages necessarily attendant on such a state of things are obvious. I do not mean to intimate that the people of New Orleans are more immoral than in city population in general. We do not think that they are more corrupt, or depraved, or worldly than those who live in Boston and its vicinity. It is not to be wondered at, that those who go South merely to buy and sell, and get gain, should say to the clergyman and his solicitations, "Go thy way for this time; when I have a convenient season I will come to thee." Upon the whole New Orleans is rising as rapidly in the scale of moral and religious improvement as could be reasonably expected.

Because of the liberality of his views, and his keen insight of humanity, he was called by some the "Heretical Pastor:" For nearly four decades he labored in his city by adoption.

On June 28, 1835, the new First Presbyterian Church was opened for divine service. It faced Lafayette Square. The edifice was large and imposing.

The Louisiana Auxiliary Bible Society was organized on the 29th of March 1813, and was recognized as an auxiliary by the American Bible Society on April 14, 1817. It had distributed about six thousand copies of the Bible, principally in the French and Spanish languages.

At a meeting held in the Episcopal Church in early January 1826, the following officers were elected: Beverly Chew, President; Rev. James F. Hull and Colonel Joseph Thomas as Vice Presidents; Rev. Theo. Clapp, Corresponding Secretary; Thomas J. Servass, Esq., Treasurer; William Ross, Agent; and Patrick Thompson, Recording Secretary. Directors: J. A. Maybin; Samuel B. Bennett; William Christy; D. R. Davidson; John W. Smith; John Nicholson; Robert W. Welman, Reverend Dr. Drake and W. W. Caldwell.

In the *Courier* of March 29, 1827, appeared the following announcement:

NOTICE: A sermon will be delivered in the French Language, by the Rev. M. DeFernex, Minister of the French Reformed Church, in the Episcopal Church of this city, on Sunday next at 1 o'clock, P.M.

And shortly after this announcement:

NOTICE: All persons interested in the foundation of a French Evangelical Church in this City are requested to attend a general meeting which will take place on Monday the 9th of April at half past six P.M., at Mr. Theo Nicolet's, corner of Royal and Canal Streets.

The *Courier* of April 12, 1827 in an article titled "The French Church" said:

The necessity of a French Evangelical Church where the principles of Christianity may be taught in a manner worthy of the age in which we live, has been long felt in this country. Obstacles, real or imaginary, have hither prevented its establishment. It belonged to the zeal of some enlightened individuals, whose Christian philanthrophy reaches amongst its most ardent followers with a bold hand to overcome the apparent difficulties, which to the present day have defeated the wishes of these devotees to the doctrine, taught by the Galilean law giver.

They have invited amongst us a minister, who brings with him the principles of the Helvetian Church in all their purity. Already has he had occasion to develop them with a force of talent, which is only equalled by the eloquent simplicity of the doctrine he professes, Those who occasionally turn their thoughts upon a future existence, will readily conceive how desirable it is to retain in among us a minister of the Gospel who can so happily direct us in that sacred path. To attain this, a meeting was held Wednesday, 9th inst. at the house of Mr. Theodore Nicolet. Mr. Urquhart was unanimously chosen President and Mr. P. Soulé, Secretary.

On motion it was unanimously resolved, that subscription lists be opened for the purpose of founding a French Evangelical Church in the City of New Orleans, and for the purpose of providing a salary for the pastor of said Church, and that Rev. D. E. Fernex be invited to officiate as Pastor of the same. That a committee be appointed to receive the above subscriptions and Messrs Whittelsey, Nicolet, Sorbé, Roumage, Frey and Babcock were named on said committee. Mr. Nicolet was appointed the Treasurer.

That Messrs Theo. Urquhart, John A. Merle and Thomas Toby appointed a standing committee to attend to the general concerns of the Church for which this meeting has been called.

We are happy to say that in less than twenty-four hours the subscriptions exceeded our greatest expectations. We venture to hope that persons of all different sects and persuasions will cheerfully come forward and contribute to the support of the Church, where our citizens may hear dispensed by an accomplished divine, the consoling doctrines of the Christian religion, from a desk erected by tolerance and brotherly affection.

Services were held by its Minister Mr. DeFernex, every Sunday at 1:00 P.M. in the Episcopal Church. The following April the corner stone of the French Evangelical Church was laid at the corner of Bienville and Rampart by J. F. Canonge, Esq. Grand Master of the Grand Lodge of Louisiana, he was assisted and attended by a numerous body of Masonic Brothers and citizens.

The *Courier* of April 13, 1829, gave the following report of the ceremony:

The procession marching from the Cathedral up Chartres to Bienville, thence out to Rampart. The Consistory of the Church was composed of the Reverend J. L. DeFernex, P. H. Clamageron, John A. Mule, H. Theodore Nicolet, Thomas Toby. Address by Duncan. Corner stone laid by Canonge. Box deposited containing the charter of the Society, a scroll containing the names of the President and Vice-President of the United States, the Governor and the Secretary of the State of Louisiana. Name of consistory of the Church and American coins.

On May 28, 1831, the *Courier* reported that the Reverend Caliste Leiris of the Evangelical Church preached in the French Church of that denomination, situated on Bienville and Rampart, and would continue to do so during the month of June.

The Reverend Caliste Leiris was installed as pastor of the French Protestant Church on December 25, 1831.

Mr. Leiris succeeded Mr. DeFernex, who, judging from the following article in the *Courier* of June 11, 1831, must have been a victim of yellow fever, it said:

Mr. Leiris has preached before the society several times, has satisfied all expectation. Young and well educated, eloquent and modest, well fitted as successor to the accomplished DeFernex, who we all remember and lament, and whose history and fate so much resembled that of the gifted Larned. An eloquent preacher in the French language is a great desideratum in this city; and if it be true, as circumstances authorize us to believe, that there are in the city and state many of the descendants of the Protestants driven from France during the reign of the proud bigoted, Louis XIV signalized in history by the revocation of the edict of Nantes, then we have great reasons to rejoice, that on the banks of the Mississippi they may worship in the language of their forefathers each under his own vine and fig tree, and without any to molest or make afraid, and that they will hear the lessons of wisdom and instruction from the lips of one who drew his last breath in the fair field in France once distinguished for ruthless persecution, but now most remarkable for tolerance, liberality and purity of religious feeling.

On the first day of January 1833, a lottery was drawn for the benefit of the French Evangelical Church. The tickets sold for $4.00 and the highest prize was $10,000.00.

On September 6th 1833, Reverend Leiris passed away, and his corpse was exposed in the presbytery of his Church.

The venerable Rector of Christ Church, the Reverend J. F. Hull died on the 6th of April 1833.

To mention a few among the many Protestant ministers who visited and held religious services in New Orleans are: Rev. Zrilfels from Philadelphia who held services in the Episcopal Church on Christmas day 1825. The German citizens were most cordially invited to attend service in their own language.

On January 6th 1830, the Rev. Wm. McMahon preached at the Methodist Church in Gravier Street.

The Rev. Henry B. Mascon delivered a discourse in the Presbyterian Church on Sunday evening April 3, 1831.

The Rev. Mr. Wheeler performed Divine Services in Christ Church on the Sunday morning of February 22, 1932.

In 1830, the first German Protestant Church was organized, and shortly afterwards the First Congregational Church was incorporated.

In 1828, an organization of the Mariner's Church Society was formed. That church was situated at the foot of Canal Street on public property. It was poorly built and not kept in good repair, and there was a popular demand that it should be demolished. The following excerpt is from the *Bee* of May 5, 1835. "For some period past the condition of the building connected with the partially built church has become a perfect nuisance. But the trustees have not only redeemed their establishment from debt, but are in a fair way of obtaining the building." And it added that the Trustees are not empowered to build and rent stores on public ground. Again on May 13, it editorially commented about the Mariner's Church "being a disgrace and nuisance, and as occupying unconstitutionally and uselessly the public grounds." And on November 10th, it again returned to the charge, by saying that "it broods like an evil genius of feudalism on the custom house square and must be thrown down. The wretched ruins are an eyesore and a nuisance."

Shortly afterwards it was demolished to make way for progress.

Cartouche from the famous Tanesse Map of 1815.

CHAPTER XXVII

REVEREND JOEL PARKER

Soon after the Louisiana Purchase when communications became more facile, both within the nation itself as well as transoceanic, the propagandists of obloquy and defamation spread their libelous distortions of conditions in New Orleans. Many of the visiting authors who enjoyed the munificent hospitality of the city, each according to his mood, his prejudices, nationality or religion, would write about the impiety and lack of morals of its population.

The press of the country, especially of New England, was replete with maligning communications from visitors to the city who were there for no other purpose than to exploit its commercial possibilities. Ministers of the Gospel, dupes of that insidious propaganda, made the alleged godlessness of New Orleans the theme of their sermons, and the emancipationists were the continuous expounders of these libels for the furtherance of their cause. Both the Gallic and Anglo-Saxon residents smarted under this campaign of exaggeration, vilification and lies; but there was nothing they could do to controvert the unjust ill repute of their city. New Orleans was soon known as the most infamous city, not only in the Union, but in the World. It was the vogue of that period to malign the city. It was the popular thing to do, for it sold books and increased the number of subscribers to newspapers and magazines.

The people of New Orleans were hardly surprised then when rumors reached them that one of its ministers, preaching in a New England pulpit, had reviled the city's inhabitants. Indignation rose to a high pitch and resentment was voiced in no uncertain terms.

The following communication appeared in the *Louisiana Advertiser* on November 12, 1834:

> The undersigned having been appointed a committee by the Presbyterian Church and congregation of this city, beg leave most respectfully to address their fellow citizens in relation to their pastor, the Rev. Joel Parker. They are aware of the excitement which has prevailed in the city, aroused by the statement alleged to have been made by him in an address delivered last

August in Hartford, Conn., that of the Catholics of New Orleans, the men are almost without exception atheists and that the Protestants can hardly be said to be in a much better state.

The undersigned fully appreciate the motives which have so agitated our fellow citizens, created by the statement — they are honorable and worthy of applause — they evince a high regard for the character and prosperity of our city and an earnest desire to stand deservedly well in the estimation of their fellow citizens elsewhere. Such a sensitiveness is always entitled to approbation and great respect.

As soon as the declaration ascribed to Mr. Parker appeared in this city, which was first published in the *Bulletin* of September 4, inst., a meeting of nearly all the male members of his church, then in New Orleans, (but few in number being here) was convened, at which it was resolved that if Mr. Parker had thus slandered the community, they requested that the pastoral relation between him and that church and its congregation be at once dissolved. This decision was published at the time in the *Bulletin* and was forwarded to Mr. Parker by the first mail succeeding. This step was adopted as an act of justice to this community, of which the undersigned are a part, and to which they are very much attached, to which nearly all that they possess is centered and for whose reputation and welfare they trust that they in common with their fellow citizens feel a deep regard. The opinion and wish at the meeting were expressed by the committee held for that purpose to Mr. Parker, in strong and decided language accompanied, however, with an earnest wish which to his friends and members of his Church, they most naturally entertained — that he was entirely innocent of the alleged statement.

The friends of Mr. Parker have received from the North certain documents relative to the subject of his address at Hartford, to the character of the address in our Northern cities concerning this place, and to the charge which has also been brought against him of being one of the abolitionists or of being friendly to their measures. The course which some gentlemen, not connected with Mr. Parker's Church or congregation, recommended to be adopted in relation to these documents was, to submit them to several of our fellow citizens who are not members of Mr. Parker's society and unprejudiced for or against him and in whose intelligence, candor and judgement, reliance was to be placed, to present their decision to the public and have the documents [posted] at some public place where they could be exposed to the inspection of all. . . . . They are now presented together with the certificate from one of our highly respected legal gentlemen, Lucius C. Duncan, Esq., as part of the evidence. . . . . The undersigned have seen several charges preferred in our public prints against Mr. Parker in addition to the one which has created the excitement in our city. They will only say and they do it in respectful terms, that they believe them to be without foundation. If their Pastor has been guilty of anything unworthy of him as a man, or as a Christian minister, they most assuredly will not justify it. Their own self respect and a proper respect for the community, independent of higher motives, should not permit them to defend him in such a case. But in the piety of Mr. Parker, in his integrity and veracity as a man, they place very high confidence; his talents,, humility, self-denial and entire devotion in the sacred cause in which he embarked, have commanded from the undersigned their approbation, esteem and confidence.

The undersigned hope that after an examination of the documents now published, their fellow citizens will agree with them in the opinion of the innocence of Mr. Parker, and that the same honorable and high-minded feelings which prompted this community to express their indignation against him, on the supposition that he had been guilty of the alleged slander will equally prompt them to do him justice, consider him in this instance as a misrepresented man and restore him to their confidence and support.

Signed: John R. Moore, Samuel H. Harper, F. R. Southmayd, Dan F. Relf, R. A. Streker, Louis Littlefield, J. A. Maybin, Alfred Hennen, T. Parmele, Charles Gardiner, L. J. Robbins.

New Orleans, November 10, 1834.

To this communication was appended a statement by Rev. Mr. Parker, setting forth his defense.

In the first place what was said in my speech of the moral and religious condition of New Orleans was intended to be a very guarded statement. In the preliminary part, I avowed the intention to make it of such a character, that those of whom I spoke should not be offended if present. I also alluded to the fact that the best influences of our northern friends had often been destroyed by a censorious representation of the moral condition in New Orleans. Some of my hearers who resided there have testified their conviction that such a statement would have given no offense before a New Orleans audience. There was an intermingling of generous, noble and high-minded traits in the character of the southern people, and their neglect of religion and their destitution of Protestant institutions; and your selections from this part of my subject so appear in the article, I think, so to wound the sensibilities of a people whom I have much reason to love and who were neither degraded nor injured by my statements.

The other objectionable part of the article respects the cause of colonization and abolition. The indication that I was once on one side and am now on the other side in the fierce battle [emancipation] is very wrong in two respects. I am not now and never was a partisan on either side of the question. I am now and always have been on the whole, friendly to the Colonization Society — but have never had as high an opinion of the capabilities of such an organization as many others of its friends. Nor have I felt myself called on to denounce the members of the anti-Slavery Society.

I said nothing disrespectful to them in the statement to the Centre Church, a respected father to the ministry who has been from the first a member of the Anti-Slavery Society, has since assured me that there was nothing in my remarks adapted to sustain or inspire either party. This was certainly my intention and I trust my remarks were generally so understood.

There are too many, already employed in fanning the fire of angry excitement and I should feel myself guilty, if I did not use what little influence I possess in conciliating rather than inflaming the public mind.

To which Rev. Joel Parker appended the following appeal to the Editor of the Hartford, Conn. paper:

Mr. Rhea: Sir:

I beg leave only to say, through your paper that I did not use the objectionable language imputed to me in the *Connecticut Observer*. Nor I did say anything disrespectful of either Catholics or Protestants in that address.

I am a citizen of New Orleans; and do not think myself less sensible to injurious representations of our city than any of its most devoted friends.

Very Respectfully Yours,
Joel Parker

Again on October 13, 1834, he protested to Rhea that "I am not now and never was an immediate abolitionist. If it be asked why I have never publicly denounced them, my reply is denunciation is not my business."

Among others he presented a letter from Lucerne Rhea, which stated: "I do not know that you made use of the word 'atheist' in reference to the Roman Catholics at New Orleans. It may have been inferred of my own frame of mind from your remarks upon the prevalence of French philosophy in that City. . . . . In speaking of the Protestants being scarcely in a better state, nothing was maintained except that all the evils of New Orleans were not to be charged upon the Catholics."

Apparently L. C. Duncan was the apologist and the defender of the Rev. Mr. Parker, but it would seem that his efforts were futile, for the Minister was found guilty in the Court of public opinion. The pent-up resentment in all its fury broke out all over the city.

In the *Bee* of December 15, 1834 appeared the following article with the head line:

IMMENSE MEETING

One of the largest meetings ever held here [took place] at Bishop's Hotel last evening, for the purpose of taking into consideration certain obnoxious language imputed to the Rev. Parker in speaking of this community during a visit which he made last summer at Hartford, Conn.

It was presided over by E. Yorke, but James H. Caldwell was called to the chair.

Notwithstanding the excitement was very great, no great riot took place and what is perhaps an unexampled circumstance and one which certainly speaks greatly for the moderation of our citizens, the individual himself, who was the cause of all the disquietude and dissatisfaction was brought before the assembled multitude (indiscreetly we thought) and permitted not only to have a hearing, but when the hearing was over, which was generally deemed to be a lame apology, not the least sign of outrage or disturbance was shown in so great a mass comprising all classes of society, and under the greatest possible degree of excitement. This fact deserved to be recorded as an evidence that reason and not passion were concerned in what took place. Admitting Mr. Parker to have been innocent, the presumption of his being guilty was so prevalent and so deeply founded, that even this would in no way lessen the credit which is due.

As chroniclers of events, we feel it our duty to notice these proceedings of our citizens, otherwise we should never have mentioned the name of Joel Parker in our columns. We deprecated introducing in a journal any discussion by which religion may be involved, and besides we hold it improper for an editor to influence the minds of the public in which their feelings are so sensibly alive as the one to which we have referred.

The following is a report of that meeting:

Called to order by Samuel P. Moore.

Resolved, that as it is unprecedented to condemn any man without a hearing, that this meeting assures Mr. Parker of protection, provided he will appear and make his defense.

Mr. Parker spoke sometime in his defense.

Then resolved: that the Reverend Joel Parker had not succeeded in exculpating himself from the charges alleged against him.

The following resolutions were then drawn and **unanimously** adopted:

"Whereas, the Rev. Joel Parker, pastor of the First Presbyterian Church of this city, in an address delivered before an audience in Hartford, Conn., in the month of August last, did most grossly calumniate the citizens of New Orleans, by saying "that of the Catholics, the men are with hardly any exception, atheists, they regard religion only as intended for women and servants and do not give themselves any trouble on the subject; the Protestants can hardly be said to be in a much better state" — and

Whereas the said Joel Parker, notwithstanding the excitement thereby occasioned, has returned to this city with the intention of resuming his ministry in the aforesaid Church, without having exculpated himself — and

Whereas: the people of New Orleans have too long suffered, both in reputation and in their interests by the calumnies of "Clerical villains" and hirelings and interested writers who visit our city; and

Whereas: a committee of Mr. Parker's Church, after the above charges were made in the *Bulletin* of the 4th of September last, pledged themselves that if Mr. Parker had thus slandered this community, the pastoral relations between him and his Church and congregation should be at once dissolved; and

Whereas: the said committee published an attempted defense of the Rev. Mr. Parker in the *Louisiana Advertiser* —

Therefore, as the sense of this meeting it is resolved that the Rev. Mr. Parker has incurred the just displeasure and indignation of this community for the slanders against the population, in his address uttered before an audience in Connecticut, in the month of August last,

Resolved: That in their defense of their pastor, published in *Louisiana Advertiser* of the 12th of November, the committee of Mr. Parker's Church have not succeeded in exculpating him from the charge of having slandered the population of this city, and

Resolved, that the attempt on the part of the Rev. Joel Parker to resume his ministry without exculpating himself of the above charge, can be considered in no light than as a contempt for the feelings and opinions of this community, and

Resolved, that the conduct of the Elders of the First Presbyterian Church in attempting to force so obnoxious a person as Mr. Parker upon the community, should be considered as a contempt of public opinion, and

Resolved, that the future residence of Joel Parker in this city is fraught with danger to the peace and quietness of the population, and

Resolved, that the Chairman and Secretary of this meeting furnish the Rev. Joel Parker and each of his elders with a copy of the proceedings of this meeting and request Mr. Parker to leave the city, and

Resolved, that notwithstanding the people of New Orleans should be pleased to enjoy the favorable opinion of their Northern brethren, yet they will never consent to sacrifice their own self respect by adopting their opinions, and by becoming the dupes of a fanatical and aspiring priesthood. — That the tolerant feelings and social happiness that prevail among us, are mainly to be attributed to the absence of that pernicious influence of priestcraft that at this moment weighs so heavily on the intelligence and energies of our Northern brethren, and

Be it further resolved, that the proceedings of this meeting be published in the different papers of the city.

Jas. H. Caldwell, Chairman

H. Bogart and Thos. Duplessis, Secretaries.

Harriet Martineau reported this incident as follows:

> Half a year before my visit to New Orleans a great commotion had been raised in the city against a Presbyterian clergyman, the Rev. Joel Parker, on account of some expressions which he had been reported to have used, while on a visit in New England, respecting the morals of New Orleans, and specially the desecration of the Sunday. A public meeting was called, opinions were divided. Some determined to be present at the meeting and support the pastor's right of speech.
>
> Matters were proceeding fast towards a condemnation of the accused and a sentence of banishment when these gentlemen demanded that he be heard in his own defense — a guarantee for his personal safety being first passed at the meeting. This was agreed to and Mr. Parker appeared in the meeting. Unfortunately, he missed the opportunity — a particularly favorable one — of making a moral impression which should never have been lost. A full declaration of what he had said, the grounds of it, and his right to say it, would have turned the emotions of the assemblage, already softened in his favor, towards himself and right. As it was, he did nothing very right, but there was a want of judgment and taste in his address which was much to be regretted. He was allowed to go free for the time, but the newspapers reported all the charges against him, suppressed his replies, and lauded the citizens for not having pulled the offender to pieces: and Mr. Parker's congregation were called upon, on the grounds of the resolutions passed at the public meeting to banish their pastor. They refused, and appealed to all the citizens to protect them from such oppression as was threatened.

She further stated that nothing was done and that a new edifice rose up to care for the increasing number of the congregation. She also said that "Mr. Parker was not a highly educated man."

New Orleans, the city of iniquity, infamy and godlessness, that pest hole of immorality — what a text for a sermon! What an inspiration for the preachers! No infamous place of the Bible could inspire them to greater heights of oratory. They slandered with impunity, whilst the Pharisees in their congregations, basking in self-righteousness, uttered a fervent prayer of thanks that they alone were devout Christians.

The Reverend Mr. Clapp, in his autobiography, voiced his indignation as follows: "I have never seen a letter, published in the Northern religious newspaper purporting to be a picture of the moral state of things in New Orleans, which was not a gross libel."

CHAPTER XXVIII

QUADROONS AND QUADROON BALLS

The place of quadroons in the social history of New Orleans has to a certain extent been ignored by our historians, and we are indebted mainly to tradition and legend for information about them. Some of the chroniclers and diarists, who visited the City during the first four decades of the nineteenth century, wrote accounts — less factual and more sensational to better delight their readers— that endowed the quadroon women with grace, beauty, intellectuality, education, and devotion and loyalty to their paramours. Their adulation was, to say the least, fantastic.

The courtesans of Rome may be said to have been their prototype, for they sought the devotion and the attention of renowned poets to be immortalized in odes and sonnets, which were sung and recited in the remotest corners of the Empire, and sculptors who would mould their divine beauty into marble and proclaim them deities. Temples were erected for them and new cults originated in their honor — new Venuses were born. Some of these statues now adorn our art galleries, and a few of these odes, which fortunately have survived the ravages of time, are the gems of classical literature.

The quadroons of New Orleans did not consort with poets or artists; they were actuated by more sordid considerations — the quest of ease and prestige which only money could procure. Their names have not been engraved in bronze, inscribed on marble or immortalized in verse. In fact their fame ended in the grave. They were exhibited on a flimsy pedestal which crumbled with their fading youth. As individuals, they are practically unknown today.

Not all the quadroon women were paramours. Among them were some of deep religious conviction, of unimpeachable morals, who although they deplored their destiny, feeling a resentment for that fraction of Negro blood which coursed through their veins, maintained their dignity and retained their virtue to their dying days. In a society dedicated to maintain the purity of the white race, as a social and moral principle, and from which there could be no deviation, or compromise, these unfortunate people were disdained and ostracized. Despite which, many of them maintained a respectful demeanor as ladies and were well considered by the white population. Many married in their own caste, others sought solace in the sanctuary of a convent. A few were more fortunate. Some fathers, because of sympathy, regret, or a qualm of conscience, endowed their illegitimate daughters and even their sons, and provided for their education in Europe where their daughters often married. And it is said, a few formed alliances with the nobility. Few ever returned to New Orleans, and of these there is very little known.

The words *mulatto* and *mulattress* signify the offspring of a white father and a Negro mother, or vice versa. A person born of a mulattress and a white father is a quadroon. Evidently it is a derivative of the French word *quarteron*, which means a quarter or one fourth, and it may be presumed that the term originated in Louisiana. The issue of a white man and a quadroon is called an *octoroon*. A *griff*, or *griffe*, a word seldom heard in New Orleans, means a child of a mulattress and a Negro. Those who have a less amount of Negro blood, no matter how small the proportion, are called *des jens de couleur*, persons of color.

There is no doubt that many of these women of mixed breed, with the hue of their skins ranging from dark brown to a light tan, were all classified as quadroons for it would have been difficult to trace their genealogies. Some refinement of features, some shades lighter than black, and being the mistress of an influential white man, would assure them an entreé in their own select society, whether a mulattress, a quadroon or an octoroon. These people would have passed unnoticed in the history of New Orleans were it not for some European visitors, who in writing their impressions, extolled their culture with superlative exaggeration. The local press was practically silent on the subject, and any mention was derogatory and generally concerned the ribaldry which took place at their balls.

If it is taken into consideration that the white male, according to the census of 1820, nearly doubled the number of white females, or 10,090 to 6,318, and that the discrepancy would be increased three-fold during the cold months, as it has already been pointed out, the young visitors (and they were nearly all young) craving the companionship of the decent women of the city denied to so many of them, *faute de mieux*, they patronized the Quadroon balls.

The fibers with which the fabric of the glamorous vestal quadroons was woven were taken from reports of the Duke of Saxe-Weimar Eisenach, the Governor of the Dutch East Indies, who visited the city in 1825; James Stuart, an Englishman, who wrote the book, "Three Years in the United States," who was in New Orleans in 1829; Mrs. Trollope in 1827, and Harriet Martineau, a guest in late 1830, both English ladies; and Isidore Lowenstern from Leipsig in 1937. All were foreigners, who visited New Orleans for only a few days, and who frankly admitted that some of their reports were based on hearsay. They were confronted with a racial question, such as they had never met before, and they poured out all their sympathy for these people of lighter color by extolling their virtues and extravagantly praising their beauty.

We read the legend of these gorgeous cratures, arrayed in all their splendor, promenading on the levee facing the city — the only promenade in New Orleans at that time — chaperoned by their black mothers, sometime slaves, but generally free-persons-of-color, appraising the young blades with an eagle eye, in the hope of finding a suitable companion for their daughters. A dropped handkerchief, a sly glance, a smile — an acquaintance was formed, and frequently, so it was said, there was love at first sight. With all the reserve and shyness of a Spanish maiden, she would introduce him to her chaperone who would survey him from head to foot. The mother would question him as to his financial status with all the acumen of a Shylock, bargain with him with all the shrewdness of a merchant, and when a bargain was negotiated to her satisfaction, she would give her blessing. He could either make his domicile with them or visit at his pleasure. Such we are told. It made a fantastic story, but is it true? Stuart wrote: "The tales, which have been told of the assembly of beauties on the levee at sunset where the mother or female relation makes the best bargain she can for her daughter or her ward, are, I am quite satisfied, merely travelers' stories."

It is evident that Stuart was correct. And many other stories relative to the quadroons must be classified as "travelers' stories."

There were many quadroon balls. They were held in various sections of the city, and most of their locations are unknown today. There were but a few places large enough to hold a ball unless at a residence with large rooms. Saxe-Weimar reported that he had attended such a place of amusement at the St. Philip Theater. That theater could not survive the competition of the Theatre d'Orlean, and had to discontinue its presentations and be transformed into a ballroom, which soon became the notorious Washington Ball Room.

Saxe-Weimar frankly acknowledged having been there and that he found them more enjoyable than the sedate and refined balls of the respectable society. He wrote that "Most of the gentlemen did not remain long at the ball (Theatre d'Orleans) but hastened away to the quadroon ball, so called, where they amused themselves more and were more at their ease. This was the reason why there were more ladies than gentlemen present at the ball [at the Orleans Theater] and that many were obliged to form 'Tapestry.' When a lady is left sitting it is said to be *bredouille*." And he further commented that "like many others, I find the quadroon balls more entertaining than those of a more decorous nature." Yet in the same work he stated: " a quadroon ball at St. Philip Theatre, many ladies left early, and the gentlemen, a motley society, were for the most part drunk." And in describing a masquerade ball at the same place, he wrote:

> There were but few masks, and among the tobacco-chewing gentry, several Spanish visages slipped about, who carried swordcanes, and seemed to have no good design in carrying them. Some of these visitors were intoxicated and then appeared a willing disposition for disturbance. The whole aspect was that of a den of ruffians. I did not remain but a half hour, and learned the next day that I was judicious in going home early, as later, battles with fists, with canes and dirks had taken place. Twenty persons were more or less dangerously wounded.

It can be here noted that nearly a century after Weimar's visit to New Orleans, there was a grand ball known as the "Ball of Two Well Known Gentlemen" held on Mardi Gras, at the Odd Fellows Hall on Camp Street, now the site of the Post Office. It was strictly for whites. It was a ball of the denizens of Storyville, in which the elite of the courtesanship presided. Many prominent citizens would slip away from the spectacular ball of Comus, either because of curiosity, ennui, or at a time of festivity to drink a toast to their lady friends of the demi-monde. Like Saxe-Weimar many really enjoyed themselves. Human nature has not changed.

Reiser in his article on Saxe-Weimar, published in the Foreign Quarterly Review, Volume 3, 1928-1929, quotes him as having said:

> Many a female quadroon is beautiful, well educated and superior in their manners and appearance to the white female.

Their charms and accomplishments, however, render the latter only so much the more jealous of their influence.

By law they are prohibited from marrying with the whites; they are not allowed to travel in the streets in a coach by daylight. They dare not come into the chamber, or public room where a white woman is, nor sit down in her presence without her permission and if convicted, is punished same as a slave. Some are sent to Europe by their fathers and are enabled to form respectable matches; but their fate in New Orleans generally is to live as mistress to white men and in this capacity, our travellers say that they conduct themselves with a degree of fidelity, modesty and propriety which the married females of the priviledge race do not always exhibit.

Mrs. Trollope, an English lady, in her book "Domestic Manners of the Americans" recording her description of the New Orleans of 1827, stated that the quadroons

.... consist of the excluded and amiable set and such of the gentlemen (Creoles) as can, by any means escape from the high places where pure Creole blood swells the veins at the bare mention of any being tainted in the remotest degree with the Negro stain.

Quadroon girls, the acknowledged daughters of wealthy American or Creole fathers, educated with all the style and accomplishments which money can procure in New Orleans, and with the decorum that care and affection can give; exquisitely beautiful, graceful, gentle and amiable, they are not admitted, nay, are not on any terms admissible into the society of Creole families of Louisiana. They cannot marry; that is to say, no ceremony can render a union with them legal or binding; yet such is the powerful effect of their very peculiar grace, beauty and sweetness of manner, that unfortunately they perpetually become the objects of choice and affection. If the Creole ladies have privilege to exercise the awful power of repulsion, the genteel quadroon has the sweet but dangerous vengeance of possessing that of attraction. The unions formed with this unfortunate race is said to be often lasting and happy, as far as any union can be so and which certain degree of disgrace is attached.

Harriet Martineau, the novelist, made practically the same observations relative to the morals and the customs of these women. She wrote that the quadroon men "marry women of a somewhat darker color than their own; the women of their own choice objecting to them because *Ils sont si dégoutants*, they are so disgusting."

For Mrs. Trollope the reality was too prosaic, she had to yield to the temptation to be melodramatic. It made the story so much more sensational. She wrote that when "the time comes for the gentleman to take a wife, the dreadful news reaches his quadroon partner, either by letter entitling her to call the house and the furniture her own, or by the newspaper which announces the marriage." A thorough search of the journals fails to reveal, except on a very rare occasion, announcements of marriage. They simply did not have a society column at that time. Another fabrication of the whole cloth is her statement that "the quadroon women are rarely known to form a second connection. Many commit suicide; more die broken hearted."

Then she assumed the role of an ethicist, for with all the fervor of a reformer she expounded:

> What security for domestic purity and peace there can be where every man has had two connections, one of which must be concealed; and two families, whose existence must not be known to each other; where the conjugal relation begins in treachery, and must be carried on with a heavy secret in the husband's breast, no words are needed to explain. If this is the system which is boasted of as a purer than ordinary state of morals, what is to be thought of the ordinary state? It can only be hoped that the boast is an empty one.

Isidore Lowenstern, who visited New Orleans in 1837, gave us what may be considered the most sober version of the quadroons and their balls. The following is a translation from the French:

> The class which suffers the most from slavery, is the one known in New Orleans as quadroons, the issue, ordinarily, of white planters and of griffs, daughters of whites and mulattresses, or even of quadroons, they resemble, because of the light color of their skin, their fathers, so much so that only a trained eye can distinguish their African origin by the coarseness and the peculiar nature of their hair, as well as by their eyes, so black, so quick.
>
> As it is usual for all persons who find themselves excluded from society for such a cause, they employ every means to introduce themselves, so much so, that the quadroons have no other ambition than to mix with the whites, and prefer to live with them as their mistresses, rather than legitimately marry in their proper caste.
>
> I have attended one of these mask balls, called "Quadroon Balls" composed of these women of color and their white admirers. No African gentlemen were present, they are vigorously excluded by the patronesses.
>
> These ladies employed every possible care to hide their color derived from her maternal blood, so as to amplify their paternal resemblance and to do so, they apply to their faces and necks a

large dose of white powder, which when dancing, had a singular effect due to perspiration.

The admission price to these balls is $2.00. One is searched from head to foot to detect any concealed weapons. For one word may occasion sanguinary brawls, which frequently result in death.

Henry Gally Knight, Esq., the English poet and writer on architecture, who wrote his impression of New Orleans under the nom de plume of A. Singleton, Esq., remarked that "it has been rumored, it is not to be believed, much less repeated, to be a gentleman here, like foreign princes, and lords of the nobility, one must patronize a yellow miss, even if only for the name of the thing; and if a young man (buck) has one or two discarded lemons, his credit rises in proportion to the number." This is another wild and irresponsible statement by a prominent English author.

However, a prominent English author wrote:

In the twenties and even in the early thirties, these balls were strictly limited to these women and their white admirers. No white woman would risk the opprobrium for attending them, even disguised with a mask. The fear of apprehension was too great, but in the marvelous thirties, when the population, both males and females, grew to tremendous proportions, white women, either because of curiosity, for amusement, or to confirm their suspicions as to the whereabouts of their husbands, would attend these balls, where they were not welcome, in increasing numbers. At first carefully disguised, then flaunting all conventions by not attempting to hide their identity.

At a meeting of the City Council on November 20th, 1935, that abuse was discussed, and Acting Mayor Culbertson made the following report:

I am of the opinion that it would be necessary you should adopt some measures concerning the masquerade balls of free colored women, where only white men are admitted. From the most positive information, I know to a certainty, that at the last ball of that description there were in the rooms more white ladies than colored ones and that even some of them have shown themselves without a mask. I believe, gentlemen, that such a state of things cannot be tolerated in our country, and if possible, you ought to remedy this threatening evil.

On November 27, the Mayor sent the following message to the City Council:

The information which I received from all quarters on the composition of the masquerade ball, to which I alluded in one of my last letters, imposes on me the duty again to call your attention to the necessity for repressing the scandal and disorders at such balls. I know from positive information that these meetings are the sink of the most dissolute class of women; and that the spectacle of their abominations is constantly offered to the public gaze. Besides the greatest part of the white women who resort there, bring with them unprincipled men who have been expelled from other states, and who find here, in consequence of the disguise they are allowed to assume, and the protection of these females every opportunity to follow their swindling career.

Let me ask, gentlemen, do you think we ought to authorize any longer such schools of immorality; in which our impetuous youths, free from restraint are imbibing the most pernicious principles? I do not hesitate to say NO!

This impassioned plea of the Mayor met with opposition from some of the aldermen. Mr. Allard interposed by stating that "there was nothing in the law prohibiting the admittance of white women in colored balls. Nevertheless he would present an amendment in which white women would be allowed entrance to these balls, in disguise, for the purpose of surprising their husbands in *flagrante delicto*."

The *Bee* on November 30, commented editorially:

The acting Mayor has made two unsuccessful attempts to place the masked balls of the color women on a more eligible basis by preventing the entrance of white women for which he certainly deserves credit; but in which he is singularly opposed by the City Council.

On Saturday night we paid a visit to the Washington Ball Room in St. Phillip Street, and though we found great regularity prevailed, we were certainly surprised to find that two thirds, at least, of the females present, were white women; and doubly so when we were informed by one who seemed to possess experience in these matters, that there were many white ladies present who are usually considered respectable in their sphere of life; and whose curiosity, if not other motives, induced them to attend these balls, obscured as they are by their masks.

It was even asserted that many married ladies were present. Now however disposed we may be to esteem ladies and to gratify their curiosity, etc., we did not like to see them disguised in liquor or dress. What they may be permitted to do at a fancy ball respectively "got up" can scarcely afford a precedent to unrestrained freedom at masked balls for colored people two or three times a week.

That there was a notorious coterie of quadroon women is true, that they were the paramours of white men is an historical fact.

That they all had a fair skin, more pale than those of pure white blood, and that they were more educated than the ladies of the social set, possessing a far superior elegance, poise and social graces, as well as possessing great wealth, is pure fiction. Again it must be repeated that the majority of the women of color were respectable, moral and virtuous who did not condone the profligacy of their sisters.

The first apologist for the voluptuous quadroon was Saxe-Weimar. He set a pattern which was followed by subsequent writers. During his short stay he was royally feted, and doubtless, whilst enjoying the hospitality of the young gentlemen of the town — he himself was then only in his early thirties — the conversation turned to the quadroons. This was all new to him and he was intrigued and an attentive listener. His hosts boasted of the beauty of their mistresses, their fidelity, for who could acknowledge the possibility of their colored paramours being unfaithful to them? Of the lasting alliances, their superior education and social graces, they verbally built a temple in which to place their Venuses.

As is depicted in the chapter on Education, the educational facilities for both boys and girls, were neglected and greatly limited in its scope, even for the whites. As for these of the black race, there were no schools. In fact, to teach Negroes to read was against the law. The only way a quadroon could be educated, man or woman, was to be sent to the North or to Europe. There, after enjoying social equality with the whites, they remained and they certainly would not have returned to the city of their birth to subject themselves to the ignominy they had once suffered. The statement frequently made that they were the offspring of rich planters, both French and English-speaking, that they were endowed with great wealth and enjoyed the blessing of paternal love, even surpassing their tenderness for their legitimate children, borders on the ridiculous. Most of them never knew who their fathers were.

It was written that the octoroon maidens were reared in the tender devotion of a loving mother, that they were brought up in culture and refinement, that their innocence was protected with all the astuteness of an austere duenna. This makes a pretty story were it not for the fact that these mothers were either slaves or emancipated slaves. By choice they did not marry, although they were not in any way prohibited from forming alliances with their own kind, giving as a pretext that they "were so disgusting," a sentiment not shared by their brothers. They preferred to be the mistresses of white men. They sold themselves not only for a living of ease and comfort and even luxury, but also to enhance their prestige in their own society and to humiliate the respectable women in the community, whom they despised. They were not prostitutes in the full acceptance of the word, but they must be classed as concubines.

Gayarré, the historian, a contemporary of the time, wrote that "in the hybrids, those in whom the line of color no longer exists apparently will continue. . . . . It must be kept in mind, that the Negro hates the hybrid; and the hybrid despises the Negro, is more adverse than the white man to associate with him, except for political purposes. As to the female quadroon, there are few of them that would not belabor with a broomstick the leveller and the trader in new principles, who would propose to them to marry a Negro."

Although to a great extent what has been written about them is legendary, yet the octoroons and their balls are an important chapter in the history of New Orleans.

In *Niles Register* of November 5, 1825, is the following squib:

> A writer in the New Orleans *Gazette* under the signature of "Mother of a Family" complains of the insolence of the mulatto girls, who drive the white women from the walks. She calls them "Heaven's lost, worst gift to white men."

CHAPTER XXIX

SLAVES AND FREE PERSONS OF COLOR

All Negroes were not slaves. A large number enjoyed freedom, including pure blooded Africans as well as those of mixed blood. Some bought their freedom through their own initiative and industry; others were released from slavery through the generosity of their owners; some were emancipated by their masters after death through testamentary action; and a number, already free men, were refugees from San Domingo.

The 1820 census of the City of New Orleans gave the white population as 15,408, and Negroes, 14,592, of whom 6,237 were free persons of color. There were nearly as many free Negroes as slaves, or about 43%. By way of comparison, there were in the Parish of Orleans only 924 free persons of color to 7591 slaves. This was due to the fact that the plantations in the parish needed slaves and the liberated slaves deserted the soil for a life in the city. The number of free females exceeded the males by 521 to 403, whilst that of the slaves was 2,969 to 4,622, an inverse ratio to that of the city proper. Unfortunately, the free persons of color were grouped together and were not classified as pure Africans or in accordance to the degree of white blood flowing in their veins, so the proportion of mulattoes, quadroons and octoroons is not known.

With the sole exception of a relatively few notorious quadroons, the free persons of color did not wish or try to integrate with the whites. They kept their place and were respected by the community. They married with their own kind, and their children enjoyed the same freedom as their parents.

It was against the dignity of white men to engage in manual labor. There were slaves for that purpose. New Orleans was not a manufacturing city, and there was a lack of white artisans. This is attested to by the press, which continually begged for more skilled workers to settle in the city, whilst deploring the ever increasing numbers of professional men and clerks. That vacuum was filled by free-men-of-color. Those who had the necessary skill and intelligence were employed as carpenters, bricklayers and in associated crafts. Others were street vendors or had stands in the markets. They were an integral part of the business of the city. The women were sometimes peddlers, they also performed various chores, and not a few were accomplished seamstresses. They had rights and privileges which were protected by the laws of the State.

The following quotation is taken from "A History of Louisiana" by Henry Chambers:

> There was among the New Orleans militia of that day a battalion of "free men of color" — that same organization which had given Claiborne so much concern, when he first came to the Territory of New Orleans, as to whether he had better disarm and disperse them as a military organization, or not. He had not done so, but had permitted the matter to rest in status quo all these years. the battalion was now commanded by Colonel Fortier, a rich white merchant, and Major Lacoste, also white, and a rich planter. All the subordinate officers were colored. This battalion volunteered as a body at Claiborne's call and assured him that their numbers would be largely increased if necessary. What otherwise might have been a dark spot upon the escutcheon of the City of New Orleans was lightened by the action of these dark men.

They participated in the Battle of New Orleans where they acquitted themselves with honor and distinction.

Negro slavery was introduced into America by the Spaniards upon the advice of Bartholome de las Casas, a Spanish priest who accompanied Columbus to America in 1493. Observing the cruel manner in which the Indian slaves were treated, he made a trip across the ocean to plead their cause at the Spanish court. It is said that in fifteen years the Spaniards killed off a million Indians in the attempt to make them work in the mines. Indians did not make good slaves. It was found impracticable to make slaves of the American Indians. In 1517 the importation of Negro slaves began in the Spanish Colonies.

The first Negro slaves to arrive in the British Colonies were the 20 "negars" brought by a Dutch trading vessel to Jamestown, Virginia in 1620.

England later became a leader in the slave trade and by 1790 more than half the slave trade was in English hands. But while legalizing slavery in her colonies, it was not recognized in the Mother Country. The English courts decided in 1772 that as soon as a slave set his foot on the soil of Great Britain he was free, though he might be reclaimed to slavery if he returned to his master's country. Also the movement to abolish slavery began in England as early as 1729.

That Negroes were considered merchandise is shown by the wording of some contracts. One called for the delivery of "10,000 tons of Negroes." In 1713 his Britannic Majesty entered into a 30-year contract with the Spanish Government agreeing to deliver to Spanish America "114,000 pieces of India, both sexes and all ages." These various contracts or treaties all ended *El nombre del santissima Trinidad*, "in the name of the Most Holy Trinity."

From the very beginning New Orleans had slaves. They were introduced into Louisiana by John Law. A census taken in 1726 gave their number at 1540 Negroes and 229 Indians. In 1732 the estimate was over 2,000. At that time males sold for $150.00, and females for $120.00.

W. D. Warden, the American Consul at Paris, published in 1820 that the price of slaves was between $400.00 and $500.00, the more active and intelligent bringing $1,000.00.

The white population was always on the qui vive, for there was ever the potential danger of a slave uprising. The massacre of San Domingo and the few attempted insurrections in the neighboring parishes only increased the apprehension of Orleanians and impelled them to pass suitable laws for their protection.

In 1795 there was a serious insurrection of Negroes in Louisiana. It originated on the plantation of Julien Poydras in Pointe Coupee Parish. The conspiracy extended throughout the parish and the massacre of all white men was to begin on the 15th of April. The women were to be spared perhaps to be victims of a fate worse than death. Because of dissension in their ranks, one of the chief agitators ordered his wife to divulge the conspiracy to the parish commandant. The ringleaders were promptly arrested, but not without bloodshed, for before the slaves surrendered, 25 were killed, 23 were hanged along the banks of the Mississippi from that parish to New Orleans, and their bodies as a warning remained on their gallows for many days. Thirty-one were whipped and three white men were banished from the colony.

Another uprising occurred in January 1811. Its locale was St. John the Baptiste, on the left bank of the river, about fifty miles above New Orleans.

This time they were better organized for their army of nearly

View of the St. Charles Theatre, one of the finest theatres in the World. (Courtesy Howard-Tilton Library)

Interior view of St. Charles Theatre. (Courtesy Howard-Tilton Library)

Street Scene — Corner Rampart and Esplanade Streets, 1828.

500 men and women was divided into companies commanded by officers. Their objective was the sack of New Orleans. They were goaded to a frenzy by the beating of drums and iron kettles, accompanied by the barbarous shrill notes of reed quills. They destroyed buildings on several plantations on their march to the city, but fortunately their owners were warned in time to enable them to escape. Only one remained to protect his property, Trepanier, with loaded guns at hand, boldly faced the demoniacal mob which awed by his superb heroism resumed its march. The rioters were routed and subdued by the militia and soldiers from Fort Charles and at the barracks. Sixty-six were either killed in that battle or immediately hanged, others died in the swamps. Sixteen of the ringleaders were tried, condemned and executed and their heads were exhibited on poles along the river bank.

Capt. J. E. Alexander, an English chronicler, in his book published in 1833, mentioned that:

> In the beginning of September an alarm of a slave insurrection at New Orleans. Hand bills of an inflammatory nature were found, inciting the slaves to rise and massacre the whites. Several stands of arms, some said three hundred were also found in a colored man's house. Five hundred citizens were under arms every night and the Mayor solicited a detachment of four companies of regulars from the nearest garrison.

This proved to be a false alarm and was the last time that New Orleans was seriously threatened by a Negro insurrection.

In a memoir addressed to the Spanish Government in 1776, Francisco Bouligny made the following, perhaps somewhat exaggerated, report:

> The Negroes are slave only in name for in reality they are as happy as may be the laborers of Europe. The master is obliged only to give each negro a barrel of corn in the ear, a piece of ground on which to make his crop of corn, rice or whatever he may wish, a cabin like those that are made here in the orchard of Orihuela and a yard of 30 by 40 paces with a fence for him to raise chickens, hogs, etc. With his profits each Negro buys every winter a woolen coat, a pair of long breeches and two or three skirts. With what remains he buys bear's grease to cook as he pleases the corn on which they all live, and are so healthy and robust that some persons who came here lately from Havana were astonished to see Negroes so nimble, strong and bright. It is the custom here in winter, as there are sometimes heavy frosts, not to make the Negroes go to the fields before 7 or 8 o'clock in the morning. They stop work at 12 noon and return to the fields

at 2 o'clock in the evening. In the summer they go out at daybreak and remain till 11, and return to work at 3 and remain till night. This way they have the time to attend for a short while to their crops and to their poultry, hogs, etc.

He further stated that they were healthy and that a physician is annually paid $1.00 per head to attend them.

Martin, in his "History of Louisiana," stated that Carondelet, having received instructions from the King to attend to the humane treatment of slaves in the province, on July 11, 1792 established the following regulations:

1. That each slave should receive monthly, for his food, one barrel of corn at least.

2. That every Sunday should be exclusively his own, without his being compelled to work for his master except in urgent cases when he must be paid or indemnified.

3. That on other days they should not begin to work before day break nor to continue after dark. One half hour to be allowed at breakfast and two hours at dinner.

4. Two brown shirts, a woolen coat and pantaloons, and a pair of linen pantaloons and two handkerchiefs to be allowed yearly to each male slave and suitable dresses to females.

5. None to be punished with more than thirty lashes within twenty four hours.

6. Delinquents to be fined in the sum of one hundred dollars and in grave cases that slave may be ordered to be sold.

At the solicitation of the Cabildo, Carondelet issued a proclamation prohibiting the importation of Negroes from the French and British islands because it would drain the colony of its specie and because of the apprenhension of the danger of an insurrection by the slaves.

Shortly after the founding of the city a code regulating the police authority over slaves was promulgated by Bienville in the name of the King. Known as the Black Code, it was put into effect in March 1724. It provided for the spiritual welfare of the slaves, made it obligatory for the masters to instruct them in the tenets of the Catholic faith, and stipulated that they should not be made to work on Sundays and Church holidays, under severe penalties, even to the forfeiture of the slave, and that those who died in the Christian faith were to be buried in consecrated grounds. Intermarriage between the whites and blacks was absolutely prohibited, and the clergy was strictly forbidden to unite them. Concubinage between masters and slaves and free men of color with slaves was not only not tolerated, but subject to severe penalties and confiscation, but marriages between slaves were not only permitted but encouraged.

Permission to marry must be granted by the masters irrespective of the wishes of the parents. If the mother was a slave, so was the child, irrespective of the father being a free man, but if the mother was a free woman, whilst the father is a slave, the offspring is free. Most of the stipulations in this act retained their substance until the Civil War. The term "Black Code" was an opprobrious one to the propagandists of emancipation, yet it cannot be contradicted that under the circumstances it protected the slaves in their natural rights.

The code further provided in Article 43 that husbands and wives shall not be seized and sold separately when belonging to the same master; and their children under 14 years of age shall not be separated from their parents and such seizures and sales should be null and void.

The police regulations published on February 18, 1751, provided for the prohibition under severe penalties of the sale of intoxicants to Negroes, the harboring of slaves for unlawful purposes, trading only with slaves who are specifically allowed by their masters to do so. All assemblies of slaves were prohibited and no Negro was allowed to carry a stick or cane. Any white person had the right to stop a Negro night or day, slave or free, and demand to be shown his written pass.

Article 30, read:

> A private person, a soldier, or any other individual, has not the right to ill-treat a Negro who is not guilty of an offense against him. In certain cases, the person offended may arrest him and ask that he be dealt with according to the dictates of justice because the Negro is subject only to the police regulations of the country and to the tribunal of his own master. Consequently and in compliance with the orders of his Majesty, we forbid that any one should take the liberty to ill-treat slaves; and for any violence of this prohibition, the person so offending shall undergo an arbitrary punishment, according to the circumstances of the case.

Practically the same regulations were in force during the Spanish domination.

Even in the colonial times restrictions were placed on the importation of African Negroes, but like all prohibitions, they were ignored, and the traffic was uninterrupted. The slave smugglers always found a way to evade those in authority and to dispose of their cargoes. The increase in plantations in the state and the great fertility of its virgin lands, created a continuous demand for slaves. They were needed for the cultivation of the crops, and it was cheap labor. One of the principal markets for imported Africans was at Barataria, and even at points on lakes Maurepas and Pontchartrain, the slave dealers had a thriving business in human flesh. Despite all the efforts of Governor Claiborne, the Lafittes were unrestrained in their commerce. Slaves were consigned to them for distribution, and as many as four hundred at a time were openly sold to the highest bidder at a public auction held at Grande Terre. The demands were so great that Governor Roman raised the restrictions against the importation of slaves from the other states, with the exception of Mississippi, Alabama, Arkansas and Florida.

The Duke of Saxe-Weimar in his diary mentions that "Many owners of slaves in the State of Maryland and Virginia have (pardon the loathsome expression, I know not how otherwise to designate the beastly idea) stud nurseries for the slaves, whence the planters of Louisiana, Mississippi, and the other southern states draw their supplies, which increase every day in price."

Again quoting the same author: "In Chartres Street there are two establishments to sell slaves. Negroes of both sexes stood or sat the whole day in these shops or in front of them to exhibit themselves or wait for a purchaser."

It is also known that slave auctions were conducted in the rotunda of the St. Louis Hotel and in exchanges in the neighborhood. Although trading in slaves was legal, yet these traders were considered as belonging to the lowest strata of society.

The extent of that slave traffic can be appraised by the figures given in the United States census. In 1810, the white population numbered 8001 and the non-whites 16,551. In 1820, there were 22,107 blacks to 19,244 whites. An increase of 140% compared to 68.5% for the Negro.

In the ten years following 1820 the population growth was not as great, for the whites only increased their numbers to 21,281, or 10.6% and the blacks to 28,545, or by 28.7%.

The next decade showed the greatest accession of population in the history of New Orleans, for in 1840, the city had increased its white population to 59,431 or 179.1%, whilst the number of Negroes grew to 42,647, or 49.1%.

The total number of slaves in 1840 was 20,708, of whom 7,863 were males and 13,647 females. There were as nearly as many free persons of color as there were slaves. They numbered 20,294, of whom 10,852 were females and 9,616 males. Despite all the legal prohibitions, both by the State and the United States Government, the number of slaves increased in tremendous numbers and the smuggling of Negroes was a thriving business. Yet a salient fact, which is seldom or even ever mentioned, is that nearly one half of the Negroes in New Orleans were free persons of color. It is evident that originally they were all brought here to be sold as slaves except a few refugees from San Domingo, and that they were owned by white masters who generously manumitted them eventually.

A slave was a good investment, and many of the slave holders hired them out to perform tasks for which they were best suited. Warden mentioned that artisans earned from $20.00 to $30.00 per month for their masters, and negresses from $12.00 to $15.00, and the labor of a good slave brought about $200.00 a year net.

What probably was the first labor meeting held in New Orleans by a representative group of workers, took place on August 30, 1835. It was called by one hundred and fifty mechanics for the object of preventing slaves from learning any kind of mechanic arts. The *Bee* reported that "speeches were made capable of exciting minds." The police arrested and jailed the speakers and whilst that particular meeting was disbanded, it was resumed in other places, where the mob was incited to riot by rabble rousers. It was only after the Legion was called out and Acting Mayor Culbertson issued a proclamation that order was restored. The leaders were apprehended and incarcerated. An editorial in the *Bee* of September 2, was profuse in its praises of the stand Acting Mayor Culbertson took and his stern denunciation of mob law. What could have been a serious uprising was averted. The editorial continued as follows:

> The mechanics of this city are as elsewhere generally men of industry and propriety of conduct; and we must exculpate them from any participation in the proceedings on Sunday, although we do believe that the object of those who assembled on that day was to create disturbances — but giving vent to dis-

contented feelings at such a time and place under present circumstances, was imprudent and calculated to produce disturbances.

The editorial also asserted that the City Council was justified in its interference. The dissenters met the next night to exonerate themselves and resolved to enforce the law and to assist the authorities. "They know," said the *Bee*, "that their renumeration here is great and that their services are in constant demand and that they should live and let live."

The grievances of the white mechanics were not altogether without grounds of justification. The employment of slaves in the skilled trades threatened the standard of living of white artisans. They were forced to compete with cheap labor. In the *Louisiana Gazette* of May 8, 1808, appeared the following advertisement:

> PUBLIC ATTENTION! On Monday, May 9, next, will be sold at the auction store of the subscriber, without reserve — a gang of Negroes, consisting of 62 slaves, including two children, forming one of the best collections in the country; In this band are mechanics of every kind, some above the ordinary, etc.

In the same paper on April 16, 1837 appeared the following notice:

> MORE NEGROES! Received by this day's steamer from Mobile 42 likely negroes from Georgia and Virginia. Buyers are requested to call and see for themselves. All descriptions, field-hands, mechanics, cooks, washers and ironers and body servants. Among them I have a No. 1 blacksmith, two seamstresses, a No. 1 body servant and a barber.

In these years many similar advertisements were published in the local press.

Slaves, it may be said, were in Louisiana the first beneficiaries of what might be called "social security," for the code provided that slaves disabled through old age, sickness, or any other cause, whether the disease was incurable or not, were to be fed and maintained by their owners. The sick were to have all the kinds of temporal and spiritual assistance the situation might require.

In colonial times there was more encouragement of slave marriages than after the Louisiana purchase. The Supreme Court of the State in the year 1818 clarified the issue with the following decree:

> It is clear that the slaves have no legal capacity to assent to

any contract. With the consent of their masters they may marry, and their moral power to agree to such a contract or connection to that marriage cannot be doubted; but whilst in a state of slavery it cannot produce any civil effect because slaves are deprived of all civil rights. Emancipation gives to the slave his civil rights, and a contract of marriage, legal and valid by the consent of the master and the moral assent of the slaves, from the moment of freedom, although dormant during slavery, produces all the effects which results from such contract among free persons.

A large number of the slaves in New Orleans were domestics. Nearly all the women were employed in the homes of their owners as cooks, nurses, house maids and the personal attendants to the ladies of the household. Commanding the affection and respect of their mistresses, they in turn reciprocated with all the devotion and loyalty that could be manifested by a member of the family. These household slaves imbibed the family pride and by their demeanor reflected the distinction they enjoyed. From the babyhood of the girls to their wedding day their faithful servants had been nurse, their guardian and later devoted duenna. The authority they asserted over the children would not be understood today. Seldom did they have a change of masters, and were fixtures in the same families to the day of their death. They lived in a separate section of the house known today, in the vieux carré, as the slave quarters, now converted into apartments. Many of the male slaves enjoyed the same privileges, some were coachmen, others butlers and workers around the house. They lived well in comparison to the slaves of the plantations.

An interesting anecodote about the relationship of a master and his slaves is related by Judge W. W. Howe in his Memoire of Francis Xavier Martin, the basic historian of Louisiana. Martin was a penurious old bachelor whose household consisted of an old slave and his wife and a body servant and factotum named Tom. In the words of Howe: "The judge had said to the cook and her husband: 'I intend to be a generous master; I will permit you a room but you must feed yourselves and supply my table with decent fare, besides cleaning the house in which we all reside and which is yours as well as mine. This is all I require of you. The rest of the time is yours and whatever money you may make or save after having nourished me and kept my clothes in a good state of repairs is your absolute property'. Such were the peculiar idiosyncrasies of the judge, that I am convinced he thought himself very generous on that occasion. It may be easily imagined what fare he had and what an infinite variety of stains and patches adorned his garments which really were a nondescript curiosity."

Another fascinating account by the same author desrves to be quoted; it shows a not too rare relationship between the master and his slave. It reads:

Tom, the body servant of Martin, was as much of a character in his way as the personage he waited upon, and was well known throughout the State, for he never failed to accompany the judge on his annual circuit. The slave looked upon his master as a sort of helpless grown-up baby of whom he had to take care and for whose safety and welfare he was accountable to the State of which that master, as he proudly knew, was one of the highest dignitaries. Tom very naturally came to the conclusion that, notwithstanding the color of his skin, he was a man of great importance and even assumed authority over the great personage whom he considered as his ward. For instance, when at home where Tom had full sway, the judge rose from his seat, Tom would sometimes say:
"Where are you going?"
"I am going to take a walk."
"What! without consulting me? Don't you know it's raining?—er—sit down, sir, sit down."
And taking his master by his shoulders, Tom would gently force him back to his seat.

The judge was once overheard saying to his faithful companion in a hotel where he had stopped:
"Tom, have I dined today?"
"What!" replied Tom in a scolding tone. "What a question, sir. Are you getting clear out of your mind? Don't you recollect that you ate a full duck?"
"Oh, very well then, all right."
One day Tom said to him, "I want a whip for our buggy."
"Well Tom, if you want a whip, buy a whip of course. I do not see any objection to it."
After a while Tom came to him whip in hand.
"Master," he said, "I want a dollar."
"A dollar from me? Monstrous. What for? On what tenable ground do you establish your petition?"
"To pay for the whip."
"Why Tom, I thought you were a man of sense. Did you not buy the whip for your own accommodation?"
"I bought it for your buggy, sir."

"My buggy! Our buggy, you mean. You called it our buggy yourself. Don't you ride in it? Tush! Don't trouble me any more about it."

From the earliest days in New Orleans slaves were instructed in the principles of the Catholic faith by the Ursuline nuns, and in later days that task was undertaken by their mistresses. They were baptised in the faith, they attended services at the Cathedral and outwardly practiced the tenets of Christianity. Their peculiar moral code, their emotionalism, their strange psychology, their idolatry, their superstitions, their awe of fetishes and the Voudou worship which they brought with them from the wilds of Africa to the West Indies and later to the shores of America, were all so indelibly stamped upon their minds that only a relatively few could be altogether converted. Only a few subordinated their fetishism to the dogma of the white man's church. They were confused, and as an alternative, they would worship in the faith of their masters and at the same time clandestinely practice a barbaric cult. Chambers wrote that "the slaves had their dances, weird and grotesque affairs reminiscent of the African jungle, from whence they originally had come. They would be given in the open air at some surburban spot. *Congo Square* now known as Beauregard Square was a favorite place for these. Here time was kept by beating upon long crudely-made drums, the sound suggestive of those of the tom-toms in African wilds. These slave dances, starting as they did at first to give opportunities to enjoy the exhilirating effects of rhythmic bodily motions, became in time a Voudou rite — that strange fetich snake-worshipping cult introduced into the West Indies."

Latrobe in his Journal gives a vivid description of one of these Sunday gatherings in Congo Square, now Beauregard Square with the Municipal Auditorium at the back. He estimated that there were 500 or 600 persons present, all black with less than a dozen mulattoes. They grouped themselves in rings or circles in the middle of which woman danced around weird music in the center. The musical instruments were made from gourds and wooden staves and the drums were primitive. They sang songs, in a language which Latrobe says must have been African as it was not French, as they danced. He wrote, "I have never seen anything more brutally savage and at the same time dull and stupid, than this whole exhibition."

The *Louisiana Gazette* of August 16, 1820, under the headline "Idolatry and Quackery" reported a raid by the police on one of these meetings:

> Persons brought before the Mayor on the charge of holding illegal nightly meetings.
>
> For some time past, a house in the suburb Tremé has been used as a kind of temple for certain occult practices and the idolatrous worship of an African deity called Voudou. It is said that many slaves and some free people repaired there at nights to practices superstition, idolatrous rites, to dance, carouse, etc. It is also suspected that the slaves carried there the fruits of their robberies which the leaders appropriate to further their own debauches and villainy. The jugglers had collected some trumpery to aid their views: The image of a woman whose lower extremity resembled a snake and many smaller articles were seized and brought to the Mayor's office. Among the persons arrested was one white man, the others were free colored people and slaves.

The next day the French section of the same paper stated that the majority of the Negroes, slaves who participated in that interesting reunion were immediately whipped; the free-colored people were fined and the white man was put on a bond. These reunions were prohibited by law and the raids on them by the police occurred more frequently than is thought.

The voudou cult had its priests and priestesses, who because of superstition, had absolute sway over the Negroes. Also many white persons feared their conjurations. A *gris-gris* found on a door-sill or mysteriously placed in a chamber, in fact any fetish, was a sinister omen of brewing trouble. The voudou adepts were the fortune tellers of the city. Superstitious whites had great faith in them because, in collusion with household slaves, they were able to reveal secrets and make prophecies that came true. Some of their disclosures to the naive seemed to border on the supernatural. The word *gris-gris* is still used by children in playing games.

The Creole slaves had a patois typically their own, unfortunately it is a part of their folklore which has today disappeared.

Even as early as the thirties an ominous cloud darkened the political horizon. The South was enjoying great prosperity and its population was growing rapidly. It was predicted that New Orleans would surpass New York in population and commercial importance. Because of the fertility of the soil, the unlimited amount of cultivatable lands and the cheapness of slave labor, large plantations became more numerous in Louisiana. The planters lived in such splendor and accumulated such great wealth that they formed an aristocracy of their own which was not only not understood but aroused the envy of Northerners.

A movement to free the slaves now acquired momentum. The abolitionists argued that the prosperity of the South could only be due to slave labor; therefore, slavery must be abolished. The pro-slavery side pointed out that as the greater part of the Southern wealth was in slaves, to emancipate them would mean confiscation of property without compensation.

Both sides were irreconcilable. It was inevitable that this discord and hatred could only result in a fratricidal war. The emancipators were already fanning the smoldering embers of that approaching war.

On January 4th, 1836 Governor E. D. White of Louisiana, in his message to the Legislature, reported on the gravity of the situation:

> A class of persons in the northern states have arrogated to themselves the province of interference in the domestic affairs of the South. Dwelling remote from us and necessarily unacquainted with the operation of our institutions, these persons have associated themselves for their overthrow.
>
> Under the specious garb of friends to a particular class of our population, they are seeking to plunge them into unutterable misery and ruin. Where there is now peace and happiness with the obligation of service on the one hand, accompanied by the reciprocal obligation of protection and support, as well as in the weakness of infancy, as in the decreptitude of age, these infuriate zealots would sow discontent and insubordination. If successful in their machinations, they would kindle the flame of servile war, deluge the land in blood and cause the extermination of their hapless deluded victims.
>
> To promote their object, affiliated societies are formed in various parts; large sums of money are contributed, the press made auxillary to the scheme; tales of horror, having no foundation but in the heated fancy of the inventors; even the holy texts of religion are profaned, by being invoked in their disbolical purpose. By inflaming the passions of men of every age they are evidently laboring to prepare a crusade against us; while from their subsidized presses, volumes of graven form are issued; they are filled with pictures, engravings and emblems, intended to rouse the excitable imagination of infancy and of youth. The

mail, that most invaluable channel of inter communication, is perverted to a vehicle for the dissemination among ourselves of their incendiary writings.

I am glad to have it in my power to lay before you a collection of the publications referred to, which though not wholly complete, may serve to convey some adequate conception of the kind of warfare that is waging in our own country against our repose, our fortunes and our lives. These works are openly vended and distributed in other cities connected to us by the ties of commerce and kindred nationality.

Such is the case presented for your consideration. Difficult it is for us, with our habitual respect for the private concern of others, and in our wonted kindliness of such a demoniacal spirit, yet are we seriously called on to look at the painful reality as it is and to adopt the proper presentations to countervail the mischief.

In what light are these agitators to be regarded? They are traitors — traitors to humanity, traitors to their country and its constitution. It is an axiom too trite to be adjudged by each and every state in its own way. Neither the states collectively nor any state individually is invested with any right out of its own limits to intermeddle in regard to any other State without an infraction of the compact, much less can it be permitted to any number of individuals in a state to undertake to achieve what the State itself is inhibited from attempting.

CHAPTER XXX

MORALS AND VICE

New Orleans for many years was branded as the most infamous city in America. During the French and Spanish dominations the city was little known. It was a small colonial town located in a wilderness and isolated from the civilized world. Because of her limited commerce, her intercourse with the rest of the world was restricted to the occasional visit of a deep-sea vessel.

The original settlers were, as a rule, law-abiding, sober and moral, and their relationship between themselves was peaceful, amiable and friendly. They all spoke French, worshipped in the same Church, and had the same culture. Vice was to a large extent unknown among them. Practically the same conditions prevailed during the first decade of the nineteenth century. Soon after the "Purchase" New Orleans attracted the attention of the world, and it achieved fame as a city of business opportunity, an El Dorado where wealth was easily acquired. Its growth was rapid, and as is usually the case, there came a swarm of ruffians, gamblers, adventurers, men of loose morals and of easy conscience, *chevaliers d'industrie*, steeped in the way of crime and of vice, ready to pounce on guileless victims and despoil them of their hard earned gains. They were the procurers of misnamed places of amusement and operators of dens of iniquity, grop shops, gambling joints, and vulgar ball rooms. These sprang up in increasing proportion to the yearly increase of prospective customers. Brawls, robberies, fights and even murders were of daily occurrence. New Orleans was an open city, a place of amusements of all sorts, a resort which catered to the most vulgar, but at the same time provided pleasures for the most refined and cultured members of its society, both Creole and American.

It may be said that, in some respects, New Orleans was the first frontier city in the United States. It was no better and no worse than those notorious places which sprang up over night, and which were an integral part of the then Wild West. The so-called depravity of the city was not properly evaluated. Protestants, not only the ministers but many laymen as well, proclaimed it a godless, perverted, immoral and irreligious city. They wrote about it in their religious journals; it was a good theme for their sermons; and it was compared to the infamous cities of the Bible. Ministers often were dissuaded from accepting a pastorate there because of its alleged depravity. These facts are authoritatively attested to by the distinguished Minister, Theodore Clapp, in his autobiography.

The Protestants smarted because of the poor attendance at their services, and because one of their principal churches was owned by a Jew and existed only because of his bounty. They did not seem to realize that the irreligiousness of the city was due to its migrant population, for no matter how "good" these newcomers were in their home towns, when they got to New Orleans they became more interested in amassing money than in worshipping God. Besides the Protestant critics in their bigotry overlooked the fact that religion was practiced by Catholics and by most of the resident American Protestant families.

Practically the same accusations of moral depravity in New Orleans were made by some Catholics, as evidenced by Guilday, whom I have already quoted in the chapter on the Roman Catholic Church.

Many defamatory and disparaging letters about New Orleans circulated in the North and especially in the New England States. There newspapers found it profitable to calumniate the city for it made good reading. And many of the travelling authors who published their observations about New Orleans realized that the more sensational and the more exaggerated their reports, the more books they would sell.

W. Darby, in his book "Geographical Description of the State of Louisiana", said:

> Much distortion of opinion has existed, and is not yet eradicated in the other parts of the United States, concerning the public morals and manners in New Orleans.
>
> Divested of pre-conceived ideas on the subject, an observing man will find little to condemn in New Orleans, more than in any other commercial city; and will find that noble distinction of all native communities, acuteness of conception, urbanity of manners, and polished exterior.

On August 20, 1820, a letter was published in the *Baltimore Chronicle*:

I was in New Orleans but a very short time. I saw but little and heard sufficient to convince me that gambling and sensual pleasures were practiced to such a degree to destroy domestic happiness and tranquility.

Both New Orleans and Mobile are sinks of filth and hot beds of sensuality.

Such scandalous communications, for obvious reasons, must be discounted. But they were a model on which so many others have been based. It was properly refuted by the editor of the *Louisiana Gazette* on October 2, 1820:

> Two lies and truth are very well for them, indeed we have seen many letters from this city published in eastern papers. The truth is that gambling and sensual pleasure did not destroy the tranquility and happiness of a single respectable inhabitant of this city; and do not prevail to a greater extent in New Orleans than in Baltimore, Philadelphia or New York; nor are our young men more dissipated. We would recommend to the editor of the *Chroncile* and all other editors who are so fond of defaming New Orleans, and so much in the habit of publishing such lying, nonsensical and rascally letters, to publish also the names of the writers, so that they may be held up as a people subject for scorn to point her slow moving finger at, and that the citizens of this city may know and expose the authors of such abominable defamation.
>
> "Sic pergos dicere qua vis dissas non vis audies."

With the increasing floating population the number of gambling establishments increased, so much so that the respectable part of the population agitated the question of abolishing them.

"Feuilleton" wrote the following in the *Gazette* of October 29, 1821:

> Chartres Street: so famous for her magnificent establishments of that kind. Her beautiful cafés, her table covered with a green spread, and with dollars and bank notes, which present a tableau pleasing to the eye.
>
> What would become of these employees in yellow shoes, these diners away from homes? Yet they say card games are prohibited?

Again the same author, on November 29, 1821, remarked:

> A stranger passing on Jefferson Street would imagine that all the inhabitants of this place do nothing but drink and play billiards, for in every door is to be found a refreshment room and a table for that noble game.

Again "Feuillton" reported that Christmas Eve was celebrated with a great deal of restraint. There were forty drunks in the Faubourg St. Mary, twenty-five in the Fabourg Marigny, and in the city proper two hundred and sixty — a total of three hundred and twenty-five.

Despite the efforts made to limit gambling, on January 27, 1823, that journal reported that black gambling dens were in full operation in the rear of Faubourg St. Mary, and that: "The keepers of roulette and faro tables do not fail to open wherever customers may be expected — and most of them know how to blind those whose duty it is to be inquisitive."

That year a bill was introduced to allow only six gambling house to operate.

"Feuillton" again reported on July 22, 1823, that "Jefferson Street made herself remarked above all the others for her orgies and the assemblage of Negroes in the morning, and fisticuffs among the sailors in the afternoon. The Faubourg St. Mary is not better protected, and besides there are balls."

In the *Louisiana Gazette* of March 5, 1825, a communication appeared which complained:

> New Orleans, as it is well known, presents too many temptations to the young, the thoughtless and the unwary, who come among us, and with very few counterbalancing restraints.
> Seamen come here from the nothern ports, and from abroad, away from parental eyes and parental voices, young, ignorant of the world, unsuspicious, unreflecting, and are soon robbed by those hardened in the ways of vice of their scanty pittance, (but hard earned pittance), led into every kind of inquity, and then robbed of health, of money and of peace, and sent adrift upon a world's wide ocean. This is a sad but evident truth.

He proposed that "a large, neat, handsome Mariner's Church be erected so that they may go there."

That same Journal writing under the caption "Gambling Houses" observed that "those gambling houses which are no more than a catch penny contrivance of the owners, should be guarded against by every one that visits the city with produce." And it further observed "that hardly a night but these places are filled with the crews of a ship or a flat boat, not so much for the purpose of gambling as to look over, when by the interference of individuals concerned, are taken to the bottle become mellow, and set to gambling—after winning a few dollars, they persist; and when fortune frowns they have no stopping place until all is lost. Individuals from the country should be cautious and never be led into difficulties in those places."

Another example of that insidious propaganda which pervaded the country is found in the book, "Letters from the West and South", by A. Singleton, an American, published in 1824. He wrote:

> As to the morals of the city, the word is obsolete. On the Sunday we arrived, a balloon with a live lamb in the car, and aerial fireworks were to be exhibited by permission of the Mayor. It is said that there has never been an unpleasant day of Independence, which is a good omen for the country.
>
> Sunday is a busy holiday, when the theater and the circus have the most spectators, as then they least value the time.
>
> As the good people of New England are scandalized by their travel-spectators, as are the Kentuckians dreaded on account of their swaggering boatmen; and as the Western people call the Eastern travelers yankees, so do the citizens call all the up-river boatmen Kentuckians.
>
> In some streets you cannot pass a door or corner, but will see a party sitting at some game. It has been rumored, it is not to be believed, much less repeated, to be a gentleman here, like foreign princes, and lords of the nobility, one must patronize a yellow miss, even if only for the name of the thing, that if a young buck has one or two discarded lemons, his credit rises in porportion to the number!
>
> In this city are hundreds of Eastern merchants, and, notwithstanding the foreign remarks, many lovers of morality and reverers of religion.

The following article appeared in the *Chillicothe Times* which was quoted by the *Gazette* on December 24, 1825:

> The French population is I suppose, three to one American, and with them Sunday is the greatest day of the week, the morning being devoted to business and the evenings to pleasure. As a specimen I will give the following prominent feature of a Sunday in New Orleans.
>
> You see the markets much better; every branch of business is moving on a greater degree of spirit; all the uniform companies of the city elegantly equipped and on parade morning and evening, every species of gaming that human invention has discovered: congo dances; and the French theater crowded to overflowing.
>
> The Americans are gradually gaining ground, and the old forms and customs are giving place to new ones.

They now enjoy a well regulated police. The city guards are seen in all places of the city, and if perchance there happens to land an old Kentuck "a half horse, half alligator, and a little touched with the snapping turtle", he has to keep himself very cool, or else he is very soon walked in the Cabildo.

The legal prohibition of gambling places met with little success, for more than ever it thrived behind closed doors, and any one so inclined had little difficulty in finding a place to practice this vice. On June 13, 1828, the *Courier* remarked that "the opinion of all good men of sense are settled on that subject, and if the law does not entirely prohibit these establishments, it is because our Legislature was aware that the prohibition of gambling houses, licensed and opened to the public, would give rise to establishments of clandestine houses much more pernicious in their effects."

It advocated that the cost of the license should be $5,000,00, and that $2,500.00 should go to the state, and the balance to be appropriated to charitable institutions.

James Stuart who visited New Orleans in 1830 wrote:

British writings about looseness of manners among the people (of New Orleans) is false. Excepting only the appearance of lottery offices, billiard rooms, vice is much more prominent in London, and even in Edinburgh, and, I suspect, in most of the European cities, than in New Orleans. Females of light character are nowhere seen on the streets, or public resorts, or at the doors or in the lobbies of theaters; and there seems to me to be more perfect propriety of conduct at the theaters here than at any public place of that description in Britain, and more general attention to dress here than there. In fact, everybody who goes to the French Theater here must dress in the same way as if going to the opera house in London.

It is a striking fact in the manners of the people of the American cities, and is very much to their credit, that there is no appearance of light character upon any of the public streets at any time, either of the day or night.

I am quite confident that no stranger will discover, unless from conversation, that either in Philadelphia, New York or Baltimore, or in the streets or public resorts in New Orleans, he had met a female of questionable description.

But he remarked that "in one respect there is a greater laxity than in any of the American towns I have seen. The people spend the Sunday more in amusements and shopping (for the shops are generally opened on Sunday), than within the walls of their churches."

Tyrone Power, Esq., who was in New Orleans in 1834, gave also a favorable report on New Orleans. He observed:

> I have heard in the North much said about the great danger incurred by a night stroll in New Orleans, and so will the stranger who next follows after me; but do not let these bug-a-boo tales deter him from a walk upon the Levee at 10 p. m. It is not amongst these sons of industry, however rude, that he will encounter either insult or danger. I have traversed it often on foot and on horseback, and never met with the first, or had the slightest cause to apprehend the latter.
>
> I question whether London or Paris can boast of less crime in proportion; certaintly, not fewer felonies. Here, it is too true, a quarrel, in hot blood is often followed by a shot or a stroke with the ready poniard; and for the stranger, all he has to do is to keep out of low places of gambling and dissipation, and if in a large hotel, to keep his door locked; a precaution which would be as much called for at Cheltenheim or Spa, where the congregated number equally are at; although, in the latter places, I admit, the thieves might be nice men, better dressed, and not chewers of "Baccy".
>
> The streets after nightfall, are the very quietest I ever saw in any place possessing one-third of the population. The theaters, I repeat, as far as observation goes, might serve as a model to cities boasting greater claims to refinements.
>
> As a set-off, however, let the stranger visit the gambling tables, which are numerous; the low balls, masked or other, occurring every night, for whites or quadroons, or both; let him visit the low bar rooms, or even look into that of the first hotel, which bar forms a half circle of forty feet, yet is, during the hours of the twenty-four, only to be approached in turn, and whose daily receipt is said to exceed $300.00 for drams; and he will, if such be his only source of information, naturally come to conclusions anything but favorable to the moral conditions of New Orleans.
>
> The crowds so occupied, however, be it remembered, is so composed of strangers, so what is here called the transient population, at this season, counting at least 40,000 persons, the greatest proportion of whom are here without a home, except the barrooms of a public house, or a shelter, save the bed chamber which they have in common with three to twenty companions, as luck or favor may preside over their billet.

A. A. Parker, who was a visitor at approximately the same time, had a totally different point of view, for he wrote:

> It is a place of great business, bustle and bandishment; and of dissipation, disease and death.
>
> As I passed along by its muddy pavement and putrid gutters,

and saw the many gambling houses, grog shops, oyster shops, and house of riot and debauchery, surely thought I, there are many things here exceedingly offensive, both to the physical and moral man. And when I saw the motley throngs, hurrying on to these haunts of vice, corruption and crime, I almost instinctively exclaimed in the words of the immortal bard—

"Broad is the road that leads to death
and thousands walk together there."

But there, the career of the debauchee is short: The poisonous atmosphere soon withers and wastes away the polluted life's blood. Death follows close upon the heels of crime, and one need stand but a short time at the charnel house, to behold cartloads of its victims, hurried "unwept, unhonored and unsung" to their last home.

The sanction of law and religion are set at naught, the Sabbath is profaned, and they give themselves up to hilarity, dissipation and crime.

As long as crime is sanctioned in New Orleans, so long will it be the general haunt of the knaves and vagabonds of the Union and of the world.

I must say that New Orleans does not show that order, neatness and sobriety, found in other larger cities of the Union. Murders, robberies, thefts and riots, are too common hardly to elicit a passing notice.

The police is inefficient or shamefully negligent. The authorities of the city appear to stand aloof, and the populace, physically or morally, wallowing in crime. It does appear to me, that if all in authority, and all the virtuous portion of the citizens would brace themselves to the work, the city might be greatly improved in health and in morals.

Let the strong arm of the law be put forth fearlessly — let the police be active and take into custody the disorderly knaves and vagabonds — let gambling houses be put down, and Sunday theaters and circuses be suppressed, and New Orleans would wear a different aspect.

No exaggeration — wish it was — but it is indeed too true; and whoever happens to visit it, that places a decent value upon life, or the goods of life, will be glad, like me, to escape without the injury of loss of either.

I could not, however, feel at ease among such a set of plunderers and robbers. The best citizens are culpably negligent in not improving the city. As long as crime is sanctioned in New Orleans, so long will it be the general haunt of the knaves and vagabonds of the Union.

Yet gambling was a vexation to the residents of the city, and many efforts were made, if not to suppress it, at least to control it, for having found from experience that under the ban of the law, even with severe penalties, it thrived clandestinely behind closed doors.

An Act of 1823 provided a $5,000.00 license on gambling houses and $1,500.00 on each theater, which amount was to be applied to the Charity Hospital, Poydras Asylum, Boys Asylum, College of Louisiana and the primary schools of the State. An Act, passed by the Legislature in 1830, increased the licenses from $5,000.00 to $7,000.00, and for the theaters from $1,500.00 to $4,000.00, which amount was to be divided among the above mentioned institutions.

Niles Weekly Register of August 12, 1826, gave the following estimate of the expenses of the six gambling licenses authorized by law, which "is believed falls short of the actual expenditures:"

6 licenses @ $5,000.00	$30,000.00
24 journeymen, 4 to each bank @ $100.00 per month	28,800.00
Boarding same at $25.00 per month each	7,200.00
Servant's hire, one to each bank @ $25.00 per month—including board	1,800.00
House rent each bank, not less than $100 per month	7,200.00
Liquors to induce customers to play freely, for light and fuel $2.50 per day for each bank	5,475.00
A total of	$80,475.00

In 1834, the revenues from licensed gambling places amounted to $113,000.00, to be apportioned as follows:

Male Orphan Asylum	$ 6,000.00
Female Orphan Asylum	6,000.00
College of Louisiana	9,500.00
Primary Schools of N. O.	14,000.00
Charity Hospital	52,000.00
Ordinary purposes	15,000.00

A report of the State Treasurer to the Legislature, in 1835, gave the following tableau of the total revenues derived from legally operated gambling houses:

Year		Year		Year	
1824	$30,000.00	1828	$33,000.00	1832	$ 68,000.00
1825	30,000.00	1829	33,000.00	1833	94,000.00
1826	28,000.00	1830	50,500.00	1834	113,000.00
1827	33,000.00	1831	53,000.00		

The *Bee* reported on March 7, 1835, that in the State Legislature, an Act to suppress gambling houses was the Order of the day, and that "no speaker denied the necessity of passing such a law, after the second reading. It provided for a penalty of not less than $1,000.00 or more than $5,000.00 for the first offense, and not less than $10,000.00 for the second, and imprisonment in the penitentiary—not less than one or more than five years. The owners of these houses, considered as accessories, were subject to the same penalties."

Credit was given to Senator L. H. Moore, Esq., for "his philanthropic efforts for the suppression of gambling." He was honored at a banquet held at Banks Arcade Exchange, on March 13, 1835, and on April 30 the citizens paid him a tribute of respect for having eradicated the "occasions for the practice of that vice."

The *Bee* of May 7, 1835 published an editorial stating that "it is pleasing to find that the opprobrium cast on the city by some travellers will soon be left without a shadow of probability. Already have the most strenuous exertions been made to redeem it from obloquy, and render it a desirable place for residence and trade. Gambling has been abolished, or (at least) discontinued by law."

On July 13, it also expounded on the dangers threatening the city. It mentioned the riots and insurrections in the various cities of the State of Mississippi. And further warned that "when we reflect on the considerable numbers of vagabonds and scoundrels which are at present in New Orleans, and that their number increases every day by their numerous arrivals from the interior as well as from the exterior, we are really surprised a city police of only 129 men can suffice to restrain that mass of people without avowal, and composed of so many heterogeneous principles."

New Orleans had the most luxurious drinking palaces in the country. Their grandeur and their luxury far excelled those of the North. This fact is attested to by the severest and most biased critics who visited the city. Yet at the same time she had the most dissolute and vilest dens where the lowest elements of the population congregated. Every one drank according to his status and his circumstances. Drunkenness was very prevalent and drunkards could be found in every section of the city. The drinking custom varied with the nationality of the individuals. The Anglo-Saxons were addicted to hard drinks, principally whiskey, which they gulped down in a hurry, whilst the French, following the customs of their ancestors, sat at a table, and leisurely imbibed their favorite wines and liquors. It has been frequently said that inebriety was more common among the Americans than among the Creoles.

Isidore Lowenstern, who visited the city in 1837, gave an excellent pen picture of the drinking habits at that time:

> In New Orleans strong drinks are used in excess. Not only the richest and the most considered are observed to take ten or twelve tumblers of grog or whiskey punch before dinner.
>
> There are in every American hotel an antichamber where all sorts of wines and liquors are sold from early morning to midnight, and where the gentlemen rarely pass without stopping to imbibe, standing and in haste, their glass of gin or bitters, as coachmen do at home in the wine cellars. A bar is a most profitable business, so much so, it is even found on steamboats. It is especially in New Orleans where the business is most thriving, for they serve a buffet table twice a day, from one to two, and eight to eleven o'clock in the evening. The food is free for the customers, but the custom of having luncheon, and a hasty supper, amply compensates that prodigality."

New Orleans was long famous for its free lunches.

Lowenstern mentioned the drink "Tom" made with eggs, sugar, eau de vie (cognac) and hot water. He found it agreeable.

Lotteries were common. They had to have the approval of the Legislature, and they were usually run for the benefit of churches, schools, asylums and other charitable institutions. They were usually well conducted and were never a cause for scandal.

The first temperance lecture in New Orleans was delivered by Dr. Edward H. Barton, a prominent physician of the city, at Rev. Mr. Clapp's Church, on June 18, 1835; but it was not until April 21, 1836, that a temperance society was organized at a meeting held at the Presbyterian Church in Lafayette Square. It was called by the Reverend Mr. Lawrence, and Thomas N. Morgan, Esq., presided. A constitution was proposed by Seth Barton, Esq., and addresses were delivered by Barton, S. P. Andrews, J. Walton, W. W. Caldwell and Rev. Joel Parker. The following constitution was adopted:

Article (1) The Society shall be called the New Orleans Temperance Society.

Article (2) We, whose names are hereby annexed, believing that the use of ardent spirits is not only unnecessary, but hurtful to the social, civil and religious interest of men, agree that we will, in all suitable ways, discountenance the use of them throughout the community.

Article (3) The society will meet annually, on the 1st Wednesday of January, and at such other times as the executive shall appoint.

The officers were: J. W. Breedlove, Esq., President; Hon. H. A. Bullard, Dr. Barton, Dr. Meux; T. C. Cash; Joshua Baldwin; S. F. Andrews; Vice President; Thomas N. Morgan, Secretary; James S. Walton, Treasurer; Joseph Lovell, Auditor. Sixty-five signatures were attached to the constitution.

H. Didimus, in his book "New Orleans As I Found it" published in 1845, wrote:

> The city enjoys a questionable reputation for good order, whose name abroad is held synonymous with midnight robberies and assassinations.
>
> There was a time that if what is said of the dangers of New Orleans its desperate population, its inefficient police, the inactivity of the administration of criminal jurisprudence — was true, is proved by the very existence of prejudicial opinions now generally entertained, and not lightly resigned, by those who have not visited our city within ten years, and who are accustomed to see gaming tables spread by authority at the corners of our principal streets, and hear the ringing of silver, as the stakes were lost and won, at all hours of the day and night.
>
> Of the large number accused of every variety of crimes, and annually arraigned before the Criminal Court of New Orleans, but a very small portion are connected with the city by residence or business.
>
> The darker crimes are mostly perpetrated by foreigners freshly imported from the prisons of Europe, or by such of the citizens of the river states as having been long accustomed to a life subjected to little restraint, supposed that there were even such slight checks upon vice, as they have been made acquainted with, are wanting.
>
> New Orleans cannot be said to groan beneath the weight of churches. One church closed for lack of patronge — Episcopalian — is but thinly attended, and is the private property of a wealthy Jew, who, with liberality never looked for among those of his tribe, bestows the usufruct of his temple upon the natural enemies of his faith.

The immorality of New Orleans of the early nineteenth century has been greatly exaggerated. No attempt was made by most of the writers to distinguish between the good and bad portion of the population. They scrambled them in one classification, and that was the bad. They did not realize, and perhaps they did not want to, that the ungodliness, the depravity, the gambling dens, that heterogeneous mob which crowded the streets were visitors only for the winter months; and that most of the crimes were committed by unwelcome strangers who infested the city.

Yet had those writers peeped behind the curtain they would have seen the resident population as it was — social, cultured, law abiding, and above all moral — qualities which they may not themselves have possessed, and perhaps not found in their native localities. After all, it was the mode of the time for New Orleans to be defamed by American and English authors.

To sum up, it can be said that New Orleans was not as bad as it was depicted.

CHAPTER XXXI

YELLOW FEVER

New Orleans in the early part of the nineteenth century was notorious as the worst pest hole in the world. Its ill repute was well deserved. Yearly in ever increasing numbers from everywhere adventurers, home seekers, merchants and professional men would flock hither only to become the prey of that dread epidemic, yellow fever, and to fill prematurely a wet grave.

The Creoles enjoyed an immunity to "yellow jack," which Dr. Delery attributed to their having contracted the disease in childhood, and only rarely in later years. But he thought that the natives of the neighboring parishes were apt to contract yellow fever when exposed to it. Negroes, through a racial characteristic not clear to us even today, were very seldom victims of the black vomit, even if only newly imported into the city. Dr. Charles Chassaignac expressed the opinion that:

> The prognosis is better by far among the blacks and colored than among the whites, even when the former are otherwise in less favorable conditions and surroundings. Whether this is because the darkies merely possess a higher degree of resistance to this particular poison, or because their skin being tougher and their odor more repellant to the mosquito, they are less frequently bitten, we are not prepared to say. The fact remains that the majority have the disease in a mild form and the mortality among them is almost nil, so much so that they, like white children, have been supposed to be immune until comparatively recently.

Strangers, most of them originating from every part of the Union and from Europe, who possessed no immunity, were in a large part the victims of the merciless killer. It was a well established fact that after the appearance of the first frost to the beginning of the following summer, the city was relatively healthy and the strangers could live here in comparative security. All business was transacted during the cold months. The city was then a beehive of activity. The theatres reopened their doors, ballrooms thrived, gambling establishments flourished, cafes and the groggeries were crowded; money was readily made and as easily spent. Only the prudent ever thought of the probability of another epidemic. These would leave at the approach of Summer, whilst the less thoughtful would ignore warnings and refuse to take precautionary measures. Then when the first case of yellow fever occurred, they would flee in panic to any place which promised safety. Means of escape became difficult and boats and trains were crowded far beyond their capacity. Some of those in flight, who felicitated themselves on having escaped, died of the disease enroute, and their bodies were thrown into the river or buried on the wayside.

Dr. Jabez Heustis, a prominent physician of that time, maintained that the reason Americans contracted the disease much more frequently than the French was, no doubt, owing to differences in their manner of life and habits of temperance and sobriety. The French drink little or no spiritous liquors, in place of which they substitute the small acidulous wines, particularly claret. "The Americans on the other hand, influenced by taste, strangely and erroneously imagine that the use of distilled spirits is necessary to preserve them against the fogs, damps, and sickly vapors of the climate: a fatal opinion and a destructive practice, which has committed greater ravages than the sword, and sent more victims to the shades of death than ever the arms of war sacrificed at the shrine of ambition, cruelty or rapine."

From its founding in 1718 to its acquisition by the United States in 1803, the period of the French and Spanish domination, New Orleans was of slow growth. Its then isolation from the rest of the world because of the restrictions imposed on its commerce, and of the lengthy and perilous sea voyage, even from the neighboring countries bordering the Gulf of Mexico and the Caribbean Sea, resulted in an almost negligible immigration. These factors, although detrimental to the progress of the city, were conducive to its protection from devastating epidemics. In the provincial days the mortality, although great, at no time reached the exceedingly high death rate which prevailed for many decades following the Louisiana Purchase. The history of the first ninety years of Louisiana is practically silent concerning its medical aspect, and but scant definite references are made to its diseases, its hospitals and its physicians.

Long before yellow fever prevailed in New Orleans, it had attacked many of the large cities of the Eastern seaboard of the United States. There were epidemics of that disease as early as

1668 in New York, 1691 in Boston, 1693 in Philadelphia and 1699 in Charleston. It was not until 1796 that New Orleans experienced its first epidemic. Some writers have expressed the opinion that the disease had appeared in New Orleans before that time, notably in 1769 and 1791 and in 1793-1794, but careful research proves that such opinions were not based on facts.

Doctors Thomas, Delery, Barton and Carpenter as well as an anonymous writer, evidently a physician, in the *Louisiana Courier* of November 27, 1820, all have stated definitely that the first epidemic of yellow fever occurred in this city in the summer of 1796.

Dr. Carpenter maintained that "commercial intercourse between New Orleans and the West Indies, principally confined to the Spanish islands, was only interfered with by the embargo laws from 1807 to the spring of 1809, and by the war of 1812-1815, having three years of interrupted trade with the Spanish islands, during a period in which commerce with the British and French West Indies was entirely prevented. Consequently yellow fever was epidemic during two of those years. — None during the embargo and during the war."

There were epidemics in 1812, 1817, 1819, 1822, 1824, 1827, 1828, 1829, 1831 and 1832, 1837, 1839. The most deadly of all was that of 1819 when one out of every twelve inhabitants died of the pest — 2190 deaths in a population of 26,183. Even these figures do not give a clear insight of the virulence of the epidemic because of the large number of Creoles, or the indigenous element of the population, and of Negroes who had a certain degree of immunity.

In the *New Orleans Gazette* of February 3, 1818, is recorded the following dramatic episode which, unfortunately, was only one of many such tragedies. It reads:

> In 1817 whilst the yellow fever was epidemic in New Orleans, Phillip's barge left the city for St. Francisville and soon began to lose her passengers and hands. To replace the latter, new hands were continuously engaged, who took the disease in succession, so that it was with great difficulty the voyage was performed; and finally, of the captain, crew and passengers, not one survived.

Yet only eighty persons were supposed to have died of yellow fever in the epidemic of 1817. It cannot be controverted that the death rate of these epidemics must have exceeded by far that which was handed down as official. *The Niles Register*, on September 27 of that year reported that "New Orleans is sickly. The deaths are said to amount to 12 per day, exclusive of the Kentuckians and other boatmen, who are said to disappear by boat loads."

Yellow fever was much more malignant during the first half of the nineteenth century. The statistical records show that in the period of 1822 to 1844 there were 9637 cases and 3787 deaths; and that from 1847 to 1905, there were 32,678 cases and 5,019 deaths. These figures are only approximate, but are accurate enough for comparison.

The epidemics of yellow fever were not of equal virulence. In some years the yellow fever was fatal in nearly every case, in others the disease was of medium intensity, with a low death rate, and frequently the epidemics were so mild that nearly every patient recovered. Two reasons have been advanced for this disparity between the mortalities of the epidemics. One: that all great epidemics, as well as those of medium intensity, which ravaged New Orleans have always begun in May, June or July and it has taken one, two or two and a half months of incubation after the importation of the first case or cases, before the disease became epidemic or claimed many victims. The other: that all epidemics beginning in August and September have been mild, have lacked virulence and have shown only a slight mortality.

As there was no specific treatment, the physicians had to resort to empiric methods. The early medical literature of this city abounds with articles and monographs advocating and condemning the various therapeutic measures then in vogue. The remedies which would prove apparently to be beneficial in one epidemic were absolutely inert in another. It can readily be conceived the predicament of the physicians of the time, who were baffled and thwarted in their efforts to cure their patients of a malady having such a high death rate.

The formula of Dr. Musdovoi was considered so successful that it was used in the epidemics of 1796, 1817, 1819 and 1820. It contained cinchona, tartar emetic, cream of tartar and an amonia salt. The distinguished doctors Gros and Geradin treated the disease in 1817 as follows: The young and robust were bled, mild evacuants, acidulated drinks with cream of tartar, tamarind, oranges, citrous fruits, and butter milk. They preferred luke warm to cold baths. Large doses of camphor and musk were prescribed. The whole body was rubbed with slices of lemons or with vinegar.

They opined that the discovery of a specific remedy for that disease "must be classed among the chimerical illusions born of the imagination."

Dr. Jabez Heutis in his pamphlet published in 1817, asserted that the mercury treatment in vogue at that time was empirical, and disproved the belief that when salivation was produced by the drug that the safety of the patient was secured. He further commented that the sad consequences of the practice were practically exemplified in New Orleans in the year 1812. He remarked that most of the soldiers forming three companies of the first regiment of Artillery at the barracks of this city, died of yellow fever and from the effect of the mercury. Dr. Heustis advocated the use of cold baths, copious draughts of cold water and sponging of the body with cold vinegar, nitre and water. The room to be well ventilated, the floors occasionally scrubbed with vinegar or nitrous acidulated with sugar, which he said had "a tendency to correct the alkaline disposition of the fluids."

The mercurial treatment was a controversial subject among the physicians. It was frequently employed and as frequently discarded. Dr. Barton wrote in 1832 that confidence "in that means of treatment was impaired in 1820 because salivation was seldom induced and when it occurred, the patient did not always recover. A sore mouth did not always save them"

For many years quinine was considered a specific in the treatment of yellow fever. It was first advocated by Doctor A. P. Lambert in the epidemic of 1837, but he discontinued its use in 1839. It is said of him that he was the first to acknowledge the "infidelity of the therapeutic means." Drs. Bahir, S. Mart, N. H. Daret and Ed. Fortin, as early as 1839 claimed that quinine was not a specific in yellow fever.

Practically the same preventive measures were taken against the spread of yellow fever as were employed during the cholera. Cannon were shot and barrels of tar were burned in the streets to "clarify the atmosphere and to disintegrate the miasmas." The burning of the bedding and clothing of the patient, the fumigation of homes with sulphurous acid, the disinfection of privy-vaults with sulphate of iron and carbolic acid, the flushing out of gutters, the passing and repealing of quarantine regulations, the private funerals, the gruesome hauling to the graveyard of the unshrouded corpse in the "wee small hours" of the morning, the splashing of bodies thrown in shallow watery graves and the over-crowded graveyards exhaling putrid odors of decomposition — all contributed to the writing of a horrid chapter in the history of New Orleans.

In 1822 the City Council passed an ordinance prohibiting the tolling of the church bells and the chanting of the priests at funerals because of the depressing effect on the sick, and further that such doleful sounds could terrorize those who were well.

But immediately after the first frost, the prostrated city would cast away all sorrow and forget all tribulations. The mourning which hung like a pall during the summer months would disperse. Commerce would be resumed. Strangers would flock hither by thousands. Places of amusement would reopen their doors and gaiety would reign supreme again. Little thought was given to the catastrophe of the past and little done to prevent its recurrence until hope was again shattered by the announcement of another first case.

New Orleans has incurred obloquy from letter writers, chroniclers and travellers, who wrote that during the epidemics the population was callous, that their phlegmatism bordered on inhumanity, that the sick were unattended and that the lack of reverence for the dead was ghoulish. They wrote that during the days of calamity orgies and ribaldry prevailed, places of amusements thrived and that vice and crime reigned supreme. The facts are that during the summer months the city was very quiet, that the theatres and other places of amusement were closed, that the permanent residents of the city, as a rule, were immune and that the disease lashed its fury on recently arrived strangers. Yet it cannot be gainsaid that they were treated with all the care and humanity possible under the circumstances. This fact is attested by the distinguished cleric Theodore Clapp, who voiced his indignation for the fantastic and irresponsible tales in circulation at that time. He wrote:

> In the epidemics which I have witnessed, instead of unusual depravity, an extraordinary degree of benevolence has prevailed, shedding a heavenly light upon the dark scenes of the sick room, the death bed, the coffin, the funerals, etc. Yet with respect to the subject, New Orleans has been most shamefully misrepresented. In the summer of 1824 an English officer came into our city on his way to Jamaica, West Indies. He was an intrepid, well informed, interesting man who was induced to visit New

Orleans simply to gratify his curiosity. He said that he was glad to be with us in days of mourning, disaster and death, for he wished to become acquainted with all the phases of suffering humanity, and had much rather see New Orleans in the sickly season than in the healthy period of winter. He accompanied one of our physicians to the Charity Hospital and walked with him through all the yellow fever wards. He used no precautions and seemed to be entirely superior to fear. We admired his courage, equanimity and gentlemanly bearing. After a fortnight sojourn, he left us in good health.

On his return to England his travels in the United States that summer were published. A copy of his work fell into my hands. On turning to that portion of the book, a description of his experiences among us during the time just mentioned, I was astonished at the assertion that New Orleans, in the midst of a dreadful epidemic was full of merriment, intemperance and gaiety. He says the sick were neglected and abandoned; the crowds rushed every night to the balls, opera and theatrical amusements; and that the intoxicated persons were often seen uttering profane and ribald language when employed in burying the dead — in performing the last offices which humanity calls for. Words more false, defamatory, and unjust could not be written. Similar fictions are propagated in our northern cities concerning New Orleans, every time an epidemic prevails there. Yet the fact is that in its darkest days the inhabitants have deported themselves nobly and recognized the sacred claims of religion and humanity. Many of these libels are circulated in letters professedly written by persons who were eye and ear witness of the scenes which they described.

It seems to give some men particular delight to depreciate and vilify human nature. It is easy to be severe, harsh, vilify, satirical and disparaging in commenting on the behavior of our fellow-beings, but not one ever too charitable in his views of other men — the motives, principles, character, or conduct. It has been my lot for the past 40 years to reside in what is reputed to be the worst place in he civilized world; yet to this day I have not met a person so hardened, so brutal, as to be capable of treating with indifference, neglect, or levity the suffering form of humanity within his reach. In New Orleans, I have been often struck with admiration to see persons in the lowest walks of life making every possible sacrifice of time, ease and money in attending on the sick, soothing the dying and providing funds and a decent burial for those who are absolute strangers and utterly destitute. I go so far as to say that I have never in a single instance, seen poor and wicked people (as they are called) declining to perform all the offices of charity in their power to the ill and distressed around them. This most terrible form of sin has sometimes, perhaps been manifested in the higher circles of humanity, I have never beheld it even there.

I have witnessed noble and disinterested actions among all classes of mankind, not excepting the rudest and most vulgar. I have seen poor young men standing on the vestibule of mercantile life, close the stores, suspend all business, give their days and their nights, their toil and their money to the relief of the sick, indigent and helpless strangers from whom they could neither wish nor hope for the smallest renumeration. I have known them to carry on this work of charity till their health was undermined and their lives were offered up as a sacrifice on the altar of philantrophy.

The people of New Orleans are in the highest degree earnest, excited, serious, anxious, ready, one and all to pour their treasures and their heart's blood, if it could avail, to save the victims of disease from the jaws of destruction.

During these days of dire calamity, both city fathers and private citizens did every thing in their power to procure proper care and whenever possible, provided a decent burial for the unfortunates. Most of the victims were not residents of the city but were part of a floating population of helpless and friendless strangers, many of whom were in a destitute condition.

In October 1822, a county hospital was fitted up at the lower end of Common Street for the reception of yellow fever patients by the Board of Health, "where persons not domiciliated in the city or destitute of the means of medical aid and other attendance who may be certified by any licensed physician of the city to have fallen sick of the disease."

On October 2, 1822 the following ordinance was passed by the City Council:

Resolved; That the Mayor is authorized to form, in each district of this city, a board of benevolence, to be composed of the alderman of each district and two respectable inhabitants, to be named by the Mayor. That the object is to open a subscription to succor the indigent poor, to choose a physician to attend the sick in their respective districts and to indicate them to the Mayor; who upon the recommendation of said members of the respective boards, will write to the said physicians to engage them to attend the poor sick of the city, gratis; if any physicians of the city should refuse to concur in this act of humanity, the Mayor is authorized to allow them such compensation as he should think equal to the service of such physicians. The following were names of the Board of Benevolence in each district:

1st: Porter, Morse H. Landreaux, M. White.
2nd: Vigne, A. Peychaud, M. Girod.
3rd: A. Abat, A. Davezac, Chas. L. Blache, August Doucé.

4th: Lanna, Bebetaud, S. Cucullu, F. J. Giquel.
5th: E. Mance, Nabat, C. Morin, J. F. Canonge.
6th: Wm. Montgomery, F. Gaiennie, DeBuys, N. Cox.
7th: J. F. Rousseau, Chas. Genois, Fort.
8th: P. Allard, E. Blanc, H. Bebe.

In September 1824, a Benevolent Committee was appointed for each ward, "whose office it shall be to provide means for the relief of the persons laboring under want and sickness." The Mayor asked physicians to gratuitously donate their services and to inscribe their names at the Mayor's office.

"Druggists and apothecaries in each respective wards will be appointed to them who will furnish according to their orders." Signed — J. Roffignac, Mayor.

The following composed the committee:

1st Ward: W. Christy, Honoré Landreaux, Caleb Struger, Apothecary Kimbel.

8nd Ward: Wiltz, Sr., Martin Gordon, R. Relf, Apothecary Vignaud.

3rd Ward: J. A. Bernard, Louis LeRoy, Felix Arnaud, Apothecary Guilhon.

4th Ward: John Lanna, Simon Cucullu, J. Quessart, Apothecary, Delche and Kerr.

5th Ward: John Naba, B. Marigny, Jos. Sabattier, Apothecary Pironeau.

6th Ward: Nath'l Cox, J. B. Plauché, R. Linton, Apothecary Lacan.

7th Ward: Chas. Genois, J. A. Fort, Louis Lefort, Apothecary Chevallier.

Physicians donating their services: Drs. Lemonier, Conti between Dauphine and Bourbon; Sanchez, Poydras St.; Lemonier, Royal and St. Peter Sts.; Connaud, St. Louis between Royal and Bourbon; Thomas, St. Peter St.; Dupuy, St. Louis between Bourbon and Dauphine.

In September 1829, the usual committee was appointed and the Mayor issued the following proclamation:

> The Mayor, convinced of the noble disinterestedness which annimates the generality of the practicing physicians of the city, would not take upon himself to assign limits to their charitable assistance; and it is merely to comply with the above resolution that he designates officially to afford gratuitous assistance to

the patients of the several wards: Drs. Davidson, Ker, Gros, Lemonier, Halphen, Labatut, Tricou, Dupuy, Martin, Abersback, Lacroix, McFarlane, Clark, Formento, Renou, Rice and Thomas.

This assistance given by the city authorities was further supplemented by that of the citizens, either individually or in groups. There were relief societies organized by the ladies who not only provided funds, but who even visited the sick and in many instances nursed them with tender care.

The Howard association was organized during the epidemic of 1837, by a number of very young men, Virgil Boullemet, its president, was only 17 years old. About 150 youths were on the roster of the society. The other officers were D. L. Ricardo, Secretary; G. Kursheedt, treasurer; C. W. Shaw, H. W. Palfrey and J. O. Harris, finance committee. Their devotion to the afflicted bordered on the fanatical, for they faced every danger in the performance of their duties. The wealthy as well as the pauper were given the same attention and devotion. Providence must have smiled upon them for during seventeen years of constant exposure to the epidemics, not one of them contracted the disease.

Despite the malicious reports to the contrary, circulated throughout the country, New Orleans did every thing possible to alleviate suffering and succor the unfortunates, yet at times the exigencies were beyond human efforts and chaos would result.

The city grew despite the frightful ever-recurring epidemics, for the continuous influx of strangers more than supplanted the almost yearly depleted ranks of its population.

Yellow fever has contributed a horrid chapter to the history of New Orleans.

CHAPTER XXXII

THE CHOLERA EPIDEMIC OF 1832

The weather this morning was very peculiar, the heavens were covered with thick, heavy, damp, lowering clouds, that seemed like one black ceiling spread over the whole horizon. To the eye it almost touched the top of the houses. Every one felt a strange difficulty of respiration. I never looked upon such a gloomy, appalling sky before or since. Not a breath of wind stirred. It was so dark that in some of the banks, offices, and private houses, candles or lamps were lighted that day.

Immediately after breakfast, I walked down to the post office. In every corner and around the principal hotels, were groups of anxious faces. As soon as they saw me, the question was put by several persons at a time, "Is it a fact that the cholera is in the city?" I replied by describing what I had seen but two hours before. Observing that some of them appeared panic struck, I remarked, "Gentlemen, do not be alarmed. These may prove merely what the doctors have called sporadic cases. We do not yet know that it will prevail to an alarming extent. Let us trust in God and wait patiently the developments of another morning."

This happened on the 25th of October 1832. That morning two men, in a dying condition were found on the levee. They had just landed from a steamboat which had arrived the night before. They were transported in a wheelbarrow to the Charity Hospital, where it was diagnosed cholera.

This dramatic word picture from the pen of Rev. Mr. Clapp depicted the beginning of the most terrible epidemic that ever afflicted New Orleans. The people, only stunned at first, became panic stricken. It was to them something new and horrifying. They had been through many epidemics of yellow fever which killed a large number of the population, but the residents of the city knew that they were immune to that plague, and that only visitors and the unacclimated were potential victims. Furthermore, they could seek safety in flight. But cholera was different. No one was immune, natives as well as strangers were equally liable to become victims of that dreadful disease. As the realization dawned upon them that there was no way of evading it, consternation turned to fatalism.

Rev. Mr. Clapp gave the impression that the people did not

worry about the probability of cholera striking the city, but the fact is that the local press called attention many times to such a possibility and pleaded for the adoption of the proper sanitary precautions.

As early as January 7, 1832, the *Courier* reported that:

> There was a rumor yesterday afternoon, and even to this moment the report spreads through the city that a Swedish vessel which arrived the day before yesterday, has the cholera morbus abroad, and that one of the crew had died a victim of the fatal disease. Notwithstanding all our efforts, we have not been able to discover the source from whence this information is derived. We only understood from one of the Custom House officers, that one of his colleagues wishing to repair on board the vessel in the discharge of some of his duties, could not procure a boat; such was the apprehension entertained by the boatmen. We place no confidence in the report, which created so much alarm in the city; but think it is our duty to mention it in order to induce the authorities of the place to assertain its truth.
>
> The direct relation existing between this place and England, where it has made its appearance, may reasonably impress us with a dread of seeing that scourge introduced here every instant. However, our Legislature now in session for a week past, has not as yet adopted any measure calculated to prevent the introduction of so destructive a disease. Do they want to adopt these precautionary means, which in the northern cities were taken as soon as the news of the existence in Europe had reached there until it be imported amongst us and one half of our population have fallen victims of its baneful influence?

The same paper on Feb. 20, reported:

> Cholera morbus has been introduced into Mobile by the British brig *Jesse*, which sailed from Liverpool on the 25th of December.
>
> We are inclined to believe that the gentlemen of the faculty — [medical] at Mobile have mistaken the character of the disease, which they term cholera — Be this as it may, if the bad weather of last night has not retarded the progress of the steam boat which carries the mail, we will know in the course of a day what degree of confidence may be placed in the report current.

It was said that it was only a false rumor, the disease was diagnosed a billious complaint based on the fact "that they did not die after a sickness of 10 to 15 hours."

Another warning was sounded about the existence of cholera in France and England in the French section of the same paper on May 3. Again it insisted that some precautionary measures be taken.

On June 22 in the *Courier* was the following news item:

> Brig *Motion*, Capt. Rogers from Havre, sailed 18th of April. Arrived here last evening at the port, vessel 260 tons — 112 passengers, 12 of whom died on the passage. Authorities should investigate.

The following day the Captain replied that among the 12 passengers who died, 7 were children, many at the breast, for the want of their mothers' milk, the women having suffered much from sea sickness; several men died from old age, being infirm and in ill health when they came on board, and one man from dysentery. The two sailors died from the effects of hard drinking, never having been sober the whole time they were in Havre.

The Mayor appointed Drs. L. A. Tricou and Thomas to investigate the charges, and they declared it an absurd report. "Fourteen died en route, and all were in good health at the time of sailing, and only a few came from Paris where the cholera raged. There was one death on the second day of the voyage and one on the 16th and that since the 16th day (the day of the last death) the health on board had been perfectly good." The report of the doctors reads further:

> But even admitting that they had the cholera, this would be additional security for this place, since it is the opinion of the most distinguished medical authorities of Europe in which we take pride in sharing, that that scourge takes it source in a peculiar modification of the atmosphere, a modification which cannot reach across the ocean, the air of which being impregnated with saline particles and other disinfecting matters, must necessarily destroy it, and this would have been the case here, since after 16 days the evil disappeared.
>
> We conclude then and invite the public not to suffer themselves to be alarmed by light reports which might hereafter be spread of the introduction of the cholera here, convinced as we are that if it rages at any time in Louisiana, it will not be from Europe that it will be brought.

The good doctors' viewpoint was not shared by the *New York Courier and Enquirer*, which advocated that New York should take proper precautions against the cholera, for it may be brought by emigrants entering the city

In July we read that the cholera was spreading with great rapidity in Montreal, and that the New York Board of Health was taking precautionary measures.

Dr. Thomas, was so positive that the city would escape cholera, because the salt laden air of the ocean would necessarily destroy it, as chairman of the committee of public salubrity, on July 7th announced that the cholera had reached Canada, and that all sanitary measures were useless. He further asserted that all physicians agreed in declaring that this dreadful malady is not contagious, and that it would be useless to resort to the vexatory measure of establishing quaratines. The City Council passed the following resolution:

> Resolved, that there shall be chosen immediately a committee composed of seven physicians and three apothecaries, to be nominated by the Council with the title of Board of Health of the City of New Orleans. Dr. Kerr was the chairman, Drs. Davidson, Fortin, Cenas, Tricou, H. H. Bonnabel and Pierre Forestier, chemist. D. Augustin was the secretary.

The *Courier* of August 1st carried the following editorial:

The cholera continues to be the all-absorbing topic of public attention. Reports of the progress are looked for by our citizens with intense anxiety. Go where you will, you hear nothing talked of but the cholera — which seems to be thought of worse than death itself. Groups of persons are discussing the matter in our streets and "Shall we have it?" is a question which every one is asking and which none can answer.

It is a truly fearful calamity, and the terror with which it inspires every one is without parallel. Look what panic it has created in the northern cities. It has caused an entire suspension of business and depressed the money market. Hundreds of steamboats, that at this season of the year were known to carry an extensive business, have been compelled to let up — the city of New York, which has been the resort of thousands from different parts of the Union is now deserted of its own citizens. The cholera was no sooner known to exist in New York than thousands left immediately, deserting their businesses and their friends and it is said, even their wives and children, whilst they lay lingering with the direful scourge.

Such is the dreadful pestilence which is now extending itself over our fair country. If there are any that think we will be saved, that it will not visit New Orleans — we do not think it. Then comes the question, "Are we prepared for it?" The answer is NO!

Look at the condition of the streets and see whether we are prepared for it or not. They never were in a worse condition. On whom does it devolve to have them cleaned, and why are they not? The proper authorities should immediately set about putting them in a good condition, and should spare no expense to have them well cleaned, for when they are well cleaned, it will be easy to keep them so — for the health, wealth and benefit of our citizens require that it should be done immediately.

Rumors were bruited around that St. Louis was in the throes of the pestilence. From the East coast it had spread Westward, and from there along the Mississippi and its tributaries. Soon New Orleans was to be next. Yellow fever, which at first was comparatively mild, now began its ravages with unusual fury. So much so that the *Courier* of October 12, reported that the city was "extremely unhealthy, as much sickness as in 1822, and that it has increased for the last two or three days" Again it bewailed the unsanitary condition of the streets. And it decried this condition only five days before the cholera ravaged New Orleans.

The same paper on October 27, gave the following warning:

"It is with regret we notice the daily arrival of strangers — yellow fever still exists, they are in great danger. New cases daily; they should be told to leave the city for a short time." And in the same issue it had an editorial entitled CHOLERA which read:

> Our citizens will, therefore, see the necessity of being on their guard. It is admitted on all hands that immediate medical aid in the attack of the disease is necessary to its fortunate termination. Let us all who feel the premonitory symptoms call in a physician without delay. Medicine, if instantly administered, will 19 cases out of 20, check the progress of the disease in people of temperate habits; and in every family and by every person, some should be kept at hand, in case a physician cannot be immediately obtained. Fear should not be allowed to exist. We do repeat it, banish fear, which is perhaps more to be dreaded than the disease itself, since it is sufficient to produce it. Neither should credit be given to the rumors which well intentioned persons, fools or frightened individuals may spread. Take sufficient courage to meet the malady and be prepared to conquer it by leading a regular and sober life.

This advice was well intended, but impossible in application:

> Abstain from eating any unripe fruit or vegetable and also from spiritous liquors, although, however, it would not be prudent to change suddenly the mode of living. This is an advice given by enlightened physicians and, if followed, there is no danger. Poor people who have not the means of remunerating a doctor for his visits, should not on that account delay sending for aid. We have so high an opinion of the medical faculty for kindness and philantrophy, that we think they will not at a time like this, refuse to visit anyone, rich or poor. — Let all call in medical aid the moment they feel the premonitory symptoms.

The cholera has almost ceased to exist in the Eastern States of the Republic, and is now raging to a great extent in the Western Country.

The Board of Health requested that the physicians report their cases before 11 A.M. every day, and that they "afford facilities to some members of the Board of Health to visit each case, and to report to the Board the character of the cases visited." An impossible request as will be seen.

Thus began the worst calamity ever experienced in New Orleans, and it can be said to have been the worst in the history of this country.

The newspapers were unusually quiet during the epidemic, and were it not for the authentic description by Rev. Mr. Clapp, the curtain would be lowered on the greatest drama ever experienced by the people of this city. He wrote:

> That day so many persons left the city as could find the means of transportation. On my way home from the post office, I walked along the levee where the two cholera patients had been disembarked but three or four hours before. Several families in the neighborhood were making preparation to move, but in vain. They could not obtain the requisite vehicles.
>
> That same afternoon the pestilence entered their houses, and before dark, spread through several squares opposite to the point the steamer landed the first case.
>
> On the evening of the 27th of October, it had made its way through every part of the city. During the ten succeeding days, reckoning from October 27, to the 6th of November, all the physicians judged that at the lowest computation there were 5000 deaths — an average of 500 per day. Many died of whom no account was rendered. A great number of bodies, with bricks and stones tied to their feet, were thrown into the river. Many were privately interred in gardens and enclosures, on the ground where they expired, whose names were not recorded.
>
> Often I was kept in the burying ground for hours in succession by the incessant, unintermitting arrival of corpses, over whom I was requested to perform a short service. One day I did not leave the cemetery until 9 o'clock at night; the last interments were made by candle light.
>
> On my arrival, I found at the graveyard a large pile of corpses without coffins, in horizontal layers, one above the other, like cord wood. I was told that there were more than one hundred bodies deposited there. They had been brought by unknown persons, at different hours since nine o'clock the evening previous. Large trenches were dug, into which these uncoffined corpses were thrown indiscriminately. The same day, a private hospital was found deserted, the physicians, nurses and attendants were

all dead, or had run away. Not a living person was in it. The wards were filled with putrid bodies, which by order of the Mayor, were piled in an adjacent yard and burned and their ashes scattered to the winds. Could a wiser disposition have been made of them?

Many persons, even of fortune and popularity, died in their beds without aid, unnoticed and unknown, and lay there for days unburied. In almost every house might be seen the sick, the dying and the dead in the same room. All the stores, banks and places of business were closed. There were no means, no instruments for carrying on the ordinary affairs of business; for all the drays, carts, carriages, hand and common wheelbarrows, as well as hearses, were employed in the transportation of corpses, instead of cotton, sugar and passengers.

Words cannot describe my sensation when I first beheld the awful sight of carts driven to the graveyard and these upturned, and their contents discharged as so many loads of lumber or offal, without a single mark of mourning or regret, because the exigency rendered it impossible.

Most of the bodies laid in the ground had a covering of earth but a few inches in depth and through the porous dirt, there was an unimpeded emission of all the gases evolved from animal matter when undergoing the process of putrefaction.

The Minister made an observation that may sound strange to many, that he "never saw an unbeliever who died in fear," and that he "met no dying persons who were terrified except church members who had been brought up in the Trinitarian faith."

Reverend Mr. Clapp gave many striking examples of the virulence of the disease, of its insidiousness and the rapidity with which it killed. Here are a few examples:

Multitudes began the day in apparently good health and were corpses before sunset. One morning as I was going out, I spoke to a gentleman who resided at the very next house to mine. He was standing at his door and remarked that he felt very well but "I wonder," he added, "that you are alive." On my return only two hours afterwards, he was a corpse. A baker died in his cart directly before my door. Near me there was a brick house going up; two of the workmen died on a carpenter's bench but a short time after they commenced their labors for the day. Often did it happen that a person, engaged a coffin for some friend, himself died before it could be finished.

I went, on Wednesday night to solemnize the contract of matrimony between a couple of very genteel appearance. The bride was young and possessed of the most extraordinary beauty. A few hours only had elapsed before I was summoned to perform the last offices over her coffin. She had on her bridal dress and was very little changed in the appearance of the face.

One family of nine persons supped together in perfect health; at the expiration of the next twenty-hour hours, eight out of the nine were dead. A boarding house that contained thirteen inmates, was absolutely emptied; not one was left to mourn.

Persons were found dead all along the streets, particularly early in the mornings.

The minister wrote that he expected to see the city depopulated. He was of the opinion that they had premonitory symptoms the day or the night before, but labored under the delusion that they were well. He also believed that in the early stage, the disease could be easily arrested; but when the cramps and collapse set in, death was in most cases, inevitable.

There appeared many communications in the press from physicians proposing prophylactic measures. The *Courier* on July 9, published the following letter from a physician:

It is my belief that it [cholera] will not be so dangerous in our climate. Two powerful motives induce me to entertain that opinion; the season and the disproportion of population within the same extent of country, to which may be added those vast forests, it might be said the vast forest which covers the whole of the continent and which bring out such a vast quantity of oxygeneous matter indispensable to sustain animal life. It may evade the country during the warm weather because from observations made, all those in whom perspiration had been kept active, had a certain degree of immunity. It would be well to use that as a preventative.

Precautions: Wear flannel next to your skin as a certain means of keeping perspiration active.

Expose not yourself to humidity after sunset; use a wholesome diet, eat little at the time, hardly any meat, and a little salt provisions; commit no excess in drinking, take some spice, but not in abundance; it is good to keep the organs in a light stage of excitement, to avoid impressions. Bathe often, cleanliness being one of the first means to adopt against the greatest part of the disease; keep your bowels free. These who recommend medicines as a preventive are in error.

It would be prudent to carry a vial of *vinaigre des quatre valeurs*, and rub one's head and hands with it when going out.

There were many other suggestions as bizarre as this one. The means taken by the Board of Health to combat the disease enveloped the city in an eeriness worthy of Milton or Dante.

Rev. Clapp painted the following vivid picture of these hellish ten days:

> Artificial causes of terror was superadded to the gloom which covers the heavens. The burning of tar and pitch at every corner; the firing of cannons by order of the city Authorities along all the streets, and the frequent conflagrations which actually occurred at that dreadful period, — all these conspired to add a sublimity and horror to the tremendous scene. Our wise men hoped, by the combination of tar and gun powder, to purify the atmosphere. We have no doubt that hundred perished from mere fright produced by artificial noise, the constant sight of funerals, darkness and various other causes.
>
> It was an awful spectacle to see night ushered in by the firing of artillery in different parts of the city, making as much noise as arises from the engagement of two powerful armies. The sight was one of the most tremendous which was ever presented to the eye, or even exhibited to the imagination in description. After walking my night rounds, the flames from the burning tar so illuminated the city streets or river, that I could see every thing almost as distinctly as in the day time. And through many a window into which was flung the sickly flickering light of these conflagrations, could be seen persons struggling in death, and rigid, blackened corpses, awaiting the arrival of some cart or hearse as soon as dawn appeared, to transport them to their final resting place.
>
> Many are killed by medicine, starving and fright, than from eating improper food. A mistaken opinion as to this subject has arisen from the fact that multitudes have been seized with cholera directly after eating breakfast, dinner or supper and have immediately ejected their food as it was taken. Hence they have found that what they ate brought on sickness.

Cholera, which originated in Europe, travelled along the trade lanes to the Eastern seaboard, then along the Ohio and Tennessee river to St. Louis, from thence to New Orleans.

A pestilence is like a hurricane, which is comparatively mild at its point of origin, but gathers force along its course, and the longer the distance it travels the greater its violence. It seems that the cholera celebrated its journey of half way around the world when it reached New Orleans with an orgy of death; for in the space of ten days it killed one out of every six of the inhabitants. And this may be a very conservative estimate, for the actual death rate will never be known. It must be assumed that many died in flight, and others, strangers, passed away unknown and unobserved. The dead were picked up by carts making the rounds like garbage collectors in the morning. The bodies were thrown into shallow ditches, unregistered and unknown.

The city was in a state of chaos, yet everything humanly possible was done to succor the afflicted, but it was an impossible task. Many who escaped the cholera died of yellow fever, which was raging at the same time.

There was a recurrence of cholera morbus in the following year. On June 6, the *Courier* editorially commented that "it seems at least to be admitted by all that the cholera has made its appearance amongst us" and that the city council had appropriated $20,-000.00 for sanitary purposes. The following measures were proposed:

(1) The commissioner of police should visit public and private yards.

(2) Prosecute those who break sanitary laws.

(3) Depot of quick lime ought to be established at the expense of the city to correct the exhalation caused by stagnant water, etc.

(4) Water works to be kept going day and night, remove all obstruction in gutters, canals, etc.

(5) Public and private hospitals must be kept under the vigilant inspection of the police.

(6) Sextons of different grave yards should give a daily account of the situation of their cemeteries, and if any delay in burying the dead.

(7) Commissioners of police shall see if graves are kept clear of water.

On June 25, the same paper reported that "the cholera had greatly diminished. The majority of death are children who at this season of the year are afflicted with the worms, a disease which has been very fatal."

Evidently the cholera must have spent its fury the previous year for it was comparatively mild in its devastating effects. In September the first case of yellow fever was proclaimed.

Rev. Mr. Clapp wrote: "So within the space of twelve months, we had two attacks of cholera and two epidemics of yellow fever which carried off 10,000 persons that were known and many more that were not reported."

Our historians make but scant mention of this devastating pestilence, yet its record is an epic of the courage, the suffering, and the fortitude of a people.

This letter from Dr. J. S. McFarlane to the Hon. Lewis McLane, Secretary of the Treasury of the United States, is quoted in full, because it gives undoubtedly the most authoritative picture of what transpired during the cholera epidemic. This communication was written on the advice of Martin Gordon, Esq., the collector of the Port of New Orleans and an agent of the local Marine Hospital. He wrote this brief history of the epidemic and mentioned the awful scenes of horror which defied description. He related:

On the night of the 24th of October last, two steamboats arrived from the West, said to contain several cases of cholera, and that numbers of persons had died from that disease on the passage.

On the 25th, two men died on the Levee after one or two hours of sickness in the neighborhood of Rilleux's cotton press at the corner of Poydras Street and the Levee; large crowds collected around them and continued their conjectures as to the causes of their sudden death and various extraordinary reasons were assigned. As one of the Board of Health, I was called on as a member of the Corporation to investigate the character of the disease, and I could not, after deliberate examination, from the collapse and livid condition, hesitate to pronounce them "cholera." In the course of the same day a Negro man died of the same disease in the neighborhood of the upper "steam cotton press" after one or two hours sickness. On the 26th the alarm became general and reports circulated of attacks of disease and deaths, fearful in numbers, and terrifically rapid in their progress.

On the 27th, 28th, 29th, 30th, the disease raged with increasing fury, and the destroying angel appeared to spare none. Men and women were seen flying through the streets in search of medicine and medical aid wringing their hands in absolute despair. Until the last three days of the epidemic, many men sustained (at least) an appearance of fortitude — now despair gleamed on every face! No man proceeded many steps from his own door without meeting his neighbor searching for aid, with the horrific account of suffering and death in his family; the man to whom was spoke now would be taken in a few hours and die even before the more fortunate survivor had reached his home; when any man left his family (which only occurred when called upon by the most indispensible duties) he left as if he took his last leave.

During the reign of terror, despair and death, many have died in their bed without aid, unnoticed and unknown and were there found in a state of decomposition. On or about the 1st of November, many men formed themselves into small bands to aid and assist one another when taken with this horrible disease. The apothecary shops were crowded from morning till night, and no other object seem to engross all minds but to keep themselves and families clear from all scourge. Every physician in the city was worn down by excessive labor and fatigue and many so disheartened as to give up in despair, quit the field and abandon all exertion. Every face bore the marks of incipent disease and a blight appeared to have passed over the whole community — indeed, to sum up all, never could I have conceived unless I had witnessed it. When the Almighty breathes forth the blast of pestilence and the missioned destroyer is sent abroad, how feeble, how impotent, are all the exertions of Man! Such was the multitudes of dead throughout the City that the ordinary forms of sepulture were abandoned, many were hurried to the grave yards in carts, without coffins, trenches were with difficulty prepared in cemeteries and the dead were miscellaneously thrown together without a single mark of decency or respect.

Notwithstanding all this the dead accumulated to such an extent that hundreds lay days unburied, while every effort of the Mayor, Corporation and private citizens, were in vain employed to procure adequate assistance to perform the melancholy duty. Carts filled with uncoffined human bodies were driven to the grave yards and there upturned and their contents discharged as so many loads of common lumber. The grave yards being found inadequate to contain the masses of the dead bodies which hourly accumulated, and extensive excavation or trench was by dint of great exertion excavated, prepared by the city authorities, under direction of the Mayor, on the edge of the swamp in the rear of the city, in a desecrated spot where malefactors who had paid the last penalty of the law for the violated statutes of their country, have formerly been hidden from human view. In fact the city was decimated, one tenth part of the entire population having been swept off in ten days. Such was the pestiential effluvia emanating from the mass of putrifying bodies, that laborers could not be obtained at any price to excavate the earth, fearing to endanger their lives in the attempt. The occurrence of the terrible pestilence was at a most unpropitious period, the old Charity Hospital of the City, having recently been sold to the State, had been vacated and abandoned, and only one wing of the Charity Hospital was prepared to receive patients, consequently the number they could admit was but small. To have refused to receive the sick in the Marine Hospital under such circumstances would not only have subjected me to the execration of my fellow citizens, but would have been absolutely criminal. The seamen in the Hospital, being few in number, were removed to the second story of the building and entirely secluded; and the whole of the lower floor wards, with all the out-buildings and premises, were thrown open for the unhappy wretches who were hourly crowding in for relief, at that time the number of able attendants in the Marine Hospital was thirteen, a force far exceeding the ordinary demand, but as the disease progressed, they gradually fell sick and many of them died. Until the 3rd of November the last male assistant, exhausted by fatigue, gave up and died also.

During the whole period of the epidemic, as will be seen by a reference to my vouchers, which I have transmitted, through the politeness of Martin Gordon, Esq., you will perceive that my exertions were unremitting to obtain additional assistance; but such was the panic which pervaded every mind, such the dread of entering a hospital, such the disease, dismay and death which overwhelmed the whole City, that all efforts were fruitless. I was myself a sufferer from the disease and rose from my sick bed to seek for aid; I sought even in the prisons for men to assist, but they preferred captivity to that kind of labor. At length on the 4th instant, all exertion in the burial of the dead was temporarily suspended; and on temporarily suspension, on the 5th, the committee of the Council made a visit of inspection and witnessed a scene of distress and misery which was well calculated to excite the most painful sensations, which they afterwards reported in glowing colours in the City Council. We urged them to send aid, but we received none. On Wednesday the 7th instant, the dead were removed to an adjacent lot and there buried. Had the Mayor simply supplied us with four men and one cart, the whole of the dead (twelve in number) could have been removed to the public cemetery in two hours.

It is to be distinctly borne in mind that none of these painful circumstances extended themselves to the United States seamen who were located upstairs; they were confined to charity patients generally sent by the city authorities, picked up about the streets, most of whom were already in a state of collapse at the time of their arrival, and whom no human aid could have saved. When our assistants became disabled and were diminished by the disease and death, orders were given to receive no more, but in vain, such was the confusion which reigned that they were laid at the gate and must perish in the street had we not, instigated by humanity, let them in, etc.

Dr. McFarlane, in a communication in the *Courier* of November 12, 1832, depicted another horrifying scene in that drama of human desolation, he wrote:

The subscriber requested Mr. John Conn to offer any price for assistance, but he could obtain none; he also authorized his friends to proceed up and down the levee and engage assistance on any terms, but none could be obtained. He also called upon Mr. Holland and urged him to permit some of those persons who were confined for minor offences to aid him in performing the necessary duties at the infirmary. Mr. Holland sent a large number, but they never came. The dying and the dead were continually arriving. It was neither the duty nor the province of the subscriber to bury the dead sent by the Mayor, and it was but by courtesy that he originally consented to do so at his desire. Finding that the attendants were inadequate to attend on the living and bury the dead, orders were given to admit no more. Controversies arose among those who brought them but they refused to take them away. At length they accumulated, twenty frequently arriving during the day: the attendants exhausted by fatigue, sickness and a majority of them died: among whom were slaves belonging to the subscriber of the value of $5,000.00 leaving but three: two of whom were females, to supply the remaining inmates of the infirmary with food and medicine. The convalescents could not be induced by any offer of remuneration to lend their assistance. Coffins could not be obtained to receive the dead, no men to drive the vehicles in which they were to be transported to the cemetery. Thus they continued to accumulate, while the subscriber was awaiting with horrible anxiety the hourly arrival of assistance from some of the agents whom he had set in motion to procure it. Such was the condition of the infirmary when visited by the committee of the City Council.

Shortly after their visit an arrangement was made with Mr. James Lambert to bury the dead, and that duty was slowly but steadily going on, when the incendiary torch was lighted by the active exertions of an officious individual, which was intended to consume him. Such is the honest, just and true statements of facts as they occurred at the Orleans Infirmary.

When it is taken into consideration that laborers have not been obtainable for hospital duties at any price: the Secretary of State, with all the appliances of wealth, friends and popularity, lay several days unburied in his own house until two benevolent individuals who were entreated to perform the duty, could hardly endure the pestilential effluvia of his decomposing remains; when it is recollected that hundreds lay unburied many days in the cemeteries, with all the finance of a wealthy city, and all the exertions of the Mayor and corporation to facilitate their interments, can it be charged to a single unassisted individual, that a similar catastrophy should have occurred with him, and he laboring at the same time under the influence of a disease which was hurrying thousands to an untimely grave? No! it cannot be; common humanity — common magnaminity — common mercy forbid it.

Signed: J. S. McFarlane.

Again in the same newspaper of February 1st, 1833, appeared a communication from Dr. McFarlane, deploring the injustice of the charges made against him for want of proper diligence in seeing to the interment of the dead bodies in his hospital during the cholera.

Were it not for that controversy and the recorded statements concerning the difficulties under which Dr. McFarlane labored, both as surgeon of the U. S. Marine Hospital and at his private infirmary, but comparatively little would be known today of the tribulations of a people during the most agonizing ten days of that pestilence of which little is known, and that but seldom mentioned.

CHAPTER XXXIII

CITY OF THE WET GRAVE

From its very beginning and for more than a century afterwards, New Orleans was confronted by the difficult problem of finding a suitable place for the burial of its dead. Some of the obstacles then encountered were practically unsurmountable. The terrain on which the city was situated and the swamps surrounding it were most unpropitious for grave yards. Of necessity the cemetery had to be located within the limits of the city. The water level was only a couple of feet from the surface, and the bodies had to be consigned to what was in effect a watery grave.

There are many gruesome narratives by witnesses to these interments. Josiah Condon in 1833 wrote of New Orleans as "the city of the Wet Grave, where the hopes of thousands are buried." And further elaborated that "those who cannot afford to procure a vault for their dead are literally compelled to deposit them in water." During the early American period the mortality was great, out of all proportion to the population, which crowded the burial grounds beyond their capacity. Coffins would be laid one on top of the other, and were covered by only a small layer of mud.

During the Spanish Domination, the cemetery was situated in the square of Burgundy, Rampart, Toulouse and St. Peter. In the archives of the Cathedral is a letter from Father Antonio de Sedella, which reads as follows:

> I, Brother Antonio de Sedella, Capuchin Priest of the very Holy Church Cathedral of the City of New Orleans, certify on the faith that I have: Because of the epidemic which followed the great fire of the 21st of March 1789, the inhabitants suffered greatly.
>
> The Governor of these colonies, who then was Estaban Miro, after consulting those empowered and with the consent of the administration, gave the power to remove the cemetery or Holy ground to a location further back in the rear of the Charity Hospital to which I gave my consent, because of the reasons they gave and especially because it was a menace to the public health.
>
> I also wish to certify that the great fire destroyed several books and many parcels of archives of the same Church, dating from its foundation or establishment and to make this legal, I,

having superior orders, have given this in New Orleans on the 9th of April, 1801.

The following is quoted in part from another letter by the same prelate:

> Whilst passing the cemetery having myself perceived a fetid smell, I sought information from the neighbors and they affirmed that these foul odors have been very often perceived this year. — The consequence is that we are looking for another burial ground out of the city where the dead will produce no deleterious effects and the corpses could be buried there inside of eight days.
>
> We pray to our Excellency to authorize the City Administration to provide bricks so that the new cemetery may be permanent and the old one be condemned and the bones are to be removed to the new one so that in about two years homes will be built where it now stands. The old cemetery comprises twelve lots of 70 feet front 120 feet deep, which his Majesty might give away to citizens on condition to contribute to the City Treasury six dollars annually."

This letter was dated the 12th of November 1788.

The new cemetery is now St. Louis No. 1, which was bounded by St. Louis, Basin, Tremé (St. Claude) and Conti streets. It was divided into two parts, one Catholic and the other Protestant. The latter was in the rear of the former facing Tremé Street. It once extended to Bienville street, but it was narrowed down by the opening of Tremé Street to a strip of about one hundred feet wide. In 1807, the City Council assigned it to Christ Church, which was relinquished in 1821 when the Girod Street cemetery was opened and became the burial place for Protestants.

Zacharie tells us that "beyond this was a place surrounded by cypress pickets called *pieux* and reserved for the burial of Negroes."

Benjamin Henry Latrobe said that in 1819 the Catholic and Protestant cemeteries were adjacent and each about 300 feet square. The tombs were made of brick and about 8 feet long, 5 feet wide and 5 feet high. There were but few inscriptions on the tombs. He noticed that the Protestant cemetery had the same kind of tombs as the Catholic and described the Claiborne family monument.

Latrobe also asserted that the graves were filled with water up to eight or nine inches below the surface and that the bodies were buried in water. These graves were not deeper than three feet. The ground was every where perforated by crawfish, and:

"I have indeed seen some of them in their usual attitude of defense in the gutters of the streets. The French love to eat them, the Americans do not. They pretend the sellers of this fish get them from grave yards: Not true."

There were many City ordinances for the policing of the grave yards. In 1822 the law forbade any interment from September on in the cemetery situated between Conti and St. Louis Streets. The interments had to be made in Faubourg St. Mary. Graves were to be no less than four feet deep and three feet apart. The tombs had to be of brick twelve inches thick with mortar in all the joints. This insistence on the use of bricks was due to the prevailing custom of building tombs of wood, which would not only quickly deteriorate, but were from a sanitary standpoint dangerous.

In November of that year the City Council turned over the burial ground to the Episcopal Church in which Protestants of other denominations had the right to bury their dead. The charges were $6.00 for a plot.

A former superintendent of the old burial ground voiced his disapproval of that ordinance in a communication under date of November 20, 1822, which is quoted verbatim:

> The Episcopal Church has only received the New Burial Ground from the corporation in the place of the burial ground (commonly called the Protestant burial ground) that the Corporation have shut up.
>
> The Episcopal Church never had any right to the old Burial Grounds, — the United States Navy and the Army and the Charity Hospital had preference to it. Until 1811 it belonged to the United States. The City, about this time became possessed by the adjusting of the land claims in the Congress of the United States, for the territories of Orleans and Louisiana, of the old fortifications in the rear of the City and to the distance of sixty yards beyond, including the American burial ground.
>
> It was not an uncommon thing to see the Reverend Mr. Chase (while he was the pastor of the Episcopalian Church in New Orleans) attending a funeral . . . . at the same time a party of 8, 10 or 12 soldiers of the United States Army, digging, perhaps one or two graves at a time for their deceased comrades, — and at other times the United States Marine soldiers making interments at one and the same time.
>
> The above ground was nothing more than a public burial ground. A potter's field.

In 1823, the State Legislature, at the close of its session, passed a law authorizing the City Corporation to donate the Catholic

Church a piece of ground for a new cemetery. The Act also provided a penalty of $500.00 for every interment that would be made in the Basin and St. Louis streets grave yard after the first day of June.

A communication in the *Louisiana Gazette* of October 29, 1823, called attention to the fact that the law was violated, and that it was a daily practice to inter in the old Catholic cemetery on Basin street, and that many petitions were presented to the Board of Health, stating that this cemetery was a nuisance and a hot bed of infection.

In defiance of expostulations from these respectable sources, the "fabrique" of the Catholic Church hurled their denunciations upon the public, and still preserved in cruelty the wantonly infective atmosphere and jeopardize the lives of our fellow citizens by the shocking custom of exposing the contents of graves.

Public clamor finally became so indignant and general that our legislators, among one or two praiseworthy resolves, passed an act authorizing the corporation of the city to give to a large and rich "fabrique" a new piece of ground for a cemetery and causing a penalty of $500.00 to be affixed to a contempt of the same, should interments be continued after the first of June 1923.

Notwithstanding all this, dead bodies were daily deposited in the old cemetery and the regular autumnal pile, (that dreadful conflagration) is about to be kindled, which scatters the ashes of the humble poor to the four winds of heaven.

Signed: Bonum Publicum.

These accusations were denied in the same journal of October 30, which stated that: "First: The law cited, permits the opening of graves in the old cemetery as often as the Mayor may see fit to do so: Second: No new graves were dug from the first of June last — without the authorization of the Mayor, who granted it only during the time the water was so high as to prevent the interments in the new burying ground."

In 1824 the Protestant burying ground was found to be too small for the increasing number of burials, so the Mayor was authorized by the Council to sell a portion of land to Christ Church at the extremity of the Protestant Cemetery, which was reserved for a Catholic burial ground.

In 1829 the roads leading to the Protestant Cemetery were impassable. One morning several hearses broke down and the coffins had to be taken out in nearly every square. That deplorable condition forced the Council to pass a resolution for the paving of that part of Girod Street from Circus Street (Rampart) to the Protestant burial ground.

The City was fast growing beyond the confines of the cemeteries; a vexatious problem to solve. The *Courier* of June 22, 1832 carried a communication addressed to the wardens of the Cathedral which is quoted in part:

> The inhabitants comparatively young of this city have already seen three cemeteries, and at this moment there is talk of cutting streets through the Basin Street grave yard, where even today, burials take place. The cypress swamps in the rear of the new cemetery should be acquired before the saw mills and all sorts of establishments will surround it as it was previously the case.
>
> The Protestant Congregations themselves see that the Girod Street cemetery will soon be surrounded by establishments brought there by the new canal [New Basin] and they would be very happy to abandon a burying place which is not large enough to accommodate their growing population provided you would sell to them a strip of land along Canal Street.
>
> There will come a time when it will be impossible to inhume in the tombs of the ancient Catholic Cemeteries. The interest of that quarter which will soon be very populous, between the Carondelet Canal and Canal Street, would oppose it.

The *Courier* on June 26, 1832 published the following enlightening article about the wrangle between the City Council and the Wardens of the Cathedral, relative to the cutting of streets through the cemetery:

> Two years since an agreement was entered between the Mayor and A. Relf and R. M. Wellman, two of the trustees of the Protestant church, the City surveyor was instructed to lay out several streets through the old Protestant Cemetery and to cause to be removed the tombs which would be found in the way of the streets. Through the neglect of the Surveyor, the streets were not opened; only last week that work began.
>
> As soon as the land speculators on the back part of the City perceived what an increase in value would be given to their lots if the same streets were continuous through the old Cathedral burial ground, they hastened to address a memorial to the City Council to obtain from them an ordinance to that effect.
>
> The Council was not slow to act. Several alderman interested in the value of those lots and others acted uncautiously and passed the infamous ordinance, which for several days has created the greatest alarm throughout whole families and has

been the cause of the most painful sensations to them. If those of the members of the Council, who own no property in the back part of the City, on the adoption of the ordinance and if they had been a little more cautious, they would soon have detected how glaring a violation of the right of property they were about to perpetrate and they would have shrunk from the idea of assisting a handful of mercenaries who would speculate even on the profits they might reap from the sale of the ashes of their departed parents, wives and children.

The ordinance was adopted by a vote of 7 to 3.

At a meeting of the Church Wardens of the Cathedral, the following resolution was adopted:

Whereas, the City Council has issued a resolution to open the streets through the old cemetery of the Catholic Church in this City, which in the opinion of the Church Wardens they have not the right to do, therefore be it resolved unanimously: That if the said resolution should receive the sanction of the Mayor (which the Church Wardens do not believe) or if the City Council should pass it by a majority of two thirds, the President is authorized to employ counsel to resist the measure.

Signed:
Chas. Bolot, Jr., Secretary.

In the immediate rear of the cemeteries there was a cypress swamp extending from the lumber yards on the Carondelet Canal to Canal Street. Villere Street was already opened and the tombs of the old Protestant grave yard which were adjacent to the new Catholic cemetery were removed for the extension of St. Louis Street.

The *Courier* of June 28 reported that the infamous ordinance was vetoed by the Mayor and returned it to the Council with "a few objections touching on the expenses which the removal of the tombs would necessitate."

Thereupon, Mr. Freret proposed to the City Council that that body should take into consideration the resolution relative to the opening of certain streets in the old Catholic cemetery which ordinance failed of passage completely, "leaving nothing but shame to those who dared to solicit its passage."

In June 1833, the Health Committee of the City Council made the following report on the condition of the cemeteries:

The Committee in company with the Mayor visited the Catholic and Protestant burying grounds. The latter in the lower part was not such as it ought to have been. Filled up. Prices of internments $6.00, Catholic Cemetery only $2.00. A few barrels of lime should be thrown over the ground.

Your Committee have held conferences with a committe appointed on the part of the trustees of the Catholic Church of St. Louis and in pursuance with these deliberations, Messrs J. J. Mercier and Felix Labatut were appointed to take the necessary measures to prevent in future the accumulation of dead bodies.

Paid a second visit to the Presbyterian cemetery and found it in a disgusting condition. The trustees of Christ Church, in permitting the present state of things to exist there, have violated the ordinances in relation to public health in the most scandalous manner. Nothing can equal their neglect, but the contempt they have shown for the laws and their utter disregard for the usages of Society. They even refused to cause lime to be thrown over the ground as they have been directed to do and therefore, your Committee submits for your adoption the following resolutions:

Resolved: That the Mayor be requested to use all legal means to compel the members of Christ Church to keep their graveyard in the situation as required by the City ordinance:

Resolved: That on their non-compliance, the Mayor will cause the said graveyard to be closed and forbid for the future any interment therein:

Resolved: That the Mayor be requested to prosecute them before any court of competent jurisdiction.

Signed: E. A. Cannon, Chairman,
F. Buisson.
Permanent Committee of the City Council.

The report of the Committee was unanimously adopted.

The City purchased 300 barrels of lime to purify the graveyards. The accuracy of this report is verified by a distinguished Easterner, Master Brooks, the editor of the *Portland Advertiser*, who visited the City at that particular time. He painted a horrifying picture of the deplorable conditions then existing in the cemeteries. This historical account was published in the *Courier* of June 10, 1833:

> The tombs were all above the ground, those who can afford it will never be buried underground. The tombs are chiefly or all of brick, some plastered over, some not. They are from 2½ to 3 feet high and there is a little oven hole or front door into which the body is put. Some of the tombs in this, the Catholic burying ground are elegant and well walled over. The weeping willow overshadowed a few, but a very few. A few flower pots were on the summit of some. Others had little railings for a guard, and many had inscriptions.

This graveyard is on a dead level and on rainy days, inundated with water. It is a morass, a swamp partly rescued from its wilderness.

I have looked around many of the graves. A hole here and holes there, were all ready for the next comers, some six feet long or more, some three or four feet long — the water was in all the graves. The ground beneath our feet was like that of a swamp, the surface of which the sun had incrusted. I tumbled over broken coffins, pieces of which were piled in little heaps and pieces of which were placed as stakes to mark the spot of the last buried. The very earth gave way under my feet. The vegetation was that of a swamp. The rank weeds flourished roughly over many a dead body. Old sticks, old poles, such as our gardens stick peas with, white sides of coffins were put up as grave stones. What a spectacle! I tell you the plain truth in unexaggerated words.

Wandering yet further to the borders of the yard, I approached what appears like ovens (*fours*) and so they are called. They look exceedingly like the oven doors in our kitchens. They were six or seven feet deep and there were three tiers, that is, three bodies could be laid above the same spot of earth, one above the other. An oven being assigned for each. The doors of these ovens were filled with bricks and plastered over. On some of them there were inscriptions, on marble, perhaps. Many of these ovens were open mouthed — warning visitors of their fate, almost as it were, inviting them to enter. I hurried sickened from the spectable. For from the earth pestilence seemed to be issuing. In many places the odors were insufferable.

This morning (April 24) I rose with the sun so as to escape the burning rays and not to be risked without danger, for a long time, by a person non-acclimated — and curiosity again drew me to another graveyard. Curiosity is an impulse I cannot resist. It gets the better even of cowardice and all the disgust which haunted me after yesterday's stroll. I went to the Protestant, the American burying ground. The tombs there are all above ground but not any so neat as I saw in the French graveyard. It is a more shameful affair than even the scene I have described before. The tombs were badly covered. The ovens were badly plastered. There is little like neatness, prosperity and even decency. The whole is shameful; and the Americans here would not tolerate it if they made this their abiding place and not the place to alight and make money in. But no man can calculate on dying here and if he does, so far from friends, it matters not much to him how or where his body is laid.

Graves ready dug are here also kept for sale. An oven can be had for $60.00 to $70.00. A tomb must cost a large sum. The graves were all full of water. The earth we walked over sunk under our feet. More pieces of coffins are seen here than in the

Catholic yard. I have heard much of the trenches and pits in which the cholera victims were buried. Language cannot, if it were proper to array words in the description, portray the facts as they happened at that alarming season. A friend told me the worst account, but half realized the terror of those times. He himself saw bodies, without coffins, piled in masses around these pits. The draymen raced off full gallop to the yard, so brisk was their business, and then chuckled at their profits! Two of these pits were filled with victims; and dirt was thrown over them. The earth was moist and with a stick I sounded the ditches. My stick was pushed down with ease, I know not how far it would have been driven. The exhalations from these ditches were insufferable. I turned from it to catch a breath of less contaminated air. The third ditch was filled only with water. Thank God! there was no call for it. I turned from these eventful scenes, from the wilderness of the dead and in pensive thought directed my steps towards the busy and populous parts of the city.

In the fall of 1833 the Mayor was authorized by the City Council to temporarily use the lot of ground donated by Don Almonaster to the city in 1778, for a grave yard. It was situated on the road called the Leprous Road. The ordinance had the following stipulations: It was to be opened to all sects and religious denominations at a rate of $4.00 per corpse. That from and after the establishment of that grave yard, the Catholic cemetery would be available only for mural burials and that ground burials would be absolutely prohibited.

The quest for a suitable location for a grave yard by the City Administration was a matter of the most urgent importance. In 1834, many places were considered, many objections as to them were voiced in the press and by members of the City Council. The localities proposed were in the vicinity of the Bayou road and near Bayou St. John, just outside of the then city limits. The price of the land could not be agreed upon nor could they find a piece of ground high enough to be suitable for burials, the impassable roads and the distance from the city which an objector argued "would not permit the transportation of a corpse without being in putrefaction", were objections given full consideration. Objections were voiced against the joint ownership of the cemetery by the city and the St. Louis Cathedral, and the high cost of building shell roads was also considered. At long last after months of bickering and deliberations the City Council decided in July 1834 to purchase the property of Mr. Evariste Blanc, situated on the Bayou, for the sum of $46,000.00, with bonds bearing 5% redeemable in 30 years. Objections were raised to that location and it was even predicted that "there the dead would not be interred, but drowned."

In the spring of 1835, a railroad was constructed which would transport corpses to the new cemetery on Esplanade Avenue, now St. Louis number 3.

Aldermen Pedesclaux, Labatut, McCready, Schmidt, Mercier, Pritchard and Freret, cast their voes in favor, the objectors were Bermudez and Montegut.

At the end of that year the Mayor received a communication from Pedesclaux, president of the Marquilliers of the Cathedral, notifying the City Council that further burials were impossible in the Catholic Cemeteries because of the lack of room and that only interments in tombs would be permitted.

From then on, streets were paved leading to both the Protestant and Catholic cemeteries.

These shocking revelations are true and without the slightest exaggeration.

New Orleans presented a problem for the burying of its dead not encountered by any other city in the civilized world. The city was surrounded by a cypress swamp, its terrain was low and for a great part of the year was below the level of the river, besides its outskirts were frequently inundated from high tides and from storms on the lake. Water was found from one to three feet below the surface of the ground, and there was not a high spot near the city where ground burials were possible without submerging the corpses. Another factor and an important one, was the extremely high death rate from the ever recurring epidemics of yellow fever which precluded any orderly interments of the dead. The cemeteries were filled beyond their capacity.

The Creoles and the Americans, who were permanent residents of the City, had their family tombs, but the thousands of emigrants, mostly without families and frequently without friends, who died in countless numbers, were buried in unmarked graves.

No wonder New Orleans was called the "City of the wet grave where the hopes of thousands are buried."

CHAPTER XXXIV

FUNERALS AND MEMORIAL CEREMONIES

The belated arrival of the news of the death of Napoleon on his island of imprisonment created consternation in New Orleans. At that time there were many French exiles in Louisiana, many of whom had fought under the banner of the Emperor, or who through sheer frustration, or because of the fear of political reprisal, had sought refuge in the colony. To them Napoleon was France and a France without him would be unbearable. So without any hesitancy and with little regret, they sought asylum in the fabulous city of the new world. The Creoles, always proud of their French inheritance, who through the years had always treasured their cultural traditions, had a feeling of reverence and a deep admiration for the renowned soldier. There was the anguish of disappointment, for was it not bruited that an expedition was under way to liberate their hero from the clutches of the British? And it was believed that its success was assured because the expedition was to be under the command of that great cannoneer, Dominique You, the intrepid hero of the Battle of New Orleans. Plans had been made to bring Napoleon to New Orleans, and a house had been built for him, but alas, to no avail, the Emperor had passed away.

You, after the Battle of New Orleans, became a respected citizen, liked by every one. Fortier stated that he "died in 1830 and was buried with military honors at the expense of the City Council." His tomb bears the emblem of the Masonic fraternity, and an Epitaph which eulogizes him as the "intrepid hero of a hundred battles, without fear and without reproach, who will one day view, unmoved, the destruction of the world!"

The people of New Orleans expressed their grief over Napoleon's death with a memorial funeral. The *Gazette* of Tuesday, December 20, 1824 states:

NAPOLEON'S MEMORIAL

The adherents of the late Nap. Bonaparte, who reside in this city, having caused a splendid bier or catalfaque, to be erected in the Cathedral, which was hung in black for the occasion. They yesterday walked there in procession, and a funeral service was performed by the priests. Mr. Canonge delivered an oration to the crowd who attended in the Church; and the singers of the French Company of players, sang several pieces during the celebration of grand mass. The music was composed by Mr. Cheret.

"Feuillton" in the French section of the next issue, reported the ceremony as follows:

Never did that temple have such a large assembly, and perhaps never was religious decorum more rigidly observed, because of the place, the motive and the ceremony... On the lower platform [the catafalque] were depicted arts and religion in deep grief. Above was the allegory representing the Muse of History commanding Genius to engrave the high lights of Napoleon's career, and Genius had already inscribed the capture of Toulon, the first epoch of his glory. That beautiful tableau is draped with the imperial mantle, the scepter, the hand of Justice, the crown, and the eagle which still seem wishing to protect them.

Two allegorical divinities held the true immortal crown of laurels, and in short, a cinerary urn was placed on the top of the monument. Ancient tripods at each corner, and golden eagles supporting crepe surrounded the mausoleum, the standards and the banners, which have so long triumphed, added to that beautiful work, and brought back as souvenirs. On the right side were the following inscriptions:

On a foreign soil reposes
A warrior who conquered both Thebes and Memphis
Of whom Europe, one day will make its apotheosis
On the columns of Austerlitz.

* * * * * *

Albion! Albion! what a bloody page
You have just prepared for the immortal chisel!
It asks for the hero whom you were the assasin.

And the third inscription, the very words of the Emperor pronounced on the 21st of December 1804—

Soldier, general, first consul, I have had only
one thought, as well as Emperor: the prosperity
of France.

Pere Antoine officiated, assisted by the pastor of Terre aux Boeuf, and of St. John the Baptist. Mr. Canonge delivered the oration.

In this same article it was observed that "in that large cortege marching abreast were the modest artisan, the dignitary, the rich and the poor, all preoccupied by the same object, the only distinction among them were a few who were decorated with the star of honor, the warriors who shared with their Emperor, for so long, the perils of glory. The greatest order prevailed, it seemed that every individual added to the dignity of the occasion."

By a strange coincidence, the second and third presidents of the United States died on the same day, July 4, 1826 — just 50 years after the adoption of the Declaration of Independence. At that time the news traveled slowly, and it was not until July 25, that in New Orleans the newspapers appeared in mourning, as they announced the death of the two great patriots. The news was conveyed in a letter from Josiah S. Johnston, one of the Senators of Louisiana, to a local merchant.

On August 1st the City Council held a special meeting to formulate plans for a funeral procession to take place on the 8th of August. The Honorable P. Derbigny was selected to deliver an oration in French, and Samuel H. Harper, Esq. one in English. On Tuesday the 8th, a public meeting was held, at which Moreau Lislet was called to preside with L. C. Duncan, acting Secretary. The following resolution was adopted:

> Resolved: That a committee of six gentlemen be appointed to propose measures expressive of the feelings of the meeting in paying funeral honors to our late distinguished fellow citizens, Thomas Jefferson and John Adams; which committee should be authorized to confer with any Committee appointed by the City Council to determine upon the time and place of meeting, and on selection of gentlemen to pronounce the eulogies of those patriots; and to recommend such measures as may be calculated to promote the object of the meeting.

The following were nominated on the committee: J. Moreau Lislet, R. Relf, B. Chew, L. Pierce, J. B. Plauché and L. C. Duncan. At a meeting of the City Council it was decided, that the orations eulogizing Mr. Adams, would be delivered in English by Wm. Christy, Esq. and in French, by J. F. Canonge, Esq. and for Thomas Jefferson, S. H. Harper, Esq. and Peter Derbigny. A religious ceremony was held at the First Presbyterian Church at eleven o'clock, on August the 13th, presided over by Reverend Mr. Clapp.

The funeral procession was formed at the Public Square, at the foot of the Cathedral on Wednesday, the 16th, at 5 P.M., under the direction of C. W. Morgan, J. J. Mercier, D. Augustin, H. Lackett, J. DeLavillebeuve, C. W. Boyd, Esq., Grand Marshals of the day. It proceeded up Chartres to Conti St., then to Levee and Conde St., and returned to the public square, where an eulogium was pronounced in English by Samuel Harper, Esq. and in French by Peter Derbigny. Bells of all churches tolled from 2 P.M. until sunset. Minute guns were fired, all ships had flags at half mast, and all public offices and stores were closed at 2 o'clock. The procession proceeded in the following order:

United States Troops
Louisiana Legion
Louisiana Guards
Sheriff of the Parish of Orleans as first Marshal
Governor and Senate
Soldiers of the Revolution
Secretary of State and State Treasurer
Judges of the Supreme Court
Members of the Senate
Members of the House of Representatives
Mayor and Recorder
Orators of the day
Committee on Arrangement
Members of the Council
City Treasurer and Surveyor
City Officers
Judges of the District Court of the United States
Judges of the Criminal and District Courts
Judges of the Parish and City Courts
Attorney General
Members of the Bar
Notaries Public
Clerks of the Criminal and District Courts
Clerks of the Parish and City Courts
Register of Mortgages and Register of Wills
Parish Treasurer
Postmaster
Foreign Consuls
Strangers invited
Reverend Clergy
Collector and Naval Officer
Attorneys and Marshal of the United States
Surveyor and Appraisor
Officers of Custom
Presidents, Directors and Officers of the Banks
Presidents, Directors and Secretaries of Insurance Companies
President, Directors and Secretary of Navigation Co.
Officers of the United States Army
Officers of the Louisiana Militia in Uniform
Masonic Societies
Citizens

The Philharmonic Society contributed to the interest and solemnity of the occasion. Seats were provided for the ladies. All wore crepe on the left arm.

H. W. Palfrey was the Chairman of the Committee on Arrangement.

The *Louisiana Gazette,* on August 18, gave the following report of the funeral ceremonies:

> The ceremonies were imposing and solemn. The cenotaph in the public square was tasteful and appropriate — considering the shortness of the time allowed for construction, it is honorable to the genius and abilities of Mr. Pilié, who designed and finished it. The United States troops and the Legion and the Louisiana Guards never appeared to better advantage. About 130 Masons

View of Chartres Street and the Cathedral about 1830. (From an old print)

Riverfront scene, Port of New Orleans, at the time that sailing-ships predominated.
(Courtesy Louisiana State Museum)

Cenotaph. These temporary structures were used at memorial services and funeral ceremonies for illustrious dead. (From a book in possession of Frederick G. Veith and used through his courtesy.)

in grand costume and with emblem of their order, gave effect to the scene.

At about 6 o'clock, Mr. P. Derbigny, one of the orators, appointed by the City Council, rose in a rostrum covered with black, and addressed the audience in French in one of the most chaste and elegant discourses we ever had the great fortune to hear. He was followed by Mr. S. H. Harper, who spoke in English, in a more impassioned, but not less eloquent strain. Both the orations, though different in style, were equal in merit. When Mr. Harper had finished, 24 discharges of cannon announced the conclusion of the ceremonies.

The Masonic contingent made an imposing display — and added to the solemnity of the occasion. It appeared in the following order:

Tylers of Lodges No. 1 and 3, with white rods with a knot of crepe near the point.

Music

Stewards of Lodge Nos. 1 and 3, with white rods and a knot of crape near the top.

Entered apprentices
Fellow crafts
Master masons
Tylers
Stewards
Junior Deacons
Senior Deacons
Secretaries
Treasurers
Past Wardens
Junior Wardens
Senior Wardens

Past Masters
Royal Arch Masons
Knight Templars
Master of Lodges
Grand Tyler with drawn sword and crepe
Members of Grand Lodge not in office
Grand Stewards
Grand Secretary and Grand Treasurer

The Master of Lodge No. 26 carrying the Holy Bible, Square and Compass on a black cushion, supported by two Stewards
Grand Chaplain
Past Grand Wardens
Past Deputy Grand Masters
Past Grand Masters

Two past-Masters bearing two extinguished lights, and One Past Master, forming a triangle with two preceeding ones
Two Grand Wardens
Deputy Grand Warden

Master of Lodge No. 1, carrying the Book of Constitutions on a Cushion

Junior Wardens of Lodges Nos. 25 and 26 as Grand Deacons, with black rods on a line of five feet apart
Grand Master
Grand sword bearer
Two Stewards with white rods

The Masons were dressed in full suits of black clothes, white gloves, with crepe on their left arms, and were decorated with the insignia of the order, according to their respective grades.

* * * * * *

There were other funeral pageantries, perhaps not on such a grandiose scale, or presenting such ostentatious display, yet the pattern of the cenotaph, the pomp and the dignity of the procession, and the funeral orations, was always about the same.

New Orleans has always loved its parades.

FUNERALS AND MEMORIAL CEREMONIES

From the very beginning of time primitive men, with great reverence, buried their dead. As Man evolved from the primitive to a more civilized state, and his thoughts turned to the belief of a life after death, the greater grew his respect and reverence for his departed ones. His punctiliousness in the performance of this sacred rite has been one of the best indications of the growth of his culture. To a great extent the science of archeology is based not only on the exhumation of human bones in caves, but in comparatively recent times on the exploration of the tombs, pyramids and monuments. As civilization progressed, customs changed, but in death for thousands of years the poor and humble were consigned to the earth, whilst the rich and powerful erected for themselves monuments to perpetuate their memory.

Funeral ceremonies have also been subjected to constant evolution, and the greatest change was the advent of religious participation. As a rule, Man's secret desire is to maintain his dignity even after death.

In New Orleans the funeral processions of the distinguished and wealthy members of the community were grandiose. An example was the funeral pagentry of De La Ronde. He was a distinguished Creole, and a Major General at the Battle of New Orleans. He was buried on Dec. 2, 1824.

Funeral Cortege. Type used at mock funeral and memorial services. (Courtesy Frederick G. Veith.)

ORDER OF FUNERAL
Infantry
Cavalry
Music
Clergy

Pall Bearers   Pall Bearers
"   "   "   "

Corpse

"   "   "   "

Mourners
Aides de Camp of General De La Ronde
Officers of the Militia
Officers of the United States Army
Officers of the Navy
Officers of the Colombian Navy
The Presidents of the Banks
Collector and Officers of the Port
Mayor
City Council
Gentlemen of the Bar
Justices of the Peace
The Sheriff and Attorney General of the State
Judge of the Parish Court
Judge of the 1st District Court
Judges of the Supreme Court
Att'y General and Marshal
Treasurer of the State
Speaker
and Members of the House of Representatives
President of the Senate
and the Senate
General Staff of the Governor and Secretary of State
Citizens

Companies of Artillery attended the high Mass at the Cathedral. The ladies made a collection at the Mass for the widow of a soldier and her children.

The Creoles and French portion of the population conducted their funeral ceremonies with decorum. All who could in any way afford it owned a tomb for their families, which bore inscriptions of the dates of nativity and death. The Creoles insisted on having a Christian burial, and always with the benefit of the Clergy. Many of them owned tombs even when they could not afford a home, which they always maintained in good condition. Few Creoles were buried underground.

Latrobe gives a very good description of a Negro funeral, evidently that of a free man of color. He wrote: "The Coffin was carried by men of the race; none but Negroes and quadroons attended. First, there was a march, man a man, in a military uniform with a drawn sword. Then three boys in surplices with pointed caps, two carrying staves with candle sticks in the form of urns at the top, and the third in the center of a large silver cross. At some distance behind came Father Antoine and another priest, who seemed very merry at the ceremony, and were engaged in loud and cheerful conversation. At some distance further back, the coffin carried by six well-dressed black men, and to it were attached six ribbons about two yards in length, the end of which were held by six colored girls, very well dressed in white with long veils. A crowd of colored people followed confusedly, many of whom carried lighted candles—were 69 candles."

Latrobe was also an eye witness to another Negro funeral, probably that of a slave. The grave yard was situated back of the Protestant Cemetery, a sort of Potter's Field surrounded by a cypress picket fence.

Two hundred Negroes attended, the women and many of the men all dressed in white, and about one half of them carrying lighted candles. The grave dug out of earth and bones of former burials, was half filled with water and the coffin floated. While the priest was praying one Negro woman jumped onto the coffin and had to be pulled out of the water. Some boys amused themselves by throwing skulls and bones at each other. Latrobe asked one of those present why the Negro woman jumped into the grave and was answer: "Je n'en sais rien, cela est une maniere." (I do not know, that is the custom.)

There cannot be any doubt as the authenticity of these gruesome details. The usage at that time was for the mourners to carry lit candles to the grave, and after the ceremony, to place same on the tomb or the grave. The *Bee* of November 4, 1834, in its French Section had the following anecdote:

> Last Sunday, the tomb of the deceased Mr. Barbine, a pharmacist, who died on the 31st of last month, came near being

burnt to a cinder by the large quantity of candles, which grateful persons had lit to honor his memory.

In a city, where funerals were so numerous, it is evident that the undertakers enjoyed a thriving business. The press carried many of their advertisements both in their English and French sections. An establishment in the American section carried the following announcement:

> The undersigned, at No. 61 Camp St., respectfully announces to the public and his friends generally, that we have just completed a new hearse, which for taste and beauty is surpassed by none in the city. Coffins, mahogany, ebony, poplar, stained or covered to order, are constantly kept on hand. He will also undertake to furnish tombs, carriages, scarfs, gloves. All orders will be thankfully received and attended to with dispatch at any hour, day or night, and reasonable charges made. Next door to the American theater.
>
> Thomas F. Willard.
>
> To cabinet makers — two good workmen will receive regular employment; good jobs and cash payment.
>
> Apply as above.

The following advertisement was that of an undertaker in the French section:

> Juan Fernandez has the honor of informing the public, that he continues to keep his establishment at St. Ann, between Royal and Bourbon streets, for his sole account, and without partnership with anyone. There will constantly be found in his store, coffins of qualities and proportions; and from this forward his prices will be reduced as follows:
>
> First; for a simple coffin, lined with black cotton, with ribbons, and the small two wheeled hearse. No. 1: ten dollars.
>
> Second for a coffin, lined with white satin, with the four wheeled hearse, and necessary plumes, thirty dollars, other charges in proportion.
>
> Mr. Fernandez will undertake the furnishing of coaches, and the erection of tombs and monuments of every description. He will have tombs opened and closed again when applied to. He will furnish all sorts of funeral marbles and tombstones, engraved, carved and gilt; and finally will undertake the composition and inscription and epitaphs, which will be made by an able person.
>
> Persons who will apply to him for everything they may want, will obtain tapers at the rate of ten bits to a dollar; and if they are desired to be lined with paper, no more will be charged

than those without lining. He will also furnish stuff for mourning dresses, and those who may not be able to pay in cash, will be allowed a reasonable credit, and they will obtain gratis the use of the necessary chandeliers and plate.

All persons in needy circumstances, who may wish to have their friends decently buried, will be charged only with the actual cost, without any charge for work or labor. The poor will be served without any renumeration.

As to the mode of payment, Mr. Fernandez will not do as is done in certain places, where money is required forthwith, sometimes in advance; but he will make arrangements accordingly to the fortune and situation of his employers. He will distress no one; and will send his bills to be collected only when the means of his customers will allow them to pay.

Another undertaker advertised that any person who purchases a mohagony coffin will have the use of the wagon (hearse) free of charge, and that he will at the same time furnish a shroud (mortuary drapery) to cover the most ordinary coffin.

CHAPTER XXXV

MEASURING SWORDS AND EXCHANGING SHOTS

New Orleans has not only been maligned as a profligate city in the beginning of the nineteenth century, but as one addicted to dueling. Dueling was then the accepted way of settling disputes among gentlemen, not only in Louisiana, but throughout the Union and in all civilized nations. Whether that practice was more prevalent in New Orleans than in other cities of the Union is a moot question. History tells of celebrated personal encounters in the North between men of prominence who wounded or killed their adversaries on the field of honor. But it ignores many encounters or lesser importance. The relative frequency of duels which occurred in New Orleans compared to those of the North cannot be ascertained, but it may be inferred that they were more frequent in New Orleans because of differences in temperament, clashing nationalities, the quick resentment of any affront or insult and the existing high code of honor — all factors conducive to measuring swords and exchanging shots. Laws were enacted not only to eradicate dueling, but to punish the offenders; the Church interdicted it on moral grounds; but these prohibitions and even the fear of death were subordinated to the dread of the loss of honor. For not to accept a cartel, even if it meant certain loss of life, was to be branded with ignominy and cowardice. Such is the obduracy of human nature, that for hundreds of years, dueling was not only tolerated and practiced, but justified by its adherents and glorified in song and story.

The combats of the age of chivalry and the more genteel encounters with the rapier or the German colishemard or the more brutal and deadly use of the dueling pistol, the shot gun, the six shooter and the Bowie knife, have all been glorified. The extent to which dueling was practiced in New Orleans during the colonial period is not known, for history is comparatively silent on the subject. They must have been relatively few compared to a later period, for the population was small, its people were of the same temperament, the same culture, observing the same code of honor; and besides their homogeneity was intensified by intermarriage; the provocations for and the hatred conducive to dueling were therefore greatly minimized. Yet every man was a swordsman and skilled in the use of the rapier. It was a part of the education of a gentleman. Fortier asserted that at that time "duels were fought sometimes more as a test of skill with the sword than to redress a wrong or avenge an insult."

Gayarré in his "History of Louisiana" mentioned such an instance where six young French noblemen engaged in a duel on what is now one of the principal business streets of New Orleans. . . . "as they were walking along together, with no ill feeling among them, one exclaimed: 'oh! what a beautiful night! What a splendid level ground for a joust! Suppose we pair off, draw our swords and make this night memorable by a spontaneous display of bravery and skill.' The proposal was favorably received and almost instantly six swords were glittering in the light of the moon and the encounter — begun in a spirit of heroic, but foolish bravado — terminated by two of the participants being left on the field seriously injured."

Duels became much more prevalent in the twenties and the thirties when the population was then more heterogeneous. It was a period of adjustment between the French and English-speaking segments of the population, with all their incompatibility of culture, nationality, morals and of interest, which engendered distrust and even hatred — all inciting to misunderstandings and quarrels — that brought about a large number of encounters on the field of honor. It is known that duels were numerous, but not how many.

Dueling was resorted to only by gentlemen to settle their differences. A fisticuff was considered a disgrace, blows were very seldom struck, except occasionally a slap on the face with a glove, only to be retaliated by saying, "My seconds will see you." According to the code duello, the accredited seconds of both parties would meet and dispassionately discuss the situation, striving for an apology or a conciliation. In fact the matter was altogether in the hands of these gentlemen, and, if an honorable settlement could not be reached, the choice of weapons would be agreed upon as well as the place and time of the combat. Any decision reached by the seconds as a rule was binding on the principals. A cartel from an inferior, either social or because of ill-repute, was seldom accepted. In which instance it was proper for the one challenged to cane or horsewhip the challenger in public, and never soil his hands by inflicting a blow. There are many such incidents on record. Another custom was to post placards denouncing the party challenged, stating the reasons for the cartel and branding that individual as a coward, a scoundrel and with other invectives. If the refusal to give satisfaction was based on justifiable grounds, according to the code, the challenged party was justified in the court of public opinion of avenging the insult by thrashing the challenger with his cane. But if the refusal was actuated by fear, or some other inexcusable reason, he would be disgraced in the eyes of the community. Many a duel was thereby unjustifiably forced on many an unwilling victim. There was no other way to save his honor.

Like all decrees of prohibition which do not meet with public approval, the laws on dueling were ignored by the most respectable citizens and overlooked by the police and the judiciary. There were penalties attached to the practice of dueling, and they were very severe. An editorial in the *Bee* of June 29, 1835 had this to say:

> If dueling is not prevented in Louisiana it certainly is not that there are no existing laws against it — from 1805 the statutes of the state have been rigid against it, the last law 1818, which states in Section 16: "If any person shall voluntarily engage in a duel with rapiers or small swords, back swords or pistol, or other dangerous weapon to the hazard of life — and death shall ensue — the survivor shall upon conviction suffer death: and every person aiding and abetting as seconds, agent or accessories before the fact in same act, shall suffer solitary imprisonment for a term not exceeding one year and by confinement afterwards at hard labor for a term not exceeding ten years. Section 7: If any person shall voluntarily engage in a duel, etc. (as before) when no homicide shall ensue; and if any person shall by word, message or any other manner, challenge another to fight in a duel where no duel shall ensue — every such offender and every person who has knowingly been a second, agent or abettor in such duel that ensues — be a second, agent or abettor in such duels and challenge, upon due conviction of either of said offences, shall be punished as a felonious assaulter by fine not exceeding $200.00 and imprisonment not exceeding two years.
> Section 18 — If any person shall accept a challenge to a duel and shall consent to fight therein, when no duel shall ensue — every such abettor in such acceptance of challenge shall (on due conviction) be punished by a fine not exceeding $100.00 or imprisonment not more than one year."

The editorial made the categorical assertion that "unfortunately none are disposed to enforce the law." That seems to be the truth because at no time during that period can be found any prosecution for dueling, even when an encounter, bordering on brutal murder, roused the public to a high pitch of indignation.

Contrary to what has been written, the press but rarely published these encounters on the field of honor, yet there were many lampoons and communications of crimination and recrimination published in the journals, some of which were indulged in by the editors themselves, which would leave a strong impression that an encounter would either take place or most probably had taken place, but never a word about how it terminated.

Governor Henry Johnson in his message to the Legislature in January 1827, said: "The rigor of our laws on the subject of dueling renders them ineffectual; and this will most always be the case, while it is repugnant to the popular sentiment."

In the eighteen thirties the number of duels rose to formidable proportions and many steps were taken to suppress the abuse. According to the *Bee* of September 3, 1834, a meeting was called for the purpose of decreasing the number of duels and to establish a court of honor. Bernard Marigny and General Plauché were its presidents, assisted by Donatien Augustin, Doucé and Mercier. The meeting took place at Davis Hall on Monday, September 16. It was well attended and the following resolution was adopted:

> Preamble: The subscribers considering that the number of duels in New Orleans increase in frightful extent, that this barbarous custom causes the death of many victims; that families without fortune and dependent solely upon the industrious exertions of a father for support are daily reduced to the most painful misery by a compliance with this infamous prejudice; the young men entering upon life with virtues, talents and the brilliant hope that promised to embellish society; men who had fared to be worthy fathers, useful citizens, courageous defenders of their country, are daily sacrificed by this false sense of honor and disappoint the well grounded hope of society and of their community.
>
> Considering, moreover, that it is the duty of every wise man, of every citizen to impede as far as lays in his power this evil, an evil which threatens the very existence of society and social intercourse; and believing that the only means and remedy now existing are to form a society, with the view of binding firmly all of its members together by wise regulations in order to decrease the number of duels and proceed to the suppression of the practice.
>
> Be it resolved: That as soon as 100 subscribers are obtained, they shall meet at such a place as may be deemed convenient, there to adopt rules and regulations that may tend to the pros-

perity of the society, and also to designate and appoint its officers.

Committee on Resolutions and Membership

B. Marigny	Paul Bertus	Dr. McDaniel
A. Douce	Ursin Bouligny	Capitaine St. Cyr
J. J. Mercier	J. B. Plauché	Alfred Ducros
Chas. Genois	Wm. DeBuys	J. B. D. Voisin

Subscribers

Auguste Douce	J. Saint Cyr	S. Grinolt
L. Trigant de Beaumont	Felix de Armas	C. Lepousse
H. D. Peire	B. Marigny	J. Bertrand
A. W. Pichat	J. P. Desbois	J. B. Desdunes, Fils
Y. McDaniel, M.D.	Fouche Cougat	James Duplessis
Burthe	Giquel	J. Deverges
Samuel S. Relf	J. J. Mercier	F. E. Peychaud
Charles Revoile	T. Leament	J. Dupin
A. Prieur	J. P. Freret	G. A. Montmaire
Bosque	Z. B. Lebeau	Thomas Duplessis
J. B. D. Voisin	Robert Layton	J. Chastant
Antonio Ducros	A. Hoa	Charles L. Durocher
Samuel D. Dixon	P. A. Guillotte	Tullius St. Céran
Jh. Marcel Ducros	Samuel Hermann	J. B. S. St. Amand
Jn. Dufour	L. Charbonnet	Alf. J. Lewis
De St. Romes	L. Colsson	Geo. K. Rogers
S. Saint Cyr	P. E. Tricou	Alphonse Duperu
Edmond Forstall	Joh. L. Thielen	A. Blondeau
C. G. de Armas	P. P. Cogley	J. A. Durel
M. Andry	W. F. C. Duplessis	P. Delery
George J. Bright	J. Leblanc	C. E. Forstall
A. Magnin	Emile Lasére	Gustave LeGardeur
J. B. Plauché	A. Cuvillier	A. Lisle
C. Genois	Alex Cuvillier	C. J. Carriere
J. B. Blache	Jh. Cuvillier	J. F. Maxent
E. Planchard	Jos. H. Fernandez	B. O. Vignaud
Arthur Fortier	E. Nadaud	Paul Bertus
Felix Labatut	M. Bertus	G. D'Hébécourt
D. Prieur	P. H. Kernion, Jr.	A. Mazureau
J. Bermudez	Jh. Genois	Robt. Preaux
Wm. DeBuys	F. Correjolles	A. A. Peychaud
Cuvillier	J. Le Carpentier	C. de Morant

F. McCarty	Alcide Meynier	P. R. Puissan
W. Durel	Jn. Billaud	P. LeBlanc
P. L. B. Duplessis	F. Deloup	Jno. Lewis
V. L. Rabassat	J. Colsson	Joaquin Viosca
Eugene Lasére	M. Prados	J. A. Roca
J. W. Kennedy	G. Durel	Y. Garcia
Antoine St. Amant	P. H. Y. Colsson	Thomas Buya
J. Labatut	G. Bayon	Francisco Tio
Jules Dejan	Stanilas Guirot	Jose Prats
U. Bouligny, Jr.	F. Lefebvre	A. Lacoutre
J. F. Bargas	Jas. R. Sterrelt	E. Johns
B. Bouny	G. Leonard	P. F. Smith
A. Delpit	Thos. Guyol	J. M. Dixon
J. Bayon	A. Abat	General Robeson
Robert J. Ker		

The Secretaries were J. J. Mercier and Wm. DeBuys. Despite this formidable list of names of the most prominent citizens of the city, among whom were famous duelists, it appears that their efforts to suppress dueling were futile, for barely a month after that meeting, in the *Bee* of October 13, was published in its French edition the following editorial entitled "Duel — Again the Duel," which observed:

> It is a hundred times easier to tame tigers and panthers than to extirpate so general a prejudice. The Louisiana Legislature has been too severe in their acts relative to duels. At the next assembly these laws should be revised.

A duel took place on the 18th of July 1826, which created a great deal of indignation in New Orleans, and provoked condemnatory statements in the press. The participants were Theodore Preval, a youth nineteen years old, and Zephie Canonge. The provocation was an affront to the father of the young man. The agreement was that they would fight with pistols and in case that either should miss, the affray would continue with the use of the small sword. The first volley was ineffective, so they resorted to the use of cold steel and young Preval was stabbed through the abdomen from which wound he died: Here is the report of this dramatic incident which took place at the grave of the unfortunate victim:

> The friends of the family of Mr. Preval — the friends of virtue and justice are informed that Mr. Theodore Preval, aged 19 years, terminated his career yesterday afternoon at 4 o'clock, by

a frightful fatality. Over the grave of young Preval a discourse by Mr. Pierre Landreux, who alluded, in warm language to the bravery and filial piety of the youth who felt his blood heated with indignation at the sight of his father being cruelly outraged by a despicable man, dishonored for a long time in the public opinion.

The address was concluded by the following anathema upon Preval's murderer, which was unanimously repeated by all persons present.

"For us gentlemen who sigh over the grave in which the remains of our young friend repose, 1st let us all swear, in parting with him to burden forever his murderer with the weight of our contempt, to expel him forever from the bosom of society and to abandon him without pity to the torment of remorse — I swear it!"

An encounter took place which cannot be dignified by the name of duel. It was the murder of a 19-year-old Irishman. Although there was a certain amount of callousness relative to affairs on the field of honor, properly conducted under the code duello, yet any unfair advantage taken by one of the contestants aroused great public indignation. This was one of the rare occasions when the press censured editorially or in a communication any violation of the code duello. The following is quoted in part from a report in the *Bee* on June 29, and 30, 1835:

On Thursday night, Thomas G. Dunn [the victim] had been drinking with McMahon. On paying for the refreshment, laid a picaillion [6 cent piece] on the counter, which Dunn, in the gayety of unsuspecting freedom took up and gave for two cigars, offering one of them to McMahon. The act passed unnoticed at the time, but McMahon, having followed Dunn into the street, demanded the picaillion. Dunn laughed at first, but the other was in no merry mood. Dunn perceiving this, offered his friend a coin out of his pocket. No! said McMahon. Give me my own picaillion! Back went Dunn to the cabaret; but it was closed. This was expected perhaps by McMahon, who immediately commenced scurrilous reprobation, which attracted a crowd. Berry, among others interfered, and the dispute between him and Dunn proceeded to blows.

Then McMahon changed his mode of attack on Dunn, reassumed the appearance of friendship, and aware that Berry (who kept a shooting gallery for sometime) was a dead shot, he drew Dunn aside and instigated him to challenge his antagonist for the blow inflicted. Poor Dunn was *Baechus plenus* asked a respite until morning, when he should have recovered and be more collected; but McMahon would not wait. He himself wrote the challenge and having made Dunn then sign it, he immediately brought it to Berry. The rendezvous was called for the next morning.

McMahon brought Dunn to the field in a state of drunken stupor or recklessness, scarcely knowing whether or why he went. .... Berry is said to have deliberately taken his aim during the word of command on the first fire, but Dunn escaped that. Matters were then sought to be amicably adjusted, but this McMahon imperiously refused, for his friend, forsooth, must have satisfaction! and this satisfaction poor Dunn had instantly.

McMahon was a clerk of Judge Preval's Court.

The Creoles and the French were castigated as the duelists of that period. So the fictionists, in the wildest flight of their fertile imaginations, would have us believe that duelists would ride to the oaks with the same regularity that they would partake of their morning coffee, and that they would engage in mortal combat for the slightest provocation; but what are the facts?

It is true that the Creoles would settle their difficulties on the *champ d'honneur*, and that they participated in many duels. An article which appeared in the *Louisiana Recorder* and reproduced in the Bee of July 21, 1835, bearing the title the "Creoles of Louisiana," said:

> The integrity and self respect of a Creole ensure courtesy and dignity; and though he will not wantonly give an insult, it is evident that from his address that he will not tolerate one. He may possibly bear an injury; but the ardor of his temperament and energy of his actions prevent forbearance, when impertinence or folly is obtruded on his notice. His honor being to him sacred as "the immediate jewel of his soul," the maxim of his conduct is *Nemo me inpune lacessit*; and his means of redress are prompt without being puerile or petulant, yet is the Creole neither quarrelsome; for his inherent and acknowledged determination is the safeguard from insults.
>
> In very few of the honorable yet ignoble butcheries which disgrace New Orleans are Creoles engaged as principals or instigators. Such affairs of honor are generally confined to some of the vagrants or emigrants from northern climes — men who become sublimated by the heat of a southern climate; and though formerly compounded of the phlegmatic or saturnine material of barren regions, where they could little more than vegetate, labor and die, have here their tempers mercurialized, their conduct gratified, and their desires enlarged without a corresponding elevation of heart or a commensurate improvement of mind and manners. These are they who are in Louisiana the sticklers for precedence; the triflers for bastard honor, duelists from punctilio and the laws — they who seem unconscious that recti-

tude of moral conduct is as essential a component of a gentleman as is urbanity of manners and who therefore neglect the one and forfeit the other that they may with greater impunity or effrontery act as a bully, the sot or the knave — regardless of moral courage that they may display physical bravery and their own proficiency in their infidel recklessness of humanity and life.

The Creoles had a preference for the rapier or the colishemarde with which they were adept, and besides they were not as brutal or lethal as the pistol, shot gun or the broad sword. Their hatred did not extend to the point of killing their adversary. An encounter was usually stopped upon drawing blood, no matter how little; a fatality was rare. A scratch was frequently all that was necessary to satisfy their honor. Their punctilio on the field, except in very rare cases, was scrupulously observed, for they would not take any unfair advantage. Generally, unlike the Anglo-Saxon Americans, a duel would not continue until one of the participants was slain, as it was so frequently the case when dueling pistols were used and when round after round were shot till one would fall.

The combat with broad swords on horseback was introduced by European emigrants, principally from France. Many of them had been cavalry officers who had been well trained in their use and who were very proficient with that weapon. Such encounters were not only very gory, but exceedingly spectacular.

Fortier wrote that "after the cession of the province to the United States, the Americans introduced firearms upon the field of honor and pistols, rifles and sometimes shot guns were used with more deadly effect."

There were many *salle d'escrime* (fencing parlors) in the city presided over by fencing masters who had a large following of eager pupils. There was a great rivalry among them, which was shared by their admirers. It was an absolute necessity for the young gentlemen to become proficient in the use of arms, not only to be able to defend themselves should they receive a cartel, but by displaying superior skill in fencing they would be less subjected to annoyances or insults. John Augustin wrote:

> The duello, however, had a refining influence, for every gentleman was forced to be guarded in his language and behavior as he well knew that bare brutal courage was not sufficient to carry him triumphantly through. It is true that a gentleman was obliged to fight, but he had to fight well — that is, for reason and under plausible and legitimate conditions, staunch enough to hold the current of public opinion. Otherwise he was

quickly ostracized and society sustained all who refused to cross swords or exchange shot with him. The code was very strict. You could not fight a man whom you could not ask to your house.

Among the most famous duels among the Anglo-Saxon Americans must be mentioned the meeting between Governor Claiborne and Daniel Clark, then the territorial delegate in Congress, at Fort Manchac, in which Clark was severly wounded. The affair took place in 1807.

John Augustin, in his basic thesis "The Oaks," recounts some interesting duels. He wrote of the one of Thimecourt, which his copyists have written and rewritten about, always repeating the same error. For the sake of historical accuracy the name was not Thimecourt, but Marie D'Hamécourt. Captain D'Hamécourt, as he correctly stated, had been a captain in the French Cavalry. He was of noble birth and a graduate of St. Cyr and the Ecole d'Application de Cavalerie of Saumur. Whilst on a maneuver, he was accidently struck by his superior officer, and being a man of uncontrollable temper, he retaliated with a slap. Fortunately he was able to escape the country before he was court martialed. Now with the story as Augustin recounted it:

An Italian professor of counterpoint, named Poulage, a man of magnificent physique and herculean strength, was holding his own with the broadsword and bidding defiance to all comers. Captain D'Hamécourt, a former cavalry officer, opposed and defeated him. The humiliation was too much for the Italian's pride, and he remarked with a sneer that D'Hamécourt was a good *"tireur de salle."*

"Qu'a cela ne tienne!" at once exclaimed the soldier, "Let us adjourn to the field." Without further parley they took rendezvous for the oaks and there D'Hamécourt cut his adversary to pieces. D'Hamécourt was one of the most noted professors of fence of the period, his favorite weapon being the broadsword, in the management of which he excelled. This encounter took place in the spring of 1840.

Another well known and contemporaneous professor was a German swordsman, Monthiach. He was tall, fleshy and muscular, and at the same time the best natured fellow in the world, but always ready for a duel, particularly with a professor. Professors of all kinds have always been more or less jealous of each other, but the maitres d'armes of that period were peculiarly and aggressively so. Well, D'Hamécourt and Monthiach had some slight differences about a coup and naturally as they disagreed completely, the only way to come to an understanding was to fight it out.

They fought with broadswords because it was that weapon they had disagreed. The duel was short, sharp and decisive. At the first pass, Monthiach made a terrible vicious cut at his adversary evidently to cut off his head at one blow. The coup was admirably conceived and executed. D'Hamécourt, who had his own idea, did not parry with his sword, but dodged. His hat was cut clear in two, Monthiach's blade grazing his scalp. At the same time the Frenchman passing under his adversary's sword, opened his breast with a splendid *coup de pointe*. The seconds interfered. The gash was a frightful one and the blood flowed freely, yet the German professor insisted upon going on with the fight. The seconds, however, would not permit it. They had taken no surgeon with them and Monthiach, to the horror of some bystanders, pulled out some tow which he had in his pocket and packing his wound with it to stop the flow of blood, walked home in a frenzy, cursing at the seconds who had stopped the fight, for as he said, it was a beautiful coup and he would have assuredly chopped off D'Hamécourt's head if he had had a second chance to renew it. Three days after he was on parade, marching, musket in hand in the ranks of the "Fusiliers," a German militia company, then commanded by Captain Daniel Friedrich.

Augustin related another interesting account of the duel between Donatien Augustin and Hughes Pedesclaux:

Both were attached to the "Canonniers d'Orleans," a crack artillery company of those days. Augustin had just been made a Lieutenant and was rather proud of his uniform and trailing artillery saber. Parade had just been dismissed; Pedesclaux came up to his friend Augustin (a child whom he had bullied and spanked at the College d'Orleans) and jovially but irreverently gave a deprecatory kick to the swaggering sword, saying, "What could you do with this thing?"
Quick as a flash came the retort,
"Follow me a few paces to some quiet place and I will show you."

Not one more word was said; each man picked up two friends to act as seconds, and forthwith followed by the delighted crowd, eager for the sight of a scrimmage, marched to the scene of combat. A convenient spot was soon reached, the adversaries doffed their uniforms, stripped to their shirt sleeves, and drew their weapons.

Pedesclaux was in full vigor of manhood and skilled in sword play; Augustin a mere youth with little experience in arms, but very active and willing. As luck would have it, after a few passes he cut his redoubtable adversary in the sword arm. The seconds interfered; there was a great shaking of hands and the incident ended in a gay and plentiful dinner at Victor's on Toulouse Street.

Dueling was a common practice before the Civil War. It was indulged in by both the French and English-speaking portion of the population. Many laws with severe penalties were passed to suppress it, but not having public support they were ignored and men continued to maim or kill themselves for the slightest provocation which sometimes bordered on the ridiculous. But after the war the glamour of these personal encounters vanished, they met with public disapproval and even ridicule. In time, like yellow fever, duels ceased to plague New Orleans.

CHAPTER XXXVI

AMUSEMENTS — REFINED AND VULGAR

The culture of the inhabitants of New Orleans during the colonial days was always French with only slight Spanish modifications during the later years. It was altogether Latin. Their passionate love of good music, their appreciation of the theatre, their fondness for balls, the dignity of their home entertainments, and the sumptuousness of their banquets, merited the profuse praise of the more enlightened and distinguished chroniclers who visited the city during the early nineteenth century. Many regarded New Orleans as the Paris of America. The display of wealth was not ostentatious, but what added charm to their social affairs was the dignity, decorum and urbanity which prevailed. The elite of American society exhibited these same graces.

Thomas Ashe, an Englishman, described in 1809 the Creole women of New Orleans:

Those called white are principally brunettes with deep black eyes, dark hair and good teeth. Their persons are eminently lovely, and their movements indiscriminately graceful, far superior to anything ever witnessed in Europe.

Dress of white ladies, plain and simple — The robe, white, fastened under the breast with a diamond pin, and the hair in the form of a coronet, connected with small bands of precious stones and pearls.

Their principal amusement is to ride out after sunset, in small cabriolets, which they drive themselves with ease and dexterity, a Negro boy or girl elegantly dressed standing by. They are never attended by gentlemen, for the loss of reputation is dreaded here beyond the loss of everything else.

The public amusements are balls and concerts; their private, consists of music parties at home and conversations around the door.

The ladies [Creoles] are much more reserved than French women; they are even distant in their manners toward men, and it is not until they rise into friendship and descend into familiarity with him, that they kindle into love without any difficulty and give that passion more dignity and embellishment than you can conceive it susceptible of in Europe.

Zacharie mentioned that "the dress of the French revolution was the vogue. The ladies appeared in short waists and slinging skirts. The men in tight pantaloons, blue or snuff colored coats, high red colors, brass buttons and elaborate shirt and waist ruffles. Knee breeches and silk stockings gradually disappeared and were worn at balls as late as 1830. Powdering of the hair and wearing of the cue disappeared early in the century."

Lagarde de Montiezant, a Frenchman who visited New Orleans in 1817, gives the following picture of a ball he attended in New Orleans:

> The hall was lighted with 200 candles, and sixty young demoiselles, dressed in white were the ornaments of the ball. They were simply but elegantly dressed, nearly all had white roses adorning their hair which was artistically curled and plaited with taste and dropped with grace in floating elastic spirals on a virginal forehead around an alabaster neck and upon rosy cheeks. The young mothers having completed their waltz, would nurse her newly born, which the liberty afforded by her dress, was already nearly sufficiently disengaged.
>
> The ball commenced at eight o'clock and was prolonged up to three o'clock. The women retired afoot with all the dignity of a primitive epoch. Before the city had sidewalks the women had to walk barefoot to the ball room, accompanied by their slaves, carrying the costumes they were to wear at the ball.

Zacharie tells us that "the people were fond of dancing, and in going to balls were always preceded by a Negro boy sometimes nicknamed *cocodri* carrying a lantern called in creole, *Fanal*. On moonlight nights it was not lit, but served to carry away from the supper table bonbons, nougats and other most prized delicacies. Hence one sometimes still hears the mocking cry of the urchin, "Maitress conti au bal, cocodri porté fanal."

The subscription balls were very select and were only attended by the élite of society. The consensus of even of the most biased visitors at that time was that these balls because of their luxury, their decorum, the refinement and the beauty of the ladies, their chicness, and the grace of the dancers presented a spectacle not to be seen in other parts of the country, and that these affairs stood favorable comparison to similar entertainment in the capitals of Europe. To add to their picturesqueness a Negro lackey stood in the orchestra stand who played the tambourine whilst calling the figures of the dance.

At these functions a sumptuous supper was usually served, an epicure's dream, a repast which only the creole cuisine of that time could provide. The participants were served in groups because the dining salon which adjoined the ball room was not large enough to accommodate such a large assembly at one sitting. The ladies were served first and after they had all eaten the gentlemen would regale themselves.

There is a tradition in the Fortier family that one of their forebears, an elderly gentleman, displaying the exhuberant enthusiasm of youth, a favorite of the social set, was the master of ceremonies at all social functions, a distinction he greatly enjoyed, who would announce in a stentorian voice:

Mesdames! Mesdames! Au Souper! Au Souper! A Table! A Table!

This was repeated until the last guest was served.

Again we are indebted to the Duke of Saxe-Weimar for his description of the celebration of Washington's birthday, which took place late in the twenties. He stated that all vessels in the port were adorned with flags and that there was a subscription ball in the ball room of the French theater. "In former years the subscription was $10.00 but had been reduced to $3.00. Because it was Lent, the attendance was small. The salon had been decorated with Washington's portrait and a number of standards, and a splendid supper spread for the ladies." Because of the expectation of a limited attendance, "Mr. Davis, the manager of the French theater, the balls and several gambling houses, announced a masked ball at $1.00 admission for Washington's birth night. The young ladies, however, to whom a subscription ball was in anticipation, and on account of it, had prepared a fresh set of ornaments to assist their toilet, felt themselves exceedingly disappointed by this arrangement as there would be a very mixed company at the masked ball, and they would not be able to distinguish themselves by individual ornament. For this reason their parents and relations had exerted themselves, and happily brought it to pass, that instead of a ticket, there should be one of subscription. In fact the ball was very splendid so far as the dress of the ladies contributed thereto. Moreover, no battles took place."

The Duke of Saxe-Weimar in 1822 described a banquet given by John Randolph Grymes, a Virginian, and a resident of New Orleans since 1808, a brilliant lawyer and one of the participants in the Battle of New Orleans, as follows:

> After the second course large folding doors opened and we beheld another dining room in which stood a table with the des-

sert. We withheld from the first table and seated ourselves at the second, and in the same order in which we had partaken of the first. As the variety of wines began to set the tongues of the guests at liberty, the ladies rose, retired to another apartment, and resorted to music for amusement. Some of the gentlemen remained with the bottle, while others, among whom I was one, followed the ladies, and regaled ourselves with harmony. We waltzed until ten o'clock.

At that same time Charles Augustine Murray, an Englishman, wrote his impression of the Creole balls. He claimed that the music was excellent, and that the orchestra was composed of a harp, a piano, a flute, a violin and clarinet.

On entering the room and casting my eyes around me, I stood in admiration at the number of pretty faces and figures, and at the correctness of taste displayed in the dresses of the ladies.

The general character of the Creole beauty is a dark but clear and transparent complexion, black eyes, fringed with long eyelashes, and finely penciled eyebrows; a nose neither Greek nor Roman, but delicately formed, and a very fine taille, although apt to run rather early, too far into embonpoint. In manners the Creole ladies are gay, lively and unaffected, and altogether possess as much personal attraction as has fallen to the lot even of the fairest average of the fair creation. They all have fine dark hair, and what is very remarkable, they all dress it nearly in the same manner; their coiffure is not *a la greque*, but of that character, and the hair is brought rather forward on the side of the cheek; they seem to pay very good attention to this part of the toilette, and I do not remember to have seen hair more beautifully clean, fine and gracefully disposed; nevertheless that I should admire the taste of the fair Creoles more, if they arranged it with greater variety, according to the respective characters of their features.

Of course the conversations are carried on in French, and the customs of the same nation were observed during the evening; according to these, I was privileged to address and to dance with any young lady in company without going through the ceremonial ordeal of introduction; and it is impossible to conceive an assembly with more agreement and with less restraint, than this Creole coterie. I must confess that I have seen nothing so like a ball since I left Europe. The contredanses were well danced, and there was waltzing without swinging, and a gallopade without a romp.

The supper was exceedingly handsome and in some respects, superior to those given at ball suppers in London. One the whole I went away much pleased with the mirth and agreeable manners of Creole society.

Karl Pöstl, a very severe and even unjust critic, was not too punctilious in resorting to gross exaggeration. In 1826, he observed that the carnival season began towards the close of December, with society balls, masquerades or routs and a number of private balls. He wrote that the first, third and last masquerades, the Society Balls were the most splendid. "They are regularly attended by the daughters of the merchants and planters who at this time came to the city."

He wrote of a ball he attended:

There is however nothing more tiresome than a masked ball in New Orleans. Some young merchants and some planters took it into their heads to assume the character of poor paddies (Irish), and they dressed themselves accordingly. This would have been for the most unaccomplished American or English miss, a fair opportunity for displaying at least some wit. But the Creole demoiselles when addressed by their lovers, had not a word to say except, "Oh, we know that you are no paddies! Oh, you are not an Irishman — you are rich Y." This was the conversation all around.

Pöstl continued:

Still more tedious were the public balls given in commemoration of the 8th of January, and the anniversary of Washington.

Until (1825), and owing to the shyness of the Creoles towards their new brothers, the American and Creoles, with their ladies apart, neither speaking nor dancing with one another.

He further commented that "only three American homes can be said to receive good company, the rest are Creoles."

In 1829, W. Bullock observed that the people here have the French characteristic of politeness and urbanity, and that "the ladies of the highest standing will show courtesies that would almost comport with ideas of dignity entertained by the ladies of the North. In their carnival meetings there is apparently a great deal of cheerful familiarity, tempered, however, with the most scrupulous observances, and the most punctilious decorum. They are the same gay, dancing, spectacle-loving race that they are everywhere else."

Theodore Pavie, a Frenchman, wrote in 1833, his impression of New Orleans:

New Orleans is populated like a capital of Europe, rich like any city of the Indies, gay like a town in Italy, and as brilliant as one in the Orient. It is impossible during a warm spring day, to pass the vaulted cafes which are so cool, without being tempted to rest a moment to read the journals, and to sit before a glass of frozen punch, of soda, or of beer, and smoke a cigar.

That same year, Harriet Martineau wrote about a "true Louisiana day":

> We ladies carried our work bags and issued forth at 11 o'clock, calling by the way for a friend. The house we were to visit was a small shaded dwelling, with glass doors opening into a pretty garden. In a cool parlor, we sat at work, talking of things solemn and trivial, of affairs native and foreign, till dinner which was at two. We were then joined by the gentlemen. We left the dinner table early, and the gentlemen trundled rocking chairs and low stools into the garden, where we sat in the shade all afternoon, the ladies working, the gentlemen singing Irish melodies, telling good natured stories and throwing us all into such a merry mood that we positively refused the siesta. After tea, we went to the piano, and were reminded at last by darkness of the number of hours which the delightful Louisiana visit had consumed. We all walked home together through the quiet street.
>
> I had dreaded the visit to New Orleans, and went more from a sense of duty than from inclination; the friendship that I formed there left me no feeling but rejoicing that I had gone.

An interesting observation may be made here. Latrobe definitely stated that he could not see one face "that had the slightest tinge of rouge", yet, fourteen years later, in 1833, Harriet Martineau mentioned it as being a custom of the time. Evidently rouge must have become fashionable sometimes during that interval.

There were then, as well as today, many gate-crashers, who sought admittance to ball rooms where they were neither invited or wanted. The committee in charge were composed of prominent men of the city, and they saw to it that only selected guests could participate. Any unwelcome individual forcing his entry into a ball room, was most unceremoniously thrown out. Doubtless that is the reason for the fights and disturbances so frequently mentioned.

The balls for the elite were not public but were select, and in order to keep them so, they were in the nature of subscription balls. In that way it was possible to limit the attendance to only those who were eligible to attend.

At these dances a supper was always served, and the cuisine must have been excellent, but unfortunately the menus are not known to us today, but this we do know, there always was a gumbo.

The balls of the social set of New Orleans were always held at Davis' theater and ball room, situated on Orleans St, between Royal and Bourbon. Part of the original building is now occupied by the Sisters of the Holy Family Convent. The myth that this was the site where the notorious quadroons balls were held should be exploded.

In the *Bee* of February 18, 1834, it was remarked that the city enjoyed an unprecedented whirl of amusement. Despite the fact that New Orleans had but shortly before experienced the greatest calamity which had ever afflicted it, when more than one-sixth of its population were victims in a few days of simultaneous epidemics of yellow fever and cholera and despite the fact that it had experienced a financial crisis the people were in a gay mood.

Its editorial entitled "Hard Times" said:

> Despite serious pressure and great scarcity, this community has found enough spare cash to regale themselves with amusements.
>
> Several young gentlemen gave a "Bachelor Ball" which cost about $5000.00 — also a costly military ball; and on Shrove Tuesday, [Mardi Gras] two theaters, two circuses, three or four ball rooms were severally thronged to overflowing. Better houses at the American theater than ever before this season.

In 1836 more of an entente cordialle seemed to have existed between the American and Creole socialites. For, in an advertisement in the French section of the *Bee* of February 19th of that year, the following gentlemen were appointed commissioners for a ball to be given by the fathers of families: Messrs. A. B. Roman, Thomas Barrett, John Richardson, Joseph Pilié, J. V. Zacharie, Pierre Soulé, Leonard Mathews, John Lallande, B. D. Pritchard, Wm. Christy and E. A. Cannon.

In a subsequent issue the *Bee* described the "Fancy Ball." It was held at Davis' Ball Room. One of the groups represented the Lay of the Last Minstrel — the five "young Cavaliers" were Dessailes, Harman, Hogan, Slidell and Musson. The costumes of the dancers must have been gorgeous for the *Bee* summed up the arfair with: "Group them in a bright and lustrous hall, animate them by music that stirs the blood like a trumpet, and you will have some faint conception of the assemblage on that night."

Other appointed commissioners to the private balls were: Messrs. A. Musson, F. Durive, G. Miltenberger, F. A. Guyol,

Thomas Duplessis, C. Cruzat, C. Duplessis, C. Kohn, F. McNeil, F. E. Sourdes and Theo Durel.

The Creoles were a pleasure loving people with a love for the niceties of life inherited from their French and Spanish forebears. It had been instilled in them from early childhood. Breckenridge wrote in 1814 that; "children have also their balls and are taught a decorum and propriety of behavior which is preserved through life."

The Duke of Saxe-Weimar mentioned the children's balls as follows:

> For the benefit of dancing masters at the French theater, the girls from 10 to 12 were dressed and tricked off like full grown ladies. At 8 o'clock the little children left off dancing and were mostly sent home, and in their place the larger girls resumed the dance.

He mentioned that during Mardi Gras:

> All the ball rooms in the city were opened. Great masked ball at the French theater: $2.00 for gentlemen, $1.00 for ladies. There was dancing not only in the ball room, but also in the theater itself, and on this occasion the parterre was raised to a level with the stage. The illumination of the house was very good and presented a handsome view. Many of the ladies were in masks, and intrigued as well as they were able. Many of the gentlemen had dipped too deep in the glass, and several quarrels with fists and canes took place.

He further observed that "the Balls continued through Lent, but were little frequented."

As the number of Americans increased, new places of amusements were opened. There were entertainments of all sorts, and the stranger, if he had the price, could not complain of boredom. There were many public dance halls, which were opened to all for the price of admission, which was usually one dollar. The advertisements of these places were frequently found in the papers.

Feuillton, the French commentator for the *Louisiana Gazette*, reported in its issue of February 17, 1829, that at the ball held at the Union Hall there were fights after each dance. He observed that on Mardi Gras day there were "many occasions for disorder because of the disguises, but that the police was so active and the surveillance and vigilance in these balls of percherons, there were no incident's of rioting, besides no one was allowed to present himself with arms. All canes, swords or sticks were deposited at the entrance, and from the ball at the opera to the lowest dive that formality was religiously observed."

These balls were crowded, and dancing lasted till 6 A.M. He continued: "On my return home I found Ursulines Street filled with sticks and those who were beaten. I had only time to close my door, but it was impossible to sleep, for at every instant the noise from the blows by the fist, the cane, and the daggers mingled together with the cries of those assaulted and the furious shouts of those who were attacking. For once, what a pleasant Mardi Gras!"

Among others, the most notorious balls of the period were those held at the St. Philip theater, then called the Washington ball room. There were ribaldry, brawls, fights and even many murders. The Duke of Saxe-Weimar who attended a masquerade ball at the St. Philip theater, made the following comment:

> There were but few masks and among the tobacco-chewing gentry, several Spanish visages slipped about, who carried sword canes and seemed to have no good design, and there appeared a willing disposition for the disturbance.
>
> The whole aspect was that of a den of ruffians. I did not remain here a half-hour, and learned the next day that I was judicious in going home early, as later, battles with canes and dirks had taken place. Twenty persons more or less were dangerously wounded.

Among the more notorious dance halls must be mentioned La Salle Condé and the Salle de l'Harmonie, No. 185 St. Peter between Burgundy and Rampart. It advertised that every Monday and Wednesday there would be masque balls. The price of admission was $2.00.

In 1835, the press deplored the scandalous scenes and the frequent murders occurring in the Washington Ball Room.

As early as 1825, attempts were made to persuade the Aldermen to abolish all masquerades and masked balls, but such a move met with the opposition of some of the most respectable citizens. It was not until December 19, 1836 that an ordinance was passed prohibiting these balls under penalty of $500.00. Evidently this law did not meet public approval, for in October 25, 1837 a resoluction was presented to repeal that ordinance which carried the following stipulations:

> Masked balls to be permitted in the Orleans Ball Room.

Davis' Ball Room, the St. Philip Street Ball Room and the Washington Ball Room. The license for each ball to be $20.00, one-half for the 1st Municipality, and the other for the benefit for the Catholic Association for the destitute orphans of New Orleans. Masked balls which admit white and colored women fined $50.00 for the first offence — $100.00 for subsequent offence, one-half of the fine to go to the informer, and the other half to the municipality. No masked balls before November 1st or after May 1st of every year.

The most popular promenade was on the Levee facing the city. At that time it was lined with shade trees. There were no parks in the proper sense of the word. There were three squares — one in each municipality, the Lafayette, Place d'Arms and Washington. They were neither beautiful nor were they in anyway attractive.

The *Bee* in an editorial on "Public Gardens" in its issue of May 1st, 1835 announced that the Vauxhall Gardens, between Common and Canal Streets, or ten squares from the river, was nearly completed. It said:

> It may prove an agreeable plan of recreation or retirement for our citizens, but we trust that it is but the commencement of such convenient resorts.
>
> New Orleans is wretchedly off for suburban walks and attractions, yet there are a few places where health and social relations require them in a greater degree. Our public squares are few and improperly neglected. No trees adorn the walks and afford shelter and our citizens are compelled to take a railroad drive or a steamboat trip for recreation. The gardens are under the superintendence of Foster and Sowerby.

The *Bee* carried the following advertisement:

> New Vauxhall Gardens: Common below Rampart.
> Grand Gala: Military band and a Cotillion Band.
> Fire works. Admittance $1.00.

It opened on May 6th and was said to have displayed good taste, built at a great expense, and to have been very respectable.

Christmas was a day of religious observance and it was not celebrated except by the children who received a visit from Papa Noel, but New Years was a day of rejoicing and gaiety. Gifts were exchanged. Bonne Année was wished everywhere. Young blades would pay their respect to their families and relatives, and to their social acquaintances. On foot, on horseback or in cabriolets they would visit home after home where a genteel hospitality would await them. In the spacious dining room, a large table was spread with delicacies of all kinds, dragees, delicious pastries, imported liqueurs, champagne, and not least, a delectable punch. With each toast, felicitation for the New Year and exchanges of appropriate compliments, the glasses were clicked.

Despite the fact that the shooting of fireworks was forbidden by the City Fathers, the sky was illuminated by the flares of Roman candles, and the ears dinned by the noise of firecrackers. Among the younger set, the gifts were not expensive, nor were they expected to be, except in a case of bethrothal; some flowers, a cornucopia of imported dragées; for anything costly would be considered a declaration of intentions.

"Feuillton", in the issue of January 3rd, 1823 of the *Louisiana Gazette,* noticed that the confectionery shop of Matassy and M. Mioton was distinguished by its elegance, and that Mr. Matassy was a poet as well as a confectioner. Their sign is reproduced verbatim:

> Belles que voulez pour etrennes
> Bonbons sucrés et vers flatteurs
> Que mon enseigne vous apprenne
> Que l'on trouve ici ces douceurs.

They not only furnished the bonbons, but with them were included flattering verses.

Feuillton further observed that New Year is a most insipid day for the poor. Children had their trumpets, drums and dolls. Despite the strict ordinances prohibiting fireworks, the influential rich ignored the laws. Negroes contributed the most to the celebration by their door-to-door concerts and dances which would only end when they were given a few picayunes.

Another form of amusement which was occasionally indulged in by the populace, much to the mortification of the innocent newly married couple, was the charivari. It was a mock serenade at the doors of some newly-wed couples, whose union for some reason or other did not have popular approval because of a misalliance, incongruity or disparity in the ages of the couple. A boisterous crowd would gather around their home, beat on tin pans, or use anything else as a noise maker. It was customary for the bride groom to furnish refreshment for the crowd, after which it would disperse in a happy mood. But this would not always end that way, for some husbands resented the intrusion on their privacy, and a brawl would ensue.

On August 31, 1825 an advertisement appeared in the *Gazette* headed "To the Amateurs", stating that that night a charivari would take place at the home of Madame Q — whose age is about 68, who married a Monsieur F — who was 23 years old. Two days afterwards that journal stated that "the article which appeared in our last number, relative to a charivari, had in our opinion little importance, so much so, we published it without inquiring the name of the author. We believe that Mr. F. is a respectable man, but as he feels insulted by that publication we request the author, if he is a man of honor, to send his name to this office today before ten o'clock, which is the time the aggrieved party will be here to receive the information."

Henry Bradshaw Pearson, an English visitor to New Orleans in 1818, in his book "Sketches of America" quotes the following advertisement from a local newspaper:

INTERESTING EXHIBITION

On Sunday next, will be represented in the place where fireworks are generally exhibited, near the Circus, an extraordinary fight of furious animals. The place where these animals will fight is a rotunda of 160 feet in circumference, with a railing 17 feet in height, and a circular gallery well conditioned and strong, inspected by the Mayor and surveyors by him appointed.

    1st Fight—a strong Attakapas Bull, attacked and subdued by six of the strongest dogs in the country.

    2nd Fight—Six bulldogs against a Canadian bear.

    3rd Fight—A beautiful tiger against a Black bear.

    4th Fight—Twelve dogs against a strong and furious Opelousas bull.

If the tiger is not vanquished in his fight with the bear, he will be sent alone against the last bull, and if the latter conquers all his enemies, several pieces of fireworks will be placed on his back, which will produce a very entertaining amusement.

In the circus will be placed two manikins, which, notwithstanding the efforts of the bull to throw them down, will always rise again, whereby, the animal will get furious.

The doors will be opened at 3 o'clock and the exhibition will begin at 4 o'clock precisely. Admittance, one dollar for grown persons, and fifty cents for children. A military band will perform during the exhibition.

If Mr. Renault is so happy as to amuse the spectators by that new spectacle, he will use every exertion to diversify and augment it in order to prove to a generous public, whose patronage has been hitherto so kindly bestowed upon him, how anxious he is to please them.

This was not a rare form of entertainment, for many incidents of such brutality were frequently reported.

In the *Louisiana Gazette* of January 27, 1823, there was a communication protesting against the desecration of the Sabbath by such a display of cruelty. It objected:

> Over and over again we have heard New Orleans reproached with a manner in which the Sabbath evening is kept by many of the inhabitants, but never was a more brutal pastime than that in Canal Street yesterday afternoon.
>
> In sight and hearing of the two churches, during the time of the afternoon services, some 150 individuals in the garb of gentlemen, and at least 50 well dressed females, patiently sit and see a poor bull worried by a score of dogs in a narrow pen. If such cruel sports are continued, the City Hall will merit the taint of being a reproach to the Union.

Feuilleton laconically remarked that the public which frequents these kind of spectacles is not precisely the same as the one who attend the Orleans theater, but that it matters little, providing the results are the same.

New Orleans was the favored winter quarter for circuses, the mildness of the weather, the large number of visitors, and the free flow of money made the city not only comfortable for the animals, but very profitable for the promoters. In an article under the headline, "Sights in New Orleans", which appeared on the 7th of February, 1832, it was observed that:

> New Orleans is now resuming her wanted gaiety and activity; amusements attract the eye in every direction you turn, dressed in the most pleasing manner, to engage the eye and captivate the imagination.
>
> Animals from the most distant region have taken up their winter quarters among us, including the lions, tigers, camels and the feathered tribe of creation which were never brought to New Orleans before; possessing so much interest and attraction, the most interesting are a pair of African Ostriches of the richest plumage, and a pair of Ardea Dubin, etc.

Among other attractions were Mr. Finn's fancy glass blowing and Flannington's Grand Solar Microscope, etc., etc.

The Charity Hospital at 147 Canal Street between Baronne and University Place. Built in 1815 it was sold to the State of Louisiana for use as a State House. (From a drawing by J. J. Costelanos, Jr., in possession of the author)

The New Orleans waterfront in 1841. (From an old lithograph.)

One of the most popular sports was cock fighting. At all times there were many cockpits in various sections of the city. This sport was indulged in by the whites as well as the blacks. In the eighteen thirties, the most popular pit was the one in the rear of the Union Hotel, situated on Condé Street (Chartres) and Madison Street. Cock fighting was held there every evening, "either with becks, spurs or with knives." The prices of admission were 25 cents, parquet, 50 cents, gallery 25 cents and on the grounds gratis.

Horse racing was also very popular. One of the first race tracks was situated on General Hampton's Turf, four miles above the City. One of the classics was run on February 22, 1826. The purse was $600.00, the entries were Mr. Williams', "Walk in the Water," General Hampton's, Marshal Ney," and a horse belonging to J. H. Shepherd, Esq. The race was close and was won by "Walk in the Water."

That same year another course was being built and in the summer it was in operation. Called the Jackson Course, it was situated two miles below the City, and was said to be the equal of any race track in the United States. It was advertised:

> Winter races will begin the first day of January and continue four days; the first day purse; 3 mile heat, $500.00; second day, two mile heat, $300.00; third day, one mile heat, $200.00. Free to any creole horse of this State only (carrying catch weight).
>
> The fourth day race, a silver cup, valued at $100.00, for any horse owned in Louisiana or at least for one year previous to the race. Entrance 10% of the amount of the several purses.
>
> The regular Spring races will take place as usual on the third Wednesday in March every year, and will continue four days; free to any horse, mare or gelding in the United States.

These races were run under the auspices of the New Orleans Jockey Club.

In 1833 races were still held over the Jackson Course, where many well known and favorite horses had been entered, among which were Piano, Lisbon, Maid, Belle, Tracy, Fairfield, Cowdriven and Jackson.

The *Bee* of January 28, 1837 carried the following announcement:

> At a meeting of subscribers for the purpose of forming a Jockey Club, held in persuance of previous notice at the Exchange

Hotel, St. Charles Street, on Thursday evening, the 19th of January 1837. Dr. David C. Ker was, on motion, called to preside as Chairman, and J. R. Serrett, Esq., appointed Secretary.

On motion:

"Resolved that this institution be known by the name of the New Orleans Jockey Club."

"Resolved that the officers of this club consist of a President, four Vice-presidents, seven Stewards, and a Secretary to be elected annually, on the first Tuesday in January, or as soon as thereafter practicable."

"Resolved, that the President, Vice-Presidents and Stewards or any five of them shall have power to make all the regulations for the good order and decorum of the course, and to decide on all matters not provided for by these rules and regulations."

"Resolved, that seven members including the President or two of the Vice-Presidents shall be a quorum to transact any business on motion."

The following officers were elected: Hon. Alexander Porter, President, and David C. Ker, John Slidell, H. C. Camack and Cuthbert Bullit, Vice-Presidents.

In 1835, the New Orleans Chess club was organized. The headquarters of the club was above Matassy's Confectionery in Chartres Street. Its President was Dr. Dazet Senac; Gustavus Schmidt, Esq., its Vice-President, and Edward Gottschalk, the Secretary. The Committee on rules and regulations was composed of Montigny, Esq., Rousseau, Esq., and Copeland, Esq. The entrance fee was $5.00, and the monthly dues, $3.00, "for the benefit of E. A. Cohen, Professor of the game of chess, who will act as the Manager of the Club. Opened from 4 to 10 o'clock and all day Sunday."

Billiards was a very popular game and tables were to be found in hotels, cafes and exchanges. Tournaments were frequently held even in early nineteenth century.

The *Gazette* of April 1st, 1826, reported a great billiard match between Mr. Mary of New Orleans and Mr. Miller of the District of Columbia. The prize to the winner of the first ten games was $100.00. For the first twenty one games, $500.00. "Miller won ten games and Mary, nine. At the 40th game they were tied, each twenty games. Mary won the last game and $500.00."

New Orleans deserved the reputation of having been a gay city.

CHAPTER XXXVII

THE THEATRE

The love of the Creoles for spectacles and pageantry was as passionate as their fondness for the dance. They flattered themselves as being what they termed, "amateurs" in matters concerning the theatre and the opera. Their appreciation of drama and music was a trait inherited from their Latin ancestors. It was a part of their culture. During the early colonial time Louisianians were deprived of theatrical performances, but they nurtured the hope that some day it would be their good fortune to see a play and hear an opera. Many of the pioneers died without realizing that dream, yet, with each passing generation they instilled in their offspring the desire and love for good entertainment.

They had parlor recitals, for many of the ladies were accomplished musicians on the pianoforte and the harp, an accomplishment instilled in them from girlhood by the good Ursuline sisters, proficient teachers of music. At these recitals the guests would listen with rapt attention to the tales of visitors from the capitals of Europe, especially Paris. The theatre was one of the principal subjects of conversation. Listeners were told of the grandeur of the opera houses and the great singers and conductors; of the enchantment of the theatre and its famous actors; and of the elite of society, in radiant array, who attended these performances. Travellers described eloquently the plays and operas they had attended. A fervent prayer would rise from the heart of every hearer that he too might some day see and hear them.

At last these dreams of the people of the Louisiana colony were realized in a very modest way.

In 1791 a small troupe of comedians arrived in New Orleans. There was no theater to receive them, so they gave their performances in homes, sometimes under a tent and frequently in the open air. But that did not last long, for soon the first floor of a building situated on St. Peter street between Royal and Bourbon streets was converted into a playhouse — the building is still in existence, bearing the number 716. The troupe was under the management of Louis Tabary and the cast was composed of Messrs. Dringy, St.

Martin, Fontaine, Champigny and the actresses, Mesdames Alice, Josephine and Remusat. Between the years 1803 and 1818, among many others, the following plays were presented: Richard, Coeur de Lion; Pizarro, the Conqueror of Peru; Eugenie, opera in one act; La Belle Arsene; La Foret Noire; Le Distrait, a comedy in five acts; Une Heure de Menage, an opera; Chrispin Medecin; d'Auterche; Le Petit Page. It will be seen that with such an ambitious repertoire and with such a crude hall in which to stage them, these thespians must have given their performances under considerable difficulties.

From this humble beginning, in a very short while New Orleans became the theatrical center of the Union.

According to Baroncelli, on May 11, 1808, the Spectacle St. Pierre was condemned by the City Council for being in bad repair and in a dangerous state. It reopened its doors on September 14, 1808, and continued in operation for two years, presenting such plays as "La Porte Secrete"; "L'Avare"; Moliere's "Le Misanthrope"; "Ma Tante Aurore"; the opera of Boeildieu, "La Déserteur" and "Romeo and Juliette." Villois, the orchestra conductor, was also, it was said, a splendid actor. The performers were Marie Champineau, St. Martin, Duvillers, Francingue, Stanislas and Rochefort.

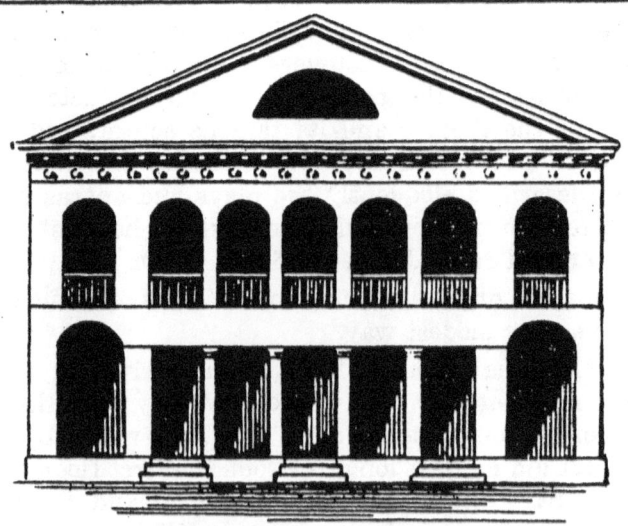

THEATRE St PHILIPPE annee 1810

St. Philip Theatre, built in 1810. (Tanesse Map.)

The St. Philip Theater, situated on St. Philip street between Bourbon and Royal, was constructed in 1810 at a cost of $100,-000.00. Its first presentation was given under the direction of Louis Tabary.

It presented a dual bill, "Les Fausses Consultations" and "Une Folle," a comic opera in two acts. On the 4th of June, it presented "L'exile en Siberie." At which time Mr. Laroque was the comptroller and Mr. Daudet the stage manager.

The St. Philip theater had a vast parquet and two rows of boxes and a seating capacity of about seven hundred. The admittance price was $7.00 for eight presentations. This theater introduced the ballet to the city and the minuet was danced there for the first time. It was damaged by fire in 1817, but was subsequently restored.

Baroncelli mentioned that in 1817 Mr. Ludlow was succeeded as director of that theatre by a Madame Coquet, "who was clever enough to make a success of an enterprise where many an impressario, nowadays, in spite of all his knowledge, loses his money." Despite competition from the Theater d'Orleans, the St. Philip Theater remained in operation until 1832, when it was transformed into a notorious dance hall. Now named the Washington Ball Room, it was the scene of many scandalous and disgraceful brawls, fights and even murders, and not long afterwards it had to close its doors.

The most celebrated and best remembered theater of that time was the Theatre d'Orleans, situated in the square, Royal, Bourbon, Orleans and St. Ann. Lacariere Latour was the architect and it was built in 1809 at a cost of $80,000.00. The promoters were Fortin, Lanuses, Tricou, Montaget and Bonamy. On November 30, 1809, at its inaugural performance, "Pataques" was presented. The leading role was played by Daudet. It was well received by the audience, thereby assuring the success of the enterprise.

This theater was burnt to the ground in 1813, but was rebuilt by John Davis at a cost of $80,000.00. Baroncelli described the architecture as being Doric and the hall as having a parquet, two rows of boxes, galaries and latticed boxes for people in mourning who did not wish to be seen by the audience. A ball room was attached to the theatre in 1817, built at a cost of $60,000.00. The policy of the theater was to employ only European actors and to import its scenery and costumes from France. Later the orchestra

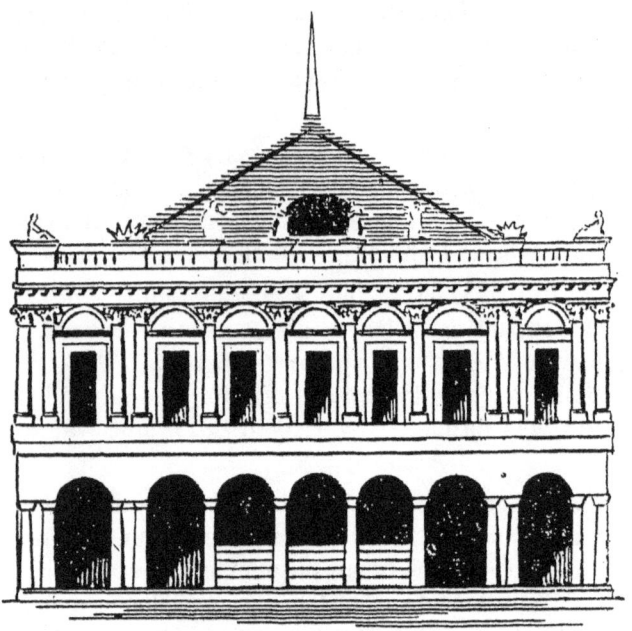

THEATRE D'ORLEANS année 1813
Orleans Theatre, built in 1813. (Tanesse Map.)

was increased to thirty-two musicians. Among the operas presented were "La Muette de Portici," "Brittanicus," "William Tell," "Neron," and "Manon." In 1837 the celebrated star, Julie Calvé, made her debut here in the "Barbier de Seville."

Sol Smith, in his book "Theatrical Management," stated:
English drama was introduced in New Orleans in December 1817, by a Commonwealth Company and that the performances were held at the St. Philip Theater. The following year Mr. Phillips took a company to that city which appeared at the Orleans Theater. Shortly afterwards Mr. Caldwell with a company from Virginia, occupied the St. Philip Theater and soon after moved to the Theatre d'Orleans. A compromise was affected with Mr. Phillips, who with the principal members of the company, enlisted under Mr. Caldwell. The great tragedian, Cooper, performed an engagement that season, receiving $333.00 per night.

The foundation of the American Theater, on Camp Street, was laid in 1821. In 1824 it was completed and opened with a company to give proper effect to the regular drama. The season was a profitable one to the manager and satisfactory to the public.

The *Louisiana Gazette* on January 3, 1824 reported the premier presentation at the American Theater of Camp Street which took place on Thursday night, New Year's Day, 1824, "to an overflowing respectable audience." It said:

> The audience part of the house, particularly, is neatly fitted up and when entirely ornamented, will, we think, be inferior to none in the United States. The chandelier is of very elegant construction and was splendidly illuminated with gas as were the floor lights of the stage.
>
> Nothing could succeed better as a first essay than the gas, and it certainly did great credit to the Engineers and will no doubt be a source of eventual benefit to the Manager and prove in the result a reward for his enterprise in this particular branch of his undertaking. The play was "Town and Country" and "Of Age To-Morrow."

The paper also admitted that "The scenery at the American Theater is deserving of praise: particularly the Roman Palace, Street Scene, Mansion House, A Wood, A Prison and a Cottage. They were painted by Mr. Mondel, an artist attached to the Theater."

1825 and 1826 were profitable seasons. Mr. Edwin Forrest, who was then 19 years old, was engaged and opened in Otway's "Venice-Preserved."

According to Sol Smith, in 1827 Caldwell "took his company to St. Louis where he converted a salt house on 2nd Street into a theatre, then to Nashville, Tenn."

In 1827, the cast was composed of Wm. J. H. Caldwell, Anderson, Jackson, Sol Smith, Lemuel, Smith, Sam Jones, R. Russell, Crampton, Gray, Lear, Hartwig, Lowery, Higgins, Cambridge, Palmer, McCafferty. And Mesdames: Hasting, Russell, Rowe, Blaxton, Johns, S. Smith, L. Smith, Jackson, Higgins, Crampton and Miss Russell. Again quoting Sol Smith:

> During the winter (1827-1828) Mr. Booth came to perform an engagement, was highly successful. I should say these were his best days. It was my luck to support him as the Physician in "King Lear" the Lord Mayor in "Richard the Third," and one of the citizens in each of the Roman pieces. After his engagement at the American Theater was finished, he performed "Orestes" twice in the French Theatre to crowded houses and to the great delight of the French population.

Pöstl, writing about the theaters of New Orleans, stated that the American playhouse opened during five months, whilst the French performed for eight months. He wrote:

> The American Theater has the advantage of becoming more and more national and popular, although at present it is only resorted to by the lower class of the American population: Boatmen, Kentuckians, Mississippi traders and backwoodsmen of every description. The late Charles Von Weber would not have been much delighted at witnessing the performance of his "Der Freyshutz," here metamorphosed into the wild huntsmen of Bohemia. Six violins which played anything but music and some voices far from being human, performed the opera which was applauded; the Kentuckians expressed their satisfaction in a hurrah, which made the very walls tremble. The interior of the theater had still a mean appearance. The curtain consists of two sail cloths and the horrible smell of whiskey and tobacco is a sufficient draw-back for any person who would attempt to frequent this place of amusement.
>
> The French theater performs the old classic productions of Corneille, Racine, Voltaire, with the addition of some new ones, such as "Regulus," "Marie Stewart," and "William Tell." The best performer of the theater is Madame Clauzel.

The Duke of Saxe-Weimar who visited the city at approximately the same time as Pöstl, gave his impression of the New Orleans theater as follows:

> Tragedy of "Regulus" and two vaudevilles. Dramatic corps was merely tolerable, such as those of the Provincial French towns, where they never presume to present tragedies and comedies of the highest class, —
>
> This is the same corps which the Philadelphians extol so highly, that one might almost suppose them equal to the artists of the Theatre Francais, if, unfortunately, one visit to the Theatre did not completely dispel the illusion.
>
> Regulus was murdered: Mr. Marchand and Madame Clauzel, whose husband performed the comic parts very well in the vaudeville, they alone distinguished themselves.
>
> The saloon is not very large — but most ornamented. Below are the pit and parquet and a row of boxes, each for four persons and before them a balcony.
>
> The boxes are not divided by walls, but only separated by a low partition so that ladies can exhibit themselves conveniently.
>
> Over the first row of boxes is a second, to which the free colored people resort and are not admitted to any other part of the theater. Above is the gallery in which slaves may go.
>
> Behind the boxes, a lobby where the gentlemen who do not wish to sit in a box, stand or walk about, where they see over the boxes.

Saxe-Weimar also attended the tragedy of "Mary Stewart" by LeBrun from Schiller, and a vaudeville, "La Demoiselle et la Dame." The first play was presented by request of several American families. He wrote:

> Madame Clauzel undertook the part of Mary Stewart and supported it in masterly style, but she was poorly supported. Unluckily, however, the machinery was not in order. At the close of the piece, when Lancaster falls in the greatest distraction into the arms of an officer of the guard, the curtain could not be lowered and several minutes elapsed before poor Lancaster could leave the painful attitude. The audience hissed.

The following communications, appearing in the *Courier*, related a disturbance attributed to Edwin Forrest, one of the greatest American actors of all times, which took place in the American Theater on November 16, 1833:

> After the curtain was dropped to the tragedy of "Brutus" on Wednesday evening, a scene of unexampled tumult took place occasioned by the non-appearance of Mr. E. Forrest in answer to a call made by a numerous portion of the audience.
>
> The manager partially succeeded in quelling the disorder by promising to send messengers to seek Mr. Forrest, who had left the theater soon after the conclusion of the play, and induce him to return. It is needless to relate the unusual expedient resorted to by the manager to allay the excitement; but the efforts were so unsuccessful as were those of the messengers employed to search for Mr. Forrest. At the suggestion of several gentlemen, the manager stopped the remainder of the entertainment and the audience peacefully retired.
>
> It was generally understood Mr. F. would appear *in propria persona*, and return his acknowledgment for the patronage of a warm and approving public — a pledge having been given on his benefit night, that on this occasion (Mrs. Russell's benefit) he would make his farewell bow to the audience. *On dit* — Mr. Forrest was aware of this public feeling and had prepared an address. We have heard several reasons assigned why he did not appear, but none sufficient to exonerate him from the charge of insulting a generous public, or at best, exhibiting a cold indifference to their good opinion. It remains for Mr. F. to vindicate his conduct on this business from any trifling and unworthy imputations.
>
> Signed: Publicola

The next day Edwin Forrest proffered his apologies:

> To the Public: An excitement having been produced on the evening of Wednesday last, on the occasion of Mre. Russell's benefit at the American Theater, originating as it is said in my

failing to obey the calls made by a portion of the audience, to appear before them after the arduous and exhausting duties of the evening and many ingenious and unjust statements having been circulated concerning the motive of non-appearance. I beg leave respectfully to assure the public that my immediate retirement from the theater was owing to fatigue and to my ignorance that on an occasion of this kind such an expression of feeling with propriety was to be expected by any one but the beneficiary.

To those who knew me it is unnecessary to say, I disclaim all intention of disrespect. To those who have so unadvisedly made my conduct the theme of cavil and misrepresentation — who said I was aware of the public feeling and had prepared an address — who have accused me of insulting a generous public — and of having exhibited a cold indifference to their good opinion — I say I repel their charges with indignation.

I am not insensible to the kindness with which I have been received, nor, while I remember that almost the first smile which gladdened my youth beamed on me in this city, can I for a moment think, without gratitude, that the same patronage rendered my recent engagement brilliant beyond expectation.

Signed: Edwin Forrest.

P.S. It has been said the announcement of my appearance, for the benefit of Mrs. Russell, was considered a pledge that I would address the audience. I sanctioned no such pledge; nor was such pledge intended to be understood in the announcement.

E. F.

The following day a communication to the *Courier* gave another version of the episode, it said:

Mr. Editor: Having been present at Mrs. Russell's benefit on Wednesday evening, when the disturbance occurred from the non-appearance of Mr. Forrest to the call of the audience, I was surprised at the extreme indecorum of Mr. Russell's deportment when addressing the house.

As Mr. Forrest has vindicated his conduct on that occasion, I beg leave to say a word respecting Mr. Russell, who it is said shortly assumes the management of the theater.

The gentleman ought to be aware of the impropriety of addressing the house with clinched hands and passionate look and ought to have governed his temper on such an emergency. I do not wish to prejudice the public mind against him at the outset of his managerial career, but I deem his manner was reprehensible; that unless he is more careful in the future in his bearing towards the audience, he cannot expect the same support and countenance which has been liberally awarded to Mr. Caldwell.

Signed (Keep Cool)

On May 24 another statement appeared defending "the indecorous conduct" by Mr. Russell.

At the end of the play, when Mr. Russell appeared in front of the curtain, there seemed to be a fixed determination in not submitting to what was then supposed a gross indignity towards the respectful and honorable calls upon Mr. Forrest for a bare "farewell" after his last performance; consequently Mr. Russell was refused a hearing, though he strenuously endeavored to make himself heard in the declaration that "Mr. Forrest was indisposed" — and finally, finding it impossible to succeed in his object, he elevated both his hands and his voice to the highest pitch and pronounced upon his honor that Mr. Forrest was not in the house, yet to little purpose, for very few heard or heeded his words. Mr. R. then retired with his "hands clinched," for ought I know and which I am not disposed to dispute, as it is the main assertion which "Keep Cool" uses as evidence in extreme decorum.

Your correspondent, Mr. Editor, has too entered upon the dignified task of depicting Mr. Russell's "looks." Now, Sir, any one who is a husband and a father, it is not to be presumed, could have any very pleasant feelings, or "looks" in beholding an amiable and inoffensive wife with her tender offspring, unprovokably and in gross violation of all gallantry and kindness, rudely driven from the stage by the hooting of some twelve or twenty persons, (not more, to the credit of an audience of five to six hundred, let it said).

Under these circumstances, Mr. R. asseverated that he was ignorant of any cause on his part that warranted the indignity of his consort and as to himself, he did not permit himself to inquire if there were any but with proper manliness, unqualifiedly asserted he was incapable of giving any. Such only was the conduct of a husband and father in protection of his wife and infant. Right or wrong, contempt to the man who would do less! Pity to him who would censure it!

The indignity, by the indecorous few, towards the lady, was severely denounced by the irresistible majority of the audience giving an affirmation to the inquiry of Mr. R. as to the pleasure of allowing Mre. Russell and child to proceed with the duet. The duet being completed without interruption, Mr. R. appeared to the calls of Mr. Forrest and after a most respectful assurance that his best efforts were ineffectual in finding Mr. F., asked if the farce should proceed without him. The audience decided in good republican style and without commotion, that the performance should cease if their wishes could not be complied with.

If there could be aught in all this, Mr. Editor, to warrant the attack made upon Mr. Russell by your correspondent, I confess my discernment is greatly at fault and I submit the statement to be disposed of as your sense of justice may dictate: and conceiving that the antidote should in the same channel through which the poison was administered, trust that the tax is not too great upon the limits of your respectable paper.

Signed: Plain Truth.

Edwin Forrest regained the good graces of his admiring public by delaying his departure for the express purpose of aiding the benefit performance for the Boys Asylum. The paper commented: "Having satisfactorily explained his recent conduct and by this unexpected zeal in the cause of the orphans, he cannot fail receiving the thanks and increased esteem of the New Orleans people."

On April 7, 1835, the *Bee* published the plans for the New American Theater to be constructed by Caldwell on St. Charles Street:

> The New American Theater! The site to be 130 ft. on St. Charles by 190 in depth. Main entrance in front will be connected with an entrance to a spacious arcade, situated on both sides of the theater — each 24 by 360 feet — running into Camp Street alongside of stores behind the theater. In the center of this theater will be a pavilion 24 ft. square and 60 ft. high, the height of the arcade.
>
> The front will be of Corinthian order — 10 columns and pilasters, projecting 12 ft. and supporting an entablature which will contain a balcony 100 by 12 feet. A balustrade over this entablature will be decorated with statues of Apollo and the Muses and a pediment supporting vases and ornaments with emblematic bas-relieves throughout the frieze — which will permit free ventilation in the grand salon. Entrance of the ground vestibule supported by fluted columns of Ionic order; staircases on either side leading to a similar vestibule above, surrounded by balustrades and leading to spacious corridors and to lobbies from 8 to 10 feet wide. Lobbies lead to the boudoirs, attached to the first tiers of boxes which hold 10 to 12 persons each. Inner staircases run from the lobbies to the second and third tier which are constructed as the first tier.
>
> Large space under the staircases in lobbies of first tier of boxes leads to an antechamber and to a small saloon, 42 by 25 feet — occupying part of the pavillion over the St. Charles Street arcade entrance, from the windows of which is a view of the whole line of the arcade — a continuation of three staircases leads to a grand saloon, 127 by 26 feet. On the South West a large entrance leading to the stage and dependencies.
>
> Through the vestibule in the main entrance and parallel to the principal doors, is the entrance to the lobbies leading to the pit — the pit parquet combined 59 feet wide and 49 feet deep,

the first will admit 700 persons seated in commodious seats with backs to them — the parquette will hold from 200 to 250 persons — orchestra, 40 to 50 musicians. On level with the pit under the first tier are private grated boxes of the same dimensions to those above. The proscenium is raised from the pit on a Corinthian order of four columns 40 feet in height over a rich pedestal resting on the stage, between columns is a stage box parallel to each tier, the proscenium is crowned by a cornice and terminates by an eleptic arch of 48 feet span by 54 feet high.

The stage is the largest in America and will rank with the largest in the world, 95 by 90 feet — clear passage of 18 feet all around the stage. The wing will be occupied as a scenery room, for managers, library, archives, properties, etc.

Double spacious staircases lead to performers' dressing rooms which are commodious — 24 of them 8 by 12 feet — with tailor shops and wardrobes, etc.

The height of the main walls — 86 feet — five tiers of boxes, including pit boxes and one for galleries — the theater would hold 5000 persons. It would contain commodiously 3000 persons.

On May 8, 1835, the corner stone was laid. The ceremonies were simple. Mr. George W. Hearsey made an appropriate address, his subject was, "Public buildings of all ages."

Besides the theater, Caldwell built a public bath with about forty tubs of marble and tin. He conducted a restaurant and a hotel of one hundred rooms for bachelors, with a reading room having all the leading periodicals, a chess room with backgammon boards, and a room where liqueurs, coffee and cigars were served. His orchestra was second to none — it included such distinguished musicians as Gambati and Norton, and also Schinotta, Maeder, Cassaloni, Myers, Kendal, Coiffi, Willis, Cherot and many others.

The cast was under the direction of Finn, a comedian as well as a stage manager. It included, Mesdames Maeder (formerly Clara Fisher) Brown, Kimlock, Crooke, Bannister, (late Stone) and the Misses Fanny Jarman, Philips, Lone, Pelham, Verity, Cushman and twelve others. The men were: Terman, J. R. Scott, Barton, Forbes, Latham, DeCamp, Webb, Larken, Hunt, Williamson, Spencer, Frimsley and Hill the Yankee.

The *Bee* of November 5, 1835, stated that the French Theater was to open on Saturday the 7th and Caldwell's on the 30th. Sol Smith claimed it opened on December 5th.

The paper predicted that Caldwell's orchestra "will be a good rival to that of the French Theater and we have no doubt of his

Camp Street in 1830, showing the American Theatre. At the right is the City Hotel. Drawing by H. Heinagle, 1830.

theater being well conducted. His boxes will be rented for $1,000.00 during the season: Tickets, first three rows of parquette $1.50, others $1.00. Miss Celeste, the celebrated danseuse, was engaged for four consecutive weeks at $5000.00; and two half-clear benefits. Russell's theater will be opened during the month."

The editor of the *Bee* stated on December 8, that he was greatly pleased with the order and decorum displayed in St. Charles Theater; — in all other theaters in this country, with the exception of the Orleans theater, the auditors are offended with graceless sights and grating sounds. The pits are usually devoted to persons of the meanest class, placed between the respectable auditors and the performers; so that immorality may have its full effect and astonish or affright the audience. This is not indeed the case at Camp Street theater; yet it, like others has its lures for ladies of a certain class and its dramshop for drunkards and smokers to excite loungers to licentiousness and disorders. Not so with the theater of Caldwell. He has no abiding places for the libidinous or disorderly; no pigeon holes or dram asylum within his theater — but a convenient place for respectable citizens according to his rank and means.

The utmost decorum is observed at all times and a mother and daughter can safely sit unmolested and unoffended in her box or boudoir at this theater, as in her parlor or drawing room at home.

And on February 28, 1836 the *Bee* said: "Caldwell's theater is now the frequent resort of the gay and fashionable. This is as it should be. He caters generously for the public; and should be substantially supported in his laudable efforts."

The Camp Street theater gave its first representation of the season on Thursday, November 19. The announcement said that the Nashville part of the Russell's Company had arrived with other actors from Louisville and Cincinnati. The cast was composed of Mr. and Mrs. and Miss Russell, Mr. and Mrs. Hodges, Miss Petrie, Mr. and Mrs. Hubbard, Mr. and Mrs. and Miss Barnes, Mesdames Knight, Sharp and Drake, and Messrs. Thorn, Farren, Pearson, Reynoldson and Parsons.

On May 22, the *Bee* announced the closing of the theaters and stated that they had a "tolerable run of business."

It also commented that "The French theater, fortunately for its manager, is conducted on the system of most European theaters, — having a good stock company without stars and producing good and new dramas." The *Bee* continued:

Russell's Theater did not succeed very well as he depended on stars for success — but when he depended on his whole Company he made money and should make $10,000.00 this season.

Caldwell's new theater not so successful — due to increased prices.

That year an Italian troupe made its appearance at the St. Charles theater at a cost to Caldwell of $20,000.00, which was claimed to be an extravagant sum. It was not a success and it was said that the theater lost $10,700.00.

At the end of November, 1836, a resolution was introduced in the Municipal Council authorizing the Mayor to subscribe $100,-000.00 in the Theater Company, stating that theatricals were indispensable to New Orleans.

It was claimed that the new St. Charles play house was the third largest in the world.

The address delivered by Mr. Caldwell on the opening night at his temporary theatre in Poydras Street was printed on posters and distributed throughout the city. It is here quoted in full.

NEW AMERICAN THEATER — NEW ORLEANS

As I am about to commence a new career in the theatrical business, a few observations may be expected from me by way of address. In attending, therefore, to that presumed expectation, although I must necessarily touch upon matters as painful to my recollection as they have been injurious to my fortunes, I hope most sincerely that the public will acquit me of any desire to awaken their sympathies.

I know that generally, addresses to the public, how much soever the writers of them may aver to the contrary, are expressly intended to excite sympathy as well as interest, for the man who says to you that he wants no sympathy asks for it in telling you so. I assert, however, that I am an exception to this general rule.

It will be generally conceded, I believe, that I am the founder of the Drama in New Orleans. I built the "American Theater" in 1822, which was really destroyed by a vile incendiary, who as yet I have not been able to bring to justice, although I still live in hopes of that event.

Such was the situation of the 6th Ward, which is now the 2nd Municipality, that the streets in which are some of the greatest monuments were scarcely even defined.

New Levee Street was then a continuous line of ponds for more than a mile, and Tchapitoulas and Magazine Streets could then boast of no better buildings than such as are denominated "shanties" with here and there the mouldering remains of a former plantation residence.

Camp Street at that time had only a few tobacco and cotton warehouses, and St. Charles Street was best known to the boys who sought in sport for snipe among the *lataniers* in the marshes, which has never been disturbed otherwise in its original growth.

The gradual raising of the walls of the first "American Theater," which walls are still standing, excited a great deal of animosity and naturally so, for people, conceiving no mercantile use for such a building, speculated jocularly on the idea of its being intended for a fortification.

For several years the people had to travel on gunwale sidewalks; and it is properly well remembered by several of our present residents, carriages could not be used after a heavy rain in places so far out of the way as Camp Street.

The success attendant on my building the American Theater rendered it the nucleus around which enterprises and commercial property first began to grow to the importance which may be said to have settled and called into existence the 2nd Municipality.

My enthusiasm in favor for the Drama and my strong feelings in favor of New Orleans, induced me in 1836 to build the St. Charles Theater and Arcade Baths. At this period I may state, merely for the purpose of explaining matters as I go along, that I had $176,000.00 — one hundred and seventy six thousand dollars, cash assets in my grasp. Circumstances of which all of us are more or less "the most humble servants" have left the St. Charles Theater; the Arcade Bath, and the Camp Street Theater among the things that were, and myself with an accumulation of losses and misfortunes almost too serious to be reflected on.

Well, however, I begin again; but instead of commanding my own large ship from my own quarter deck, I have chartered a smaller vessel to embark for sea in the search of another golden shore from which I may gather means to erect another (for so I suppose I should) REAL ST. CHARLES.

Sol Smith wrote that "this was soon followed by the end of Mr. Caldwell's career. This poster appeared early in January, six weeks after the opening of the new house in Poydras Street and one week before the St. Charles opened its doors. It appeared from his own statement that his 'new project' had not been 'profitable to his purse.' It will be for others to judge whether it had been laudatory to his character."

A few years afterwards Caldwell published what might be called a valedictory as he closed his theatre for good — the theatre he loved so passionately and for which he had risked so much. His announcement was received with deep emotion and sincere regret by the people of New Orleans.

AMERICAN THEATER

This establishment will be closed for the season, Saturday the 10th instant.

The lessee is constrained to say that the situation of the times, to which alone can be attributed the night losses, compels him in a course unavoidable as it is painful to his feelings.

It is now my painful duty to announce that I shall retire from the drama altogether — It is no longer a profession for a sensitive mind to follow; and as to pecuniary profit, the following facts, I hope, will illustrate to the world that I have done for it what few men with capital would have thought of.

From the day of the completion of the St. Charles Theater, on the 30th of November, 1835, to its conflagration of the 13th of March, 1842, I have expended in the support of its losses $100,000.00.

Had I the means I should in very pride continue on in the hope which constantly cherished me in the St. Charles, that better times would return and that the Drama would meet with a competent support. Not possessing them, I must, though reluctantly, abandon it, and seek some employment by which I may live, for loss and double ruin is the inevitable result of a managerial career in the present time.

Caldwell then devoted all his time to the promotion of the use of gas for illumination. He established gas companies in Mobile and Cincinnati and soon recouped his lost fortune.

Sol Smith, who acted with him and who knew him very well eulogized him as follows:

> I can express my opinion of Mr. Caldwell as an actor in a better way than by saying I have never yet beheld his equal in a light comedy, Murdock comes the nearest to him (of those I have seen) and Charles Mathews next.
>
> Mr. C. played the whole range of tragedy and but for some mannerism, such as drawling out certain words as if he was running the chromatic scale of the gamut in music, no actor gave better satisfaction to Southern audiences than he did. He was scrupulously guarded in giving the true text of Shakespeare when performing his characters. In the later years of his life he only appeared in Comedy, and in that he was unapproachable.

The fame of Caldwell as an actor may be dimmed with the passing years, but he will always remain a colorful personality in the history of New Orleans. His versatility, his business acumen, his promotional ability and the prominent part he played in the development of the city will long be remembered, but his greatest claim to fame is that he introduced gas light to the city.

Opera in the English language was first presented in New Orleans in 1833 by Caldwell. Sol Smith described the event as follows:

> The production of "Cinderella" at New Orleans formed an era in theatrical annals. Though a hodge-podge (made up of Rossini's original work of the same name and other productions of that composer, "William Tell" being largely drawn upon) it was the first attempt at grand opera in the English language at the South. All previous attempts had been confined to what is termed the comic opera — the "Barber of Seville" (an English adaptation), "Marriage of Figaro," "Love in a Village," "Devil's Bride," etc. The cast of "Cinderella," had the advantage of beautiful scenery and appointments, its success was very great.

Isidore Lowenstern from Leipsig, who visited the city in 1835 and who was severely critical in his chronicles of New Orleans, wrote this about its theaters:

> The St. Charles Theater presents operas with ballets, tragedies and dramas. I have attended a presentation of "La Juive" d'Halévy which was staged with a magnificence quite uncommon in America at a cost of $20,000.00.
>
> Some of the singers were fair, but the public did not appreciate them. This happens frequently in America, where all that is not extremely bad, the taste of the Americans being such that only the detestable things are applauded with frenzy.
>
> The French theater plays to a public of better taste and more competent to judge, but they are not impartial enough. It is here as elsewhere that the lesser artists give the tone with a vehemence too loud to be gracious. In "Pie Voleuse" the prima donna, who held secondary roles at the Theater Feydeau [a celebrated theater of Paris] was fairly good, the rest of the singers were mediocre, but certainly they were better than those to be found in the provincial play houses.
>
> The vaudeville which followed the opera was chosen as badly as it was executed.
>
> The American Theater specialized in comedies and other plays, to please the public. They are exaggeratedly performed.

This was the premiere representation of the grand opera "La Juive" in the United States.

With the advent of that magnificent theater, the St. Charles, the rivalry existing between the Americans and the Creoles flared up with renewed vigor. Faults and deficiencies which heretofore had been unobserved were detected about the Theater d'Orleans, and reflected in the press. The cry rose that it was too small, a fire hazard and a potential holocaust.

An editorial appeared in the French section of the *Bee* on March 24, 1837, stating that the hall was insufficient and uncomfortable. Its complaint was:

> The entrances and the exits are so small and so badly marked that one trembles at the thought of the disaster that may result from the vice of an imperfect construction. But what is more remarkable is the faulty distribution of the loges, the number of places where one can neither hear nor see and the tendency of the corridors to absorb the sound made by passers-by.
>
> What could have been tolerated some thirty years ago, in a nascent town, is not suitable in a city of so rapid growth and in which the population has increased so much that the building activity, although as great as it is, cannot accommodate the multitude of strangers, which every day reach here from every point of the globe. A new theater is badly needed.

This was the beginning of a campaign which resulted eventually in the building of the renowned French Opera House.

The following is a sample of the advertisements by the Orleans Theater.

THEATRE D'ORLEANS
Dimanche 5 Juin, 1831

Pour la troisieme et derniere representation de l'engagement de Mme. Féran.

Spectacle et Concert
Ariel del Sr Mayer, ce chi dice mal d'amore
Chanté par Mme Feran

2°-

Grand duo del Sr Mereodente "Oh non Lusciarmi"
Chanté par Mme Féran et Mme Saint Clair.

3°-

Célébres variations del Sr Paccini "Non Non ha diletto alcor:
Chanté par Mme Féran

Le Spectacle commencera par
MA TANTE AURORE
ou
LE ROMAN IMPROMPTU
Opera en deux acts de Boyeldieu
Mardi prochain 7 Juin, benefice de Mme Feran.

CHAPTER XXXVIII

PATRIOTIC CELEBRATIONS

The anniversary of the battle of New Orleans, Washington's Birthday, and the 4th of July were always observed with great patriotic fervor. On these occasions the militia participated in resplendent glory. These celebrations usually followed the same pattern except for some slight modification. It is impossible in the scope of this work to describe them all, so it must be limited to a few of the most interesting ones.

The *Louisiana Gazette* reported the celebration of the 4th of July in 1821 as follows:

> The 4th of July was celebrated in this City by a parade of volunteer uniform companies in the morning, and by public dinners, the ascension of a balloon and fireworks in the afternoon. At midday the City was remarkably stilled, no salutes from the band of naval artillery burst upon the ear, and the silence and loneliness of the streets were but little indication of so great a national holiday.
>
> The troops looked well in the morning, but the number of files to a company were very small indeed; eight of the latter were on parade, and yet the whole battalion counted no more than 140 men. It must be said to their honor that our Volunteers were more numerous in "times that tried men's souls," a company that mustered 25 men on the 4th marched 120 men to the field on December 1814.

"Feuilleton" reported the banquet which took place at Fascati's as having been a very brilliant and magnificent dinner, "where Republican toasts were proposed." There was a balloon ascension and fireworks, in fact nothing was missing. The Mayor presided at the banquet, as well as Mr. Livingston and many respectable citizens. Speeches were made and toasts drunk to Independence, the United States, the Marines, Washington, and to the Army. They were all received as they should have been, and patriotic songs and artillery salvos preceded the orators. Governor Robinson did not participate, nor did he send a representative.

In 1823 the 4th of July was celebrated in a dignified and elaborate manner with a Te Deum at the Cathedral and the reading of the Declaration of Independence in French and English. The

Church was opened to ladies accompanied by gentlemen at 10 o'clock and to the public at 11 a.m.

The procession started at the Government House and proceeded to the Cathedral where orations were delivered. The procession began at 11 a.m. and the order of march was:

Military escort
Marshal
Governor and Suite
Secretary of State and Treasurer
Members of Congress
Mexican Ambassador and Suite
Judges of the United States Supreme Court
Attorney General and United States District Attorney
Marshal and Clerk of the United States Court
Members of the Bar
Foreign Consuls
The Reverend Clergy
Committee on Arrangement
Orators of the Day
Mayor and Corporation
Collector, Naval Officer and Surveyor
Officers of the Army, Navy, and Marine Corps of the U. S.
Officers of the State of Louisiana
Physicians
Masonic Lodges
Citizens and Members of Volunteer Corps in Uniform

"Feuilleton" remarked that the Volunteer's Corps should have numbered from four hundred to five hundred men, but there were only about one hundred and forty men, and out of forty-eight officers twenty-three failed to appear.

On January 10, 1824, the *Louisiana Gazette* gave the following report of the 8th of January celebration:

> At dawn there was a discharge of artillery. The ships in the port displayed their flags. At 12 o'clock both houses of the General Assembly preceded by the Governor, and accompanied by various public authorities, and escorted by Captain Vignie's troop, proceeded to the Cathedral.
>
> Upon crossing the public square the procession was saluted with military honors by the Louisiana Legion. After a general discharge of artillery and small arms, the procession returned to

the Government House. Pious addresses to the Throne of Grace were delivered by the Rev. Mr. Clapp and by Mr. McCaleb.

The following year the Battle of New Orleans was celebrated with more than usual splendor. Again we are indebted to the *Gazette* for the following description of the oçcasion:

> All assembled at the Capitol at 12 o'clock, marched in procession under the escort of Captain Vignie's Corps of Cavalry and Captain Harper's company of the New Orleans Fencibles, to the Cathedral.
>
> The Governor and Secretary at the head of the procession, preceded by G. W. Morgan, Esq., Sheriff of the Parish of New Orleans, and his deputy.
>
> The procession was received by the Venerable Bishop Dubourg in his full episcopal robe and surrounded by the Clergy amongst whom was Father Antoine de Sedella, upon whose meek and pious brow more than four score years' had seemed to stamp the hope, the faith, and the fortitude of the Christian.
>
> There seated the Bishop meekly turning his eyes to Heaven, as if imploring the benediction of the Most High on this nation. Father Gallager delivered a most chaste, pious and classical discourse in English.
>
> Messrs. Mercier and Ducros delivered excellent discourses in French, which were highly applauded by the audience. The Te Deum was solemn and impressive — Organ — Thunder of Artillery — Musquetry. The Governor then reviewed the Legion.

The Irish Volunteers, commanded by Captain John McGrath, celebrated the 8th of January 1832 with target shooting for a medal at Tivoli Gardens, and a banquet.

A joint meeting of the Legislature and the City Council took place in February, 1832 for the purpose of formulating plans for the celebration of George Washington's birthday. E. A. Canon and C. M. Conrad were chosen to deliver orations in French and English. The committee agreed that no two gentlemen could have been chosen better able to do justice to the memory of Washington.

The following resolutions were passed at the joint meeting:

Article I: The Clergy of New Orleans are invited to join in Te Deum at the Cathedral at 11 a.m.

    All officials to attend a procession to be formed at 10 o'clock at the old Convent. G. W. Morgan, marshal; J. H. Holland, deputy marshal.

Article II: Commanding officers of the State troops and the Legion are invited to parade.

Article III: Captains of ships and steam boats to hoist their flags.
Article IV: Artillery to fire national salute at break of day, and 100 guns at 1 p.m.
Article V: House occupied by the Legislature to be illuminated and citizens to illuminate their dwellings. Railings around the public square and the trees therein to be illuminated.
Article VI: Courts and businesses to be closed that day. Committee of Senate: T. Thomas, T. Landry, T. Nichols. Committee of House; P. Landreau, A. Lacoste, D. Edwards. Committee of City Council, S. D. Dixon, T. Roby, E. Blanc.

On December 23, 1832, the anniversary of the battle fought in 1814 was observed, not in celebration, but as a memorial day for the many thousands who that year were victims of the devastating epidemic of cholera. The *Courier* gave the following interesting report of what transpired:

Funeral services were performed in honor of the memory of those who fell victim of the epidemic, and to whom military honor had not been paid. The weather was gloomy. in the midst of the Square a platform was erected, with five steps leading to it, and from them rose an obelisk of about 60 feet, on a base resembling a tomb, designed by J. Pilié. On each side was inscribed "To the Manes of our Fellow Citizens"; *"Aux manes de nos citoyens"*. Fronting the Cathedral under the obelisk rose an altar.

At ten o'clock, the Legion forming around the monument, the Governor and other superior and civil officers were admitted to the center.

At 11 o'clock de Necker, Bishop of New Orleans, accompanied by the clergy entered the Cathedral to sing the Te Deum in honor of the Anniversary of the 23rd of December, 1814. D. Augustin was the orator of the day.

In 1833 the celebration of the 4th of July was greatly curtailed because it may have been the means of again enkindling cholera, that dread disease which had then nearly disappeared.

Immediately after the Louisiana Purchase, Washington's birthday and the 4th of July were celebrated appropriately by religious services in the Cathedral, followed by the singing of the Te Deum; the delivery of patriotic orations; and military processions and the roaring of artillery; in which activities the whole population participated with due reverence. The anniversary of the Battle of New Orleans was also commemorated in solemn dignity. As the city increased in population these celebrations assumed more of a holiday spirit, while still maintaining their religious solemnity. These days were devoted to public festivities. The turning-out of the militia in all its glory, the vessels in the port bedecked with multi-colored flags, the pealing of the church bells, the salvos of artillery, the detonation of musketry, the fanfare of trumpets, the rumbling of drums, the pyrotechnic displays, the balloon ascensions, the reading of the Declaration of Independence, both in French and English, the sumptuous banquets for the elite of the city, and, not least, the outbursts of oratory — all created a patriotic fervor seldom found in any other city in the Union.

CHAPTER XXXIX

LAFAYETTE VISITS NEW ORLEANS

One of the transcendent events of the period was the visit to New Orleans of the Marquis Marie Joseph Paul Yves Roch Gilbert DuMotier de La Fayette. It was one of these rare occasions when bickerings, animosities, rivalries, and jealousies between the two elements of the population were cast aside, for all were in accord to honor the great Frenchman.

The Gallic population honored him because the patriot was of the same origin as they, and the Anglo-Saxons felt they owed him a debt of gratitude and had an unbounding admiration for the great Revolutionary hero. All were united in their love and admiration for that remarkable man.

Lafayette was the first choice of President Thomas Jefferson for the Governorship of the Territory of Louisiana; the office was his had he so wished. He was eligible, as he had been proclaimed a citizen of the United States by a grateful nation. Lafayette was the guest of the nation, and this tour of the country gave him the opportunity to observe its extraordinary growth and progress.

The people of New Orleans always did love parades and pageantry and here was an occasion for them to distinguish themselves. Plans were set on foot immediately to honor their illustrious visitor.

The General arrived in Mobile on the 5th of April 1825. The steamboat Natchez was dispatched to that city where it arrived the next day at 8:00 PM, and was placed at the disposal of the distinguished guest. On board to greet Lafayette was a deputation of three of the Governor's aides, Colonels Fort, Morse and Ducros; and four members of the Committee on Arrangement, Joseph Armand Duplantier, a comrade-in-arms of the General, Gen. Jacques Philippe Villeré, Maj. Costera Davezac and Urquhart. The Natchez left Mobile with its passengers the following day, and on the 9th at 8:00 A.M., crossed the bar, receiving a salute from the Fort of Plaquemine at noon and anchoring at Morgan's Plantation at midnight.

As early at ten o'clock in the morning, a large fleet of steamboats crowded with ladies and gentlemen, joined the Natchez and escorted her to the Chalmette Battleground where the levee was lined with thousands of greeters shouting their welcome. Again there was a salvo of artillery. Lafayette was attended by twelve grand marshals and the members of the arrangement committee. He was placed in an elegant Landau, drawn by six beautiful grey horses, and escorted to the plantation home of Mr. Montgomery, the headquarters of General Jackson, which he entered, leaning on the arms of Generals Duplessis and Villeré. The *Louisiana Gazette* reported the event:

The carriage, escorted by the General's Staff, the Governor's Aides and the cavalry, drove to the Montgomery home. The spectators who had already collected on the spacious circular galleries seemed to obstruct the entrance, but the crowd opened in respectful silence at the sight of the veteran. The Governor then advanced to meet the Guest of Louisiana. He was evidently much agitated. The scene was imposing; the field of the 8th of January was in sight; and before him stood the warriors of Brandywine and York; the emotion was universal; he remained for a moment unable to give utterance to the feelings of his heart before Governor Johnson addressed General Lafayette as follows:

"Louisiana enjoys to day the singular felicity of receiving on her soil, him, whom the Nation with one acclaim, hails as its guest; who combating in the cause of freedom and of man, shed his blood for her, long before she had risen a new star in the Federal Constellation."

"General! She did not share with you in the toil and glory of the war of Independence; but she knows and will appreciate as highly as her elder sisters in the Union, the part you bore and the signal service you rendered in the arduous struggle. Her inhabitants are as ardently attached to the principles as their brethern, and so are firmly resolved to preserve inviolate the blessings conquered by their ancestors. Nor does their love of country rest on wordy professions. They can point to a testimonial the ground on which you tread. It was here that with their companions in arms, led by the gallant Jackson, they met a haughty, experienced foe and raised a proud monument of American valor. We search in vain the annals of history for a victory achieved under the circumstances which rendered this so splendid and glorious. It relieved the soil from the tread of hostile footsteps and furnished a trophy not unworthy of arresting the eye of the warrior who reared the banner of America over the redoubt of Yorktown."

"In the name of the people of Louisiana I welcome the Veteran Patriot on a spot hallowed by the blood of patriots. We have in common with the whole people of the United

States a cheering satisfaction that the friend of our nation's youth has come in his old age, to survey the fabric his hands have contributed to rear. You have beheld with some complacency, the advancement of half a century of those states which formed the immediate theatre of action! You will find in Louisiana, one subject of consolation and delight, which no other part of the United States can present to you, and you will here percive that your generous efforts in the cause of freedom have not wholly failed in behalf of those who can boast of the same origin with you.

"This state settled by Frenchmen and principally inhabited by their descendents, enjoys as a member of the American Confederacy the full measure of their liberty for which you toiled and bled. And the wise and temperate use which Frenchmen have been made of it is a triumphant answer to those who have proclaimed them unfit for freedom and stigmatized you for laboring to confer on them the greatest of all blessings."

"In lands bathed by this magnificent river and its tributary streams, where fifty years ago civilization had not worked its luminous trade, you will see new states that have sprung into existence, strong in resources and youthful exuberance. Where then the restless Indians roamed in unproductive forests, you will see smiling fields, thriving towns, busy commerce and a free enterprising population skilled in all the arts which dignify and adorn the abode of social existence."

"In casting up the sum of happiness already attained you will be gratified, but how much will your generous soul dilate when it looks forward to the prospective increase of years to come! The ever active energies of civil and religious liberty will continue to advance."

"New states will rise and millions yet unborn will bless with the same fervor, that we feel, the illustrious philantrophist whose virtue achieved the glorious work of American liberty."

"As chief Magistrate and in behalf of the Louisianians, I again cordially bid you a welcome to this land."

After Governor Henry Johnson had delivered his address, there was a moment of subdued emotion which heightened the dramatic effect of that historical scene. As Lafayette rose to answer that warm welcome, the audience stood up spontaneously and with thunderous applause voiced the welcome of their Governor. After a few moments the distinguished guest partly regained his composure and with his voice still choaked with emotion, he began his address:

When I found myself in your magnificent river, within the limits of this commonwealth by which I have been so honorably and so affectionately invited, the emotions of French and American patriotism have united in my heart, so they have mingled in the blessed Union which have made Louisiana part of that republican confederacy that has risen for the happiness of existing millions, of numberless millions yet to come and for the example of mankind, these feelings are still forcibly executed at this, when I was in the name of the State, most affectionately welcomed by their respected chief Magistrate, on this glorious spot. Here, Sir, under the guidance of the Illustrious Jackson, and after a masterly attack of a landing enemy, the blood of the sons of revolutionary contemporaries, has mingled with the blood of the native sons of Louisiana, on that memorable and in its circumstances, unparalleled victory, which so spendidly terminated a war, just in its principles and most gallantly supported by both elements. You are pleased, Sir, to congratulate me for my enjoyments in the wonders I have hitherto witnessed, and for those that still await me, enjoyments the more delightful to an American veteran as in those wonders we find so many irresistible arguments in favor of the principles upon which have been foisted our standard of independence and freedom.

I am particularly obliged to your friendly and liberal observations, that in this state a daily evidence is given of the fitness of a French population for a wise use of the blessings of free institutions and self government, to which I must add that in the same instance you find in evidence of the great share that the intrigues of European despotism and aristocracy have had in those deplorable excesses which have hitherto retarded the establishment of freedom in France, I beg you and through you, my dear Sir, I beg the people and the Legislature of Louisiana to accept my respectful, devoted and affectionate acknowledgement.

After the exchange of compliments, a delegation of ladies headed by Bernard Marigny, braved the bad weather to pay their respects to the distinguished visitor. Marigny was not on the committee, which was very unusual, and for him not to have the chance to display his oratory on such an occasion was most disconcerting. But he was not a man to be denied, for at the request of the ladies, he was given the opportunity to welcome Lafayette. The report said that he "expressed in a short and effective address, their love and gratitude to him."

Every one present was presented to the General, and he in turn introduced his son, George Washington, and his friends, Messrs. Levasseur and Syan.

As the day drew to a close, the General was escorted to his carriage, and a procession formed according to the pre-arranged plan. The triumphal procession marched as follows:

The Grand Marshals were: C. W. Morgan (sheriff of the City) Gen. J. B. Plauché, Col. B. Shaumburg, Col. James Sterret, L. Moreau Lislet, W. Montgomery, J. R. Grymes, P. F. Dubourg, John H. Holland, Martin Duralde, J. F. Canonge, Edmond F. Fouché.

Two Marshals
A troop of cavalry
Landeau of General Lafayette

The carriage of George Washington Lafayette and Colonel Levasseur, a friend of the general's.

The carriages of the Revolutionary officers and soldiers.
The carriages of the Committee on Arrangements.
The carriages of the Secretary of State and the Governor's private Secretary.

One of the Marshals
Military escort commanded by Brigadier General Robeson
One of the Marshals
Attorney General and State Treasurer.
Mayor, Recorder, City Council and officers.
Members of Congress present.
Members of the Assembly present
Judges, Attorneys, Clerks, and Marshals of the U. S. District Court.

Judges of the Supreme Court and officers.
District Judge of 1st District Court and officers
Judge of the Criminal Court and officers
Judge of Parish Court and officers and Register of Wills
Judge of the City Court, Marshal and Clerk
One of the Marshals
Officers of the Army and Navy of the United States
Major General Lacoste and suite
Militia officers not on duty.
Ministers of Gospel
Collector of the Port and officers, harbor master and port wardens.

Members of the Bar
Register of Mortgages and Notaries Public
Presidents of the Banks and other incorporated institutions
One of the Marshals
The citizens

As the procession approached the lower portion of the City there was another national salute. The troops were drawn in order at the lower limit of the City where they were reviewed by the General and the Governor. The procession then continued under the direction of the Marshals, and marched to Esplanade, down that street to Royal, Royal to Canal, Canal to Chartres, down Chartres to Toulouse, up Toulouse to Levee, and down Levee to the front of the Public Square.

At the square an arch was erected in his honor. The *Louisiana Gazette* gave the following description of that Arch of Triumph:

It was 5 ft. 6 in. in its base in front, the span was 20 ft. by 40 ft. high, columns 15 ft., 9 ins. in front by 63 feet in height. The columns on the right represented *Liberty* bearing in her right hand *Strength,* with which she was bearing upon the many headed monster. On the left the *Cap of Liberty.* On the left of the arch where *Justice* was represented, bearing a balance in the right hand and a sword in the left. Two heralds of *Fame* surmounted these two figures and met above the arch where they united the names of Washington and Lafayette. Above these was a cornice of the Doric order, bearing the names of Revolutionary worthies: Warren, DeTousaud, Hamilton, Duportaille, Putnam, D'Estaing, Knox, Polosky, Montgomery, Degrasse, Gates, Rochambeau, Lee, DeKalb, Green and Koskiusco. The interior was decorated with the names of those who signed the Declaration of Independence.

Again at the triumphal arch there was an outburst of oratory.

Addresses of welcome were made by Mayor Roffignac and Recorder Denis Prieur, which were responded to by Lafayette.

The inclemency of the weather was such that the proposed procession through the streets had to be abandoned and the General was escorted through the arch to the Presbytery, to the quarters prepared for his reception in the Council Chambers.

All boats were decorated and the different religious societies rang their bells. The citizens illuminated their homes on the night of the General's arrival. The Committee on Arrangements wore a blue badge on their left lapel.

Although the weather continued wet and uncomfortable throughout the day, it did not in any way dampen the enthusiasm of the crowd. In fact, one of the reporters stated that "the turnout was more general than any we have ever witnessed in the State."

During his stay in the City, Lafayette received visitors every day between the hours of 10 A.M. to 2 P.M. He was entertained both at the American and the French Theater, where he received a most enthusiastic reception. And the Grand Masonic Lodge of Louisiana gave in his honor a sumptuous banquet at the John Davis Hotel.

On the 15th at nine o'clock in the morning, he embarked on the steamboat *Natchez* for Baton Rouge.

The State appropriated $15,000.00 to defray the expenses of a reception "worthy of the patriotic warrior whom the American people delight to honor."

Thus came to an end the most magnificent display of hospitality ever seen in New Orleans.

CHAPTER XL

NAPOLEON'S DEATH MASK

On Saturday, November 8, 1834, an immense crowd gathered on the Levee. The word had spread in the French section of the City that a distinguished visitor would disembark, that he would be their guest for an indefinite period, and perhaps that he would make the city his permanent domicile.

At no time has there been in New Orleans a greater display of enthusiasm for a private individual, not a dignitary nor a national hero, but for one whose only claim to fame was that he had attended Napoleon Bonaparte in his exile at St. Helena. Bonapartists who had participated in the Emperor's hour of triumph and who after the debacle chose exile rather than remain in their native land ruled by a monarch; Frenchmen who remembered with nostalgia their ancestral homes under the Empire; and Creoles, though true Americans, thrilled with the fame and glory of Napoleon, assembled at the landing to welcome his doctor. It was reported that a "large concourse of citizens, without previous concert, immediately assembled for the purpose of adopting measures expressive of their feelings at the event."

Francesco Antommarchi was born in Corscia on July 5, 1789. He acquired his medical education in Pisa and Florence, and at the age of nineteen was the favorite student of the great Florentine anatomist, Mascagni. At that time his work "Planches Anatomique du Corps Humain" appeared in Paris. It was predicted that he would succeed to the chair of his great teacher. During the years 1817 and 1818, Antommarchi devoted himself exclusively to his scientific studies, which were interrupted when he was called to act as surgeon to Napoleon at St. Helena.

Dr. Antommarchi left Rome in 1819, after receiving verbal instructions from Napoleon's family. Accompanied by the Abbé Buonaviti, the Abbé Vignalli, a cook and a butler, he reached London, and embarked at Gravesend on his sad mission.

For two years Dr. Antommarchi attended the Emperor on his island of exile. His deportment there, his opposition to Dr. Gall, his relationship with the Emperor, have all been the subject of historical conjecture. But this fact is accepted, he was the one who presided at the death bed of the great warrior, closed his eyes, made the autopsy, preserved his heart in an urn, and prepared the remains for burial.

After the death of the Emperor, the doctor returned to England in July 1821, and proceeded to Italy to resume his research in Anatomy and to publish the works of Professor Mascagni. But for some reason or other he failed in that enterprise. He then returned to Paris, where he published his "Planches Anatomique." He contributed at least eight works on Anatomy and on the history of Napoleon. Antommarchi not only basked in the reflected glory of having served the Emperor during the last years of his life, but he also achieved distinction in his own right.

As soon as his ship had docked at New Orleans Dr. Antommarchi came ashore and was escorted by a deputation led by Judge Maurian to Davis' Ball Room, where a reception was held in his honor. Judge Maurian made the address of welcome, appropriately answered by the distinguished guest, "who expressed the most lively gratitude for the hospitality with which the citizens of New Orleans had received him." Dr. Formento, on behalf of the physicians of the City welcomed Dr. Antommarchi "and tendered him whatever services he might require."

That same evening Dr. Antommarchi was serenaded at his home by the artists of the Theatre d'Orleans. Popular airs were sung, hilarity prevailed, and many toasts were proposed. It was the hope of his friends that he would reside permanently in the city. During the evening the doctor related some new incidents in the life of the great Corsican, which were listened to with rapt attention.

Dr. Antommarchi had come to New Orleans because of the many frustrations, and especially because of the ingratitude of the French government which injustice he resented. In New Orleans he hoped he would find peace and tranquility in the practice of his profession. The following letters give one of the motives which induced his expatriation:

Paris, August 25, 1834

To Mr., the President of the Consul des Ministeres:
Mr. Mareshal:

I have already renewed the offer for my services, made to the King, to transfer the mortal remains, to France, of the Emperor Napoleon, now resting at St. Helena.

Although on the eve of leaving France, my offer still holds, although far away I will always be ready to execute the orders transmitted to me by the Government. I consider it a formal obligation. In thus acting, I am fulfilling a pious duty of gratitude, and the happiest day of my life, would be the one, when I will be able to give a new evidence of my devotion to the memory of Emperor Napoleon, and to deserve the respect of my fellow citizens.

        Signed: F. Antommarchi   Medecin de
                                              l'Emperor Napoleon.

* * * * * *

Monsieur the Grand Mareshal:

As I am on the eve of leaving France for New Orleans, I feel obligated to let you know the reason for my departure.

The Emperor Napoleon, had, in his will, assured my destiny and my fortune. Because of obstacles which he could not foresee his benevolent intentions in my respect have not been fulfilled. They have ignored the conservative measures which I had taken to assure their fulfillment. My rights, as well as my letters, have been ignored, so I am today obliged to resort to the tribunals. It would be very painful for me to assist in those judicial debates.

To my great regret, I am leaving France, and I would love to think, Monsieur le Mareshal, that you do not disapprove of the motives which induced me to make that resolution. I hope that you will continue to do justice to the one who had the advantage to have met you on the soil of exile, and who had the sad honor to assist in the long agony of the greatest man of centuries, and to have closed his eyes.

A letter from Havre, dated September 24, announced that Dr. Antommarchi had left France so that "he will not assist in these sad debates destined to assure him of the fortune willed to him by the Emperor, which is still being disputed a long time after the death of the testator. He goes to New Orleans, at last, to put to profit his science and his profession."

On November 28, Antommarchi, in a letter to the Editor of the *Bee* announced his intention to practice medicine in New Orleans, he wrote:

Sir: When yielding to honorable and generous solicitations, I have always acted with the philantropic principles which have always been the guide of my actions — Happy, if in the discharge of my professional duties, I can alleviate suffering humanity, and to rendered myself useful to some few Louisianans, who may suffer from infirmity or from disease.

In order to do this, I respectfully inform the public that I will give medical advice at the following places, viz: At Mr. Girod's corner, St. Louis and Chartres, from 10 O'clock A.M. until noon; for the poor (gratuitously) every Monday and Thursday in each week; at Mr. R. Trodeunix's No. 13 Royal Street, for all other persons, every day between the hours of 12 and 1 O'Clock P.M.; and if any persons request it, I will visit patients at their residences.

He also offered his memoirs for sale at the book store of Alfred Moret on Royal Street.

With this announcement the renowned doctor, the man who had been bequeathed a large legacy by a great Emperor, which the country he had served well and faithfully denied him, at the age of forty-five, began the practice of medicine in a foreign land.

Antommarchi, touched by the cordial reception with which he was received, decided that he would show his appreciation by donating the death mask of Napoleon to the City. The City Council passed a resolution of acceptance, and the date for that ceremony was set for Thursday, the 20th of November. A Committee was deputized to call on the Doctor to inform him that the City Council had decided to accept the precious glift he had so generously offered.

The *Bee* of November 17, editorially commented in its French section:

... for us, Napoleon is a man worthy of the greatest excellence. We must see Napoleon as a man of war, and what people more than a republican one, can have the feeling of the greatest gratitude for the one, whose origin was so low that he could rise to such great height. .

His image should not be covered, nor should there be any fear to expose it to the public, it should be exposed in a place where anyone may contemplate at leisure."

The ceremony of acceptance of the mask of Napoleon was held on Saturday, the 22nd of November. The Recorder delivered the address of acceptance, which was answered by Dr. Antommarchi. It was exhibited in the chamber of the City Council.

Immediately after the death of Napoleon, Antommarchi made a plaster mold of his head, but it was not until 1833 that the bronze casts were cast. It is claimed that there were but five: two are in Vienna, one in the Louvre and the other in New Orleans. The fifth is supposed to have been donated by Antommarchi to a German physician, a brother-in-arms in the Russian war.

The mask bears the following inscription: "Dr. F. Antommarchi — Fondé par S. Richard deQuesnel de Paris." On a medal attached are these words surrounding an engraved head of the Emperor: "Napoleon Empereur et Roi—Dr. Antommarchi—1833."

In general the portraits of Napoleon convey the impression that his head was unusually large, but the mask shows that this was not the case for his head was beautiful in its conformation.

Since 1840 the mortal remains of Napoleon have rested in stately grandeur in a sarcophagus of porphyry under the dome of the Hotel des Invalides in Paris. By a strange coincidence, and through the vagaries of chance, New Orleans has the only death mask of Napoleon in the Western Hemisphere, and that its repository should be the Cabildo, the building in which he transferred Louisiana to the United States. It is fitting that the mask be in the city that named one of his principal avenues after Napoleon, as well as a series of streets commemorating his victories, Berlin, Milan, Marengo, Jena and Austerlitz. During the first World War, the hysterical frenzy of patriotic fervor caused the changing of the name of Berlin Street to General Pershing Street, thereby breaking the street sequence of the Emperor's victories. And in this same city admirers purchased an elegantly furnished home, still known as the Napoleon House, in the hope that a blockade running expedition under the command of the privateer, the lieutenant of the Lafittes, Dominique You, would not only rescue the ex-emperor from his prison island, but would bring him to New Orleans. This idea became useless at the news of Napoleon's death. If by any chance that expediton could have succeeded, what a chapter in history it would have made!

Francesco Antommarchi, smarting under the ingratitude of his country, a disappointed and frustrated man, after a comparatively short stay, left New Orleans. The last heard of him was in 1838 when he died in Cuba.

He will long be remembered here as the man who presented the death mask of Napoleon to the City of New Orleans.

CHRONOLOGICAL TABLE

1800	October	Signing of the secret treaty of San Ildefonso.
1802	October 25	Signing of the Spanish Royal order for the delivery of the Province of Louisiana to France.
1903	March 26	Arrival of Pierre Clement DeLaussat.
1803	April 30	Conclusion of the Treaty of Paris ceding Louisiana to the United States.
1803	December 20	Transfer of Louisiana to the United States.
1804	March 25	Claiborne appointed Governor of the Territory of Louisiana.
1804	July 27	The Louisiana Gazette, the first newspaper published in English, made its appearance.
1804	October 2	Oath of office administered to Claiborne.
1804	October 2	James Pitot was appointed Mayor of New Orleans.
1804	December 4	The Legislative Council was organized — Julian Poydras was elected its President.
1805	February 17	City of New Orleans was incorporated.
1805	March 4	First election held for Aldermen.
1805	March 5	Schism in the Catholic Church.
1805	March 12	The first bank in New Orleans, the Bank of Louisiana, was formally organized.
1809	September 29	Charity Hospital destroyed by fire.
1811	January	The last territorial legislature was convened.
1811	February 20	Congress of the United States authorized the forming of a State Government for Louisiana.
1811		The City Charter was amended to provide for the election of the Mayor. Nicholas Girod was the first Mayor to be elected in New Orleans.
1811	November 11	The first constitutional Convention of Louisiana was assembled.

1812	January 10	Arrival of the first steamboat in New Orleans.
1812	January 22	The constitution of the State of Louisiana was adopted.
1812	April 3	Louisiana became the 18th State of the Union.
1812	April 8	The Constitution of the State of Louisiana was approved by the President of the United States.
1812	July 31	Claiborne was inaugurated the first Governor of the State of Louisiana.
1815	January 8	Battle of New Orleans.
1816	May 5	Crevass at Macarty's plantation, part of the city was inundated.
1820		Financial crash.
1825	April 9	General Lafayette visited New Orleans.
1825		Ribbon Sugar cane was introduced in Louisiana.
1826	October 14	Corner stone of Mortuary Chapel was laid.
1826	August 13	Tornado struck City, many houses demolished.
1827		First coal barge reached the city.
1829	January 19	Death of Pére Antoine.
1831	March 5	Act passed by the State Legislature authorizing the digging of the New Basin Canal.
1831	April 23	Pontchartrain Railroad inaugurated its passenger service.
1832	September 19	First steam propelled train in New Orleans.
1832	October 9	First railroad accident.
1832	October 24	First appearance of Cholera.
1833		J. H. Caldwell was granted the exclusive privilege for street illumination by gas.
1833		Incorporation of the City of Lafayette.
1833	January 28	First attempted derailment of a railroad train.
1833	July 29	First race riot because of segregation on the railroad.
1835		Exchange Hotel (St. Charles Hotel) under construction.

1835	January	Medical College of Louisiana inaugurated First Monday of its first lectures.
1835	May	United States Mint under construction.
1835	September 26	Carrollton Railroad began operation.
1836		City Exchange (St. Louis Hotel) under construction.
1836	March 13	Opening of the new St. Charles Theater (Caldwell's).
1836	March 8	Governor signed the Legislative Act which divided the city into three separate municipalities.
1836	April 6	First graduating exercises of the Medical College of Louisiana.
1837	May 13	Panic — 14 banks suspended payment.
1842	March 13	Caldwell's theater destroyed by fire.

GOVERNORS OF LOUISIANA
(THE TERRITORY OF LOUISIANA)

W. C. C. Claiborne	October 2, 1804 to April 12, 1812

(THE STATE OF LOUISIANA)

W. C. C. Claiborne	July 31, 1812 to December 8, 1816
Jacques Philippe Villeré	December 8, 1816 to December 18, 1820
Thomas Bolling Robertson	December 18, 1820 to November 15, 1824 (resigned to accept the judgeship of the United States District Court)
Henry S. Thibodaux (Acting Governor)	November 15, 1824 to December 12, 1824
Henry Johnson	December 12, 1824 to December 15, 1828
Pierre Derbigny (Died in office)	December 15, 1828 to October -, 1829
A. Beauvais (Acting Governor)	October 1, 1829 to January 15, 1830
Jacques Dupre (Acting Governor)	January 15, 1830 to January 30, 1831
André Bienvenu Roman	January 30, 1831 to February 2, 1835
Edward Douglas White	February 2, 1835 to January 7, 1839
André Bienvenu Roman	January 7, 1839 to January 30, 1843

SENATORS AND REPRESENTATIVES OF THE LOUISIANA STATE LEGISLATURE FROM THE CITY OF NEW ORLEANS

First Legislature (July 27, 1812)

Senators:	Samuel Winter	Thomas Urquhart
Representatives:	Guichard	Bonfignac
	J. B. Labatut	Zenon Cavalier
	L. Duncan	

Second Legislature (Nov. 10, 1814)

Senators:	E. Mazureau	Thomas Urquhart
Representatives:	Jean Blanque	Marigny
	Rouquette	Guichard
	Bonfignac	Morel

Third Legislature (Nov. 18, 1816)

Senators:	Etienne Mazureau	Moreau Lislet

2nd Session (Jan. 5, 1818)

Senators:	Denis de la Ronde	Bernard Marigny
Representatives:	Armas	Guichard
	Bouligny	Morel
	J. Ducros, Jr.	Bonfignac
	Forstal	

Fourth Legislature (Jan. 4, 1819)

Senators:	Denis de la Ronde	Bernard Marigny
Representatives:	Albin Michel	L. Moreau Lislet
	Pierre Lacoste	St. Blancard
	Jos. Roffignac	David Ker
	L. D. Macarty	Etienne Coraby

Fifth Legislature (Jan. 7, 1822)

		J. Ducros, Jr.
		Bernard Marigny
Representatives:	J. B. Macarty	Louis St. Blancard
	Martin Duralde	L. Moreau Lislet
	Ferdinand Percy	John R. Grymes

Sixth Legislature (January 6, 1823)
Senators: R. J. Ducros, Jr. L. Moreau Lislet
Representatives: Stephen Mazureau Felix Grima
John R. Grymes Charles Maurian
Augustin A. Davezac P. E. Foucher

Seventh Legislature (Jan. 7, 1826)
Senators: R. J. Ducros, Jr. Moreau Lislet
Representatives: J. Grymes Alonzo Murphy
J. B. Labatut Cristobal deArmas
Thomas Urquhart John Mercier

Eight Legislature (Jan. 1, 1827)
Senators: Moreau Lislet R. J. Ducros, Jr.
Representatives: Charles Maurian Pierre Landreau
George Waggaman Anthony Ducros, Jr.
Alonzo Murphy John R. Grymes
F. Gaiennie Louis Allard

Ninth Legislature (Nov. 17, 1828)
Senators: P. Lacoste Moreau Lislet
Representatives: Pierre Landreau D. F. Burthe
Antonio Ducros, Jr. Martin Duralde
J. H. Shepherd

Tenth Legislature (Jan. 3, 1831)
(Session held in Donaldsonville at the home of Valery Blanchard)
Senators: Pierre Lacoste D. Burthe
Representatives: Louis Allard Charles E. A. Gayarré
W. C. C. Claiborne Pierre Landreaux
James P. Freret James Workman
Francois Gaiennie Etienne Mazureau

November 14, 1931. Extraordinary Session held at New Orleans
Eleventh Legislature (Jan. 5, 1833)
Senators: Casimir Lacoste D. F. Burthe
Representatives: R. Z. Canonge J. R. Grymes
E. A. Canon A. Hoa
C. F. Daunoy B. Marigny
W. F. C. Duplessis

Twelfth Legislature (Jan. 5, 1835)
Senators: Albert Hoa   C. Lacoste
Representatives: D. Augustin   Dixon
                 Freret   F. Labatut
                 A. Ducros   Montegut
                 Debuys

Thirteenth Legislature (Jan. 2, 1837)
Senators: Ducros   Hoa
Representatives: E. A. Canon   J. Grymes
                 G. R. Rogers   J. Slidell
                 E. J. Forstall   L. M. Kennedy

Fourteenth Legislature (Jan. 7, 1839)
Senators: J. M. Ducros   Albert Hoa
Representatives: W. C. C. Claiborne   L. V. Gaiennie
                 Charles Conrad   W. DeBuys
                 H. Lockett   C. K. Rogers
                 A. W. Pichot

MAYORS OF NEW ORLEANS

Etienne De Boré	November 30 to May 26, 1804
James Pitot	June 2, 1804 to July 26, 1805
John Watkins	July 27, 1805 to March 8, 1807
James J. Mather	March 9, 1807 to May 16, 1812
Charles Trudeau (Acting Mayor)	May 16, 1812 to October 8, 1812
Nicholas Girod (First elected Mayor)	October 8, 1812 to November 6, 1812
Lebreton Dorgenois (Acting Mayor)	November 6, 1812 to December 4, 1812
Nicholas Girod	December 4, 1812 to September 4, 1815
August Macarty	September 4, 1815 to May 13, 1820
Joseph Roffignac	May 14, 1820 to May 10, 1828
Dennis Prieur	May 12, 1828 to April 9, 1838
Paul Bertus (Acting Mayor)	April 19, 1838 to May 12, 1838
Charles Genois	May 12, 1838 to April 6, 1840
William Freret	May 4, 1840 to April 4, 1842

COUNCILMEN OF NEW ORLEANS

First Municipal Council of New Orleans established by Laussat, Colonial Prefect and Commissioner of the French Government, dated November 30, 1803 — Boré as Mayor; Derbigny as Recording Secretary; Destrehan, first deputy mayor; Sauvee, second deputy mayor.
Aldermen: Livaudais, Sr., Petit, Cavelier, Villere, Johns Sr., Fortier Sr., Donaldson, Faurie, Allard Jr., Tureaud, Jean Watkins, and Labatut, Treasurer.

ALDERMEN FROM 1803 TO 1840

— A —

Antonio Abat—1816, 1827
Louis Allard—1825, 1826, 1827

Antoine Argotte—1805
Felix Arnaud—1805, 1806

— B —

Bacas—1826
J. Baldwin—1832
S. Beauregard—1824
Bagoutin Bellechasse—1805
F. Benetaud—1824
E. A. Bermudez—1827, 1834
J. A. Bernard—1824
Pierre Bertonniere—1805, 1806, 1807, 1808, 1809, 1810, 1811
J. Bertrand—1827
Joseph V. Beville—1805

Thomas Bickel—1825
Evariste Blanc—1805, 1806, 1820, 1821, 1822, 1833, 1835
Sauvinier Blanc, Sr.—1824
S. F. Blancard—1816
J. Blanquet—1808, 1809, 1810, 1811, 1812, 1813, 1815
J. Boulié—1815
Louis Bouligny—1808, 1809
Thomas Bryant—1816, 1817, 1819
Burthe—1826

— C —

E. A. Canon—1832, 1833
J. F. Canonge—1828
Antoine Carraby—1807, 1813
Etienne Carraby—1819, 1820, 1821
Jno. Castanedo—1812
Zenon Cavelier—1816, 1835
B. Cenas—1807
Charbonnier—1818, 1819

Chauveau—1826
William Christy—1824, 1826, 1827, 1833
Coleson—1809, 1811
Nathaniel Cox—1814, 1827
N. J. Cucullu—1828
John Culbertson—1832, 1833

— D —

Auguste Davezac—1818, 1819, 1820, 1821, 1822, 1824, 1826, 1827
G. DeBuys—1804
Deflechier—1807, 1808
Denis de la Ronde—1806
J. B. Dejan—1813
Delarme—1805
Wm. A. Depeyster—1815, 1816
LeBreton Deschapelles—1807
S. D. Dizon—1830, 1831, 1934

William Donaldson—1804
J. Lebreton Dorgenois—1804, 1813
Chevalier Doriocourt—1813
Francis J. Dorville—1805, 1810, 1811
François Dreux, Sr.—1816
Guy Dreux—1805
Ducros—1831
François Duplessis—1805, 1809, 1810, 1811

— E —

Emerson—1831

— F —

J. B. Faget—1826, 1828
Joseph Faurié—1804, 1805, 1806
E. Fleytas—1825, 1826
L. S. Fontaine—1812
J. A. Fort—1825

M. Fortier—1804, 1808
Fortin—1809
J. B. Foucher—1825
James Freret—1813, 1816, 1817, 1818, 1819, 1830, 1831, 1833, 1834

— G —

François Gaiennie—1812, 1820, 1821, 1824, 1826, 1827, 1830
Jaques Garrick—1804, 1805
Charles Genois—1824
Nicholas Girod—1824
Martin Gordon—1820, 1821, 1828
J. R. Grymes—1813, 1825
Francis M. Guerin—1805, 1809, 1810, 1812
Gurley—1804

— H —

J. H. Harper—1828
Samuel H. Harper—1825
Guillet Hazeur—1805
J. Henderson—1810, 1811, 1812
Thomas L. Herman—1810, 1811
J. H. Holland—1830
William E. Hulings—1804
L. G. Hull—1822
T. H. Hyde—1831

— L —

Felix Labatut—1832, 1833, 1834, 1835
Alexandre Lacoste—1825, 1826
Lafon—1808, 1809
J. Lalande—1831, 1832, 1833
Honoré Landreaux—1813
Jean Lanna—1808, 1810, 1812, 1813, 1817, 1819, 1821, 1824, 1825, 1826, 1827
Paul Lanusse—1813
Nicholas Lauve—1813
Eugene Lavaud—1816, 1817
Pierre Lavergne—1805
Henri Lavigne—1808, 1809, 1810, 1812
Fanny Laverty—1828
Jules Leblanc—1831
Lee—1833
John Linton—1836
François Livaudais—1809
J. Livaudais, Sr.—1804, 1805
Livermore—1826

— M —

JN Bte. Macarty—1805, 1806
McDonogh—1805
Macready—1834
Arnaud Magnon—1806, 1807
Bernard Marigny—1811, 1812, 1813, 1818, 1819, 1825, 1826
Mayronne—1806, 1812
E. Méance—1816, 1817, 1822, 1824, 1825, 1826, 1827
J. F. Mericult—1804
J. F. Miller—1830
C. Miltenberger—1821, 1822
Pierre Misotierre—1811, 1812
Montagnet—1834
William N. Montgomery—1822, 1825
Bartholomew Montreuil—1825, 1826
Benjamin Morgan—1807, 1809, 1810
M. Morgan—1832
S. Morgan—1811, 1812
Nathan Morse—1816, 1817, 1818, 1819
V. Morse—1827
T. Mosey—1825

— P —

Parks—1807
Charles Patton—1806
Carnelius Paulding—1822
Manuel Paxton—1825
Pedeselaux—1805, 1834
Ferdinand Percy—1812, 1813, 1815, 1816, 1818, 1819
Peres—1807
S. J. Peters—1830
Pierre Petit—1804, 1805
Anathole Peychaud—1822
L. Pierce—1832
A. Pitot—1830
J. Pitot—1804
Jean Baptiste Plauché—1816
Pollock—1805
Charles Porée—1804, 1808, 1809, 1810, 1811, 1812
Thomas Poree—1804, 1805, 1806
Benjamin J. Port—1822
Porter—1820, 1821
T. Preston—1830
Gallien Preval—1818, 1819, 1820, 1821
Thomas Price—1807
Proffit—1805

— Q —

J. L. Quessart—1818, 1819, 1820, 1821, 1822

— R —

Richard Relf—1812
Reynes—1826
Rippley—1826
Roblot—1806, 1807

Roche—1818, 1819
Joseph Rodriguez—1825, 1826, 1828
Joseph Roffignac—1817
F. A. Rosseau—1819, 1820, 1821

— S —

St. Blancard—1820, 1821
J. A. Shepherd—1825
Al R. Smith—1815

Soniat Dufossat—1808
Soulé—1831
Soulié—1812

— T —

Doctor Thomas—1831, 1832, 1833
Toby—1831
Tricou—1818, 1819

Charles Trudeau—1806
Turner—1826

— U —

David Urquhart—1806, 1807, 1815, 1826

— V —

J. B. Vigné—1820, 1821, 1822, 1827

— W —

John Watkins—1804, 1805
Charles W. West—1825
Maunsel White—1813, 1818
Wiliams—1818, 1819

L. G. Willigsberg—1820, 1821
J. B. Wiltz—1824, 1825, 1827
Samuel Winter—1804, 1806, 1807, 1808, 1809

— Y —

Samuel C. Young—1816, 1817

FIRST ALDERMEN OF THE THREE MUNICIPALITIES (1837)

1st Municipality: J. A. Armitage, P. H. Colson, F. Correjolles, A. D. Crossman, M. Cruzat, Edward Duplessis, W. F. C. Duplessis, F. B. Faures, Charles Guesnard, Joseph Guillet, Jr., F. Lambert, A. P. Lanaux, Charles Lesseps, Dr. C. A. Luzenberg, P. Lefebre, P. Phillips, J. M. W. Picton, F. Prados, F. Roy, H. Vigne, V. Wiltz.

2nd Municipality: James Caldwell, John Hall, Henry Lockett, Spencer Lloyd, T. O. Meux, John Nixon, Samuel Peters, Ed Sewell, B. Whitney, Edward Yorke.

3rd Municipality: M. S. Cucullu, J. Giquel, J. Kilshaw, Bernard Marigny, G. Montomat, R. Preux, L. Rigaud.

REFERENCES

Alexander, Capt. Sir James Edward: *Transatlantic Sketches, Visits To North and South America and West Indies.* London, 1835.

Alliffe, Charles: *Dixhuit mois dans la Nouvelle Orleans.* Paris, 1853.

Antommarchi, Francesco: *Last Days of the Emperor Napoleon.* London, 1830.

Augustin, John: *The Oaks — The Old Duelling Grounds of New Orleans,* in "The Louisiana Book" by Thomas M'Caleb, New Orleans, 1894.

Bache, Richard: *View of the Valley of the Mississippi, or the Emigrant's and Travellers Guide to the West.* 1834.

deBaroncelli, J. C.: *Le Theatre Français á la Nouvelle Orleans.* New Orleans. 1906.

Bispham, St. M., Clarence Wyatt: *Louisiana Historical Review.* October, 1912.

Brackenbridge, Henry Marie: *Views of Louisiana.* 1814.

Brown, Samuel R.: *The Western Gazette,* Auburn, New York. 1817.

Bullock, W.: *Sketches of a Journey Through the Western States of North America in 1827.*

Castellanos, Henry C.: *New Orleans as it Was.* New Orleans 1895.

Catholic Encyclopedia.

Chambers, Henry E.: *A History of Louisiana.* The American Publishing Society, Inc. Chicago and New York. 1925.

Clapp, Theodore: *Autobiographic Sketches and Recollections During a Thirty-five Year's Residence in New Orleans.* Boston 1857.

Condon, Josiah: *Modern Traveller: a Description, Geographical, Historical and Topographical.* London, 1830.

Darby, William: *The Emigrant's Guide to the Western and Southwestern States and Territories. A Geographic Description of the State of Louisiana with an Account of the Character and Manners of the Inhabitants,* etc. Philadelphia, 1818.

Davis, Mathew Livingston: *Memoirs of Aaron Burr,* Vol. II. New York, 1836-37.

Debouchel, Victor: *Historie de la Louisiane.* New Orleans, 1841.

Deiler, J. Hanno: *The Settlement of the German Coast of Louisiana and the Creoles of German Descent.* Philadelphia, 1900.

Didimus, H. ("pseudo" Durell, Henry Edward): *New Orleans as I found it.* New York, 1845.

Sketches of some of the Incidents of my First Visit to New Orleans in the Winter of 1835-36. New Orleans Social Life and Customs.

Dowler, Bennett: *Graveyards and Cemeteries.* DeBows Review, XX X 111, 1852.

Duvallon, Berquin: *Vive de la Balonie Expagnale.* Paris, 1802.

Evans, Estwick: *A Pedestrian Tour of 4000 Miles in Western and Southwestern States and Territories.* Concord N. H., 1819.

Faye, Stanley: *The Schism in 1805 in New Orleans.* The Louisiana Historical Quarterly. January, 1939.

Ficklen, John R.: *History of Education in New Orleans,* from Rightor's History of New Orleans.

Flint, Timothy: *The History and Geography of the Mississippi Valley.* Cincinnati, 1832.

Fortier, Alcée: *Louisiana.* Century Historical Association. 1914.

Fossier, A. E.: *The Charity Hospital of Louisiana.* New Orleans Medical & Surgical Journal, May to Oct. 1923.
History of Medical Education in New Orleans from its Birth to the Civil War. Annals of Medical History. Vol. 6, No. 4, and No. 5, 1924.
Charles Aloysius Luzenberg. A History of Medicine in New Orleans During the Years 1830 to 1848. Louisiana Historical Quarterly. Vol. 26, No. 1. 1943.

Flugel, Felix: *Pages from a Journal of a Voyage Down the Mississippi in 1817.* Louisiana Historical Quarterly. Vol. 7, 1924.

French, Benjamin Franklin: *Historical Collection of Louisiana.* New York.

Gayarré, Charles Etienne Arthur: *History of Louisiana.* New York, 1854.
The New Orleans Bench and Bar in 1822, from Thomas M'Caleb's The Louisiana Book, New Orleans, 1894.
Essai historique sur la Louisiane. New Orleans, 1930-31.

Gould, E. W.: *History of River Navigation.* St. Louis, 1839.

Guilday, Peter: *The Life and Times of John Carroll.* Vol. II. The Encyclopedia Press. New York, 1922.

Gurley, Ralph Randolf: *Life and Eloquence of the Rev. Sylvester Larned — First Pastor of the First Presbyterian Church in New Orleans.* New York. 1844.

Hall, Capt. Basil: *Travels in North America in the Years 1827 and 1828.* Philadelphia, 1837.

Hall, James: *Statistics of the West at the Close of the Year 1836.* Cincinnati, 1837.

Hall, Oakley: *The Manhataner in New Orleans — Phases of "Crescent City Life."*

Heustis, Dr. Jabez Wiggins: *Physical Observations of Medical Traits and Researches on the Topography and Diseases of Louisiana.* New York, 1817.

Hodgson, Adam: *Letters from North America Written During a Tour in the United States and Canada.* London, 1824.

Hunt, Gaillard: *Life in America One Hundred Years Ago.* New York, 1914.

Jones, Dr. Joseph: *Medical and Surgical Memoires.* New Orleans, 1890.

Kendall, John Smith: *History of New Orleans.* Lewis Publishing Co. Chicago, 1922.

Ker, Henry: *Travels Through the Western Interior of the United States.* 1816.

Lafon, R.: *Annuaire Louisianais.* 1808.

Lagarde, P. deMontlezon: *Voyage fait dans les années 1816 et 1817, de New York à la Nouvelle Orleans et de l'Orénoque au Mississippi.* Paris, 1818.

Latour, Arcéne Lacarriere: *Historical Memoirs of the War in West Florida and Louisiana in 1814-1815.* Philadelphia, 1816.

Latrobe, Benjamin Henry: *The Journal of Latrobe.* New York, 1905.

Logan, James D., Esq.: *Notes on a Journay Through Canada, the United States of America and the West Indies.* Edinburgh, 1838.

Lowenstern, Isidore: *Les Etats Unis et la Havane — Souvenir d'un Voyageur.* Paris, 1842.

M'Caleb, Thomas: *The Louisiana Book.* New Orleans, 1894.

Marbois, M. Barbé: *Histoire de la Louisiane.* Paris, 1829.

Martin, François Xavier: *The History of Louisiana from the Earliest Period.* New Orleans, 1827.

Martineau, Harriet: *Retrospect of Western Travel — Society in America.*

Marvat, Capt. C. B.: *A Diary in America.* 1839.

Montules: *New Voyages and Travels — Consisting of Originals and Translations.*
Voyages in North America and West Indies.

Moody, Valton: *Slavery on American Plantations.* Louisiana Historical Quarterly. Vol. 7, 1934.
Murray, Charles Augustus: *Travels in North America During the Years 1834-35-36.* 1841.
Pavie, Theodore: *Souvenirs Atlantique, etc.* Braunschweig, 1834.
Pearson, Henry Bradshaw: *Sketches of America.* London, 1818.
Pöstl, Karl Anton (Sealsfield Charles): *The Americans as They Are — Described in a Tour Through the Valley of the Mississippi,* by the author of "Austria As It Is." London, 1828.
Power, Tyrone: *Impression of America During the Years 1833-34-35.* Philadelphia, 1836.
Schlarman, J. H.: *From Quebec to New Orleans.* Buechler Publishing Co. Belleville, Illinois, 1929.
Schultz, Christian: *Travels on an Inland Voyage through the States of New York, Pennsylvania, Virginia, Kentucky and Tennessee and Through the Territories of Indiana, Mississippi and New Orleans Performed in the Years 1807 and 1808.* New York, 1810.
Shea, John Dawson Gilmary: *History of the Catholic Church in the United States.* New York, 1888.
Singleton (Knight, Henry Cogswell): *Letters from the South and West.* Boston, 1824.
Smith, Solomon Franklin: *Theatrical Management in the West and South for Thirty Years.* New York, 1868.
Soniat, DuFossat, Chevalier Guy: *Synopsis of the History of Louisiana,* translated by Soniat, Charles T. New Orleans, 1903.
Stoddard, Major Amos: *Sketches Historical and Descriptive of Louisiana.* Philadelphia, 1812.
Stuart, James: *Three Years in America.* Edinburgh, 1833.
Trollope, Mrs. Frances: *Domestci Manners of the Americans.* London, 1832.
Warden, W. B.: *Statistiques, Histoire et Politique des Etats Unis.* 1810.
Zacharie, James S.: *New Orleans — Its Old Streets and Places.*
The Louisiana Historical Quarterly.
The Niles Weekly Register. Baltimore.
Files of contemporary newspapers.
Official Messages of Governors of Louisiana and the Mayors of the City of New Orleans.
Transactions of the State Legislature and the City Council.
Court records.

INDEX

A

Abat, A.—401, 405
Abers, Doctor—408
Alcard, A.—203
Allard, F.—402
Allard, Louis—76, 110, 112
Architecture, American—3, 8
American Settlers, extent of—257
Andrews, S. F.—242, 391, 392
Antoine, Pere—250, 314, 315, 329, 331
Anglo-Saxon animosity against French-speaking population—285
Antommarchi's Death Mask of Napoleon—500
Arnaud, Felix—219, 402
Association of Native Louisianians—291
Associates of New Orleans—115
Asylum, Ursulines Convent—247
Aubert, F. A.—203
Augustin, Donatien—113, 135, 290, 407, 431, 443, 444
Aury, Commodore—115

B

Baldwin, Captain C. J.—41
Baldwin, Joshua—130, 392
Balls, description of — 452, children's, 459
Banks Arcade—15
Banks, failures—72
Bank of Louisiana—60, 65
Bar in Chamber of City Council—84
Barenheidt, A.—203
Bargas, J. F.—445
Barker, Captain C. B.—29
Barrett, Thomas—290, 458
Barton, Doctor Edward—211, 212, 215, 216, 245, 391, 396, 398
Barton, Seth, Esq.—242
Batture case—152
Bayon, J.—190, 191
Beardslee, Doctor—177, 179
Beardslee, James—192, 196
Beardslee, William—196
Beaujeon, Ané—79
Beaumarais, Lalaune—79
Beauvais—252
Bell, Robert—196
Bell, Thomas—308
Bellechase—219
Bennett, H. S.—196
Bennett, S. Bretton—250, 343
Bermudez, Judge—150
Bermudez, J.—306, 390, 428, 444
Bernard, J. A.—402
Berton, Mrs.—250
Bertrans, J.—306, 444
Bertus, Paul—203, 290, 444
Bickle, Tobias—68
Bigot, Lieutenant—200
Billaud, Jr.—445
Billiard tournaments—460
Biron, P. N.—189
Blache, Charles L.—401
Blache, Jos. T.—163
Blache, J. H.—79
Black Code—370

Blanc, Monseigneur Anthony—303, 307
Blanc, E.—112, 127, 402
Blanc, F. A.—306
Blandeau, A.—444
Blanquet, Doctor—218
Board of Health of City of New Orleans, 407
Bocas, G.—110, 127
Bolot, Charles J.—427
Bonnabel, Doctor H. H.—407
Booth, Captain Ben—30
Bordeaux, A.—79
Boria, J.—196
Boré—76
Boulemet, Vergil—403
Bourbon Street, proposal to enlarge—57
Bouligny, F.—41
Bouligny, L.—41
Bouligny, Ursin—444
Bouligny, Ursin, Jr.—444
Bouny, B.—445
Bourg, J.—79
Boyd, D. W., Esq.—431
Bradford, James M.—187
Breadlove, A. W.—196
Breadlove, J. W., Esq.—392
Bridge to span Mississippi River—21
Bright, G. W.—196
Brown, William—41, 60, 92, 102
Bull and dog fights—462
Burials in Protestant cemetery—421
Business, phenomenal growth of—54

C

Caldwell, J. H.—76, 133, 343, 354, 391, 469, 471, 481
Caleb, T. F.—234
Calender, Thomas—60
Callien, Fred—130
Calvo, Casa—317
Cammack, H. G.—186
Camp Street—13
Camp Street Theater—470, 478
Canal Street, cleaning and widening of Canal—88
Canal Street, improvement of—21
Cannon, A. E.—90, 155, 158, 182, 183, 234, 254, 425
Cannon, Doctor—290
Cannon, L. C.—242
Canonge, Judge J. F.—127, 170, 234, 290, 345, 430, 494
Canonge, Zenie—445
Cantrelle—76
Carpenter, Doctor—396
Carpenter, M. M.—216
Carrol, Miss, Book Store—241
Carlston, H.—123
Caressol, Edward—200
Carriere, C. J.—444
Carter, John F.—189
Cashman, Madame—57
Castanedo, Juan de—320
Casteret, J. E.—200
Cathedral, services in—298
Catholic Priests, zeal of—298
Cavalier, Jonnier—60
Cavalier, Xavier—76, 250, 334
Cemeteries—cost of plots, 421; roads impassable, 422

Cenas, August H.—212, 214, 217
Cenas, Doctor—407
Cenas, H. R.—132
Chabaud, J.—239
Chalaron—198
Chapotin—178, 235
Charity Hospital—12; Founding of, 218; Revenues of, 221
Charivaries—462
Chase, Rev. Philander—336
Chassaignac, Doctor Charles—384
Chastant, J.—444
Chess Club—466
Chew, Beverly—60, 238, 251, 303, 431
Christ Church—336
Christmas Day observances—461
Christy, Wm., Jr.—402
Circuses—464
City Bank—13, 69
Citizens Bank—69
Civil Code of Louisiana, 143
Claiborne, W. C. C.—93, 97
Clapp, Rev. Theodore—340, 343
Clark, Washington—196, 403
Clauzel, Madame—472
Claw, Jr., Clem—196
Clay, Curtis—196
Coal Barges, first to arrive—25
Cock fighting—464
Cogley, P. P.—444
Cohen, E. A.—466
Cohen, S. M., Lieutenant—200
Colgue, R.—123
Coleson, J.—445
Coleson, L.—444
Coleson, P. H. Y.—445
College of Orleans, 229; closing of, 131
Commercial Bank—131
Commune, M.—116
Confield, Robert E.—196
Congregational Church, First—346
Conn, John—416
Connaud, Doctor—402
Conrad, C. M.—234
Consolidated Assn. of Planters—67
Constitutional Convention, First—97
Correjolles, Lieutenant F.—200
Correjolles, M. G.—116
Cotter, Daniel F.—196
Cotton—7
Coubrough, James—196
Cougat, Fauché—203, 444
Coulter, A. S.—79
Court, docket of District—150
Courts, organization of Municipal—150
Covens, William—196
Cowley, William H.—196
Cox, Nath'l—402
Cox, S.—402
Creoles, allegiance to France by, 269; charitable work of, 276; clanishness of, 278; definition of word, 266; dislike for Anglo-Saxon Ameri-

cans by, 272; morals of, 276; purity of language of, 273
Creole women, use of powder and rouge—277
Coton, cultivation of, 49; cost of plantation, 49; number of bales exported, 50; Presses, 52; price of, 50, 55, 70
Crimes, prevalence of—387
Crosey, G.—138
Crozat, Professor A.—235
Crozat, C., Prof.—235
Cruzat, Manuel—127, 192
Cucullu, Simon—112, 306, 402
Cuddy, J. N.—290
Culbertson, John—133, 188
Curfew—167
Cuvellier, Alex—444
Cuvellier, Colonel C.—198
Cuvellier, Joseph—444

D

Dame, C.—196
Dandreau, H.—138
Daret, Doctor N. H.—298
Daudet, Alexis (Feuilton), First Newspaper Commentator in New Orleans—177
D'Aufossy, E.—198
Daunoy, Chas. E.—116, 200
Daunoy, Favre—112, 182
Daunoy, J. S., Lieutenant—200
Daunoy, Louis—37
Davezac, Esq. A.—79, 108, 110, 401, 447, 448
Davezac, Major Costera—490
Daverac, Jules—230
Davidson, Doctor—135, 227, 238, 343, 403, 407
Davidson, Richard—233
Davis, John—78, 82, 83
d'Autrive, Marigny—79
D'Hamécourt, G.—444
D'Hamécourt, Marie J. A.—449, 450
Dawson, John E.—116, 213
DeArmas, Felix—290, 444
DeArmas, G. C.—110, 112
DeArmas, Octave—203
deBeaumont, L. Trigant—290, 444
Debret, Professor—235
DeBuys, P.—203
DeBuys, William—95, 444
De Fernex, Reverend—344
Dejan, Jules—445
Delachaise, F.—41
DeLaronde, D.—135, 203; Funeral of, 435
Delassus, Aug.—290
Delatule, M. A.—216
DeLavillebeuve, J.—431
Delaup, Francois—192
De laPlaine—242
Delavigne, Alphonse—216
Delery, Doctor Paul—290, 394, 396
Delpit, A.—445
deMorani, C.—444
deNeckere, V. M. Very Reverend Bishop—303
Derbigny, C.—41
Derbigny, Pierre—76, 84, 91, 95, 99, 111, 143, 289, 431, 435
Delche—402
Desbois, J. P.—444
Desdunes, J. B.—238, 444
Desforges, Adolphe—200
De St. Romes—203
Destrehan, J. N.—76, 96, 99

Deverges, J.—444
Deverges, P.—112, 194
Delery, P.—444
Diamond, Chas.—130
Districts, boundaries of—55
Dickinson—96
Dixon, J. M.—445
Dixon, Robert G.—84, 196
Dixson, S. D.—113, 135, 196, 444
Doherty, Patrick—290
Doisiere, Widow—65
Donaldson—63, 70
Dorciere—95
Dow—95, 219
Drainage—84
Drinking customs—390
Drake, Reverend—343
Drama, introduction of English—470
Droz, A.—203
Dubertrand, P.—203
Dubois—203
Dubourgh, Judge A.—150
Dubourg, L.—130
Dubourg, P. F.—490
Dubourg, Very Reverend Bishop Louis W.—302
Ducros, Captain Alfred—444, 490
Ducros, J. Marcel—444
Dueling — Laws prohibiting, 442; Meeting held to discourage, 442
Dufour, Captain J.—200
Duhy, Charles Guillaume—177
Duncan, Esq., L. Abner—99, 113, 241, 242, 345, 431
Dupenceau—95
Duperu, Alphonse—444
Duplessis, C.—185, 459
Duplessis, Edward—253
Duplessis, James—444
Duplessis, Pierre LeBreton—115, 445
Duplessis, Thomas—444, 459
Duplessis, W. F. C.—306, 354, 444
Dupre, Francois—45, 403
Dupre, Governor—290
Dupre, Jacques—290
Dupin, J.—444
Dupuy—203
Durdie, J.—200
Durel C.—113, 116
Durel, G.—445
Durel, Justin A.—290, 444
Durel, Thomas—459
Durel, W.—445
Durive, F.—458
Durocher, Charles L.—444
Dutillet, Charles—79
Dutillet, F.—113
Dutilet, J.—116
Duvillers—468
Duverges, Pre—79

E

Eustis, Doctor—94
Eustis, George—213, 216, 234
Eustis, James B.—94
Evans, Whitten—61, 242
Eyratta, M. P.—116

F

Faubourg, St. Mary—8, 57
Faurie, R.—76
Fenno, Edward—196
Fernandez, Jos. H.—444
Ferrier, L. D.—196
Fireworks—461, 462

Financial depression of 1822—66, 67
Fitzgerald, J. B.—64
Flatboats—24
Fletcher, Professor—235
Fleytas—83, 110
Flood—95
Folwell, J. N.—146
Forestier, Pierre—407
Formento, Doctor—213, 403, 498
Forrest, Edwin—472, 473
Forstall, J. N.—146
Fort, Captain John A.—122, 196, 396, 402, 490
Fort St. Charles—9
Fortier, Author—76, 219, 444
Fortin, Doctor—215, 398, 409
Foucher, A.—110, 130, 203
Foucher, P. Edmond—109, 494
Foundling Asylum, necessity for—250
Fountains in Squares, dispute over—133
Franklin Infirmary—225
Franklin Typographical Society—344
French Evangelical Church—344
French, Daniel—30
Freret, J. F.—110, 112, 135, 178, 418, 444
Frey, H.—83, 344
Friend of the Law (newspaper)—192
Fromentin, Eligius—97
Funeral of a free Negro—437; of a slave, 437

G

Gaiennie, Colonel Francis—83, 110, 112, 195, 198, 402
Guillard—203
Gallagher, Father—250, 305
Gallen, F.—200
Gally, Major L.—198, 200
Galvez, Professor—235
Gambling, prevalence of—384; Taxes on, 399
Garcia, Y.—445
Garnier, Lieutenant—200
Gas Light and Banking Co.—69
Gas light street illumination—86
Gastor, H.—306
Gayarré, Charles E. A.—230, 245
Geordy, Lieutenant—203
George, Richard S. H.—196
Gener, F. Captain—200
Generally, Fleury, Lieutenant—200
Genois, Charles—130, 402, 444
Genois, J. P.—130
German immigration—261; redemptioners, 261
Genole, J. H.—444
Gibson, John—183, 190, 191, 203
Gili, Father Don Sabastian—313
Giquel, P. J.—402
Girod, E.—306
Girod, F.—81, 108
Girod, M.—401, 447
Girod, Nicholas—65, 77, 97, 203, 302
Girod Street Cemetery—420
Goguet, F.—116
Gordon, Martin—68, 110, 127, 290

Gottschalk, Edward—460
Griff or Griffe, definition of term—357
Griffith, David—176
Griffon, L. D.—79
Grima, B.—108, 183
Grima, Esq., Felix—97, 111, 234
Grinault, S.—444
Grivat, Judge—290
Gros, Doctor—397, 403
Grymes, John R.—110, 112, 115, 146, 152, 155, 157, 290, 471, 494
Guadiz, J.—204
Guerrero, Canors—316
Guilhon—402
Guillot, Jr., Jos.—290, 306
Guillot, P.—183
Guillotte, P. A.—444
Guirot, Stanislas—444
Guyol, F. A.—458
Guyol, Thos.—445
Gumble, Captain—112
Gurley, John W.—60

H

Halbrau, L.—203
Hale, Fornell—124
Hall, D. A.—96
Hall, Justice—102
Halphen—403
Harman—64, 65
Harang, Judge—150
Harlequin, first literary journal in Louisiana—159
Harper, Aaron—196
Harper, Judge—123, 129
Harper, Captain Samuel H.—31, 168, 172, 176, 350, 481
Harper, Samuel H.—130
Harris, J. D.—403
Harrison, A.—203
Harrison, Doctor John—205, 212, 216
Harrison, Esq., J. Burton—243
Hart, Alexander—216
Hart, Jacob—43, 79
Hart, M.—116
Hasset, Canon—316
Hartwig—471
Hearsey, George W.—477
Hearsey, Colonel Thomas H.—129, 196
Henderson, L.—123
Henderson, Stephen—130
Hennen, Esq., Alfred — 103, 122, 123, 145, 152, 159, 288, 350
Hermann, Samuel—444
Herr, Louis—94
Herty, C.—203
Heustis, Doctor Jabez—395, 398
Heury, F. D.—112
Hewes, Wm. G.—290
Hilperens, Chas.—290
Historical Society of Louisiana—243
Hoa, Albert—105, 152, 160, 290, 444
Hoa, Pierre—290
Hoffman, W. M.—37, 41
Hogan, John—123, 252
Holland, John J.—80, 168, 188, 290, 494
Hopkins, D. R.—139
Hopkins, James—37
Horse racing—Jackson course, 465; Jockey Club, 465
Hosey, Captain C. F.—203

Hospitals, Charity—52; King's, 3
Hotchkiss, D. C.—130
Hotels—City Exchange, 15; Exchange Hotel, 14; Orleans, 13; Strangers, 13; Verandah, 14
Houses, description of—8
Howard Association, for yellow fever relief—403
Howard—178
Hubert, J.—112
Hull, Reverend J. F.—241, 250, 346
Hunt, Doctor Thomas—204, 206, 212, 213, 214
Hunter, William H.—196
Hyde—84

I

Illumination of streets—8
Immorality of New Orleans—160, 292, 382
Improvement Bank—13
Imports from abroad—46
Improvement Company of New Orleans—69
Indigo, failure of crops—47
Ingalls, Doctor Thomas R.—201, 212, 214
Interment, cost of —425
Irish emigration—180

J

Jacobs, L.—282
Jackson, C. P.—132, 471
Jacquelin, H.—208
Jeanfreau, A.—290
Jefferson College—Faculty and enrollment—234
Johnson, Governor—104, 105, 126
Johnson, Josiah S.—109, 431
Johnston, Thomas—196
Jones, Doctor James—216
Jones, Sam—471
Jorda, Pierre—290
Jourdon, N. J.—290
Journal of Commerce—180
Jph, Jean, Bishop of Havana —317

K

Kahn, C.—459
Kahn, J.—41
Kennedy, A. M.—68
Kennedy, J. W.—445
Kenner, William—60, 95
Kentucks, portrait of—33
Ker, Doctor David C.—108, 225, 403, 407, 466
Ker, Robert J.—159, 191
Kerr, William H.—141
Kernion, Jr., F. H.—444
Kindall, William—191
Kimball, Professor—235
Kinderlon, Father Adam—254
Kirby—96
Koune, Father Pedro Juan—305, 315, 318
Kostki, Albert Simon—216
Kursheedt, G.—403

L

Labatut, Felix—85, 133, 135, 171, 200, 290, 306, 403, 428
Labatut, General J. B.—31, 108, 132, 250, 308, 324, 334, 444, 445

Labatut, Doctor Isidor—213
Labranche, Alcée—154, 157
Labranche, Lucien—40
Lacoste, General—40, 193, 197, 275
Lacroix—403
Ladaviere, Father—303
Lafargue—203
Lafayete, General—arrival in New Orleans, 490; reception, 491; address, 491; order of procession, 494.
Lafayete, George Washington —493
Lafferranderie, A.—79
Lafittes—155
Lakanal, Professor—230
Lallande, John—458
Landreau or Landreaux, Pierre S.—113
Lacroix—403
Laidlow, Peter—130, 138, 139, 235, 254
Laidlow, Samuel—129
La Lannterne, Magique—192
Lambert, Doctor A. P.—213, 398
Lambert, T.—203
Landry, Trasimond—290
Lanaux, Armond—290
Langley—178
Lanna, J.—127, 402
Larned, Reverend Sylvester—337, 338, 339, 340
Lasere, Emile—444, 445
Laussat, Pierre Clement—76
Lavergne, Hugh—234
Lavillebeuve, J. W.—180
Laverty, Kenny—331
Lawyer's fees—151
Lawhon, John C.—216
Lawrence, Reverend—391
Layton, Robert—444
Leaumont, H.—170
Leaumont, T.—444
Lebeau, Z. B.—444
Lear—471
LeCarpentier, Joseph — 113, 138, 444
Lacontre, A.—445
Lee, Frank W.—130
LaGardeur, Gustave—444
Legendre, H.—203
Legislature, Council—88
Lemonier, Doctor Yves—402, 403
Lemuel—471
Leblanc, P.—445
Leonard, Henry F.—242
Leonard, G.—290
Leonard, Judge Gilbert—290, 445
Lepousse, C.—444
Lepretre, J. B.—173
LeRoy, Louis—402
Lesassier, Esq., L.—138
Levees, description of—27
Lewin, Phillipe—176
Lewis, Alfred J.—444
Lewis, John H.—216, 331, 445
Lewis, Judge Joshua—95, 189
Lewis, Stuart Hillhouse—196
Lewis, Wm. Y.—138, 196
Liautaud, Lieutenant, L.—200
Libraries—Commercial Library Society, 230; New Orleans Law, 239; New Orleans Public, 239; News and Reading Room, 239; Public, 239; Society Library, 238; Touro Free, 238
Linton, John—123, 180

Linton, R.—402
Lisle, A.—444
Litterfield, Louis—350
Lislet, L. Moreau—65, 79, 82, 131, 143, 147, 152, 157, 168, 431
Livaudais—76
Livermore, Samuel—110, 130, 250
Livingston, Edward—102, 109, 110, 115, 143, 147, 152, 330
Lloyd—104
Lockett—431
Longstaff, Ogden H.—216
Lorrain, Charles—188
Louisiana Gazette, first English newspaper—176, 192
Louisiana Guards—176, 192
Louisiana Whig—192
Ludlow—469
Lyceums—141

MC

McCaleb—13
McCall, John T.—196
McCarty, F.—445
McConnell, Doctor—221
McCoy, Amos M.—196
McCoy, L. L.—113
McCrady—428
McDaniel, Doctor—444
McDonogh, John—60
McFarlane, Doctor J. S.—84, 133, 184, 225, 407, 414
McKarsher, James—179, 187
McNeil, F.—459
McNeil, Joseph—60
McQueston, Wm.—113

M

Mail deliveries—139
Mance, E.—402
Magnin, A.—444
Maher, Michel—290
Maison de Sante, Dr. Stone's Infirmary—228
Mardi Gras disorders—459
Martyrs of Louisiana, execution of—270
Miller—460
Malard, Alfred—239
Manseau, J. B.—239
Marigny, Bernard—37, 104, 107, 110, 113, 125, 132, 178, 180, 290, 443, 444
Mathews, Leonard—458
Martin, historian—345
Mather—95
Maurian, Judge M.—110, 149, 150, 178, 498
May, Charles—113
Maybin, J. A.—41, 238, 242, 343, 350
Mazureau, E.—113, 145, 152, 153, 290
Mead, Joe H.—185
Mead, Lowel K.—177
Mechanics and Traders Bank—203
Medical College of Louisiana—204; Board of Trustees, 213; Faculty, 205, 212; First graduation, 215, 216; Incorporation of, 212; Tuition, 216
Medical College of New Orleans—213
Meilleur—112
Meilleur, Simon—79, 113
Mercier, J: J:. Esq.—110, 290, 428, 431, 443, 444

Mieux, Doctor—392
Militia—Age of conscription, 195; Company of free men of color, 193; lack of discipline, 202; law of 1820, opposition to naturalized citizens and foreigners as officers, 196; uniforms of, 203
Meynier, Alcide—445
Millaudon, L.—41
Miller, John J.—83
Miltenberger, G.—458
Mioton, Lieutenant N.—200
deMiropaix, Esq.—79, 112
Moller, A.—203
Mondel—471
Moni, Father—306
Moniteur de la Louisiana, first paper published in New Orleans—176
Monseigneur, B.—113
Montegut, Edgard—79, 173, 306, 428
Montegut, Felix—219
Montegut, M. R.—112, 116
Montgomery, B.—81, 123
Montgomery, T. W.—37
Mackie, Doctor J. Monroe—205, 206, 212, 216
Maenhaut, Foher—307
Montmaire, G. A.—203, 444
Montreuil, Theo.—290
Moore, John R.—350
Moore, John R.—350
Moore, Esq., L. H.—390
Moore, Samuel P.—350
Morse, N.—123, 127
Morgan, Benjamin—60, 95, 115, 123.
Morgan, Doctor C. W.—117, 257, 404
Morgan, George W.—251
Morgan, Matthew—37
Morgan, Esq., Thomas N.—391, 392
Marin, C.—402
Murphy, B.—402
Mosey, T.—306
Morphy, Alonzo—110, 234
Morse, Colonel—490
Morse, Esq., N.—37, 78
Mossey, T.—113
Mowry, Eugene—192
Mule, John A.—345
Mullen, Father James Ignatius—308
Musson, A.—458
Mulligan, G.—213

N

Naba, John—402
Nadaud, E.—444
Napoleon, Memirial celebration—426
Native American Association—238, 201; Oath of, 288
New Orleans Banking and Canal Co.—60
New Orleans, City of—Charter amended, 77; Debts, 77, 80; First Council, 76; Guards, salaries and uniforms, 164, 166, 182; Improvements, 78, 87; Incorporation, 76; Ordinance prohibiting funerals in Cathedral, 308; Regulation of funerals; Revenues, 80; Street Lamps, 82; Taxes receivable, 83; Value of property for taxation, 90; Suit against Presbyterian Church, 340; Libraries, 230, 238,

239;; Immortality, 160, 292, 382; Population growth 287
Newspapers—Advertising rates 192; Subscription Price, 270
New Year, observance of—462
Nicholson, John—130, 251 343
Nicolet, Theodore—344
Noret, A.—203
Norton, Henry—130
Nott, Doctor A. G.—64, 257

O

Oakey, S. W.—70
Octoroon, definition—357
Orleans Bank—161
Orleans Theater—82, 469
Orphan Asylum for boys—250 252
Orphanages, regulations for admittance and discharge—253

P

Pacaud—64
Palfrey, George—106, 110
Palfrey, H. W.—127, 403, 43:
Palfrey, Jones—60
Palfrey, Lieutenant R. C.—20
Palfrey, William T.—196, 47
Panic—beginning of, 70; Bank suspended payment, 72 Monday, May 13, 1837, 72 excessive rates of interest 73
Parker, Reverend Joel—391
Parlee, A.—250, 251
Parmele, J.—350
Patterson, Daniel Tod—105
Paving of upper suburb—88
Paxton, John A.—196
Pedesclaux, H.—306, 428
Peire, H. D.—113, 114, 118 444
Penalver, Bishop—315
Penas, J.—200
Pendagast, J. C.—191, 285
Penn, Alfred—196
Penn, F.—79
Penniman, A. T.—179, 182 187
Pepin—242
Peralta, M.—79
Perry, F.—306
Penrice, John—179, 192
Perdonville, Rene—192
Perrault, J. B.—68
Perry, Captain Henry—115
Peuve, F.—102
Peters, S. J.—113, 165, 173
Petit—76
Phillips, A.—290
Picayune, The—88, 191
Picton, Doctor William—221
Pichot, A. W.—444
Pierce, L.—431
Pierce, Levi—130
Pilie, M. J.—79, 83, 85, 8: 112, 116, 432, 458
Pinerom—402
Pitcher, L.—196
Pitot, Armond—290, 306
Pitot, James—76, 83, 96, 14 239
Plummer, Senator—95
Planchard, E.—444
Planter's Bank—13, 61
Plauché, Gerald—290
Plauché, J. B., General—10, 112, 123, 200, 402, 43

443, 444, 494
Plauché, P. E.—123
Peychaud, A. A.—401, 440.
Peychaud, P. E.—444
Peyraud, Josephine—86
Pollock—95
Pontchartrain Railroad, banking privileges granted to—69
Porée, Charles—321, 324
Porter, Judge Alexander—149, 244, 304, 401
Powell, Doctor W. Byrd—214, 215
Poydras Orphan Asylum—448, 449
Poydres, Julian—60, 63, 64, 76, 79, 83, 95, 97, 448
Poutz, Victor—290
Prados, M.—445
Pratz, Jose—445
Preaux, Robert—444
Prentiss, Hon. S. S.—156
Preval, Judge Gallien—79, 112, 113, 150, 182, 254
Preval, Theodore—445
Presbyterian Church, First—334; indebtedness of, 841; City's suit against, 340; new church on Lafayette Square, 343
Preston,, Isaac T.—152, 158
Preston, J. T., Esq.—108, 290
Prevost, J. B.—60, 96
Prices of commodities—56
Prisons—Cost of maintaining prisoners, 170; Crowded condition of, 169; New Parish Prison, 171; Report of Grand Jury concerning, 170; Lock up house, 1st Municipality, 173; Temporary Jail of 2nd Municipality, 172

Q

Quadroons, definition of 247; Balls, 358; exclusion of white women from balls, 359
Quessart, J.—402

R

Railroad—first accident on, 38; race riot on Pontchartrain, 38, 39; description of a train, 38; meeting for the organization of the Carrollton, 40; exhibition of miniature, 87; first round trip from city to lake, 37; speed limit of, 37
Rea, P. R.—190, 191
Real Estate—speculation in, 70; soaring value of, 70
Redemptioners—261
Relf, Dan F.—350
Relf, Richard—68, 138, 402, 423, 431
Relf, Major Samuel S.—200, 290
Renau—403
Reveille, Chas.—200, 444
Reynolds, F.—196
Reynolds, J. M.—123
Ricardo, D. L.—403
Richardson, R. D.—177, 182, 183
Riddell, Doctor John J.—216
Ripley, General—108, 110, 122

Ripley, Leonard—123
Riviere, P.—130
Roach, James—203, 308
Robert, Williams—450
Robertson, Guy—250
Robertson, Thomas B.—99, 102
Robin, Professor—235
Robeson, General William L.—41, 47, 135, 196, 405, 445
Roca, J. A.—445
Rochefort—230
Rodriguez—112
Roffignac, Joseph—68, 78, 198, 259, 495
Rogers, George K.—444
Rogers, William—196
Rollins, Doctor John—220, 221
Rollinson, Charles R.—196
Roman, A. B.—95, 458
Roman, F. G.—216
Roosevelt, Nicholas—29
Rose, William—238
Roselius, Esq., Christian—152, 159, 290
Rosillon, Abbé—307
Ross, William—343
Roumage—344
Rousseau, J. F.—402, 466
Rousset, Eugene—79
Royal Street—56, 57
Ruelle, Jean—79
Russel, C. E.—138
Russell, Mrs.—472, 473
Russell, R.—471, 473

S

Sabbath—observance of—297
St. Amant, Antoine—445
St. Armand, J. H. S.—444
St. Ceran, Tulliens—444
St. Charles Street—13
St. Cyr, Jr., Captain—200, 444
St. Cyr, S., Major—200
St. Martin (actor)—468
St. Mary Orphanage—308
St. Patrick Church—305
St. Peter Theater—468
St. Philip Theater—469
St. Romes, J. C.—290
St. Vilmer, M. G.—116
Sabattier, Jos.—402
Salary and wages, 1837—68
Sampson, J. P. C.—183
Sanchez, Doctor—402
Sanderson, John T.—196
Sauvé—76, 95
Savings Bank, first in New Orleans—68
Schmidt, H. C.—40, 85, 448
Schools, central and primary—234; board of regents, 234
Scott—81
Seghers, Dominique—82, 146, 147, 152
Senac, Doctor David—466
Servass, Thomas B.—238, 343
Shade, A. H.—196
Shaumburg, Colonel B., 116, 182, 494
Shaw, C. W.—403
Sheldon, William A.—196
Shenson, A. D.—290
Shephard, J. H.—123
Shreve, Captain Henry M.—29
Shute's School—232
Sickles, S. V.—239
Sigg, J. J.—203
Sinnott, Nicholas—290
Skipwith, Esq., Pulman—139
Slaves—as a good investment, 873; occupation of, 375;

public auction of, 374; religion of, 377
Slidell, J.—41, 247
Smith, Colonel—200
Smith, Judge E.—150
Smith, Doctor Edwin E.—205, 211
Smith, John H.—343
Smith, Sol—471
Smith, T. P.—445
Society dinners—455
Soniat—112
Sorbé—340
Soule, Jean—63, 64
Soulé, Pierre—152, 158, 290, 344, 458
Soulet, Thomas—130
Sourdes, F. E.—454
Southmayd, F. R.—350
Sparks, W. H.—213
Speed violations, 165; demand for speed laws, 166
Spot s, Major—41
Spring Hill College—235
Steamboat, first to arrive in New Orleans—28, 29
Stem, Albert—133
Sterret, James R.—445, 494
Stone, Doctor Warren—216
Stores, women owners of—57
Strawbridge, George—234
Street illumination—8
Story, Benjamin—214
String, E.—116
Stringer, Caleb—402
Sugar—value of, 61; introduction of ribbon cane, 49; price of, 48, 55; tariff on, 52, 53
Sugar plantations—capital investment, 47, 48; failures of, 50
Surgi—203
Swan, William—196
Syan—493

T

Taney, Charles H.—8
Taxes on chimneys—8
Temperance society—constitution of, 391; first lecture, 391
Theater, American (Camp St.)—470; description of, 476; price of admission, 478
Theater, Italian troupe—479
Theatrical troupe, first in New Orleans, 467
Thierry—178
Thomas, Doctor—110, 200, 396, 402, 406
Thomas, Joseph—104, 123, 138, 238, 343
Thomas, General Philemon—105, 106
Thompson, Lieutenant J.—200
Tio, Francisco—290, 445
Tobacco exports—560
Tobin, M. C.—308
Toby, Thomas—344
Toledano, M.—123
Toledano, R.—203
Tourné, J. P.—130
Touro, Judah—341
Tracy, William L.—196
Traffic accidents—166, 167
Tratour—203
Traweek, Cornelius—216
Tremoulet Hostelry—6
Tricou, F.—113
Tricou, Doctor L. A.—213, 403, 406, 407

Tricou, P. G.—290
Tug boats of river—25
Tulane, Louis—196
Turner, F. L.—127
Turner, Judge S. H.—123, 144, 158, 196

U

Undertakers advertisements—438
Union Bank of Louisiana—13, 69
Urquhart, G.—123
Urquhart, Thomas—64, 234, 344
Ursulines Convent—3, 235
Ursulines Orphanage — report of inspection, 247, 448
Urban Guards, roster of—204

V

Verner, Doctor—280
Vice, prevalence of—163
Vieux Carré, description of houses—7
Vignie, Coloney—200
Vignaud, B. D.—79, 402, 444
Vignie—401
Villere, Governor Jacques Philip—76, 98, 99, 104, 106, 181, 260, 490
Villois—468
Viosca, Joaquin—200, 290, 445
Voisin, J. B. D.—79, 402, 444
Voodooism, cult of—378

W

Wages of journey-men printers—188
Waggaman—110
Walsh, Father Patrico—311, 312, 313, 314, 315, 316, 325, 328
Wales, J.—116
Walton, Jr.—391
Walden, D. T.—41
Walton, S. F.—392
Ward, James B.—188
Washington Guards—203
Watkins, James—76, 77, 95
Watkins, Doctor John—96
Watts, Judge Charles—149
Welman, Robert M.—343, 423
West, Frederick W.—196
West, John W.—115
Wharton—242
Wharves—building of, 88; size of, 88
Whiske (Le Whiski), satire on Mazureau—117
White, Judge E. D.—110, 150

White, Maunsel—40, 46, 112, 235, 401
White, Samuel—37
Willard, C.—196
Wilson, H.—196
Williams, Henry—196
Wiltz—402, 447
Withers, W.—105
Wogan, P. K.—184
Wooster, Boswell—196
Workman, Judge James—150, 231, 238, 250
Worthington, A. G.—196

X

Ximens, Juan—2, 9

Y

You, Dominique—429
Yellow Fever—epidemic years, 396; mortality rate, 397; benevolent committee to succor victims, 401

Z

Zacharie, J. V.—420, 452, 453, 458
Zacharie, S.—63, 64
Zimple, Charles F.—40, 41

www.ingramcontent.com/pod-product-compliance
Lightning Source LLC
Chambersburg PA
CBHW022005300426
44117CB00005B/40